תנ"ך קורן ארץ ישראל
The Koren Tanakh of the Land of Israel

ירושלים
KOREN

THE GOLDMAN EDITION OF GENESIS

תנ״ך קורן ארץ ישראל

THE KOREN TANAKH OF THE LAND OF ISRAEL

GENESIS • בראשית

EDITOR IN CHIEF

David Arnovitz

TORAH TRANSLATION BY

Rabbi Lord Jonathan Sacks, z"l

KOREN PUBLISHERS JERUSALEM

The Koren Tanakh of the Land of Israel
Genesis
First Hebrew/English Edition, 2024

Koren Publishers Jerusalem Ltd.
POB 4044, Jerusalem 91040, ISRAEL
POB 8531, New Milford, CT 06776, USA

www.korenpub.com

The Publishers wish to acknowledge the assistance of Stacey and Amir Goldman and the Jewish Book Trust, Inc. in the creation of this volume.

Printed in PRC

Hardcover, ISBN 978-965-7766-70-5

The Goldman Edition is dedicated to the memory of

Herbert Marshall Goldman (Chaim ben Shmuel)

Born in Brooklyn, New York in 1945 to two Depression-era orphans, Herbert was the cherished second child of his loving parents. In 1967, Herbert married his beloved wife, Jeralyn Schecter, and together they embarked on a life full of love, adventure, and dedication to their shared values. They moved to Israel in 1971, where they played a pivotal role in the establishment of Moshav Neve Ilan, a testament to their unwavering commitment to the Jewish state.

Later, they raised their three devoted sons in Albuquerque, New Mexico, and Las Vegas, Nevada, instilling in them a deep love for their heritage, the Jewish people, and Jewish texts. This love was passed down from generation to generation, as Herbert's children in turn shared these cherished values with his beloved grandchildren.

Herbert Marshall Goldman's memory will forever be a source of inspiration and blessing to those who were fortunate enough to know him.

The Goldman Family
Jerusalem, Merion Station, Las Vegas, and Houston

Editor in Chief
David Arnovitz

Rabbinic Adviser
Rabbi Dr. Tzvi Hersh Weinreb

Academic Contributors
Prof. Shawn Zelig Aster, *Biblical History and Geography*
Dr. Yigal Bloch, *Ancient Near East*
Dr. Michael Carasik, *Ancient Near East, Languages*
Dr. Yitzhaq Feder, *Biblical and Ancient Near East Ritual*
Dr. Kristine Henriksen Garroway, *Biblical Scholarship, Archaeology*
Dr. Elaine Adler Goodfriend, *Biblical Scholarship, Ancient Near East*
Dr. Shalom E. Holtz, *Biblical Scholarship, Ancient Near East*
Dr. Gilad Itach, *Archaeology, Geography*
Dr. Lea Jacobsen, *Ancient Near East*
Dr. Jill C. Katz, *Biblical Archaeology*
Dr. Shirly Natan-Yulzary, *Ancient Near East*
Dr. Dvir Raviv, *Archaeology, Geography*
Rabbi Dr. Zvi Ron, *Biblical Scholarship*
Rabbi Dr. Jeremiah Unterman, *Biblical Scholarship, Ancient Near East*

Contributors
David Arnovitz

Design & Typesetting
Tomi Mager, *Layout and Typesetting*
Tani Bayer, *Art Director*
Estie Bryk, *Photo Enhancement*
Eliyahu Misgav, *Art Director*
Esther Be'er, *Typography*
Dov Abramson Studio, *Design*

Academic Editor
Rabbi Dr. Jeremiah Unterman

Translation of Genesis
Rabbi Lord Jonathan Sacks, z"l

Content Editors
Doron Chitiz
Rabbi Alan Haber
Ilana Sobel

Language Editor
Carolyn Budow Ben-David

Proofreader
Carolyn Budow Ben-David

Maps
A. D. Riddle
J. Rosenberg
Dr. Chris McKinny

Bibliographic Editor
Marc I. Sherman

Indexer
Marc I. Sherman

Contents

Publisher's Preface

The Koren Tanakh of the Land of Israel
The Vision

The messages of the Tanakh, the Hebrew Bible, have always been universal. From the Church Fathers of Rome to the early Muslims of Arabia, from the medieval Christians of Europe to the Pilgrims to America – the Tanakh has resonated across lands and throughout history, a voice for people's struggles, an expression of their dreams.

Yet despite the Tanakh's universal message, it is also deeply grounded in the Land. The events it chronicles took place in Israel and its neighboring kingdoms; the region is littered with inscriptions and archaeology that attest to the events behind its dramas – the Merenptah Stele, the Mesha Stele, the Tel Dan Stele, the excavations of the City of David are but a few examples. Its language and the cultural background against which it reacts reflect its ancient Near East context, and in that sense, the Tanakh is a product of its time and place. The geography, architecture, politics, culture, technology, and poetry of the Tanakh are, fundamentally, those of the land of Israel.

The use of Tanakh's ancient Near Eastern background as a basis for interpreting Tanakh has a long history in Jewish thought. The most salient example of this is the famous statement of Maimonides, who thought that Sabian texts might reflect practices of the ancient Near East:

> I say that my knowledge of the belief, practice, and worship of the Sabians [i.e., an ancient idolatrous nation] has given me an insight into many of the divine precepts, and has led me to know their reason… I will mention to you the works from which you may learn all that I know of the religion and the opinions of the Sabians; you will thereby obtain a true knowledge of my theory as regards the purpose of the divine precepts… **The knowledge of these theories and practices is of great importance in explaining the reasons of the precepts. For it is the principal object of the Law and the axis round which it turns, to blot out these opinions from man's heart and make the existence of idolatry impossible.** (*Guide of the Perplexed* III:29)

◂ To understand

To understand the text, we must understand its context. This is true of any work, but is particularly true of the Tanakh, whose laws and narrative can only be appreciated against the backdrop of its socio-political realities. Thus, the significance of the Ninth Plague cannot be fully grasped unless we know that, in Egyptian theology, the sun god Re was reborn every morning. Throwing Egypt into perpetual darkness, God was essentially "killing off" the principle deity of ancient Egypt.

One also cannot begin to comprehend the radical ethical revolution of the Torah without knowledge of the reality into which it entered. While the rest of the world, then and for thousands of years thereafter, treated slaves as expendable merchandise, the Torah speaks of their rights; while neighboring nations made women fully subservient to their husbands, the Torah is explicit in delineating their prerogatives; and while kings were considered above the rule of law, the Torah firmly subjects them to it. Human rights and dignity of all people have their very origins in the Torah.

Acknowledgments

A project of this scope and depth could not have been undertaken without the support of those who shared in our vision and enabled its realization. Susan and Roger Hertog, who have supported the project's first volumes, have been enthusiastic and creative partners, especially with their concrete suggestions for the design in the earliest stages. We thank you both, not only on behalf of the scholars, artists, and editors who created this groundbreaking work, but also on behalf of the generations of readers who will benefit from using it. We also thank Stacey and Amir Goldman for their generous sponsorship of this volume and for their support of Koren over the years.

We thank our rabbinic authority and *posek*, Rabbi Tzvi Hersh Weinreb, *Shlita*, for his profound knowledge and wisdom. In a project with such great potential for error, we are so grateful for his understanding of the world of Torah. Further we thank Rabbi Dr. Jeremiah Unterman, academic editor for this series, for his unique knowledge, insights, guidance, and commitment to religious and academic integrity.

Our editor in chief, David Arnovitz, is uniquely qualified to have led this project. In the best tradition of the Renaissance Man, he combines a love of Tanakh with a love of the land of Israel, and possesses the experience and abilities to get things done. From the get-go, David understood the vision of this project, and together with his assembled team, worked tirelessly to implement it.

A project of this uniquely multidisciplinary nature required the cooperation of over a dozen academic, religious, and specialized institutions. We thank our partners for their invaluable cooperation and contributions.

Matthew Miller
December, 2023

Introduction to the Series

What is the Tanakh?

The word Tanakh is an acronym comprised of the Hebrew letters *t n kh*, referring to the fundamental collection of writings on which Judaism is based: *Torah* (the Five Books of Moses), *Nevi'im* (the Prophets), and *Ketuvim* (the Writings). The Tanakh is a literary collection composed over the course of a millennium. It has had more influence on humankind than any other work – it has had more interpretation, commentary, analysis, and scholarship written about it than any other piece of literature. Originally written in Hebrew, with some portions in Aramaic (notably in Daniel and Ezra), the text we have today has been translated over the centuries into many hundreds of languages.

Contrary to modern scholarship that posits that the first part of the Tanakh, the Torah, was edited from multiple ancient sources by a later "redactor," Jewish tradition holds that the Torah is a unified text from a single divine author. The Torah itself (Deut. 31:10–13) describes the importance of transmitting this text to future generations.

One anecdote which describes the process of transmission of the text of the Torah appears in the Talmud Yerushalmi (Ta'anit, chapter 4) and in other rabbinic works (*Avot de Rabbi Natan* chapter 46 and Mishna Soferim 6:4). It speaks of three scrolls found in the Temple courtyard that differed from each other in three separate places in the text. A master copy was then created by taking the majority text in each of those three places (i.e., two against one), thereby creating a fourth text which was promulgated to all of Israel.

The traditional Jewish rabbinic text of the Tanakh is called the Masoretic Text, codified between the 7th and 10th centuries CE by a group called the Masoretes, who added vocalization markers (*nikkud*) and punctuation markers (*te'amim*) to the consonantal text. It is well known that alternate versions of some of the books of Tanakh exist: the Septuagint, for example, attests a text of Jeremiah that is substantially shorter than that of the Masoretic Text. But it is the Masoretic Text that achieved the status of "authorized version," both by virtue of rabbinic support for the Masoretes' work and by the use of this text in Jewish communities.

The Koren Jerusalem Hebrew Tanakh version of the Masoretic Text was published in 1962, based on printed Hebrew Bibles and discussions of generations of Masoretic scholars. Eliyahu Koren designed a new font and painstakingly prepared the text

◂ with the

with the assistance of A. M. Habermann, D. Goldschmidt, and M. Medan. The Koren Tanakh text is considered one of the most reliable in the Jewish world. The text itself, its layout and custom-designed font, are used in a myriad of Koren publications.

The Koren Tanakh of the Land of Israel includes the original texts with a new English translation that is designed to be accurate and loyal to the Hebrew, yet still flows smoothly using modern conventions, idioms, and vocabulary.

Why is Koren publishing this series?

An endless sea of literature is derived from, and related to, the Tanakh. In the last two centuries, modern scholarship in multiple fields has developed new perspectives in allowing the Tanakh to be viewed in its historic, literary, religious, social, legal, political, and geographical contexts. We aim to allow our readers to access new insights on the text from this scholarship.

The events and geography of Tanakh (like those of nearly every narrative) are set in specific places and times, and its text uses the literary techniques of long-lost cultures. But few works, particularly those written for an English-speaking Jewish audience, have tried to relate the Tanakh to its milieu – comparing its history, literary style, geography, cultural interactions, and political relationships to those that existed at the time.

The empires of Egypt, Sumer, Assyria, Hatti, Babylonia, and Persia – as well as the smaller surrounding civilizations of Moav, Edom, Midyan, Amon, Phoenicia, Philistia, Aram, Ugarit, Canaan, and others – all interacted with, ruled over, influenced, or had conflicts with the Israelites. In the last two hundred years, scholarship about those civilizations, based upon archaeological discoveries and ancient texts, have revolutionized the way that the Tanakh is studied. We have attempted to popularize and summarize this recent scholarship to help the lay reader better understand the Tanakh.

Who is the series for?

The Koren Tanakh of the Land of Israel does not assume any background on the part of its readers, although readers may be familiar with many of the biblical stories and may have heard of the major personalities.

The series is written from a Jewish perspective and is consistent with an Orthodox Jewish worldview. Yet, the series has relevance for everyone, irrespective of whether the reader knows the Tanakh as the Jewish Bible, the Old Testament, or the Hebrew Bible – or calls it by another name.

All scholars would admit that modern knowledge about the ancient world is limited; we have only a tiny fraction of the material culture and literature of that world, and what we do not know far surpasses what we do know. New discoveries and reevaluations take place constantly. This series strives to present the most up-to-date scholarship in order to connect the Tanakh and its events, concepts, language, and cultural interactions to the ancient Near East – in a way that is accessible to a contemporary audience.

◂ How to

How to read the series

The books in the series are meant for browsing and surveying. By no means is this a series of books that must be read cover to cover. The articles are self-contained, allowing readers to look through the topics, images, and sections and focus on whatever is of interest. For your convenience, there is a graphic "How to read this book" introduction on the following pages.

The articles are related to a specific verse or sequence of verses, while the section introductions explain topics that are related to a larger section of the biblical text. For example, the section introduction on "Creation in the ancient Near East" contrasts the creation story in Genesis with other ancient Near East creation epics, noting the theological and ethical differences between them.

The books in this series are visually appealing, with photographs, reconstructions, and maps that complement the text to help readers understand and visualize concepts from surrounding societies, geographic relationships, and physical objects.

The series draws on previous Koren publications, incorporating images that appear in other Koren works – such as images that help readers visualize aspects of the time of the patriarchs, and pictures of the plants, animals, and archaeological finds from that time.

The Tanakh and contemporary scholarship

The Koren Tanakh of the Land of Israel discusses the text's relationship to its time and milieu – from early recorded history until the beginning of the Second Temple period (approximately the 5th century BCE). Where parallels between the descriptions in the Tanakh and contemporary religion and culture exist, the series highlights them; when there is a clear conflict between current knowledge and some element in the text, the series notes the conflict and leaves the question open.

The multidisciplinary academic research that surrounds the Tanakh is a constantly moving target, reflecting Rashbam's quote of a conversation he had with his grandfather, Rashi, in which the latter "acknowledged to me that if he had more time, he would need to produce more commentaries in accord with the new meanings that are uncovered every day" (commentary on Genesis 37:2). This is particularly true in an era of intense archaeological, literary, and historical research. Debates about the Tanakh arouse passions among scholars in so many disciplines, and it is fascinating to watch issues rise, fall, and reemerge as academic research and archaeology continue to reveal new finds. In this series, Koren is proud to present a window into some of the key questions that are debated in academic circles, sharing these issues and new understanding with a more general audience.

Religious orientation

Koren Publishers Jerusalem is an Orthodox Jewish publishing house, having produced texts for over fifty years. *The Koren Tanakh of the Land of Israel* is a delicate balance between the scholarship of academia over the last two centuries and the traditions of the Jewish Sages that have come down to us over the last two millennia.

◂ As a

As a series that is consistent with the beliefs and traditions of Orthodox Judaism, Koren Publishers Jerusalem assumes that the Tanakh is a testament to God's providence over the history of the Jewish people, from the creation of the world to the return of the Jewish people to the land of Israel and the building of the Second Temple. As the first Jewish edition of the Tanakh in English which approaches the biblical text with a keen interest in the historical reality of its events, it is essential to articulate the series' religious and scholarly points of departure:

- The series assumes the divine authorship of the Torah, rejecting theories of multiple authorship which disregard its fundamental unity.
- The series assumes divine inspiration of the Prophets and Writings.
- The series does not address questions of biblical chronology which cannot be resolved and, more importantly, are not required for understanding and appreciating the meaning of the text.
- Certain idiomatic elements of biblical language, such as some numbers, cannot be read literally. They must be considered through the lens of contemporaneous literary usages, which the series attempts to explain.
- The series does not justify, explain, deny, or rationalize the presence of miracles in the Tanakh. While presenting the historical circumstances of biblical events, the articles in the series recognize the reality of miracles as God's intervention in human affairs.

It is our hope that the new understandings of the Tanakh gained by reading it in the context of our current understanding of the surrounding civilizations at the time will give the reader new insights into the meaning of the text as it would have been understood by an ancient Israelite or Judahite reader. We also hope that this approach will draw an entirely new audience of readers to the Tanakh's timeless messages.

Translation, transliteration, and terminology

The Koren Tanakh of the Land of Israel series uses a new translation of the entire Tanakh, produced by a team of scholars who remained true to the original text while also being consistent with modern language, idioms, and readability expectations. Any translation is a commentary, and the Koren translation is no exception. The translations of the books of the Tanakh used in this series attempt to be true to the initial Hebrew text and also present the Tanakh in a form that flows and is accessible to the modern reader. The late Rabbi Lord Jonathan Sacks was the primary contributor to the Torah translation, while other scholars and professional translators produced the translations of the Prophets and the Writings.

Transliterations in this series follow conventions designed to make them easy to read. The emphasis is placed on modern Hebrew pronunciation of the words of the text rather than on the spelling of the original Hebrew words.

Each book contains a glossary of common vocabulary, including terms from the biblical text as well as terms, sources, and scholars that are referenced in the ◂ articles.

articles. The maps and timelines at the front of the book provide easy reference to locations and time periods. A bibliography appendix includes both general topic bibliographies on biblical commentaries and ancient Near East material, as well as bibliographical references used to compose the individual articles. Image credits are listed in a separate appendix.

David Arnovitz, Editor in Chief
Jeremiah Unterman, Academic Editor

The Torah and Its Ancient Near Eastern Context

The ancient Near East (ANE) before the Sinai revelation

The Israelite people, including the patriarchs and matriarchs, were born in the region of the cradle of civilization, where civilization was already ancient and highly advanced. By the 3rd millennium BCE, many Near Eastern civilizations had undergone significant cultural and technological progress, principally, the Sumerians and Egyptians. The main advances achieved by these two societies during this time include:

- *Writing*. The Sumerians are credited with inventing the first writing system, cuneiform, which they used to keep records of their economic transactions, their religious beliefs, and other important information. The Egyptians developed a complex writing system known as hieroglyphics, which they used to record everything from religious beliefs to day-to-day events. The system involved the use of pictograms and ideograms, as well as a more abstract phonetic component.

- *Irrigation and Agriculture.* The Sumerians were among the first to develop advanced irrigation systems, which enabled them to grow crops in the fertile land between the Tigris and Euphrates rivers. They used canals and levees to control the flow of water and maximize agricultural output. The Egyptians developed advanced agricultural techniques, such as the use of the Nile River to irrigate their crops through numerous canals, the creation of specialized tools such as plows and sickles, and the development of crop-rotation practices.

- *Urbanization.* The Sumerians were among the first to establish large, permanent settlements with sophisticated infrastructure and public works, such as temples, palaces, and defensive walls.

- *Architecture*: The Egyptians were famous for their monumental architecture, including pyramids, temples, and other grand structures. They developed sophisticated building techniques, such as the use

◂ of massive

of massive stone blocks and the creation of complex internal systems to ensure stability. The Great Pyramids of Egypt were constructed during the Old Kingdom period of ancient Egyptian history, which spanned from around 2686 BCE to 2181 BCE (the largest is the Pyramid of Khufu, which was built around 2560 BCE and stands at a height of 147 meters/481 feet). The construction of these massive edifices was a tremendous feat of engineering and required the labor of thousands of workers over many years.

- *Mathematics.* The Sumerians developed a number system based on the number 60, and performed complex mathematical calculations. They also developed a system of weights and measures, facilitating trade and commerce.

- *Astronomy.* The Sumerians were among the first civilizations to make and record systematic observations of the night sky. They tracked the movements of the stars, the planets, and the moon, and they developed methods to predict their positions. This enabled them to develop the lunar calendar, as well as the concept of the zodiac, which divided the sky into twelve equal parts, each associated with a particular constellation. They were then able to track the movements of the planets against the background of the stars.

- *Medicine.* Egyptian medical knowledge was highly advanced for its time. Physicians sutured wounds, set broken bones, and performed basic surgeries.

- *Metalworking.* The Egyptians were skilled metalworkers, particularly in the use of copper and bronze. They used these materials to fashion a wide range of objects, from jewelry to tools to weapons.

By the 2nd millennium BCE, different regions of the world were connected by several major trade routes. Such routes facilitated the exchange of goods, information, and ideas, and thus shaped the cultural, economic, and political landscape of the ancient world. The Near East was linked to many of these trade routes, some of which were:

- *The Silk Road* – a network of trade routes that connected China and other parts of Asia with the Mediterranean world. Perhaps the most famous trade route in history, it was crucial for the exchange of silk, spices, precious metals, and other luxury goods.

- *The Mediterranean trade routes* – the Mediterranean Sea was a major hub of trade during this period, with various ports and cities along its coast serving as important trading centers. Key goods traded in the Mediterranean included olive oil, wine, grain, and pottery.

◂ The Red

- *The Red Sea trade routes* – goods sailed on the Red Sea between Egypt, the Arabian Peninsula, and East Africa. These shipping routes were particularly important for the exchange of spices and incense.

- *The Trans-Saharan trade routes* – connected North Africa with West Africa, and were important for the exchange of salt, gold, ivory, and other goods.

- *The Indus Valley trade routes* – the Indus Valley civilization in what is now Pakistan was a major trading power. Goods such as cotton, spices, and precious stones were exchanged along routes that linked the Indus Valley with other parts of South Asia and the Persian Gulf coast.

The Torah and its ancient Near East (ANE) context

In order to fully understand the Torah (and each of its books separately – Genesis, Exodus, Leviticus, Numbers, and Deuteronomy), it needs to be apprehended within its ANE context. The Torah's phraseology, narrative and poetic style, legal materials, rituals, treaties, genealogies, and even prophecies share similarities with those in other ANE literature, including non-Semitic works, such as those of the Sumerians, Egyptians, and Hittites. In terms of language, the Torah (with the exception of two words written in Aramaic in Gen. 31:47), is written in Biblical Hebrew – itself a Semitic language. It belongs to the family of Northwest Semitic languages – comprising Aramaic, Ugaritic, Phoenician, Moabite, Edomite, and Ammonite (plus other Canaanite tongues) – with unquestionable commonalities to other more Eastern Semitic languages such as Akkadian and Amorite, and even South Semitic Arabic.

Furthermore, understanding the Torah within its historical, cultural, literary, and geographic context underscores that from beginning to end, it is truly exceptional. No other text is a continuous historical narrative from the creation of the world and humans to the development of humanity before the flood and its dispersion throughout the Middle East, the Levant, North Africa, and the Mediterranean. No other text tells the story of one small people within the context of all of human history. Indeed, no other single text is a narrative which also includes genealogies, treaties, civil and ritual laws, poetry, and prophecy. No other text is so large – 5,845 verses. Even excluding Deuteronomy, most of which recapitulates Exodus through Numbers, the Torah's first four books would still be the largest single literary work created in the entire ancient Near East.

More significantly, the Torah's monotheism represents a revolution against ANE thought. The Hebrew word *torah* (meaning "teaching" or "instruction") epitomizes that rebellion, as all appearances of the word in the Pentateuch refer to God's instructions to the Israelites (starting with Avraham in Gen. 26:5). No other ANE text portrays a deity instructing a people. No other text portrays the relationship of a deity to the world and to humanity, on the macro level, as well as to one family and to the people generated by that family, on the micro level. No other text describes a deity taking a people out of slavery in one land and leading

◂ them to

them to another, or making a treaty with that people (or making a treaty with their ancestors), or giving them their laws.

It is important to recognize that metaphors (and, to a lesser extent, similes) are the primary ways in which the Tanakh conveys God's interrelationships with nature, humanity, and Israel. These metaphors are articulated in images based on observable natural and social phenomena (including politics, family, law, etc.). Every image of God produces a counter-image. So, when God is called "king" or "father" or "shepherd," there must be a "subject," "child," and "sheep." In other words, these images are not portrayals of God, but of God's relationships. Thus, the God-Israel relationship is variously depicted as that of king-subject, parent-children, husband-wife, eagle-nestling, shepherd-sheep, and so on.

Therefore, it must then be asked: To what image of the God-Israel relationship does the noun *torah* allude? In other words, from what social phenomenon is *torah* derived? As more than ninety-five percent of the occurrences of *torah* (208 times, and the plural, *torot* – 12 times) refer either directly or indirectly in the Tanakh to the instructions of God to the people originating at Sinai, to answer this question we must seek out those biblical texts which provide evidence of nontheological understanding of the term. Only a handful of such texts exist, primarily in the book of Proverbs. Outside of 28:4–5, 9 (apparently in reference to God's *torah*; possibly also 29:18), Proverbs explicitly expresses *torah* as coming from one of two sources – the sage (once in 13:14; compare Ps. 78:1), and parents (eight times: 1:8, 3:1, 4:1–2, 6:20, 23, 7:1–2, 28:7, 31:26). Representative examples of the latter are: "Heed (*shema*), my son, your father's instruction (*musar*), and do not forsake your mother's teaching (*torat emecha*)" – 1:8; "My son, do not forget my teaching (*torati*), and let your heart guard my precepts (*mitzvotai*)" – 3:1.

It is noteworthy that the sage's teachings in Egypt – *Instructions for Merikare*; *Instructions of Amenemope* – are written respectively by a sage/king and a sage/scribe, each for his son, and a sage also writes for his son in Mesopotamia (*Instructions of Shuruppak, Instructions of Shupe-Ameli*). Proverbs (compare 1:1–4 with 1:8–15) presents a similar milieu. Logically, then, *torah* refers originally to the particular parental teaching to a child, with the particular addition of the significance of a mother's *torah* added to the father's. The usage of *torah* as a key theological term in the Tanakh testifies that a key aspect of God's relationship to Israel is that of a parent to a child – an idea explicitly stated in the Torah in Exodus 4:22–23 and in Deuteronomy 1:8, 8:5, 14:1, 32:11, etc.

This concept implies an eternal bond between God and Israel, for when a child is punished for disobeying the parent, such punishment is inevitably seen as temporary, with the purpose being to correct the child and to restore the proper relationship to the parent. That is why the very prophets who will portray God's anger at His rebellious son – the people – still depict, after a temporary punishment, God's redemption of that child.

At the heart of the Torah's revolution is its *sui generis* ethical ideology and content. The following are just some of the Torah's major ethical innovations in its effort to create a just society:

◂ Humans

- Humans were conceived to emulate God as good rulers of the earth, not as slaves to the gods' physical needs and self-centered desires. Further, men and women were created equally in the "image of God," which meant that all human life is sacred. Moreover, since human life is sacred, human life and property are not commensurable.

- God's rest on the Sabbath was transformed into the first universal labor law. The Sabbath, in which all members of society, even slaves, ceased work one day a week, was a unique, democratizing enactment.

- God rules the world with justice. Moral evil is not demonic but is the result of unrestrained human selfishness. Nonetheless, humans are capable of exercising their free will to behave ethically, and are called upon to do so.

- In God's unique treaty with the Israelites at Sinai, the treaty's stipulations are the laws of the nation. Therefore, the Torah's laws have an importance which exists in no other society, for the destiny and fate of the people rest on their obedience – bringing divine blessing – or disobedience – resulting in divine punishment. As every adult Israelite is a party to the treaty, each person is behaviorally responsible for the future of the society. At the same time, the community is responsible for ensuring that each individual is law-abiding and treated justly. The result is the innovation of two new mutual concepts: individual and communal responsibility.

- As God is the source of goodness, ethical values are holy and become law – one is required to help others, and even to act lovingly toward them. Such love is implicit in the understanding that God's instruction (*torah*) to Israel signifies a parent-child relationship, in which the relationship is permanent and divine punishment for misbehavior is only corrective. Thus, hope for the future becomes a fixture of the relationship.

- The Torah, unlike all other ANE legal collections, presents a host of laws on behalf of the two most disadvantaged categories of people in society – the resident alien and the poor. The resident alien was transformed into a member of society who was protected both divinely and legally, with wide-ranging benefits and with significant parity with the average citizen. The Torah's legislation, thus, acts to counter xenophobia. Similarly, each member of society is obligated to care for and sustain the poor, including needy widows and orphans. Laws are established for their benefit which are not only unattested in any other ancient law code, but also do not find expression in even the most ethical considerations of ANE wisdom literature.

- The Torah legislates numerous ethical innovations concerning repentance for civil misdeeds, including that the wrongdoer – *before* he or

◂ she is

> she is apprehended – must not only confess his or her crime but must make restitution and pay a penalty to the victim (which is considerably less than the wrongdoer would have to pay if already caught). Further, since every crime against a human is also a crime against God, a reparation offering is made by the perpetrator at the Sanctuary. However, as restitution to the victim *precedes* the reparation offering, compensation to the victim takes priority over reparation to God (!) – an unthinkable concept in ancient Near Eastern paganism.

Eventually, many of the Torah's revolutionary ethical concepts and precepts transformed much, if not most, of the world – from the idea that people must rest at least one day a week, to the necessity of providing subsistence living to the disadvantaged, to the social and political foundations of modern democracy. All of the above, and more, will be addressed in the Torah volumes in this series.

Jeremiah Unterman, Academic Editor

Introduction to the Book of Genesis

Names of the book

The original names of the five books of the Torah (the compilation known in English as the "Pentateuch") come from one of the first Hebrew words in each book. It was common practice in the ancient Near East to title a text by its first phrase or word, e.g., *enuma elish* ("when on high") for the Babylonian creation epic and *sha nagba imuru* ("he who experienced all") for the *Epic of Gilgamesh*. Similarly, the first book of the Torah is named after its first word, *bereshit,* which is a prefixed noun in the construct form meaning "in the beginning of." Here, syntactically, it refers to the beginning of God's creation of the cosmos (elsewhere, the word *bereshit* refers to the beginning of the reign of a king, as in Jer. 26:1, 28:1).

Although *Bereshit* became the common Jewish title of the book, in both the Talmud Yerushalmi (Sota 1:10) and the Babylonian Talmud (Avoda Zara 25a) it is called *Sefer Hayashar* ("the book of the upright;" compare Josh. 10:13; II Sam. 1:18).

The English name, Genesis, is derived from Old Latin, ultimately tracing back to the Greek translation of the Tanakh known as the Septuagint. Genesis means "origin," and is first used in the Septuagint of Genesis 2:4, "This is the book of the origin (*geneseos*) of heaven and earth." Genesis may well have already become the title of the book in the 3rd century BCE Jewish community of Alexandria, Egypt.

Overview and outline

Genesis, as the first book of the Torah, lays the historical foundation for God's unique relationship with the people called "the children of Israel," whose early existence is documented in Exodus. This foundation is essential for introducing the Torah's unique concept of divinity, known as ethical monotheism. It begins with God's creation of the world, from every blade of grass on earth to the stars in the sky, concluding with its pinnacle, humanity. Yet, God's work is more than the technicalities of creation, as it is coupled with the ethical act of providing sustenance for all life on the earth (1:29–30). God's beneficence, caring, justice, and mercy will be manifested throughout Genesis in His relationship with humanity, from the first humans through Noaḥ and his descendants to Avraham and his descendants, who eventually relocated to Egypt. With Avraham, God takes on another role in addition to being the Creator and ultimate Judge – He becomes the personal Deity of a particular family (Gen. 26:24, 28:13, etc.). In Exodus, that

◂ personal

personal relationship will be transformed as God becomes the national Deity of the Israelite people (Ex. 6:7; Lev. 26:12; Num. 15:41; Deut. 29:12, etc.).

Genesis is divided into two primary literary sections – before Avraham and from Avraham through Yosef. The major theme of the first section, from chapter 2 through chapter 11, is the gradual moral decline of humanity. From Adam and Ḥava's disobedience and refusal to take responsibility for their actions, to Kayin's murder of Hevel to the violent dominance of human evil, takes merely ten generations (albeit stretching over 1,650 years). After the flood's destruction, God renewed His beneficent relationship to humans in His covenant with Noaḥ, but again humanity rebelliously refused to follow His commandment – this time to "fill the earth" (Gen. 9:1; see Rashbam's comment to 11:4; note that the Tower of Bavel episode appears to chronologically precede chapter 10's Table of Nations).

The overarching theme of the larger, second section of Genesis is the details of God's third attempt at a positive relationship with humanity – this one with Avraham and his descendants. This section is bookended by two migrations: of Avraham's family to Canaan and of Yaakov's to Egypt. Although God acknowledged at the time of the flood that humans are ethically flawed (see 6:5 and 8:21), His relationship with Avraham, Yitzḥak, Yaakov, and Yosef ultimately succeeded because, throughout their trials and tribulations, these forefathers, despite occasional morally questionable behavior, *always* obeyed God. The permanent transference of the land of Canaan to their descendants is the patriarchs' reward (13:14–16, 15:16–21, 26:3–5, 28:13–14, 35:11–12, 48:4, 50:24–25).

The book's outline is as follows:

- I. Before Avraham (1:1–11:26)
  - A. Creation and the Sabbath, including instructions to humans (1:1–2:3)
  - B. The Garden of Eden and the expulsion (2:4–3:24)
  - C. Kayin's killing of Hevel and its aftermath (4:1–26)
  - D. The genealogy from Adam to Noaḥ (5:1–32)
  - E. Prelude to the flood (6:1–8)
  - F. Noaḥ and the flood (6:9–9:29)
    - 1. Preparations and embarkation (6:9–7:9)
    - 2. The flood (7:10–8:12)
    - 3. Exiting the ark and sacrifice (8:13–21)
    - 4. God's blessing, instructions, and covenant (9:1–17)
    - 5. Noaḥ and his sons (9:18–29)
  - G. The Table of Nations (10:1–32)
  - H. The Tower of Bavel (11:1–9)
  - I. The Genealogy from Shem to Avram (11:10–26)
- II. From Avraham through Yosef (11:27–50:26)
  - A. The Avraham narrative (11:27–25:18)
    - 1. Teraḥ and his sons (11:27–32)
    - 2. God's revelation and promises to Avram (12:1–13:18)
      - a. God's call and Avram's Canaan journeys (12:1–9)
      - b. Avram and Sarai in Egypt (12:10–20)

◂ c. Avram's

   c. Avram's return and separation from Lot; the eternally Promised Land (13:1–18)
3. Avram's rescue of Lot (14:1–24)
4. The covenant between the parts (15:1–21)
5. Hagar and Yishmael (16:1–16)
6. Name changes; circumcision; the promises of Yitzḥak (17:1–18:15)
7. Sedom and Amora: Avraham's pleas; God's justice (18:16–19:36)
8. Avraham and Sara in Gerar (20:1–18)
9. Birth of Yitzḥak; exile of Yishmael and Hagar; pact with Avimelekh(21:1–34)
10. The binding of Yitzḥak (22:1–19)
11. The birth of Rivka (22:20–24)
12. The death of Sara and purchase of the cave of Makhpela (23:1–19)
13. Arranging a wife for Yitzḥak (24:1–67)
14. The end of Avraham's life; Yishmael's genealogy (25:1–18)

B. The Yitzḥak narrative (25:19–28:9)
   1. Birth of Esav and Yaakov; beginning of a rivalry (25:19–34)
   2. Yitzḥak in Gerar and Be'er Sheva (26:1–33)
      a. Transfer of God's promise to Yitzḥak (26:1–5)
      b. Troubles with Philistines and pact with Avimelekh (26:6–33)
   3. Esav's Hittite wives (26:34–35)
   4. Yaakov's deceitful appropriation of Yitzḥak's blessing (27:1–41)
   5. Sending Yaakov off to find a wife (27:42–28:5)
   6. Esav's marriage to Yishmael's daughter (28:6–9)

C. The Yaakov narrative (28:10–36:43)
   1. God's promise at Beit El (28:10–22)
   2. Marriages and children in Padan Aram (29:1–30:24)
   3. Dealings with Lavan, flight to Gilad, pact at Galed (30:25–32:1)
   4. Name change and meeting with Esav (32:2–33:17)
   5. The rape of Dina at Shekhem (33:18–34:31)
   6. Transfer of God's promise to Yaakov at Beit El (35:1–15)
   7. Birth of Binyamin; death of Raḥel; death of Yitzḥak (35:16–29)
   8. Esav's descendants and kings of Edom (36:1–43)

D. The Yosef narrative (37:1–50:26)
   1. Yosef's slanders and dreams; Yaakov's favoritism; the brothers' enmity; sale of Yosef for servitude to Egypt (37:1–36)
   2. The story of Tamar and Yehuda, who acknowledges his wrong (38:1–25)
   3. Yosef: from prisoner to vizier (39–41)
   4. Yosef and his brothers in Egypt (42–45)
   5. The descent of the entire family, with God's blessing, to join Yosef in Egypt (46:1–30)
   6. The meeting with Pharaoh; settlement in the region of Ramesses (46:31–47:12)
   7. Yosef's food distribution policies; Israel in Goshen (47:13–27)
   8. Yaakov's final days, death, and burial (47:28–50:14)
      a. Burial preparation; words to Yosef; blessing of Efrayim and Menashe (47:28–48:22)

◂ b. Yaakov's

   b. Yaakov's testament to his sons (49:1-32)
   c. Yaakov's death, burial in the cave of Makhpela, return of mourning party to Egypt (49:33–50:14)
9. The brothers' fear of Yosef's revenge; Yosef's reassurance (50:15–21)
10. Yosef's last years; the oath of the Israelites to bury him in the Promised Land; Yosef's death, embalmment, and placement in a coffin (50:22–26)

Genesis in its ancient Near Eastern context

Geography and History

Three separate regions of the ancient Near East comprise the primary geographical setting of Genesis, as stated in the book itself: The Mesopotamian background of the Tower of Bavel and the itinerary of Avraham's family in chapter 11 (the Tigris and Euphrates, the two principal Mesopotamian rivers, are mentioned firstly in the Garden of Eden story – 2:14); the Greater Canaanite background of the patriarchs (and the Aramean/Amorite one of the Yaakov story); and the Egyptian background of most of the Yosef story. These are supplemented by brief references to other geographic areas such as Ararat in Anatolia (8:4) and the regions mentioned in the Table of Nations (chapter 10).

Based upon both internal and external evidence, it is probable that the patriarchal narrative – from Avraham through Yosef – correlates historically with the Middle Bronze Age in Canaan (ca. 2000–1500 BCE), and perhaps also the beginning of the Late Bronze Age (ca. 1500–1200). Two different sets of data lead convincingly to this conclusion: personal names and place names. Concerning the first set, ancient Semitic personal names often included a deity's name. However, *none* of the names in Genesis have either a theophoric beginning or ending that includes a reference to the Tetragrammaton (God's four-letter name: *y h v h*), by which, according to Exodus 6:3, God did not make Himself known to the patriarchs. Indeed, only starting in Exodus does one find names such as Yokheved and Yehoshua. Almost all the theophoric names in Genesis are compounded with *el*, e.g., Meḥiyael, Metushael (4:18), Mahalalel (5:12), Yishmael (16:11), Eldaa (25:4), and, of course, Yisrael. The presence of *el*-names indicates a commonality with such personal names and the name of a deity from inscriptions throughout the Middle Bronze Age and Lower Bronze Age – from Sinai to Shekhem, Ugarit, and Hatti (the land of the Hittites). While polytheists in Greater Canaan and Sinai originally used *el* in reference to a pagan deity, in Genesis the name was adapted and adopted to the worship of God. That no personal names in Genesis have a theophoric beginning or ending based upon the Tetragrammaton indicates a pre-Exodus historical background in the Bronze Age.

The second body of evidence relates to the place names of the homeland of Avraham's ancestors in what Genesis terms Aram Naharayim (24:10) or Padan Aram (28:2), the area of the Euphrates and Habur rivers in Syro-Mesopotamia. All the names of Avraham's immediate forefathers – Serug, Naḥor, Teraḥ – match up with places in this region, as well as the city of Ḥaran (11:31–32, 24:10, 29:4–5). From the

◂ time

time of the early Israelite monarchy, this was Aramean enemy territory, but in the Middle Bronze Age, Ḥaran was a center of Amorite (Akkadian *amurru*) tribes. A few inscriptions refer to this group as pastoralists who spoke a Northwest Semitic dialect, that is, a sister language to Hebrew (or even, perhaps, an antecedent to Hebrew). Consequently, the Genesis narratives' emphasis on a close family relationship between Avraham's descendants and his relatives in Padan Aram fits a Middle Bronze Age setting.

Other data from Genesis also suit the Middle Bronze Age, as opposed to earlier and later developments in Mesopotamia: (a) During the Old Babylonian period, the *Laws of Hammurabi*, Mari texts, and others from the 19th and 18th centuries BCE, attest to the price of a slave as approximately twenty shekels – which is the price of Yosef's sale (37:28). In the late 3rd millennium, though, the price was cheaper; in the late 2nd millennium it was higher; (b) Parity treaties, frequently preceded by negotiations, from the 19th and 18th centuries in Mari and Tell Leilan exhibit a certain form not found earlier or in the Late Bronze Age: deities are invoked, oaths are taken, stipulations are made, witnesses and a curse are stated, and treaties are accompanied by a ceremony often entailing a feast and/or sacrifice and gift-giving. Most of these features (including negotiations) are found in Genesis 21 and 26, where first Avraham and then Yitzḥak made treaties with Avimelekh, and in chapter 31, when Lavan made one with Yaakov.

Other linguistic, literary, mythological, and cultural elements in Genesis indicative of a Middle Bronze Age or early Late Bronze background are found in numerous articles throughout this volume, including on creation, the Sabbath, the Garden of Eden, Kayin and Hevel, the flood, the Tower of Bavel, the God-Avraham relationship, the historicity of the patriarchal narratives, the war of the four and five kings, the covenant between the parts, Sedom and Amora, the Philistines, the cave of Makhpela, the bride-price, inheritance rights, vows to a deity, herding pacts, sheep shearing, teraphim, and many more. These articles are based primarily upon information provided in studies by academic scholars, including archaeologists and specialists on the Tanakh and the ancient Near East. We have been particularly aided by research done by Nahum Sarna in his commentary on Genesis and other earlier and more recent scholarship, particularly by those scholars who, in the words of Moshe Greenberg, are "animated by a respect" for the text.

Polytheism versus Monotheism

In modern times, the discoveries of an abundance of ancient Near Eastern writings from many cultures – myths, law codes, treaties, temple inscriptions, prayers, wisdom instructions, etc. – have provided us with a wealth of information about the belief in the gods and their relationships with the world and its inhabitants. Certain key universal characteristics of this type of polytheism can be confirmed by published texts:

- The ancient Near Eastern gods are *natural* beings. In that sense, they are no different from humans. They eat, drink, sleep, fornicate, make war, are born, and even, sometimes, die (or can be killed). They are part and parcel of nature. However, while they are not supernatural,

◂ they are

they *are* superhuman in such characteristics as strength, longevity (some can even be resurrected), and other powers.

- While possessed of superhuman powers, the gods are not almighty. As natural beings, they are affected by nature. Other forces also limit them – the gods are subject to and cannot completely control forces such as time, magic, divination (trying to ascertain the gods' plans that will affect humans, often, in order to circumvent them), and destiny.

- *Ethically*, the gods are capricious. Sometimes they behave justly, and sometimes they do not. Nor do these ancient texts view the gods as ethical paragons. Their attitudes to humans are notably problematic. On the one hand, Mesopotamian kings saw their divine charge as ensuring justice in society. On the other, humans were created as slaves to the gods and to enable them to rest, as befits their divine royalty. As slaves, the gods rarely show care for them, other than what is necessary to ensure that these slaves provide for the gods' needs and wants.

In contrast, Genesis presents the only God, who is not only supernatural but both creator and sustainer of all of nature. He is omnipotent, and controls both time and destiny. Further, He is entirely good and, accordingly, always acts justly to humanity. What emerges, then, is that the difference between ancient Near Eastern polytheism and Genesis' ethical monotheism is much more than numerical – it's not merely about how many gods there are; it's about a completely different concept of what divinity is.

The contribution of Genesis to humanity

From its very first sentence, Genesis represents a revolution in thought and ethics against ancient Near Eastern amoral polytheism. In attempting to understand Genesis within its ancient Near Eastern context, this volume illuminates that revolution. Originally, Genesis (and the rest of the Torah) was an unknown text carried by a seemingly insignificant people who eventually precariously occupied a small piece of land buffeted between empires. In the course of human events, all the other civilizations of the ancient Near East – from Babylon to Assyria to the Hittites to Egypt – died out and, although their knowledge was eventually resurrected, they were relegated to obscurity in libraries and a few university courses attended by a sparse number of students. But that unknown text and seemingly insignificant people survived, and its vision of ethical monotheism has never ceased to challenge humanity to do better. It is the aim of this volume to help bring that vision into greater focus.

Jeremiah Unterman, Academic Editor

The books in the series are visually appealing, meant for browsing and surveying. By no means is this a book or series of books that must be read cover-to-cover. The articles are self-contained, allowing readers to skip around among topics, images, and sections that interest them. Each article has a category, indicated by a color and an icon:

ARCHAEOLOGY
A connection between the text and what has been found by archaeologists

EGYPTOLOGY
Related to ancient Egypt

NEAR EAST
Comparison with one of the surrounding civilizations, primarily Mesopotamia (Iraq and Iran), the Levant (Israel, Lebanon, Syria, Jordan, Saudi Arabia), and the Hittite Empire (Turkey)

MISHKAN
Comparing the Tabernacle in the desert or the Temple in Jerusalem to parallel ancient Near East temples and rites or helping the reader visualize how the Tabernacle and Temple might have looked

LANGUAGE
A related language construct from one of the surrounding civilizations

GEOGRAPHY
Placing a term or region mentioned in the text to a location on the map

FLORA AND FAUNA
Understanding the plants and animals to which the text refers

HALAKHA
A well-known Jewish law that is based on the text

As each article is related to a verse or sequence of verses, section introductions appear to help explain topics that are developed over a larger section of the text. For example, there were many other "creation stories" in the literature of the surrounding cultures either before or concurrent with the traditional date of the reception of the Torah. Comparing elements of the Genesis creation story to parallel literature in other cultures shows a different view of creation than the Israelite monotheistic account.

Concepts, such as the mysterious purity process using a red cow in Numbers 19, that are referenced by multiple articles, are introduced in the section introductions that appear throughout the book.

This book is very visual. Pictures and images that accompany the articles and the section introductions are meant to complement the articles and help the reader understand and visualize concepts from surrounding societies.

Where there are actual artifacts, inscriptions, museum objects, or images that illustrate a concept, term, or historical figure, the book includes pictures. Maps and reconstructions help visualize some of the objects described by the text. The series draws from previous Koren publications, for example those that visualize the Tabernacle and the plants, animals, and precious stones that were used in the Tabernacle and Temple service.

How to Read This Book

Page headers indicate book name and chapter number in Hebrew and in English

Articles are divided into color-coded categories with corresponding icons

Hebrew Tana text, in clea Koren font with vowels punctuatior and cantillati marks

Article verse number(s) and article title

New English translation

Vibrant color images help bring the narrative to life

Tanakh page

Author's initials appear after each article (see List of Contributors appendix)

Tanakh pages are read right to left honoring the authenticity of original Hebrew texts

Section introductions indicate significant themes in the biblical narrative

Highlighted text helps the reader understand a main point made in the section introduction

Section Introduction page

A section introduction occupies a full-page spread. The text reads from left to right across the spread, even though the page numbers go from right to left.

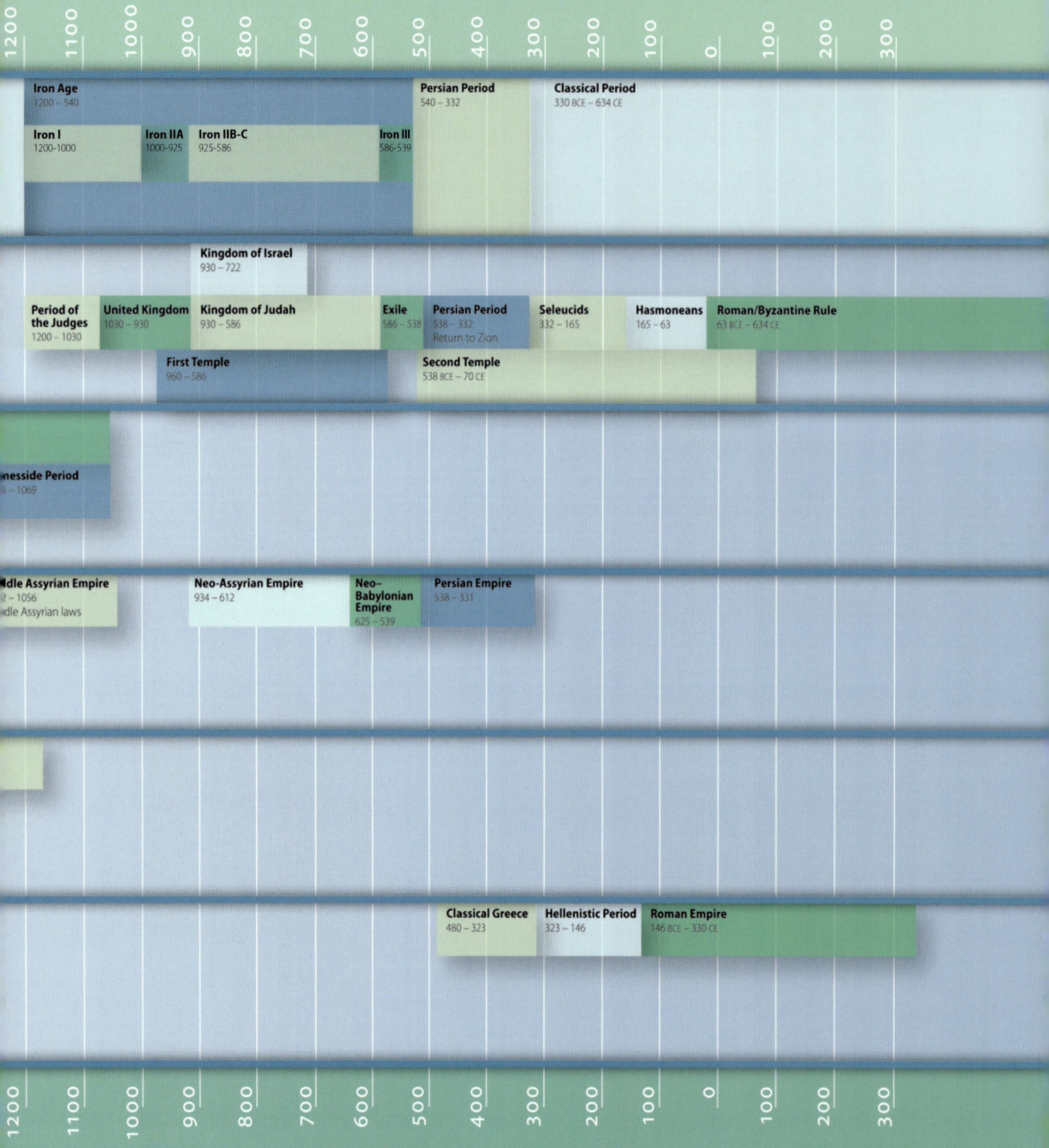
1200 1100 1000 900 800 700 600 500 400 300 200 100 0 100 200 300
Iron Age
1200 – 540
Persian Period
540 – 332
Classical Period
330 BCE – 634 CE
Iron I
1200-1000
Iron IIA
1000-925
Iron IIB-C
925-586
Iron III
586-539
Kingdom of Israel
930 – 722
Period of the Judges
1200 – 1030
United Kingdom
1030 – 930
Kingdom of Judah
930 – 586
Exile
586 – 538
Persian Period
538 – 332
Return to Zion
Seleucids
332 – 165
Hasmoneans
165 – 63
Roman/Byzantine Rule
63 BCE – 634 CE
First Temple
960 – 586
Second Temple
538 BCE – 70 CE
nesside Period
– 1069
dle Assyrian Empire
– 1056
dle Assyrian laws
Neo-Assyrian Empire
934 – 612
Neo-Babylonian Empire
625 – 539
Persian Empire
538 – 331
Classical Greece
480 – 323
Hellenistic Period
323 – 146
Roman Empire
146 BCE – 330 CE
1200 1100 1000 900 800 700 600 500 400 300 200 100 0 100 200 300

Ancient Near East Timeline

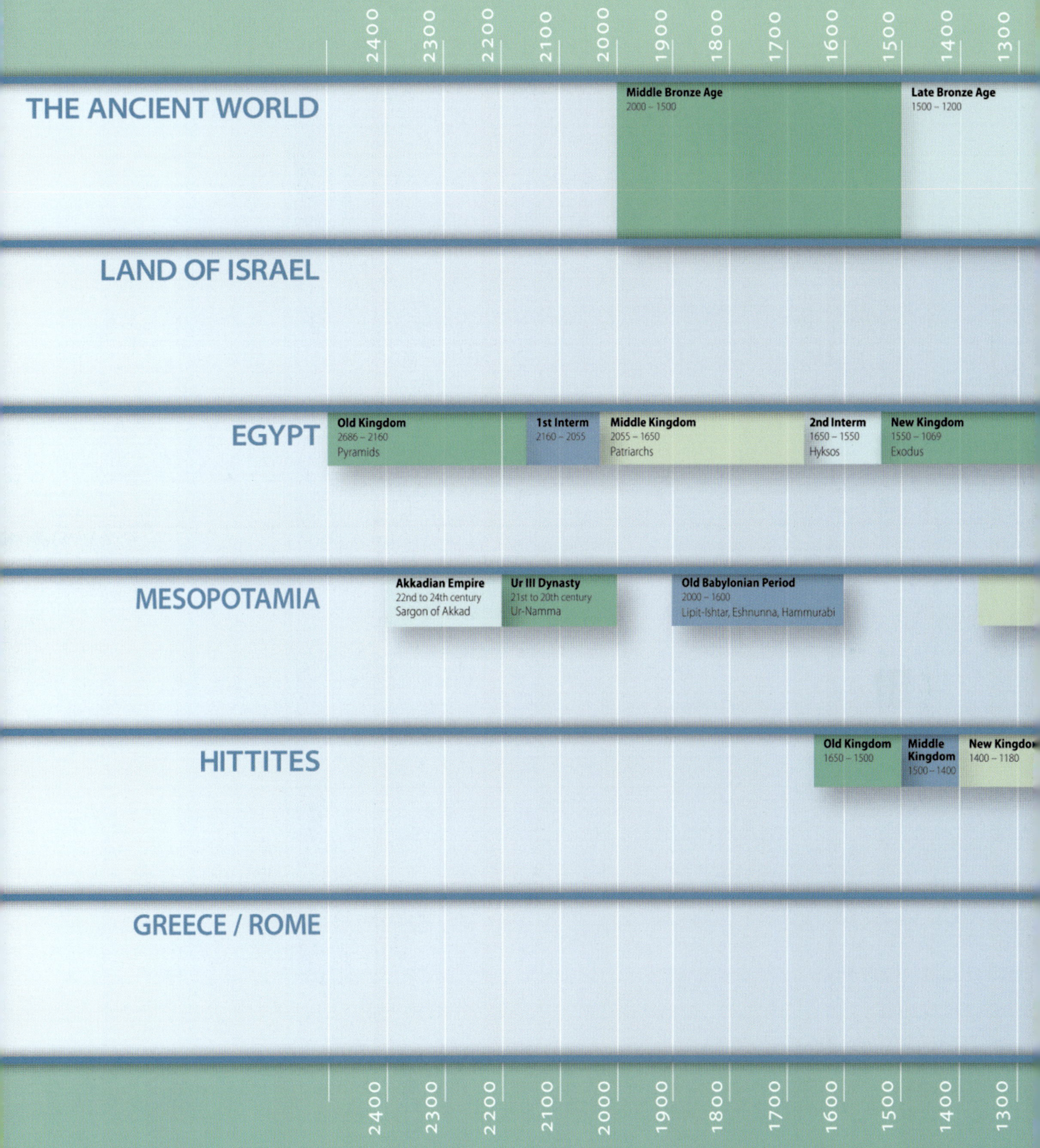

Karkemish
Ḥaran
Nineveh
Kalah
Erbil
Assyria
Ashur
Nuzi
Euphrates River
Tigris River
Tadmor
Mari
Babylonia
Babylon

Map of the Ancient Near East
Tell Tayinat
Alepp
Ugarit
Neo-Hittites
Hamat
Cyprus
Byblos
Levo Hamat
MEDITERRANEAN
SEA
Sidon
Arameans
Damascus
Tyre
Phoenicians
Dan
Hatzor
Megiddo
Israel
Raba
Jerusalem
Amon
Yehudah
Philistines
Lakhish
Aza
Be'er Sheva
Moav
Khirbet Nahash
Kadesh
Barnea
Edom
Timna
Saqqara
Memphis (Mof)
Egypt
Mount Sinai(?)
Midyan

בראשית
GENESIS

traditions. For example, the *Epic of Atrahasis* tells why humans were created (to relieve the gods from their labor), and relates the gods' efforts to control human population via plagues, the flood, and the like, resulting in the diminution of humanity.

Creation occurs as a process of construction or of generating seed (a divine, sexual act). Some texts describe creation as a series of divine acts, whereas others see a sequential process: a god creates the heavens, the heavens create the earth, the earth creates rivers, etc. As Mesopotamia, unlike Egypt, was generally not unified until the 1st millennium BCE, cosmogonies were much more varied, and the differences in the stories between locales were far greater.

By far the best-known ancient Near Eastern cosmogony is the Babylonian *Enuma Elish Epic*, named for its first two words, meaning, "When on high" in Akkadian. It shares significant commonalities with the biblical creation narrative, both in content and in sequence:

- In the beginning, nothing identifiable exists.
- The first words mention both heaven and earth.
- Water is present as part of creation.
- Tiamat (the water monster-goddess at the beginning of creation) and the Hebrew word *tehom* ("deep" water in Gen. 1:2) are probably from the same linguistic root.
- Creation of the heavens, the firmament to keep the upper waters in place, the dry land, the luminaries, and humans all occur in the same sequence.
- Divine rest follows creation.

Instruction of Merikare

Well tended is mankind – god's cattle. / He (the sun god) made sky and earth [Gen. 1:1] for their sake, / He subdued the water monster [Gen. 1:2], / He made breath for their noses to live [Gen. 2:7]. / They are his images [Gen. 1:26–27], who came from his body. / He shines in the sky for their sake; / He made for them plants and cattle, / Fowl and fish to feed them [Gen. 1:26, 28–29, 9:2–3]. / He slew his foes… / He makes daylight for their sake [Gen. 1:14–15], / He sails by to see them. / He has built his shrine around them, / When they weep he hears. /… He made for them magic as weapons / To ward off the blow of events, / Guarding them by day and by night. / He has slain the traitors among them, / As a man beats his own son for his brother's sake, / For god knows every name. (lines 131–138; square brackets indicate verses which are particularly similar to or divergent from the creation accounts in Genesis 1 and 2.)

Enuma Elish Epic – a summary

Before heaven and earth were created, only the two original gods – the male Apsu (the primeval sweet-water ocean) and the female Tiamat (the salt-water ocean) – existed. The commingling of their waters brought forth several divine offspring who, in turn, gave birth to others. As typical of exuberant teenagers, the clamor of the younger generation of gods disturbs the ancestors who are unable to sleep. The older generation of gods decides to kill the younger ones. Ea, the younger generation's "wise" god, kills Apsu and engenders the future savior (and real focus of the epic), Marduk.

Tiamat gathers her divine and monstrous allies, with Kingu as commander, and goes to war against the younger gods. The latter's assembly appoints Marduk their sovereign, and he goes out to meet Tiamat. "When Tiamat opened her mouth to devour him…he shot off an arrow…it split her heart." Having killed her, "he split her open…into two parts; half of her he set in place and formed the sky as a roof. He fixed the crossbar and posted guards…not to let her waters escape." With the other half of Tiamat, Marduk established the earth. He takes possession of the tablet of destinies, sets up the stars in constellations to define the twelve-month calendar, fixes the path of the sun, creates the moon, delineates the month into days, and arranges abodes for the gods. Marduk then kills Kingu and out of his blood creates humankind to serve the gods. Finally, he is lavishly praised by the gods. Humans are urged to remember Marduk's fifty names and rejoice in them, so that humanity's land shall be fruitful and it shall go well with them.

However, the contrasts between the two stories are remarkably revealing:

- Creation occurs through violent, unjustified conflict in the *Enuma Elish Epic* – are the noisy activities of youngsters really a good reason to kill them? By contrast, the Torah depicts a universe in which creation takes place in complete harmony as God's commands bring cosmic order into being. Not only is there no violence, the biblical ideal (Gen. 1:29–30) is that both animals and humans should be vegetarian.
- The gods are part of nature and subject to it: they are born, engage in sexual relations, give birth, and die. God in the Torah is not only above nature, but He alone rules it.
- The gods are subject to magic. In the Torah, magic can never affect God.
- The gods create humans to be their slaves. In Genesis, God creates humans to rule the earth (1:28).
- In *Enuma Elish*, humans are made out of the blood of the evil god. In Genesis 1, the human being is made in the image of God (1:26–27).
- God's day of rest at the end of creation is sanctified (Gen. 2:3).

In the end, the primary difference between creation in Mesopotamian literature and the Torah may be encapsulated in an observation by the famed Assyriologist and Bible scholar Alexander Heidel: "In Genesis, man is created in the image of God; but the Babylonians created their gods in the image of man." ▪ JU

Creation in the ancient Near East

Diverse accounts of the creation of the universe, known as cosmogonies, have been found in the remnants of polytheistic civilizations throughout the ancient Near East, originating from as far back as the 3rd millennium BCE, in both Sumer and Egypt.

Egyptian cosmogonies

In Egypt, no standard cosmogony exists to which others had to conform. Cosmogonies were developed locally – in the cities of Hermopolis (Egyptian, *Khemenu*), Heliopolis (Hebrew, *On*), Memphis (Hebrew, *Mof*), and Thebes (Hebrew, *No*). Nonetheless, some elements are commonly found:

- "Non-existence" as the state of the pre-created world, where all was one without differentiation and without even the existence of gods. This state was often described in negative terms, "before x existed," where "x" is replaced by sky, earth, men, gods, death, etc. Similar phraseology appears in both Akkadian texts and the Tanakh (Gen. 2:5; Prov. 8:24–26). In other instances, this state was described as utter darkness and limitless waters (compare Gen.1:2).
- One creator god creates many gods: The creator god is different and has a different manifestation in each cosmogony, although the sun god (under diverse names, each representing a particular phase of the sun's daily manifestation) becomes the chief god everywhere. Everything is created out of Nun, the god of primeval waters. Creating is often accomplished by separating into pairs, such as heaven and earth, light from darkness, even pairs of gods.
- Out of the waters emerged the primordial mound of earth. Sometimes the element of a cosmic egg replaces either this mound or the primeval waters.
- Depending on the given cosmogony, the process of creation occurs in three diverse ways: through a god's spittle or semen; through a god's plan and utterance; or through a god's fabricating and building, like an artisan.

The closest Egyptian parallel to Genesis 1 and 2 is the *Instruction of Merikare* (see sidebar). This selection is intriguingly similar to creation in Genesis: creation of heaven and earth by one deity, immediately followed by mention of water; breathing life into humankind; humans made in the god's image; the placement of plants, animals, fish and fowl under human control; and making daylight for human benefit. Nevertheless, there are significant divergences, as these texts place the god squarely within the norms of ancient Near Eastern paganism: the god as the sun (though here he is clearly benefactor to humanity); his battle with the "water monster" (as in *Enuma Elish*, below); humans created as carnivores; magic; and the origination of humanity in the god's body.

It is noteworthy that even though polytheism abounds in all other aspects of Egyptian life, Egyptian wisdom literature generally speaks of just one deity. The purpose of this instruction is not to describe how heaven, earth, stars, and the moon were created. Rather, it is to encourage reverence for the divinity, represented by the sun god, upon whom the king depends.

Mesopotamian cosmogonies

Most Mesopotamian cosmogonies are preserved in brief ritual texts. The principal actors and the chronology of creation are not uniform. For example, different texts attribute the primary act of creation to one god (Anu), two gods (Anu and Enlil), three gods (Anu, Enlil, and Ea), or to the divine assembly as a whole. A Sumerian tradition in Nippur speaks of the marriage of heaven and earth. Sometimes planning is mentioned, sometimes not, although most such texts assume that the gods designed the world for human benefit. Sometimes creation is mentioned briefly only as a prelude to another account, such as how agricultural tools were given to humans by the gods.

In Genesis, man is created in the image of God; but the Babylonians created their gods in the image of man.

Very few cosmogonies are found in large compositions that incorporate several

בראשית בְּרֵאשִׁית בָּרָא אֱלֹהִים אֵת הַשָּׁמַיִם וְאֵת הָאָרֶץ׃ וְהָאָרֶץ הָיְתָה ב א א
תֹהוּ וָבֹהוּ וְחֹשֶׁךְ עַל־פְּנֵי תְהוֹם וְרוּחַ אֱלֹהִים מְרַחֶפֶת עַל־פְּנֵי

1 1 2 When God began creating heaven and earth, the earth was
void and desolate, there was darkness on the face of the deep,

NEAR EAST

1:1 The beginning of what

The first three Hebrew words are translated as "when God began creating" – due to the first word, *breisheet*, appearing in the construct state, i.e., its literal meaning is, "at the beginning of." In the Tanakh, *breisheet* only appears elsewhere in Jeremiah (26:1, 27:1, 28:1, 49:34; compare Hos. 9:10), always referring to the beginning of a time period. Hence, the common translation "In the beginning, God created" is incorrect; the phrase discusses the beginning *of* God's creation.

The Akkadian cognate *reshtu* and the Egyptian *sp tpy* are used similarly in reference to time. Indeed, the Egyptian phrase is used to speak about the primordial period of time when existence was first established. ▪ JL'

NEAR EAST

1:1 Heaven and earth

The phrase "heaven and earth" appears multiple times throughout Tanakh (for example, Gen. 14:19; Ex. 20:11; Deut. 3:24; II Kings 19:15). In the context of the creation story, it is found here as well as in Genesis 2:1 and 2:4.

Many scholars understand the expression as a merism, a figure of speech in which the two contrasting extremities of a range are used to refer to the entire entity. Thus "heaven and earth" would indicate heaven, earth, and everything in between – meaning the entire universe.

Other scholars argue that the phrase is not a merism, but rather describes two separate realms or categories of matter. "Heaven and earth" also appear, for example, in Psalms 115:16 as the two basic entities in creation: "The heavens are the Lord's, but He has granted the earth to mankind." In the biblical view, everything is either part of the heavens or the earth (which also includes the seas, as seen in Psalms 148:7, "Praise the Lord from the earth: sea monsters and all the deep seas.") with nothing in between.

Similar terminology is found in ancient Egyptian and Mesopotamian literature, and the phrase itself has a direct cognate in the Akkadian *shamu u ertzetu* – for example, "to build heaven and earth" (of the gods, CAD B 88a, b). An Egyptian example from 2100–1650 BCE is: "I am the one who stills the sky for him, I am the one who silences the earth for him" (the god Shu referring to the god Atum concerning the calming of chaos after the world was created, *Coffin Texts Spell* 75). ▪ ZR

Amulet of the god Shu with arms raised to separate the sky from the earth, Egypt, faience, 7th to 1st century BCE

NEAR EAST

1:2 Pre-existence: void and desolate

The terms *tohu va-vohu* appear together only here and in Jeremiah 4:23, used as a depiction of the future destruction of Yehuda, in a passage that also mentions darkness (in that verse) and desert (v. 26). The two terms also appear as parallels in Isaiah 34:11. *Tohu* appears alone in other verses, always in the sense of uselessness, nothingness, or a wasteland or confusion (see, for example, Deut. 32:10; I Sam. 12:21; Is. 49:4; Ps. 107:40).

Mesopotamian texts do not describe the state of the cosmos before creation, with the exception of a Sumerian text mentioning darkness. At the inception of the Babylonian creation epic, *Enuma Elish* (I:5), the primeval gods Apsu and Tiamat – both personifications of watery depths – "were mingling their waters together." In ancient Egyptian texts, the time before creation is described by the phrase "before there were two things"; an era before boundaries and function were established, when nothing had yet been differentiated and brought into existence. In the Egyptian conception, this time was characterized by complete darkness and limitless waters, personified as the god Nun, whose name means "primeval waters." After creation, the primeval realm still existed at the boundaries of the current world. For example, the underworld is described in the *Book of the Dead* as "utterly deep, utterly dark, utterly endless" (ch. 175).

Thus, although Genesis does not personify or deify the elements of darkness and water as did the pagan cultures of the ancient Near East, it refers to similar conceptions and uses analogous imagery. ▪ ZR

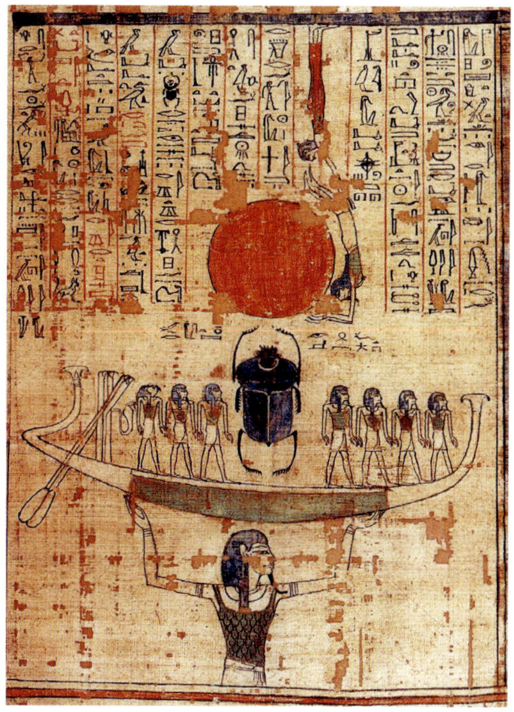

↗ God of waters of chaos, Nun, lifts the barque of the sun god Ra into the sky at the beginning of time, 11th century BCE

NEAR EAST

1:2 The deep

The translation of *tehom* as "the deep" in this verse follows a long tradition in English renderings of the Torah, but it conceals something of major significance: the definite article "the" does not appear in the text. This suggests that Biblical Hebrew used the word "deep" as a proper noun personifying the waters that covered the earth at the beginning of the creation story. Job 28:14 also does this: when asked where wisdom can be found, *tehom* says, "It is not in me!"

Though no other Hebrew word derives from it, the Semitic root *t h m*, meaning "ocean," is clearly the source of *tehom*. Ugaritic dictionaries tell us plainly how the word is used in that language to mean "ocean" or "Ocean" – the sea personified as a god who plays a role in the story of creation. In Akkadian, the word is *tamtu*, but the root also produced a name: Tiamat, the ocean-goddess, is mentioned in the Akkadian *Enuma Elish* creation story. Tiamat was the mother of the gods, who was killed in battle and split in two (as the water in Genesis 1 is split by the firmament) by Marduk to create the world. In Genesis, of course, God has no rivals and, therefore, the splitting of the water is a planned act of God as part of creation.

One thing that Ugaritic, Akkadian, and Hebrew sources share is the idea that the primordial water had to be somehow overcome by force for humans to populate the land. In the Tanakh, those stories echo in Isaiah (e.g., 51:9–10), Psalms (89:9–10), and Job (26:12). Genesis 1 alludes to them in literary fashion to debunk the notion that creation involved a battle. When "God created the great sea creatures" (v. 21), knowledgeable Israelites would understand that Rahav, the mythical monster of the sea mentioned in the Isaiah, Psalms, and Job verses, was simply another of God's creatures. ▪ MC

↗ According to some scholars, Marduk (with thunderbolt) fighting Tiamat. Temple of Ninurta, Nimrud, 9th century BCE

הַמָּיִם׃ וַיֹּאמֶר אֱלֹהִים יְהִי־אוֹר וַיְהִי־אוֹר׃ וַיַּרְא אֱלֹהִים אֶת־ ג ד
הָאוֹר כִּי־טוֹב וַיַּבְדֵּל אֱלֹהִים בֵּין הָאוֹר וּבֵין הַחֹשֶׁךְ׃ וַיִּקְרָא ה
אֱלֹהִים ׀ לָאוֹר יוֹם וְלַחֹשֶׁךְ קָרָא לָיְלָה וַיְהִי־עֶרֶב וַיְהִי־בֹקֶר
יוֹם אֶחָד׃

3 and the spirit of God moved over the waters. God said, "Let
4 there be light." And there was light. God saw the light: it was
5 good; and God separated the light from the darkness. And
God called the light "day," and the darkness He called "night."
There was evening, and there was morning – one day.

NEAR EAST

1:2 *Meraḥefet*

Meraḥefet is a rare verbal root which appears in the Tanakh only here and in Deuteronomy 32:11 in the intensive or causative *pi'el* verb form (and once in Jer. 23:9 in the simple, *qal*, verb form). In Deuteronomy, it is translated in accordance with its primary meaning, "hovers," although the translation here is "moved".

Rashi describes this action as being "like [that of] a dove" – or in Hebrew, a *yona*. While he knows that the verb in Deuteronomy 32:11 refers to an eagle, here the verb is in the feminine, so he identifies it with a dove. *Yona*, like *ruaḥ* ("spirit"), the subject, can take either a masculine or feminine verb, whereas *nesher* ("eagle"), can take only a masculine verb. In another words, Rashi is choosing a bird which, like the *ruaḥ* of God, fits either the masculine or feminine.

The verb appears six times in Ugaritic in the *Tale of Aqhat*, always in reference to eagles (as in Deut. 32:11) or to the goddess Anat flying with (or like) eagles. There, too, the eagles and Anat are hovering above something – in this case, the hero Dan'el.

From the Ugaritic tale, which mentions eagles hovering, and from Deuteronomy 32:11, where the eagle hovers over its young in a parental, caring, protective sense, we may understand that here the spirit of God is hovering over the stuff of creation, like a mother bird hovering over its young. In other words, in the last clause of this verse, where God is about to create the world, He is represented not as a sculptor or painter, but as the "mother" of creation. Thus, when God sees that each step of creation is "good" and at the completion "very good," He is not referring to an aesthetic perspective, but to a morally compassionate one, like that of a mother watching her baby emerge from the womb. ▪ JU

Young doves (*Columba palumbus altricials*) in their nest

NEAR EAST

1:3 God said, "Let there be..."

The idea that spoken words have creative power is also found in Egyptian texts. The most famous Egyptian account of creation, the *Memphite Theology*, from the temple of Ptah at Memphis, describes the creator god Ptah "who gave life to all the [gods] and their *kas* [principal aspect of the soul] as well through his heart and this tongue...in this mouth that pronounced the identity of everything, and from which Shu and Tefnut emerged and gave birth to the Ennead" (a group of nine deities in Egyptian mythology). ▪ ZR

Ramesses II and the god Ptah, Temple of Ptah, Memphis, 13th century BCE

ו וַיֹּאמֶר אֱלֹהִים יְהִי רָקִיעַ בְּתוֹךְ הַמָּיִם וִיהִי מַבְדִּיל בֵּין מַיִם
ז לָמָיִם׃ וַיַּעַשׂ אֱלֹהִים אֶת־הָרָקִיעַ וַיַּבְדֵּל בֵּין הַמַּיִם אֲשֶׁר מִתַּחַת

6 Then God said, "Let an expanse stretch through the water;
7 let it separate water from water." So God made the expanse,
and it separated the water beneath the expanse from the water

NEAR EAST

1:3–4 Light – time and quality

The fact that "light" is called "day" and "darkness," "night" indicates that a primary significance of light is its use in the demarcation of a period of time.

The association of light with time can also be seen in other cultures of the ancient Near East. In the Babylonian creation myth *Enuma Elish*, the god Marduk is described as creating time, for example, "He made the moon appear, entrusted (to him) the night. He assigned to him the crown jewel of nighttime to mark the day (of the month): Every month, without ceasing, he exalted him with a crown" (V:12–14). Similarly, the Egyptian sun god Re, with his regular rising and setting, is considered the creator of time and of the ordered universe.

As opposed to other ancient Near East cultures, only the Tanakh characterizes the light as "good." In Tanakh, light represents life (as in Ps. 56:14, "You have saved me from death, my feet from stumbling, that I may walk before God in the light of life"), joy (as in Ps. 97:11, "Light is sown for the righteous, and joy for the upright of heart"), justice (as in Zeph. 3:5, "The Lord, righteous within her midst, does no wrong; morning after morning, unfailingly, His judgment comes to light"), and deliverance (as in Is. 9:1, "The people who walked in darkness have seen abounding light; those who live in a land of death's shadow – light now bathes them"). ▪ ZR

NEAR EAST

1:6–7 The expanse

The term *rakia* as a noun is used in Hebrew only to refer to the boundary that separates earth from the heavens. In Tanakh, the verb form of this word is used for hammering metal into flat sheets (as in Ex. 39:3, "They hammered out thin sheets of gold", and Jer. 10:9, "Beaten silver is brought from Tarshish") or stamping on the ground, thus flattening it (as in Ezek. 6:11, "stamp with your feet"). This term is found in reference to God stretching out the earth over the sea (as in Ps. 136:6, "Who spread the earth upon the waters, His loving-kindness is forever").

The noun form is used in Phoenician for a gold plate (*mrq' hrs*). Here, it has the sense of a barrier stretched out and flattened, which separates the waters above from those below. Once this separation is effected, the upper waters are called "heavens," *shamayim*.

Other ancient Near Eastern societies also described heaven as separated from the earth. The Hittite *Song of Ullikummi* states that the gods "came and cut heaven and earth apart with a copper cutting tool" (A iii 40–43). Some of these myths also include a barrier separating the two. The Egyptians understood that Shu, the primordial god of the air, supports the sky (sometimes pictured as the goddess Nut), separating the primeval waters of chaos that are above the sky from the earth. The Babylonian creation epic, *Enuma Elish*, relates that Marduk killed Tiamat, the primordial goddess of the sea, and "He split her in two, like a fish for drying. Half of her he set up and made as a cover, heaven. He stretched out the hide and assigned watchmen, and ordered them not to let her waters escape" (IV:137–140). The waters on either side of the barrier, made of the hide of Tiamat, are the remnants of her body. This barrier was kept in place by cables, "leadlines, entrusted to Ea" (V:68), the god of ritual purification, responsible for ritual cleansing waters (Ea's water).

Crown, gold relief, stamped and hammered, Phoenician, reported to be from near Latakia, 10th century BCE

While the Israelite description of the separation between the waters above and below shares some elements with the ancient Near Eastern mythology, in Tanakh it is God alone who divides the waters and sets a barrier made of unspecified material between them. ▪ ZR

The sun god, with the head of a falcon crowned by the sun disc, with Akhenaten wearing a crown, Karnak, Temple of Aton, Thebes, 14th century BCE

לָרָקִ֔יעַ וּבֵ֣ין הַמַּ֔יִם אֲשֶׁ֖ר מֵעַ֣ל לָרָקִ֑יעַ וַֽיְהִי־כֵֽן׃ וַיִּקְרָ֧א אֱלֹהִ֛ים ח
לָֽרָקִ֖יעַ שָׁמָ֑יִם וַֽיְהִי־עֶ֥רֶב וַֽיְהִי־בֹ֖קֶר י֥וֹם שֵׁנִֽי׃
וַיֹּ֣אמֶר אֱלֹהִ֗ים יִקָּו֨וּ הַמַּ֜יִם מִתַּ֤חַת הַשָּׁמַ֙יִם֙ אֶל־מָק֣וֹם אֶחָ֔ד ט •
וְתֵרָאֶ֖ה הַיַּבָּשָׁ֑ה וַֽיְהִי־כֵֽן׃ וַיִּקְרָ֨א אֱלֹהִ֤ים ׀ לַיַּבָּשָׁה֙ אֶ֔רֶץ וּלְמִקְוֵ֥ה י
הַמַּ֖יִם קָרָ֣א יַמִּ֑ים וַיַּ֥רְא אֱלֹהִ֖ים כִּי־טֽוֹב׃ וַיֹּ֣אמֶר אֱלֹהִ֗ים תַּֽדְשֵׁ֤א יא •
הָאָ֙רֶץ֙ דֶּ֗שֶׁא עֵ֚שֶׂב מַזְרִ֣יעַ זֶ֔רַע עֵ֣ץ פְּרִ֞י עֹ֤שֶׂה פְּרִי֙ לְמִינ֔וֹ אֲשֶׁ֥ר
זַרְעוֹ־ב֖וֹ עַל־הָאָ֑רֶץ וַֽיְהִי־כֵֽן׃ וַתּוֹצֵ֨א הָאָ֜רֶץ דֶּ֠שֶׁא עֵ֣שֶׂב מַזְרִ֤יעַ יב

8 above. And so it was. God called the expanse "heavens." There
was evening, and there was morning – a second day.
• 9 Then God said, "Let the water beneath the heavens be
gathered to one place, and let dry ground appear." And so
10 it was. God called the dry ground "earth," and the gathered
• 11 waters He called "seas." And God saw: it was good. Then God
said, "Let the earth produce vegetation: seed-bearing plants
and trees of all the kinds on earth that grow seed-bearing fruit."
12 And so it was. The earth produced vegetation: plants bearing
seeds, each of its kind, and trees bearing fruit containing

NEAR EAST

1:9 The gathering of waters and the appearance of dry land

In the introduction to the Sumerian myth *Bird and Fish* (ca. 2064–1955 BCE), the god Enki creates the world by raising underground waters to fertilize the land: "Collecting all the waters, established their dwelling places…Suspended at his side the Tigris and Euphrates, brought them into the waters of land. Cleansed the small canals, made furrow ditches alongside them. Father Enki spread wide the stalls, provided them with shepherd and herdsmen" (lines 5–10). Although that account is like our passage, in that the water is collected in its appropriate place, it does not describe the land emerging from the water. However, Egyptian creation myths do feature a primeval hillock, a solitary island that emerges from the water. ▪ ZR

Relief of the Ogdoad, eight primordial deities worshipped in the Egyptian town that was renamed Hermopolis by the Greeks, Temple of Hathor, 1st century CE ↙

NEAR EAST

1:11–12 Let the earth produce vegetation…and so it was

Although the previous elements in creation were brought into existence directly by the word of God, here the earth produces vegetation using the powers God had imbued in it. These powers are activated by the word of God, with the earth producing the plant life needed for agriculture.

The idea that the gods establish the system by which vegetation can grow is also seen in the Sumerian creation text KAR 4 (copied ca. 1100 BCE) where in order "to prepare the irrigation system" the gods "determined the course of the Tigris and Euphrates," (lines 5–6) where the created humans will do their agricultural work. People can then "install the irrigation system to provide water everywhere and thus make all kinds of plants grow" (lines 26–29).

As Nahum Sarna points out, in the ancient Near East, the natural sources of power were individually deified and developed into fertility cults, such as that of the Sumerian god Dumuzid. In Genesis, this pagan viewpoint is negated, as all of nature's productive forces are created by God and exist only by His will. ▪ ZR

זֶ֤רַע לְמִינֵ֔הוּ וְעֵ֧ץ עֹֽשֶׂה־פְּרִ֛י אֲשֶׁ֥ר זַרְעוֹ־ב֖וֹ לְמִינֵ֑הוּ וַיַּ֥רְא אֱלֹהִ֖ים
יג כִּי־טֽוֹב׃ וַֽיְהִי־עֶ֥רֶב וַֽיְהִי־בֹ֖קֶר י֥וֹם שְׁלִישִֽׁי׃
• יד וַיֹּ֣אמֶר אֱלֹהִ֗ים יְהִ֤י מְאֹרֹת֙ בִּרְקִ֣יעַ הַשָּׁמַ֔יִם לְהַבְדִּ֕יל בֵּ֥ין הַיּ֖וֹם
טו וּבֵ֣ין הַלָּ֑יְלָה וְהָי֤וּ לְאֹתֹת֙ וּלְמ֣וֹעֲדִ֔ים וּלְיָמִ֖ים וְשָׁנִֽים׃ וְהָי֤וּ לִמְאוֹרֹת֙

seeds, each of its kind. And God saw: it was good. There was 13
evening, and there was morning – a third day.
Then God said, "Let there be lights in the heavens' expanse 14 •
to separate day from night and to serve for signs and seasons,
days and years. They shall be lights in the heavens' expanse, 15

NEAR EAST

1:14 Signs and seasons, days and years

The idea that astronomical bodies enable the measuring of time, days, months, and years echoes a theme found in many ancient Near Eastern creation narratives. The Sumerian version of the prologue to the *Great Astrological Treatise* begins, "When An, Enlil, and Enki, the great gods, in their ineffable counsel, among the great laws of heaven and earth, had established the crescent of the moon, which brought forth day, established the months and furnished the omens drawn from heaven and earth…." The Akkadian version of the omen series *Enuma Anu Elil* ("When Anu and Elil") opens with, "When Anu, Elil and Ea, the great gods, by their decision laid down the design of heaven and earth, and assigned to the great gods their functions, to create the day, to renew the month for mankind to behold, they saw Shamash (the sun god) in (his) gate, they made him appear regularly in heaven and earth." Similarly, the Egyptian *Morning Hymn to Amun-Re* (the Egyptian god Amun fused with the sun god Ra) states, "You who create the years, join months together – days, nights, and hours occur according to your footsteps." ▪ ZR

Shrine of Amun-Re, mortuary temple of Hatshepsut, Deir el-Bahari (northwest of Luxor), 15th century BCE

טז בִּרְקִיעַ הַשָּׁמַיִם לְהָאִיר עַל־הָאָרֶץ וַיְהִי־כֵן׃ וַיַּעַשׂ אֱלֹהִים
אֶת־שְׁנֵי הַמְּאֹרֹת הַגְּדֹלִים אֶת־הַמָּאוֹר הַגָּדֹל לְמֶמְשֶׁלֶת הַיּוֹם
יז וְאֶת־הַמָּאוֹר הַקָּטֹן לְמֶמְשֶׁלֶת הַלַּיְלָה וְאֵת הַכּוֹכָבִים׃ וַיִּתֵּן
יח אֹתָם אֱלֹהִים בִּרְקִיעַ הַשָּׁמָיִם לְהָאִיר עַל־הָאָרֶץ׃ וְלִמְשֹׁל בַּיּוֹם
וּבַלַּיְלָה וּלֲהַבְדִּיל בֵּין הָאוֹר וּבֵין הַחֹשֶׁךְ וַיַּרְא אֱלֹהִים כִּי־טוֹב׃
יט וַיְהִי־עֶרֶב וַיְהִי־בֹקֶר יוֹם רְבִיעִי׃
כ וַיֹּאמֶר אֱלֹהִים יִשְׁרְצוּ הַמַּיִם שֶׁרֶץ נֶפֶשׁ חַיָּה וְעוֹף יְעוֹפֵף עַל־
כא הָאָרֶץ עַל־פְּנֵי רְקִיעַ הַשָּׁמָיִם׃ וַיִּבְרָא אֱלֹהִים אֶת־הַתַּנִּינִם
הַגְּדֹלִים וְאֵת כָּל־נֶפֶשׁ הַחַיָּה ׀ הָרֹמֶשֶׂת אֲשֶׁר שָׁרְצוּ הַמַּיִם
כב לְמִינֵהֶם וְאֵת כָּל־עוֹף כָּנָף לְמִינֵהוּ וַיַּרְא אֱלֹהִים כִּי־טוֹב׃ וַיְבָרֶךְ
אֹתָם אֱלֹהִים לֵאמֹר פְּרוּ וּרְבוּ וּמִלְאוּ אֶת־הַמַּיִם בַּיַּמִּים וְהָעוֹף
כג יִרֶב בָּאָרֶץ׃ וַיְהִי־עֶרֶב וַיְהִי־בֹקֶר יוֹם חֲמִישִׁי׃
כד וַיֹּאמֶר אֱלֹהִים תּוֹצֵא הָאָרֶץ נֶפֶשׁ חַיָּה לְמִינָהּ בְּהֵמָה וָרֶמֶשׂ
כה וְחַיְתוֹ־אֶרֶץ לְמִינָהּ וַיְהִי־כֵן׃ וַיַּעַשׂ אֱלֹהִים אֶת־חַיַּת הָאָרֶץ
לְמִינָהּ וְאֶת־הַבְּהֵמָה לְמִינָהּ וְאֵת כָּל־רֶמֶשׂ הָאֲדָמָה לְמִינֵהוּ

16 shining upon the earth." And so it was. God made the two
great lights – the greater light to rule by day and the lesser light
17 to rule by night – and the stars. God set them in the heavens'
18 expanse to shine upon the earth, to rule by day and by night
and to separate light from darkness. And God saw that it was
19 good. There was evening, and there was morning – a fourth
day.
20 Then God said, "Let the water teem with swarms of living
creatures, and let birds fly over the earth across the heavens'
21 expanse." So God created the great sea serpents, and all the
kinds of crawling, living things that swarm in the water, and
all the kinds of winged, flying creatures. And God saw that it
22 was good. God blessed them, saying: "Be fertile and multiply
and fill the waters of the seas, and let flying creatures multiply
23 on earth." There was evening, and there was morning – a fifth
day.
24 Then God said, "Let the land produce every kind of living
thing: all the different species of cattle, crawling things and
25 wild animals of the earth." And so it was. God made the
different kinds of wild animals of the earth, and cattle, and
all the species of creature that creep upon land. And God saw

NEAR EAST

1:16 Stars

In this verse, God creates the stars, places them, and gives them their functions.

Significantly, while Mesopotamian accounts also speak of the gods establishing the stars in their positions and assigning them functions, they did not attribute to the gods the creation of the stars. For example, in the Akkadian version of the second prologue to the *Great Astrological Treatise*, the great gods Anu, Enlil, and Ea "installed the stars." The Mesopotamian astronomical collection *Mul Apin* (ca. 1000 BCE) divides the stars into the paths of Anu, Enlil, and Ea, representing the equatorial, northern and southern sections of the sky. Similarly, in the Babylonian epic *Enuma Elish*, the god Marduk is stated to have "established (in) constellations the stars…He set up twelve months of three stars each" (V:2–4). Of course, ancient Near Eastern civilizations were not aware of the physical compositions of the stars. ▪ ZR

Fragment of a tablet from the *Mul Apin* astrological series, Neo-Babylonian, 7th to 6th century BCE

NEAR EAST

1:21 The great sea creatures (*taninim*)

In this verse, "the great sea creatures" (*taninim*) are mentioned as one of the species that God created on the fourth day. In context, the verse raises two questions: First, all other animals are described by collective nouns signifying entire zoological groups (*sheretz*, *of hashamayim*, *degat hayam*, *ḥaya*, *behema*, *remes*, and even *adam*). Why then is *taninim* the only species mentioned specifically? Second, why are the *taninim* – a term that usually refers to crocodiles, which are not singularly large or fierce – designated as "great"?

The appearance of *tanin* or *taninim* in other passages in the Prophets and Writings may help answer these questions. In some instances, the *tanin* is used as a symbol of the forces of evil and chaos, or of God's enemies. For example, Iyov questions God "Am I Yam or the sea monster (*tanin*)? Why do You place me under guard?" (Job 7:12). Medieval Jewish interpreters viewed *tanin* or *taninim* in the same way. For example: "Rise, rise, and don your dress of might, the Lord's strong arm. Rise as long ago in the earliest time – was it not You who cleaved Rahav, beat the Serpent (*tanin*) down?" (Is. 51:9). Rashi interprets "Rahav" as Egypt and *tanin* as a reference to Pharaoh – Israel's and God's enemy.

One of the most important Ugaritic discoveries was the myths about the Canaanite gods Baal and Anat, who fought against the god Yamm (literally, "The Sea") and his sea monsters – *tunnanu* (*tanin*), *bathnu bariḥu* ("The Fleeing Serpent"), and *bathnu 'aqallatanu* ("The Twisty Serpent"; compare Is. 27:1). In the Ugaritic *Baal Cycle* myth, Anat cries out:

> What enemy rises against Baal,
> What foe against the Cloud-Rider?
>
> Surely I fought Yamm,
> the Beloved of El,
> Surely I finished off River,
> The great God,
>
> Surely I fought Tunnan (*tunnanu*) and destroyed him.
> I fought the Twisty Serpent (*bathna 'aqallatana*),
> The Potent with Seven heads...
> (KTU 1.3 iii 37–42).

In light of this Ugaritic tradition, some researchers hypothesized that the reference in our verse serves a polemical purpose, combatting a similar ancient tradition that may have existed in Israel (with echoes in various passages in the Prophets and Writings) of God's conquest of the sea and the great sea creatures. This ancient tradition, probably transmitted as an oral epic song, proclaimed the triumph of God in primordial combat over the forces of chaos (great sea monsters). Only when God vanquished the resistance of Yamm and his assistants (the sea monsters), did God turn to create the universe (compare Ps. 74:12–17).

A talmudic passage may also reflect this ancient Israelite tradition: "At the time when the Holy One, blessed be He, sought to create the world, He said to the minister of the sea: Open your mouth and swallow all the waters of the world so that there will be room for land. The minister of the sea said before Him: Master of the Universe, it is enough that I will stay within my own waters. God immediately struck him and killed him; as it is stated: 'With His might He strikes Yam; by His guile He crushes Rahav' (Job 26:12)" (Bava Batra 74b).

The specific mention of the *taninim hagedolim*, then, would contextualize the tradition by emphasizing that God is the sole creator and ruler of the world, thus erasing the mythic theme in which the great monster *tanin* was one of God's adversaries before creation. The text stresses that they were created by God. Thus, the *taninim* are like other animals; they did not predate or resist creation. The plural form of the noun adds to the notion that the *taninim* are one of God's created animals. ▪ SNY

Chest depicting king making offering to the crocodile god Sobek, Egypt, ca. 1st century BCE

וַיַּרְא אֱלֹהִים כִּי־טוֹב׃ וַיֹּאמֶר אֱלֹהִים נַעֲשֶׂה אָדָם בְּצַלְמֵנוּ כו
כִּדְמוּתֵנוּ וְיִרְדּוּ בִדְגַת הַיָּם וּבְעוֹף הַשָּׁמַיִם וּבַבְּהֵמָה וּבְכָל־הָאָרֶץ
וּבְכָל־הָרֶמֶשׂ הָרֹמֵשׂ עַל־הָאָרֶץ׃ וַיִּבְרָא אֱלֹהִים ׀ אֶת־הָאָדָם כז
בְּצַלְמוֹ בְּצֶלֶם אֱלֹהִים בָּרָא אֹתוֹ זָכָר וּנְקֵבָה בָּרָא אֹתָם׃ וַיְבָרֶךְ כח
אֹתָם אֱלֹהִים וַיֹּאמֶר לָהֶם אֱלֹהִים פְּרוּ וּרְבוּ וּמִלְאוּ אֶת־הָאָרֶץ
וְכִבְשֻׁהָ וּרְדוּ בִּדְגַת הַיָּם וּבְעוֹף הַשָּׁמַיִם וּבְכָל־חַיָּה הָרֹמֶשֶׂת עַל־
הָאָרֶץ׃ וַיֹּאמֶר אֱלֹהִים הִנֵּה נָתַתִּי לָכֶם אֶת־כָּל־עֵשֶׂב ׀ זֹרֵעַ זֶרַע כט
אֲשֶׁר עַל־פְּנֵי כָל־הָאָרֶץ וְאֶת־כָּל־הָעֵץ אֲשֶׁר־בּוֹ פְרִי־עֵץ זֹרֵעַ
זָרַע לָכֶם יִהְיֶה לְאָכְלָה׃ וּלְכָל־חַיַּת הָאָרֶץ וּלְכָל־עוֹף הַשָּׁמַיִם ל
וּלְכֹל ׀ רוֹמֵשׂ עַל־הָאָרֶץ אֲשֶׁר־בּוֹ נֶפֶשׁ חַיָּה אֶת־כָּל־יֶרֶק עֵשֶׂב

26 that it was good. Then God said, "Let us make humankind
in our image, our likeness, that they may rule over the fish
of the sea and the flying creatures of the heavens, the cattle
and all the earth, and every living creature that moves upon
27 the earth." So God created humankind in His image: in the
image of God He created him; male and female He created
28 them. God blessed them, saying, "Be fertile and multiply. Fill
the earth and subdue it. Rule over the fish of the sea, and the
flying creatures of the heavens, and every living thing that
29 moves upon the earth." Then God said, "I give you all these
seed-bearing plants on the face of the earth and every tree
30 with seed-bearing fruit. They shall be yours to eat. And to all
the beasts of the earth and birds of the heavens and everything
that crawls over the earth and has within it living spirit – I give

NEAR EAST

1:26–30 The creation and role of humans in the ancient Near East

In most Mesopotamian sources of the 2nd millennium BCE, such as the Babylonian creation epic, humans were created from the blood of an evil god. Their purpose was to serve as slaves to the gods, providing them with food, drink, and housing (temples) so they could rest. Even if the gods created food for humans, it was in order for the humans to be able to provide for the gods, as in the Sumerian composition *Bird and Fish*. In Genesis, by contrast, God gives the Earth to humanity as a fiefdom, to "fill the earth and subdue it" and to "rule over" all living creatures. Since He is supernatural, God has no need of physical sustenance (e.g., Ps. 50:8–15).

In the ancient Near East, an image could have one of three purposes:

1. an idol represented a deity – once an idol was consecrated, this physical image of the deity was thought to contain his spirit or essence.
2. a king's sculpted image would be depicted in monuments to be placed in lands that his army had conquered;
3. the king was understood as the image of a god. For example, among Egyptian pharaohs, the name Tutankhamun means "the living image of (the god) Amun," and Thutmose IV was designated "the likeness of Re." A Mesopotamian salutation states, "the king, my lord, is the very image of Bel."

Thutmose IV, granite statue, Médamoud, early 14th century BCE

In ancient Near Eastern literature, the only text that has been discovered which mentions a god creating humanity in his image is the Egyptian *Instruction of Merikare*, which speaks of the sun god's relationship to humans (see "Creation in the ancient Near East" on page 3): "They are his images, who came from his body." The reference to humans as the product of the god's body emphasizes his physical nature.

The Mesopotamian *Epic of Atrahasis* illustrates the gods' opposition to human overpopulation, to the extent that they send plagues, drought, and famine to diminish humanity's numbers. In contrast, God blesses people to "be fertile and multiply" and "fill the earth."

Verse 26 of the epic states, "Let us make humankind in our image, our likeness, that they may rule over" the earth and all living creatures. The implication is that humans are made to be rulers in God's image. As God is metaphysical, any image of God must point to a non-physical quality, such as virtue; God is the best possible ruler, so humans also have to be good rulers. That explains why the Genesis creation story alone, out of the entire ancient Near East literature, portrays humans as ideally created to be vegetarians (v. 29). After all, good rulers do not eat their subjects! It is not until the end of the flood story that humanity is permitted by God to eat animals (9:2–3).

The Torah here presents a revolutionary idea: while in Mesopotamia only the king is made in the image of a deity, in Genesis the image of God as ruler is at the essence of *every* human being – a democratization of humanity unlike anything else known in the world. ▪ JU

לא לְאָכְלָה וַיְהִי־כֵן׃ וַיַּרְא אֱלֹהִים אֶת־כׇּל־אֲשֶׁר עָשָׂה וְהִנֵּה־טוֹב
מְאֹד וַיְהִי־עֶרֶב וַיְהִי־בֹקֶר יוֹם הַשִּׁשִּׁי׃
ב ••א ב וַיְכֻלּוּ הַשָּׁמַיִם וְהָאָרֶץ וְכׇל־צְבָאָם׃ וַיְכַל אֱלֹהִים בַּיּוֹם הַשְּׁבִיעִי

31 every green plant for food." And so it was. Then God saw all
that He had made: and it was very good. There was evening,
and there was morning – the sixth day.
2 1•• So the heavens and the earth were finished, and all their vast
2 array. On the seventh day God finished the work that He had

NEAR EAST

2:1–3 The Sabbath in contrast to Mesopotamian divine rest

These verses underscore three items: God finished His work on the seventh day; on that day, He rested from His work of creation; and He blessed and sanctified the seventh day. Interestingly, the proper noun for the seventh day, the Sabbath (in context, literally, "cessation" from work) is not found in this narrative (indeed, it does not appear in the Torah until Exodus 16:23, 25, 26, 29), although the verb form appears twice. The laws commanding the Israelites to observe the Sabbath are first mentioned in Exodus, with particular emphasis in the Ten Commandments on the verses here as providing the reason for its observance (Ex. 20:8–11).

The idea of creation and its subsequent divine rest taking place in a seven-day period (or even in seven parts) is unique to the Torah. No other ancient Near Eastern culture conceived of anything similar. To be sure, ancient Mesopotamia recognized particular seven-day cultic observances, such as the Sumerian king Gudea's dedication of the Lagash temple in a seven-day festival (compare. Shlomo's dedication festival, which probably included Sukkot, I Kings 8:65–66), and a seven-day Old Babylonian ritual at Larsa. However, these were one-time affairs and not comparable to the Genesis creation narrative, or to the biblical week.

In the aftermath of Marduk's creation of the world after killing the older gods, he does provide rest for the gods by creating humankind to relieve the deities of their burdens (*Enuma Elish Epic* VI:5–8). The gods, in return, build his great temple for him to live in, where they too can rest when visiting him (VI:49–74). Of course, that temple, and those for other deities, are designed for the care and feeding of the gods – who are required to eat and sleep due to their inability to escape their essence as natural beings.

In the Torah, the supernatural, one God needs no rest. Rather, His "rest" at the end of the creation narrative is there only to serve as a model for the Israelites, who will be required to create a just society in which all members – even slaves – must rest one day a week. That ethical practice was absent everywhere else in the ancient Near East, as Near Eastern polytheism viewed humans as continual slaves to the gods. In contrast, in the Torah, humans were required to imitate God, not to provide for Him.

Numerous academic scholars have tried to (unsuccessfully) link the biblical weekly Sabbath with ancient Mesopotamia by pointing to three primary similarities:

- There may be a linguistic link in the Akkadian, Old Babylonian *Epic of Atrahasis*, where Sumerian terms for moon phases were translated as *arḫu* (new moon), *sebutu* (quarter moon, seventh day), and *shapattu* (full moon, 15th day; *shapattu* – which itself may have entered Akkadian as a loanword, for it has no attached Akkadian verbal root – may possibly refer to the cessation of the growth of the moon).
- However, while the cultic and civil calendar of Mesopotamia was tied to the phases of the moon, the biblical week is revolutionary in the ancient world, as it is wholly independent of lunar (or solar) calculation. The Mesopotamian month and year were dependent upon the moon, and the day, of course, upon the sun, but the biblical week was not in the least part of any phenomenon in nature.
- In the late 1st millennium BCE – around the time of the beginning of the Second Temple period – in Achaemenid texts from Uruk, the Neo-Babylonian lunar sacrifices typically fell on the 7th, 14th, 21st, and 28th days of the month, sometimes a day or two earlier.
- By contrast, in the Tanakh, no holidays are mentioned as connected with the moon except for Rosh Ḥodesh ("the head/beginning of the month"), and possibly *kesseh* (Ps. 81:4; also, the first of the month of Tishrei, but it is not designated as Rosh Hashana – "the head/beginning of the year" in the Bible, but only in later Judaism). Furthermore, it is impossible to align the biblical week with the days of the lunar month, since the latter takes approximately 29¼ days.
- In the Third Dynasty of Ur (Sumer, 22nd to 21st century BCE), certain groups were given days of rest and holidays. These occasions, however, were tied to the lunar calendar, and none occurred at weekly intervals. ▪ JU

↗ Sacred basin, extensively reconstructed, dedicated by Gudea to the Temple of Ningirsu, Girsu (Iraq), 22nd century BCE

מְלַאכְתּוֹ אֲשֶׁר עָשָׂה וַיִּשְׁבֹּת בַּיּוֹם הַשְּׁבִיעִי מִכָּל־מְלַאכְתּוֹ אֲשֶׁר
עָשָׂה: וַיְבָרֶךְ אֱלֹהִים אֶת־יוֹם הַשְּׁבִיעִי וַיְקַדֵּשׁ אֹתוֹ כִּי בוֹ שָׁבַת ג
מִכָּל־מְלַאכְתּוֹ אֲשֶׁר־בָּרָא אֱלֹהִים לַעֲשׂוֹת:
שני אֵלֶּה תוֹלְדוֹת הַשָּׁמַיִם וְהָאָרֶץ בְּהִבָּרְאָם בְּיוֹם עֲשׂוֹת יְהוָה ד
אֱלֹהִים אֶרֶץ וְשָׁמָיִם: וְכֹל ׀ שִׂיחַ הַשָּׂדֶה טֶרֶם יִהְיֶה בָאָרֶץ וְכָל־ ה
עֵשֶׂב הַשָּׂדֶה טֶרֶם יִצְמָח כִּי לֹא הִמְטִיר יְהוָה אֱלֹהִים עַל־הָאָרֶץ
וְאָדָם אַיִן לַעֲבֹד אֶת־הָאֲדָמָה: וְאֵד יַעֲלֶה מִן־הָאָרֶץ וְהִשְׁקָה ו
אֶת־כָּל־פְּנֵי הָאֲדָמָה: וַיִּיצֶר יְהוָה אֱלֹהִים אֶת־הָאָדָם עָפָר ז
מִן־הָאֲדָמָה וַיִּפַּח בְּאַפָּיו נִשְׁמַת חַיִּים וַיְהִי הָאָדָם לְנֶפֶשׁ חַיָּה:

done, and on the seventh day He rested from all the work that
3 He had done. God blessed the seventh day and sanctified it,
because on it He rested from all His work, from all that God
had created and done.
4 This is the story of the heavens and the earth when they
were created, on the day the Lord God made earth and
5 heaven. No shrub of the field yet grew on earth, and no
plant had yet sprouted, for the Lord God had not yet
brought rain upon the earth, and there was no one to work
6 the land. A mist would rise up from the earth and water
7 all the face of the land. Then the Lord God formed man
from the dust of the land[1] and breathed the breath of
life into his nostrils, and the man became a living being.

1 | The Hebrew *adam* (man) resonates with *adama* (land).

NEAR EAST

2:1 Array

The "vast array" (v. 1) of the heavens and the earth is literally *tsava*, "army" (and indeed the English word "array" originally had military connotations). However, *tsava* also refers to a workforce, as in, e.g., Ex. 38:8; see also Is. 40:2; Job 7:1).

In Akkadian, the related word *tsabu* can refer to soldiers or to a city work crew rebuilding the embankment of the Tigris River, or even simply to the people of a town. In Deuteronomy 4:19, the *tsava* of heaven is identified as consisting of the sun, moon, and stars. Here, the implication is that all creation on earth is a team arrayed in service of God, just as the heavenly bodies are. ▪ MC

NEAR EAST

2:5 No plant had yet sprouted, for the Lord God had not yet brought rain upon the earth

Descriptions of the primitive world and humankind in a state without agriculture or watering are also found in ancient Near Eastern texts. The earliest recorded Sumerian creation myth, *Eridu Genesis* (ca. 1600 BCE), describes how man was created by the gods to cultivate the land, care for flocks, and worship the gods. Restored sections of this myth describe the miserable condition people were in before attaining the benefits of civilization, "In those days no canals were opened, no dredging was done at dikes and ditches on dike tops." There were years of suffering and famine, with no food being produced, "no (one of) all the countries was planting in furrows."

Note that in our verse, the reason that nothing was growing was that God had not yet watered the land, and man had not yet been created. There was no period of hardship, though, after man was created. In Genesis, man is sophisticated from the outset, as demonstrated by his ability to name the animals (v. 20). ▪ ZR

↖ Agricultural scenes, tomb of Nakht's offering chapel, facsimile by Norman de Garis Davies, original Thebes, 14th century BCE

LANGUAGE

2:6 *Ed*

The "mist" of this verse is *ed*, a word found only one other time in the Tanakh, in Job 36:27 – a usage that does not help clarify the meaning here. Since land from which a mist rises would not seem to need watering, a common alternative understanding (offered by Rashi) is that *ed* refers to a "stream" or "flow" of water, perhaps from underground.

Akkadian *edu*, ("onrush of water,") suggests that the latter meaning is correct. The Hebrew word cannot refer to an "onrush," but neither *ed* nor *edu* is originally Semitic; both words seem to be related to the Sumerian *adea* ("flooding") and *id* ("river course,") which can refer to the Abzu, the Sumerian name for the cosmic, subterranean waters that will play a significant role in the flood (Gen. 7:11). Perhaps, then, *ed* is best understood as an "upsurge" of subterranean waters which drenched the earth. ▪ MC

NEAR EAST

2:7 The creation of man from the dust of the earth

Here, man is described as being formed by God from "the dust of the land." In Job, the parallel term "clay" is used, "You kneaded me like clay" (Job 10:9) and "I too was cut from clay" (Job 33:6).

The idea of man being formed from clay is also found in Egyptian art, with the god Khnum making human beings with a potter's wheel. He was believed to create the bodies of babies at this potter's wheel, and then place them in their mothers' wombs. The Egyptian *Instruction of Amenemope* (ca. 1300–1075 BCE), containing advice for a successful life, states "Man is clay and straw, and God is his potter" (ch. 25). "God" in Egyptian wisdom literature is a reference to the concept of deity in Egyptian polytheistic religion, not to a specific deity.

Similarly, the Mesopotamian myth *Enki and Ninmah* relates that "Ninmah took in her hand clay from the top of the Abzu (the primeval subterranean ocean), she fashioned from it the first man" (ll 58–59). In the ancient world, clay was a familiar natural resource, abundantly and easily available in alluvial plains, particularly in Mesopotamia. People used clay as the raw material for bricks, pottery, figurines, and tablets.

The idea that a deity breathes life into man through his nostrils can also be seen in Egyptian literature. Shu, the god who symbolizes dry air and preservation, states that he gives life "through my mouth, which is Life in their nostrils, I will lead my breath into their throats" (*Coffin Texts Spell* 2 40c–43h). In the *Instruction of Merikare* (ca. 2000 BCE), the god Re is also said to have given man life because he "made breath for their noses to live." ▪ ZR

↗ The god Amun-Re (right) holding the ankh, symbolizing life, to the nose of Ramesses II, mortuary temple of Ramesses II, Luxor, 13th century BCE

The epic of gilgamesh – a summary

The powerful Gilgamesh, although human in appearance, is actually half-man, half-god, born of the union of a man and a goddess. As king of the great city of Uruk, he takes the damsels for himself and puts the men to hard labor. His tyranny results in the townspeople beseeching the gods for relief, who respond by creating a hairy, wild man of great strength named Enkidu, who runs, grazes, and drinks with the animals. Enkidu is to be a companion to Gilgamesh, "an equal to his stormy heart," thereby diverting Gilgamesh from his despotic rule. Gilgamesh, upon learning of this wild man, sends a courtesan to seduce him, to alienate the animals from him. She lays with Enkidu for six days and seven nights, at the end of which the animals flee from him. Although he himself was somewhat physically diminished, Enkidu's "understanding had broadened." The courtesan says to him, "You are beautiful… you are become like a god," and dresses him and takes him to Uruk. There he has a mighty wrestling match with Gilgamesh, to whom he loses. Enkidu pledges his friendship to the victor, and the two become inseparable.

After several dangerous adventures, including displeasing the gods by killing the ogre Humbaba and "the bull of heaven," the gods decide that one of the two friends should perish. The lot falls upon Enkidu, who takes ill and dies. Gilgamesh is devastated with sorrow, but also comes to an even more distressing conclusion: if Enkidu could die, so could he. He then goes on a search for immortality. After traversing a beautiful garden made of precious stones and sailing across the sea of death, he finds Utnapishtim, who, together with his wife, had been the only two humans to survive the flood (see "The flood story in the Bible and ancient Mesopotamia" on pages 40–41), and were granted immortality by the gods. Utnapishtim informs Gilgamesh that the gods will not grant that same boon to him. Nevertheless, Utnapishtim does tell him about a plant at the bottom of the sea, which will make him young again if he eats of it. Gilgamesh finds the plant, but when he bathes in a spring, "a snake…silently came up and carried off the plant. While going back, it sloughed off its casing" due to the effect of the plant. This element of the story reflected the ancients' belief that snakes were immortal because they sloughed their skin. His last hope for immortality gone, Gilgamesh returns to Uruk, where he takes solace in the enduring walls of his city. If even he, who had a divine parent, could not achieve immortality, then all humans must die.

The capriciousness of ancient Near Eastern deities rendered its polytheism incapable of producing a foundational story which revolved around divine and human morality.

ked, and they immediately sew belts (the literal meaning of Hebrew *ḥagorot*; compare I Kings 2:5; Ezek. 23:15) of fig leaves to cover their genitals (see "Fig leaves" on page 23). The next time the word "knowledge" is used is in 4:1: "the man knew his wife Ḥava." The informed reader comprehends that "knowledge of good and evil" is a euphemism for puberty or for sexual knowledge, understanding, and ability, and is so used elsewhere in Tanakh (Deut. 1:39; II Sam. 19:36; Is. 7:15–16). In the Garden of Eden story, "knowledge of good and evil" has the further, logical connotation of creative abilities (3:22). This is the reason that when God punishes the humans for both their disobedience and their refusal to admit guilt by accepting responsibility for their actions (3:12–13), they are sentenced in regard to their individualized creative abilities, the woman concerning childbirth and the man in farming (3:16–19). Additionally, they are banished from the Garden of Eden, because God understands that "Now that man has become like one of us, knowing good and evil, he must not be allowed to…take also of the Tree of Life, eat, and live forever" (3:22).

In other words, the first humans were given a choice – they could either be immortal or be creators. To be both would make them divine. However, due to their immoral behavior, it would also make them a rebellious rival to God. Thus, once they have gained creative abilities, they lose their chance at immortality and are banished from the Garden of Eden. Nonetheless, God still cares for them (He "made garments of skins for Adam and his wife and clothed them," 3:21) and for their moral development (4:6–7). In contrast, the capriciousness of ancient Near Eastern deities rendered its polytheism incapable of producing a foundational story which revolved around divine and human morality. Only the Torah's ethical monotheism could do so. ▪ JU

The ethics of the Garden of Eden versus the quest for immortality in ancient Babylon

The Garden of Eden story explains, among other elements of the natural world, how human death became a reality, and why all humans eventually die. Indeed, until the possibility of human death is first mentioned in Genesis 2:17, no death of any kind makes an appearance in the text. In contrast, in the ancient Near East, death is part and parcel of the world before the earth is even created. In the Babylonian creation epic, *Enuma Elish*, the primordial gods are killed by the younger ones before creation occurs. In the Old Babylonian version of the *Epic of Gilgamesh*, the divine barmaid Siduri tells Gilgamesh, "When the gods created mankind, they allotted death to mankind" (Tablet X.3, 3–4). Death is recognized as part of natural existence. By contrast, God, as described in the Torah, is not only metaphysical, He is beyond time. He "lives," but He cannot die. Moreover, God provides the first humans with the means to be immortal through the Tree of Life, which is not forbidden until after the human couple disobeys God by eating from the Tree of Knowledge of good and evil.

The closest connections in the ancient Near East to the Garden of Eden story appear in the *Epic of Gilgamesh*, which, however, has far different concerns than Genesis 2 and 3. While the Garden of Eden story introduces us to death, it also explains why a man marries a woman, why men and women are so companionable, why people cannot live forever, and why hardship is inescapable, as well as exploring the relationship of humans to the divine authority. The *Epic of Gilgamesh* on the other hand, focuses primarily on the human search for immortality.

A number of elements connect the stories of Gilgamesh and the Garden of Eden: both feature a man who spends time with the animals and is familiar with them; his true companionship is discovered to be with another human, and he leaves the animals; his comprehension of human sexuality changes his fate and gives him greater understanding; the phrases "you are become like a god" or "you will be like God"; a beautiful garden and the mention of precious stones (Gen. 2:12); a tree or plant that enables one to be immortal; and a serpent that prevents the human(s) from achieving immortality.

While the emphasis in Mesopotamia is on the futile human quest for immortality, the Garden of Eden story has a much different concern, derived from the fact that Genesis does not conceive of humans as slaves to benefit the gods, but as rulers of the earth, made in God's image (1:26–28): Will humans demonstrate the ethical thinking and behavior needed to be good rulers? That is why the story centers on the human response to God's command not to eat of the Tree of Knowledge of good and evil. It is noteworthy that the humans are given the reason for the command: "you may not eat from that, for on the day you eat of it, you shall die" (2:17; compare 3:3). In contrast, they are permitted to eat from the Tree of Life (2:9, 16), which enables them to be immortal!

However, they disobey God and eat of the fruit of the Tree of Knowledge of good and evil, thereby gaining an understanding of the sexual purpose of their genitals – the first thing they realize is that they are na-

ח וַיִּטַּע יְהוָה אֱלֹהִים גַּן בְּעֵדֶן מִקֶּדֶם וַיָּשֶׂם שָׁם אֶת־הָאָדָם אֲשֶׁר
ט יָצָר: וַיַּצְמַח יְהוָה אֱלֹהִים מִן־הָאֲדָמָה כָּל־עֵץ נֶחְמָד לְמַרְאֶה
וְטוֹב לְמַאֲכָל וְעֵץ הַחַיִּים בְּתוֹךְ הַגָּן וְעֵץ הַדַּעַת טוֹב וָרָע:

8 The LORD God planted a garden in Eden, in the east, and
9 there he put the man He had formed. And from the land, the
LORD God caused all kinds of trees to grow, pleasant to look at
and good to eat from, and the Tree of Life stood in the middle

NEAR EAST

2:8 Garden

While no exact parallel to the entire Garden of Eden story exists in ancient Near Eastern literature, the idyllic setting of the garden shares common elements with the setting in the Sumerian myth *Enki and Ninmah* (ca. 18th century BCE, Old Babylonian tablets). That story tells of a "pure," "clean," and "bright" island in the Persian Gulf, Dilmun, where "a lion did not slay, a wolf did not carry off lambs"; that is, tame cattle and wild animals lived together in harmony. In Dilmun, sickness and death were unknown, and nature was at peace. However, the rest of the myth has no obvious parallels to the Garden of Eden narrative. ▪ JU

LANGUAGE

2:8 Eden

The Hebrew *eden* seems to be connected to the Old Aramaic cognate usage of the root *e d n*, which, according to the Tel Fekhariya bilingual inscription (ca. 850 BCE), means "to enrich, to make abundant (in water supply)." A Ugaritic description of the fertility god Baal as providing an abundance of water also uses the root *e d n* (KTU 51 v 68–69; 14th century BCE). The Torah states that the Garden of Eden is well watered; see Gen. 2:10, 13:10. ▪ JU

↗
Lion-headed eagle, symbol of the Sumerian god Ningirsu, Temple of the goddess Ninhursag, Tell Al-Ubaid, ca. 2500 BCE

NEAR EAST

2:9 The Tree of Life

The only other mention of specifically a "tree of life" in ancient Near Eastern literature is in Egypt, in *The Great Cairo Hymn of Praise to Amun-Re* (ca. 15th century BCE; Amun-Re was the chief god and sun god): "… unique one, like whom among the gods?...who made mankind, who created the flocks, lord of what exists, who created the tree of life, who made the herbage…" (COS 1.88). However, nothing more is said of it.

Aside from the plant of life mentioned in the *Epic of Gilgamesh* (see "The ethics of the Garden of Eden versus the quest for immortality in ancient Babylon" on pages 16–17), a food that can make one immortal is also found in the *Tale of Adapa* (fragments from Amarna, 14th century BCE, plus finds from the Royal Library of Ashurbanipal). The sage Adapa offended the great god Anu and is summoned before the god to defend his behavior. Before the sage departs for heaven, the god Ea advises him not to eat or drink there. Once there, Adapa is offered food and water but rejects them. Afterward, Adapa is informed that he had refused the "food of life" and the "water of life," through which he would have become immortal.

The *Tale of Adapa*, then, is another example in which a human loses the chance to become immortal, but there it is due to divine trickery. In contrast, the loss of immortality in the Garden of Edeb is due to just punishment for human sin. ▪ JU

י וְנָהָר֙ יֹצֵ֣א מֵעֵ֔דֶן לְהַשְׁק֖וֹת אֶת־הַגָּ֑ן וּמִשָּׁם֙ יִפָּרֵ֔ד וְהָיָ֖ה לְאַרְבָּעָ֥ה
יא רָאשִֽׁים׃ שֵׁ֥ם הָאֶחָ֖ד פִּישׁ֑וֹן ה֣וּא הַסֹּבֵ֗ב אֵ֚ת כָּל־אֶ֣רֶץ הַחֲוִילָ֔ה

of the garden, and the Tree of Knowledge of good and evil.
10 A river flows from Eden to water this garden, and from there
11 divides into four headwaters. The name of the first is Pishon.

NEAR EAST

2:10 Four headwaters

Fertile headwaters flowing from a deity is a theme in ancient Near Eastern artwork. Egyptian art shows either two or four rivers flowing out of Nun, the deification of the primordial watery abyss. The waters are received by two other gods, apparently representing the northern and southern Nile, who spit them out further. A panel from the fresco on the wall of Zimri-lim's palace at Mari portrays two deities standing opposite each other holding pots, each with four streams of water flowing from it in different directions. Also from Mari, a cylinder depicts a god sitting on a mountain top, at the base of which are two serpents with rivers flowing from their mouths. A Middle Assyrian plaque (13th century BCE) portrays a divine figure with four rivers streaming from him in four directions. He is standing between two trees and next to each tree is a winged guardian.

In contrast, in our verse, the four rivers are described as flowing naturally from the Garden of Eden. ▪ ZR

↗ Two gods facing each other, each with a pot with four streams flowing out of them, fresco of the investiture of Zimri-lim, royal palace of Mari, 18th century BCE

↗ Fountain of the Four Rivers, Gian Lorenzo Bernini, Piazza Navona, Rome, 1651

NEAR EAST

2:11–14 Pishon, Giḥon, Tigris, and Euphrates

The Pishon and Giḥon rivers do not appear in ancient sources; various attempts have been made to identify them. Since Pishon is described as a river that "surrounds the land of Ḥavila, where there is gold" it may be connected to one of the two ancient rivers identified by that name. One is Nubia, a region along the Nile River that was a source of gold and bdellium (v. 12) in ancient Egypt. Based on this, Pishon might be the Nile. The other possibility is in Arabia, where satellite images and analysis of sand patterns have revealed an old riverbed called Wadi al-Batin that appears to have dried up sometime between 3500 and 2000 BCE. It runs from the Hijaz mountains – an area rich in gold – to the Persian Gulf, near the mouth of the Tigris and Euphrates.

The root *g y ḥ* indicates "gushing" – and indeed, the spring in the Kidron Valley outside Jerusalem is also called Giḥon. This river is "the one that surrounds the land of Kush," which refers to Nubia (for further information on Kush, see "The Kushite woman" on page 70 in the Numbers volume of this series). This region encompasses the area between the first cataract of the Nile and the confluence of the Blue and White Niles, so it is possible that Pishon and Giḥon refer to these two rivers.

The Tigris River, mentioned only here and in Daniel 10:4, is called Ḥidekel, which appears to be an early form of the name of this river, called *idiqlat* in Akkadian and *deqlat* in Aramaic.

The Euphrates is the only river named without accompanying geographic information; apparently, it was well known to the Israelites. In the Tanakh, it is usually identified as "the great river" or just "the river" (e.g., Gen. 15:18, 31:21). ▪ ZR

NEAR EAST

2:15 To work it and safeguard it

The idea that human beings were created as slaves to work and provide for the gods was common throughout the ancient Near East. The Sumerian creation text KAR 4 describes the purpose of the creation of humankind, "the corvée (forced labor) of the gods will be their corvée: They will fix the boundaries of the fields once and for all, and take in their hands hoes and baskets, to benefit the House of the great gods" (lines 21–23). The Mesopotamian myth *Enki and Ninmah* states that before man was created, "the great gods labor, the young gods carry baskets, the gods dig canals…the gods grind away, grumble about their life" (lines 9–11). Nammu, the primeval mother goddess, tells her son Enki to "create servants for the gods, let them throw their baskets away" (line 23), which he does, and "the corvée of the gods has been forced on it" (line 30).

In sharp contrast, man is placed in the garden "to work it and safeguard it," assumedly for his own needs, not God's. ▪ ZR

אֲשֶׁר־שָׁם הַזָּהָב: וּזֲהַב הָאָרֶץ הַהִוא טוֹב שָׁם הַבְּדֹלַח וְאֶבֶן יב
הַשֹּׁהַם: וְשֵׁם־הַנָּהָר הַשֵּׁנִי גִּיחוֹן הוּא הַסּוֹבֵב אֵת כָּל־אֶרֶץ כּוּשׁ: יג
וְשֵׁם הַנָּהָר הַשְּׁלִישִׁי חִדֶּקֶל הוּא הַהֹלֵךְ קִדְמַת אַשּׁוּר וְהַנָּהָר יד
הָרְבִיעִי הוּא פְרָת: וַיִּקַּח יהוה אֱלֹהִים אֶת־הָאָדָם וַיַּנִּחֵהוּ בְגַן־ טו •
עֵדֶן לְעָבְדָהּ וּלְשָׁמְרָהּ: וַיְצַו יהוה אֱלֹהִים עַל־הָאָדָם לֵאמֹר טז
מִכֹּל עֵץ־הַגָּן אָכֹל תֹּאכֵל: וּמֵעֵץ הַדַּעַת טוֹב וָרָע לֹא תֹאכַל יז
מִמֶּנּוּ כִּי בְּיוֹם אֲכָלְךָ מִמֶּנּוּ מוֹת תָּמוּת: וַיֹּאמֶר יהוה אֱלֹהִים יח
לֹא־טוֹב הֱיוֹת הָאָדָם לְבַדּוֹ אֶעֱשֶׂה־לּוֹ עֵזֶר כְּנֶגְדּוֹ: וַיִּצֶר יהוה יט
אֱלֹהִים מִן־הָאֲדָמָה כָּל־חַיַּת הַשָּׂדֶה וְאֵת כָּל־עוֹף הַשָּׁמַיִם וַיָּבֵא
אֶל־הָאָדָם לִרְאוֹת מַה־יִּקְרָא־לוֹ וְכֹל אֲשֶׁר יִקְרָא־לוֹ הָאָדָם
שלישי נֶפֶשׁ חַיָּה הוּא שְׁמוֹ: וַיִּקְרָא הָאָדָם שֵׁמוֹת לְכָל־הַבְּהֵמָה וּלְעוֹף כ •

12 It surrounds the land of Ḥavila, where there is gold. And the
gold of that land is good; bdellium and rock crystal are there
13 also. The name of the second river is Giḥon; it is the one that
14 surrounds the land of Kush. The name of the third river is the
Tigris, and it flows to the east of Assyria. The fourth river is
• 15 the Euphrates. The LORD God took the man and placed him
16 in the Garden of Eden to work it and safeguard it. And the
LORD God commanded the man: "You are free to eat from
17 any tree in the garden. But the Tree of Knowledge of good
and evil – you may not eat from that, for on the day you eat
18 of it, you shall die." Then the LORD God said, "It is not good
for man to be alone. I will make a fitting partner for him."
19 The LORD God formed all the wild animals, and all the birds
of the heavens, out of the land. He brought them to the man
to see what he would call them, and whatever he called each
• 20 living thing, that became its name. So the man gave names
to all the animals, the birds of the heavens, and all the wild

Reclining cow, part of facade frieze, Temple of Ninhursag (Ninmah), Tell Al-Ubaid (Iraq), ca. 2500 BCE

כא הַשָּׁמַיִם וּלְכֹל חַיַּת הַשָּׂדֶה וּלְאָדָם לֹא־מָצָא עֵזֶר כְּנֶגְדּוֹ: וַיַּפֵּל
יְהוָה אֱלֹהִים ׀ תַּרְדֵּמָה עַל־הָאָדָם וַיִּישָׁן וַיִּקַּח אַחַת מִצַּלְעֹתָיו
כב וַיִּסְגֹּר בָּשָׂר תַּחְתֶּנָּה: וַיִּבֶן יְהוָה אֱלֹהִים ׀ אֶת־הַצֵּלָע אֲשֶׁר־לָקַח
כג מִן־הָאָדָם לְאִשָּׁה וַיְבִאֶהָ אֶל־הָאָדָם: וַיֹּאמֶר הָאָדָם זֹאת הַפַּעַם

creatures. But he found no fitting partner for himself. Then 21
the LORD God made the man fall into a deep sleep, and while
he was sleeping He took one of his ribs and closed the flesh
in its place. And the LORD God built the rib He had taken 22
from the man into a woman. He brought her to the man. And 23
the man said: "This, at last, is bone of my bones and flesh of

NEAR EAST

2:20–24 The creation of woman

Genesis 1:26–27 emphasizes humankind's relationship with God; both male and female were created in God's image. In the Garden of Eden, God first observed that man's solitary existence is "not good" (2:18) and that he needed an *ezer kenegdo*, which Robert Alter translates as "a sustainer (rather than the conventional 'helper,' or 'helpmeet') alongside him", emphasizing that the noun form *ezer* "connotes active intervention…as often in Psalms" (Ps. 33:20, 70:6, 115:9–11, 146:5). God then proceeded to create pairs of animals, male and female, to which the man assigned names, a process which impressed upon him his lonely uniqueness. Verse 20 reports that man's new perception agreed with God's – that his solitary existence is undesirable – so God placed the man in an anesthetic sleep, removing his "rib" (*tsela*), "built" it into a woman, and presented her to man. His reaction was enthusiastic: this one "finally" (*zot hapa'am*) corresponded to him so perfectly that he labeled her "woman" (*isha*) in accord with his own identity, "man" (*ish*).

Verse 24 affirms that the institution of marriage is based on the preceding narrative, emphasizing that man's incompleteness can only be remedied by the companionship of a woman, with whom he forms "one flesh" (a complete flesh). Interestingly, verse 24 says that a man must leave his parents and join his wife, which can be seen as contrasting with the dominant "patrilocal" model in which women leave their families to join their husbands' clans. Conversely, perhaps the verse, rather than describing a physical departure, describes a new psychological reality for the man: he creates a new unity by clinging (*davak*) to his wife as opposed to his parents.

The narrative of Genesis 2 offers a richer and more detailed version of creation than we find in any ancient Near Eastern myth. Genesis' story of humankind begins with a single male and female, which suggests that they serve as archetypes, indicating the universal applicability of monogamous heterosexual marriage. Further, the Torah's description of monogenesis (creation from one couple) allows for later ethical teachings about the common origins of humanity, their equality, and the infinite value of a single life. By contrast, in Greek myth, Deucalion and Pyrrha, survivors of the great flood, threw stones behind them which sprang up as males and females. The origins of women in particular are nowhere found in ancient creation myths, which do, however, include the sexual origins of multiple generations of gods and goddesses. In these myths, divine birthing assistants or "womb goddesses" play a prominent role in the creation of humankind; they shape and nurture the clay lumps that later become humans. By contrast, the single non-gendered God of Genesis needs no assistance.

In terms of similarities, two Hebrew terms that are prominent in Genesis 2 are also used in Akkadian literature. The Hebrew *tsela* is usually translated as "rib" although elsewhere in the Bible it means "side" (for example, regarding the building of the Tabernacle, Ex. 26:20–35; I Kings 6:5, 8). In Akkadian, the cognate *tselu* (or *ṣelu*) is also used in anatomic and architectural contexts: for Siamese twins joined at the side, a cut of meat that includes the rib, and the wing or side of a building complex. Its use for both bones and flesh together may also be reflected here, as Adam states in verse 23 that the woman is "bone of my bones and flesh of my flesh." Also, the text says that God "builds" (*vayyiven*) the rib into a woman – the only time this root is used in the creation chapters (but it is sometimes associated with procreation; see Deut. 25:9; Ruth 4:11). The Semitic cognate *banu* is commonly used for architecture but also in references to the creation of humankind. ▪ EG

Deucalion and Pyrrha throwing stones
that turn into men,
sketchbook of Jacob Toorenvliet, 1701

עֶצֶם מֵעֲצָמַי וּבָשָׂר מִבְּשָׂרִי לְזֹאת יִקָּרֵא אִשָּׁה כִּי מֵאִישׁ לֻקְחָה־
זֹּאת: עַל־כֵּן יַעֲזָב־אִישׁ אֶת־אָבִיו וְאֶת־אִמּוֹ וְדָבַק בְּאִשְׁתּוֹ וְהָיוּ כד
לְבָשָׂר אֶחָד: וַיִּהְיוּ שְׁנֵיהֶם עֲרוּמִּים הָאָדָם וְאִשְׁתּוֹ וְלֹא יִתְבֹּשָׁשׁוּ: כה •
וְהַנָּחָשׁ הָיָה עָרוּם מִכֹּל חַיַּת הַשָּׂדֶה אֲשֶׁר עָשָׂה יהוה אֱלֹהִים א • ג
וַיֹּאמֶר אֶל־הָאִשָּׁה אַף כִּי־אָמַר אֱלֹהִים לֹא תֹאכְלוּ מִכֹּל עֵץ
הַגָּן: וַתֹּאמֶר הָאִשָּׁה אֶל־הַנָּחָשׁ מִפְּרִי עֵץ־הַגָּן נֹאכֵל: וּמִפְּרִי ב ג
הָעֵץ אֲשֶׁר בְּתוֹךְ־הַגָּן אָמַר אֱלֹהִים לֹא תֹאכְלוּ מִמֶּנּוּ וְלֹא תִגְּעוּ

my flesh. This shall be called Woman, for from Man was this
24 one taken."[2] That is why a man leaves his father and mother
• 25 and cleaves to his wife and they become one flesh. The man
and his wife were both naked, but they were not ashamed.
3 • 1 The serpent was the slyest of all the wild animals the Lord
God had made. "Did God say," it asked the woman, "that you
2 must not eat from any tree in the garden?" The woman told
the serpent, "We may eat the fruit of the trees in the garden,
3 but God did say, 'You must not eat fruit from the tree in the

2 | *Isha* (woman) resonates with *ish* (man).

NEAR EAST

2:25 Naked

The nakedness of the first humans is representative of their innocence before eating from the Tree of Knowledge of good and evil; it is not portrayed as primitive or uncivilized. This stands in contrast to the understanding of nakedness in early Mesopotamian texts. The 3rd millennium BCE Sumerian creation myth *Ewe and Wheat* describes the primitive state of uncivilized humanity: "The people of those distant days, they knew no cloth to wear; they went about with naked limbs in the land, and like sheep they ate grass with their mouth, drinking water from the ditches" (lines 20–25). Similarly, in the *Epic of Gilgamesh*, the character of Enkidu is presented as a wild and primitive beast-like man. Part of the civilizing and taming process that he undergoes is being clothed by the prostitute Shamhat. The Old Babylonian version describes the transformation of Enkidu: "the barber groomed his body so hairy, anointed with oil he turned into a man. He put on a garment, became like a warrior..." (ll.108–110).

In contrast, when God exiles Adam and Ḥava from the Garden of Eden, He provides them with clothing to protect them from the elements (3:21), as an act of compassion even though they had just sinned. ▪ ZR

Bust of Thutmose III wearing crown with a uraeus cobra, Karnak, Thebes, 15th century BCE

NEAR EAST

3:1 Slyest

The Hebrew term *arum* indicates "cunning," "slyness," or "craftiness."

The term for snake, *naḥash*, is related to the verbal root *n ḥ sh*, "to give omens," "to divine." Ancient Egyptian iconography also associates snakes with occult wisdom. The uraeus, the image of an upright cobra, was positioned in the middle of the pharaoh's forehead. The ancient Egyptians believed that the gods imbued this object with magical power, which empowered the pharaoh who wore it with magical abilities. The goddess of this object is referred to in some Egyptian texts as "The Magician."

In Genesis, the snake, although able to speak like the snakes and other animals in Egyptian literature, does not possess occult power. ▪ ZR

ה בּוֹ פֶּן תְּמֻתוּן: וַיֹּאמֶר הַנָּחָשׁ אֶל־הָאִשָּׁה לֹא־מוֹת תְּמֻתוּן: כִּי
יֹדֵעַ אֱלֹהִים כִּי בְּיוֹם אֲכָלְכֶם מִמֶּנּוּ וְנִפְקְחוּ עֵינֵיכֶם וִהְיִיתֶם
ו כֵּאלֹהִים יֹדְעֵי טוֹב וָרָע: וַתֵּרֶא הָאִשָּׁה כִּי טוֹב הָעֵץ לְמַאֲכָל
וְכִי תַאֲוָה־הוּא לָעֵינַיִם וְנֶחְמָד הָעֵץ לְהַשְׂכִּיל וַתִּקַּח מִפִּרְיוֹ
ז וַתֹּאכַל וַתִּתֵּן גַּם־לְאִישָׁהּ עִמָּהּ וַיֹּאכַל: וַתִּפָּקַחְנָה עֵינֵי שְׁנֵיהֶם
וַיֵּדְעוּ כִּי עֵירֻמִּם הֵם וַיִּתְפְּרוּ עֲלֵה תְאֵנָה וַיַּעֲשׂוּ לָהֶם חֲגֹרֹת:
ח וַיִּשְׁמְעוּ אֶת־קוֹל יְהוָה אֱלֹהִים מִתְהַלֵּךְ בַּגָּן לְרוּחַ הַיּוֹם וַיִּתְחַבֵּא
ט הָאָדָם וְאִשְׁתּוֹ מִפְּנֵי יְהוָה אֱלֹהִים בְּתוֹךְ עֵץ הַגָּן: וַיִּקְרָא יְהוָה
י אֱלֹהִים אֶל־הָאָדָם וַיֹּאמֶר לוֹ אַיֶּכָּה: וַיֹּאמֶר אֶת־קֹלְךָ שָׁמַעְתִּי

middle of the garden, and you must not touch it, or you will
die.'" But the serpent told the woman, "You will not die; 4
God knows that on the day you eat from it your eyes will be 5
opened, and you will be like God, knowing good and evil."
The woman saw that the tree was ripe for eating, enticing 6
to the eyes, and desirable too for granting insight. She took
some of its fruit and ate, and she gave some to her husband
and he too ate. The eyes of both of them were opened, and 7
they realized that they were naked. So they sewed fig leaves
together and made coverings for themselves. They heard the 8
sound of the Lord God walking in the garden in the cool of
the day, and the man and his wife hid from the Lord God
among the trees of the garden. The Lord God called to the 9
man: "Where are you?" He answered, "I heard Your voice in 10

GEOGRAPHY

3:8 The cool of the day

This phrase, literally "at the wind (*ruaḥ*) of the day" appears only here. It refers to the late afternoon or evening when cool breezes bring relief from "the heat of the day" (Gen. 18:1). Late afternoon breezes coming from the west are familiar to anyone living in Israel and would have been familiar to the ancient Israelites. They are caused by the differential between the land and sea temperatures, which enables the cool maritime air to penetrate inland. In sub-tropical regions, such as the East Mediterranean, this phenomenon is most pronounced in the summer when the temperature differences between the land and sea are greatest. ▪ ZR

↗ Sun rays shine on Jerusalem, late afternoon, February 6, 1942

FLORA AND FAUNA

3:7 Fig leaves

Figs trees have particularly large leaves: around 12–25 centimeters (4.7–10 inches) long and 10–18 centimeters (4–7 inches) wide. Figs would have been familiar to the Israelites as the edible fig tree is indigenous to the land of Israel and was one of the earliest plants to be cultivated by humans; partially fossilized figs were found in the early Neolithic village Gilgal I in the Jordan Valley, dating to around 9400–9200 BCE, thus predating the domestication of wheat by a thousand years. ▪ ZR

↖ Fig and fig leaf, etching, Batty Langley, 1729

בַּגָּן וָאִירָא כִּי־עֵירֹם אָנֹכִי וָאֵחָבֵא׃ וַיֹּאמֶר מִי הִגִּיד לְךָ כִּי עֵירֹם יא
אָתָּה הֲמִן־הָעֵץ אֲשֶׁר צִוִּיתִיךָ לְבִלְתִּי אֲכָל־מִמֶּנּוּ אָכָלְתָּ׃ וַיֹּאמֶר יב
הָאָדָם הָאִשָּׁה אֲשֶׁר נָתַתָּה עִמָּדִי הִוא נָתְנָה־לִּי מִן־הָעֵץ וָאֹכֵל׃

the garden, and I was afraid, because I was naked. So I hid."
11 "Who told you," God asked, "that you were naked? Have
you eaten from the tree from which I commanded you not
12 to eat?" The man said, "The woman You put here with me –

NEAR EAST

3:14–15 The snake's curse

The Egyptian *Pyramid texts* are the oldest religious writings in the world; the most ancient ones are the inscriptions on the sarcophagi and walls of the pyramids at Saqqara from the Fifth and Sixth Dynasties of the Old Kingdom (ca. 2613–2181 BCE). They make up the principal funerary literature of ancient Egypt, used to assist the pharaohs on their journey to the afterlife.

Among the hundreds of recitations found in these texts are many spells and curses designed to be used against the snakes that were thought to impede the pharaoh on his way to the afterlife. These utterances include curses of the snakes reminiscent of those in our verses, declaring that the snake will crawl on its belly, eat dirt and that its head will be stricken, as in the following tomb inscriptions: Pepi II (23rd century BCE) – "Monster snake, lie down!...crawl away!"; Unas (24th century BCE) – concerning the "accursed snake," the goddess Mafdet will "jump on the neck of the snake…striking you on your face… so that you fall in your excrement and crawl in your urine. Fall down, lie down, crawl away…"; Teti (ruled 2323–2291 BCE) – "Horus's sandal has stepped" on the snake, and declares to it, "you have no feet and you have no arms…."

All of this reflects a negative view of snakes, which was common throughout the ancient Near East. ▪ ZR

↗ Relief fragment with spells from the *Pyramid texts*, pyramid of Pepi II, Saqqara, 23rd century BCE

NEAR EAST

3:16–19 Punishment of the humans – an etiology

Etiological stories explain the origin of natural or social phenomena. The creation and flood stories in the ancient Near East seek to answer questions about the inception of humanity and the world in which we live. The instinct for asking how things came to be the way they are is universal and is a major part of the literature of the ancient Near East.

The Tanakh provides its own unique answers to all these questions. In 1901, the German scholar Hermann Gunkel showed that much of Genesis is composed of etiological narratives and gave a detailed description of the different types of such narratives.

These verses describing the punishment of humans explain why women suffer in childbirth, a phenomenon mostly unknown in other female mammals: the sin has turned the blessing "Be fertile and multiply" (Gen. 1:28) into a painful process. Similarly, the difficulty of extracting food from the ground is explained as a fitting punishment for eating forbidden food.

Verse 3:19 emphasizes the reality of human mortality: "You are dust, and you will return to dust." The punishment befits the human desire to fulfill the snake's tempting statement, "you will be like God" (3:5). As Nahum Sarna comments, "Human beings had attempted to elevate themselves to the level of the divine. All they achieved was to condemn themselves to a ceaseless, brutal struggle for subsistence, with the consciousness of the fragility of life ever hanging over them." ▪ ZR

↗ Adam and Eve banished from the Garden of Eden, William A. Foster, from *The Bible Panorama*, or *The Holy Scriptures in Picture and Story*, 1891

יג וַיֹּאמֶר יְהוָה אֱלֹהִים לָאִשָּׁה מַה־זֹּאת עָשִׂית וַתֹּאמֶר הָאִשָּׁה
יד הַנָּחָשׁ הִשִּׁיאַנִי וָאֹכֵל: וַיֹּאמֶר יְהוָה אֱלֹהִים ׀ אֶל־הַנָּחָשׁ כִּי
עָשִׂיתָ זֹּאת אָרוּר אַתָּה מִכָּל־הַבְּהֵמָה וּמִכֹּל חַיַּת הַשָּׂדֶה עַל־
טו גְּחֹנְךָ תֵלֵךְ וְעָפָר תֹּאכַל כָּל־יְמֵי חַיֶּיךָ: וְאֵיבָה ׀ אָשִׁית בֵּינְךָ וּבֵין
הָאִשָּׁה וּבֵין זַרְעֲךָ וּבֵין זַרְעָהּ הוּא יְשׁוּפְךָ רֹאשׁ וְאַתָּה תְּשׁוּפֶנּוּ
טז עָקֵב: אֶל־הָאִשָּׁה אָמַר הַרְבָּה אַרְבֶּה עִצְּבוֹנֵךְ
וְהֵרֹנֵךְ בְּעֶצֶב תֵּלְדִי בָנִים וְאֶל־אִישֵׁךְ תְּשׁוּקָתֵךְ וְהוּא יִמְשָׁל־
יז בָּךְ: וּלְאָדָם אָמַר כִּי שָׁמַעְתָּ לְקוֹל אִשְׁתֶּךָ וַתֹּאכַל
מִן־הָעֵץ אֲשֶׁר צִוִּיתִיךָ לֵאמֹר לֹא תֹאכַל מִמֶּנּוּ אֲרוּרָה הָאֲדָמָה
יח בַּעֲבוּרֶךָ בְּעִצָּבוֹן תֹּאכֲלֶנָּה כֹּל יְמֵי חַיֶּיךָ: וְקוֹץ וְדַרְדַּר תַּצְמִיחַ לָךְ
יט וְאָכַלְתָּ אֶת־עֵשֶׂב הַשָּׂדֶה: בְּזֵעַת אַפֶּיךָ תֹּאכַל לֶחֶם עַד שׁוּבְךָ
אֶל־הָאֲדָמָה כִּי מִמֶּנָּה לֻקָּחְתָּ כִּי־עָפָר אַתָּה וְאֶל־עָפָר תָּשׁוּב:
כ כא וַיִּקְרָא הָאָדָם שֵׁם אִשְׁתּוֹ חַוָּה כִּי הִוא הָיְתָה אֵם כָּל־חָי: וַיַּעַשׂ
יְהוָה אֱלֹהִים לְאָדָם וּלְאִשְׁתּוֹ כָּתְנוֹת עוֹר וַיַּלְבִּשֵׁם:

she gave me fruit from the tree and I ate." Then the LORD 13
God said to the woman, "What is this you have done?" The
woman said, "The serpent beguiled me and I ate." And the 14
LORD God said to the serpent, "Because you have done
this, you are accursed more than all the animals and all wild
beasts. You will creep on your belly and dust will you eat all
the days of your life. I will plant hostility between you and 15
the woman, between your children and hers. And man will
strike your head, and you will strike his heel." To the 16
woman He said, "I will make your pain in pregnancy searingly
great; in sorrow will you bear children. You will long for
your husband, but he will rule over you." To Adam[3] 17
He said, "Because you listened to your wife and ate of the tree
from which I commanded you not to eat – cursed will be the
land on your account. By painful toil you will eat from it all
the days of your life. It will sprout thorns and thistles for you, 18
and you shall eat plants of the field. By the sweat of your brow 19
will you eat bread until you return to the land, for from there
you were taken. You are dust, and you will return to dust."
Then the man named his wife Ḥava, for she would become 20
the mother of all life.[4] Then the LORD God made garments 21
of skins for Adam and his wife and clothed them.

3 | The Hebrew *adam* can be read, depending on usage, as a common noun (man; cf. 2:7) or as a proper name.

4 | The name Ḥava resonates with *ḥai* (life).

NEAR EAST

3:20 Ḥava – mother of all life

The name Ḥava appears to be closely related to the Hebrew term for a living thing, *ḥayyah*, although the form has a different connotation, as *ḥayyah* is used for animals. Specifically, the name Ḥava means "giver of life."

In Ugaritic, the common term for life is *ḥwt*, which, as in Hebrew, is also used for an animal, while *ḥyt* is rarely used. The term "mother of all life" also resembles the epithets given to the Ugaritic chief goddess Athirat (Hebrew, *Ashera*), who was called the "mother" and "the creator/progenitor of the gods." Hence, Ḥava may simply be an archaic Hebrew form of the word for life, of Canaanite/Phoenician origin, which was chosen to preserve the sense of "progenitor of life" while at the same time erasing any association with animals or connections to mythology.

Also, a play on words may be involved since in Aramaic, *ḥivyah* means "snake," and this word appears as *ḥvvh* in a Sefire stele (8th century BCE). This connection was noted in the midrashic literature: "Said Rav Aḥha: *Ḥivyah* [the snake] is your snake, and you are the snake of Adam" (Bereshit Rabba 20:11, 22:2), meaning that the snake caused Ḥava to sin, and Ḥava acted like the snake to Adam, as she caused him to sin. ▪ ZR

Decorated jug with trees representing the goddess Ashera and a Proto-Canaanite inscription, Lakhish, 13th century BCE

רביעי וַיֹּאמֶר ׀ יְהוָה אֱלֹהִים הֵן הָאָדָם הָיָה כְּאַחַד מִמֶּנּוּ לָדַעַת טוֹב כב
וָרָע וְעַתָּה ׀ פֶּן־יִשְׁלַח יָדוֹ וְלָקַח גַּם מֵעֵץ הַחַיִּים וְאָכַל וָחַי

22 The Lord God then said, "Now that man has become like one of us, knowing good and evil, he must not be allowed to reach out his hand and take also from the Tree of Life,

NEAR EAST

3:24 Flaming, whirling sword

In ancient Near Eastern texts, fire and sword can both be understood as divine weapons. Various ancient gods carried mythological weapons. Ashur had a dagger and Shamash had a toothed sword. Baal even had his own blacksmith to create magical weapons. Understood this way, the sword with its flame could be an image representing God's power, His weapon.

In some ancient Near Eastern texts, "Flame/Fire" is also found as a name for a divine being. In West Semitic texts, "Flame" is known as Reshep, while Akkadian texts call him Ishum. The *Epic of Erra* describes, "Fire, the famous slayer, whose hands are suited to wield his terrible weapons and to make his fierce swords flash."

Here, the flaming sword could refer either to an item (sword) or a natural phenomenon (fire) viewed as an agent of God. For example, Psalm 104:4 calls "flames of fire" God's ministers.

Nonetheless, even though "the flaming, whirling sword" appears here as separate from the cherubim (who are not said to be wielding it), it is not personified. Rather, in contrast to other ancient Near Eastern texts, it is demythologized in Genesis and is simply a defensive weapon to ensure that humans will not eat of the Tree of Life. ▪ KG

Sickle-shaped sword with inscription commemorating the construction of a palace by King Adad-Nirari I, Middle Assyrian, 13th century BCE

NEAR EAST

3:24 Cherubim (*keruvim*)

The Hebrew *keruvim* seems to be a cognate to the Akkadian noun *kuribu*, which generally refers to composite figures of human-headed bulls with eagles' wings that were placed at the entrance to Mesopotamian temples. For example, the Assyrian king Esar Ḥadon states, "I placed (at the entrance of the inner area of the temple of Ashur)...kuribus made of reddish gold facing each other" (CAD K 559b). However, this figure was not uniform, as a text written in Standard Babylonian states, "Namtartu [a god of death], his female (counterpart) has the head of a kuribu [but human hands and feet]" (CAD K 559b).

Although no description is given of the cherubim here, we know that the ones fashioned for the Ark of the Covenant each had one face and two wings (Ex. 25:20). By contrast, the cherubim in Yeḥezkel's vision of the Divine Chariot (Ezek. 1:6–11, 10:1–22) seem closer to those in Mesopotamia: each had four faces, four wings, and human hands; their feet were like a calf's hoof; their faces were that of a man, a lion, an ox, and an eagle. On the other hand, the cherubim decorating the walls of the prophet's vision of the Temple had two faces each – a man's and a lion's (Ezek. 41:18–19).

The cherubim at the edge of the Garden of Eden were similar to those in Mesopotamian temples in that they were served as fearsome guards. Nahum Sarna comments, "The motif of the composite human-animal-bird figure is widespread in various forms in art and religious symbolism throughout the Fertile Crescent." Thus, the cherubim in Genesis did not need any detailed description, as the ancient Israelites would have been familiar with this Near Eastern artistic motif. ▪ JU

Human-headed winged bulls, guarding the gate of Sargon II's palace, Dur Sharrukin, 8th century BCE

כג לְעֹלָם: וַיְשַׁלְּחֵהוּ יְהוָה אֱלֹהִים מִגַּן־עֵדֶן לַעֲבֹד אֶת־הָאֲדָמָה
כד •• אֲשֶׁר לֻקַּח מִשָּׁם: וַיְגָרֶשׁ אֶת־הָאָדָם וַיַּשְׁכֵּן מִקֶּדֶם לְגַן־עֵדֶן
אֶת־הַכְּרֻבִים וְאֵת לַהַט הַחֶרֶב הַמִּתְהַפֶּכֶת לִשְׁמֹר אֶת־דֶּרֶךְ
ד • א עֵץ הַחַיִּים: וְהָאָדָם יָדַע אֶת־חַוָּה אִשְׁתּוֹ וַתַּהַר
ב • וַתֵּלֶד אֶת־קַיִן וַתֹּאמֶר קָנִיתִי אִישׁ אֶת־יְהוָה: וַתֹּסֶף לָלֶדֶת
אֶת־אָחִיו אֶת־הָבֶל וַיְהִי־הֶבֶל רֹעֵה צֹאן וְקַיִן הָיָה עֹבֵד אֲדָמָה:

eat, and live forever." So the LORD God sent him away from 23
the Garden of Eden to work the land from which he had
been taken. He drove out the man, and east of the Garden 24 ••
of Eden He placed the cherubim and the flaming, whirling
sword to guard the way to the Tree of Life. The man 1 • 4
knew[5] his wife Ḥava, and she conceived and gave birth to
Kayin. She said, "With the LORD's help I have made a man."[6]
Later, she gave birth to his brother Hevel.[7] Hevel became 2 •

5 | A euphemism for sexual relations.
6 | The name Kayin resonates with *kaniti* (I have made).
7 | *Hevel* means "breath" and carries connotations of transience.

LANGUAGE

4:1 With the Lord's help I have made (*kaniti*)

In this verse, when Ḥava says she has "made a man," it does not use the same Hebrew verb as when God "made" the expanse (1:7). Instead, it is *k n h*, the same root with which Avraham "bought" the cave of Makhpela (25:10).

But Ḥava certainly did not "buy" Kayin. How can this be the appropriate verb to give him his name? The answer lies in Genesis 14:19 (and 22), where God is called "Maker [*koneh*] of heaven and earth." The verb means more generally "to acquire," and one way to acquire something is by making it.

An 8th century BCE Phoenician inscription from Karatepe has the formula *el qn artz*, "El creator of earth," and Ugaritic uses *k n y* for "procreate," as in our verse. ▪ MC

NEAR EAST

4:2 Shepherds and farmers

In ancient times, when people were few and land was plentiful, there was no inherent conflict between shepherds (or cattlemen) and farmers. The conflict here concerns God's acceptance of Hevel's offerings as opposed to Kayin's.

A conflict between shepherds and farmers also occurs in the Sumerian poem, called by the great Sumerologist Samuel Noah Kramer, *Inanna Prefers the Farmer* (ca. 20th to 18th century BCE). In this poem, the shepherd-god Dumuzid (after whom the month Tamuz is named) and the farmer-god Enkimdu compete to marry the goddess Inanna. She prefers the farmer, but Dumuzid aggressively details how his flock is superior to the farmer's produce. The farmer tries to appease him, inviting the shepherd to pasture his sheep on the farmer's land, and for the sheep to drink water from the farmer's canal. The shepherd, for his part, adjures the farmer not to impede the shepherd's wedding to Inanna. The farmer then offers to bring gifts to the shepherd and to Inanna.

It appears that both the shepherd and the farmer rely on the quality of their produce to attract Inanna. While it is unclear from the poem (pieces of which are missing) whom Inanna marries, other mythological tales speak of the union of Inanna and Dumuzid. As Inanna is associated with fertility, these stories are part of the Sumerian fertility cult – in which it is important that the gods provide the conditions for successful harvests, which benefit both humans and animals.

Inanna Prefers the Farmer, with mentions of Enkimdu (god of farming) and Dumuzid (shepherd god), Nippur, first half of 2nd millennium BCE

In Genesis, Hevel is a peaceful shepherd, while the farmer Kayin shows his adverse temperament. While both bring offerings to God in an apparent show of appreciation for His beneficence, Kayin's is, literally, "of the fruit of the land" (verse 3); that is, the fruit are not chosen for their excellence, but are of average quality. Hevel's offering, in contrast, is "fat portions from the firstborn of his flock" (verse 4, literally, "from the firstborn of his flock and from the fat of them"). Here "fat" (Hebrew, *ḥelev*) is used as in the English expression "fat of the land," that is, the "best" (for example, Gen. 45:18 concerning land; Num. 18:12 concerning wine/grapes; Ps. 81:17, 147:14– concerning wheat). In other words, apparently Hevel's offering is accepted because he brings the choicest of his flock's firstborn. Perhaps Kayin's offering indicates that he sees himself in partnership with God, while Hevel's symbolizes his understanding that he succeeds only because of God's beneficence.

The resemblance between the Sumerian text and Genesis revolves around a shepherd and a farmer as "contestants" for divine favor, and the quality of their proffered gifts, but there the similarity ends. The former is a pagan myth focused on divine suitors for a goddess. The latter is part of a lesson on moral behavior. ▪ JU

![NEAR EAST icon]

NEAR EAST

4:3–4 Offering

The Hebrew *minḥa* is translated here as "offering," and is the name of the afternoon prayer service in Judaism. Literally, it means "gift" or "tribute," as do the cognate *mnḥ* in Ugaritic and the plural *manaḥatu* in Akkadian.

Throughout the Torah's laws, *minḥa* in the context of an offering to God refers only to a grain offering (e.g., Lev. 2, 7:9–10; Num. 15:4, 6, 9; see "Grain offering" on page 40 of the Leviticus volume in this series). Here the term indicates that Hevel's sheep offerings were not a burnt sacrifice, as opposed to, for example, Noaḥ's sacrifice (Hebrew, *ola*, Gen. 8:20). It may be that Hevel's *minḥa* was comparable in kind (but not in thought) to Yaakov's tribute to Esav, which is also described as a *minḥa* (Gen. 32:13–14).

וַיְהִי מִקֵּץ יָמִים וַיָּבֵא קַיִן מִפְּרִי הָאֲדָמָה מִנְחָה לַיהוָה: וְהֶבֶל ג ד
הֵבִיא גַם־הוּא מִבְּכֹרוֹת צֹאנוֹ וּמֵחֶלְבֵהֶן וַיִּשַׁע יהוה אֶל־הֶבֶל
וְאֶל־מִנְחָתוֹ: וְאֶל־קַיִן וְאֶל־מִנְחָתוֹ לֹא שָׁעָה וַיִּחַר לְקַיִן מְאֹד ה
וַיִּפְּלוּ פָּנָיו: וַיֹּאמֶר יהוה אֶל־קָיִן לָמָּה חָרָה לָךְ וְלָמָּה נָפְלוּ ו
פָנֶיךָ: הֲלוֹא אִם־תֵּיטִיב שְׂאֵת וְאִם לֹא תֵיטִיב לַפֶּתַח חַטָּאת ז

3 a shepherd, while Kayin was a worker of the land. Time
passed, and Kayin brought fruit of the land as an offering
4 to the Lord. Hevel too brought an offering: fat portions
from the firstborn of his flock. The Lord looked favorably
5 on Hevel and his offering, but upon Kayin and his offering
He did not look with favor. Kayin became very angry, and
6 his face downcast. The Lord said to Kayin, "Why are you
7 angry; why is your face downcast? If you act well, will you
not be uplifted? If you fail to act well, sin is crouching at the

It was common throughout the ancient Near East to make offerings to deities from what was grown, in appreciation of the gods' ensuring the land's fertility. In Mesopotamia, the grain offering (Akkadian, *mashatu*) was the offering of the poor, for instance: "The widow makes her offering to you with cheap flour, the rich man with a lamb" (CAD M:331). A similar view is expressed in rabbinic tradition in Vayikra Rabba 8:4, in which a wealthy individual brings a sacrifice from the herd but a poor person brings a grain offering (a *minḥa*). ▪ JU

Rekhmire and his mother receiving offerings, artist copy by Charles K. Wilkinson ca. 1928, original from tomb of Rekhmire, Thebes, 15th century BCE

ח רֹבֵץ וְאֵלֶיךָ תְּשׁוּקָתוֹ וְאַתָּה תִּמְשָׁל־בּוֹ׃ וַיֹּאמֶר קַיִן אֶל־הֶבֶל
אָחִיו וַיְהִי בִּהְיוֹתָם בַּשָּׂדֶה וַיָּקָם קַיִן אֶל־הֶבֶל אָחִיו וַיַּהַרְגֵהוּ׃
ט וַיֹּאמֶר יהוה אֶל־קַיִן אֵי הֶבֶל אָחִיךָ וַיֹּאמֶר לֹא יָדַעְתִּי הֲשֹׁמֵר
י אָחִי אָנֹכִי׃ וַיֹּאמֶר מֶה עָשִׂיתָ קוֹל דְּמֵי אָחִיךָ צֹעֲקִים אֵלַי מִן־
יא הָאֲדָמָה׃ וְעַתָּה אָרוּר אָתָּה מִן־הָאֲדָמָה אֲשֶׁר פָּצְתָה אֶת־פִּיהָ
יב לָקַחַת אֶת־דְּמֵי אָחִיךָ מִיָּדֶךָ׃ כִּי תַעֲבֹד אֶת־הָאֲדָמָה לֹא־תֹסֵף
יג תֵּת־כֹּחָהּ לָךְ נָע וָנָד תִּהְיֶה בָאָרֶץ׃ וַיֹּאמֶר קַיִן אֶל־יהוה גָּדוֹל
יד • עֲוֺנִי מִנְּשֹׂא׃ הֵן גֵּרַשְׁתָּ אֹתִי הַיּוֹם מֵעַל פְּנֵי הָאֲדָמָה וּמִפָּנֶיךָ

door; it longs to have you, but you must rule over it." Then 8
Kayin said to his brother Hevel[8] – and when they were in the
field, Kayin rose up against his brother Hevel and killed him.
The LORD asked Kayin, "Where is your brother, Hevel?" "I 9
do not know," he said. "Am I my brother's keeper?" He said, 10
"What is it you have done? The voice of your brother's blood
cries out to Me from the land! Now you are cursed, more 11
so than the land[9] that has opened its mouth to receive your
brother's blood from your hand. When you work the land, 12
it will no longer grant you its powers. You will be a fugitive
wanderer over the land." Kayin said to the LORD, "My sin is 13
more than I can bear. You have banished me today from the 14 •
face of the land, and from Your face too I will be hidden. I
will be a fugitive wanderer over the land, and whoever finds

8 | It is not specified what Kayin told Hevel.

9 | Cf. 3:17.

LANGUAGE

4:7 Sin is crouching at the door

The Hebrew for "crouching" is from the root *r b tz*. The Akkadian cognate is the noun *rabitzum*, a type of demon. These demons could be either good protectors or, alternatively, evil attackers, who would lurk at doorways or gates to assault the inhabitants within. For example, "he who enters his living quarters, the demon will strike him," and the god Nergal "placed the demon Rabitzu at the sixth gate" (CAD R 23a, c).

As is normal in the Tanakh, this term is removed from its ancient Near Eastern pagan context, so that the meaning conveyed is that sin is like an evil predator crouching at the doorway. A human being desires to sin, but at the same time he has the power to act with goodness and to rule over his evil inclination. ▪ JU

Plaque of the god Nergal flanked by two human figures, Nippur, 20th to 17th century BCE

NEAR EAST

4:14 Whoever finds me will kill me

Genesis 5:4 reports that "After Shet was born, Adam lived eight hundred years and had other sons and daughters." This could explain how Kayin found a wife (4:17), as well as his fear that someone – another member of his victim's family – would kill him. Nahum Sarna suggests that this concern would thus anticipate and prefigure the institution of the blood avenger (Num. 35:12–28).

The idea of the blood avenger – although called by various titles – appears in the law codes of the ancient Near East. For example, the proclamation of the Hittite King Telipinu states, "And the procedure in case of bloodshed (is) as follows: whoever commits bloodshed, only (that) which the next-of-kin (literally, "lord of the blood") says (will happen): if he says, 'He shall die,' let him die, but if he says 'He shall pay,' let him pay" (§49). Similarly, in the *Middle Assyrian Laws*, "If a man, who has not yet received his inheritance share, takes a life, they shall hand him over to the next-of-kin (literally, "owner of life"). Should the next-of-kin so choose, he shall kill him, or, if he chooses to come to an accommodation, then he shall take his inheritance share" (MAL B §2; see "Blood avenger (*goel*)" on page 216 of the Numbers volume in this series). ▪ ZR

אֶסָּתֵר וְהָיִיתִי נָע וָנָד בָּאָרֶץ וְהָיָה כָל־מֹצְאִי יַהַרְגֵנִי׃ וַיֹּאמֶר טו
לוֹ יהוה לָכֵן כָּל־הֹרֵג קַיִן שִׁבְעָתַיִם יֻקָּם וַיָּשֶׂם יהוה לְקַיִן אוֹת
לְבִלְתִּי הַכּוֹת־אֹתוֹ כָּל־מֹצְאוֹ׃ וַיֵּצֵא קַיִן מִלִּפְנֵי יהוה וַיֵּשֶׁב טז
בְּאֶרֶץ־נוֹד קִדְמַת־עֵדֶן׃ וַיֵּדַע קַיִן אֶת־אִשְׁתּוֹ וַתַּהַר וַתֵּלֶד אֶת־ יז

15 me will kill me." The LORD said to him, "Whoever then kills
Kayin will suffer vengeance seven times over." Then the LORD
put a mark on Kayin so that none who found him would kill
16 him. So Kayin departed from the LORD's presence and lived
17 in the land of Nod,[10] east of Eden. Kayin knew his wife, and
she conceived and gave birth to Ḥanokh. He built a city,

10 | "Land of Nod" bears the simultaneous meaning "land of wandering."

NEAR EAST

4:17–22 Kayin and the beginnings of civilization

These verses credit Kayin and his immediate descendants with four major developments associated with civilization: cities, living in tents and raising livestock, music, and metalworking. Hevel had already pastured sheep, but his livelihood died when he was killed.

In ancient Near Eastern and Greek traditions, the advancements of civilization were achieved by the gods, or, sometimes, semi-divine beings. For example, in Mesopotamia the air god Enlil formed an agricultural tool, apparently a mattock, and the water god Enki/Ea, who was the patron of arts and of crafts, innovated the use of irrigation. In Egypt, the god Osiris showed humans how to farm, and Ptah was the patron of artists and craftsmen. In Ugarit, the god Kothar was an architect, a smith, and the inventor of beautiful furniture. In Greece, Athena created the rake and the plough, Apollo established towns, and he or Hermes invented the lyre, while Pan or Apollo created the flute.

In Genesis 4, all the advancements of civilization are achieved by humans. Thus, as is consistent with monotheism in the Torah, these developments are demythologized and are placed in historical context. ▪ JU

Remains of an ancient irrigation system, near Hierapolis (Turkey)

יח חֲנ֑וֹךְ וַֽיְהִי֙ בֹּ֣נֶה עִ֔יר וַיִּקְרָא֙ שֵׁ֣ם הָעִ֔יר כְּשֵׁ֖ם בְּנ֥וֹ חֲנֽוֹךְ׃ וַיִּוָּלֵ֤ד
לַחֲנוֹךְ֙ אֶת־עִירָ֔ד וְעִירָ֕ד יָלַ֖ד אֶת־מְחֽוּיָאֵ֑ל וּמְחִיָּיאֵ֗ל יָלַד֙ אֶת־
• יט מְת֣וּשָׁאֵ֔ל וּמְתוּשָׁאֵ֖ל יָלַ֥ד אֶת־לָֽמֶךְ׃ וַיִּֽקַּֽח־ל֥וֹ לֶ֖מֶךְ שְׁתֵּ֣י נָשִׁ֑ים חמישי

18 naming it Ḥanokh after his son. Ḥanokh had a son Irad, and
Irad had a son Meḥuyael. Meḥiyael had a son Metushael,
19 • and Metushael had a son Lemekh. Lemekh married two

NEAR EAST

4:17 The first city

The phrasing of this verse that Kayin was *boneh ir*, literally, "a city builder," implies that he introduced the construction of cities, as his descendants listed in Genesis 4:20–22 innovated other professions. The Torah's description of Kayin, "a worker of the land" (Gen. 4:2), as the initiator of the construction of cities is consistent with our understanding of the pre-historic progression from the domestication of plants and agricultural village life to urbanization, with fields extending outward from the city's edge.

The verse is understood as meaning that Kayin names the city, literally, "after the name of his son, Ḥanokh." It is interesting to note that in the Sumerian King List and in the Sumerian flood story (late 3rd to early 2nd millennium BCE), Eridu is listed as the first of five antediluvian cities where kingship was received. Eridu, close to the mouth of the Euphrates River, is known to be one of the earliest settlements in southern Mesopotamia (founded ca. 5400 BCE). Eridu is very similar to the name of the son of Ḥanokh, Irad (v. 18); both names are composed of the same consonants. This raises the possibility that this verse might conceivably be read as, "Kayin knew his wife, and she conceived and gave birth to Ḥanokh. He (Ḥanokh) built a city, naming the city after the name of the son of Ḥanokh." Thus, the name of the city would be Irad, i.e., Eridu. ▪ ZR

Inscription with the name of King Amar-Sin of Ur, Eridu, 21st century BCE

NEAR EAST

4:19 Married two women

In the ancient Near East, polygamy was never outlawed and was not very unusual. However, only rich men were able to afford more than one wife; among common people, monogamy was the norm.

The most common reason for taking on a second wife was infertility. In some Nuzi marriage contracts, a man may not take another wife if his first wife bears him children. Other reasons given in ancient texts for taking a second wife are if the first wife was ill or was perceived to be engaging in misconduct. For example, the *Laws of Hammurabi* give the husband the option to either divorce his wife or take on a second wife in case his wife "appropriates goods, squanders her household possessions or disparages her husband" (LH §141). ▪ ZR

Legal dispute over land, cuneiform tablet, Nuzi, 15th to 14th century BCE

שֵׁם הָאַחַת עָדָה וְשֵׁם הַשֵּׁנִית צִלָּה: וַתֵּלֶד עָדָה אֶת־יָבָל הוּא כ
הָיָה אֲבִי יֹשֵׁב אֹהֶל וּמִקְנֶה: וְשֵׁם אָחִיו יוּבָל הוּא הָיָה אֲבִי • כא
כָּל־תֹּפֵשׂ כִּנּוֹר וְעוּגָב: וְצִלָּה גַם־הִוא יָלְדָה אֶת־תּוּבַל קַיִן • כב

20 women, one named Ada and the other Tzila. Ada gave birth
to Yaval. He was the ancestor of those who live in tents and
• 21 raise livestock. His brother's name was Yuval. He was the
• 22 ancestor of all those who play the lyre and the pipe. Tzila,
too, had a son, Tuval-Kayin, who forged all kinds of bronze

NEAR EAST

4:21 The lyre and the pipe

The lyre (*kinor*) and the pipe (*ugav*) are paired together also in Job 21:12, "singing with the drum and lyre, rejoicing to the sounds of the pipe" and 30:31, "My lyre is given over to mourning and my pipe to the sounds of weeping." These examples represent two main classes of musical instruments, the stringed (*kinor*) and wind (*ugav*) instruments.

The *kinor* is one of the earliest instruments found in the ancient Near East. It is the only string instrument mentioned in the Torah, and the instrument mentioned most often in Tanakh. An etching from a floor stone in Megiddo, dated to 3300–3000 BCE, shows a female figure adjacent to a classic triangular harp having eight or nine strings.

The exact identification of *ugav* is unclear. The Targums translate it as *abuva*, an instrument similar to an oboe, but the word may simply be a general term for wind instruments. The earliest flutes, found in the Hohle Fels cave near Ulm, Germany and dating from the Upper Paleolithic period, were made of bone. The oldest musical instrument ever found in Mesopotamia is a silver flute from Ur with a gold mouthpiece, dated to the 27th to 26th century BCE. ▪ ZR

↗ Tel Megiddo, aerial view

NEAR EAST

4:22 Forged…bronze and iron tools

Bronze, an alloy of copper and tin, was produced in Mesopotamia and in the Sinai area as early as the 3rd millennium BCE. The widespread use of bronze from about 3300–1200 BCE led archaeologists to label that period of human history "the Bronze Age."

Iron was used sporadically even in the Bronze Age, since it can be extracted in small quantities, for example, by hammering meteoric iron which did not need the technology to produce the high temperatures required for smelting. However, the widespread use of iron in the ancient Near East dates to around 1200 BCE when that technology was invented. This led to the Iron Age, from about 1200–550 BCE, when iron tools replaced bronze ones. Thus, the order in which the different metals are mentioned in Genesis (gold in 2:11, bronze and iron here) matches the progression of metallurgy in the ancient world.

The verse refers to forging, from the Hebrew root *l t sh* which has the sense of sharpening, a term equally applicable to making tools or weapons. Both bronze and iron can be worked by hammering at cold or low temperatures; the earliest metal tools were not made by melting or casting.

The earliest copper artifact discovered so far is an awl dating to the 7th millennium BCE found at Tell Maghzaliya in northern Iraq. A copper awl set in a bone handle was discovered in Be'er Sheva, dating to the 4th millennium BCE, the Chalcolithic period. The oldest sharpened iron artifact was found in a grave in Samarra, on the east bank of the Tigris in Iraq, dated to 5000 BCE. It was formed by carefully hammering naturally occurring iron. ▪ ZR

↗ Chalcolithic copper mine, Timna
5th to 4th millennium BCE

כג לֹטֵשׁ כָּל־חֹרֵשׁ נְחֹשֶׁת וּבַרְזֶל וַאֲחוֹת תּוּבַל־קַיִן נַעֲמָה׃ וַיֹּאמֶר
לֶמֶךְ לְנָשָׁיו עָדָה וְצִלָּה שְׁמַעַן קוֹלִי נְשֵׁי לֶמֶךְ הַאְזֵנָּה אִמְרָתִי כִּי
כד אִישׁ הָרַגְתִּי לְפִצְעִי וְיֶלֶד לְחַבֻּרָתִי׃ כִּי שִׁבְעָתַיִם יֻקַּם־קָיִן וְלֶמֶךְ
• כה שִׁבְעִים וְשִׁבְעָה׃ וַיֵּדַע אָדָם עוֹד אֶת־אִשְׁתּוֹ וַתֵּלֶד בֵּן וַתִּקְרָא
אֶת־שְׁמוֹ שֵׁת כִּי שָׁת־לִי אֱלֹהִים זֶרַע אַחֵר תַּחַת הֶבֶל כִּי הֲרָגוֹ
כו קָיִן׃ וּלְשֵׁת גַּם־הוּא יֻלַּד־בֵּן וַיִּקְרָא אֶת־שְׁמוֹ אֱנוֹשׁ אָז הוּחַל

and iron tools. Tuval-Kayin's sister was Naama. Lemekh 23
said to his wives: "Ada and Tzila, listen to my voice; wives
of Lemekh, heed my words. I killed a man for wounding
me, killed a boy for bruising me. If Kayin will be avenged 24
seven times, then Lemekh, seventy-seven." Adam knew his 25 •
wife again, and she gave birth to a son and named him Shet,
"because God has granted[11] me another child in place of
Hevel," for Kayin had killed him. And Shet too had a son, and 26
named him Enosh. That was when people began to pray in

11 | The name Shet resonates with *shat* (granted).

NEAR EAST

4:25–26 When people began to pray in the name of the Lord

The lineage of Kayin ends with the words of Lemekh in verse 24. Our verse represents a new beginning with the line of Shet and his son Enosh, from whom present-day humanity descends. In the time of Enosh, people began to pray, or literally, "to call in the name of the Lord." This term is used in reference to the patriarchs when God's presence is invoked at a cultic site (Gen. 12:8, 13:4, 21:33, 26:25).

Prayer is presented as disconnected from other rituals, and not limited to a particular place or time. As with the offerings in Genesis 4:3–4, prayer here is initiated by humans, not commanded by the deity – in contrast with other ancient Near Eastern cultures where the gods establish temples for themselves and create people to serve them. ▪ ZR

Temple of Baalat Gebal (Jbeil), Byblos, originally built in 2800 BCE

ששי לִקְרֹא בְּשֵׁם יְהוָה׃ זֶה סֵפֶר תּוֹלְדֹת אָדָם בְּיוֹם בְּרֹא א • ה
אֱלֹהִים אָדָם בִּדְמוּת אֱלֹהִים עָשָׂה אֹתוֹ׃ זָכָר וּנְקֵבָה בְּרָאָם ב
וַיְבָרֶךְ אֹתָם וַיִּקְרָא אֶת־שְׁמָם אָדָם בְּיוֹם הִבָּרְאָם׃ וַיְחִי אָדָם ג •
שְׁלֹשִׁים וּמְאַת שָׁנָה וַיּוֹלֶד בִּדְמוּתוֹ כְּצַלְמוֹ וַיִּקְרָא אֶת־שְׁמוֹ

5 • 1 the name of the Lord. This is the book of Adam's
descendants: On the day God created humankind, He made
2 them in the likeness of God. Male and female He created
them, and on the day they were created, He blessed them
• 3 and called them Humankind.[12] Adam lived one hundred and
thirty years and then had a son in his own likeness and image,

12 | Hebrew *adam*.

NEAR EAST

5:1–32 Ten generations

The genealogy list in chapter 5 details ten generations from Adam to Noaḥ. One of the extraordinary elements of this list is the astonishing length of the lives reported – Ḥanokh's 365 years represent a comparatively short life on this list; most of the other individuals lived closer to the 969 years of Metushelaḥ!

An intriguing parallel appears in the Sumerian list of antediluvian kings first recorded by Berossus – a Babylonian author, historian, and astronomer who wrote in Greek – in the early 3rd century BCE. He lists ten semi-divine kings who came before the flood, whose reigns ranged from 10,800 years to 72,000 years! A more recently discovered Sumerian inscription lists eight kings reigning between 18,600 and 43,200 years. These lists are based upon the Sumerian sexagesimal (base 60) number system; hence all the reigns are multiples of sixty years. The total of all the reigns in the Berossus list is 432,000 years. In comparison, the total number of years in the Bible from creation until the flood is 1656.

The significant similarity between the biblical genealogy and the Sumerian list is that the ten generations before the flood consist of a list of the longest-lived people in their respective histories. Here as well, the Torah's account parallels an ancient Near Eastern tradition, but without the mythological elements. Unlike the Sumerian lists, all the male progenitors of Noaḥ are simply long-lived humans with no divine ancestors. ▪ JU

King List, Sumerian, Larsa (Iraq), ca. 1800 BCE

ד שֵׁת׃ וַיִּהְיוּ יְמֵי־אָדָם אַחֲרֵי הוֹלִידוֹ אֶת־שֵׁת שְׁמֹנֶה מֵאֹת שָׁנָה
ה וַיּוֹלֶד בָּנִים וּבָנוֹת׃ וַיִּהְיוּ כָּל־יְמֵי אָדָם אֲשֶׁר־חַי תְּשַׁע מֵאוֹת שָׁנָה
ו וּשְׁלֹשִׁים שָׁנָה וַיָּמֹת׃ וַיְחִי־שֵׁת חָמֵשׁ שָׁנִים וּמְאַת
ז שָׁנָה וַיּוֹלֶד אֶת־אֱנוֹשׁ׃ וַיְחִי־שֵׁת אַחֲרֵי הוֹלִידוֹ אֶת־אֱנוֹשׁ שֶׁבַע
ח שָׁנִים וּשְׁמֹנֶה מֵאוֹת שָׁנָה וַיּוֹלֶד בָּנִים וּבָנוֹת׃ וַיִּהְיוּ כָּל־יְמֵי־שֵׁת
ט שְׁתֵּים עֶשְׂרֵה שָׁנָה וּתְשַׁע מֵאוֹת שָׁנָה וַיָּמֹת׃ וַיְחִי
י אֱנוֹשׁ תִּשְׁעִים שָׁנָה וַיּוֹלֶד אֶת־קֵינָן׃ וַיְחִי אֱנוֹשׁ אַחֲרֵי הוֹלִידוֹ
אֶת־קֵינָן חֲמֵשׁ עֶשְׂרֵה שָׁנָה וּשְׁמֹנֶה מֵאוֹת שָׁנָה וַיּוֹלֶד בָּנִים
יא וּבָנוֹת׃ וַיִּהְיוּ כָּל־יְמֵי אֱנוֹשׁ חָמֵשׁ שָׁנִים וּתְשַׁע מֵאוֹת שָׁנָה
יב וַיָּמֹת׃ וַיְחִי קֵינָן שִׁבְעִים שָׁנָה וַיּוֹלֶד אֶת־מַהֲלַלְאֵל׃
יג וַיְחִי קֵינָן אַחֲרֵי הוֹלִידוֹ אֶת־מַהֲלַלְאֵל אַרְבָּעִים שָׁנָה וּשְׁמֹנֶה
יד מֵאוֹת שָׁנָה וַיּוֹלֶד בָּנִים וּבָנוֹת׃ וַיִּהְיוּ כָּל־יְמֵי קֵינָן עֶשֶׂר שָׁנִים
טו וּתְשַׁע מֵאוֹת שָׁנָה וַיָּמֹת׃ וַיְחִי מַהֲלַלְאֵל חָמֵשׁ
טז שָׁנִים וְשִׁשִּׁים שָׁנָה וַיּוֹלֶד אֶת־יָרֶד׃ וַיְחִי מַהֲלַלְאֵל אַחֲרֵי הוֹלִידוֹ
אֶת־יֶרֶד שְׁלֹשִׁים שָׁנָה וּשְׁמֹנֶה מֵאוֹת שָׁנָה וַיּוֹלֶד בָּנִים וּבָנוֹת׃
יז וַיִּהְיוּ כָּל־יְמֵי מַהֲלַלְאֵל חָמֵשׁ וְתִשְׁעִים שָׁנָה וּשְׁמֹנֶה מֵאוֹת שָׁנָה
יח וַיָּמֹת׃ וַיְחִי־יֶרֶד שְׁתַּיִם וְשִׁשִּׁים שָׁנָה וּמְאַת שָׁנָה וַיּוֹלֶד
יט אֶת־חֲנוֹךְ׃ וַיְחִי־יֶרֶד אַחֲרֵי הוֹלִידוֹ אֶת־חֲנוֹךְ שְׁמֹנֶה מֵאוֹת

and named him Shet. After Shet was born, Adam lived eight 4
hundred years and had other sons and daughters. Altogether 5
Adam lived nine hundred and thirty years, and then he
died. Shet lived one hundred and five years and 6
then had a son, Enosh. After Enosh was born, Shet lived eight 7
hundred and seven years and had other sons and daughters.
Altogether, Shet lived nine hundred and twelve years, and 8
then he died. Enosh lived ninety years and then 9
had a son, Keinan. After Keinan was born, Enosh lived eight 10
hundred and fifteen years and had other sons and daughters.
Altogether, Enosh lived nine hundred and five years, and 11
then he died. Keinan lived seventy years and had a 12
son, Mahalalel. After Mahalalel was born, Keinan lived eight 13
hundred and forty years and had other sons and daughters.
Altogether, Keinan lived nine hundred and ten years, and then 14
he died. Mahalalel lived sixty-five years and had a 15
son, Yered. After Yered was born, Mahalalel lived eight 16
hundred and thirty years and had other sons and daughters.
Altogether, Mahalalel lived eight hundred and ninety-five 17
years, and then he died. Yered lived one hundred 18
and sixty-two years and had a son, Ḥanokh. After Ḥanokh 19

NEAR EAST

5:3 Adam...had a son in his own likeness and image

Enuma Elish, the Babylonian creation epic, uses similar phraseology in its list of the generations of the gods: "Anshar made his son Anu like himself, and Anu begot Nudimmud in his likeness."

Due to the surrounding cultural context, it is not surprising that the language and syntax used in the Genesis genealogical lists are comparable to those in the ancient Near Eastern mythologies. However, the Babylonian myth views the gods as natural beings who are born generation after generation – an impossibility in the Torah's view of metaphysical monotheism. In Genesis, such language can be applied only to human generations.

"Had a son" in our verse is the translation of the verbal root *y l d*, literally "gave birth to." While such language is used in a literal fashion in polytheistic genealogies, in the Tanakh it is applied to God only rarely and always metaphorically, never literally (e.g., Deut. 32:18; Is. 66:9; Ps. 2:7). ▪ JU

שָׁנָה וַיּוֹלֶד בָּנִים וּבָנוֹת׃ וַיִּהְיוּ כָּל־יְמֵי־יֶרֶד שְׁתַּיִם וְשִׁשִּׁים שָׁנָה כ
וּתְשַׁע מֵאוֹת שָׁנָה וַיָּמֹת׃ וַיְחִי חֲנוֹךְ חָמֵשׁ וְשִׁשִּׁים כא
שָׁנָה וַיּוֹלֶד אֶת־מְתוּשָׁלַח׃ וַיִּתְהַלֵּךְ חֲנוֹךְ אֶת־הָאֱלֹהִים אַחֲרֵי כב
הוֹלִידוֹ אֶת־מְתוּשֶׁלַח שְׁלֹשׁ מֵאוֹת שָׁנָה וַיּוֹלֶד בָּנִים וּבָנוֹת׃ וַיְהִי כג
כָּל־יְמֵי חֲנוֹךְ חָמֵשׁ וְשִׁשִּׁים שָׁנָה וּשְׁלֹשׁ מֵאוֹת שָׁנָה׃ וַיִּתְהַלֵּךְ כד •
שביעי חֲנוֹךְ אֶת־הָאֱלֹהִים וְאֵינֶנּוּ כִּי־לָקַח אֹתוֹ אֱלֹהִים׃ וַיְחִי כה
מְתוּשֶׁלַח שֶׁבַע וּשְׁמֹנִים שָׁנָה וּמְאַת שָׁנָה וַיּוֹלֶד אֶת־לָמֶךְ׃
וַיְחִי מְתוּשֶׁלַח אַחֲרֵי הוֹלִידוֹ אֶת־לֶמֶךְ שְׁתַּיִם וּשְׁמוֹנִים שָׁנָה כו

was born, Yered lived eight hundred years and had other
20 sons and daughters. Altogether, Yered lived nine hundred
21 and sixty-two years, and then he died. Ḥanokh lived
22 sixty-five years and had a son, Metushelaḥ. Ḥanokh walked
faithfully with God for three hundred years after Metushelaḥ
23 was born, and had other sons and daughters. Altogether,
• 24 Ḥanokh lived for three hundred and sixty-five years. Ḥanokh
walked faithfully with God and then he was no more, for
25 God took him. Metushelaḥ lived one hundred and
26 eighty-seven years and had a son, Lemekh. After Lemekh
was born, Metushelaḥ lived seven hundred and eighty-
27 two years and had other sons and daughters. Altogether,

NEAR EAST

5:24 Ḥanokh walked faithfully with God...God took him

An ancient rabbinic tradition states that "All sevenths are favored...Of the generations, the seventh is favored: Adam, Shet, Enosh, Keinan, Mahalalel, Yered, Ḥanokh" (Pesikta Derav Kahana, 154b–155a; perhaps composed as early as the 5th century CE). This tradition dovetails with those in Mesopotamia. In the Babylonian list of pre-flood sages, the seventh, Utuabzu, is said to have "ascended to heaven." An inscription about Enmeduranna, the seventh in the Sumerian lists of pre-flood kings, relates that he was beloved by some of the chief gods, who revealed to him the secrets of heaven and earth. ▪ JU

NEAR EAST

5:29 This one will bring us comfort

The name Noaḥ apparently comes from the Hebrew root *n v ḥ*, meaning "rest." It cannot be etymologically derived from the root *n ḥ m* (comfort), so the explanation of the name given in the verse should be viewed more as a kind of play on words, involving two unrelated words with similar sounds. This was already noted by the Sages: "The name does not correspond to the interpretation [given to it], nor does the interpretation correspond to the name. The text should either have stated, 'This one Noaḥ will bring us rest (*yaniḥenu*),' or, 'And he called his name Naḥman, saying: This one will bring us comfort'" (Bereshit Rabba 25:2).

While there are no extra-biblical parallels for this name, it may be related to a name found in a fragment of the Hurrian version of the *Epic of Gilgamesh*. The Hurrians were an ancient Near Eastern people who flourished in the Bronze Age. They influenced other societies, particularly the Hittites. In their version of the *Epic of Gilgamesh*, the character of Gilgamesh is called Glagamishul, and there is a figure called Naḥmolel (or Naḥmasulel), who appears to be the Hurrian version of Utnapishtim, the character told by the deity to build a large boat before the flood. This name bears some resemblance to Noaḥ, which may possibly be an abbreviated version of the Hurrian name. ▪ ZR

Incense container, central temple of Tell-Basmosian (Iraq), Hurrian, 2nd millennium BCE

כז וּשְׁבַע מֵאוֹת שָׁנָה וַיּוֹלֶד בָּנִים וּבָנוֹת: וַיִּהְיוּ כׇּל־יְמֵי מְתוּשֶׁלַח
כח תֵּשַׁע וְשִׁשִּׁים שָׁנָה וּתְשַׁע מֵאוֹת שָׁנָה וַיָּמֹת: וַיְחִי־לֶמֶךְ
• כט שְׁתַּיִם וּשְׁמֹנִים שָׁנָה וּמְאַת שָׁנָה וַיּוֹלֶד בֵּן: וַיִּקְרָא אֶת־שְׁמוֹ נֹחַ
לֵאמֹר זֶה יְנַחֲמֵנוּ מִמַּעֲשֵׂנוּ וּמֵעִצְּבוֹן יָדֵינוּ מִן־הָאֲדָמָה אֲשֶׁר
ל אֵרְרָהּ יהוה: וַיְחִי־לֶמֶךְ אַחֲרֵי הוֹלִידוֹ אֶת־נֹחַ חָמֵשׁ וְתִשְׁעִים
לא שָׁנָה וַחֲמֵשׁ מֵאֹת שָׁנָה וַיּוֹלֶד בָּנִים וּבָנוֹת: וַיְהִי כׇּל־יְמֵי־לֶמֶךְ
לב שֶׁבַע וְשִׁבְעִים שָׁנָה וּשְׁבַע מֵאוֹת שָׁנָה וַיָּמֹת: וַיְהִי־
נֹחַ בֶּן־חֲמֵשׁ מֵאוֹת שָׁנָה וַיּוֹלֶד נֹחַ אֶת־שֵׁם אֶת־חָם וְאֶת־יָפֶת:
ו • א וַיְהִי כִּי־הֵחֵל הָאָדָם לָרֹב עַל־פְּנֵי הָאֲדָמָה וּבָנוֹת יֻלְּדוּ לָהֶם:

Metushelaḥ lived nine hundred and sixty-nine years, and then
he died. Lemekh lived one hundred and eighty-two 28
years and had a son. He named him Noaḥ, saying, "This one 29 •
will bring us comfort[13] after all our labor and the sorrow of
our hands on the land the Lord has cursed." After Noaḥ 30
was born, Lemekh lived five hundred and ninety-five years
and had other sons and daughters. Altogether, Lemekh 31
lived seven hundred and seventy-seven years, and then he
died. After Noaḥ was five hundred years old, Noaḥ 32
had three sons: Shem, Ḥam, and Yefet. Humans began to 1 • 6

13 | *Noaḥ* resonates with *yenaḥamenu* (will bring us comfort).

NEAR EAST

6:1–4 *Benei ha'elohim*

In his commentary on Genesis, Rabbi David Tzvi Hoffman summarizes the three main, distinct interpretations found in the Jewish tradition of the expression "the sons of God" – Hebrew, *benei ha'elohim*:

- They are angels (this explanation also appears in pre-rabbinic sources, such as Philo, Enoch, and the book of Jubilees);
- they are the descendants of Shet; those who are God-fearers; or
- they are the descendants of the "great ones," that is, heroes, rulers, or judges (in the sense of the kind of leaders mentioned in the book of Judges).

After detailed argumentation in which Hoffman develops the angel explanation, he concludes that the "sons of God" are humans who had been imbued with supernatural powers by satanic beings (a type of "fallen" angel), and who, therefore, acted against God's wishes (but with God's knowledge). The progeny of these humans brought enough evil to humanity for God to bring destruction upon the world by the flood and start human civilization again with Noaḥ and his descendants.

Rabbi Moshe David (Umberto) Cassuto wrote, among other works, important studies on Ugarit and the Tanakh, as well as commentaries on Exodus and the first twelve chapters of Genesis. He states that the Tanakh "concentrates in the Lord or in His messengers all the forces and tasks that the pagan peoples used to attribute to the various deities.... Since the angels...take the place of the Canaanite deities, the terms that formerly denoted the collectivity of gods...changed their meaning in conformity with this trend. The expression *benei elim* or *benei (ha) elohim*...became in the Bible designations for the heavenly household" (see Ps. 29:1, 89:7; Job 1:6, 2:1, 38:7; compare Ps. 103:20–21, 148:2).

Due to the bad behavior here of the "sons of God," Cassuto determines that the reference is not to the ministering angels but to the lowest order, the shedim – demonic beings who eat, drink, procreate, and die (as in BT Ḥagiga 16a; the idea that some angels are corruptible may also be implied in Is. 14:12 and Job 4:18–19). The "sons of god" in Genesis are, thus, similar to many references in ancient Near Eastern literature (for example, numerous Mesopotamian kings claimed divine sonship), and particularly to Ugaritic texts, which describe the gods having progeny with human partners. Like the Ugaritic great god El who had two sons by two different women, the "sons of God" in Genesis procreate with women.

Cassuto concludes that Genesis here, as in many other places, is counteracting polytheistic legends by reducing "to a minimum the content of the ancient traditions concerning the giants...only so much was retained as was innocuous to Israel's monotheistic faith and did not in the least detract from the glory of God...." ▪ JU

Egyptian god Seth (right), a man (center), and the Canaanite god Reshef (left), cylinder seal of Addumu, king of Sidon, 13th century BCE

NEAR EAST

6:4 Nefilim

Nefilim were apparently giants, as reported by the spies in Numbers 13:32–33. As the progeny of angels (see *"Benei ha'elohim"* on the previous page), they resemble such mythological characters as Gilgamesh, who was the son of a king but whose mother was the wise cow-goddess, Ninsun. The Hittite version of the *Epic of Gilgamesh* describes him as eleven cubits (over 5 meters, about 16 feet) tall.

Anne Kilmer suggested that the image of the nefilim here may be parallel to the *apkallu* of Mesopotamian literature – semi-divine beings who lived mostly before the flood, occasionally behaved in ways that angered the gods, and were sometimes linked with human wickedness. ▪ JU

ב וַיִּרְאוּ בְנֵי־הָאֱלֹהִים אֶת־בְּנוֹת הָאָדָם כִּי טֹבֹת הֵנָּה וַיִּקְחוּ
ג לָהֶם נָשִׁים מִכֹּל אֲשֶׁר בָּחָרוּ׃ וַיֹּאמֶר יהוה לֹא־יָדוֹן רוּחִי בָאָדָם
ד לְעֹלָם בְּשַׁגַּם הוּא בָשָׂר וְהָיוּ יָמָיו מֵאָה וְעֶשְׂרִים שָׁנָה׃ הַנְּפִלִים
הָיוּ בָאָרֶץ בַּיָּמִים הָהֵם וְגַם אַחֲרֵי־כֵן אֲשֶׁר יָבֹאוּ בְּנֵי הָאֱלֹהִים
אֶל־בְּנוֹת הָאָדָם וְיָלְדוּ לָהֶם הֵמָּה הַגִּבֹּרִים אֲשֶׁר מֵעוֹלָם אַנְשֵׁי
הַשֵּׁם׃

2 multiply on earth, and daughters were born to them. When
the sons of God[14] saw that the daughters of man were lovely,
they began to take whomever they chose to be wives to them.
3 Then the Lord said, "My spirit will not forever judge man;
he is of flesh. His life shall be but one hundred and twenty
4 years." In those days the Nefilim[15] were on earth, and later
also, for the sons of God had gone to the daughters of man
and had children with them. These were the heroes of old,
men of legends.

14 | Opinions vary regarding the meaning and proper translation of this phrase.

15 | Apparently giants (see Num. 13:33).

↗ Ninsun, mother of Gilgamesh, bas-relief, Sumer, 24th to 21st century BCE

↖ Noah's Ark on Mount Ararat, Simon de Myle, 1570

Statue of Ea, Akkadian god of water, holding a cup, Old Babylonian, 20th to 17th century BCE

icant ideological and ethical differences:

- In contrast to the *Epic of Gilgamesh*, God only acted to destroy humanity for a clear ethical reason – when its evil had become so great that violence had polluted the entire earth (Gen. 6:5, 11–13).
- Utnapishtim was saved because he was a god's favorite, but God saved Noaḥ due to his righteousness (Gen. 6:9, 7:1).
- Ea showed no care for the boat's passengers, but God showed His care for all the passengers aboard the ark by instructing Noaḥ to take enough food on the ark for all to survive (6:21), and by closing its door Himself (7:16).
- The gods, as natural beings, were terrified by the outpouring of nature. One is almost moved to pity the poor little gods who, like frightened children, ran up to the "attic" to escape the rising flood waters. On the other hand, the biblical God serenely controlled every-

In contradistinction to Enlil or Ishtar, God's behavior was motivated by justice, so He did not regret His decision to flood the earth.

thing and was constantly solicitous of the ark's inhabitants (Gen. 6:18, 8:1, 17).
- Unlike the gods who were starving for food, God is never hungry. Anthropomorphically, He "smelled the fragrant aroma," but that only prompted Him to ethical reflection (8:21–22). In contradistinction to Enlil or Ishtar, God's behavior was motivated by justice, so He did not regret His decision to flood the earth.
- The Utnapishtim story illustrates the gods' capriciousness. In contrast, in Genesis, when God began humanity anew with a righteous man and his family, and with the elucidation of natural human selfishness (6:5, 8:21), He guaranteed that He would never again mete out such an all-encompassing catastrophe. Further, He established a permanent covenant with humankind and blessed humanity's future procreation in the same manner as in Genesis 1, with the acquiescence that humanity's selfish nature demands carnivorous behavior, and with laws to control that selfishness. Thus, God reminded Noaḥ and his family that they were made in His image, and that taking human life must be punished (9:5).

Epic of Gilgamesh tablet, Megiddo, 14th century BCE

The close relationship, in both details and sequence, of the Genesis flood story to that of the earlier *Epic of Gilgamesh* testifies to the influence of the latter, and thus begs the question, "What is the Torah's purpose in telling the flood story?" The conclusion seems inescapable: the Torah refutes and corrects the amoral Mesopotamian account which was circulating (in one version or another) throughout the ancient Near East (a fragment of the *Epic of Gilgamesh*, ca. 14th century BCE, was even found near Megiddo).

Here, unlike in the *Epic of Gilgamesh* all is the work of the single, ethical, God, and the flood occurs because man has brought destruction upon himself. Indeed, the unprecedented biblical idea of the one and only God counteracts the possibility of conflicting divine interests (as seen in Mesopotamia). The Noaḥ narrative thus highlights the ideology of ethical monotheism and thereby shapes the ancient Israelites' moral consciousness. ▪ JU

The flood story in the Bible and ancient Mesopotamia

It is well known that many ancient cultures had flood stories. Two Mesopotamian stories in particular – the *Epic of Atrahasis* (Akkadian; ca. 17th century BCE) and Tablet XI of the *Epic of Gilgamesh* (see "The ethics of the Garden of Eden versus the quest for immortality in ancient Babylon" on pages 16–17) – show closer similarities to the Torah's narrative than any other.

The most significant piece of information in the Atrahasis story, which does not appear in the *Epic of Gilgamesh,* is the motivation for the gods' decision to destroy humanity. In the *Epic of Atrahasis* the noise people make, due to overpopulation, disturbs the gods' rest, and they decide to destroy humanity. By contrast, in the *Epic of Gilgamesh,* the only motivation for the gods' decision to destroy humanity is "their heart prompted the great gods to bring the deluge" (XI.14).

As the *Epic of Gilgamesh* provides the closest ancient Near Eastern parallel to the Noaḥ narrative, a summary of its flood story follows:

In a council, the great gods made their decision to bring the flood (to be kept secret from man). The god Ea repeated this secret to a man who was apparently his favorite – Utnapishtim. Ea urged him to save himself by building a ship of equal length and width, and, upon questioning, Ea told him to hide what he was doing from the townsfolk. Utnapishtim built the ship as a cube using workmen and pitch, asphalt, and oil. When the ship was completed, Utnapishtim loaded it with his silver and gold, his relatives, whatever he had of "the seed of all living creatures," the game and beasts of the field.

As it began to rain, Utnapishtim entered the ship and closed the door. The storm was so strong that "even the gods were terror-stricken at the deluge. They fled and ascended to the heaven of Anu (the sky god). The gods cowered like dogs…." The goddess "Ishtar cried out like a woman in labor…(and) lamented…'Because I commanded evil in the assembly of gods…how could I command war to destroy my people, for it is I who give birth to these my people!' The …gods wept with her." The gods then regretted their hasty decision.

It rained for six days and nights. The ship landed on Mount Nisir. Utnapishtim sent out a dove which found no resting place and returned. He then sent out a swallow and the same thing happened. Finally, he sent out a raven, which ate and did not return. Utnapishtim then left the boat and offered a sacrifice. "The gods smelled the sweet savor. The gods gathered like flies over the sacrificer." Ishtar lifted up the jewels around her neck as a reminder of the flood.

The instigator of the flood, Enlil, joined the gods late. Ishtar accusingly said, "without reflection he brought on the deluge and consigned my people to destruction." Enlil became angry when he saw that some mortals escaped. One of the gods tattled on Ea. Ea defended himself by attacking Enlil, "How could you without reflection bring on this deluge? On the sinner lay his sin, on the transgressor lay his transgression." However, the story identifies no particular sinner or sinners, so Ea's after-the-fact ethical principle is hypothetical.

Ea then suggested that Enlil would have done better by bringing a lesser punishment, such as wild animals or pestilence, on humankind. Ea further defended himself by prevaricating. He stated that he did not reveal the gods' secret to Utnapishtim, but simply showed it to him in a dream. Finally, Enlil, having apparently calmed down, made Utnapishtim and his wife immortal.

While the Noaḥ narrative shares a number of details with this story, it evinces signif-

Fragment of the *Epic of Atrahasis,* Akkadian, Mesopotamia, 17th century BCE

מפטיר וַיַּרְא יהוה כִּי רַבָּה רָעַת הָאָדָם בָּאָרֶץ וְכָל־יֵצֶר מַחְשְׁבֹת לִבּוֹ רַק ה
רַע כָּל־הַיּוֹם׃ וַיִּנָּחֶם יהוה כִּי־עָשָׂה אֶת־הָאָדָם בָּאָרֶץ וַיִּתְעַצֵּב ו
אֶל־לִבּוֹ׃ וַיֹּאמֶר יהוה אֶמְחֶה אֶת־הָאָדָם אֲשֶׁר־בָּרָאתִי מֵעַל ז
פְּנֵי הָאֲדָמָה מֵאָדָם עַד־בְּהֵמָה עַד־רֶמֶשׂ וְעַד־עוֹף הַשָּׁמָיִם כִּי
נִחַמְתִּי כִּי עֲשִׂיתִם׃ וְנֹחַ מָצָא חֵן בְּעֵינֵי יהוה׃ ח

5 The LORD saw how great man's wickedness was upon the
earth, and that his thoughts constantly inclined toward evil.
6 Then the LORD regretted that He had made man on earth,
7 and His heart was touched with sorrow. The LORD said,
"I will erase My creation, humankind, from the face of the
land – man, even animals and creeping things, even birds of
8 the heavens – for I regret having made them." But Noaḥ found
favor in the LORD's sight.

NEAR EAST

6:14–16 The ark and boats in the ancient Near East

The term *teva*, used for the ark, signifies a box, made to float on the water but without any navigational system such as sails, oars, a rudder, or even a crew of sailors. The same word describes the container into which Moshe was placed as a baby (Exodus 2:3–5). Use of this term emphasizes that only the will of God determines the fate of those on board. By contrast, the vessels of Atrahasis in the Akkadian flood story and Utnapishtim in the flood story in the *Epic of Gilgamesh* have crews of sailors on board.

The size of the ark, based on the standard measurement of a cubit (around 45 centimeters), is 157 meters long, 23 meters wide and 14 meters high (75.5 x 46 feet), resulting in a displacement of 43,000 tons (39,000 metric tons) and a capacity of about 15,000 tons (13,600 metric tons). In the *Epic of Gilgamesh*, Utnapishtim's vessel is a cube, 120 cubits on each side, making it much larger than Noaḥ's ark. Additionally, Noaḥ's ark had three decks, while Utnapishtim's had seven, with nine compartments each. The ship of Atrahasis was made of reeds and had only two decks. The pitch (*kofer*) used by Noaḥ to prevent leakage on his ark is identical with the Akkadian *kupru* which is mentioned with regard to both Atrahasis and Utnapishtim.

The earliest watercraft were made of skins and reeds or dugout logs. These were small boats, suitable for rivers. A large vessel such as Noaḥ's ark would need to be made of planks of wood, as described in verse 14. These planks had to be joined together using wooden pegs; nails were invented only much later. The earliest plank ships were from Egypt in the middle of the 3rd millennium BCE. Larger plank ships appeared later in the 3rd millennium BCE in Mesopotamia, with more advanced technology used to make bigger and bigger ships over time. However, even the Roman ship *Isis*, a famous and very large vessel that operated in the Mediterranean around 150 CE, was less than a quarter the size of the ark. ▪ ZR

↗ Ancient Egyptian boat, found near the pyramid of Senusret III, Dahshur, 19th century BCE

ט אֵלֶּה תּוֹלְדֹת נֹחַ נֹחַ אִישׁ צַדִּיק תָּמִים הָיָה בְּדֹרֹתָיו אֶת־הָאֱלֹהִים נח
י הִתְהַלֶּךְ־נֹחַ׃ וַיּוֹלֶד נֹחַ שְׁלֹשָׁה בָנִים אֶת־שֵׁם אֶת־חָם וְאֶת־יָפֶת׃
יא יב וַתִּשָּׁחֵת הָאָרֶץ לִפְנֵי הָאֱלֹהִים וַתִּמָּלֵא הָאָרֶץ חָמָס׃ וַיַּרְא
אֱלֹהִים אֶת־הָאָרֶץ וְהִנֵּה נִשְׁחָתָה כִּי־הִשְׁחִית כָּל־בָּשָׂר אֶת־
יג דַּרְכּוֹ עַל־הָאָרֶץ׃ וַיֹּאמֶר אֱלֹהִים לְנֹחַ קֵץ כָּל־בָּשָׂר
בָּא לְפָנַי כִּי־מָלְאָה הָאָרֶץ חָמָס מִפְּנֵיהֶם וְהִנְנִי מַשְׁחִיתָם אֶת־
• יד הָאָרֶץ׃ עֲשֵׂה לְךָ תֵּבַת עֲצֵי־גֹפֶר קִנִּים תַּעֲשֶׂה אֶת־הַתֵּבָה
טו וְכָפַרְתָּ אֹתָהּ מִבַּיִת וּמִחוּץ בַּכֹּפֶר׃ וְזֶה אֲשֶׁר תַּעֲשֶׂה אֹתָהּ שְׁלֹשׁ
מֵאוֹת אַמָּה אֹרֶךְ הַתֵּבָה חֲמִשִּׁים אַמָּה רָחְבָּהּ וּשְׁלֹשִׁים אַמָּה
טז קוֹמָתָהּ׃ צֹהַר ׀ תַּעֲשֶׂה לַתֵּבָה וְאֶל־אַמָּה תְּכַלֶּנָּה מִלְמַעְלָה
יז וּפֶתַח הַתֵּבָה בְּצִדָּהּ תָּשִׂים תַּחְתִּיִּם שְׁנִיִּם וּשְׁלִשִׁים תַּעֲשֶׂהָ׃ וַאֲנִי
הִנְנִי מֵבִיא אֶת־הַמַּבּוּל מַיִם עַל־הָאָרֶץ לְשַׁחֵת כָּל־בָּשָׂר אֲשֶׁר־
• יח בּוֹ רוּחַ חַיִּים מִתַּחַת הַשָּׁמָיִם כֹּל אֲשֶׁר־בָּאָרֶץ יִגְוָע׃ וַהֲקִמֹתִי
אֶת־בְּרִיתִי אִתָּךְ וּבָאתָ אֶל־הַתֵּבָה אַתָּה וּבָנֶיךָ וְאִשְׁתְּךָ וּנְשֵׁי־

9 This is the story of Noaḥ. Noaḥ was a righteous man, a person
10 of integrity in his generation; Noaḥ walked with God. And
11 Noaḥ had three sons: Shem, Ḥam, and Yefet. The earth had
12 become corrupt in God's sight, full of violence. And when
God saw how corrupt the earth had become, all flesh
13 corrupting its ways upon the earth, God said to
Noaḥ, "The end of all flesh has come before Me, for the earth
is full of violence because of them. I am about to destroy
14 • them, along with all the earth. So make yourself an ark of
cypress wood. Make it with compartments and coat it in pitch
15 inside and out. This is how you shall make it: the ark shall be
three hundred cubits long, fifty cubits wide, and thirty cubits
16 high. Make a window for the ark, and taper the latter to within
a cubit of the top.[16] Put a door in the side of the ark and make
17 lower, middle, and upper decks. And I – I am about to bring
floodwaters over the earth to destroy all flesh that has within
it the breath of life under the heavens. Everything on earth
18 • will die. But I will establish My covenant with you, and you
will enter the ark – you, your sons, your wife, and your sons'

16 | That is, the ark should slant upward, becoming narrower as it approaches the top.

The Egyptian/Hittite Kadesh peace treaty, Temple of Karnak, Luxor, 13th century BCE

NEAR EAST

6:18 Covenant

This is the first mention in Tanakh of the term *brit*, literally, "treaty" – an important concept that appears throughout the Tanakh, for political relationships between people, here for the relationship between God and man, and, particularly, between God and the Israelites. Since the term was not used previously with relation to Adam, this covenant does not seem to be a fulfillment of the blessings given in Genesis 1:28, but rather it envisions the covenant detailed later (after the flood is over), in Genesis 9:8–17.

By contrast, the other flood stories of the ancient Near East do not mention a covenant or treaty between the deity and the person tasked with building the ship, and more generally, no ancient Near Eastern document records any god making a covenant with any individual or group of humans (see "God's eternal covenant with life on Earth" on page 51). ▪ ZR

בָּנֶיךָ אִתָּךְ: וּמִכָּל־הָחַי מִכָּל־בָּשָׂר שְׁנַיִם מִכֹּל תָּבִיא אֶל־הַתֵּבָה יט
לְהַחֲיֹת אִתָּךְ זָכָר וּנְקֵבָה יִהְיוּ: מֵהָעוֹף לְמִינֵהוּ וּמִן־הַבְּהֵמָה כ
לְמִינָהּ מִכֹּל רֶמֶשׂ הָאֲדָמָה לְמִינֵהוּ שְׁנַיִם מִכֹּל יָבֹאוּ אֵלֶיךָ
לְהַחֲיוֹת: וְאַתָּה קַח־לְךָ מִכָּל־מַאֲכָל אֲשֶׁר יֵאָכֵל וְאָסַפְתָּ אֵלֶיךָ כא
וְהָיָה לְךָ וְלָהֶם לְאָכְלָה: וַיַּעַשׂ נֹחַ כְּכֹל אֲשֶׁר צִוָּה אֹתוֹ אֱלֹהִים כב
שני כֵּן עָשָׂה: וַיֹּאמֶר יהוה לְנֹחַ בֹּא־אַתָּה וְכָל־בֵּיתְךָ אֶל־הַתֵּבָה א ז
כִּי־אֹתְךָ רָאִיתִי צַדִּיק לְפָנַי בַּדּוֹר הַזֶּה: מִכֹּל ׀ הַבְּהֵמָה הַטְּהוֹרָה ב •
תִּקַּח־לְךָ שִׁבְעָה שִׁבְעָה אִישׁ וְאִשְׁתּוֹ וּמִן־הַבְּהֵמָה אֲשֶׁר לֹא
טְהֹרָה הִוא שְׁנַיִם אִישׁ וְאִשְׁתּוֹ: גַּם מֵעוֹף הַשָּׁמַיִם שִׁבְעָה שִׁבְעָה ג
זָכָר וּנְקֵבָה לְחַיּוֹת זֶרַע עַל־פְּנֵי כָל־הָאָרֶץ: כִּי לְיָמִים עוֹד שִׁבְעָה ד •
אָנֹכִי מַמְטִיר עַל־הָאָרֶץ אַרְבָּעִים יוֹם וְאַרְבָּעִים לָיְלָה וּמָחִיתִי

19 wives with you. And you shall take two of each living creature,
20 male and female, into the ark to keep alive with you. Of every
kind of bird, animal, and wild beast, bring two to keep alive.
21 As for you, take all the food to be eaten and store it: it will be
22 for food for you and for them." Noaḥ did so: all that God
7 1 commanded him, he fulfilled. Then the LORD said to Noaḥ,
"Enter the ark, you and all your household, for I have seen
• 2 you alone to be righteous before Me in this generation. Take
seven and seven of every pure animal, seven pairs, and two of
3 every animal that is not pure, of each kind a pair. Also take
seven pairs of each kind of bird, male and female, to keep their
• 4 kind alive across the earth. For in seven days' time I will send
rain on the earth for forty days and forty nights, and I will
wipe from the face of the earth every living creature I have

NEAR EAST

7:2–3 Pure animals and birds

These verses comprise the first mention of the concept of pure and impure animals (and birds, Gen. 8:20) in the Tanakh, indicating that these categories existed before dietary laws were given to the Israelites. Here, purity does not imply permission to eat, as meat was prohibited until after the flood (Gen. 9:2–3), and even once permission was granted, no distinction was made between pure and impure creatures. Rather, as can be inferred from Noaḥ's later actions (Gen. 8:20), purity refers to the animal's suitability for sacrifice.

Other cultures of the ancient Near East had their own views about which kinds of animals were suitable for sacrifice. Based on the widespread understanding that the sacrifice was a meal to feed the god, the types of animals offered reflected each society's conception of what was edible and tasty. In Mesopotamia, those were domesticated animals, while in Egypt, wild animals, such as antelopes and gazelles, were preferred.

The flood story of the *Epic of Atrahasis* also contains a reference to the sacrifice of pure animals (ii 32–33), but in that fragmentary section, it appears that the sacrifices took place before the flood, as the animals were being brought on board the vessel. Accordingly, it appears that Atrahasis's and Noaḥ's sacrifices had different purposes. The former was a gift to the gods to protect Atrahasis from danger, while the latter was a thanksgiving offering. ▪ ZR

↗
Butchering a cow,
Saqqara, 3rd millennium BCE

ה אֶת־כׇּל־הַיְקוּם אֲשֶׁר עָשִׂיתִי מֵעַל פְּנֵי הָאֲדָמָה: וַיַּעַשׂ נֹחַ כְּכֹל
ו אֲשֶׁר־צִוָּהוּ יהוה: וְנֹחַ בֶּן־שֵׁשׁ מֵאוֹת שָׁנָה וְהַמַּבּוּל הָיָה מַיִם
ז עַל־הָאָרֶץ: וַיָּבֹא נֹחַ וּבָנָיו וְאִשְׁתּוֹ וּנְשֵׁי־בָנָיו אִתּוֹ אֶל־הַתֵּבָה
ח מִפְּנֵי מֵי הַמַּבּוּל: מִן־הַבְּהֵמָה הַטְּהוֹרָה וּמִן־הַבְּהֵמָה אֲשֶׁר
ט אֵינֶנָּה טְהֹרָה וּמִן־הָעוֹף וְכֹל אֲשֶׁר־רֹמֵשׂ עַל־הָאֲדָמָה: שְׁנַיִם
שְׁנַיִם בָּאוּ אֶל־נֹחַ אֶל־הַתֵּבָה זָכָר וּנְקֵבָה כַּאֲשֶׁר צִוָּה אֱלֹהִים
י אֶת־נֹחַ: וַיְהִי לְשִׁבְעַת הַיָּמִים וּמֵי הַמַּבּוּל הָיוּ עַל־הָאָרֶץ:
יא בִּשְׁנַת שֵׁשׁ־מֵאוֹת שָׁנָה לְחַיֵּי־נֹחַ בַּחֹדֶשׁ הַשֵּׁנִי בְּשִׁבְעָה־עָשָׂר
יוֹם לַחֹדֶשׁ בַּיּוֹם הַזֶּה נִבְקְעוּ כׇּל־מַעְיְנֹת תְּהוֹם רַבָּה וַאֲרֻבֹּת

made." Noaḥ did all that the Lord commanded him. Noaḥ 5 6
was six hundred years old when the floodwaters came upon
the earth. Noaḥ, with his sons, his wife, and his sons' wives, 7
came into the ark to escape the waters of the flood. The pure 8
animals, the animals that were not pure, the birds, and all that
walked the earth came two by two to Noaḥ into the ark, male 9
and female, as God had commanded Noaḥ. Thus, after seven 10
days the floodwaters came upon the earth. In the six 11
hundredth year of Noaḥ's life, in the second month, on the
seventeenth of the month – on that day, all the wellsprings of

NEAR EAST

7:4–12 The numbers seven, forty, six hundred

The numbers seven, forty and six hundred appear many times in Tanakh. Rather than representing an exact or historical quantity, these numbers have allegorical and typological meaning.

"Forty days" is used in Tanakh to indicate a period longer than a month, such as with the time required for embalming (Gen. 50:3), the number of days Moshe was on Mount Sinai (Ex. 24:18), and the number of days Golyat taunted Sha'ul's army (I Sam. 17:16). However, Rabbi Moshe David (Umberto) Cassuto showed that the forty days of the rain during the flood (Gen. 7:4) and the forty days after the mountaintops became visible until Noaḥ sent the raven (Gen. 8:6) fit exactly with the dates given in the text.

The number forty appears occasionally in the literature of other ancient Near East cultures, but not as frequently. It is found, for example, in the Mesha Stele stating that the North Israelites oppressed Moav for forty years, "Now Omri took the land of Madeba, and occupied it in his day, and in the days of his son, forty years." In the Tanakh, the term "forty years" generally refers to a generation – for example, the book of Judges uses the phrase "the land rested for forty years" to indicate a generation of peace (Judges 3:11, 5:31, 8:28).

The significance of the number seven in ancient times has been explained as related to the seven heavenly bodies which the ancient astronomers deified, associating the number seven with holiness and perfection. Additionally, according to Old Babylonian mathematics, seven was considered a unique number because it was not divisible by 2, 3, or 5.

"Seven days" appears in the Noaḥ narrative as an exact number. However, it is also found in Tanakh in many contexts as a symbolic number used to indicate completion, perfection, and holiness (best expressed in the concept of the Sabbath). In Mesopotamia we see this idea, too. The *Epic of Gilgamesh* describes Gilgamesh weeping over his friend Enkidu for seven days and seven nights. The Gudea cylinders (ca. 2125 BCE) contain the Sumerian myth of the *Building of Ningirsu's Temple* to Eninnu at Girsu, a ritual play to be enacted during the annual dedication of the temple which lasted for seven days.

Six hundred is a basic number in Mesopotamia's sexagesimal (base sixty) system, where large numbers were counted in units of sixty. The length of the reigns of the antediluvian kings in the Sumerian King List are all within the sexagesimal system. They range from 18,600 (600 x 31) to 43,200 (600 x 72) years – all the reigns totaling 241,200 years (600 x 402). Noaḥ's age of six hundred when the flood began may be related to this symbolic Mesopotamian unit, even if it is meant literally (compare Gen. 7:6 with 8:13). ▪ ZR

↗ Votive stele of King Gudea of Lagash, dedicated to the Temple of Ningirsu, Girsu (Iraq), 22nd century BCE

יב הַשָּׁמַיִם נִפְתָּחוּ׃ וַיְהִי הַגֶּשֶׁם עַל־הָאָרֶץ אַרְבָּעִים יוֹם וְאַרְבָּעִים
יג לָיְלָה׃ בְּעֶצֶם הַיּוֹם הַזֶּה בָּא נֹחַ וְשֵׁם־וְחָם וָיֶפֶת בְּנֵי־נֹחַ וְאֵשֶׁת
יד נֹחַ וּשְׁלֹשֶׁת נְשֵׁי־בָנָיו אִתָּם אֶל־הַתֵּבָה׃ הֵמָּה וְכָל־הַחַיָּה לְמִינָהּ
וְכָל־הַבְּהֵמָה לְמִינָהּ וְכָל־הָרֶמֶשׂ הָרֹמֵשׂ עַל־הָאָרֶץ לְמִינֵהוּ
טו וְכָל־הָעוֹף לְמִינֵהוּ כֹּל צִפּוֹר כָּל־כָּנָף׃ וַיָּבֹאוּ אֶל־נֹחַ אֶל־הַתֵּבָה
טז שְׁנַיִם שְׁנַיִם מִכָּל־הַבָּשָׂר אֲשֶׁר־בּוֹ רוּחַ חַיִּים׃ וְהַבָּאִים זָכָר וּנְקֵבָה
מִכָּל־בָּשָׂר בָּאוּ כַּאֲשֶׁר צִוָּה אֹתוֹ אֱלֹהִים וַיִּסְגֹּר יהוה בַּעֲדוֹ׃
יז וַיְהִי הַמַּבּוּל אַרְבָּעִים יוֹם עַל־הָאָרֶץ וַיִּרְבּוּ הַמַּיִם וַיִּשְׂאוּ אֶת־ שלישי
יח הַתֵּבָה וַתָּרָם מֵעַל הָאָרֶץ׃ וַיִּגְבְּרוּ הַמַּיִם וַיִּרְבּוּ מְאֹד עַל־הָאָרֶץ
יט וַתֵּלֶךְ הַתֵּבָה עַל־פְּנֵי הַמָּיִם׃ וְהַמַּיִם גָּבְרוּ מְאֹד מְאֹד עַל־הָאָרֶץ
כ וַיְכֻסּוּ כָּל־הֶהָרִים הַגְּבֹהִים אֲשֶׁר־תַּחַת כָּל־הַשָּׁמָיִם׃ חֲמֵשׁ
כא עֶשְׂרֵה אַמָּה מִלְמַעְלָה גָּבְרוּ הַמָּיִם וַיְכֻסּוּ הֶהָרִים׃ וַיִּגְוַע כָּל־
בָּשָׂר ׀ הָרֹמֵשׂ עַל־הָאָרֶץ בָּעוֹף וּבַבְּהֵמָה וּבַחַיָּה וּבְכָל־הַשֶּׁרֶץ
כב הַשֹּׁרֵץ עַל־הָאָרֶץ וְכֹל הָאָדָם׃ כֹּל אֲשֶׁר נִשְׁמַת־רוּחַ חַיִּים בְּאַפָּיו
כג מִכֹּל אֲשֶׁר בֶּחָרָבָה מֵתוּ׃ וַיִּמַח אֶת־כָּל־הַיְקוּם ׀ אֲשֶׁר ׀ עַל־פְּנֵי
הָאֲדָמָה מֵאָדָם עַד־בְּהֵמָה עַד־רֶמֶשׂ וְעַד־עוֹף הַשָּׁמַיִם וַיִּמָּחוּ
כד מִן־הָאָרֶץ וַיִּשָּׁאֶר אַךְ־נֹחַ וַאֲשֶׁר אִתּוֹ בַּתֵּבָה׃ וַיִּגְבְּרוּ הַמַּיִם
ח א עַל־הָאָרֶץ חֲמִשִּׁים וּמְאַת יוֹם׃ וַיִּזְכֹּר אֱלֹהִים אֶת־נֹחַ וְאֵת כָּל־
הַחַיָּה וְאֶת־כָּל־הַבְּהֵמָה אֲשֶׁר אִתּוֹ בַּתֵּבָה וַיַּעֲבֵר אֱלֹהִים רוּחַ
ב עַל־הָאָרֶץ וַיָּשֹׁכּוּ הַמָּיִם׃ וַיִּסָּכְרוּ מַעְיְנֹת תְּהוֹם וַאֲרֻבֹּת הַשָּׁמָיִם
ג וַיִּכָּלֵא הַגֶּשֶׁם מִן־הַשָּׁמָיִם׃ וַיָּשֻׁבוּ הַמַּיִם מֵעַל הָאָרֶץ הָלוֹךְ וָשׁוֹב
ד וַיַּחְסְרוּ הַמַּיִם מִקְצֵה חֲמִשִּׁים וּמְאַת יוֹם׃ וַתָּנַח הַתֵּבָה בַּחֹדֶשׁ •

the great deep burst, and the
12 heavens' floodgates opened. The
rain fell on the earth for forty
13 days and forty nights. On that
very day, Noaḥ, his sons, Shem,
Ḥam, and Yefet, Noaḥ's wife,
and his sons' three wives entered
14 the ark. With them came every
kind of wild beast, every kind of
animal, every creeping, crawling
creature of the land, every kind
15 of flying creature, every bird, and each winged thing. They came to Noaḥ, to the ark, two by two, of all
16 flesh that had within it the breath of life. They came, male and female of all flesh, as God had commanded
17 him. Then the Lord shut him in. For forty days the flood came upon the earth. The waters swelled,
18 lifting the ark so that it rose above the land. The waters surged, swelling enormously on the earth, and
19 the ark began to drift on the surface of the water. The waters surged ever more, until all the high mountains
20 beneath all the heavens were covered. Fifteen cubits above them the waters surged as the mountains
21 were covered. All flesh that moved upon the earth perished – birds, animals, wild beasts, and all the
22 creatures that swarm on the earth, and all humankind. Everything on dry land that had breath of life in
23 its nostrils died. Every living thing on the face of the earth was wiped out: from humans to animals, from
creeping creatures to winged birds of the heavens, all were wiped from the earth. Only Noaḥ and those
8 24 1 with him in the ark survived. For one hundred fifty days, the waters surged over the earth. Then God
remembered Noaḥ and all the wild beasts and animals with him in the ark. God sent a wind over the
2 earth, and the waters began to subside. The wellsprings of the deep and heavens' floodgates closed, and
3 the heavens' rains were reined in. The water steadily receded from the earth, and by the end of one
• 4 hundred fifty days, the water had abated. In the seventh month, on the seventeenth day of the month,

ה הַשְּׁבִיעִי בְּשִׁבְעָה־עָשָׂר יוֹם לַחֹדֶשׁ עַל הָרֵי אֲרָרָט׃ וְהַמַּיִם הָיוּ
הָלוֹךְ וְחָסוֹר עַד הַחֹדֶשׁ הָעֲשִׂירִי בָּעֲשִׂירִי בְּאֶחָד לַחֹדֶשׁ נִרְאוּ
ו רָאשֵׁי הֶהָרִים׃ וַיְהִי מִקֵּץ אַרְבָּעִים יוֹם וַיִּפְתַּח נֹחַ אֶת־חַלּוֹן
ז הַתֵּבָה אֲשֶׁר עָשָׂה׃ וַיְשַׁלַּח אֶת־הָעֹרֵב וַיֵּצֵא יָצוֹא וָשׁוֹב עַד־
ח יְבֹשֶׁת הַמַּיִם מֵעַל הָאָרֶץ׃ וַיְשַׁלַּח אֶת־הַיּוֹנָה מֵאִתּוֹ לִרְאוֹת
ט הֲקַלּוּ הַמַּיִם מֵעַל פְּנֵי הָאֲדָמָה׃ וְלֹא־מָצְאָה הַיּוֹנָה מָנוֹחַ לְכַף־
רַגְלָהּ וַתָּשָׁב אֵלָיו אֶל־הַתֵּבָה כִּי־מַיִם עַל־פְּנֵי כָל־הָאָרֶץ וַיִּשְׁלַח
י יָדוֹ וַיִּקָּחֶהָ וַיָּבֵא אֹתָהּ אֵלָיו אֶל־הַתֵּבָה׃ וַיָּחֶל עוֹד שִׁבְעַת יָמִים

the ark came to rest on the mountains of Ararat. The water 5
continued to abate until the tenth month, and on the first day
of the tenth month, the mountaintops became visible. After 6
forty days Noaḥ opened the window he had made in the ark
and sent a raven forth. It flew to and fro until the water on the 7
earth had dried. After that he sent forth a dove to see whether 8
the water had subsided from the face of the land. But the dove 9
found no resting place to plant its foot, and so it returned to
him, to the ark, for water still covered the face of the earth
completely. He reached out his hand and brought the dove
back to him, into the ark. Then he waited another seven days, 10

NEAR EAST

8:4 The mountains of Ararat

In contrast to other ancient Near East flood accounts, this verse does not identify a specific mountain upon which the ark came to rest – only the Ararat mountain range. This area, called Urartu in Assyrian inscriptions, covers the expanse between the Aras River and Lake Van, in today's eastern Turkey. The area was known to the ancient Israelites and is mentioned a few times in the Tanakh (II Kings 19:37; Is. 37:38; Jer. 51:27). The mountain called Mount Ararat today (Masis in Armenian, Agrı Dagı in Turkish) is a dormant volcano which has been identified by that name, at least since the Middle Ages. *Ararad* is the Western Armenian pronunciation for a kingdom that existed in the Armenian highlands in the 9th to 6th century BCE. ▪ ZR

↗ The large peak of the traditional site of Mount Ararat, view from Yeravan, Armenia

NEAR EAST

8:11 Freshly picked olive leaf

The olive is one of the earliest trees cultivated in the ancient Near East, going back to the Early Bronze Age. It is a very strong and long-lasting evergreen, producing fruit for hundreds of years. The locals claim that the al Badawi olive tree in Beit Leḥem is over 4,000 years old, but no scientific evidence has been produced to support this claim. However, carbon-dating tests have demonstrated that olive trees in Malta are 2,000 years old, and one in Croatia that still produces fruit is 1,600 years old. Some olive trees in Israel may well go back to talmudic times.

Olive trees can grow in rocky soil and on hillsides, but not at high elevations. Thus, a freshly cut olive leaf indicates that the water had receded enough for the trees that grow at lower elevations to have regenerated, indicating that the land was sufficiently dry. ▪ ZR

Olive tree purported to be 1,600 years old, Olive Gardens Nature Reserve, Lun, Croatia

אֲחֵרִים וַיֹּסֶף שַׁלַּח אֶת־הַיּוֹנָה מִן־הַתֵּבָה׃ וַתָּבֹא אֵלָיו הַיּוֹנָה יא •
לְעֵת עֶרֶב וְהִנֵּה עֲלֵה־זַיִת טָרָף בְּפִיהָ וַיֵּדַע נֹחַ כִּי־קַלּוּ הַמַּיִם
מֵעַל הָאָרֶץ׃ וַיִּיָּחֶל עוֹד שִׁבְעַת יָמִים אֲחֵרִים וַיְשַׁלַּח אֶת־הַיּוֹנָה יב
וְלֹא־יָסְפָה שׁוּב־אֵלָיו עוֹד׃ וַיְהִי בְּאַחַת וְשֵׁשׁ־מֵאוֹת שָׁנָה יג
בָּרִאשׁוֹן בְּאֶחָד לַחֹדֶשׁ חָרְבוּ הַמַּיִם מֵעַל הָאָרֶץ וַיָּסַר נֹחַ אֶת־
מִכְסֵה הַתֵּבָה וַיַּרְא וְהִנֵּה חָרְבוּ פְּנֵי הָאֲדָמָה׃ וּבַחֹדֶשׁ הַשֵּׁנִי יד
רביעי בְּשִׁבְעָה וְעֶשְׂרִים יוֹם לַחֹדֶשׁ יָבְשָׁה הָאָרֶץ׃ וַיְדַבֵּר טו
אֱלֹהִים אֶל־נֹחַ לֵאמֹר׃ צֵא מִן־הַתֵּבָה אַתָּה וְאִשְׁתְּךָ וּבָנֶיךָ טז
וּנְשֵׁי־בָנֶיךָ אִתָּךְ׃ כָּל־הַחַיָּה אֲשֶׁר־אִתְּךָ מִכָּל־בָּשָׂר בָּעוֹף יז
הַיְצֵא וּבַבְּהֵמָה וּבְכָל־הָרֶמֶשׂ הָרֹמֵשׂ עַל־הָאָרֶץ הוצא אִתָּךְ וְשָׁרְצוּ
בָאָרֶץ וּפָרוּ וְרָבוּ עַל־הָאָרֶץ׃ וַיֵּצֵא־נֹחַ וּבָנָיו וְאִשְׁתּוֹ וּנְשֵׁי־בָנָיו יח
אִתּוֹ׃ כָּל־הַחַיָּה כָּל־הָרֶמֶשׂ וְכָל־הָעוֹף כֹּל רוֹמֵשׂ עַל־הָאָרֶץ יט
לְמִשְׁפְּחֹתֵיהֶם יָצְאוּ מִן־הַתֵּבָה׃ וַיִּבֶן נֹחַ מִזְבֵּחַ לַיהוָה וַיִּקַּח כ •
מִכֹּל ׀ הַבְּהֵמָה הַטְּהֹרָה וּמִכֹּל הָעוֹף הַטָּהוֹר וַיַּעַל עֹלֹת בַּמִּזְבֵּחַ׃
וַיָּרַח יְהוָה אֶת־רֵיחַ הַנִּיחֹחַ וַיֹּאמֶר יְהוָה אֶל־לִבּוֹ לֹא אֹסִף לְקַלֵּל כא
עוֹד אֶת־הָאֲדָמָה בַּעֲבוּר הָאָדָם כִּי יֵצֶר לֵב הָאָדָם רַע מִנְּעֻרָיו

• 11 and again he sent the dove forth from the ark. The dove came
back to him in the evening – and in its beak was a freshly
picked olive leaf. Noaḥ knew then that the water had subsided
12 from the earth. He waited another seven days and again sent
13 forth the dove – and it returned to him no more. So it was
that, by the first day of the first month of Noaḥ's six hundred
and first year, the water on the earth dried up. Noaḥ removed
the covering of the ark and saw that the face of the land was
14 dry. By the twenty-seventh day of the second month, the earth
15 had dried completely. Then God said to Noaḥ,
16 "Leave the ark – you, and your wife, your sons, and your sons'
17 wives with you. And every living thing with you – birds,
animals, and all wild beasts that walk the earth – bring them
out with you. Let them swarm again on the earth and be
18 fertile and multiply upon it." So Noaḥ came out with his sons,
19 his wife, and his sons' wives. Every beast, creeping thing,
winged creature, everything that creeps across the earth,
• 20 emerged from the ark by families. Then Noaḥ built an altar
to the Lord and, taking of each of the kinds of pure animals
21 and pure birds, sacrificed burnt offerings on the altar. The
Lord smelled the fragrant aroma and said in His heart,
"Never again will I curse the land because of man;[17] the

17 | Cf. 3:17, 5:29.

כב וְלֹא־אֹסִף עוֹד לְהַכּוֹת אֶת־כָּל־חַי כַּאֲשֶׁר עָשִׂיתִי׃ עֹד כָּל־יְמֵי
הָאָרֶץ זֶרַע וְקָצִיר וְקֹר וָחֹם וְקַיִץ וָחֹרֶף וְיוֹם וָלַיְלָה לֹא יִשְׁבֹּתוּ׃

devisings of the human heart are evil from its youth. And
never again will I destroy all life as I have done. As long as 22
earth and time endure – sowing time and harvest, cold and

NEAR EAST

8:20–21 Noaḥ's sacrifice and God's response

In the *Epic of Gilgamesh*, the gods are starving because they have not eaten for a week, so they "smelled the sweet savor" and "gathered like flies around the sacrificer." Utnapishtim not only makes fourteen sacrifices but also pours out a libation, as the gods were not only hungry but also thirsty. In the immediate aftermath of the sacrifice, as the gods come to partake of it and recriminations ensue: the great goddess Ishtar wants to stop the great god Enlil from joining the meal because he is the one who instigated humanity's death. The implication is that Enlil deserves to go hungry!

In contrast, Noaḥ sacrifices one of every permitted animal and bird as a thanksgiving offering. As God is metaphysical, He never is hungry (Ps. 50:8–15). In verse 21, God's smelling the fragrant aroma metaphorically indicates His acceptance of the sincerity of the sacrificer (also, Ex. 29:18, 25, 41, etc., but contrast Lev. 26:31).

Maimonides (in the *Guide of the Perplexed* I: 47), notes that although Tanakh uses anthropomorphic terminology in connection with God, it never attributes taste to Him. Smell, however, was considered appropriate because, "While these two senses, namely, taste and touch, only act when in close contact with the object, by sight, hearing, and smell, even distant objects are perceived. These, therefore, were considered...appropriate expressions [to be figuratively applied to God]" (see "A pleasing aroma" on page 8 in the Leviticus volume of this series). ▪ JU

The goddess Ishtar standing on a lion and holding a bow, Mesopotamia, 19th to 17th century BCE

וַיְבָרֶךְ אֱלֹהִים אֶת־נֹחַ וְאֶת־בָּנָיו וַיֹּאמֶר לָהֶם פְּרוּ וּרְבוּ וּמִלְאוּ א • ט
אֶת־הָאָרֶץ: וּמוֹרַאֲכֶם וְחִתְּכֶם יִהְיֶה עַל כָּל־חַיַּת הָאָרֶץ וְעַל ב
כָּל־עוֹף הַשָּׁמָיִם בְּכֹל אֲשֶׁר תִּרְמֹשׂ הָאֲדָמָה וּבְכָל־דְּגֵי הַיָּם
בְּיֶדְכֶם נִתָּנוּ: כָּל־רֶמֶשׂ אֲשֶׁר הוּא־חַי לָכֶם יִהְיֶה לְאָכְלָה כְּיֶרֶק ג
עֵשֶׂב נָתַתִּי לָכֶם אֶת־כֹּל: אַךְ־בָּשָׂר בְּנַפְשׁוֹ דָמוֹ לֹא תֹאכֵלוּ: ד

9 • 1 heat, summer, winter, day, and night will not cease." Then God
blessed Noaḥ and his sons, saying to them, "Be fertile,
2 multiply, fill the earth. Fear and dread of you shall fall upon
all beasts of the earth, upon all winged creatures of the
heavens, upon all that creeps upon the land and all fish of the
3 sea. Into your hand they are given. Every moving thing that
lives shall be food for you; I allow them all to you, like green
4 plants. But flesh with its lifeblood still in it you may not eat.

NEAR EAST

9:1–7 God's new blessing to humanity

God's blessing to humanity in these verses replaces the earlier one in 1:28–30. In both passages, humans are told "be fertile, multiply, and fill the earth" – a sharp contrast to the *Epic of Atrahasis*, in which the increase in humanity disturbs the gods to the extent that it becomes the reason for the flood!

Even though humans are given sovereignty over all living creatures in the first two chapters of Genesis, they were meant to live in harmony with the animals. Now, though, the latter shall live in "fear and dread" of humans because God granted them permission to eat animal life (vv. 2–3). The idea that animals live in fear of humans has no counterpart in the rest of the ancient Near East, where humans fear wild beasts. To be sure, the Tanakh describes individual humans frightened by wild beasts (for example, Amos 3:8, 5:19), and such fear lies at the basis of the curse of Leviticus 26:22. Nonetheless, the Torah understands something that has become obvious to us only in modern times: that animals are helpless in the face of human desires.

↗ Hunting scene, cave painting, Mongolia, ca. 3000 BCE

It is highly doubtful that the laws in this section are designed to prevent the extinction of animals and humans. Indeed, for thousands of years until the invention of modern refrigeration techniques, most humans ate animals infrequently, generally as part of religious rituals. Only the nobility and royalty could afford to eat meat daily.

Rather, the Torah is addressing the carnivorous brutality of humans. In order to limit that brutality, God adds the caveat that "flesh with its lifeblood still in it you may not eat" (v. 4). As indicated by Shadal and Nahum Sarna, the plain sense of this commandment seems to refer to the prohibitions of eating an animal's blood, whether after slaughtering it or eating part of an animal while it is still alive (the latter interpretation is the traditional rabbinic reading of these words). There is no evidence of similar proscriptions or customs in any other ancient Near Eastern society. The logic of the law shows that God's permission to eat animal life is a privilege granted to humans, which must be respected by not consuming blood – for blood is the symbol of life, which only God creates. This prohibition is reiterated many times concerning Israelite society (Lev. 3:17, 7:26–27, 17:10–14, 19:26; Deut. 12:16, 23–25, 27, 15:23; compare I Sam. 14:32–34).

The law concerning the shedding of human blood is apparently introduced to reduce the level of human violence which led to the flood (Gen. 6:11–13). Now, all men or beasts who kill a human forfeit their lives because they have destroyed the image of God (9:5–6; regarding an animal killing a person, see Ex. 21:28).

Unlike various ancient Near Eastern laws (for example, Edict 49 of the Hittite king Telipinu; *Laws of Hammurabi* LH §§116, 210, 230), the intentional murderer is not allowed to ransom his life nor to have another life substituted for his, as Numbers 35:31 states, "You may not accept a ransom for the life of a murderer found guilty of a capital crime; he must be put to death" (note that the Torah treats accidental homicide due to negligence differently, for example, Ex. 21:12–13). The sanctity and inestimable value of human life in the Torah also gives rise to the principle that no amount of property can equal a human life. Therefore, again in contrast to ancient Near Eastern laws (for example, *Laws of Hammurabi* LH § 6, 7, 8, etc.; *Middle Assyrian Laws* MAL A §3), theft of property can never result in the death penalty.

This legislation concerning homicide is highly significant for another reason. Since humans are obligated to punish the murderer with execution (vv. 5–6), this law, perforce, requires the institution of a judicial system. ▪ JU

ה וְאַךְ אֶת־דִּמְכֶם לְנַפְשֹׁתֵיכֶם אֶדְרֹשׁ מִיַּד כָּל־חַיָּה אֶדְרְשֶׁנּוּ וּמִיַּד
ו הָאָדָם מִיַּד אִישׁ אָחִיו אֶדְרֹשׁ אֶת־נֶפֶשׁ הָאָדָם׃ שֹׁפֵךְ דַּם הָאָדָם
ז בָּאָדָם דָּמוֹ יִשָּׁפֵךְ כִּי בְּצֶלֶם אֱלֹהִים עָשָׂה אֶת־הָאָדָם׃ וְאַתֶּם
ח פְּרוּ וּרְבוּ שִׁרְצוּ בָאָרֶץ וּרְבוּ־בָהּ׃ וַיֹּאמֶר אֱלֹהִים חמישי
ט אֶל־נֹחַ וְאֶל־בָּנָיו אִתּוֹ לֵאמֹר׃ וַאֲנִי הִנְנִי מֵקִים אֶת־בְּרִיתִי אִתְּכֶם
י וְאֶת־זַרְעֲכֶם אַחֲרֵיכֶם׃ וְאֵת כָּל־נֶפֶשׁ הַחַיָּה אֲשֶׁר אִתְּכֶם בָּעוֹף
בַּבְּהֵמָה וּבְכָל־חַיַּת הָאָרֶץ אִתְּכֶם מִכֹּל יֹצְאֵי הַתֵּבָה לְכֹל חַיַּת

5 And for your own lifeblood I will demand account; I will
demand it from every wild beast. For human life I will demand
6 account, of every man toward his fellow man: One who sheds
the blood of man – by man shall his blood be shed, for in
7 God's image man was made. As for you, be fertile and multiply,
8 abound on earth and become many on it." Then God
9 said to Noaḥ and to his sons with him: "I – I am about to
establish My covenant with you and your descendants after
10 you, and with every living creature that is with you – the birds,
the animals, and all the wild beasts of earth that are with you,

NEAR EAST

9:8–17 God's eternal covenant with life on Earth

No similar divine promise or treaty exists in the other ancient flood stories known to us. Indeed, no record has ever been found of another ancient Near Eastern civilization mentioning a god making a treaty with a human, in any context. Also, "eternal" treaties are rare, even between kings. The most famous of these was between the Hittite Hattushili and the Egyptian Ramesses II (1259 BCE, fifteen years after the battle of Kadesh). On the other hand, God's "eternal treaty" described here is followed by several others later in the Tanakh: with the Israelites (Gen. 17:4; Ex. 31:16; Lev. 24:8; etc.), with the priests (Num. 25:12–13), and with David (II Sam. 23:5; see "An eternal covenant" on page 374 in the Samuel volume of this series).

Of particular interest is the reference to the rainbow in this passage – literally, "the bow in the cloud(s)" (vv. 13, 14, 16). "Bow" here, and in other biblical passages, refers to the archer's bow, often a symbol of the hunter or warrior in the ancient Near East. In the *Enuma Elish Epic*, after the god Marduk's defeat of Tiamat, the great god Anu places Marduk's bow in the heavens (as a star or constellation; VI:82–90), presumably as an eternal sign of his victory. In the Ugaritic *Tale of Aqhat*, the god of crafts, Kotharu wa-Khasis, gives a bow to the human hero, Dan'el, who gives it to his son, Aqhat. The war and huntress-goddess Anat covets the bow, although Aqhat will not give it to her at any price. She has Aqhat murdered, but the bow is accidentally broken and she mourns its loss.

In imagery reminiscent of the flood, God's bow is mentioned in Habakkuk 3:9–11, where it appears as a symbol of God fighting on behalf of Yehuda. In Lamentations 2:4 and 3:12, it is the opposite. In our passage, as Ramban comments (to v. 12), God places His bow in the sky as a symbol of His treaty of peace. That positioning of God's bow fits the idea of it hanging at rest, facing upward – no longer positioned to shoot destruction down at the world.

In verses 15 and 16, God promises to remember this eternal covenant whenever He sees the rainbow. In contrast, in the *Epic of Gilgamesh* flood story, the goddess Ishtar lifts up her necklace of jewels fashioned for her by Anu, and vows never to forget the devastation of the flood. As Nahum Sarna pointed out, Ishtar's "oath is not accompanied by any promise or assurance about mankind's future, and it issues from the lips of that member of the Mesopotamian pantheon most notorious for perfidy."

The divine covenant with Noaḥ and his descendants, confirmed for all time by the beautiful appearance of the rainbow, addressed human concern for the preservation of the species in the face of natural disasters. Unlike ancient Near Eastern polytheists, the Israelites knew that whatever catastrophes may occur will be temporary and limited; life will go on afterward. Thus, Genesis brought hope to humanity. ▪ JU

Kadesh treaty fragment, Hittite copy in Akkadian, Hattusa, 1269 BCE

הָאָרֶץ׃ וַהֲקִמֹתִי אֶת־בְּרִיתִי אִתְּכֶם וְלֹא־יִכָּרֵת כָּל־בָּשָׂר עוֹד יא
מִמֵּי הַמַּבּוּל וְלֹא־יִהְיֶה עוֹד מַבּוּל לְשַׁחֵת הָאָרֶץ׃ וַיֹּאמֶר אֱלֹהִים יב
זֹאת אוֹת־הַבְּרִית אֲשֶׁר־אֲנִי נֹתֵן בֵּינִי וּבֵינֵיכֶם וּבֵין כָּל־נֶפֶשׁ חַיָּה
אֲשֶׁר אִתְּכֶם לְדֹרֹת עוֹלָם׃ אֶת־קַשְׁתִּי נָתַתִּי בֶּעָנָן וְהָיְתָה לְאוֹת יג
בְּרִית בֵּינִי וּבֵין הָאָרֶץ׃ וְהָיָה בְּעַנְנִי עָנָן עַל־הָאָרֶץ וְנִרְאֲתָה יד
הַקֶּשֶׁת בֶּעָנָן׃ וְזָכַרְתִּי אֶת־בְּרִיתִי אֲשֶׁר בֵּינִי וּבֵינֵיכֶם וּבֵין כָּל־ טו
נֶפֶשׁ חַיָּה בְּכָל־בָּשָׂר וְלֹא־יִהְיֶה עוֹד הַמַּיִם לְמַבּוּל לְשַׁחֵת כָּל־
בָּשָׂר׃ וְהָיְתָה הַקֶּשֶׁת בֶּעָנָן וּרְאִיתִיהָ לִזְכֹּר בְּרִית עוֹלָם בֵּין טז

11 everything that left the ark, every living creature on earth. I
will establish My covenant with you, that never again may all
life be destroyed by the waters of a flood; never again will
12 there be a flood to destroy the earth." God said, "This is the
sign of the covenant I am making between Me and you – and
every living creature with you – for all generations to come.
13 I have laid down My bow in the clouds to be the sign of the
14 covenant between Me and the earth. Whenever I bring clouds
15 over the earth and the rainbow appears in the clouds, I will
remember My covenant that binds Me and you and every
living creature of all flesh so that never again will the waters
16 become a flood to destroy all life. The rainbow will be there
in the cloud, and I will see it, remembering the eternal
covenant between God and every living creature, all flesh

NEAR EAST

9:18–19 Regeneration of humanity

After the flood, humanity is regenerated from Noaḥ's three sons, as detailed in chapter 10. This natural method stands in contrast to the magical way the world is repopulated after the flood in the myths of other ancient cultures. For example, in the Greek story of Deucalion and his wife Pyrrha, after surviving the flood, they are instructed to throw stones (called the "bones of their mother," meaning stones from Mother Earth) over their shoulders. The stones thrown by Deucalion became men, and those thrown behind Pyrrha became women.

In the Akkadian *Epic of Atrahasis,* the gods actively work against humanity being too fertile after the flood by having a she-demon "snatch the baby from the lap of her who bore it" (iii 5) and "establish high priestesses and priestesses, let them be taboo, and so cut down childbirth" (iii 6–7).

These distinctions highlight the difference in perspective between pagan beliefs in selfish deities and the God of the Torah, who wants humans to multiply and fill the earth (9:1). ▪ ZR

Deucalion and Pyrrha (detail), Peter Paul Rubens, 1636

יז אֱלֹהִים וּבֵין כָּל־נֶפֶשׁ חַיָּה בְּכָל־בָּשָׂר אֲשֶׁר עַל־הָאָרֶץ: וַיֹּאמֶר
אֱלֹהִים אֶל־נֹחַ זֹאת אוֹת־הַבְּרִית אֲשֶׁר הֲקִמֹתִי בֵּינִי וּבֵין כָּל־
בָּשָׂר אֲשֶׁר עַל־הָאָרֶץ:
יח וַיִּהְיוּ בְנֵי־נֹחַ הַיֹּצְאִים מִן־הַתֵּבָה שֵׁם וְחָם וָיָפֶת וְחָם הוּא אֲבִי ששי
יט כ כְנָעַן: שְׁלֹשָׁה אֵלֶּה בְּנֵי־נֹחַ וּמֵאֵלֶּה נָפְצָה כָל־הָאָרֶץ: וַיָּחֶל נֹחַ
כא אִישׁ הָאֲדָמָה וַיִּטַּע כָּרֶם: וַיֵּשְׁתְּ מִן־הַיַּיִן וַיִּשְׁכָּר וַיִּתְגַּל בְּתוֹךְ

upon the earth." So said God to Noaḥ: "This is the sign of the 17
covenant that I have established between Me and all flesh that
is on earth."
Noaḥ's sons who came out from the ark were Shem, Ḥam, 18
and Yefet. Ḥam was the father of Kenaan.[18] These three were 19
Noaḥ's sons; and from them all the world branched out. Noaḥ 20
began to be a man of the land, and he planted a vineyard. He 21

18 | The ancestor of the Canaanites, whose land would ultimately be given to Israel, descendants of Shem.

ARCHAEOLOGY

9:20–21 Viticulture and viniculture

This is the first mention in the Tanakh of the science of growing grapes (viticulture) and their cultivation for making wine (viniculture). The earliest evidence of grapevine cultivation dates from the Early Bronze Age, with the Levant and the Aegean being the earliest centers of this science. Excavations in Israel from Yeriḥo and Lakhish have unearthed grape seeds from around 3000 BCE. Grape presses carved in bedrock found in the Levant date to the 3rd millennium. It takes about three years until vines are able to produce high quality grapes that can be used for wine, so the production of wine is a sign of a stable society. ▪ ZR

Remains of a grapevine, Akrotiri, Santorini, 2nd millennium BCE

אָהֳלֹה: וַיַּרְא חָם אֲבִי כְנַעַן אֵת עֶרְוַת אָבִיו וַיַּגֵּד לִשְׁנֵי־אֶחָיו • כב
בַּחוּץ: וַיִּקַּח שֵׁם וָיֶפֶת אֶת־הַשִּׂמְלָה וַיָּשִׂימוּ עַל־שְׁכֶם שְׁנֵיהֶם כג
וַיֵּלְכוּ אֲחֹרַנִּית וַיְכַסּוּ אֵת עֶרְוַת אֲבִיהֶם וּפְנֵיהֶם אֲחֹרַנִּית וְעֶרְוַת
אֲבִיהֶם לֹא רָאוּ: וַיִּיקֶץ נֹחַ מִיֵּינוֹ וַיֵּדַע אֵת אֲשֶׁר־עָשָׂה לוֹ בְּנוֹ כד
הַקָּטָן: וַיֹּאמֶר אָרוּר כְּנָעַן עֶבֶד עֲבָדִים יִהְיֶה לְאֶחָיו: וַיֹּאמֶר כה כו
בָּרוּךְ יְהוָה אֱלֹהֵי שֵׁם וִיהִי כְנַעַן עֶבֶד לָמוֹ: יַפְתְּ אֱלֹהִים לְיֶפֶת כז
וְיִשְׁכֹּן בְּאָהֳלֵי־שֵׁם וִיהִי כְנַעַן עֶבֶד לָמוֹ: וַיְחִי־נֹחַ אַחַר הַמַּבּוּל כח
שְׁלֹשׁ מֵאוֹת שָׁנָה וַחֲמִשִּׁים שָׁנָה: וַיְהִי כָּל־יְמֵי־נֹחַ תְּשַׁע מֵאוֹת כט
שָׁנָה וַחֲמִשִּׁים שָׁנָה וַיָּמֹת:

drank some of the wine, became drunk, and lay uncovered in
• 22 his tent. Ḥam, father of Kenaan, saw his father's nakedness and
23 told his two brothers who were outside. Shem and Yefet then
took a cloak and put it over both their shoulders. They walked
backward and covered their father's nakedness, averting their
24 faces so as not to see the nakedness of their father. Noaḥ woke
from his wine and realized what his youngest son had done to
25 him. He said, "Cursed be Kenaan! The lowest of slaves shall
26 he be to his brothers." Then he said, "Blessed be the Lord,
27 God of Shem; Kenaan shall be his slave. May God enlarge
Yefet, and let him dwell in the tents of Shem; Kenaan shall
28 be his slave." After the flood Noaḥ lived three hundred and
29 fifty years. Noaḥ lived a total of nine hundred and fifty years,
and he died.

Stele commemorating Seti I's military campaign against rebellious towns near Beit She'an, 13th century BCE

NEAR EAST

9:22–27 Characteristics of Ḥam and Kenaan

In Genesis 10:6, Mitzrayim (Egypt) and Kenaan (Canaan) are listed as children of Ḥam. Egypt is associated with Ḥam himself in Psalms 78:51, "He struck down every firstborn in Egypt, the first fruits of manhood in the tents of Ḥam," and in Psalms 105:23, 27, 106:22 where Egypt is called "the land of Ḥam."

Rabbi Yosef Bekhor Shor notes that the curse that Kenaan will be a slave to his brothers is based on a play on his name, connecting it to the Hebrew root indicating subjugation (*k n a [ayin]*). One of the features of Genesis is the use of genealogical lists to represent political relationships between nations. This connection reflects the historical situation in the Late Bronze Age (ca. 1550–1200 BCE) when Egypt (represented by Ḥam, the father, or by his second son Mitzrayim) ruled over Canaan (the youngest son of Ḥam), as well as the reality that Canaan would be invaded by the Sea Peoples, associated with Yefet's son Yavan (Greece) and grandson Kitim (Cyprus), and the Israelites, descendants of Shem.

Additionally, the immodesty of Ḥam, specifically identified here as father of Kenaan, establishes the trait of sexual depravity associated with these two nations elsewhere in the Bible, as in Pharaoh's kidnapping of Sarai (Gen. 12:10–20) and the behavior of the Canaanites in Leviticus 20:23 that concludes a long list of forbidden relationships, "Do not follow the practices of the nation I am driving out before you, for they did all these things and I was disgusted with them." Egypt and Canaan are also connected in the warning concerning forbidden sexual practices, "You shall not do as they do in the land of Egypt where you lived. Nor shall you do as they do in the land of Canaan where I am bringing you; do not follow their practices" (Lev. 18:3). ▪ ZR

Noah with grapes, Mausoleum of Joseph Sec, Pierre Pavillon, Aix-en-Provence (France), 17th century

ASHKENAZ
GOMER
RIFAT?
MESHEKH?
MAGOG
LUD?
YAVAN
TUVAL
Togarma
DODANIM
KAFTORIM
KASLUḤIM?
ELISHA
Kitim
ARAM
EVER?
ASHUR
ARPAKHSHAD?
MADAI
ELAM
KENAAN
See inset map
PUT
Naftuḥim?
MITZRAYIM
PATRUSIM
SHEVA?
DEDAN
HAVILA?
YOKTAN?
KUSH
HAVILA?
Raama?
Avimael?
Yovav?
SHEVA
Oval?
Hadoram?
Dikla?
HATZARMAVET
Savta?
Savtekha?
Ofir?
SEVA?
Uzal?
Shelef?
UNKNOWN LOCATIONS
Anamim
Shelaḥ
Peleg
Almodad
Yeraḥ
Mash

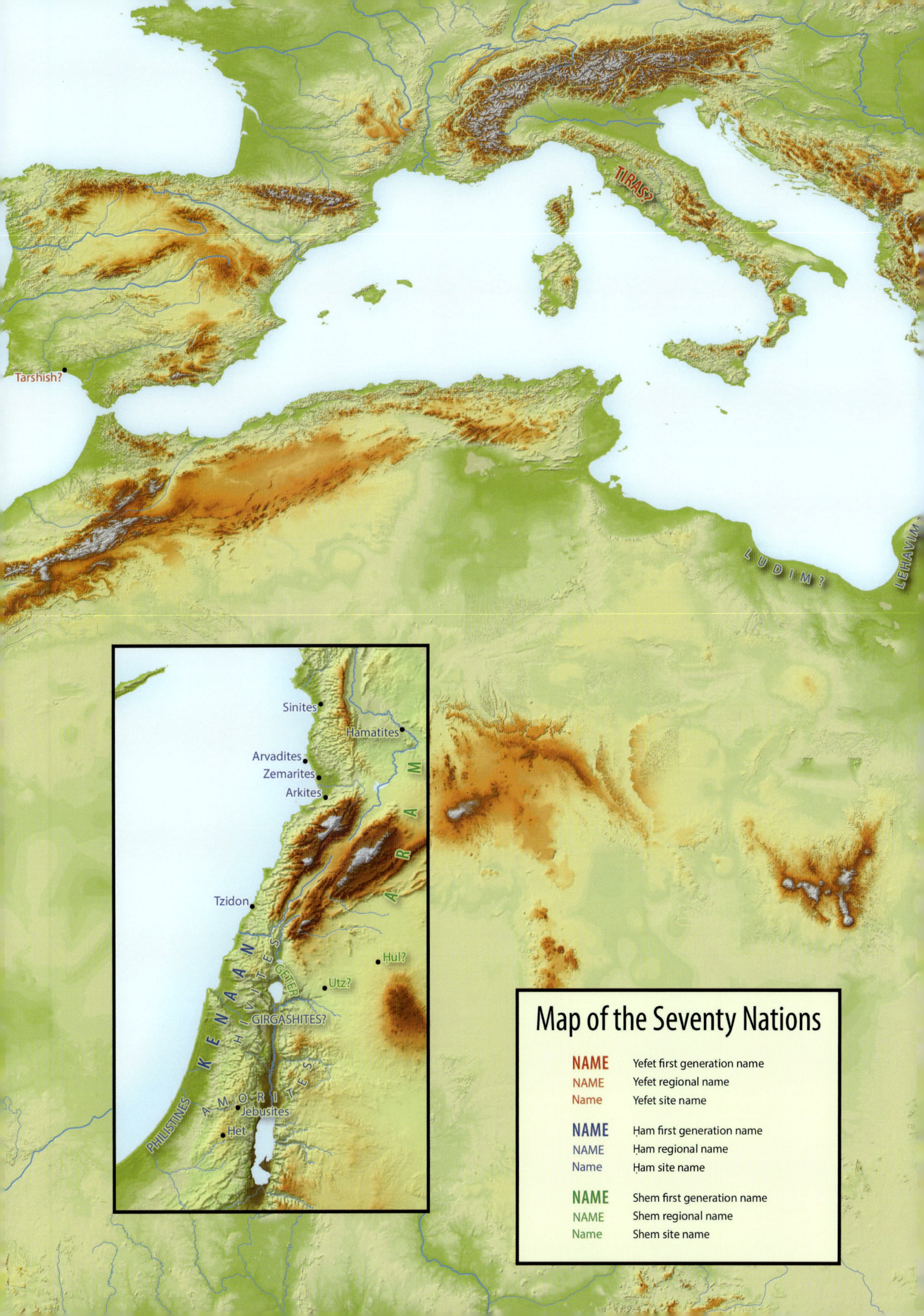

Map of the Seventy Nations
NAME Yefet first generation name
NAME Yefet regional name
Name Yefet site name
NAME Ḥam first generation name
NAME Ḥam regional name
Name Ḥam site name
NAME Shem first generation name
NAME Shem regional name
Name Shem site name
TIRAS?
Tarshish?
LUDIM?
LEHAVIM
Sinites
Hamatites
Arvadites
Zemarites
Arkites
ARAM
Tzidon
Ḥul?
Utz?
GETER
HIVITES
KENAAN
GIRGASHITES?
AMORITES
Jebusites
Ḥet
PHILISTINES

GEOGRAPHY

10:1–32 The seventy nations

This chapter, traditionally called "the Table of Nations," presents the fulfillment of God's command to Noaḥ and his three sons to "be fertile and multiply, abound on earth and become many on it" (Gen. 9:7). It emphasizes the common origins of humankind and, consequently, its unity and equality. The geographic horizons of the chapter extend from Iran in the east (v. 21, Elam) to possibly Spain or Sardinia (Tarshish, v. 4) in the west, and from the Black and Caspian Seas in the north (vv. 2–3) to Sudan in the south (v. 6, Kush). At the center lies the land of Canaan, the borders of which are offered in v. 19, along with the most complete list of the various ethnic groups that inhabited it (vv. 16–17; compare Deut. 7:1).

The peoples on the list number seventy (although the sum is not explicit), with fourteen for Yefet, thirty for Ḥam, and twenty-six for Shem. The number seventy is a symbolic number, frequently used in the Tanakh to convey the concept of completeness or totality. It is the number of the descendants of Yaakov who went down to Egypt (Gen. 46:27; Ex. 1:5; Deut. 10:22), and the number of elders that represent Israel in its covenant with God (Ex. 24:1; Num. 11:24). Seventy was the number of palms (along with twelve springs) at Eilim, an oasis in the wilderness (Ex. 15:27). Perhaps as a critique of extreme polygyny, Gidon and King Aḥav have seventy sons (Judges 8:30; II Kings 10:1). In the *Baal Cycle* from Ugarit, the great god El and his consort Athirat (Hebrew, *Ashera*) have seventy sons and in the same text, animals (wild bulls, deer, asses, etc.) are slaughtered in groups of seventy. As the number associated with completeness, seventy years is a lifespan which is both realistic and satisfactory (Ps. 90:10; not ideal like 120 years). The assumption that there are seventy nations with their languages continues into rabbinic literature (BT Sanhedrin 17a–b, BT Shabbat 88b), as well as Christian scriptures (Luke 10:1).

וְאֵלֶּה תּוֹלְדֹת בְּנֵי־נֹחַ שֵׁם חָם וָיָפֶת וַיִּוָּלְדוּ לָהֶם בָּנִים אַחַר א • י
הַמַּבּוּל: בְּנֵי יֶפֶת גֹּמֶר וּמָגוֹג וּמָדַי וְיָוָן וְתֻבָל וּמֶשֶׁךְ וְתִירָס: ב •
וּבְנֵי גֹּמֶר אַשְׁכְּנַז וְרִיפַת וְתֹגַרְמָה: וּבְנֵי יָוָן אֱלִישָׁה וְתַרְשִׁישׁ ג ד
כִּתִּים וְדֹדָנִים: מֵאֵלֶּה נִפְרְדוּ אִיֵּי הַגּוֹיִם בְּאַרְצֹתָם אִישׁ לִלְשֹׁנוֹ ה
לְמִשְׁפְּחֹתָם בְּגוֹיֵהֶם: וּבְנֵי חָם כּוּשׁ וּמִצְרַיִם וּפוּט וּכְנָעַן: ו •

10 • 1 These are the descendants of Noaḥ's sons, Shem, Ḥam,
and Yefet; after the flood, children were born to them.[19]
• 2 Yefet's sons were Gomer, Magog, Madai, Yavan, Tuval,
3 Meshekh, and Tiras. Gomer's sons were Ashkenaz, Rifat,
4 and Togarma. Yavan's sons were Elisha, Tarshish, Kitim, and
5 Dodanim. From these the seagoing nations spread out to
their territories, each with its own language, by their clans
• 6 and their nations. Ḥam's sons were Kush, Mitzrayim,[20] Put,

19 | The following are the eponymous ancestors of various nations.

20 | In this translation, Ḥam's son is rendered "Mitzrayim," while the nation is called "Egypt"; see introduction.

The names in Genesis 10 are understood to be eponyms, a legendary person or primordial ancestor who gave his name to a people or place. Some of the names have plural endings (4, 13–14) or end with a gentilic "i" (vv. 16–18), both of which indicate an ethnic group. The criteria that the Torah uses for expressing relationships is not racial nor linguistic, but rather a combination of ethnic, geographic, historical, and perhaps socio-political. The use of kinship language as symbolic of other kinds of associations is found elsewhere in the Tanakh (Judges 17:10; I Kings 9:13, 20:32; II Kings 5:13; Amos 1:9). For example, Genesis 10:6 assigns Canaan (along with Egypt) to the line of Ḥam, even though Canaanite is (like Hebrew) a Semitic language (Is. 19:18). Perhaps the linkage reflects Egypt's political hegemony over Canaan in the 2nd millennium BCE or the Torah's disdain toward both cultures (Lev. 18:3). Verse 22 lists Elam as a son of Shem even though Elamite is an isolated language and not Semitic; both Elam and its "brother" Assyria were great powers far to the east of Israel. The only name which can assuredly be identified as an individual (and not a nation) is Nimrod, whose prowess as a hunter and empire builder is extolled in verses 8–11 and is associated with Assyria or Babylon as the "land of Nimrod" in Micah 5:5. ▪ EG

↗ Early cylinder seal from Susa III or Proto-Elamite culture, 32nd to 29th century BCE

GEOGRAPHY

10:2–5 Yefet's sons

The Yefetites comprise the peoples settled around the Mediterranean in Anatolia, the Aegean area, and further north.

Gomer is identified with the Gimmiraya people in Assyrian sources, called Cimmerians in later classical sources. These were a nomadic Indo-European people who migrated from the area beyond the Caucasus Mountains into western Asia, and central and southeastern Europe.

The term Magog itself has not been identified in ancient Near Eastern sources. In Tanakh, Magog is famously the land of Gog (Ezek. 38:2) associated with the final war that precedes the messianic era, located in "the far edges of the north" (Ezek. 38:15). The name Magog may be connected to the Assyrian *mat Gugi*, land of Gyges, king of Lydia in western Asia Minor.

Madai refers to the Medes, who lived in what is now northwestern Iran, known from archaeological sites dating from the Iron Age as well as from records of Assyrian kings.

Yavan refers to the Ionians, one of the Greek tribes, who colonized the western coast of Asia Minor, and are referred to in Isaiah 66:19 as "the distant coastlands where none ever heard tell of Me." Yavan is associated with Meshekh (Ezek. 38:2) and Tuval (Is. 66:19) or both (Ezek. 27:13), places identified with the countries Tabal, located in southeastern Anatolia, and Mushku, associated with King Mita (i.e., King Midas) which was centered at Gordion in the west central part of Anatolia, both mentioned in Assyrian sources.

Tiras has sometimes been associated with one of the Sea Peoples, either the Tursha, mentioned in Egyptian sources at the time of pharaohs Merenptah and Ramesses II, or the Tyrsenoi, the Greek term for the Etruscans.

Ashkenaz is identified with the Ashkuzi found in Assyrian texts, known as Scythians by the Greeks, a group of ancient tribes of nomadic warriors who originally lived in what is now southern Siberia. They are mentioned in Jeremiah 51:27, "the kingdoms of Ararat, Mini, and Ashkenaz."

Rifat, called Difat in I Chronicles 1:6, remains unidentified.

Togarma is found in Ezekiel 27:14 and 38:6 as Beit Togarma, a place mentioned in cuneiform texts as Tegarama, a city in east-southeast Anatolia during the Bronze Age.

Elisha is identified with Alashiya, the term used in the ancient Near Eastern world for the island of Cyprus.

Tarshish is the place to which Yona sought to flee (Jonah 1:3). Its identity is the subject of much speculation; it is generally identified with one of three cities on the Mediterranean coast that have similar sounding names: the Greek Tartessos (on the south coast of the Iberian Peninsula), Tarsus, in south-central Turkey, or Tharros, on the west coast of Sardinia (some suggest that it is a name for Sardinia itself).

The Kittim are the people of a kingdom located in the area of modern-day Larnaca, called Kitti by the Phoenicians and Kition by the Greeks.

The Dodanim are identified with the island of Rhodes, based on the spelling Rodanim in I Chronicles 1:7. ▪ ZR

Amarna letter, correspondence between Pharaoh Amenhotep III and the king of Alashiya (Cyprus), Tell el-Amarna, ca. 1380 BCE

GEOGRAPHY

10:6 The four Hamatite groups

The Hamites are divided into four groups: Kush, Mitzrayim, and Put are located in Africa proper, and Kenaan is at the connection point of Africa and Asia.

Kush, called Kash or Kesh in Egyptian, was the region south of Egypt called Nubia, where one of the earliest civilizations of Africa, the Kerma culture, ruled until being conquered by Egypt in the New Kingdom period (ca. 1500 BCE). In the 8th century BCE, the kingdom of Kush conquered Egypt and ruled it as the Twenty-Fifth Dynasty, until being replaced by the Egyptian Twenty-Sixth Dynasty a century later.

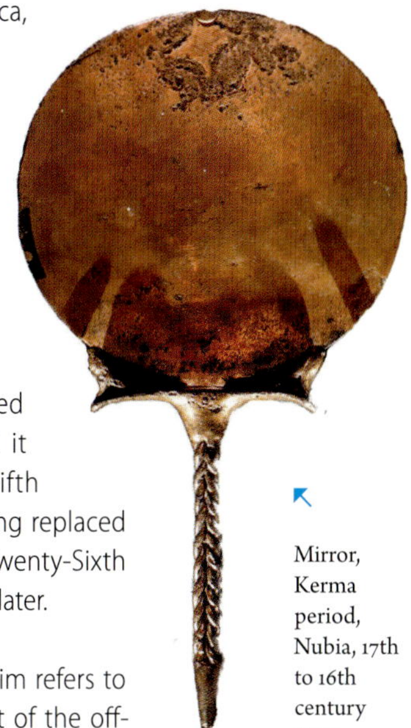

Mirror, Kerma period, Nubia, 17th to 16th century BCE

In Tanakh, Mitzrayim refers to Egypt, but in light of the offspring of Mitzrayim listed in verse 14, here it indicates Lower Egypt, the northernmost region of Egypt, which includes the Nile Delta between Memphis and the Mediterranean Sea.

Put refers to ancient Libya, the Latin term for North Africa west of Egypt. This region was called Putaya in Persian and Puṭa in Neo-Babylonian.

Kenaan's descendants lived in the area of Canaan from the time of the New Kingdom of Egypt (Late Bronze Age), when the small kingdoms there functioned as vassals of the pharaohs. The borders as described in verse 19 correspond to those fixed in the peace treaty between Ramesses II and the Hittite king Hattushili III ca. 1267–1237 BCE. These borders would have been familiar to the ancient Israelites. ▪ ZR

וּבְנֵי כוּשׁ סְבָא וַחֲוִילָה וְסַבְתָּה וְרַעְמָה וְסַבְתְּכָא וּבְנֵי רַעְמָה ז
שְׁבָא וּדְדָן: וְכוּשׁ יָלַד אֶת־נִמְרֹד הוּא הֵחֵל לִהְיוֹת גִּבֹּר בָּאָרֶץ: ח
הוּא־הָיָה גִבֹּר־צַיִד לִפְנֵי יהוה עַל־כֵּן יֵאָמַר כְּנִמְרֹד גִּבּוֹר צַיִד ט
לִפְנֵי יהוה: וַתְּהִי רֵאשִׁית מַמְלַכְתּוֹ בָּבֶל וְאֶרֶךְ וְאַכַּד וְכַלְנֵה י
בְּאֶרֶץ שִׁנְעָר: מִן־הָאָרֶץ הַהִוא יָצָא אַשּׁוּר וַיִּבֶן אֶת־נִינְוֵה וְאֶת־ יא
רְחֹבֹת עִיר וְאֶת־כָּלַח: וְאֶת־רֶסֶן בֵּין נִינְוֵה וּבֵין כָּלַח הִוא הָעִיר יב
הַגְּדֹלָה: וּמִצְרַיִם יָלַד אֶת־לוּדִים וְאֶת־עֲנָמִים וְאֶת־לְהָבִים יג
וְאֶת־נַפְתֻּחִים: וְאֶת־פַּתְרֻסִים וְאֶת־כַּסְלֻחִים אֲשֶׁר יָצְאוּ מִשָּׁם יד
פְּלִשְׁתִּים וְאֶת־כַּפְתֹּרִים: וּכְנַעַן יָלַד אֶת־צִידֹן בְּכֹרוֹ טו

7 and Kenaan. Kush's sons were Seva, Ḥavila, Savta, Raama,
8 and Savtekha. Raama's sons were Sheva and Dedan. Kush
was the father of Nimrod, the first mighty warrior on earth.
9 He was a mighty hunter before the Lord, which is why
people still say, "Like Nimrod, a mighty hunter before the
10 Lord." His kingdom began with Babylon, Erekh, Akad, and
11 Kalneh in the land of Shinar. From that land, Ashur went out
12 and built Nineveh, Reḥovot Ir, Kalaḥ, and Resen between
13 Nineveh and Kalaḥ; that is the great city. Mitzrayim fathered
14 the Ludim, Anamim, Lehavim and Naftuḥim, Patrusim,
Kasluḥim – from whom the Philistines descended – and the
15 Kaftorim. Kenaan fathered Tzidon, his firstborn,

Sphinx head of Shabaka, king of Kush, ruled 705–690 BCE

GEOGRAPHY

10:7 The descendants of Kush: Arabia and Africa

The descendants of Kush include Arabian as well as African groups. The two are listed together due to trade relations – and the resulting cultural exchanges – between the two regions. Seva is also associated with Kush and Mitzrayim in Isaiah 43:3 and 45:14, indicating a place in or at least near Africa. It appears to be related to the Sabeans, an ancient group of South Arabians who founded the kingdom of Saba in what is today southern Yemen. For Ḥavila, see "Pishon, Giḥon, Tigris, and Euphrates" on page 19. It is unclear where Savta was located, but it may refer to Shabwah, which was the ancient capital of Hadhramaut, on the eastern coast of the Arabian Peninsula. Raama, a group mentioned in Ezekiel 27:22 as merchants, may correspond to Ramat, which was a prosperous trading center in the 1st and 2nd centuries BCE, in the area of Najran in southwestern Saudi Arabia. While Savtekha is unknown in finds from the 2nd millennium BCE, in a later period it appears to correspond with Shebitku, also known as Shabataka, who was the second pharaoh of the Twenty-Fifth Dynasty of Egypt (ruled 714–705 BCE), when the kingdom of Kush ruled Egypt. During that time, Savta may have been associated with Shabaka, the third Kushite pharaoh of the Twenty-Fifth Dynasty (ruled 705–690 BCE).

Dedan is the term used in cuneiform texts for the kingdom of Lihyan, a major center for the spice trade, located in the northwestern Arabian Peninsula, with Al-'Ula as its capital. Since here and in Ezekiel 38:13 it is mentioned along with Sheva, probably the Sheva listed here is in the same area, a different Sheva than the one with which King Shlomo had trade relations, which is listed in verse 28. ▪ ZR

GEOGRAPHY

10:8–12 The descendants of Kush: Asia

Nimrod has not been positively identified, but may be a version of Naram-Sin, the ruler of the Akkadian empire (ca. 2254–2218 BCE), who brought it to the height of its power. He was the first Mesopotamian king known to refer to himself as a god, using the title "God of Akkad," and called himself "King of the Four Quarters, King of the Universe." The Hebrew appellation may be an intentional corruption of his name, casting him as a rebel (from the root *m r d*). Alternatively, Nimrod could be Naram-Sin's grandfather, Sargon the Great (ca. 2334–2284 BCE), the first ruler to use the title "King of the Universe." The parts of his kingdom listed in verses 10–12 are all in Mesopotamia.

Babylon was the well-known city on the Euphrates, called *bab-il* ("the gate of god") in Akkadian. Erekh is Uruk, the Sumerian city that in mythology served as the capital of the legendary king, Gilgamesh. Akad was a Sumerian city that served as the center of the kingdom of Sargon the Great (ca. 23rd to 24th century BCE), who is considered the first historical figure to rule an empire, but the term came to refer to the northern part of Babylonia. No archaeological evidence links Kalneh to any known Akkadian location, but the Talmud identified it with the ancient Sumerian city of Nippur (BT Yoma 10a). In the Samaritan tradition, the word is vowelized to read *kulana* ("all of them"), so that the verse would end by saying that all of these places are in the land of Shinar (see "Shinar" on page 66).

Verse 11 may be referring to Nimrod going out to Ashur (Targum Yonatan, Bekhor Shor), here designating Upper Mesopotamia. Alternatively, it can mean that the individual called Ashur went out and then built Nineveh, and the verse is no longer discussing Nimrod (Rashi quoting Bereshit Rabba 37:4, Ibn Ezra, Radak). Beyond being the designation for a region, Ashur was a city west of the Tigris River. It was one of the three main cities of Assyria, the other two being Nineveh and Kalaḥ, both located east of the Tigris. Reḥovot Ir is not known to be the name of an Assyrian city. It means "broad places of the city" and may refer to Rebit-Ninua, the less-densely populated suburb of Nineveh. No major city has yet been identified with Resen. ▪ ZR

Ishtar gate in its original context, Babylon, photograph, from 1932

GEOGRAPHY

10:13–19 The Hamatites: Mitzrayim and Kenaan

The offspring of Mitzrayim seems to refer to regions or tribes under Egyptian control. The ones that can be reliably identified include the Patrusim, the people of Pathros, derived from the Egyptian term *pꜣ tꜣ-rsy*, meaning "the southern land," and referring to Upper Egypt. As well, the Kaftorim are identified as the people of Crete, called *keftiu* in Egyptian and *kaptaru* in Akkadian.

Some of Kenaan's offspring are identified with well-known locations. Tzidon is the famous Phoenician port city of Sidon. Until the 10th century BCE, it was the most powerful of the Phoenician cities, reflected in being designated the firstborn here. The list also includes the inhabitants of the five Syrian cities of Arka, Sin, Arvad, Zemar and Hamat.

Ḥet represents the Hittites, who lived in Canaan. This group is not the same as the Hittites of the kingdom of Hatti in Anatolia (see "Hittites" on page 169). The Hittites, Jebusites, Amorites, Girgashites and Hivites are found in lists of the pre-Israelite inhabitants of Canaan (for example, Deut. 7:1). Nothing is known of the Jebusites, Girgashites or Hivites outside of references in Tanakh. The Amorites are found in Akkadian and Sumerian texts, where the term *Amurru* (meaning "west") was used to designate any of the Semitic-speaking nomadic tribes who lived west of the Euphrates in what is today Syria, Lebanon, Jordan, and Israel. The territory of Kenaan includes Gerar, which seems to be referring to Tel Haror, northwest of Be'er Sheva, one of the largest urban centers in the area during the Middle Bronze Age, and Aza (modern-day Gaza), the capital of the Egyptian province of Canaan. ▪ ZR

Pottery with white painted patterns, Minoan, Crete, 26th to 20th century BCE

וְאֶת־חֵת׃ וְאֶת־הַיְבוּסִי וְאֶת־הָאֱמֹרִי וְאֵת הַגִּרְגָּשִׁי׃ וְאֶת־ טז יז
הַחִוִּי וְאֶת־הַעַרְקִי וְאֶת־הַסִּינִי׃ וְאֶת־הָאַרְוָדִי וְאֶת־הַצְּמָרִי יח
וְאֶת־הַחֲמָתִי וְאַחַר נָפֹצוּ מִשְׁפְּחוֹת הַכְּנַעֲנִי׃ וַיְהִי גְּבוּל הַכְּנַעֲנִי יט
מִצִּידֹן בֹּאֲכָה גְרָרָה עַד־עַזָּה בֹּאֲכָה סְדֹמָה וַעֲמֹרָה וְאַדְמָה
וּצְבֹיִם עַד־לָשַׁע׃ אֵלֶּה בְנֵי־חָם לְמִשְׁפְּחֹתָם לִלְשֹׁנֹתָם בְּאַרְצֹתָם כ
בְּגוֹיֵהֶם׃ וּלְשֵׁם יֻלַּד גַּם־הוּא אֲבִי כָּל־בְּנֵי־עֵבֶר אֲחִי • כא
יֶפֶת הַגָּדוֹל׃ בְּנֵי שֵׁם עֵילָם וְאַשּׁוּר וְאַרְפַּכְשַׁד וְלוּד וַאֲרָם׃ וּבְנֵי כב כג
אֲרָם עוּץ וְחוּל וְגֶתֶר וָמַשׁ׃ וְאַרְפַּכְשַׁד יָלַד אֶת־שָׁלַח וְשֶׁלַח יָלַד כד
אֶת־עֵבֶר׃ וּלְעֵבֶר יֻלַּד שְׁנֵי בָנִים שֵׁם הָאֶחָד פֶּלֶג כִּי בְיָמָיו נִפְלְגָה כה

16 17 and Ḥet, and the Jebusites, Amorites, and Girgashites, the
18 Hivites, Arkites, and Sinites, the Arvadites, Zemarites, and
19 Hamatites. Later, the Canaanite families were dispersed. The
Canaanite borders were from Sidon toward Gerar near Aza,
and toward Sedom, Amora, Adma, and Tzevoyim, near Lasha.
20 These were the descendants of Ḥam, by their clans and their
• 21 languages, with their lands and their nations. Sons
were also born to Shem. The older brother of Yefet, he was the
22 ancestor of all the sons of Ever. Shem's sons were Elam, Ashur,
23 Arpakhshad, Lud, and Aram. Aram's sons were Utz, Ḥul,
24 Geter, and Mash. Arpakhshad was the father of Shelaḥ, and
25 Shelaḥ was the father of Ever. To Ever, two sons were born.
One was named Peleg, for in his time the earth was divided.[21]

21 | Peleg evokes the Hebrew *niflega* (divided). This is often understood to refer to the dispersion recounted in 11:1–9.

GEOGRAPHY

10:21–30 The Shemites

The genealogy of the Shemites begins by mentioning Ever, even though he is Shem's great-grandson, because he is the ancestor of the Israelites. The text then lists Shem's five sons, but focuses only on the descendants of Aram, the youngest, and Arpakhshad, the third son. Aram receives special treatment because of the significance of the Arameans for the Israelites; the patriarchs maintained close ties with Rivka's family, who are identified as Arameans (for example, Gen. 25:20; see "Aramean" on page 177). The genealogy of Arpakhshad is presented in the greatest detail, as he is Ever's grandfather.

Elam (v. 22) is the easternmost area found in this list, an ancient civilization centered in southwestern Iran, called *elamtu* in Akkadian. Although the Elamite language is not related to Semitic or Indo-European languages, the Elamites are listed here due to their geographical proximity to and political relations with the other places mentioned in this verse. Ashur, the city on the western bank of the Tigris that had been included in verse 11 as part of Nimrod's empire, is here listed as an offspring of Shem. Arpakhshad is not currently identified with any known place. The consonants making up the first part of the name, *Arip*, are found as an element in Hurrian personal names. If this prefix is separated from the rest of his name, we are left with Kesed (Gen. 22:22), ancestor of the Chaldeans. Jubilees 9:4 states that Arpakhshad was given the land of the Chaldeans (see also Josephus, *Antiquities*, 1.6.4). Lud is not found in texts from the 2nd millennium BCE, but the Lydians were a later Iron Age kingdom located in modern western Turkey.

The children of Aram are not identified, except for Utz (see "Descendants of Naḥor" on page 138). Mash may be the same as Mashu, a great cedar mountain in the *Epic of Gilgamesh* "whose peaks [reach to] the vault of heaven" (IX.2.4), and which may refer to the mountains of Lebanon. Mash has also been identified with Maacah, an Aramean tribe south of Mount Hermon.

While Shelah is not identified with a particular region or group, the name of his son, Ever, is connected to the term "Hebrew," *ivri* (see "Avram the Hebrew" on page 88). Peleg, whose name is based on the term meaning division, is so named "for in his time the earth was divided" (v. 25), understood by the Sages to be a reference to the dispersal of humanity resulting from the Tower of Bavel incident. The name may also be related to the Akkadian *palgu*, meaning "canal" or "irrigation ditch," and thus refers to the development of agriculture and to the division of land by irrigation canals. Yoktan has been associated with the Qahtanites, Arabs who originate from the southwest corner of the Arabian Peninsula.

The sons of Yoktan who can be identified are all connected to various Arabian locations. Ḥatzarmavet is the Hadhramaut region in South Arabia, comprising eastern Yemen and southern Saudi Arabia. Sheva here is the southern Arabian kingdom of Saba, which had connections with King Shlomo, known also from Assyrian inscriptions. Identification of other names here is more speculative. For example, Shelef may be the town of As-Salif in western Yemen, prominently involved in the salt trade. ▪ ZR

כו הָאָרֶץ וְשֵׁם אָחִיו יָקְטָן׃ וְיָקְטָן יָלַד אֶת־אַלְמוֹדָד וְאֶת־שָׁלֶף
כז וְאֶת־חֲצַרְמָוֶת וְאֶת־יָרַח׃ וְאֶת־הֲדוֹרָם וְאֶת־אוּזָל וְאֶת־דִּקְלָה׃
כח כט וְאֶת־עוֹבָל וְאֶת־אֲבִימָאֵל וְאֶת־שְׁבָא׃ וְאֶת־אוֹפִר וְאֶת־חֲוִילָה
ל וְאֶת־יוֹבָב כָּל־אֵלֶּה בְּנֵי יָקְטָן׃ וַיְהִי מוֹשָׁבָם מִמֵּשָׁא בֹּאֲכָה סְפָרָה
לא הַר הַקֶּדֶם׃ אֵלֶּה בְנֵי־שֵׁם לְמִשְׁפְּחֹתָם לִלְשֹׁנֹתָם בְּאַרְצֹתָם
לב לְגוֹיֵהֶם׃ אֵלֶּה מִשְׁפְּחֹת בְּנֵי־נֹחַ לְתוֹלְדֹתָם בְּגוֹיֵהֶם וּמֵאֵלֶּה
נִפְרְדוּ הַגּוֹיִם בָּאָרֶץ אַחַר הַמַּבּוּל׃

His brother was named Yoktan. Yoktan was the father of 26
Almodad, Shelef, Ḥatzarmavet, Yeraḥ, Hadoram, Uzal, Dikla, 27
Oval, Avimael, Sheva, Ofir, Ḥavila, and Yovav; all these were 28 29
Yoktan's sons. Their settlements extended from Mesha toward 30
Sefar, in the eastern hill country. These were the descendants 31
of Shem, by their clans and their languages, with their lands
and their nations. These, then, are the clans of the sons of 32
Noaḥ, by their lines, in their nations. And from these, the
nations spread out across the earth after the flood.

↗ Linear Elamite inscription, detail, perforated stone of Puzur-Inshushinak, Susa, ca. 2100 BCE

Tower of Babel, Pieter Bruegel the Elder, 1563

the lookout tower in Yizre'el"; Isaiah 2:15, "for each tall tower, each impenetrable wall," etc. Cities fortified "to heaven" are also mentioned in Deuteronomy 1:28, 9:1.

This "city and a tower that reaches the heavens" was built particularly because the people feared that they would "be scattered across the face of the earth." Why did they think they would be so dispersed? Rashbam comments that the people of Bavel were trying to defend themselves against an attack from Heaven, since they knew they were defying God's command after the flood to "fill the earth" (9:1, 7).

According to this interpretation, their tower was not designed as a ziggurat to encourage God to descend to the people. Quite the opposite – it was a defensive fortification which, in their arrogance, they thought could prevent God from compelling them to fulfill His command. God, in turn, went "down to see," that is, to investigate what the people are doing (an ominous turn of phrase; the next time God went down to see what people were doing, it was to observe the behavior of Sedom and Amora, Genesis 18:21). His conclusion (11:6) was that human unity, when motivated by power and selfishness, is an evil enterprise.

Remains of ziggurat from Borsippa (Iraq)

Interestingly, the *Summa Alu* omen series (Akkadian, from the Royal Library of Ashurbanipal) records that "If a city lifts its head to the midst of heaven, that city will be abandoned" (1:15), and "If a city rises like a mountain peak to the midst of heaven, that city will be turned into a ruin" (1:16). The implication may be that the Mesopotamians recognized that a city should not try to replace a sacred structure in importance.

As Sarna notes, the Lord's reaction illustrates the rebels' helplessness before His incomparable transcendence and supremacy. The text uses heavy irony to depict God, as it were, taking the stairs all the way down from the top floor to ground level, just to see what the people were doing. He did not need to destroy anything in order to enforce His will; He merely exercised power that only He has, to impose a diversity of languages upon the humans to prevent their coordination, making it impossible for them to do evil on a grand scale (at least until the rise of empires).

Against their will, the people's fears were realized. God's plan for humanity cannot be averted. ▪ JU

Tower of Bavel

This etiological narrative seeks to explain why people have so many languages that it inhibits communication, and how the great city of Babylon got its name (for other such narratives, see "Punishment of the humans – an etiology" on page 24). Last, but not least, the story focuses on the sin of those who reconstituted humanity after the flood – their rebellion against God. That rebellion and God's squelching of it form the immediate background for God's choice of Avraham and his descendants to carry His message to humanity.

The Mesopotamian context

No other ancient Near Eastern story accounts for the spread of humankind throughout the Earth. Nonetheless, as Nahum Sarna points out, the episode here evinces "an intimate acquaintance with Babylonian construction techniques, a familiarity with characteristic royal building inscriptions, and a knowledge of certain Mesopotamian traditions."

The statement that Babylon had an extraordinarily tall tower is surely based on the ziggurat (derived from the Akkadian verb, *zaqaru*, "to build high"), approximately twenty-five of which have been discovered in Mesopotamia. Ranging from some sixty to nearly two hundred feet square, the ziggurat was a sacred space, but not a temple. While its outside was made of kiln-fired brick, its inside was packed with dirt. Each ziggurat was dedicated to a particular deity. Its primary architectural feature was an external stairway or ramp that rose to the top (see illustrations on pages 66 and 67). Apparently, at the top, the god's bed and table were housed in a small room. However, no rituals took place at the ziggurat itself. Typically, worship took place at a temple adjoined to the ziggurat at its base.

Mesopotamian inscriptions reflect the height of the ziggurat accompanied by its temple. So, at Larsa, "He [the king]… made its head touch heaven. On account of this deed the gods Nanna and Ningal rejoiced." Hammurabi was said to have built a temple tower "whose top is sky high." Esar Ḥadon of Assyria (7th century BCE) tells that he "made high its [the temple of Ashur] top up to heaven."

The names given to some of the ziggurats are the best clues to their function: the ziggurat at Larsa, was called "The House of the Link between Heaven and Earth"; at Sippar, it was "The Temple of the Stairway to Pure Heaven" (apparently, a reference to the myth of the stairway that the divine messenger traversed between heaven, the earth, and the underworld); at Babylon, the name (Etemenanki) meant, "The House of the Foundation of Heaven and Earth." Thus, the ziggurat expressed the people's hope that the god would favorably descend to the ziggurat to accept the people's devotion.

In Genesis, the people also felt that success in their building project would result in their fame, "let us make a name for ourselves." This prideful desire evokes an ancient Mesopotamian tradition. An inscription of the Sumerian king, Gudea of Lagash, relates that "on account of the great name that he made for himself, he was received among the gods into their assembly." Similarly, an inscription commemorating Nevukhadnetzar's building projects states, "The fortifications of Esagila [the temple and ziggurat] and Babylon I strengthened, and made an everlasting name for my reign."

No other ancient Near Eastern story accounts for the spread of humankind throughout the Earth.

The biblical perspective

While the ancient Israelites could well have heard of Babylon's famous tower, the cultic purpose of the ziggurat does not appear in Genesis. Further, the biblical narrative includes no reference to a temple or to the worship of a deity. Here, the Tower of Bavel reflects the ordinary purpose of a city tower (Hebrew, *migdal*) built in the midst of a city or atop the wall or gate, for defense against attackers. The Tanakh includes many examples of such towers: Judges 9:51–52, "There was a stronghold [*migdal-oz*] in the town… Avimelekh reached the tower [*migdal*] and attacked it"; II Kings 9:17, "the watchman stationed in

Baked brick fragment stating "Nevukhadnetzar, king of Babylon, provider for Esagila and Ezida, ...", 6th century BCE ↗

שביעי וַיְהִי כָל־הָאָרֶץ שָׂפָה אֶחָת וּדְבָרִים אֲחָדִים: וַיְהִי בְּנׇסְעָם מִקֶּדֶם א ב יא
וַיִּמְצְאוּ בִקְעָה בְּאֶרֶץ שִׁנְעָר וַיֵּשְׁבוּ שָׁם: וַיֹּאמְרוּ אִישׁ אֶל־רֵעֵהוּ ג
הָבָה נִלְבְּנָה לְבֵנִים וְנִשְׂרְפָה לִשְׂרֵפָה וַתְּהִי לָהֶם הַלְּבֵנָה לְאָבֶן
וְהַחֵמָר הָיָה לָהֶם לַחֹמֶר: וַיֹּאמְרוּ הָבָה | נִבְנֶה־לָּנוּ עִיר וּמִגְדָּל ד
וְרֹאשׁוֹ בַשָּׁמַיִם וְנַעֲשֶׂה־לָּנוּ שֵׁם פֶּן־נָפוּץ עַל־פְּנֵי כׇל־הָאָרֶץ:

11 1 The whole world spoke the same language, the same words.
2 And as the people migrated from the east they found a valley
3 in the land of Shinar and settled there. They said to each other,
"Come, let us make bricks, let us bake them thoroughly."
4 They used bricks for stone and tar for mortar. And they said,
"Come, let us build ourselves a city and a tower that reaches
the heavens, and make a name for ourselves. Otherwise we

GEOGRAPHY

11:2 Shinar

Shinar is the term used in Tanakh to refer to Babylonia (for example, Is. 11:11; Zech. 5:11; Dan. 1:2), although it is not the Akkadian name for any area of Babylon and was not used in Mesopotamia itself. However, this term is associated with Babylonia in other languages. Shinar is equivalent to the Egyptian *Sngr* and Hittite *Shanḫar(a)*, used for the Kassite kingdom of southern Mesopotamia (16th to 12th century BCE), which included the cities of Babylon and Nippur. ▪ ZR

Kassite-era ziggurat, Aqar-Quf (Dur-Kurigalzu), Iraq, 16th to 12th century BCE

Mud brick with cuneiform inscription mentioning Amar-Sin, son of Shulgi, Mesopotamia, 21st to 20th century BCE

LANGUAGE

11:2–3 Making bricks in the valley of Shinar

"A valley in the land of Shinar" (v. 2) refers to the large plain between the Tigris and Euphrates rivers in southern Mesopotamia, which encompasses ancient Babylon and Sumer. Verse 3 reflects the reality that the paucity of stones in that plain required the creation of bricks out of molded, baked clay as the basic building material. The bricks were greatly strengthened by the use of bitumen (tar) for mortar. The combination of clay bricks and bitumen allowed for the architecture of multistoried buildings. Indeed, a common phrase in building inscriptions in southern Mesopotamia is "with bitumen and burnt-brick."

The translation "Let us make bricks" is, in literal Hebrew, "let us brick bricks" (*nilbina levainim*), the precise equivalent of the Akkadian expression, *labanu libittu*. The *Enuma Elish Epic* (VI:60) relates that "for one whole year they [the gods] made (literally, 'bricked') bricks" in order to build Babylon. ▪ JU

ה וַיֵּרֶד יְהוָה לִרְאֹת אֶת־הָעִיר וְאֶת־הַמִּגְדָּל אֲשֶׁר בָּנוּ בְּנֵי הָאָדָם׃
ו וַיֹּאמֶר יְהוָה הֵן עַם אֶחָד וְשָׂפָה אַחַת לְכֻלָּם וְזֶה הַחִלָּם לַעֲשׂוֹת
ז וְעַתָּה לֹא־יִבָּצֵר מֵהֶם כֹּל אֲשֶׁר יָזְמוּ לַעֲשׂוֹת׃ הָבָה נֵרְדָה וְנָבְלָה
ח שָׁם שְׂפָתָם אֲשֶׁר לֹא יִשְׁמְעוּ אִישׁ שְׂפַת רֵעֵהוּ׃ וַיָּפֶץ יְהוָה אֹתָם
ט מִשָּׁם עַל־פְּנֵי כָל־הָאָרֶץ וַיַּחְדְּלוּ לִבְנֹת הָעִיר׃ עַל־כֵּן קָרָא שְׁמָהּ
בָּבֶל כִּי־שָׁם בָּלַל יְהוָה שְׂפַת כָּל־הָאָרֶץ וּמִשָּׁם הֱפִיצָם יְהוָה
עַל־פְּנֵי כָּל־הָאָרֶץ׃

will be scattered across the face of the earth." But the Lord 5
came down to see the city and the tower being built by the
children of men. The Lord said, "If, as one people with one 6
language, they have begun to do this, nothing they plan to
do will be impossible for them. Let us go down and confuse 7
their language so that one will not understand the speech of
another." From there the Lord scattered them all over the 8
earth, and they abandoned the building of the city. That is 9
why it was called Bavel, because it was there that the Lord
confused[22] the language of all the earth; and from there the
Lord scattered them all across the face of the earth.

22 | The name Bavel (Babylon) resonates with *balal* (confused).

LANGUAGE

11:9 Bavel...because the Lord confused the language

"Bavel," the location of the famous tower, is simply the Hebrew name of Babylon, occurring more than 250 times in the Tanakh. The Akkadian name is *Bab-ilu*, "Gate of god," a meaning mocked by the biblical story.

The tower was a ziggurat, and the term "reaches the heavens" (v. 4) is actually an Akkadian cliché, like the modern "skyscraper."

Dictionaries relate English "babble" to the *ba-ba-ba* sounds made by babies, but the traditional English rendering of Bavel as "Babel" reflects the Hebrew pun in our story, when God "confused" [*balal*] their language. The Akkadian cognate of *balal* is *balalu*, "to mix" – or "mix up." ▪ MC

NEAR EAST

11:8 They abandoned the building of the city

The image of the abandoned original construction of the city of Babylon may well have resonated with the Israelites who, at a much later date, read or listened to the Torah.

Long after the Genesis narrative of the abandonment of the original city would have taken place, a modest Babylon was built in the latter part of the 3rd millennium BCE. In the 18th century, Hammurabi transformed it into a major city and made it the capital of the Old Babylonian empire he founded – complete with impressive walls, towers, and temples. Nonetheless, in 1595 BCE, the Hittite king Mursili I raided and sacked the city, ending the Amorite dynasty, of which Hammurabi was the sixth king. This event is recorded in the *Telipinu Proclamation*, "And then he [Mursili I] marched to Aleppo, and he destroyed Aleppo and brought captives and possessions of Aleppo to Ḫattusa. Then, however, he marched to Babylon, and he destroyed Babylon, and he defeated the Hurrian troops, and he brought captives and possessions of Babylon to Ḫattusa" (§9–10, I 28–31). Prior to that, Babylon (which has been extensively excavated in modern times) had become probably the world's largest city (dozens of times the size of David's Jerusalem), and its fame was widespread.

The early Israelites, who would have certainly heard of the Hittite destruction of Babylon, would have understood the Genesis narrative as presenting one of the underlying reasons for both the original abandonment and the much later destruction – the extreme hubris of its inhabitants. Indeed, the monotheistic Israelites may well have interpreted Babylon's destruction as also the work of God. ▪ ZR, JU

↗ Ziggurat of Ur, Sumerian, reconstructed, original from 21st century BCE

אֵלֶּה תּוֹלְדֹת שֵׁם שֵׁם בֶּן־מְאַת שָׁנָה וַיּוֹלֶד אֶת־אַרְפַּכְשָׁד י
שְׁנָתַיִם אַחַר הַמַּבּוּל: וַיְחִי־שֵׁם אַחֲרֵי הוֹלִידוֹ אֶת־אַרְפַּכְשָׁד יא
חֲמֵשׁ מֵאוֹת שָׁנָה וַיּוֹלֶד בָּנִים וּבָנוֹת: וְאַרְפַּכְשַׁד חַי יב
חָמֵשׁ וּשְׁלֹשִׁים שָׁנָה וַיּוֹלֶד אֶת־שָׁלַח: וַיְחִי אַרְפַּכְשַׁד אַחֲרֵי יג
הוֹלִידוֹ אֶת־שֶׁלַח שָׁלֹשׁ שָׁנִים וְאַרְבַּע מֵאוֹת שָׁנָה וַיּוֹלֶד בָּנִים
וּבָנוֹת: וְשֶׁלַח חַי שְׁלֹשִׁים שָׁנָה וַיּוֹלֶד אֶת־עֵבֶר: יד
וַיְחִי־שֶׁלַח אַחֲרֵי הוֹלִידוֹ אֶת־עֵבֶר שָׁלֹשׁ שָׁנִים וְאַרְבַּע מֵאוֹת טו
שָׁנָה וַיּוֹלֶד בָּנִים וּבָנוֹת: וַיְחִי־עֵבֶר אַרְבַּע וּשְׁלֹשִׁים טז

10 These are the descendants of Shem. When Shem was one
hundred years old, he had a son, Arpakhshad, two years after
11 the flood. After Arpakhshad was born, Shem lived five hundred
12 years and had other sons and daughters. When
Arpakhshad was thirty-five years old, he had a son, Shelaḥ.
13 After Shelaḥ was born, Arpakhshad lived four hundred and
14 three years and had other sons and daughters. When
15 Shelaḥ was thirty years old, he had a son, Ever. After Ever
was born, Shelaḥ lived four hundred and three years and
16 had other sons and daughters. Ever lived thirty-four

GEOGRAPHY

11:10–29 From Shem to Avram

A significant aspect of the genealogy in these verses is the shorter lifespans compared to Genesis 5, where the ages ranged from 365 to 969 with seven individuals living into their tenth century. In contrast, in the line from Shem to Avram, only Shem, a transitional figure, has a lifespan reminiscent of Genesis 5 (600 years), while his descendants' lifespans range from 464 down to 148 years. In this regard, Genesis 5 and 11:10–26 reflect a theme similar to the Sumerian King List, where lifespans before the cataclysmic flood were far longer than lifespans afterward. That said, the difference between the two periods is more pronounced in the King List than in Genesis, as before the flood the semi-mythological kings of southern Mesopotamia reigned for tens of thousands of years, but afterward relatively normal regnal years dominate. Regarding the age of siring one's firstborn, only Shem (at 100) and Teraḥ (the last, at 70) stand out, while those in between father their firstborn at ages 29 to 34. Teraḥ's relatively advanced age at the birth of his firstborn may hint at the infertility that characterizes the next several generations of his line.

While Avram's place of origin, Ur Kasdim, is linked by some scholars with southern Mesopotamia, other aspects of the genealogy list point to a northern location in the general vicinity of Ḥaran (see "Ur Kasdim" on page 70). Sites with names similar to Ur appear in the area, and a cluster of names in the genealogy are associated with the region of the Balikh River, a northern tributary of the Euphrates River in modern-day Syria. The name Serug (vv. 22–23), which is connected to the place-name, Sarug (just north of Ḥaran (v. 31), is known from Assyrian inscriptions for its location along an important trade route. A text from the Ur III period (ca. 2100 BCE) mentions a personal name, Sarug, and the modern Turkish toponym Suruç is thought to preserve the ancient name.

Serug's son and grandson are both named Naḥor, and a city by that name, mentioned in the Mari archive (mid-2nd millennium BCE), was located near Ḥaran on the Balikh River. Personal names with the Semitic root *n ḥ r* are found over a wide spectrum of ancient Near Eastern history.

Teraḥ, Avraham's father, has a parallel to his name in *Til Turakhi*, "the mound of Teraḥ," a toponym near Ḥaran. The name "Teraḥ" is similar to *yare'aḥ*, Hebrew for "moon"; both Ur (Teraḥ's point of departure) and Ḥaran (his destination) share an association with the worship of Sin, the moon god.

The city Ḥaran (v. 31) was located about 100 kilometers (62 miles) north of the junction of the Euphrates and Balikh rivers and served as an intersection for trade routes. The name is derived from the Akkadian *ḥarranu*, and its various meanings – "highway," "caravan," and "business venture" – reflect the nature of ancient commerce. Ḥaran is identified with Padan (Gen. 28:2, see also "Padan Aram" on page 155), to which Yaakov flees and there marries into Naḥor's line; the Akkadian *padanu* also means "road."

The name Reu (vv. 19–20), with its root letters *r a* [*ayin*] *h* appears as an element in Semitic personal names from a wide variety of times and places. It has two semantic associations in those languages: with shepherding and with friendship. The element *reu* may be compounded with a divine name to describe a characteristic of the deity (God as a shepherd) or to describe the name bearer as a "friend of God." An example is the biblical name Reuel, given to three individuals in the Tanakh, the most famous of whom is Moshe's Midianite father-in-law (Exodus 2:18).

In Genesis 17:15, Sarai's name is changed to Sara. The form "Sarai" in v. 29 represents a more archaic feminine termination preserved in other Semitic languages. Both forms are associated with royalty (from the root *sh r h*, meaning "rule") and can be translated "princess" or "noblewoman."

The name Milka (v. 29), a variant of Malka, is a feminine form of the root *m l kh*, meaning "ruling," and denotes "queen," similar to Sarai. She is the mother of Betuel and grandmother of Lavan and Rivka. ▪ EG

יז שָׁנָה וַיּוֹלֶד אֶת־פָּלֶג׃ וַיְחִי־עֵבֶר אַחֲרֵי הוֹלִידוֹ אֶת־פֶּלֶג שְׁלֹשִׁים
יח שָׁנָה וְאַרְבַּע מֵאוֹת שָׁנָה וַיּוֹלֶד בָּנִים וּבָנוֹת׃ וַיְחִי־פֶלֶג
יט שְׁלֹשִׁים שָׁנָה וַיּוֹלֶד אֶת־רְעוּ׃ וַיְחִי־פֶלֶג אַחֲרֵי הוֹלִידוֹ אֶת־רְעוּ
כ תֵּשַׁע שָׁנִים וּמָאתַיִם שָׁנָה וַיּוֹלֶד בָּנִים וּבָנוֹת׃ וַיְחִי
כא רְעוּ שְׁתַּיִם וּשְׁלֹשִׁים שָׁנָה וַיּוֹלֶד אֶת־שְׂרוּג׃ וַיְחִי רְעוּ אַחֲרֵי
הוֹלִידוֹ אֶת־שְׂרוּג שֶׁבַע שָׁנִים וּמָאתַיִם שָׁנָה וַיּוֹלֶד בָּנִים
כב וּבָנוֹת׃ וַיְחִי שְׂרוּג שְׁלֹשִׁים שָׁנָה וַיּוֹלֶד אֶת־נָחוֹר׃
כג וַיְחִי שְׂרוּג אַחֲרֵי הוֹלִידוֹ אֶת־נָחוֹר מָאתַיִם שָׁנָה וַיּוֹלֶד בָּנִים
כד וּבָנוֹת׃ וַיְחִי נָחוֹר תֵּשַׁע וְעֶשְׂרִים שָׁנָה וַיּוֹלֶד אֶת־
כה תָּרַח׃ וַיְחִי נָחוֹר אַחֲרֵי הוֹלִידוֹ אֶת־תֶּרַח תְּשַׁע־עֶשְׂרֵה שָׁנָה
כו וּמְאַת שָׁנָה וַיּוֹלֶד בָּנִים וּבָנוֹת׃ וַיְחִי־תֶרַח שִׁבְעִים

years and then had a son, Peleg. After Peleg was born, Ever 17
lived four hundred and thirty years and had other sons and
daughters. Peleg lived thirty years and then had a 18
son, Reu. After Reu was born, Peleg lived two hundred and 19
nine years and had other sons and daughters. Reu 20
lived thirty-two years and then had a son, Serug. After 21
Serug was born, Reu lived two hundred and seven years
and had other sons and daughters. Serug lived 22
thirty years and then had a son, Naḥor. After Naḥor was 23
born, Serug lived two hundred years and had other sons
and daughters. Naḥor lived twenty-nine years and 24
then had a son, Teraḥ. After Teraḥ was born, Naḥor lived 25
one hundred and nineteen years and had other sons and
daughters. Teraḥ lived seventy years and fathered 26

Possible predecessor of Sin temple, excavations at Tel Haran, 3rd millennium BCE

שָׁנָ֑ה וַיּ֙וֹלֶד֙ אֶת־אַבְרָ֔ם אֶת־נָח֖וֹר וְאֶת־הָרָֽן׃ וְאֵ֙לֶּה֙ תּוֹלְדֹ֣ת כז
תֶּ֔רַח תֶּ֚רַח הוֹלִ֣יד אֶת־אַבְרָ֔ם אֶת־נָח֖וֹר וְאֶת־הָרָ֑ן וְהָרָ֖ן הוֹלִ֥יד
אֶת־לֽוֹט׃ וַיָּ֣מָת הָרָ֔ן עַל־פְּנֵ֖י תֶּ֣רַח אָבִ֑יו בְּאֶ֥רֶץ מוֹלַדְתּ֖וֹ בְּא֥וּר כח •

27 Avram, Naḥor, and Haran. These are the descendants of
Teraḥ. Teraḥ was the father of Avram, Naḥor, and Haran, and
• 28 Haran had a son, Lot. While his father Teraḥ was still alive,

↗ Aerial view of the excavation site of Ur (Tell el-Muqayyar), March 1927

GEOGRAPHY

11:28 Ur Kasdim

Ur was an important Sumerian city-state in southern Mesopotamia, located at modern-day Tell el-Muqayyar in Iraq. The history of this city goes back to the prehistoric Ubaid period in Mesopotamia (ca. 6500–3800 BCE), becoming one of the dominant city-states in the 3rd millennium BCE. The city has been well excavated and is documented in many ancient Near Eastern sources. It contains the best-preserved ziggurat from ancient Mesopotamia.

However, identifying this Ur with the biblical Ur Kasdim is problematic in light of the fact that the Chaldeans (from the Greek translation of Akkadian *kaldu* or *kashdu*) are not recorded in southern Babylonia before the 1st millennium BCE, when they emigrated from the northern Levant. Furthermore, they only came into prominence in Babylonia in 780 BCE when the Chaldean Marduk-apla-uṣur became king of Babylonia. Additionally, the city of Ur was so well known that there would be no need to describe it further by associating it with Chaldeans.

Another complication is that if Teraḥ and Avram were traveling to Canaan from Ur, they would not pass through Ḥaran as described in 11:31; Ḥaran, located in southeastern Turkey, is far to the north of any of the ancient trade routes connecting Ur to Canaan.

Sites with names similar to Ur are found in the general vicinity of Ḥaran, possibly due to the fact that *uru* means "city" in Sumerian. Therefore, other sites have been suggested as the birthplace of Avram. These include the city of Ur in northern Mesopotamia, which is the modern Urfa, located in southeastern Turkey north of Ḥaran. This place would be identified with the Chaldeans, who were understood by ancient Greek historians to have come from the area of Armenia north of Ḥaran.
▪ ZR

כט כַּשְׂדִּים: וַיִּקַּח אַבְרָם וְנָחוֹר לָהֶם נָשִׁים שֵׁם אֵשֶׁת־אַבְרָם שָׂרָי מפטיר
וְשֵׁם אֵשֶׁת־נָחוֹר מִלְכָּה בַּת־הָרָן אֲבִי־מִלְכָּה וַאֲבִי יִסְכָּה:
ל לא וַתְּהִי שָׂרַי עֲקָרָה אֵין לָהּ וָלָד: וַיִּקַּח תֶּרַח אֶת־אַבְרָם בְּנוֹ
וְאֶת־לוֹט בֶּן־הָרָן בֶּן־בְּנוֹ וְאֵת שָׂרַי כַּלָּתוֹ אֵשֶׁת אַבְרָם בְּנוֹ
וַיֵּצְאוּ אִתָּם מֵאוּר כַּשְׂדִּים לָלֶכֶת אַרְצָה כְּנַעַן וַיָּבֹאוּ עַד־חָרָן
לב וַיֵּשְׁבוּ שָׁם: וַיִּהְיוּ יְמֵי־תֶרַח חָמֵשׁ שָׁנִים וּמָאתַיִם שָׁנָה וַיָּמָת
תֶּרַח בְּחָרָן:

Haran died in the land of his birth, Ur Kasdim. Avram and 29
Naḥor married; the name of Avram's wife was Sarai, and the
name of Naḥor's wife was Milka. She was the daughter of
Haran, father of Milka and Yiska. And Sarai was barren – she 30
had no child. Teraḥ took his son Avram, and his grandson Lot, 31
son of Haran, and his daughter-in-law Sarai, his son Avram's
wife, and together they set out from Ur Kasdim to go to the
land of Canaan. But when they arrived at Ḥaran, they settled
there. Teraḥ lived two hundred and five years, and he died 32
in Ḥaran.

↗ Abraham Leaves Harran, attributed to Francesco Bassano the Younger, 1560–1592

son's action and initiative. An Akkadian proverb states: "When you plan ahead your god is yours; when you do not plan ahead your god is not yours." In other words, such gods may be the personification of one's right and wrong actions, that is, the power of decision-making. That said, a Mesopotamian deity could fail in his guidance. For example, an Akkadian private letter (ca. 17th century BCE) rebukes the addressee for where he settled: "May the name of your god and whosoever encouraged you (in this) and caused you…to settle down there, perish." Nonetheless, an Old Babylonian text from the same period asserts, "without the (personal) god, man eats no bread." According to another Assyriologist, Tzvi Abusch, Mesopotamians psychologically "objectified and externalized major aspects of [the] self…[and] could thus be surrounded by a series of divine beings who represented aspects of self," who would then be viewed as personal deities.

Only in Israel does the personal-family God of the Israelites' ancestors become the national God of the entire people.

Head of a god, probably from Thebes, 15th century BCE

The family would identify its personal god as "the god of the father(s)" – a description used often in Genesis (for example, 26:24, 28:13, 31:5, 29, 42, 53). Worship of the personal god in Mesopotamia would be carried on from generation to generation as a kind of inheritance – always determined by the god worshipped by the man of the household, who had in turn inherited the obligation to worship the god from his father. A girl in her father's household would worship his god, but upon entering her husband's household she would worship her husband's god. Worship of this god would not in any way be exclusive to one family or clan, and it would still be accompanied by worship of other deities, such as the great gods. Such family gods are perhaps represented in the Tanakh by the teraphim, assuming that those were not part of ancestor worship.

Female fertility figurine, Mesopotamia (Neo-Assyrian or Neo-Babylonian), 10th to 6th century BCE

As the family god was a lower-ranked deity in terms of placement in the pantheon, many scholars assume that it became associated with a family because it was generally a local deity with a temple or shrine nearby. A city god, which was of higher rank though not usually one of the great gods, would thus not be the personal god of local citizens. However, a great god would be a personal god to a highly ranked individual, such as a king.

One of the achievements of the Torah's ethical monotheism is its complete revolutionary restructuring of divinity in the ancient world. Whereas in the pagan pantheons multiple gods assumed roles in relation to people, families, cities, and political entities (kingdoms), the Torah presents just the one transcendent, metaphysical deity who fulfills all the roles: provider of nature, creator and ruler of the cosmos, and the judge and caregiver of humanity. Furthermore, out of the entire world, only in Israel does the personal-family God of the Israelites' ancestors become the national God of the entire people. In this historical transformation, God preserves a personal bond with each Israelite and, simultaneously, maintains ultimate sovereignty of the universe and all it contains. ▪ JU

The religious revolution of God's personal relationship with Avraham

Although previously in Genesis God did speak directly to Adam, Ḥava, Kayin, and Noaḥ and his sons, a new stage of God's relationship with humans ensues with Avraham. The earlier divine communications to humans were concerned either with all humanity (and, in the case of Noaḥ and his sons, even all life on earth), now and in the future (1:28–30, 3:16–19, 9:1–17), or, conversely, with the particular lifetime of a single human being (2:16–17, 4:6–7, 9–15). However, the preceding God-human contacts ended in failure. Rather than follow God's beneficial plans, the first humans disobeyed God, the next generation committed fratricide, and humanity then devolved into violence. Following a new beginning with the righteous Noaḥ, humanity disobeyed God again and rebelled against Him with the Tower of Bavel.

With the advent of His contact with Avraham (then, Avram) in verse 1, God embarks on an innovation. In a world already populated far and wide with people, He will work with a single man, his family, and their descendants. Even though He is the transcendent Master of the cosmos, He also becomes the personal God of a tiny segment of humanity.

Famed Sumerologist and Assyriologist Thorkild Jacobsen identified three stages in the development of polytheism in Mesopotamia, with each approach to the role of the gods attached to a particular time period: the gods as providers, through natural fertility – 4th millennium BCE; the gods as rulers, exerting power and authority – 3rd millennium BCE; the personal gods – 2nd millennium BCE.

In the Mesopotamian imagination, the fertility gods coexisted with, but were transcended by, the ruling gods. The ruling deities were the great gods who comprised the supreme "divine assembly." In contrast, the "personal god" was a minor deity – neither a ruling god nor a fertility god. This polytheistic element reflects a personal relationship with a deity to whom the family was devoted and who, in turn, would be the family's patron. Jacobsen defined this idea as a "religious attitude in which the religious individual sees himself as standing in close personal relationship to the divine, expecting help and guidance in his personal life and personal affairs, expecting divine anger and punishment if he sins, but also profoundly trusting to divine compassion.... In sum: the individual matters to God, God cares about him personally and deeply." The representative expression is that the individual and his family have "acquired a god."

Some texts describe this god as a personified power of good fortune and achievement which functions according to a per-

↗ The god Ashur inside a winged disc, Northwest Palace of Ashurnasirpal II, Nimrud, 9th century BCE

Map of Avraham
in the Land of Israel
Dan
Haran, Hova, and
Damascus
SEA OF
GALILEE
MEDITERRANEAN SEA
Shekhem
hills east of
Beit El
Beit El
Ai
Mount Moria
Shalem
Shaveh Valley
DEAD SEA
Oaks of Mamre
Makhpela, Hevron
Gerar
Be'er Sheva
NEGEV
Sedom?
Amora?
Tzoar
Tzevoyim?
to Kadesh
and Shur

לך לך וַיֹּאמֶר יהוה אֶל־אַבְרָם לֶךְ־לְךָ מֵאַרְצְךָ וּמִמּוֹלַדְתְּךָ וּמִבֵּית א • יב
אָבִיךָ אֶל־הָאָרֶץ אֲשֶׁר אַרְאֶךָּ׃ וְאֶעֶשְׂךָ לְגוֹי גָּדוֹל וַאֲבָרֶכְךָ ב •

The Lord said to Avram, "Go – from your land, your 1 • 12
birthplace, and your father's house – to the land that I will
show you. I will make you a great nation, and I will bless you 2 •

NEAR EAST

12:1 Go – from your land, your birthplace, and your father's house

God commands Avram to leave his land, his *moledet*, and his *beit av*. The term *moledet* has a connotation of family, as in "The man kept asking about us and our family (*moladeteinu*)" (Gen. 43:7), so in addition to the reference to his geographical birthplace, it indicates that Avram left his extended family, in addition to leaving his immediate family (*beit av*).

The emphasis on leaving both land and family is significant in the context of the theology of Mesopotamia at the time, where people believed in a god that looked after the needs of a particular family. Individuals worshipped the god of their family and larger kin group, as can be seen in seals that have been discovered in which different generations within the same family always refer to the same god: the family deity which was passed down from father to son.

Generally, the family deity was also the local god who had a sanctuary in the district where the family lived. Each Mesopotamian city had a patron deity (for example, Marduk was the patron god of Babylon). Unless a deity was one of the chief gods of an area, he or she was not perceived to have any power in faraway places. Avram's journey at God's command would thus sever him from the god of his family and of the place where they lived. ▪ ZR

NEAR EAST

12:2 I will make you a great nation, and I will bless you and will make your name great

While ancient Near Eastern literature tells of deities promising kingship, prosperity, and offspring to individuals, it has no parallel to this promise to Avram – to make him into a great nation. This unique promise is made more incredible by the fact of Avram's advanced age and childlessness. By following the word of God, Avram thus demonstrated his great faith.

In the ancient Near East, a person's name represented his essence. For example, a hymn of praise to the Egyptian god Horus states, "Your mother Nut has spread herself over you in her name of Shetpet…Horus has filled you with his eye in his name of Divine Offering." Therefore, the promise to "make your name great" means to make Avram an exalted figure, one whose character would personify the concept of a blessing (as detailed in verse 3).

This stands in contrast to the people of Bavel, whose selfish goal was to "make a name for ourselves" (Gen. 11:4). ▪ ZR

Image of Horus with the double crown of Egypt, Temple of Horus, Edfu, 3rd to 1st century BCE ↘

וְאֲגַדְּלָה שְׁמֶךָ וֶהְיֵה בְּרָכָה׃ וַאֲבָרְכָה מְבָרְכֶיךָ וּמְקַלֶּלְךָ אָאֹר ג
וְנִבְרְכוּ בְךָ כֹּל מִשְׁפְּחֹת הָאֲדָמָה׃ וַיֵּלֶךְ אַבְרָם כַּאֲשֶׁר דִּבֶּר ד
אֵלָיו יהוה וַיֵּלֶךְ אִתּוֹ לוֹט וְאַבְרָם בֶּן־חָמֵשׁ שָׁנִים וְשִׁבְעִים שָׁנָה
בְּצֵאתוֹ מֵחָרָן׃ וַיִּקַּח אַבְרָם אֶת־שָׂרַי אִשְׁתּוֹ וְאֶת־לוֹט בֶּן־אָחִיו ה •
וְאֶת־כָּל־רְכוּשָׁם אֲשֶׁר רָכָשׁוּ וְאֶת־הַנֶּפֶשׁ אֲשֶׁר־עָשׂוּ בְחָרָן וַיֵּצְאוּ

3 and make your name great. You will become a blessing. And
I will bless those who bless you, and those who curse you I
will curse. And through you, all the families of the earth will
4 be blessed." So Avram went, as the Lord had told him, and
with him went Lot. Avram was seventy-five years old when
• 5 he left Ḥaran. Avram took Sarai his wife, and Lot his nephew,
and all the wealth they had acquired and the people they had
gathered in Ḥaran. They set out to go to the land of Canaan,

GEOGRAPHY

12:5 Canaan

"Canaan" in the Tanakh is a broad term roughly covering the area of modern-day Israel, with the addition of Lebanon and the southwestern parts of Syria. In Late Bronze Age literature such as the *Amarna letters* and Ugaritic texts, the term is used by the Egyptians, Babylonians, Hittites, and Mitanni to designate the Asiatic areas under the rule of the pharaoh. Thus, it is the name of a territorial-political entity, also called the "land of the king (pharaoh)."

The boundaries of the Promised Land as delineated in Numbers 34 – the most detailed description in the Torah – correspond to the borders of the Egyptian province of Canaan from the time of the New Kingdom until the early 12th century BCE. The eastern border of Egyptian territory was the Jordan River; the western border was the Mediterranean Sea. The northern border was in the area of the al-Kabir River, which today constitutes the Lebanese northern border with Syria. This border was established by the peace treaty between Ramesses II and the Hittites after the stalemate at the battle of Kadesh (ca. 1275 BCE). The southern border extends from Wadi el-Arish, which is the largest dry wadi in Egypt and a natural barrier between the Negev and the Sinai, northeast to the bottom tip of the Dead Sea. The term Canaan excluded Transjordan, which was a peripheral area of little significance for Egypt.

Semitic peoples first appeared in this area in the Early Bronze Age, and textual references to this area already appear in *Mari letters* dated to around the mid-18th century BCE, where the Canaanites are called *Kinahnum*, named for an area south of the Syrian city of Qatna. This area basically corresponds to the northern border of the land designated as Canaan in the Late Bronze Age, indicating continuity of the area of Canaan throughout the Middle and Late Bronze Age.

Canaan was never united under one king, but was instead composed of many small kingdoms and city-states which were vassals of Egypt in the Late Bronze Age. The inhabitants of this area would identify themselves and were seen by others both as Canaanites in a general sense, and as citizens of the smaller kingdom to which they belonged. The most important of these city-states was Ḥatzor.

The *Amarna letters* which mention Canaan mainly address Egyptian control of this region and the relationship between the pharaoh and his Canaanite vassals. For example, Burnaburiash, king of Babylonia, complained in a letter to Pharaoh Akhenaten (14th century BCE) that his merchants were robbed in Canaan: "Canaan is your country, and [its] kings [are your servants]. In your country I have been despoiled. Bring [them] to account…" (EA 8). Rib-Hadda, king of Byblos, sent a similar letter to the reigning pharaoh during the mid-14th century BCE: "If he does not send archers, they will take [Byblos] and all the other cities, and the lands of Canaan will not belong to the king" (EA 131). Egyptian dominance in this area diminished by the end of the 13th century BCE. ▪ ZR

Statue of a Canaanite ruler, basalt, Ḥatzor, 15th to 13th century BCE

ו לָלֶכֶת אַרְצָה כְּנַעַן וַיָּבֹאוּ אַרְצָה כְּנָעַן: וַיַּעֲבֹר אַבְרָם בָּאָרֶץ

6 and they entered the land of Canaan. Avram traveled through
the land to the region of Shekhem, to the Oak of Moreh. The

— FLORA AND FAUNA —

12:6 Oak of Moreh

The oak of Moreh may have been a single large tree that served as a landmark to indicate this site.

Several kinds of oak grow in Israel. The most common are *Quercus ithaburensis* (Mount Tabor oak) and *Quercus calliprinos* (called the common oak in Israel). Both of these can reach a height of 10 meters (33 feet) and live for hundreds of years. The deep roots of the oak enable it to survive harsh and dry conditions. In Tanakh, the oak (*elon*) is always used in conjunction with another descriptive term, as in Judges 9:6, "the Monumental Oak at Shekhem."
▪ ZR

Israel common oak (*Quercus calliprinos*)

NEAR EAST

12:6 Canaanites

The phrase "The Canaanites were then (*az*) in the land" may well mean that at the time that Avram came to the land, the Canaanites were already there. The phrase thus explains why Avram was unable to take possession of the land promised to him by God right away: because it was inhabited by Canaanites.

The earliest reference to Canaanites is in a letter written by Yasmah-Adad, king of Mari (ruled 1796–1775 BCE), discussing conflict due to "thieves and Canaanites." Numerous mentions of Canaan and Canaanites appear in correspondence between Egyptian pharaohs and other rulers found in the *Amarna letters* (14th century BCE).

All this indicates that in the Middle and Late Bronze Age (ca. 2000–1200 BCE), there was a region in the southern Levant referred to as Canaan, populated by Canaanites, who may have been a single ethnic group or a combination of a number of different societies living in the same geographical area.

Extensive archaeological investigations were carried out at Ugarit (which provided major insights into Canaanite mythology), Megiddo, Ḥatzor, and other sites that have greatly increased our understanding of Canaanite culture during the Middle and Late Bronze Age. The Canaanites disappear from written and archaeological records in the early Iron Age. ▪ ZR

Canaanite tower, Tel Gezer, Karmei Yosef

NEAR EAST

12:6 Shekhem and the patriarchs

Shekhem is mentioned several times throughout the patriarchal narratives. Not only was it Avraham's first stop in Canaan, but Yaakov camped near Shekhem after his reunion with Esav and later bought land there from Ḥamor, the father of Shekhem. Yaakov then built an altar there (33:18–20) and buried pagan ritual items that were in the family's possession under a tree near Shekhem (35:2–4). The rape of Dina (ch. 34) caused a conflict with the residents of Shekhem. Hundreds of years later, Yehoshua even ensured that Yosef would be buried in Shekhem (Josh. 24:32).

The earliest extra-biblical mentions of Shekhem are from the Middle Bronze Age, in the 19th century BCE, in the Egyptian execration texts, and the Khu-Sebek inscription. These texts identify a city and a region, indicating a city-state that controls the surrounding territory. The *Amarna letters* reference a ruler named Lab'ayu who interacted with city-states such as Jerusalem, Megiddo, Gezer, and Pella (across the Jordan River).

The location of ancient Shekhem has been identified by archaeologists at Tell Balata, inside the modern city of Nablus, at the eastern end of the pass between Mount Eival and Mount Gerizim (see Deut. 11:29). Ample water sources are found nearby, and it overlooks fertile land. It lies in a strategic location with roads going south to Jerusalem, west to the coastal plain, northwest to Shomron and Dotan, and northeast to the Yizre'el or Jordan Valleys. A nearby site known in Arabic as Qubur Yusef (Yosef's Tomb) and another called Jacob's Well echo patriarchal memories.

The archaeological remains from the 19th and early 18th centuries BCE show the beginning of settlement, and late 18th century to early 16th century Middle Bronze Age remains include walls and monumental architecture of a walled city. The city apparently reached its largest and most fortified size starting about the mid-17th century, with gates, massive walls, towers, large temples and other sizeable buildings reflecting a powerful Canaanite entity. A gap in occupation occurred between the mid-16th to the mid-15th century, after which the site began to be developed again. Destruction took place in the late 14th century, followed by a lesser occupation preceding a vast destruction about 1100 BCE, which took place considerably after the conquest described in the book of Joshua. Curiously, the book of Joshua never mentions a conquest of Shekhem!

As noted elsewhere, it is very difficult to place the precise time in which the patriarchs lived. However, significant remains from the Middle Bronze Age exist at all the locations mentioned in these narratives along the main highway (today known as the "Way of the Patriarchs") that traverses the watershed of the central hill country – Shekhem, Beit El, Salem (Jerusalem), and Ḥevron. Avraham and the other patriarchs would have thus encountered Shekhem at a time during which it was settled, although it would be difficult to conceive that the two brothers, Shimon and Levi, could defeat an entire fortified city with walls, towers, and monumental architecture without using deception, as later attested in the book of Genesis. However, the strategic location of Shekhem, as well as its settlement history reflected in its architecture, might have been appropriate for patriarchal interaction when "the Canaanites were then in the land" (this verse), depending on the dating of the patriarchal period (which, as noted, is heavily contested among academic scholars). ▪ DAA

Middle Bronze Age wall, Shekhem excavations

ז עַד מְקוֹם שְׁכֶם עַד אֵלוֹן מוֹרֶה וְהַכְּנַעֲנִי אָז בָּאָרֶץ׃ וַיֵּרָא יהוה
אֶל־אַבְרָם וַיֹּאמֶר לְזַרְעֲךָ אֶתֵּן אֶת־הָאָרֶץ הַזֹּאת וַיִּבֶן שָׁם מִזְבֵּחַ

Canaanites were then in the land. Then the LORD appeared to 7
Avram and said, "To your descendants I will give this land."
There he built an altar to the LORD, who had appeared to him.

NEAR EAST

12:7 Promise of land

In Genesis 12:2–3, God promised Avram nationhood and blessings; here, for the first time, he is also promised land.

Ancient Near Eastern literature includes the motif of a deity promising to allow a king to retain and even increase the land under his control. For example, the *Mari letters* (FM 7 39) include the prophecy of Nur-Sin in the name of the god Adad to the king of Mari, Zimri-lim (ca. 1775–1761 BCE): "Am I not Adad, lord of Aleppo, who raised you in my lap and restored you to your ancestral throne?... If you do what I have written to you and heed my word, I will give you the land from the rising of the sun to its setting, [your] land [greatly in] creased." However, the promise to Avram is unique in that he was granted possession of land to which he had no prior connection.

This is also the first time in Tanakh that the text states that God "appeared" to a person. Until now, God spoke to people, but it does not say that he appeared to them. The term *vayera* ("appeared") might not refer to an actual visual experience, but rather to a type of prophetic interaction. Similarly, I Samuel 3:15 describes a prophecy experienced only as speech (I Sam. 3:11–14) with the term *mareh* ("vision"). This usage is similar to the term *ḥazon* used by prophets, which also means "a vision," but is sometimes used for purely verbal prophecies (Is. 1:2; Amos 1:1; Mic. 1:1; compare Gen. 15:1). ▪ ZR

NEAR EAST

12:7 There he built an altar to the Lord

This is the first of four altars that Avraham would build, and only the second one mentioned in Tanakh (the first was built by Noaḥ for his sacrifices; Gen. 8:20). This practice was to be followed by Yitzḥak (Gen. 26:25) and Yaakov (Gen. 33:20, 35:3, 7).

With the exception of the altar he built at Moria (Gen. 22:9), the text never says that Avraham offered sacrifices at any of his altars. They may, therefore, have had other purposes. The altar he built between Beit El and Ai was where he "called on the name of the Lord" (Gen. 12:8, 13:3–4), a phrase indicating worship and invoking of God's presence.

Pagan altars found in Bronze Age Canaan, like other altars in the ancient Near East, were built in proximity to a temple. It was understood that sacrifices were only meaningful if offered in the presence of a deity, who was assumed to reside in his or her temple. Hence, Avram's altars can be seen as the opposite of contemporary pagan practices: whereas Avram used the altar to establish God's presence in a particular location, the pagan altars were built specifically where the deity was believed to reside. ▪ ZR

Canaanite altar, Tel Megiddo, ca. 3000 BCE

Tablet of Zimri-lim, Mari, 18th century BCE

ח לַיהוָה הַנִּרְאֶה אֵלָיו׃ וַיַּעְתֵּק מִשָּׁם הָהָרָה מִקֶּדֶם לְבֵית־אֵל וַיֵּט
אָהֳלֹה בֵּית־אֵל מִיָּם וְהָעַי מִקֶּדֶם וַיִּבֶן־שָׁם מִזְבֵּחַ לַיהוָה וַיִּקְרָא
ט בְּשֵׁם יְהוָה׃ וַיִּסַּע אַבְרָם הָלוֹךְ וְנָסוֹעַ הַנֶּגְבָּה׃
י וַיְהִי רָעָב בָּאָרֶץ וַיֵּרֶד אַבְרָם מִצְרַיְמָה לָגוּר שָׁם כִּי־כָבֵד הָרָעָב

8 And from there he moved on to the hills east of Beit El, and
pitched his tent with Beit El to the west and Ai to the east.
There he built an altar to the Lord and called on the name
9 of the Lord. Then Avram journeyed on, traveling toward
the Negev.
10 There was a famine in the land. Avram went down to Egypt

Decorative lintel from Burj Beitin, probably from the Byzantine church, 4th century CE

GEOGRAPHY

12:8 Beit El and Ai

The biblical site of Beit El (Hebrew, "the house of God"), is situated within the Arab village Beitin, in the southern part of Shomron, 16 kilometers (10 miles) north of Jerusalem. The site is located at an altitude of 880 meters (a little more than half a mile elevation), next to the main highland road from Shekhem to Jerusalem.

Besides Jerusalem, Beit El is the site most frequently mentioned in the Tanakh, attesting to its great importance as a religious center. In Beit El, Yaakov dreamed of a ladder reaching the sky and angels of God climbing up and coming down (Gen. 28). When the Israelites entered Canaan, Beit El was captured by the tribes of Yosef (Judges 1:22–26), but it was eventually included in the territory of the tribe of Binyamin (Josh. 18:22). The city served as a religious center during the days of the judges (I Sam. 7:15–16), after the kingdom was divided (I Kings 12:32–33), and, after the destruction of the Kingdom of Israel, as part of a Neo-Assyrian province (II Kings 17:28–41).

Beit El is not mentioned in any Middle or Late Bronze Age Egyptian written sources. Thus, unlike Shekhem and Jerusalem, which are mentioned in several of the *Amarna letters*, the city of Beit El apparently did not serve as a regional center. Archaeological excavations conducted at the site exposed a Middle Bronze II fortified city, as well as more limited remains from several historical periods including the Late Bronze Age, Iron Age I, and Iron Age II.

In contrast to Beit El, the location of the site named Ai is disputed among scholars. Several suggestions have been made, but scholarly consensus identifies it with Khirbet et-Tell, 2 kilometers (1.2 miles) southeast of Beit El, based on its location and finds. Although the site is mentioned here in the first journey of Avram to Canaan, it is mostly known from the description of the conquest of Canaan by Yehoshua. According to Tanakh, Yehoshua destroyed the city and left it abandoned for good (Josh. 8:28). In the excavations at Khirbet et-Tell, large-scale, impressive remains of an Early Bronze Age city were found, but it was abandoned afterward for more than a thousand years and was not settled in the Late Bronze Age. During the Iron Age I, only a rural village was established there, and it was abandoned again by the end of the 11th century BCE. Therefore, the suggestion that this is the site of Ai runs counter to Joshua 8, which depicts a major battle during which Yehoshua conquered and set fire to the city. Other scholars suggest that Deir Dibwan was the biblical Ai. According to archaeological surveys, it has Middle Bronze Age remains.

According to Byzantine tradition, the cultic site that Avram built, situated between Beit El and Ai, is identified with Burj Beitin, 500 meters (0.3 miles) southeast of Beit El. The Byzantines built a church there commemorating the place of Yaakov's dream. A second possibility identifies the cultic site with the mount of Baal Ḥatzor, located 7 kilometers (4.4 miles) northeast of Beit El, as high mountains were often worshipped in ancient times and this is the highest point in the hills of Shomron. A third, recent, suggestion, based also on archaeological surveys, locates the cultic site about 1 kilometer (0.62 miles) east of Beit El. Additional archaeological data is needed to identify the site's location more definitively. ▪ GI

NEAR EAST

12:9 Negev

The name Negev, from the Hebrew root meaning "dry," refers in the Tanakh to the rocky desert area in the southern part of Yehuda to the Wilderness of Tzin (Num. 13:17, 21–22; Josh. 15:21–32). It is located just below the hill country of Yehuda and northeast of the Sinai Peninsula, with Be'er Sheva and Arad its principal cities. It is west of the long and narrow Arava Valley along the border with modern Jordan. Its northwestern border is the Mediterranean coast (Num. 34:3; Josh. 15:2). It roughly correlates with the northern Negev today which receives about 200 millimeters (approximately 8 inches) of rainfall annually and has some fertile soil.

The first urban settlements in this area were established in the Bronze Age by Canaanite, Amorite, and nomadic groups (copper mining was carried out south and east of the biblical Negev). Among the tribes who lived there were the Amalekites (Num. 13:29), the Jerahmeelites, the Kenites (I Sam. 27:10), the Keretites and the Kalev clan (I Sam. 30:14). Settlement in the Negev during the early biblical period was unstable due to the difficult desert conditions, changes in climate, and shifts in Egyptian control.

Due to the Negev as the name of the southern part of the Promised Land, *negev* became a general synonym for "the South" or "south of" (Gen. 13:14, 28:14; Josh. 17:9, 10, etc.). ▪ ZR, JU

View over the Ramon Crater at sunset, Negev desert

GEOGRAPHY

12:10 Famine in the land

The famine described here impacted the entire land of Canaan; Avram could not simply relocate to another nearby area – he had to journey all the way to Egypt. The Negev area is known to have a very small amount of rainfall, making the availability of vegetation for grazing and agriculture precarious even under normal circumstances. The widespread famine in the entire land of Canaan would result from a drought, a failure of seasonal rains over a prolonged period of time.

Archaeologists have found evidence of a three hundred-year drought in the ancient Near East lasting from about 2200–1900 BCE, a widespread environmental crisis which resulted in abandoned towns and mass migrations. This drought led to the downfall of the Akkadian empire in Mesopotamia and disrupted societies in the Middle East during this time, including in Canaan. ▪ ZR

Famine stele, inscription describing a seven-year drought and famine during the reign of Pharaoh Djoser (27th century BCE), Sehel Island (near Aswan), inscribed 4th to 1st century BCE

NEAR EAST

12:10 Egypt

This is the first mention of Egypt in relation to Israelite history, foreshadowing the complex relationship of Israelites with this land – a place fraught with danger that also functioned as a shelter in times of famine.

Since Egyptian agriculture depended on the annual flooding of the Nile, not rain, for its agriculture, it was reasonable to turn to Egypt in times of famine. A report by an Egyptian frontier official from the late 13th century BCE relates that they "have finished letting the Shasu (Egyptian for Semitic nomads or semi-nomads) tribes of Edom pass the fortress...to keep them alive and to keep their cattle alive." ▪ ZR

בָּאָרֶץ׃ וַיְהִי כַּאֲשֶׁר הִקְרִיב לָבוֹא מִצְרָיְמָה וַיֹּאמֶר אֶל־שָׂרַי יא
אִשְׁתּוֹ הִנֵּה־נָא יָדַעְתִּי כִּי אִשָּׁה יְפַת־מַרְאֶה אָתְּ׃ וְהָיָה כִּי־יִרְאוּ יב
אֹתָךְ הַמִּצְרִים וְאָמְרוּ אִשְׁתּוֹ זֹאת וְהָרְגוּ אֹתִי וְאֹתָךְ יְחַיּוּ׃ אִמְרִי־ יג
נָא אֲחֹתִי אָתְּ לְמַעַן יִיטַב־לִי בַעֲבוּרֵךְ וְחָיְתָה נַפְשִׁי בִּגְלָלֵךְ׃
שני וַיְהִי כְּבוֹא אַבְרָם מִצְרָיְמָה וַיִּרְאוּ הַמִּצְרִים אֶת־הָאִשָּׁה כִּי־יָפָה יד
הִוא מְאֹד׃ וַיִּרְאוּ אֹתָהּ שָׂרֵי פַרְעֹה וַיְהַלְלוּ אֹתָהּ אֶל־פַּרְעֹה טו
וַתֻּקַּח הָאִשָּׁה בֵּית פַּרְעֹה׃ וּלְאַבְרָם הֵיטִיב בַּעֲבוּרָהּ וַיְהִי־לוֹ טז
צֹאן־וּבָקָר וַחֲמֹרִים וַעֲבָדִים וּשְׁפָחֹת וַאֲתֹנֹת וּגְמַלִּים׃ וַיְנַגַּע יז

to stay there for a while because the famine in the land was
11 severe. And as his arrival in Egypt drew close, he said to Sarai
12 his wife, "I know what a beautiful woman you are. When the
Egyptians see you, they will say, 'She is his wife'; they will kill
13 me and keep you alive. Please, say you are my sister. Then I
will be treated well for your sake, and because of you my life
14 will be spared." When Avram came to Egypt, the Egyptians
15 saw the woman, saw that she was very beautiful indeed. And
when Pharaoh's officials saw her, they praised her to Pharaoh,
16 and the woman was taken into Pharaoh's palace. He treated
Avram well for her sake: he acquired flocks, herds, donkeys,
17 male and female servants, she-donkeys, and camels. But

NEAR EAST

12:13 The sister-wives

This episode is one of three stories in Genesis where one of the patriarchs entered a foreign land and, fearing for his life, described his wife as his sister. Avram did so with his wife Sarai upon entering Egypt (Gen. 12) and Gerar (Gen. 20), and Yitzḥak also used this stratagem at Gerar with Rivka (Gen. 26).

In Hebrew, the word *aḥoti*, ("my sister,") can refer not only to a female born to the same mother, but to any female relative, and even to one's beloved: the male lover in the Song of Songs 4:9–10 uses the phrase *aḥoti kalla* ("my sister bride"). Similarly, in ancient Egyptian, the word meaning "sister" was another way, alongside the word for "wife," to refer to one's female spouse. In all three of the biblical narratives, however, the ambiguity is strategic; explicitly calling her his "wife" would leave the patriarch vulnerable in a way that calling her his "sister" would not.

Biblical and extra-biblical ancient sources show that the patriarchs' decision reflects a special conception of the brother-sister relationship. Dina's maternal brothers, Shimon and Levi, were the ones who fought against Shekhem (Gen. 34). Also, after Tamar was raped by Amnon, she turned to her brother, Avshalom, to act on her behalf (II Sam. 13).

Cuneiform records demonstrate that, in the absence of a father, responsibility for an unmarried woman could devolve upon her brother. In one record from Nuzi, a woman states that her adoptive brother "will ward off her attackers…, treat her as a sister, and come to her aid." By calling their wives "sisters", the patriarchs invoke a version of this special relationship and the protections it is meant to afford. The brother's legal position may also explain Pharaoh's gifts to Avram, who, in the absence of a father, would have been empowered to contract Sarai's marriage and receive her bride-price.

↗ Cuneiform tablets, Nuzi (modern Yorghan Tepe, Iraq), 2nd millennium BCE

Pharaoh's actions constitute attempted adultery, a punishable offense. However, a *Middle Assyrian Law* provides exceptions for the unwitting adulterer: "If an unrelated man…should arrange to have a man's wife travel with him, then he shall swear an oath to the effect that he did not know that she is the wife of a man and he shall pay 7,200 shekels of lead to the woman's husband. If [he knows that she is the wife of a man], he shall pay damages and he shall swear, saying 'I did not fornicate with her'" (MAL A §22). There are no such oaths in these stories, but Avimelekh's protestation of innocence and God's acknowledgment (Gen 20:5–6) serve a similar purpose. ▪ SH

יהוה ׀ אֶת־פַּרְעֹה נְגָעִים גְּדֹלִים וְאֶת־בֵּיתוֹ עַל־דְּבַר שָׂרַי אֵשֶׁת
יח אַבְרָם׃ וַיִּקְרָא פַרְעֹה לְאַבְרָם וַיֹּאמֶר מַה־זֹּאת עָשִׂיתָ לִּי לָמָּה
יט לֹא־הִגַּדְתָּ לִּי כִּי אִשְׁתְּךָ הִוא׃ לָמָה אָמַרְתָּ אֲחֹתִי הִוא וָאֶקַּח
כ אֹתָהּ לִי לְאִשָּׁה וְעַתָּה הִנֵּה אִשְׁתְּךָ קַח וָלֵךְ׃ וַיְצַו עָלָיו פַּרְעֹה

the Lord struck Pharaoh and his household with terrible
afflictions because of Avram's wife Sarai. Pharaoh summoned 18
Avram and said, "What have you done to me? Why did you
not tell me she was your wife? Why did you say 'She is my 19
sister,' so that I took her as a wife? Now – here is your wife.
Take her. Go." Pharaoh gave orders to his men about him, and 20
they sent him on his way, together with his wife and all that

NEAR EAST

12:16 Domestication of camels

Camels are mentioned in the list of livestock in this verse, and also play a prominent role in several other stories in Genesis. Camels were domesticated for a variety of resources, including their meat and milk, but above all, their ability to carry goods and people long distances across arid landscapes.

The appearance of camels in Genesis is dismissed by some as anachronistic, because of the claim that the widespread use of camels did not begin until the end of the 2nd millennium BCE, and that they came into general use as domestic beasts of burden only in the 1st millennium BCE.

It is important to realize that the camel's natural habitat lies outside of the normal range of archaeologists, who concentrate on more densely populated areas. The one-humped dromedary, as opposed to the two-hump Bactrian camel, is the type most likely found in the Genesis narratives, although the Hebrew *gamal* (like the Akkadian *gammalu*) is ambiguous.

Several kinds of evidence suggest that the mention of camels in the Genesis narrative does, in fact, accurately reflect the reality during Avraham's lifetime (ca. early 2nd millennium BCE):

- References to the one-humped dromedary appear in lexical texts from Emar and Ugarit (both in Syria) dating from the Middle Babylonian period (1500–1000 BCE), but some scholars assume that these lists reflect a tradition that goes back to the early 2nd millennium BCE. The Akkadian term for dromedary, *ibilu*, is found in texts dating to the Old Babylonian period (1894–1595 BCE).
- Examples of dromedaries are found in Mesopotamian art from the 3rd millennium or even earlier, with definite signs of domestication, such as a rider, harness, and saddle, depicted.
- On the island of Umm an-Nar near Abu Dhabi, two hundred camel bone fragments were found, belonging to the first half of the 3rd millennium BCE, as were depictions of dromedaries at the site. Scholars assume this reflects the first steps toward domestication.
- The importation of Arabian spices, such as myrrh and frankincense, to Egypt in the 3rd millennium BCE suggests that camels were already in use, because donkey caravans (the primary means of transport in the Levant), could not have handled such long-distance trips through the desert.
- Artistic representations of camels date from the First Dynasty in Egypt and are interspersed throughout the 2nd millennium. These include clay figurines of camels, an ointment vessel in the form of a recumbent dromedary, and a rock carving showing a man leading a dromedary by a rope.
- Further evidence of early domestication is provided by a camel-hair rope almost a meter (approximately 39 inces) in length, dated to the Third or Fourth Egyptian Dynasty (2650–2494 BCE).

Therefore, multiple lines of textual and artistic evidence testify to the exploitation of the domesticated camel as far back as the 3rd millennium BCE. Furthermore, the Genesis narratives do not necessarily portray the camel in common use. It informs us that Avraham's great wealth included camels and that he later sent his servant with camels to obtain a bride for his son, perhaps in order to convey an impression of great prosperity.

Avraham and Yaakov were both wealthy semi-nomadic pastoralists who traveled to and from Upper Mesopotamia, thus their use of camels was exceptional rather than usual. Ephraim Speiser observes that "the camel may have come into limited use at an earlier time, but required centuries before it ceased to be a luxury." Thus, the Genesis account accords with the available evidence; there is no legitimate reason for some academics to reject them as inauthentic or anachronistic. ▪ EG

↗ Dromedary camel, Sahara desert, Morocco

אֲנָשִׁים וַיְשַׁלְּחוּ אֹתוֹ וְאֶת־אִשְׁתּוֹ וְאֶת־כָּל־אֲשֶׁר־לוֹ׃ וַיַּעַל אַבְרָם א יג
מִמִּצְרַיִם הוּא וְאִשְׁתּוֹ וְכָל־אֲשֶׁר־לוֹ וְלוֹט עִמּוֹ הַנֶּגְבָּה׃ וְאַבְרָם ב
כָּבֵד מְאֹד בַּמִּקְנֶה בַּכֶּסֶף וּבַזָּהָב׃ וַיֵּלֶךְ לְמַסָּעָיו מִנֶּגֶב וְעַד־בֵּית־ ג
אֵל עַד־הַמָּקוֹם אֲשֶׁר־הָיָה שָׁם אָהֳלֹה בַּתְּחִלָּה בֵּין בֵּית־אֵל וּבֵין
הָעָי׃ אֶל־מְקוֹם הַמִּזְבֵּחַ אֲשֶׁר־עָשָׂה שָׁם בָּרִאשֹׁנָה וַיִּקְרָא שָׁם ד
שלישי אַבְרָם בְּשֵׁם יְהוָה׃ וְגַם־לְלוֹט הַהֹלֵךְ אֶת־אַבְרָם הָיָה צֹאן־וּבָקָר ה
וְאֹהָלִים׃ וְלֹא־נָשָׂא אֹתָם הָאָרֶץ לָשֶׁבֶת יַחְדָּו כִּי־הָיָה רְכוּשָׁם ו •
רָב וְלֹא יָכְלוּ לָשֶׁבֶת יַחְדָּו׃ וַיְהִי־רִיב בֵּין רֹעֵי מִקְנֵה־אַבְרָם וּבֵין ז
רֹעֵי מִקְנֵה־לוֹט וְהַכְּנַעֲנִי וְהַפְּרִזִּי אָז יֹשֵׁב בָּאָרֶץ׃ וַיֹּאמֶר אַבְרָם ח
אֶל־לוֹט אַל־נָא תְהִי מְרִיבָה בֵּינִי וּבֵינֶךָ וּבֵין רֹעַי וּבֵין רֹעֶיךָ כִּי־
אֲנָשִׁים אַחִים אֲנָחְנוּ׃ הֲלֹא כָל־הָאָרֶץ לְפָנֶיךָ הִפָּרֶד נָא מֵעָלָי ט

13 1 he had. Then Avram went up from Egypt to the Negev with
2 his wife and all he had, and with him went Lot. And Avram
3 had become very wealthy in cattle, silver, and gold. From
the Negev he continued on his journey to Beit El, to the site
between Beit El and Ai where his tent had previously been,
4 and where he had first made an altar. There Avram called on
5 the name of the Lord. Lot, who went with Avram, had flocks,
• 6 herds, and tents as well, and the land could not support them
living together; so many were their possessions that they
7 were unable to live side by side. A dispute broke out between
Avram's herdsmen and those of Lot; and the Canaanites and
8 the Perizzites were then too living in the land. Avram said to
Lot, "Please, let there be no friction between me and you,
and between my herdsmen and yours, for we are brothers.
9 The whole land lies before you; please separate yourself from
me. If you go to the left, I will go to the right; if you go to the

NEAR EAST

13:6–7 Dispute between shepherds

The text blames the dispute between Avram's and Lot's shepherds on the great size of their flocks (v. 6). Sheep and goats require grazing land with sufficient vegetation. The semi-arid nature of the land in the area, in addition to the scarcity of rain, which in any case only falls during part of the year, means that a large quantity of land is needed per animal. The additional comment, "the Canaanites and the Perizzites were then too living in the land" (v.7) indicates that the availability of resources for these pastoral nomads was further limited – the people already settled in the area also had animals that needed grazing land. This situation is the reason that both Avram and Lot had to leave the area – staying there was not an option even for one of the groups of herdsmen (v.9). ▪ ZR

↗ Sheep grazing, Tel Yodfat, Israel

י אִם־הַשְּׂמֹאל וְאֵימִנָה וְאִם־הַיָּמִין וְאַשְׂמְאִילָה: וַיִּשָּׂא־לוֹט
אֶת־עֵינָיו וַיַּרְא אֶת־כָּל־כִּכַּר הַיַּרְדֵּן כִּי כֻלָּהּ מַשְׁקֶה לִפְנֵי ׀ שַׁחֵת
יהוה אֶת־סְדֹם וְאֶת־עֲמֹרָה כְּגַן־יהוה כְּאֶרֶץ מִצְרַיִם בֹּאֲכָה צֹעַר:
יא וַיִּבְחַר־לוֹ לוֹט אֵת כָּל־כִּכַּר הַיַּרְדֵּן וַיִּסַּע לוֹט מִקֶּדֶם וַיִּפָּרְדוּ אִישׁ
יב מֵעַל אָחִיו: אַבְרָם יָשַׁב בְּאֶרֶץ־כְּנָעַן וְלוֹט יָשַׁב בְּעָרֵי הַכִּכָּר
יג וַיֶּאֱהַל עַד־סְדֹם: וְאַנְשֵׁי סְדֹם רָעִים וְחַטָּאִים לַיהוה מְאֹד:

right, I will go to the left." Lot raised his eyes and saw that the 10
whole plain of the Jordan up to Tzoar was well watered. It
was like the garden of the LORD, like the land of Egypt; this
was before the LORD destroyed Sedom and Amora.[23] So Lot 11
chose for himself the entire plain of the Jordan. He traveled
eastward, and the two men separated. Avram settled in the 12
land of Canaan while Lot settled in the cities of the plain,
pitching his tent near Sedom. But the people of Sedom were 13

23 | See chapter 19.

GEOGRAPHY

13:10 Sedom, Tzoar, and the "Five Cities"

The location of Sedom and the other four cities of the plain is unclear. The question has preoccupied scholars of the Tanakh, most of whom have placed it in the general area of the southern part of the Dead Sea. However, we lack clear evidence of a cataclysmic destruction in that area during the relevant period.

Recently, Tell el-Hammam, located about 10 kilometers (6.2 miles) northeast of the Dead Sea, has been proposed as the site of Sedom, due to evidence of extensive destruction of the site in the Middle Bronze Age. While it may be interesting to find out how and why Tell el-Hammam was destroyed, its identification with ancient Sedom is improbable, because Tell el-Hammam is too far away from the only one of the five cities whose location is known with relative certainty: Tzoar.

Throughout the narratives in Genesis, five towns are mentioned together: Sedom, Amora, Adma, Tzevoyim, and Tzoar. Of these, only the last, Tzoar, is said to have been saved. A site called Tzoar was known in the classical and medieval periods, which has since been conclusively identified. Located directly south of the Dead Sea near the modern Bedouin town of As-Safi, Tzoar was inhabited by orchard-owning Jews and gentiles from the Roman period into the period of Byzantine rule, and was known as Tzoar throughout this period and even in the earlier Hellenistic period. It is likely that this town is in the same location as the town of the same name on the shore of the Dead Sea in biblical times.

Assuming that Tzoar is in fact near As-Safi, Sedom must be located nearby, as stated clearly in Genesis 19:20. About 25 kilometers (15 miles) northeast of Tzoar is the site of Bab edh-Dhra, and nearby is an additional ancient site known as Numeira. Both were settled and then destroyed somewhere between 2400 BCE and 2000 BCE, and their destruction has led many to identify them as two of the four cities of Sedom, Amora, Adma, and Tzevoyim. But the dating of their destruction does not fit well with the rest of the Avraham narratives, which are much better suited to the period between 2000 and 1550 BCE. Therefore, according to current research, the story of Sedom does not match the current theories of its location.

It is possible that the story of Sedom's destruction and Lot's salvation occurred at a smaller and unknown site, somewhere on the southeastern shore of the Dead Sea. The bitumen soil in the region fits with what we are told in Genesis 14:10, and there are well-known caves which accord with the story of Lot and his daughters in Genesis 19:30.

While we cannot identify Sedom with certainty, we can identify the general region in which the narrative is placed. ▪ SZA

↗ Cave near the Dead Sea

יד וַיהוָה אָמַר אֶל־אַבְרָם אַחֲרֵי הִפָּרֶד־לוֹט מֵעִמּוֹ שָׂא־נָא עֵינֶיךָ
וּרְאֵה מִן־הַמָּקוֹם אֲשֶׁר־אַתָּה שָׁם צָפֹנָה וָנֶגְבָּה וָקֵדְמָה וָיָמָּה׃

14 evil, great sinners against the LORD. After Lot had separated from him, the LORD said to Avram, "Raise your eyes and look around from where you are to the north, south, east, and west.

NEAR EAST

13:14–17 Gift of land to Avram

As Moshe Weinfeld pointed out, the promise of land to Avram is reflective of the themes and formulae found in royal land grants throughout the ancient Near East. These grants were bestowed by rulers upon faithful vassals and included curses directed to anyone who would violate the right of the vassal to the land. Just as in our verses, these land grants did not include any obligation of the vassal to the king; the grant represents a reward for past acts of loyalty. Thus, the Torah views God's relationship with Avram as that of a king to his loyal vassal, not only as that of a god to his devoted worshipper.

Tablet with a list of diplomatic gifts, Hittite, Ras Shamra (Ugarit), 13th century BCE

For example, the language in Genesis 26:3–5, "Bide in this land and I will be with you and bless you, for I am going to give all these lands to you and your descendants, fulfilling the oath I swore to Avraham your father…because Avraham listened to My voice and kept My charge…," recalls the land grant of the Neo-Assyrian king Ashurbanipal (ruled 669–631 BCE) to his servant Baltya, "Baltya…served me with truthfulness, acted perfectly in my palace…and kept the charge of my kingship" (*Neo-Assyrian Royal Grants and Decrees*, text no. 32).

The phrase "All the land you see I will give to you and your descendants forever" (v. 15) is analogous to the idea that the royal land grant is an unconditional gift that passes on through generations. A grant bestowed by the Hittite king Hattushili III (ruled ca. 1275–1245 BCE) states, "After you, your son and grandson will possess it, nobody will take it away from them. If one of your descendants sins, the king will prosecute him at his court. Then when he is found guilty…if he deserves death he will die. But nobody will take away from the descendant of Ulmi-Tesup either his house or his land in order to give it to a descendant of somebody else" (KBo IV. 10).

The practice of walking around the land to demonstrate ownership is found in various forms throughout the ancient Near East. In both ancient Egyptian and Hittite societies, the king would demonstrate his sovereignty by touring his realm or taking a ceremonial walk around a field. In this context, it may be understood that God instructs Avraham to already now act as the "king" of the land, on behalf of his "subjects" – i.e., his future descendants. ▪ ZR

Tel Rumeida excavations, Ḥevron

ARCHAEOLOGY

13:18 Ḥevron

Ḥevron, identified with Tel Rumeida in the modern-day city of the same name, is in the southern part of the hill country of Yehuda, about halfway between Jerusalem and Be'er Sheva, at the junction of a north/south route connecting these two cities and an east/west road from the coastal plain. Due to its high elevation (930 meters/about 3000 feet), it receives more rainfall than the surrounding areas and is surrounded by fertile land. The tel also has a spring on its eastern side. Thus, the city is significant both strategically and economically.

The name Ḥevron may be connected to the Hebrew root *ḥ b r*, indicating "joining" or "unity," perhaps a reference to a confederacy of four settlements, as implied by its other name, Kiryat Arba ("city of four"; Gen. 23:2), although Kiryat Arba may have been named after a giant who might have been a previous resident (Josh. 14:15, 15:13, 21:11). Archaeological remains there date back to the Early Bronze Age when it was a Canaanite royal center fortified by a wall made of large uncut stones and high towers. ▪ ZR

טו כִּי אֶת־כׇּל־הָאָרֶץ אֲשֶׁר־אַתָּה רֹאֶה לְךָ אֶתְּנֶנָּה וּלְזַרְעֲךָ עַד־
טז עוֹלָם: וְשַׂמְתִּי אֶת־זַרְעֲךָ כַּעֲפַר הָאָרֶץ אֲשֶׁר ׀ אִם־יוּכַל אִישׁ
יז לִמְנוֹת אֶת־עֲפַר הָאָרֶץ גַּם־זַרְעֲךָ יִמָּנֶה: קוּם הִתְהַלֵּךְ בָּאָרֶץ
• יח לְאׇרְכָּהּ וּלְרׇחְבָּהּ כִּי לְךָ אֶתְּנֶנָּה: וַיֶּאֱהַל אַבְרָם וַיָּבֹא וַיֵּשֶׁב בְּאֵלֹנֵי
מַמְרֵא אֲשֶׁר בְּחֶבְרוֹן וַיִּבֶן־שָׁם מִזְבֵּחַ לַיהוָה:
יד • א וַיְהִי בִּימֵי אַמְרָפֶל מֶלֶךְ־שִׁנְעָר אַרְיוֹךְ מֶלֶךְ אֶלָּסָר כְּדׇרְלָעֹמֶר רביעי
ב מֶלֶךְ עֵילָם וְתִדְעָל מֶלֶךְ גּוֹיִם: עָשׂוּ מִלְחָמָה אֶת־בֶּרַע מֶלֶךְ סְדֹם

All the land you see I will give to you and your descendants 15
forever. I will make your descendants like the dust of the 16
earth: if anyone could count the dust of the earth, then could
your descendants be counted. Get up and walk through the 17
length and breadth of the land, for to you shall I give it." So 18 •
Avram took his tent and came to settle by the Oaks of Mamre,
in Ḥevron. There he built an altar to the Lord.
In the days of Amrafel, king of Shinar, Aryokh, king of Elasar, 1 • 14
Kedorlaomer, king of Eilam, and Tidal, king of Goyim, they 2

likely period for the ancestors of Israel, the Middle Bronze Age.

As for the cities of the five rebellious local monarchs, the first four are associated with the southern border of Canaan in Genesis 10:19. The fifth, Bela, is used elsewhere in Tanakh as a personal name, not a geographic term (a Moabite in Gen. 36:32, a Benjaminite in Gen. 46:21). The city identified with Bela, Tzoar, is linked with Sedom and Amora in Genesis 19, and with southern Canaan in Genesis 13:10 and Deuteronomy 34:3. None of these cities are mentioned in texts outside of Tanakh. As for the four named rulers, the first two, Bera and Birsha, are clearly symbolic as they allude to the Hebrew terms for evil (*ra*) and wicked (*rasha*). The following two, Shinav and Shemever, are otherwise unknown.

Like the patriarchal narratives as a whole, the story fits into the Middle Bronze period in a very general way but cannot be pinned down to a specific century. ▪ EG

NEAR EAST

14:1 War of the four and five kings

Genesis 14 provides a unique portrayal of Avram as a pivotal figure on the international scene, as he successfully led a small battalion to intervene when a coalition of four kings from as far as modern-day Iran attempted to suppress a rebellion by five local rulers. The chapter is especially intriguing because of the wealth of names included: ten individuals, nine ethnicities, and twenty-two place names, many of which are doubled.

Verse 1 introduces four kings who cannot be identified with certainty as specific monarchs known from the ancient Near East. Nevertheless, their names are similar to others known from 2nd millennium BCE inscriptions. The first, Amrafel, while without a close parallel, contains two elements, Amar and Apil, both of which are known from Akkadian names. Apil could be derived from *apilu*, a kind of cultic functionary at Mari or *aplu*, Akkadian for "son." The royal names Amar-Sin and Apil-Sin are found in the same early 2nd millennium BCE Babylonian inscription called *The Weidner Chronicle*. The geographic name Shinar is synonymous with Babylonia in Genesis 10:10 and 11:2. While the place name Elasar is not found elsewhere, it could refer to the city of Ashur (*al assur* in Akkadian). Another possibility is mentioned in the texts from Mari (mid-2nd millennium BCE Syria), the geographic name *Ilanzura*. The king's name, Aryokh, is identified with the Hurrian name *Arriwuk* or *Ariukki*, also known from the Mari texts. The third king, Kedorlaomer of Eilam, has a "good Elamite name": the term *kudur* could mean "servant," while *Lakamar* is a divine name. Eilam refers to the ancient civilization of Elam, located east of Babylonia, corresponding to western Iran; the term is used for the region as far back as the 3rd millennium BCE. Tidal, king of Goyim, corresponds to Tudhalias, the name of several kings from mid-2nd millennium BCE Hittite inscriptions. The term *goyim* is Hebrew for "peoples" and perhaps serves here as an honorific title for a ruler for many nations. In sum, the names offered in verse 1 align well with known ancient Near Eastern appellatives from the most

↗ Foundation nail figurine of king Amar-Sin carrying a builder's wicker tray-basket, and a cuneiform dedication tablet, Mesopotamia, 21st century BCE

וְאֶת־בִּרְשַׁע מֶלֶךְ עֲמֹרָה שִׁנְאָב ׀ מֶלֶךְ אַדְמָה וְשֶׁמְאֵבֶר מֶלֶךְ
צְבוֹיִם צביים וּמֶלֶךְ בֶּלַע הִיא־צֹעַר׃ כָּל־אֵלֶּה חָבְרוּ אֶל־עֵמֶק הַשִּׂדִּים ג
הוּא יָם הַמֶּלַח׃ שְׁתֵּים עֶשְׂרֵה שָׁנָה עָבְדוּ אֶת־כְּדָרְלָעֹמֶר ד
וּשְׁלֹשׁ־עֶשְׂרֵה שָׁנָה מָרָדוּ׃ וּבְאַרְבַּע עֶשְׂרֵה שָׁנָה בָּא כְדָרְלָעֹמֶר ה
וְהַמְּלָכִים אֲשֶׁר אִתּוֹ וַיַּכּוּ אֶת־רְפָאִים בְּעַשְׁתְּרֹת קַרְנַיִם וְאֶת־
הַזּוּזִים בְּהָם וְאֵת הָאֵימִים בְּשָׁוֵה קִרְיָתָיִם׃ וְאֶת־הַחֹרִי בְּהַרְרָם ו
שֵׂעִיר עַד אֵיל פָּארָן אֲשֶׁר עַל־הַמִּדְבָּר׃ וַיָּשֻׁבוּ וַיָּבֹאוּ אֶל־עֵין ז
מִשְׁפָּט הִוא קָדֵשׁ וַיַּכּוּ אֶת־כָּל־שְׂדֵה הָעֲמָלֵקִי וְגַם אֶת־הָאֱמֹרִי

all waged war against Bera, king of Sedom, Birsha, king of
Amora, Shinav, king of Adma, and Shemever, king of
3 Tzevoyim, and the king of Bela – that is, Tzoar. These had all
4 come together in Siddim Valley – now the Dead Sea; for
twelve years they had served Kedorlaomer, but in the
5 thirteenth year they had rebelled. In the fourteenth year
Kedorlaomer and his allied kings came and defeated the
Refaim in Ashterot Karnayim, the Zuzim in Ham, the Eimim
6 in Shaveh Kiryatayim,[24] and the Horites in the hill country
7 of Se'ir as far as Eil Paran by the wilderness. Then they swung
back and came to Ein Mishpat – that is, Kadesh – conquering

24 | Concerning these peoples, see Deuteronomy 2:10–11, 20.

NEAR EAST

14:13 Avram the Hebrew

The term "Hebrew" (*ivri*) is generally understood as either a geographic or ethnic term. Geographically, it would indicate someone from beyond (from the other side of) a river (see Gen. 50:10 and Num. 21:13). As an ethnic term, it would be used here in contrast to "Mamre the Amorite." Similarly, the term *ivri* is usually found in Tanakh as identifying Israelites as an ethnic group distinct from the Egyptians (for example, Gen. 39:14; Ex. 1:19, 2:11), Philistines (for example, I Sam. 4:9, 13:19), or non-Israelites in general (Jonah 1:9).

Some scholars identify the term *ivri* with the designation *hapiru* (*b* and *p* sounds are often interchangeable in regional languages) and its variants, known from Sumer, Babylon, Anatolia, and Egypt, which refer to various groups throughout the 2nd millennium BCE (see "Are Israelites *hapiru*?" in the Exodus volume of this series on page 114). Throughout the region, the term always carried a derogatory meaning; the Akkadian form means a violent person, and the West Semitic root means someone restless. The term refers to a lower-class group made of migrants who disrupt the social order. In this understanding, the term *ivri* is not a geographical or ethnic designation, but rather a social one, which natives use to refer to a bothersome underclass of outsiders. This identification has been disputed on the grounds that the words *ivri* and *hapiru* are not very similar, and that extra-biblical references to Israelites do not identify them as *hapiru*.

If indeed *ivri* here simply identifies Avram as a foreign migrant, it might explain the more international orientation of this chapter, presented as a documentary account of a war involving foreign marauders and the hero, Avram – a resident alien with positive relationships in his adopted milieu. ▪ ZR

↗ Letter from Abdi-Hepa of Jerusalem to the Egyptian pharaoh Amenhotep III, Tell el-Amarna, 14th century BCE

ח הַיֹּשֵׁב בְּחַצְצֹן תָּמָר: וַיֵּצֵא מֶלֶךְ־סְדֹם וּמֶלֶךְ עֲמֹרָה וּמֶלֶךְ אַדְמָה
וּמֶלֶךְ צביים וּמֶלֶךְ בֶּלַע הִוא־צֹעַר וַיַּעַרְכוּ אִתָּם מִלְחָמָה בְּעֵמֶק צְבוֹיִם
ט הַשִּׂדִּים: אֵת כְּדָרְלָעֹמֶר מֶלֶךְ עֵילָם וְתִדְעָל מֶלֶךְ גּוֹיִם וְאַמְרָפֶל
מֶלֶךְ שִׁנְעָר וְאַרְיוֹךְ מֶלֶךְ אֶלָּסָר אַרְבָּעָה מְלָכִים אֶת־הַחֲמִשָּׁה:
י וְעֵמֶק הַשִּׂדִּים בֶּאֱרֹת בֶּאֱרֹת חֵמָר וַיָּנֻסוּ מֶלֶךְ־סְדֹם וַעֲמֹרָה
יא וַיִּפְּלוּ־שָׁמָּה וְהַנִּשְׁאָרִים הֶרָה נָּסוּ: וַיִּקְחוּ אֶת־כָּל־רְכֻשׁ סְדֹם
יב וַעֲמֹרָה וְאֶת־כָּל־אָכְלָם וַיֵּלֵכוּ: וַיִּקְחוּ אֶת־לוֹט וְאֶת־רְכֻשׁוֹ בֶּן־
יג •• אֲחִי אַבְרָם וַיֵּלֵכוּ וְהוּא יֹשֵׁב בִּסְדֹם: וַיָּבֹא הַפָּלִיט וַיַּגֵּד לְאַבְרָם
הָעִבְרִי וְהוּא שֹׁכֵן בְּאֵלֹנֵי מַמְרֵא הָאֱמֹרִי אֲחִי אֶשְׁכֹּל וַאֲחִי עָנֵר

the whole territory of the Amalekites, as well as the Amorites
8 living in Ḥatzetzon Tamar. Then the kings of Sedom, Amora,
Adma, Tzevoyim, and Bela – that is, Tzoar – marched out and
9 drew up their battle lines in Siddim Valley against
Kedorlaomer, king of Eilam, Tidal, king of Goyim, Amrafel,
king of Shinar, and Aryokh, king of Elasar: four kings battling
10 five. The Siddim Valley was riddled with tar pits, and when
the kings of Sedom and Amora tried to flee, they fell into
11 them. The others fled to the mountains. The victors seized all
the possessions of Sedom and Amora and all the food, and
12 they left, taking with them – since he had been living in
13 •• Sedom – Avram's nephew, Lot, and his possessions. A fugitive
came and reported this to Avram the Hebrew, who was then

Legal text with an impression of the dynastic seal of King Niqmepa describing a gift and counter-gift, Ras Shamra (Ugarit), 13th century BCE

NEAR EAST

14:13 Mamre, Eshkol, Aner

The term for Avram's "allies," *ba'ale brit*, is unique in Tanakh. It indicates participants in some type of treaty, a common feature of interpersonal relationships in the ancient Near East, usually made under oath. For example, the Middle Babylonian (ca. 2nd millennium BCE) treaty between two city-states, "The seal of Ir-Addu king of Tunip: The text of the divine oath of Niqmepa king of Mukis, and of Ir-Adda king of Tunip. In this manner, Niqmepa and Ir-Addu [...] have now made an agreement between them…." In this context, the most probable treaty was a parity treaty (a treaty among equals), which included mutual military obligations.

Mamre, one of Avram's allies, is found as a local place name, "the Oaks of Mamre, in Ḥevron" (Gen. 13:18). Although "the Eshkol Ravine," where the spies "cut down a vine branch and on it one cluster (*eshkol*) of grapes" (Num. 13:23), bears the same name as one of the allies, it is in a different geographical region and, according to the Torah, was named much later (Num. 13:24). ▪ ZR

וְהֵם בַּעֲלֵי בְרִית־אַבְרָם: וַיִּשְׁמַע אַבְרָם כִּי נִשְׁבָּה אָחִיו וַיָּרֶק יד
אֶת־חֲנִיכָיו יְלִידֵי בֵיתוֹ שְׁמֹנָה עָשָׂר וּשְׁלֹשׁ מֵאוֹת וַיִּרְדֹּף עַד־דָּן:
וַיֵּחָלֵק עֲלֵיהֶם ׀ לַיְלָה הוּא וַעֲבָדָיו וַיַּכֵּם וַיִּרְדְּפֵם עַד־חוֹבָה אֲשֶׁר טו
מִשְּׂמֹאל לְדַמָּשֶׂק: וַיָּשֶׁב אֵת כָּל־הָרְכֻשׁ וְגַם אֶת־לוֹט אָחִיו טז

living near the Oaks of Mamre the Amorite, a kinsman of
14 Avram's allies, Eshkol and Aner. When Avram heard that his
own kinsman had been taken captive, he marshaled the three
hundred eighteen trained men born in his household, and
15 went in pursuit as far as Dan. He divided his forces against
the captors at night and defeated them, pursuing them to
16 Ḥova, north of Damascus. He recovered all the plunder, as
well as his kinsman Lot and his possessions, the women, and

HALAKHA

14:14 Redemption of captives

Avram's rescue of Lot is the first example in the Tanakh of the mitzva of *pidyon shvuyim*, the obligation to ransom a Jewish person from captivity, which the Talmud calls "a great mitzva" (Bava Batra 8b), one of the few things for which one may raise funds by selling a Torah scroll (Tosafot, s.v. *pidyon*). Maimonides writes, "The redemption of captives held for ransom takes precedence over sustaining the poor and clothing them. You do not find a mitzva greater than the redemption of captives, for captivity is in the same category as famine, drought, or exposure, and one stands in danger to one's life" (*Mishneh Torah*, *Laws of Gifts to the Poor* 8:10). ▪ ZR

Gravestone of Rabbi Meir of Rothenberg, who was held as a captive but died before his release was negotiated, Germany, 1293

NEAR EAST

14:14 Three hundred eighteen trained men

The term for Avram's trained men, *ḥanikhim*, is unique in Tanakh but there are cognates in extra-biblical sources. An Akkadian letter from the 15th century BCE mentions *ḫanaku* in a garrison; from the context, it refers to military retainers, who would fight when necessary in return for protection and land. It may also be related to the term *ḫnk* used for the armed retainers employed by Canaanite rulers in the Egyptian execration texts (19th to 18th century BCE).

The number of these retainers, 318, is oddly specific and has no known symbolic value or parallel. However, the *Mari letters* indicate that three hundred was a standard number of soldiers for military expeditions. For example, Iddiyatum, a diplomat of Zimri-lim (ruled ca. 1775–1761 BCE) talks about "the three hundred troops that my lord had assigned me" (*Letters to the King of Mari*, letter 26, line 527). A letter to Sumu-dabi, chief of the Yaḫruru who married Atrakatum, sister of Zimri-lim, requesting military assistance states, "Now our lord must not disregard our word. He must speak to his brothers, and they must enlist three hundred good troops..." (*Letters to the King of Mari*, letter 26, line 171). ▪ ZR

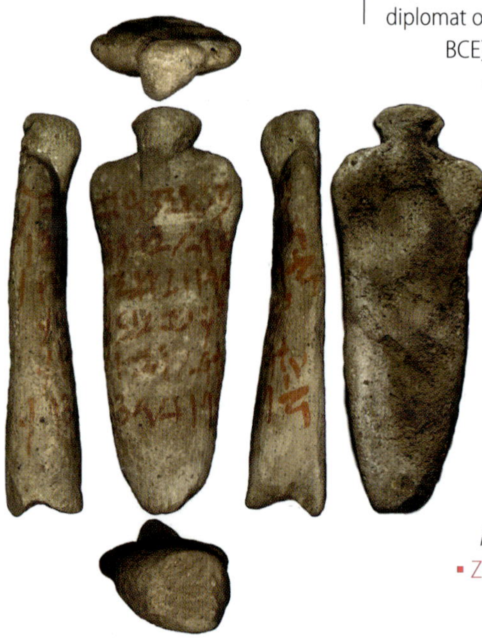

Execration figurines of prisoners with hieratic texts, Egypt, 19th to 18th century BCE

LANGUAGE

14:14 Pursuit as far as Dan

The city of Dan represents the northern border of the land of Israel (Judges 20:1; I Kings 5:5). The ancient city, identified with Tel Dan, lies not far from the base of Mount Hermon on the headwaters of the Jordan River. The tribe of Dan, the source of the site's name, was originally allotted land along the southern coastal plain (Josh. 19:40–48). According to the Tanakh, they failed to conquer it because of nearby Philistine and Amorite settlements. Judges 18 recounts that Dan relocated to northern Israel and seized a town called Layish (vv. 7, 14, 27, 29), which it renamed Dan. Joshua 19:47 offers a variant name, Leshem. In the Israelite period, Dan became an important religious site for the northern Kingdom of Israel due to the golden calf installed there by King Yorovam (I Kings 12:28–30).

Tel Dan is an important archaeological site because of several highly significant finds. From the presumed period of Avraham, the Middle Bronze Age (1800–1550 BCE), the triple-arched gateway represents the earliest preserved mudbrick arched gate in the world. Layish, its pre-Israelite name, is mentioned in the Middle Bronze Age Egyptian execration texts (lists of peoples or cities inscribed on clay tablets which were ritually broken to represent their anticipated destruction). Pharaoh Thutmose III (1479–1425 BCE) lists Layish as one of the cities from which he took prisoners during his campaign into Canaan. Late Bronze Age layers (1500–1200 BCE) reveal a treasure-filled Mycenaean tomb. In the Iron Age II period, when the city was already Israelite, it included major fortifications and a "high place" for sacrificial use. Furthermore, the "House of David" inscription found there from the mid-9th century BCE offers the only reference to King David outside of the Bible (with the possible exception of the Mesha Stele). This Aramaic text records the victory of a non-Israelite king (perhaps Ḥazael or his son Ben Hadad II of Aram) over the kings of both Israel and Yehuda (see II Kings 9:14–15, 15:20). Only after the Assyrian conquest of Israel in 733 BCE does Dan loses its significance.

Genesis 14:14–15 relates that Avram and his posse of 318 men chased the four kings from Ḥevron until Dan, the northern border of the land of Israel, and even beyond, to Ḥova, north of Damascus. Commentators, both medieval and modern, note that the use of the name Dan in Avraham's time is anachronistic, as Layish is not renamed Dan until the period of Joshua or the Judges. Rabbi David Kimḥi (Radak, 1160–1235) suggests that the later name was used for the benefit of later generations, "for when Moshe our rabbi wrote this, it was not yet called Dan." However, he holds out the possibility that the Dan of Genesis 14 is "another place that was called Dan in those days."

Shmuel David Luzzatto (Shadal, 1800–1865) concurs that the Dan of Genesis 14:14 should not be identified with Dan/Layish of Judges 18. He bases this on the extraordinary series of double names in Genesis 14: verse 2 – Bela/Tzoar; verse 3 – Siddim Valley/the Dead Sea; verse 5 – Ashterot/Karnayim; Shaveh/Kirytayim; verse 7 – Ein-Mishpat/Kadesh; Hatzetzon/Tamar; verse 17 – Shaveh Valley/ the Valley of the King. Luzzatto reasons that if this town named Dan were indeed the Layish/Dan of Judges 18, then Genesis 14:14 would say, "as far as Layish, which is Dan." The omission of Layish in Genesis 14, otherwise replete with double names, suggests that this town may be a different Dan, similarly derived from the common Semitic root meaning judgment.

Notwithstanding Shadal's opinion, the location of Dan/Layish does make geographic sense in the narrative. What route did Avram use to catch up with the four kings from Ḥevron? If they went due north along the Jordan River valley, he would have had to travel along the central highlands and head northeast and would eventually have intercepted them at Dan/Layish – a well-fortified Canaanite city that later became the extreme border of ancient Israel (see also Deut. 34:1). ▪ EG

Canaanite gate from the Middle Bronze Age, Tel Dan, 18th to 16th century BCE

וּרְכֻשׁוֹ הֵשִׁיב וְגַם אֶת־הַנָּשִׁים וְאֶת־הָעָם׃ וַיֵּצֵא מֶלֶךְ־סְדֹם יז
לִקְרָאתוֹ אַחֲרֵי שׁוּבוֹ מֵהַכּוֹת אֶת־כְּדָרְלָעֹמֶר וְאֶת־הַמְּלָכִים
אֲשֶׁר אִתּוֹ אֶל־עֵמֶק שָׁוֵה הוּא עֵמֶק הַמֶּלֶךְ׃ וּמַלְכִּי־צֶדֶק מֶלֶךְ יח
שָׁלֵם הוֹצִיא לֶחֶם וָיָיִן וְהוּא כֹהֵן לְאֵל עֶלְיוֹן׃ וַיְבָרְכֵהוּ וַיֹּאמַר יט
בָּרוּךְ אַבְרָם לְאֵל עֶלְיוֹן קֹנֵה שָׁמַיִם וָאָרֶץ׃ וּבָרוּךְ אֵל עֶלְיוֹן כ

17 the other survivors as well. When he returned from defeating
Kedorlaomer and the kings with him, the king of Sedom came
out to greet him at Shaveh Valley – that is, the Valley of the
18 King. And Malki Tzedek, king of Shalem, offered bread and
19 wine. He was a priest of God Most High, and he blessed
Avram, saying: "Blessed be Avram by God Most High, Maker
20 of heaven and earth, and blessed be God Most High who
delivered your foes into your hand." Then Avram gave him a

GEOGRAPHY

14:17 Shaveh Valley

The Shaveh Valley is mentioned only here and once more by its alternate name "Valley of the King" in II Samuel 18:18 (the site of the monument that Avshalom erected for himself). Josephus writes that the valley is located two stadia (350–400 meters/about 380–437 yards) from Jerusalem (*Antiquities*, 7.10.3), and Targum Onkelos calls it "the leveled [the literal meaning of *shaveh*] valley, that is the racecourse of the king." Jeremiah 31:39 mentions "the meadows up to the Kidron Valley, up to the corner of the Horse Gate to the east" which seems to be referring to this same general area, leading to the location of the Shaveh Valley in the little plain formed by the meeting of the Valley of Hinom and the Kidron Valley. ▪ ZR

View down the Valley of Hinom toward the place where it meets the Kidron Valley

Yehimilk inscription, Phoenician, Byblos, 10th century BCE

GEOGRAPHY

14:18 Malki Tzedek, king of Shalem

No extra-biblical information has been found about Malki Tzedek, but *tzdk*, the name of the Canaanite god who personifies justice, is a common component of West Semitic names. The title "righteous king" (*mlk tzdk*) is used in inscriptions praising the Phoenician kings Yehimilk (ca. 950 BCE) and Yehawmilk (ca. 450 BCE), so it may not be a personal name. This term appears only one other time in Tanakh, in Psalms 110:4, as part of a description of David or a Davidic king, "The Lord has sworn and will never retract: You are a priest forever by My decree, a rightful king (*malki tzedek*)."

The name Shalem appears as another name for Jerusalem in Psalms 76:3, "His tent is set in Salem [Hebrew is actually Shalem], His abode in Zion." A rabbinic tradition states that Shalem was the ancient name of Jerusalem (Bereshit Rabba 56:10), which is mentioned as early as the Egyptian execration texts (19th to 18th century BCE) as *urashalimu* and in the *Amarna letters* (14th century BCE) as *urusalim*. ▪ ZR

כא אֲשֶׁר־מִגֵּן צָרֶיךָ בְּיָדֶךָ וַיִּתֶּן־לוֹ מַעֲשֵׂר מִכֹּל: וַיֹּאמֶר מֶלֶךְ־סְדֹם חמישי

tenth of everything. And the king of Sedom said to Avram, 21
"Give me the people, and keep the possessions for yourself."

NEAR EAST

14:18 Priest of God Most High

Malki Tzedek is described both as a king and a priest, roles that were combined in some ancient Near Eastern societies, such as those of the Egyptians, Assyrians, Hittites, and Phoenicians.

In Ugaritic texts, El is the supreme god, husband of the goddess Ashera, and *el* is a common term in Semitic languages for a god in general. An 8th century BCE Aramaic treaty inscription on one of the Sefire steles states that the treaty is made "before El and Elyon, before Heaven [and Earth, before A]byss and Sources, and before Day and Night," evidence of a god called Elyon, who in the polytheistic cultures may have referred to the supreme deity in their pantheon of gods. This is supported by Eusebius' account of Philo of Byblos' (ca. 64–141 CE) record of the Phoenician priest Sanchuniathon's discussion of deities, which includes the statement, "In their time is born a certain Elyon, called the Most High" (*Praeparatio Evangelica,* 1:10). Thus, El and Elyon both function as names of specific deities for different cultures in the ancient Near East.

Both El and Elyon are used in Tanakh to refer to God, with the compound term El Elyon appearing in Israelite literature only in these verses in Genesis and in Psalms 78:35. These verses are examples of the Tanakh adapting names of pre-Israelite polytheistic deities, and even phrases used about those deities in pagan cultures and consolidating them as references to the one true God. The term Elyon is used on its own to refer to God in a number of poetic contexts in Tanakh (Deut. 32:8; Is. 14:14; Ps. 9:3, 18:14, 77:11, 87:5, 91:1; Lam. 3:35, 38), and is also found in conjunction with other names of God (for example, Ps. 7:18, 47:3, 57:3, 78:56). ▪ ZR

Figurine of the Canaanite god El, bronze with gold leaf, Megiddo, 14th to 13th century BCE

NEAR EAST

14:20 A tenth

After Malki Tzedek blessed him, Avram gave Malki Tzekek "a tenth of everything."

In the Torah, God commands the Israelites to tithe their produce "whether seed from the ground or fruit of the tree belong to the Lord" (Lev. 27:30), as well as their flocks and herds (Lev. 27:32). The Israelite king also has the power to tithe "your seeds and vineyards and give them to his officials and his staff" (I Sam. 8:15). Similarly, Ugaritic texts talk about a tithe, called by the cognate *ma'asharu* or *meshertu*, using the same term for what was given to both temples and kings.

The tithe to Malki Tzedek can be understood as a gift to the king (political tribute) or to a priest. Since Avram gave the tithe after receiving a blessing from Malki Tzedek, perhaps the priestly role is the defining factor.

We do not have any extra-biblical evidence of tithing from spoils of war. In the most similar case in Tanakh, after a battle against the Midianites, God levies tribute from the war's spoils, but a smaller percentage (Num. 31:28–30, 37–41). ▪ ZR

Melchizedek gives bread and wine to Abraham, Thomas Christian Wink, 1770

אֶל־אַבְרָם תֶּן־לִי הַנֶּפֶשׁ וְהָרְכֻשׁ קַח־לָךְ׃ וַיֹּאמֶר אַבְרָם אֶל־ כב
מֶלֶךְ סְדֹם הֲרִמֹתִי יָדִי אֶל־יהוה אֵל עֶלְיוֹן קֹנֵה שָׁמַיִם וָאָרֶץ׃
אִם־מִחוּט וְעַד שְׂרוֹךְ־נַעַל וְאִם־אֶקַּח מִכָּל־אֲשֶׁר־לָךְ וְלֹא כג
תֹאמַר אֲנִי הֶעֱשַׁרְתִּי אֶת־אַבְרָם׃ בִּלְעָדַי רַק אֲשֶׁר אָכְלוּ הַנְּעָרִים כד
וְחֵלֶק הָאֲנָשִׁים אֲשֶׁר הָלְכוּ אִתִּי עָנֵר אֶשְׁכֹּל וּמַמְרֵא הֵם יִקְחוּ
חֶלְקָם׃ אַחַר ׀ הַדְּבָרִים הָאֵלֶּה הָיָה דְבַר־יהוה אֶל־ א טו
אַבְרָם בַּמַּחֲזֶה לֵאמֹר אַל־תִּירָא אַבְרָם אָנֹכִי מָגֵן לָךְ שְׂכָרְךָ

22 But Avram said to the king of Sedom, "I raise my hand in oath
to the Lord, God Most High, Maker of heaven and earth,
23 that I will not accept anything of yours, not even a thread or
a shoe strap, so that you never shall say, 'I made Avram rich.'
24 I will accept nothing but what my young men have eaten and
the share that belongs to the men who went with me – Aner,
15 1 Eshkol, and Mamre; let them have their share." After
these events the word of the Lord came to Avram in a vision,
saying: "Do not be afraid, Avram. I am your shield. Your

NEAR EAST

14:22 Maker of heaven and earth

In verse 19, Avram uses the term "God Most High, Maker of heaven and earth," employed here by Malki Tzedek in his blessing. This term also appears in Psalms (for example, Ps. 115:15, 121:2, 124:8), but the word *koneh*, used here as well as in Ugaritic to mean "maker," is replaced in Psalms by *oseh*, as by that time *koneh* in the sense of "making" was an archaic form.

A very similar formula was found in a Phoenician building inscription from the 8th century BCE, "let Ba'lshamem and El-the-Creator-of-the-Earth (*el qn rtz*) and the Eternal-Sun and the whole Group of the Children of the gods (El) wipe out that ruler." Note also the 13th century BCE Hittite myth featuring a god called Elkunirsha, a distortion of the phrase *el qonh eretz*. This indicates that both Avram and Malki Tzedek appropriated a known pagan formula and used it in a monotheistic way. Note also that in Tanakh, this formula includes the fact that God is the creator of heaven as well as the earth, while the heavenly element does not appear in the pagan expression. This further illustrates the way in which the phrase was amended to reflect the idea that one God created the entire cosmos. The fact that Malki Tzedek also used the expanded form indicates that he – like Avram – is to be viewed as a monotheist. ▪ ZR

Temple of Baal Shamin, Palmyra, 2nd century BCE to 2nd century CE ↘

NEAR EAST

14:24 Sharing the spoils

Descriptions of the division of spoils appear only in a few places in Tanakh. Numbers 31:26–47 mentions that after the Israelite victory over the Midianites, half the sheep, cattle, donkeys, and captives were divided among the combatants and the other half was divided among the rest of the community. This was beyond the spoils that the troops plundered (Num. 31:32) for themselves. I Samuel 30:25 indicates that there was a completely equal division of spoils between those who went into battle and whoever stayed behind.

In our verse, we see that Avram divided spoils among combatants and allies who did not go out to war; although Aner, Eshkol, and Mamre did not join Avram in combat (according to Bereishit Rabba 43:9 they were guarding the military camp), they did get a portion of the spoils. Here, Avram forgoes the spoils of his own accord and chooses to give them to his allies, though this was not legally mandated.

The *Mari letters* show that spoils were divided among allies based on the size of the troops contributed to combat. There are references to the noncombatants getting a share as well, as found in the Akkadian inscription of Idrimi the ruler of Alalakh where he speaks of dividing the plunder after his invasion of Hittite territory (lines 75–77): "I took prisoners from them, plundered their riches, possessions, and property, and distributed it to my soldiers, my auxiliary troops, my brothers, and friends. I myself took a share like theirs." This contrast illustrates the selflessness of Avram's refusal to take any booty for himself, going against the conventions of the time. ▪ ZR

NEAR EAST

15:1 A vision

The term *maḥazeh* appears in only a few places in Tanakh (Num. 24:4, 16; Ezek. 13:7); the more common form is *ḥazon*.

In the ancient Near East, communications from deities could be received in several ways. The Hittite king Mursili II (ruled ca. 1330–1295 BCE), when trying to ascertain the reason for a plague, prays to the storm god of Hatti and requests, "if people have been dying because of some other reason, then let me either see it in a dream, or let it be established through an oracle, or let a man of god declare it, or, according to what I instructed all the priests, they shall regularly sleep holy" (CTH 378). The options listed include a layperson's dream, an oracle, a pronouncement from a prophet ("man of god") or "sleeping holy," a ritual sleep in a holy place with the intention of receiving divine communication. Different terms in the ancient world represent the various prophetic experiences, some of which are difficult to precisely distinguish from one another. For example, in Akkadian, *munattu* refers to a "waking dream" and *purussu amaru* refers to an oracular pronouncement made in a trance-like state.

The *maḥazeh* does not just mean seeing something. In our verse, the word of God comes in a *maḥazeh*, although only an auditory statement is reported in the text; we are not told of a visual component. Similarly, the term *roeh* (literally, "seer"), used as a synonym for a prophet (for example, to describe Shmuel in I Sam. 9:9; I Chr. 9:22, 29:29), is not limited to visual experiences. ▪ ZR

Tablet containing prayer of Mursili II to the gods to end a plague, Hattusa, 13th century BCE

NEAR EAST

15:1 Do not be afraid

The phrase "do not be afraid" appears in the literature of the ancient Near East in the genre of "oracles of assurance," where, before going out to battle, a king is given an oracle that his victory is assured. For example, the Akkadian oracle of Ishtar-latashiat of Arbela to Esar Ḥadon, king of Assyria (ruled 681–669 BCE), "King of Assyria, fear not (*la tapallah*)! The enemy of the king of Assyria I deliver to slaughter!" and the early 8th century BCE Aramaic inscription of King Zakur of Ḥamat and Lu'ath, "Be'elshamayn [spoke] to me through seers and through diviners. Be'elshamayn [said to me]: Do not fear (*al tizḥhal*), for I made you king, and I shall stand by you and deliver you from all [these kings who] set up a siege against you."

In similarity to ancient Near Eastern texts, sometimes in the Tanakh, "Do not be afraid" is said by God to the leader or king who is facing enemies, as in Numbers 21:34; Joshua 8:1; II Kings 19:6; Isaiah 7:4. However, unlike the other cultures, the phrase is divinely spoken here to a patriarch in difficulty (Gen. 26:24, 46:3), to Hagar (21:17), and elsewhere to prophets and to the Israelites at large. The Tanakh, then, uniquely reveals a God who is compassionate and caring not only to a king, but to an entire people – starting with their ancestors. ▪ ZR, JU

Royal Stele of Zakur, Aramaic, Tell Afis, in the territory of the ancient kingdom of Ḥamat, 8th century BCE

ב הַרְבֵּה מְאֹד׃ וַיֹּאמֶר אַבְרָם אֲדֹנָי יֱהוִה מַה־תִּתֶּן־לִי וְאָנֹכִי הוֹלֵךְ

2 reward shall be very great." But Avram said, "My Lord God, what will You have given me if I remain childless, and the one who will take charge of my household is Eliezer of

NEAR EAST

15:2 Childless

The term used here for childless, *ariri*, is a harsh term that appears elsewhere in Tanakh only as a divine punishment. In Leviticus 20:20–21, it is the punishment for forbidden relationships, "If a man lies with his aunt, he has exposed his uncle's nakedness. Both parties shall bear their guilt; they shall die childless (*aririm*). For a man to marry his brother's wife – that is taboo. He has exposed his brother's nakedness; both parties shall be childless (*aririm*)," and, in Jeremiah 22:30, it is part of the punishments of the disobedient Judahite kings, "This is what the Lord said: Write this man down as sterile (*ariri*), a person who will not succeed in his lifetime, for none of his descendants will rise to sit upon the throne of David, to reign ever again in Yehuda."

In Tanakh and in the ancient Near East, children are seen as a divine reward. For example, Psalms 127:3, "Children are a gift from the Lord, the fruit of the womb His reward." In the Ugaritic *Tale of Aqhat*, Dan'el gives sacrifices and libations to the gods for seven consecutive days to beseech them for a son. Finally, the god Baal enters the picture: "Then on the seventh day, Baal approached, having had mercy on the lamenting of Dan'el…the groaning of the valiant Harnamite [man], who had no son like his brothers, no scion like his kinsmen/ may he, like his brothers, have a son, like his kinsmen, a scion…please bless him please pronounce a benediction upon him, O creator of creatures (the god El), so that he may have a son in his house, a scion within his palace" (CTA 17), and the god El accedes to Baal's request. Similarly, childlessness was understood as divine punishment. An Akkadian text states that "pestilence was laid upon the people, so the womb was constricted and could not give birth to a child" (CAD R 260a). ▪ ZR

↗ *Tale of Aqhat*, House of the Great Priest, Ras Shamra (Ugarit), 14th to 13th century BCE

GEOGRAPHY

15:2 Damascus

Damascus is in southwestern Syria on a plateau along the banks of the Barada River, at the crossroads of the north-south trade route from Asia Minor to Egypt and the east-west route connecting the Euphrates Valley to Lebanon. Although the immediate area was settled already in the 7th millennium BCE, the earliest mention of Damascus (*tmsq*) is in a list of cities captured by Thutmose III (15th century BCE), inscribed on the walls of the temple of Amun in Karnak. As it was located at the northeastern edge of the area under Egypt's control, it was often part of regional power struggles in the Late Bronze Age. Though probably established by non-Semites, in Semitic languages the first syllable of the city's name (*di*) was understood to be a relative pronoun, making Meshek a term used for Damascus – as in the Aramaic inscription of the Melqart Stele of Ben Hadad Ezer II (845 BCE), "The stele which Bir-Hadad, son of Ezer, the Damascene (*msh[k]y*), son of the king of Aram, set up to his lord Melqart." ▪ ZR

↗ Thutmose III, Temple of Karnak, Luxor, 15th century BCE

ג עֲרִירִי וּבֶן־מֶשֶׁק בֵּיתִי הוּא דַּמֶּשֶׂק אֱלִיעֶזֶר׃ וַיֹּאמֶר אַבְרָם הֵן
ד לִי לֹא נָתַתָּה זָרַע וְהִנֵּה בֶן־בֵּיתִי יוֹרֵשׁ אֹתִי׃ וְהִנֵּה דְבַר־יהוה
אֵלָיו לֵאמֹר לֹא יִירָשְׁךָ זֶה כִּי־אִם אֲשֶׁר יֵצֵא מִמֵּעֶיךָ הוּא יִירָשֶׁךָ׃

Damascus?"[25] Avram said, "You have given me no children. 3
A man of my household will be my heir." Then the word of 4
the LORD came to him: "That man will not be your heir; one

25 | Eliezer is understood to have been a prominent servant of Avram.

NEAR EAST

15:2–3 Adopting Eliezer

Offspring was important in the ancient world for various reasons. Without a child, a man would have no one to inherit his name, property, and money, or provide for his funerary needs. This appears to be the basis for Avraham's complaint in Genesis 15:2. To solve this problem, a man might choose to adopt either a kinsman or a non-kinsman as an heir.

Mesopotamian adoption contracts attest to such a practice. The phrase *ana marutim lequm* or *ana marutim nadanum* means "taken for sonship" or "given for sonship" respectively. The following example comes from the city of Nuzi in northeastern Iraq: "The tablet of adoption belonging to Ehelteshup son of Puhiya; he adopted Zigi son of Akuya. Accordingly, all my lands, my buildings, my earnings, my domestics, one (part) of all my property, I have given to Zigi."

When choosing whom to adopt, couples (usually the husband) might look close to home. For families with servants, the manumission and subsequent adoption of a faithful servant would provide the man not only with an heir, but a loyal one. Such practices would be beneficial not only to the man, but also to the manumitted slave, who could remain in the household as a free man. Manumission documents contain declarations on behalf of the owner as to the manumission and protection against re-enslavement and oaths of obligation and support from the freed slaves.

Avraham's declaration concerning Eliezer – "the one in charge of my household.... A man of my household will be my heir" – seems to indicate that Avraham was feeling forced to manumit Eliezer and make him his heir. As an early 2nd millennium BCE letter from Larsa states, "A father does not adopt his slave if he has sons." ▪ KG

Adoption contract, Aramaic, archive of Ananiah and Tamut, a Jewish family, Elephantine Island, 5th century BCE

ה וַיּוֹצֵא אֹתוֹ הַחוּצָה וַיֹּאמֶר הַבֶּט־נָא הַשָּׁמַיְמָה וּסְפֹר הַכּוֹכָבִים
ו אִם־תּוּכַל לִסְפֹּר אֹתָם וַיֹּאמֶר לוֹ כֹּה יִהְיֶה זַרְעֶךָ׃ וְהֶאֱמִן בַּיהוָה

5 who comes forth from your own loins will be your heir." He
took him outside and said, "Look at the heavens and count
the stars – if indeed you can count them." He said to him,
6 "That is how your descendants will be." And because Avram
put his trust in the LORD, He reckoned it to him as

NEAR EAST

15:5 Innumerability of the stars in Mesopotamia

Ancient Mesopotamian astrologers listed and tracked the constellations as well as individual stars and planets. They divided the stars into three groups based mainly on where they rose on the eastern horizon. The horizon was divided into the Paths of Anu (in the middle), Enlil (in the south), and Ea (in the north), all named for the main cosmic deities responsible for establishing the laws governing the heavenly bodies. These paths were used to describe the location of the stars and other phenomena. The stars themselves were believed to be engraved into the heavens.

As in Genesis, the stars were used in Old Babylonian literature as an example of something innumerable. For example, a prayer from the Royal Library of Ashurbanipal (ca. 7th century BCE) states, "Enter, Ninsianna (Venus), Great Lady, and the innumerable neighboring stars," and the line "my gossipy women, more numerous than the stars of heaven" found in an Old Babylonian love poem known as "A Dialogue Between Hammurabi and a Woman." ▪ ZR

Fragment of *Mul Apin,* "Constellation of the plow," Babylonia, 7th century BCE

"A deep sleep fell upon Abram and a horror seized him," Gerard Hoet, illustration from *Figures de la Bible,* 1728

ז ויחשבה לו צדקייה: ויאמר אליו אני יהוה אשר הוצאתיך ששי
ח מאור כשדים לתת לך את־הארץ הזאת לרשתה: ויאמר
• ט אדני יהוה במה אדע כי אירשנה: ויאמר אליו קחה לי עגלה
י משלשת ועז משלשת ואיל משלש ותר וגוזל: ויקח־לו את־
כל־אלה ויבתר אתם בתוך ויתן איש־בתרו לקראת רעהו
יא ואת־הצפר לא בתר: וירד העיט על־הפגרים וישב אתם
יב אברם: ויהי השמש לבוא ותרדמה נפלה על־אברם והנה

righteousness.[26] And He told him, "I am the Lord who 7
brought you out from Ur Kasdim to give you this land to
possess it." And he said, "My Lord God, how shall I know that 8
I will possess it?" And He said to him, "Take for Me a three- 9 •
year-old heifer, and a three-year-old goat, and a three-year-old
ram, and a turtledove, and a young pigeon." And he took all 10
these and cut them in two and put each half opposite its other
half, but the birds he did not cut.[27] Birds of prey descended 11
on the carcasses, but Avram drove them away. And so it was 12

26 | Alternatively, Avram recognized the righteousness of God.

27 | This was a covenant ceremony (cf., e.g., Jer. 34:18).

NEAR EAST

15:9–17 The ritual acts of the covenant between the parts

The rituals described in 15:9–17 find several partial parallels in the Tanakh and in ancient Near Eastern documents. While these shed light on certain aspects of the text, its overall message has remained enigmatic. Particularly, scholars have struggled to explain the significance of cutting the animals into halves. Likewise, there is disagreement regarding the oven and torch that pass between them: do these represent Israel or God?

First, it has been proposed that the cutting (*b t r*) of the animals relates to the biblical expression for making – literally, "cutting" (*k r t*) – a covenant, as in verse 18: "On that day the Lord cut (*karat*) a covenant with Avram." Although this literal rendering of *krt* is somewhat speculative, it finds support in the expression "kill a donkey" (*ḥayaram qaṭalu*) in 18th to 17th century BCE letters from Mari in ancient Syria, where the killing of a donkey accompanied the sealing of an agreement. The implication is that anybody who violates the agreement will suffer the fate of the donkey. A parallel appears when the prophet Yirmeyahu rebukes the Judahites who had made (*karat*) a covenant to release their Hebrew slaves and then took them back (in contradiction to the law in Ex. 21:2): "all the people who violated My covenant…the calf that they cut in two, the sections of which they passed between…I will deliver them into the hands of their enemies" (Jer. 34:18–20; the context is the Babylonian siege of Jerusalem – vv. 7–22 there, see also I Sam. 11:7).

Second, scholars have called attention to symbolic acts that are mentioned in multiple ancient Near Eastern treaties, in which the vassal expresses a self-curse that is to befall him if he breaks the agreement. For example, in the vassal treaty between Ashurnirari V of Assyria and Mati-ilu of Arpad (8th century BCE), the severing of the head of a lamb is accompanied by a statement that Mati-ilu's head will likewise be severed if he violates the treaty. While such evidence might fit the ominous mood of Genesis 15, there is no mention in the latter of either oaths or curses, nor is it clear how it explains the passing of the fire between the pieces. Furthermore, this chapter does not fit the form of a vassal treaty, but rather, represents a divine promise.

A third parallel is a Hittite ritual for a defeated army. This ritual involves building a gate next to a river, marked on both sides by fire and by the severed remains of a human, a billy-goat, a puppy, and a piglet. The crossing through the gate and across the river was believed to purify the army of the negative force that caused its defeat.

While these parallels indicate that the biblical ritual displays similarities to existing traditions, it remains clear that Genesis 15 can only be fully explained by reference to its own context. As mentioned, a central problem that has puzzled commentators is how to understand the oven and torch that cross between the animal parts. Ramban suggested that the fire represents God (compare I Kings 19:12). Somewhat differently, biblical scholar Yair Zakovitch understands that the torch and the oven foreshadow God's protection of Israel through the pillar of fire that accompanied the Israelites during their nighttime exodus from Egypt (Ex. 13:21–22). The passage of fire between the parts (*gezarim*) in verse 17 corresponds to the Israelites' passing through the Sea of Reeds, whose two sides are described using the same term in Psalms 136:13–14: "He who split apart the Sea of Reeds [to pieces] (*gezarim*)…and made Israel pass through it." The three split animals (each three years old according to many commentators) represent the three generations of Egyptian servitude, while the two birds, left intact, symbolize the fourth generation of Israelites who will leave Egypt. Accordingly, this vision offers a precise answer to Avraham's doubts (v. 7) through its vivid premonition of the future exodus leading to the inheritance of the land.

For similarities of the covenant between the parts to ancient Near Eastern royal land grants see "Gift of land to Avram" on page 86. ▪ YF

אֵימָה חֲשֵׁכָה גְדֹלָה נֹפֶלֶת עָלָיו׃ וַיֹּאמֶר לְאַבְרָם יָדֹעַ תֵּדַע כִּי־ יג
גֵר ׀ יִהְיֶה זַרְעֲךָ בְּאֶרֶץ לֹא לָהֶם וַעֲבָדוּם וְעִנּוּ אֹתָם אַרְבַּע מֵאוֹת

that, as the sun went down, a deep sleep fell upon Avram and
13 a deep, dark dread came upon him. And God said to Avram,
"Know with certainty that your descendants will be migrants

GEOGRAPHY

15:18 The River of Egypt to... Euphrates

The southwest boundary of the land of Israel is usually designated "the Ravine of Egypt" (e.g., Num. 34:5; Josh. 15:4), which is identified with Wadi el-Arish, near the modern-day city of Arish in northeastern Sinai. The term used here, "River of Egypt," is unique. It does not seem to mean the Nile, which is always called *yeor* in Tanakh (Gen. 41:1; Ex. 1:22). Rather, it seems to refer to the easternmost tributary of the Nile which flows into Lake Sirbonis on the northern coast of the Sinai Peninsula, which is probably the same as "the Shiḥor, which is close to Egypt" (Josh. 13:3). Note that the boundaries given in this verse represent maximal borders; in practice, Israelite kingdoms never expanded this much. ▪ ZR

NEAR EAST

15:19–21 The ten nations of the covenant between the parts

The Torah underscores that the Israelites were not native to their land; it was God who granted it to them. God's promise of the land to Avraham (Gen. 15:18–21), the first statement of this grant, also lists the native populations that the Israelites will displace. Similar lists recur in the Torah and in Joshua, but they normally contain from five to seven nations, while the promise to Avraham here records ten.

The first three are the most intriguing, as they do not appear in other lists. The Kenites were related by marriage to Moshe and settled in the Negev beside the tribe of Yehuda (Judges 1:16; I Sam. 15:6, 27:10), but at least one of their families pitched its tents near Ḥatzor in the Upper Galilee (Judges 4:11, 17). Their eponymous ancestor may be identical with Tuval-Kayin, the forefather of iron and copper smiths (Gen. 4:22). Thus, the Kenites may have been itinerant metalworkers who moved across Canaan. The Kenizzites stemmed from Kenaz, a clan of Edom (Gen. 36:11, 15, 42). The Kadmonites' name derives from Hebrew *kedem* "east;" they are probably generic "easterners" inhabiting the eastern desert fringes of Canaan. Another exceptional group is the Refaim, mentioned elsewhere as ancient giants (*anakim*) living in the land of Bashan in the Golan (Deut. 2:11, 20, 3:13); by the time of the Israelite conquest of Canaan, they were mostly extinct.

The remaining six peoples mentioned in the promise can be divided into two groups. One consists of populations whose names are known from ancient Near Eastern sources. The Canaanites derive their name from Canaan – a geographical term for the entire settled region along the eastern shore of the Mediterranean. A dominant tendency, starting with the Tanakh itself, is to refer to the entire pre-Israelite population of the land as Canaanites, but some biblical references limit them to a more specific area, such as Numbers 13:29, which places them along the Mediterranean Sea and the Jordan River. The Amorites' name derives from the Akkadian designation for the west, *amurru* (Sumerian *mar.tu*), used from around 2000 BCE with reference to West Semitic nomadic populations from Syria and Canaan, some of which migrated into Mesopotamia and founded several royal dynasties there. The Hittites lived in the land of Hatti in Anatolia, which eventually became an empire extending into northern and central Syria. When the Hittite empire collapsed around 1200 BCE, some of its inhabitants may have migrated to southern Canaan, but explicit evidence for this is still lacking. In the 1st millennium BCE, the terms Amurru and Hatti became generic Akkadian designations for the region west of the Euphrates.

The final group of peoples in the promise to Avraham consists of the Perizzites, the Girgashites, and the Jebusites, unknown outside of the Tanakh. The name Perizzites, while often seeming to represent a distinct ethnic group, may be related to a term for the inhabitants of unfortified towns (*perazot*; for example, Deut. 3:5; Judges 5:7; I Sam. 6:18), although the connection is not clear. The origin of the Girgashites' name and the area they inhabited are unclear, although *grgsh* appears as a personal name in Ugaritic texts. The Jebusites lived in Yebus – another name for Jerusalem before it was conquered by David (Josh. 15:63; Judges 19:10–11; II Sam. 5:6–8). Thus, the list in God's promise of the land to Avraham covers the entire territory of Canaan, and culminates with the city that would become the seat of David's dynasty. ▪ YB

Letter from Akhenaten to Aziru, prince of Amurru, Tell el-Amarna, 14th century BCE

יד שָׁנָה: וְגַם אֶת־הַגּוֹי אֲשֶׁר יַעֲבֹדוּ דָּן אָנֹכִי וְאַחֲרֵי־כֵן יֵצְאוּ בִּרְכֻשׁ
טו גָּדוֹל: וְאַתָּה תָּבוֹא אֶל־אֲבֹתֶיךָ בְּשָׁלוֹם תִּקָּבֵר בְּשֵׂיבָה טוֹבָה:
טז יז וְדוֹר רְבִיעִי יָשׁוּבוּ הֵנָּה כִּי לֹא־שָׁלֵם עֲוֺן הָאֱמֹרִי עַד־הֵנָּה: וַיְהִי
הַשֶּׁמֶשׁ בָּאָה וַעֲלָטָה הָיָה וְהִנֵּה תַנּוּר עָשָׁן וְלַפִּיד אֵשׁ אֲשֶׁר
• יח עָבַר בֵּין הַגְּזָרִים הָאֵלֶּה: בַּיּוֹם הַהוּא כָּרַת יְהוָה אֶת־אַבְרָם
בְּרִית לֵאמֹר לְזַרְעֲךָ נָתַתִּי אֶת־הָאָרֶץ הַזֹּאת מִנְּהַר מִצְרַיִם
• יט עַד־הַנָּהָר הַגָּדֹל נְהַר־פְּרָת: אֶת־הַקֵּינִי וְאֶת־הַקְּנִזִּי וְאֵת
כ כא הַקַּדְמֹנִי: וְאֶת־הַחִתִּי וְאֶת־הַפְּרִזִּי וְאֶת־הָרְפָאִים: וְאֶת־הָאֱמֹרִי
טז א וְאֶת־הַכְּנַעֲנִי וְאֶת־הַגִּרְגָּשִׁי וְאֶת־הַיְבוּסִי: וְשָׂרַי
אֵשֶׁת אַבְרָם לֹא יָלְדָה לוֹ וְלָהּ שִׁפְחָה מִצְרִית וּשְׁמָהּ הָגָר:
• ב וַתֹּאמֶר שָׂרַי אֶל־אַבְרָם הִנֵּה־נָא עֲצָרַנִי יְהוָה מִלֶּדֶת בֹּא־נָא

in a land not their own, and there they will be enslaved and
oppressed for four hundred years. But I will bring judgment 14
on the nation they will serve, and afterward they will go free
with great wealth. As for you, you will join your ancestors in 15
peace; you will be buried in ripe old age. And the fourth 16
generation will return here, for the guilt of the Amorites is
not yet resolved."[28] And when the sun set and it was very dark, 17
a smoking furnace appeared and a blazing torch passed
between these pieces. On that day the Lord made a covenant 18 •
with Avram: "To your descendants I will give this land, from
the River of Egypt to the great river Euphrates, the land of the 19 •
Kenites, the Kenizzites, the Kadmonites, the Hittites, the 20
Perizzites, the Refaim, the Amorites, the Canaanites, the 21
Girgashites, and the Jebusites." Sarai, Avram's wife, 1 16
had borne him no children; but she had an Egyptian
maidservant named Hagar. Sarai said to Avram, "The Lord 2 •

28 | The accumulated guilt of the inhabitants of Canaan does not yet warrant their displacement.

NEAR EAST

16:2 Concubinage for the purpose of childbearing

In the ancient Near East, the husband of an infertile wife might take a concubine for the purpose of producing an heir. Barrenness was a disgraceful state understood as a sign of divine punishment – it was common for tensions to arise between the offspring-bearing woman and the barren wife.

The Sumerian *Laws of Lipit-Ishtar* (ca. 1934–1924 BCE) presents a case where a harlot was brought in for this purpose, "If a man's wife has not borne him children (but) a harlot (from) the public square has borne him children, he shall provide grain, oil, and clothing for that harlot; the children which the harlot has borne him shall be his heirs, and as long as his wife lives the harlot shall not live in the house with his wife" (§27).

A text from Nuzi implies that it was the responsibility of the barren wife to find a foreign concubine for her husband (as Sara did with Hagar): "Further, Gilimninu as wife to Sennima has been given. If Gilimninu bears (children), Sennima shall not take another wife; and if Gilimninu does not bear, Gilimninu, a woman of the Lullu as wife for Sennima shall take." However, unlike in Genesis 21, the Nuzi text states that the husband may not send away the foreign woman or her children.

Some marriage contracts require a barren wife to provide a slave to produce offspring. For example, an Old Assyrian (19th century BCE) marriage contract states, "If within two years she (the wife) does not provide him with offspring, she herself will purchase a slave woman, and later on, after she will have produced a child by him, he may then dispose of her by sale wheresoever he pleases."

While she cannot be sent away, some of the law collections allow the first wife to punish the slave woman for impertinence. The *Laws of Ur-Namma* (§22), it stipulates that the woman's mouth should be scoured with one quart of salt if she speaks insolently to or compares herself to her mistress. The *Laws of Hammurabi* state, "if later that female slave has claimed equality with her mistress because she bore children, her mistress may not sell her; she may mark her with the slave-mark and count her among the slaves" (LH §146).
▪ KG, ZR

Foundation cones mentioning Gudea, Ur-Namma, and Lipit-Ishtar, from Ur, Kish, and Warka, late 3rd to early 2nd millennium BCE ↙

ג אֶל־שִׁפְחָתִ֔י אוּלַ֥י אִבָּנֶ֖ה מִמֶּ֑נָּה וַיִּשְׁמַ֥ע אַבְרָ֖ם לְק֥וֹל שָׂרָֽי׃ וַתִּקַּ֞ח
שָׂרַ֣י ׀ אֵֽשֶׁת אַבְרָ֗ם אֶת־הָגָ֤ר הַמִּצְרִית֙ שִׁפְחָתָ֔הּ מִקֵּץ֙ עֶ֣שֶׂר שָׁנִ֔ים
לְשֶׁ֥בֶת אַבְרָ֖ם בְּאֶ֣רֶץ כְּנָ֑עַן וַתִּתֵּ֥ן אֹתָ֛הּ לְאַבְרָ֥ם אִישָׁ֖הּ ל֥וֹ לְאִשָּֽׁה׃
ד וַיָּבֹ֥א אֶל־הָגָ֖ר וַתַּ֑הַר וַתֵּ֙רֶא֙ כִּ֣י הָרָ֔תָה וַתֵּקַ֥ל גְּבִרְתָּ֖הּ בְּעֵינֶֽיהָ׃

has kept me from having children. Come now to my maid.
Perhaps through her I might build a family." And Avram
3 listened to Sarai. So it was that, after living in Canaan for ten
years, Avram's wife Sarai took Hagar, her Egyptian
maidservant, and gave her to her husband Avram to be his

GEOGRAPHY

16:7 Geography of Hagar's journey

Hagar was on the road to Shur, which is in the direction of her homeland, Egypt. This can be determined from Genesis 25:18, "Shur, up against Egypt," and I Samuel 15:7, "Shur, which is east of Egypt."

The road to Shur is identified with the southern of the two routes connecting Egypt to the Levant. This route goes from Egypt through Wadi Tumilat, located east of the Nile Delta, across the Sinai all the way to Be'er Sheva, and from there to Ḥevron, and points further north. The name Shur may be connected to "wall" (Aramaic *shura*), which could be a reference to the fortifications built by the Egyptians to defend the entry to Wadi Tumilat against Asiatic tribes.

The place where the angel found Hagar is called a spring in verse 7 and a well in verse 14. Strictly speaking, a spring is a place where groundwater comes out through a natural opening, whereas a well is an excavated hole used to reach an underground water source (usually an aquifer). Apparently, the terms are used interchangeably here and in Genesis 24:11 and 13, as wells were often dug near springs.

The well called Be'er Laḥai Ro'i has not been definitively identified. Many scholars associate it with Ein Muweileh, a spring located in the general area of Kadesh Barnea (if that is indeed the Kadesh mentioned here in verse 14 – see the articles on "Kadesh" in the Numbers volume of this series on pages 82 and 121; the location of Bered in the same verse, although some scholars claim is associated with Ramon Crater, is also unclear). It is likely to be found in the Quesima area, the location of the largest water supply in the Sinai desert, at the intersection of four ancient roads. ▪ ZR

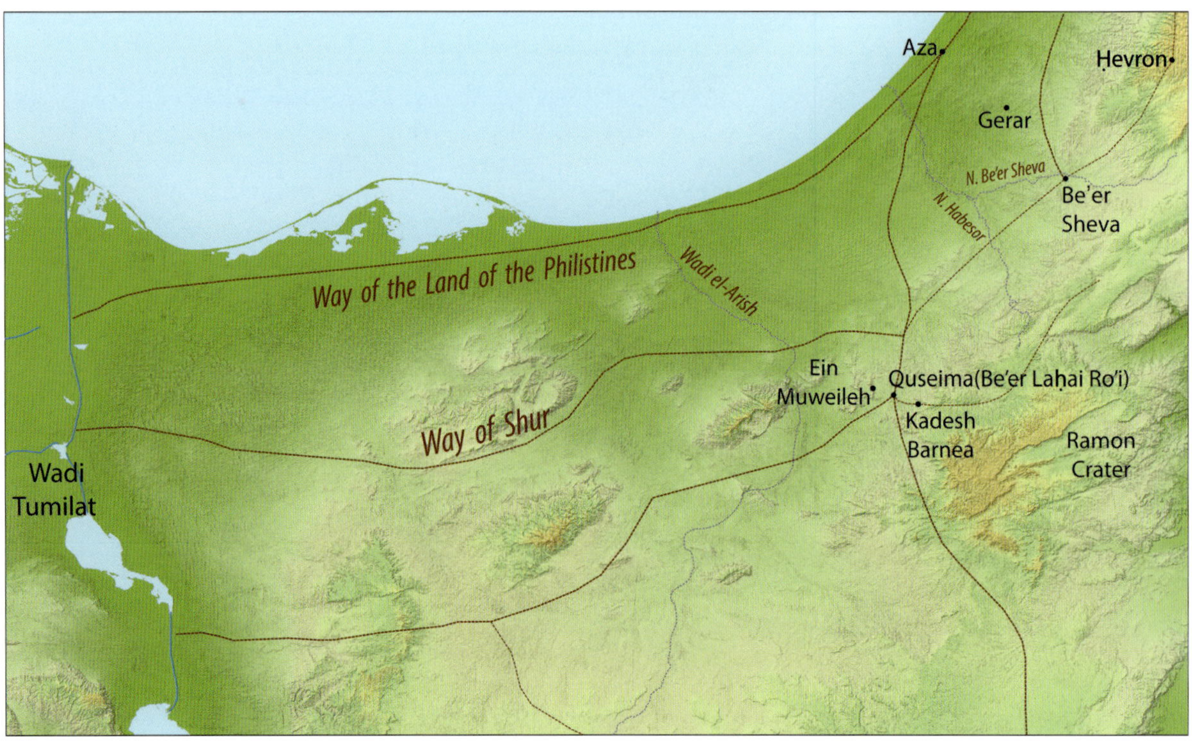

↗ Routes between Canaan and Egypt

ה וַתֹּאמֶר שָׂרַי אֶל־אַבְרָם חֲמָסִי עָלֶיךָ אָנֹכִי נָתַתִּי שִׁפְחָתִי בְּחֵיקֶךָ
ו וַתֵּרֶא כִּי הָרָתָה וָאֵקַל בְּעֵינֶיהָ יִשְׁפֹּט יְהוָה בֵּינִי וּבֵינֶיךָ׃ וַיֹּאמֶר
אַבְרָם אֶל־שָׂרַי הִנֵּה שִׁפְחָתֵךְ בְּיָדֵךְ עֲשִׂי־לָהּ הַטּוֹב בְּעֵינָיִךְ
ז וַתְּעַנֶּהָ שָׂרַי וַתִּבְרַח מִפָּנֶיהָ׃ וַיִּמְצָאָהּ מַלְאַךְ יְהוָה עַל־עֵין הַמַּיִם

wife. He came to Hagar and she conceived. And when she 4
realized that she was pregnant, she began to look upon her
mistress with contempt. Sarai said to Avram, "The abuse I 5
suffer is your fault. I laid my servant in your arms and now
that she knows she is pregnant, she looks upon me with
contempt. Let the Lord judge between me and you!" Avram 6
said to Sarai, "Your maid is in your own hands. Do with her
whatever you think best." Sarai treated her harshly – and

NEAR EAST

16:7 Angel of the Lord

The Hebrew term *malakh* means "messenger"; it can refer to a human messenger (e.g., Gen. 32:3; Judges 9:31; I Kings 19:2) or to a supernatural being sent by God (e.g., Gen. 21:17, 22:11–12, 15–18; Judges 13:3, 6, 16, 20). Sometimes these beings take on a human appearance (e.g., Gen. 18:1, 16, 19:2, 5, 10, 12, 15–16).

In the ancient Near East, it was rare for important figures to communicate directly with each other, and messengers functioned as their representatives. These messengers were accorded the respect due to whomever they were representing. When relaying their messages, they would even use the first person as if the sender of the message was speaking. Thus, the angel here speaking in God's name is not unusual. However, unlike in these verses, the messenger usually began by reporting who sent him. For example, when Baal sends messengers to Mot, they open by saying "Message of Puissant Baal" and then go on to speak as if they are Baal: "My house I have built of silver; My palace, indeed, of gold" (ANET, *Poems about Baal and Anath*, II AB, viii).

In Ugaritic, *ml'ak* is the term used for the supernatural attendants of the gods who act as messengers going back and forth between them. This concept may have been refined in the Torah and put into a monotheistic context by using the term for God's emissaries to humans. Alternatively, some scholars think the term could have been borrowed to indicate a personified manifestation of God's will. ▪ ZR

Hagar and the Angel, Cecco Bravo, 1650

בַּמִּדְבָּר עַל־הָעַיִן בְּדֶרֶךְ שׁוּר׃ וַיֹּאמַר הָגָר שִׁפְחַת שָׂרַי אֵי־מִזֶּה ח
בָאת וְאָנָה תֵלֵכִי וַתֹּאמֶר מִפְּנֵי שָׂרַי גְּבִרְתִּי אָנֹכִי בֹּרַחַת׃ וַיֹּאמֶר ט
לָהּ מַלְאַךְ יהוה שׁוּבִי אֶל־גְּבִרְתֵּךְ וְהִתְעַנִּי תַּחַת יָדֶיהָ׃ וַיֹּאמֶר י
לָהּ מַלְאַךְ יהוה הַרְבָּה אַרְבֶּה אֶת־זַרְעֵךְ וְלֹא יִסָּפֵר מֵרֹב׃ וַיֹּאמֶר יא
לָהּ מַלְאַךְ יהוה הִנָּךְ הָרָה וְיֹלַדְתְּ בֵּן וְקָרָאת שְׁמוֹ יִשְׁמָעֵאל
כִּי־שָׁמַע יהוה אֶל־עָנְיֵךְ׃ וְהוּא יִהְיֶה פֶּרֶא אָדָם יָדוֹ בַכֹּל וְיַד יב
כֹּל בּוֹ וְעַל־פְּנֵי כָל־אֶחָיו יִשְׁכֹּן׃ וַתִּקְרָא שֵׁם־יהוה הַדֹּבֵר אֵלֶיהָ יג
אַתָּה אֵל רֳאִי כִּי אָמְרָה הֲגַם הֲלֹם רָאִיתִי אַחֲרֵי רֹאִי׃ עַל־כֵּן יד
קָרָא לַבְּאֵר בְּאֵר לַחַי רֹאִי הִנֵּה בֵין־קָדֵשׁ וּבֵין בָּרֶד׃ וַתֵּלֶד הָגָר טו
לְאַבְרָם בֵּן וַיִּקְרָא אַבְרָם שֶׁם־בְּנוֹ אֲשֶׁר־יָלְדָה הָגָר יִשְׁמָעֵאל׃
וְאַבְרָם בֶּן־שְׁמֹנִים שָׁנָה וְשֵׁשׁ שָׁנִים בְּלֶדֶת־הָגָר אֶת־יִשְׁמָעֵאל טז
לְאַבְרָם׃ וַיְהִי אַבְרָם בֶּן־תִּשְׁעִים שָׁנָה וְתֵשַׁע שָׁנִים א יז
וַיֵּרָא יהוה אֶל־אַבְרָם וַיֹּאמֶר אֵלָיו אֲנִי־אֵל שַׁדַּי הִתְהַלֵּךְ לְפָנַי

Hagar ran away from her. An angel of the Lord found her
near a spring of water in the desert, the spring by the road to
8 Shur. He said, "Hagar, maidservant of Sarai, where have you
come from and where are you going?" She said, "I am running
9 away from my mistress Sarai." The angel of the Lord said to
her, "Go back to your mistress; submit yourself under her
10 hand." And the angel of the Lord added: "I will greatly
multiply your descendants; they will be too many to count."
11 Said the angel of the Lord: "You are pregnant and will give
birth to a son. You shall name him Yishmael, for the Lord
12 has heard your affliction.[29] He will become a wild donkey of
a man; his hand will be against everyone, and everyone's hand
13 against him. He will live up against all his brothers." She gave
a name to the Lord who had spoken to her: "You are the God
who sees me," for she said: "Have I not here seen Him who
14 sees me?" That is why the well is called Be'er Laḥai Ro'i.[30] It
15 is still there between Kadesh and Bered. So Hagar bore Avram
a son, and Avram gave the name Yishmael to the son that she

29 | The name Yishmael means "God hears."

30 | Meaning "Well of the Living One Who Sees Me."

— FLORA AND FAUNA —

16:12 Wild donkey

The wild donkey (*pere*), the onager, is native to the Near East and is not related to the domesticated donkey (*ḥamor*).

The temperament of this species is not suitable for manipulation by man, and it has never been domesticated. In Tanakh, the onager is used as a symbol of something free and undisciplined. For example, "Like a wild ass accustomed to the wilderness; inhaling wind as she pleases, her wailing cannot be silenced" (Jer. 2:24) and "Who set the wild ass free? Who cut the reins of the onager, whose home I made in the wilderness, whose dwellings lie in salt lands? He scoffs at the clamoring city and does not hear the taskmaster's shouts. He roams the mountain pastures in search of anything green" (Job 39:5–8). ▪ ZR

Onager (*Equus hemionus*), brown Asian wild donkey

ב וְהְיֵ֥ה תָמִֽים׃ וְאֶתְּנָ֥ה בְרִיתִ֖י בֵּינִ֣י וּבֵינֶ֑ךָ וְאַרְבֶּ֥ה אוֹתְךָ֖ בִּמְאֹ֥ד
ג מְאֹֽד׃ וַיִּפֹּ֥ל אַבְרָ֖ם עַל־פָּנָ֑יו וַיְדַבֵּ֥ר אִתּ֛וֹ אֱלֹהִ֖ים לֵאמֹֽר׃ אֲנִ֕י הִנֵּ֥ה

had borne. Avram was eighty-six years old when Hagar bore 16
him Yishmael. When Avram was ninety-nine 1 17
years old, the Lord appeared to him and said, "I am El
Shaddai. Walk before Me in integrity, and I will establish My 2
covenant between Me and you, and make you exceedingly

NEAR EAST

17:1 El Shaddai

Shaddai is understood as an ancient name of God, used in patriarchal times: "As El Shaddai I appeared to Avraham, Yitzḥak, and Yaakov" (Ex. 6:3). It appears multiple times in Genesis in prose (Gen. 17:1, 28:3, 35:11, 43:14, 48:3, 49:25). In later parts of Tanakh, it generally appears only in poetic texts, which tend to employ archaic forms (for example, Ps. 91:1; Job 5:17).

Various attempts have been made to connect this word with an ancient Near Eastern counterpart. One suggestion is the Akkadian *shadu*, meaning "mountain," which was sometimes used as an epithet for gods and multiple times in reference to Enlil, one of the supreme deities of the Mesopotamian pantheon. For example, in *Hymn to Enlil, the All-Beneficent*, "Without Enlil, the Great Mountain, no cities would be built, no settlements founded" (lines 109–110) and "O' Great Mountain Enlil, exalted is your praise" (line 170). Another suggestion is that it is a cognate of the Ugaritic *shd*, "field," used for the Mesopotamian god, Amurru, *bel shade*, "lord of the steppe." Based on these derivations, Shaddai would be a shorthand term for the titles used for gods in Akkadian or Ugaritic; the original meaning may well have been lost by the time it was in common Israelite monotheistic usage. The plural form is used as a generic parallel for gods in the beginning of the Deir 'Alla inscription (Combination I, line 5) where Bilam tells his audience, "Sit, I shall tell you what the Shaddayin have done, and come see the deeds of the gods."

These usages illustrate that the term Shaddai was understood elsewhere in the ancient Near East to be a general term for divinity, or a certain significant deity. In Genesis, it is used in a monotheistic context as a name of God (also Ex. 6:3). ▪ ZR

LANGUAGE

17:1 Walk before Me

The use of the verb "walk" is found in Assyrian land grants in phrases describing the loyal service in return for which the land was gifted. For example, the land grant of the Neo-Assyrian king Ashurbanipal (ruled 669–631 BCE) to his servant Baltya, "Baltya…served me with truthfulness, acted perfectly (literally, "walked in perfection") in my palace…" (*Neo-Assyrian Royal Grants and Decrees*, text no. 32).

While the Akkadian expression was a technical term used specifically in the context of land grants, both here and in reference to Noaḥ (Gen. 6:9; compare. 5:22), it has the more comprehensive meaning of behaving in accordance with God's wishes. Malachi 2:6 provides the most detailed expression of this meaning, "True teaching [in Hebrew, *torat emet*] was in his mouth, no sin from his lips; he walked with Me in peace and uprightness, and returned many from iniquity." ▪ ZR

Statue of the god Enlil, seated, Scribal Quarter, Nippur, 18th to 17th century BCE

בְּרִיתִי אִתָּךְ וְהָיִיתָ לְאַב הֲמוֹן גּוֹיִם: וְלֹא־יִקָּרֵא עוֹד אֶת־שִׁמְךָ ה
אַבְרָם וְהָיָה שִׁמְךָ אַבְרָהָם כִּי אַב־הֲמוֹן גּוֹיִם נְתַתִּיךָ: וְהִפְרֵתִי ו
שביעי אֹתְךָ בִּמְאֹד מְאֹד וּנְתַתִּיךָ לְגוֹיִם וּמְלָכִים מִמְּךָ יֵצֵאוּ: וַהֲקִמֹתִי ז
אֶת־בְּרִיתִי בֵּינִי וּבֵינֶךָ וּבֵין זַרְעֲךָ אַחֲרֶיךָ לְדֹרֹתָם לִבְרִית עוֹלָם
לִהְיוֹת לְךָ לֵאלֹהִים וּלְזַרְעֲךָ אַחֲרֶיךָ: וְנָתַתִּי לְךָ וּלְזַרְעֲךָ אַחֲרֶיךָ ח
אֵת ׀ אֶרֶץ מְגֻרֶיךָ אֵת כָּל־אֶרֶץ כְּנַעַן לַאֲחֻזַּת עוֹלָם וְהָיִיתִי לָהֶם
לֵאלֹהִים: וַיֹּאמֶר אֱלֹהִים אֶל־אַבְרָהָם וְאַתָּה אֶת־בְּרִיתִי תִשְׁמֹר ט

3 4 numerous." Avram fell facedown. And God said to him, "As
for Me – this is My covenant with you: you shall be father to
5 a multitude of nations. No longer shall you be called Avram.
Your name will be Avraham, for I have made you father to a
6 multitude of nations.[31] I will make you exceptionally fertile,
7 I will turn you into nations; kings will come from you. I will
establish My covenant between Me and you and your
descendants after you throughout the generations: an eternal
covenant. I will be God to you and your descendants after
8 you, and I will give you and your descendants after you the
land where you now live as strangers, the whole land of
Canaan, an everlasting possession, and I will be their God."

31 | The name Avraham resonates with *av hamon* (father of a multitude).

NEAR EAST

17:5 Your name will be Avraham

In the world of the ancient Near East, names were viewed as a reflection of the essence of a person's identity. Knowing a person's name indicated a relationship and closeness with that person, as in Exodus 33:12, "And You said, 'I have known you by name, and you have found favor in My sight.'" A name could also be used in incantations or curses to harm another person.

A name change thus indicated a change in character and personal destiny. For example, the Egyptian pharaoh Amenhotep IV (14th century BCE) changed his name, in the fifth year of his reign, to Akhenaten to demonstrate his shift from association with the god Amun to devotion to the Aten, the disc of the sun – the sole focus of worship during the rest of his reign.

Since a name indicated a person's destiny, to assign a name indicates the power to control their identity and direct their destiny – a special role reserved for parents naming their children, or rulers naming those in their charge (e.g., Gen. 41:45; Dan. 1:7). Here, God changes Avraham's destiny, making him the "father to a multitude of nations." This name change is especially pronounced here, as "Avram" literally means "my father is exalted" indicating veneration for his ancestors, while "Avraham" indicates that he himself will be the exalted ancestor of many descendants. The addition of an extra syllable to his original name also serves as a literal fulfillment of God's promise, "I will bless you and make your name great" (Gen. 12:2). ▪ ZR

Colossal statue of Amenhotep IV (Akhenaten), Karnak, 14th century BCE

י • אַתָּה וְזַרְעֲךָ אַחֲרֶיךָ לְדֹרֹתָם: זֹאת בְּרִיתִי אֲשֶׁר תִּשְׁמְרוּ בֵּינִי
יא וּבֵינֵיכֶם וּבֵין זַרְעֲךָ אַחֲרֶיךָ הִמּוֹל לָכֶם כָּל־זָכָר: וּנְמַלְתֶּם אֵת
יב בְּשַׂר עָרְלַתְכֶם וְהָיָה לְאוֹת בְּרִית בֵּינִי וּבֵינֵיכֶם: וּבֶן־שְׁמֹנַת
יָמִים יִמּוֹל לָכֶם כָּל־זָכָר לְדֹרֹתֵיכֶם יְלִיד בָּיִת וּמִקְנַת־כֶּסֶף מִכֹּל
יג בֶּן־נֵכָר אֲשֶׁר לֹא מִזַּרְעֲךָ הוּא: הִמּוֹל ׀ יִמּוֹל יְלִיד בֵּיתְךָ וּמִקְנַת
יד כַּסְפֶּךָ וְהָיְתָה בְרִיתִי בִּבְשַׂרְכֶם לִבְרִית עוֹלָם: וְעָרֵל ׀ זָכָר אֲשֶׁר
לֹא־יִמּוֹל אֶת־בְּשַׂר עָרְלָתוֹ וְנִכְרְתָה הַנֶּפֶשׁ הַהִוא מֵעַמֶּיהָ אֶת־

Then God said to Avraham, "As for you, you shall keep My 9
covenant, you and your descendants after you throughout
their generations. This is My covenant, kept between Me and 10 •
you and your descendants after you: every male among you
shall be circumcised. You must circumcise the flesh of your 11
foreskin – this shall be the sign of the covenant between Me
and you. Throughout the generations, every male among you 12
shall be circumcised at the age of eight days, including the
slave born in your household, including one acquired from a
stranger not descended from you. All must be circumcised – 13
those born in your household, those acquired with your
money – and My covenant in your flesh will be a covenant

NEAR EAST

17:10 Circumcision

Circumcision was common throughout much of the Levant and Egypt. Archaeological evidence of circumcision in the Levant exists from early in the 3rd millennium BCE; bronze figurines from the Amuq Valley in northern Syria from the Early Bronze Age show circumcised males. Circumcision was practiced in ancient Egypt starting in the 4th millennium BCE – human remains from as early as the pre-Dynastic period show that most, if not all, males were circumcised. On the other hand, in the extensive Babylonian medical texts in our possession, there is no record of circumcision from southern Mesopotamia and no Akkadian term for the practice. The fact that our text provides no specific instructions regarding the procedure also indicates that Avraham was familiar with the practice, possibly from his interactions with Canaanites and Egyptians.

In other cultures, circumcision generally took place as a rite of passage into the adult male community, at puberty or before marriage. The command of circumcision on the eighth day is unparalleled in other societies and invests it with a new and distinct meaning: a divinely commanded sign of the covenant between God and Avraham's descendants. The everlasting nature of this covenant is emphasized multiple times (vv. 7, 8, 13, 19).

This sign of the covenant is for males only, thus avoiding the "female circumcision" (clitorectomy), carried out in other cultures. However, it does include male slaves (v. 12), indicating that they become members of the Israelite people, a phenomenon found nowhere else in the ancient Near East. The implication is that these slaves adopt Israelite monotheistic religion (compare Ex. 12:48).

As opposed to the covenant of the rainbow made by God (Gen. 9:8–17), here Avraham and his descendants are responsible for *making* the sign of the covenant. Divine punishment for disobedience is severe: one who refuses circumcision "shall be severed from his people, he has broken My covenant." ▪ ZR

Priest performing ritual circumcision on a young boy, plaster copy of a relief, detail, tomb of Ankhmahor, Saqqara, 24th century BCE ↘

בְּרִיתִי הֵפַר׃ וַיֹּאמֶר אֱלֹהִים אֶל־אַבְרָהָם שָׂרַי טו
אִשְׁתְּךָ לֹא־תִקְרָא אֶת־שְׁמָהּ שָׂרָי כִּי שָׂרָה שְׁמָהּ׃ וּבֵרַכְתִּי אֹתָהּ טז
וְגַם נָתַתִּי מִמֶּנָּה לְךָ בֵּן וּבֵרַכְתִּיהָ וְהָיְתָה לְגוֹיִם מַלְכֵי עַמִּים
מִמֶּנָּה יִהְיוּ׃ וַיִּפֹּל אַבְרָהָם עַל־פָּנָיו וַיִּצְחָק וַיֹּאמֶר בְּלִבּוֹ הַלְּבֶן יז
מֵאָה־שָׁנָה יִוָּלֵד וְאִם־שָׂרָה הֲבַת־תִּשְׁעִים שָׁנָה תֵּלֵד׃ וַיֹּאמֶר יח
אַבְרָהָם אֶל־הָאֱלֹהִים לוּ יִשְׁמָעֵאל יִחְיֶה לְפָנֶיךָ׃ וַיֹּאמֶר אֱלֹהִים יט
אֲבָל שָׂרָה אִשְׁתְּךָ יֹלֶדֶת לְךָ בֵּן וְקָרָאתָ אֶת־שְׁמוֹ יִצְחָק וַהֲקִמֹתִי
אֶת־בְּרִיתִי אִתּוֹ לִבְרִית עוֹלָם לְזַרְעוֹ אַחֲרָיו׃ וּלְיִשְׁמָעֵאל כ
שְׁמַעְתִּיךָ הִנֵּה ׀ בֵּרַכְתִּי אֹתוֹ וְהִפְרֵיתִי אֹתוֹ וְהִרְבֵּיתִי אֹתוֹ
בִּמְאֹד מְאֹד שְׁנֵים־עָשָׂר נְשִׂיאִם יוֹלִיד וּנְתַתִּיו לְגוֹי גָּדוֹל׃ וְאֶת־ כא
בְּרִיתִי אָקִים אֶת־יִצְחָק אֲשֶׁר תֵּלֵד לְךָ שָׂרָה לַמּוֹעֵד הַזֶּה
בַּשָּׁנָה הָאַחֶרֶת׃ וַיְכַל לְדַבֵּר אִתּוֹ וַיַּעַל אֱלֹהִים מֵעַל אַבְרָהָם׃ כב
וַיִּקַּח אַבְרָהָם אֶת־יִשְׁמָעֵאל בְּנוֹ וְאֵת כָּל־יְלִידֵי בֵיתוֹ וְאֵת כג
כָּל־מִקְנַת כַּסְפּוֹ כָּל־זָכָר בְּאַנְשֵׁי בֵּית אַבְרָהָם וַיָּמָל אֶת־בְּשַׂר

14 everlasting. Any uncircumcised male, whose foreskin has not
been circumcised, shall be severed from his people; he has
15 broken My covenant." God then said to
Avraham, "As for Sarai your wife, you shall no longer call her
16 Sarai. Her name will be Sara.[32] I will bless her and give you a
son by her. I will bless her so that she shall birth nations; kings
17 of peoples shall descend from her." Avraham fell on his face
and laughed. "Can a hundred-year-old man become a father?"
18 he said to himself. "Can Sara, at ninety, bear a child?" To God
19 Avraham said, "If only Yishmael might live before you!" God
said, "Nonetheless, Sara your wife will bear you a son, and
you shall name him Yitzhak.[33] I will establish My covenant
with him as an everlasting covenant for his descendants after
20 him. As for Yishmael – I have heard you.[34] I will bless him
and make him fertile and multiply him exceedingly. He will
become father of twelve princes, and I will make of him a great
21 nation. But I will establish My covenant[35] with Yitzhak,
22 whom Sara will bear to you this time next year." When He
23 finished speaking with him, God went up from Avraham. On
that very day, Avraham took his son Yishmael, along with all

32 | Meaning "noblewoman."

33 | The name Yitzhak derives from the verb *vayitzhak* (to laugh), referring to Avraham's mirth in verse 17.

34 | The name Yishmael means "God hears" (cf. 16:10).

35 | The covenant affirming that Avraham's progeny will take possession of the land of Canaan.

LANGUAGE

17:15–16 Sara...kings of peoples shall descend from her

The text does not explain the meaning of Sara's name.

It may be connected to the Ugaritic and Hebrew *sar* ("ruler") and Akkadian *sharru* ("king"). In Tanakh, the term *sar* appears together with a king in a few places, for example, "kings will see and rise to their feet, ministers (*sarim*) bow low for the sake of the Lord..." (Is. 49:7). Since God blesses Sara that "kings of peoples shall descend from her" (v. 16), this could be an example of a *midrash shem*, where the name's explanation appears in connection with the name (as in v. 5 in connection with Avraham). The new name indicates that her destiny has changed; instead of being barren, she will be the progenitor of kings. ▪ ZR

כד עָרְלָתָם בְּעֶצֶם הַיּוֹם הַזֶּה כַּאֲשֶׁר דִּבֶּר אִתּוֹ אֱלֹהִים׃ וְאַבְרָהָם מפטיר
כה בֶּן־תִּשְׁעִים וָתֵשַׁע שָׁנָה בְּהִמֹּלוֹ בְּשַׂר עָרְלָתוֹ׃ וְיִשְׁמָעֵאל בְּנוֹ
כו בֶּן־שְׁלֹשׁ עֶשְׂרֵה שָׁנָה בְּהִמֹּלוֹ אֵת בְּשַׂר עָרְלָתוֹ׃ בְּעֶצֶם הַיּוֹם
כז הַזֶּה נִמּוֹל אַבְרָהָם וְיִשְׁמָעֵאל בְּנוֹ׃ וְכָל־אַנְשֵׁי בֵיתוֹ יְלִיד בָּיִת
וּמִקְנַת־כֶּסֶף מֵאֵת בֶּן־נֵכָר נִמֹּלוּ אִתּוֹ׃

those born in his house or acquired with money, every male
in Avraham's household, and circumcised the flesh of their
foreskins as God had instructed him. Avraham was ninety- 24
nine years old when he was circumcised, and his son Yishmael 25
was thirteen. That very day, Avraham and his son Yishmael 26
were circumcised; and all the men of his household, whether 27

NEAR EAST

17:16 I will...give you a son by her

In the ancient Near East, offspring were believed to be provided by the deity, and the theme of a god providing a child to an infertile couple appears in the literature. Sometimes, the deity instructs the man what procedure to undergo to have a child. For example, in the Hittite story *Appu and His Two Sons*, the sun god tells the childless Appu, "Get drunk, go home, and sleep with your wife. The gods will give you a son." In the Mesopotamian story of Etana, Sumerian king of Kish, the god Shamash tells him, "Go along the road, cross the mountain, find a pit and look carefully at what is inside it. An eagle is abandoned down there. It will show you the plant of birth," which will allow him to have children.

Conversely, Avraham is not instructed to do something specific to have a child with Sara; merely to "walk before Me in integrity" (v. 1). This is similar to the Ugaritic *Tale of Aqhat*, where King Dan'el is promised a son by the god El on the basis of his past devotion to the gods and the future devotion of his son, "He will have a son [in his house, a scion] within his palace. [Someone to raise up the stele of] his father's god, in the sanctuary [the votive emblem of his clan]; to send up from the earth [his incense, from the dust the] song of his place."

Of course, once Avraham has a son, he must circumcise him (v. 10) to signify his entrance into the covenant with God. ▪ ZR

↗ Etana seated on a lion-headed eagle, cylinder seal, Kish, 24th to 22nd century BCE

וירא וַיֵּרָא אֵלָיו יְהוָה בְּאֵלֹנֵי מַמְרֵא וְהוּא יֹשֵׁב פֶּתַח־הָאֹהֶל כְּחֹם א יח
הַיּוֹם׃ וַיִּשָּׂא עֵינָיו וַיַּרְא וְהִנֵּה שְׁלֹשָׁה אֲנָשִׁים נִצָּבִים עָלָיו וַיַּרְא ב
וַיָּרָץ לִקְרָאתָם מִפֶּתַח הָאֹהֶל וַיִּשְׁתַּחוּ אָרְצָה׃ וַיֹּאמַר אֲדֹנָי ג
אִם־נָא מָצָאתִי חֵן בְּעֵינֶיךָ אַל־נָא תַעֲבֹר מֵעַל עַבְדֶּךָ׃ יֻקַּח־נָא ד
מְעַט־מַיִם וְרַחֲצוּ רַגְלֵיכֶם וְהִשָּׁעֲנוּ תַּחַת הָעֵץ׃ וְאֶקְחָה פַת־לֶחֶם ה
וְסַעֲדוּ לִבְּכֶם אַחַר תַּעֲבֹרוּ כִּי־עַל־כֵּן עֲבַרְתֶּם עַל־עַבְדְּכֶם
וַיֹּאמְרוּ כֵּן תַּעֲשֶׂה כַּאֲשֶׁר דִּבַּרְתָּ׃ וַיְמַהֵר אַבְרָהָם הָאֹהֱלָה אֶל־ ו
שָׂרָה וַיֹּאמֶר מַהֲרִי שְׁלֹשׁ סְאִים קֶמַח סֹלֶת לוּשִׁי וַעֲשִׂי עֻגוֹת׃
וְאֶל־הַבָּקָר רָץ אַבְרָהָם וַיִּקַּח בֶּן־בָּקָר רַךְ וָטוֹב וַיִּתֵּן אֶל־הַנַּעַר ז
וַיְמַהֵר לַעֲשׂוֹת אֹתוֹ׃ וַיִּקַּח חֶמְאָה וְחָלָב וּבֶן־הַבָּקָר אֲשֶׁר עָשָׂה ח
וַיִּתֵּן לִפְנֵיהֶם וְהוּא עֹמֵד עֲלֵיהֶם תַּחַת הָעֵץ וַיֹּאכֵלוּ׃ וַיֹּאמְרוּ ט
אֵלָיו אַיֵּה שָׂרָה אִשְׁתֶּךָ וַיֹּאמֶר הִנֵּה בָאֹהֶל׃ וַיֹּאמֶר שׁוֹב אָשׁוּב י
אֵלֶיךָ כָּעֵת חַיָּה וְהִנֵּה־בֵן לְשָׂרָה אִשְׁתֶּךָ וְשָׂרָה שֹׁמַעַת פֶּתַח
הָאֹהֶל וְהוּא אַחֲרָיו׃ וְאַבְרָהָם וְשָׂרָה זְקֵנִים בָּאִים בַּיָּמִים חָדַל יא
לִהְיוֹת לְשָׂרָה אֹרַח כַּנָּשִׁים׃ וַתִּצְחַק שָׂרָה בְּקִרְבָּהּ לֵאמֹר אַחֲרֵי יב
בְלֹתִי הָיְתָה־לִּי עֶדְנָה וַאדֹנִי זָקֵן׃ וַיֹּאמֶר יְהוָה אֶל־אַבְרָהָם לָמָּה יג
זֶּה צָחֲקָה שָׂרָה לֵאמֹר הַאַף אֻמְנָם אֵלֵד וַאֲנִי זָקַנְתִּי׃ הֲיִפָּלֵא יד
שני מֵיְהוָה דָּבָר לַמּוֹעֵד אָשׁוּב אֵלֶיךָ כָּעֵת חַיָּה וּלְשָׂרָה בֵן׃ וַתְּכַחֵשׁ טו
שָׂרָה ׀ לֵאמֹר לֹא צָחַקְתִּי כִּי ׀ יָרֵאָה וַיֹּאמֶר ׀ לֹא כִּי צָחָקְתְּ׃
וַיָּקֻמוּ מִשָּׁם הָאֲנָשִׁים וַיַּשְׁקִפוּ עַל־פְּנֵי סְדֹם וְאַבְרָהָם הֹלֵךְ עִמָּם טז
לְשַׁלְּחָם׃ וַיהוָה אָמָר הַמְכַסֶּה אֲנִי מֵאַבְרָהָם אֲשֶׁר אֲנִי עֹשֶׂה׃ יז
וְאַבְרָהָם הָיוֹ יִהְיֶה לְגוֹי גָּדוֹל וְעָצוּם וְנִבְרְכוּ־בוֹ כֹּל גּוֹיֵי הָאָרֶץ׃ יח

home-born or acquired from strangers, were circumcised together with him.

18 1 The LORD appeared to him by the Oaks of Mamre as he was sitting at the entrance to his tent in the
2 heat of the day. Avraham looked up and saw three men standing nearby. The moment he saw them, he ran from the opening of his tent to greet them, and bowed down
3 low to the ground. He said, "My
4 Lord, if I have found favor in your sight, please do not pass your servant by. Let a little water be brought
5 so that you can wash your feet and rest under the tree. Since you are passing by your servant, let me bring
a morsel of bread so that you can be refreshed before you go on your way." They replied, "Do just as you
6 say." Avraham rushed to Sara in the tent and said, "Hurry – three *se'a*[36] of fine flour; knead it and bake
7 bread." Avraham himself ran to the herd and took a tender choice calf and gave it to the young man, who
8 hurried to prepare it. He brought curds and milk and the calf that had been prepared, and set them before
9 them, standing by them as they ate, under the tree. They asked him, "Where is your wife Sara?" "There,
10 in the tent," he replied. Then one of them said, "I will return to you this time next year, and your wife
11 Sara will have a son." Sara was listening at the opening of the tent behind him. Avraham and Sara were
12 already old, advanced in years; the way of women no longer visited Sara. So Sara laughed to herself,
13 saying, "Now that I am worn out, can I have this pleasure? With my lord an old man?" Then the LORD
14 said to Avraham, "Why did Sara laugh and say, 'Can I really have a child, now that I am old?' Is anything
15 beyond the LORD's powers? At the due time next year I will return to you, and Sara will have a son." Sara,
16 because she was afraid, denied it: "I did not laugh," she said. But He said, "Not so. You laughed." The
men got up to leave and looked down toward Sedom. Avraham accompanied them to see them on their

36 | See note on I Kings 18:32.

יט כִּי יְדַעְתִּיו לְמַעַן אֲשֶׁר יְצַוֶּה אֶת־בָּנָיו וְאֶת־בֵּיתוֹ אַחֲרָיו וְשָׁמְרוּ
דֶּרֶךְ יהוה לַעֲשׂוֹת צְדָקָה וּמִשְׁפָּט לְמַעַן הָבִיא יהוה עַל־
כ אַבְרָהָם אֵת אֲשֶׁר־דִּבֶּר עָלָיו: וַיֹּאמֶר יהוה זַעֲקַת סְדֹם וַעֲמֹרָה
כא כִּי־רָבָּה וְחַטָּאתָם כִּי כָבְדָה מְאֹד: אֵרְדָה־נָּא וְאֶרְאֶה הַכְּצַעֲקָתָהּ
כב • הַבָּאָה אֵלַי עָשׂוּ | כָּלָה וְאִם־לֹא אֵדָעָה: וַיִּפְנוּ מִשָּׁם הָאֲנָשִׁים
כג וַיֵּלְכוּ סְדֹמָה וְאַבְרָהָם עוֹדֶנּוּ עֹמֵד לִפְנֵי יהוה: וַיִּגַּשׁ אַבְרָהָם

way. The Lord said, "Shall I hide from Avraham what I am 17
about to do? Avraham is about to become a great and mighty 18
nation, and through him all the nations on earth will be
blessed. For I have chosen him so that he may direct his 19
children and his household after him to keep the way of the
Lord by doing what is right and just, that the Lord may
bring about for Avraham what He spoke of for him." Then the 20
Lord said, "The outcry against Sedom and Amora is great,
and their sin is very grave. I shall go down now and see if they 21
have really done as much as the outcry that has reached Me.
If not, I will know." The men turned from there and went 22 •
toward Sedom, while Avraham still stood before the Lord.

↖ Sun god of heaven (left) with the moon god, relief, Hittite, Yazılıkaya, 13th century BCE

NEAR EAST

18:22–33 Avraham intercedes for Sedom and Amora

Intercession on behalf of others by prayer before God is a significant characteristic of prophecy in the Tanakh. The first examples are Avraham's intercession on behalf of Sedom and Amora here, and on behalf of Avimelekh, king of Gerar (20:7), where God specifically juxtaposes Avraham's functions as a prophet and an intercessor. The archetype of the prophet who intercedes on behalf of the Israelites will become Moshe – at the Golden Calf episode (as in Ex. 32:10–14, 31–32), and several other times in the book of Numbers (Num. 11:2, 14:13–19, 16:22 – with Aharon, 21:7). Moshe will be notably followed by Shmuel (I Sam. 7:8–9, 12:19, 23; compare Jer. 15:1).

In the ancient Near East, prophecy was almost always a one-way street; the perceived role of the prophets was to deliver divine messages, which were usually directed to kings. Kings never requested that any other person intercede on their behalf with gods. However, kings, and others, sometimes requested from minor deities to plead on their behalf with the great gods.

In a few ancient Sumerian laments – *Lament on the Destruction of Ur*, *Lamentation over the Destruction of Sumer and Ur*, and *Lament for Isin* (ca. 2000 BCE) – the chief god or goddess of a destroyed city pleads with the major gods to restore it. Although most Assyrian texts (7th century BCE) relating to intercession speak of minor deities pleading on their own to great gods on behalf of kings, two examples exist of a human – one a priest, another a queen mother – praying on behalf of a king to a god. In one Assyrian cultic ritual concerning persons made ill by evil spirits or demons, cultic officials and, apparently, prophets are instructed to pray on behalf of the ailing individual.

The closest ancient Near Eastern parallel to Avraham's entreaty of God, and the only ancient Near Eastern example we have of an individual pleading with a god on behalf of a people, comes from the Hittite king, Mursili II (reigned 1330–1295 BCE). During a time of widespread plague and enemy invasions, he complains of the gods unleashing indiscriminate disaster on the people and prays via the sun goddess, "O gods, what is this that you have done? You have allowed a plague into Hatti, and the whole of Hatti is dying.... Whoever is a cause of rage and anger to the gods, and whoever is not respectful to the gods, let not the good ones perish with the evil ones. Whether it is a single town, a single house, or a single person, O gods, destroy only that one!" (CTH 376 A ii).

Although both Avraham and Mursili II are concerned that good people should not be killed along with the bad, the latter is speaking about the extensive calamity that has already come upon the Hittites, which he attributes to the gods' unprincipled judgment. While ancient Near Eastern people often viewed the gods as demanding that kings be just, the gods themselves did not always act justly. In contrast, Avraham expects God to act justly (v. 25), but he will now learn that "to keep the way of the Lord by doing what is right and just" (v. 19) goes beyond both his expectations and all of ancient Near Eastern ethics – for not only will God not kill the righteous along with the wicked, but He will save all the wicked if there are but ten righteous people. ▪ JU

וַיֹּאמַר הַאַף תִּסְפֶּה צַדִּיק עִם־רָשָׁע: אוּלַי יֵשׁ חֲמִשִּׁים צַדִּיקִם כד
בְּתוֹךְ הָעִיר הַאַף תִּסְפֶּה וְלֹא־תִשָּׂא לַמָּקוֹם לְמַעַן חֲמִשִּׁים
הַצַּדִּיקִם אֲשֶׁר בְּקִרְבָּהּ: חָלִלָה לְּךָ מֵעֲשֹׂת ׀ כַּדָּבָר הַזֶּה לְהָמִית כה
צַדִּיק עִם־רָשָׁע וְהָיָה כַצַּדִּיק כָּרָשָׁע חָלִלָה לָּךְ הֲשֹׁפֵט כָּל־הָאָרֶץ
לֹא יַעֲשֶׂה מִשְׁפָּט: וַיֹּאמֶר יהוה אִם־אֶמְצָא בִסְדֹם חֲמִשִּׁים כו
צַדִּיקִם בְּתוֹךְ הָעִיר וְנָשָׂאתִי לְכָל־הַמָּקוֹם בַּעֲבוּרָם: וַיַּעַן כז
אַבְרָהָם וַיֹּאמַר הִנֵּה־נָא הוֹאַלְתִּי לְדַבֵּר אֶל־אֲדֹנָי וְאָנֹכִי עָפָר
וָאֵפֶר: אוּלַי יַחְסְרוּן חֲמִשִּׁים הַצַּדִּיקִם חֲמִשָּׁה הֲתַשְׁחִית בַּחֲמִשָּׁה כח
אֶת־כָּל־הָעִיר וַיֹּאמֶר לֹא אַשְׁחִית אִם־אֶמְצָא שָׁם אַרְבָּעִים
וַחֲמִשָּׁה: וַיֹּסֶף עוֹד לְדַבֵּר אֵלָיו וַיֹּאמַר אוּלַי יִמָּצְאוּן שָׁם אַרְבָּעִים כט
וַיֹּאמֶר לֹא אֶעֱשֶׂה בַּעֲבוּר הָאַרְבָּעִים: וַיֹּאמֶר אַל־נָא יִחַר לַאדֹנָי ל

23 Then Avraham stepped forward and said: "Would You really
24 sweep away the righteous with the wicked? What if there are
fifty righteous people in the city? Would You really sweep it
away and not spare the place for the sake of the fifty righteous
25 people in it? Far be it from You to do such a thing – to kill the
righteous with the wicked, treating the righteous like the
wicked. Far be it from You! Shall the judge of all the earth not
26 do justice?" The LORD said, "If I find fifty righteous people in
the city of Sedom, I will spare the whole place for their sake."
27 Then Avraham spoke up again and said, "Now that I have
dared to speak to the Lord, though I am mere dust and ashes,
28 what if the righteous are five less than fifty? Will You destroy
the whole city for the lack of five people?" He said, "If I find
29 forty-five there, I will not destroy it." He spoke to Him yet
again, saying, "What if only forty are found there?" He said,

ARCHAEOLOGY

19:1 In the city gate

In biblical times, the gate and its adjacent open area served as the city's commercial center and place of public assembly, where disputes were settled and justice was administered, as in Amos 5:15, "Hate evil, love good; present justice at your gates."

Archaeological excavations have found stone benches near the gates of Be'er Sheva, Gezer, Lakhish, and Dan. These appear to be where the elders would meet and conduct the affairs of the community. During the negotiations with Avraham for the cave to bury Sara, "Efron the Hittite answered Avraham in the hearing of all the Hittites who had come to the city gate" (Gen. 23:10). Legal documents from Nuzi often conclude with the formula, "The tablet was written after the proclamation in the entrance of the gate."

Since the gate was also the weakest part of the wall surrounding a fortified city, it had to be well secured, with multiple chambers, towers, guard posts, and turning passages, so that the gate house itself was like a small fortress. Since Sedom had recently been involved in a war (Gen. 14), the statement, "Lot was sitting in the city gate" might indicate that he was entrusted with a kind of guard duty, to make sure that hostile elements did not enter the city. When Lot invited the strangers in, this may have aroused the suspicions of the local inhabitants.

It is also possible, though, that Lot, aware as he was of the immorality of the city's inhabitants, might have simply been trying to protect strangers (note the similarity of vv. 1–2 here to 18:2–4). ▪ ZR

↗ Reconstructed city gate, Canaanite, Ashkelon, Middle Bronze Age, 19th century BCE

וַאֲדַבֵּרָה אוּלַי יִמָּצְאוּן שָׁם שְׁלֹשִׁים וַיֹּאמֶר לֹא אֶעֱשֶׂה אִם־
לא אֶמְצָא שָׁם שְׁלֹשִׁים׃ וַיֹּאמֶר הִנֵּה־נָא הוֹאַלְתִּי לְדַבֵּר אֶל־אֲדֹנָי
אוּלַי יִמָּצְאוּן שָׁם עֶשְׂרִים וַיֹּאמֶר לֹא אַשְׁחִית בַּעֲבוּר הָעֶשְׂרִים׃
לב וַיֹּאמֶר אַל־נָא יִחַר לַאדֹנָי וַאֲדַבְּרָה אַךְ־הַפַּעַם אוּלַי יִמָּצְאוּן
לג שָׁם עֲשָׂרָה וַיֹּאמֶר לֹא אַשְׁחִית בַּעֲבוּר הָעֲשָׂרָה׃ וַיֵּלֶךְ יהוה
יט • א כַּאֲשֶׁר כִּלָּה לְדַבֵּר אֶל־אַבְרָהָם וְאַבְרָהָם שָׁב לִמְקֹמוֹ׃ וַיָּבֹאוּ שלישי
שְׁנֵי הַמַּלְאָכִים סְדֹמָה בָּעֶרֶב וְלוֹט יֹשֵׁב בְּשַׁעַר־סְדֹם וַיַּרְא־לוֹט
• ב וַיָּקָם לִקְרָאתָם וַיִּשְׁתַּחוּ אַפַּיִם אָרְצָה׃ וַיֹּאמֶר הִנֶּה נָּא־אֲדֹנַי
סוּרוּ נָא אֶל־בֵּית עַבְדְּכֶם וְלִינוּ וְרַחֲצוּ רַגְלֵיכֶם וְהִשְׁכַּמְתֶּם

"I will refrain for the sake of the forty." Then he said, "Please, 30
may the Lord not be angry, but let me speak. What if only
thirty are found there?" He answered, "I will refrain if I find
thirty there." "Now that I have dared to speak to the Lord," he 31
said, "what if only twenty are found there?" He said, "I will
not destroy, for the sake of the twenty." Then he said, "Please, 32
may the Lord not be angry, but let me speak just once more.
What if only ten are found there?" He said, "I will not destroy,
for the sake of the ten." When the Lord had finished speaking 33
with Avraham, He left. And Avraham went back to his place.
The two angels arrived at Sedom in the evening, while Lot 1 • 19
was sitting in the city gate. Lot saw them, and rose to greet
them, bowing with his face to the ground. He said, "Please, 2 •
my lords, turn aside to your servant's house, stay the night,

Model of a two-story Iron Age Israelite house with a courtyard in front, based on archaeology from the 12th to the 6th century BCE

NEAR EAST

19:2 House...square

Lot had initially "settled in the cities of the plain, pitching his tent near Sedom" (Gen. 13:12), but by now, he has moved into a house inside urban Sedom.

In the Middle Bronze Age, large houses were built with small rectangular rooms surrounding a central courtyard. Finds at Megiddo and Beit El show that over time more rooms were added, and some houses had two floors, using the lower floor as a storage area. Late Bronze Age finds from Beit She'an, Gerar and other sites show that square mud-brick houses also existed in Canaan even before the Iron Age. Their designs parallel Egyptian homes and may be remnants of Egyptian garrisons in the area.

The Biblical Hebrew term *reḥov* means a broad open area (from *raḥav*, meaning "wide"), an open square where groups could assemble: "He appointed battle officers over the people and gathered them to him by the square at the city gate" (II Chr. 32:6) and "All the people assembled together in the open plaza opposite the Water Gate" (Neh. 8:1). ▪ ZR

וַהֲלַכְתֶּם לְדַרְכְּכֶם וַיֹּאמְרוּ לֹּא כִּי בָרְחוֹב נָלִין׃ וַיִּפְצַר־בָּם מְאֹד ג •
וַיָּסֻרוּ אֵלָיו וַיָּבֹאוּ אֶל־בֵּיתוֹ וַיַּעַשׂ לָהֶם מִשְׁתֶּה וּמַצּוֹת אָפָה
וַיֹּאכֵלוּ׃ טֶרֶם יִשְׁכָּבוּ וְאַנְשֵׁי הָעִיר אַנְשֵׁי סְדֹם נָסַבּוּ עַל־הַבַּיִת ד
מִנַּעַר וְעַד־זָקֵן כָּל־הָעָם מִקָּצֶה׃ וַיִּקְרְאוּ אֶל־לוֹט וַיֹּאמְרוּ לוֹ ה
אַיֵּה הָאֲנָשִׁים אֲשֶׁר־בָּאוּ אֵלֶיךָ הַלָּיְלָה הוֹצִיאֵם אֵלֵינוּ וְנֵדְעָה
אֹתָם׃ וַיֵּצֵא אֲלֵהֶם לוֹט הַפֶּתְחָה וְהַדֶּלֶת סָגַר אַחֲרָיו׃ וַיֹּאמַר ו ז
אַל־נָא אַחַי תָּרֵעוּ׃ הִנֵּה־נָא לִי שְׁתֵּי בָנוֹת אֲשֶׁר לֹא־יָדְעוּ אִישׁ ח
אוֹצִיאָה־נָּא אֶתְהֶן אֲלֵיכֶם וַעֲשׂוּ לָהֶן כַּטּוֹב בְּעֵינֵיכֶם רַק
לָאֲנָשִׁים הָאֵל אַל־תַּעֲשׂוּ דָבָר כִּי־עַל־כֵּן בָּאוּ בְּצֵל קֹרָתִי׃
וַיֹּאמְרוּ ׀ גֶּשׁ־הָלְאָה וַיֹּאמְרוּ הָאֶחָד בָּא־לָגוּר וַיִּשְׁפֹּט שָׁפוֹט ט

wash your feet, and then go on your way early in the morning."
• 3 "No," they said, "we will spend the night in the square." But
he was so insistent that they followed him to his house and
came in. He made a feast for them and baked unleavened
4 bread, and they ate. They had not yet gone to bed when all
the townsmen, the men of Sedom – young and old, all the
5 people from every quarter – surrounded the house. They
called to Lot, "Where are the men who came to you tonight?
6 Bring them out to us so that we may know them."[37] Lot went
7 out to speak to them, shutting the door behind him, and said,
8 "My brothers, please do not do this evil. I have two daughters
who have never known a man. Let me bring them out to you;
you may do what you like with them. But do not do anything

37 | That is, violate them.

NEAR EAST

19:3 Unleavened bread

Unleavened bread could be prepared quickly for an unexpected guest, since the dough was baked immediately, without allowing time for it to rise. Similarly, when the woman from Ein Dor prepared a meal quickly for Sha'ul and his servants, we find, "The woman had a fattened calf at home, which she quickly slaughtered; she took flour, kneaded it, and baked unleavened bread" (I Sam. 28:24).

The simplest method of baking unleavened bread was to make a fire on top of a flat stone, then remove the ashes and place the dough on the heated stone, which would then be covered with the ashes. After the dough was baked enough, the ashes would be removed and the flat bread could be eaten. This is the "stone-baked cake" mentioned in I Kings 19:6. ▪ ZR

↗ Flat bread baking on a stone floor in a brick oven

עַתָּה נָרַע לְךָ מֵהֶם וַיִּפְצְרוּ בָאִישׁ בְּלוֹט מְאֹד וַיִּגְּשׁוּ לִשְׁבֹּר
י הַדָּלֶת: וַיִּשְׁלְחוּ הָאֲנָשִׁים אֶת־יָדָם וַיָּבִיאוּ אֶת־לוֹט אֲלֵיהֶם
יא הַבָּיְתָה וְאֶת־הַדֶּלֶת סָגָרוּ: וְאֶת־הָאֲנָשִׁים אֲשֶׁר־פֶּתַח הַבַּיִת
יב הִכּוּ בַּסַּנְוֵרִים מִקָּטֹן וְעַד־גָּדוֹל וַיִּלְאוּ לִמְצֹא הַפָּתַח: וַיֹּאמְרוּ
הָאֲנָשִׁים אֶל־לוֹט עֹד מִי־לְךָ פֹה חָתָן וּבָנֶיךָ וּבְנֹתֶיךָ וְכֹל אֲשֶׁר־
יג לְךָ בָּעִיר הוֹצֵא מִן־הַמָּקוֹם: כִּי־מַשְׁחִתִים אֲנַחְנוּ אֶת־הַמָּקוֹם
הַזֶּה כִּי־גָדְלָה צַעֲקָתָם אֶת־פְּנֵי יהוה וַיְשַׁלְּחֵנוּ יהוה לְשַׁחֲתָהּ:

to these men, for they have come under the protection of my
roof." "Get out of our way," they replied. "This fellow came 9
here as a migrant and now he is setting himself up as a judge!
We will treat you worse than them." They pressed hard against
Lot and moved forward to break down the door. But the men 10
inside reached out and pulled Lot back into the house and
shut the door behind him. Then they struck the men at the 11
door, young and old, with blindness so that they wore
themselves out trying in vain to find the door. The visitors 12
said to Lot, "Who else do you have here – children-in-law,
sons, daughters, or anyone else in the city? Bring them out of

NEAR EAST

19:11 Struck...with blindness

The word used here for blindness (*sanverim*) is a rare term, used again in Tanakh only when the Aramean army was struck by blindness by God in response to Elisha's prayer (II Kings 6:18). This biblical term for possible temporary blindness is related to the Akkadian *sinlurma*, a medical term used for the partial blindness experienced by someone who can either see during the day but not at night, or the opposite. The usual cause of night blindness is vitamin A deficiency, which is why the ancient Assyrian medical texts prescribed eating liver, which has high levels of vitamin A, for this condition. Reduced daylight vision can result from corneal scars or infections that can distort the higher levels of light in the daytime.

Blindness appears as a form of divine punishment in Deuteronomy 28:28–29. It also appears similarly in curses from ancient Near Eastern cultures. For example, in the Hittite *Soldier's Oath* (late 15th century BCE), "Who transgresses these oaths and takes deceptive action against the king of Hatti, and sets (his) eyes upon the land of Hatti as an enemy, may these oath deities seize him and [may they] blind his army too" (§3). Similarly, in the Ugaritic *Tale of Aqhat*, Dan'el curses the inhabitants of the three towns near where his son was murdered, "May Baal make you blind, at this very moment and forever more, now and for all generations" (4, line 5).

Here, however, the blindness caused by the angels is not a punishment, but merely a device to prevent the townspeople from carrying out their evil desires. ▪ ZR

Blind musician playing a harp, tomb painting, tomb of the Egyptian scribe Nakht, Thebes, 15th century BCE

וַיֵּצֵא לוֹט וַיְדַבֵּר ׀ אֶל־חֲתָנָיו ׀ לֹקְחֵי בְנֹתָיו וַיֹּאמֶר קוּמוּ צְּאוּ יד
מִן־הַמָּקוֹם הַזֶּה כִּי־מַשְׁחִית יהוה אֶת־הָעִיר וַיְהִי כִמְצַחֵק בְּעֵינֵי
חֲתָנָיו׃ וּכְמוֹ הַשַּׁחַר עָלָה וַיָּאִיצוּ הַמַּלְאָכִים בְּלוֹט לֵאמֹר קוּם טו
קַח אֶת־אִשְׁתְּךָ וְאֶת־שְׁתֵּי בְנֹתֶיךָ הַנִּמְצָאֹת פֶּן־תִּסָּפֶה בַּעֲוֺן
הָעִיר׃ וַיִּתְמַהְמָהּ ׀ וַיַּחֲזִיקוּ הָאֲנָשִׁים בְּיָדוֹ וּבְיַד־אִשְׁתּוֹ וּבְיַד טז
שְׁתֵּי בְנֹתָיו בְּחֶמְלַת יהוה עָלָיו וַיֹּצִאֻהוּ וַיַּנִּחֻהוּ מִחוּץ לָעִיר׃
וַיְהִי כְהוֹצִיאָם אֹתָם הַחוּצָה וַיֹּאמֶר הִמָּלֵט עַל־נַפְשֶׁךָ אַל־תַּבִּיט יז
אַחֲרֶיךָ וְאַל־תַּעֲמֹד בְּכָל־הַכִּכָּר הָהָרָה הִמָּלֵט פֶּן־תִּסָּפֶה׃ וַיֹּאמֶר יח
לוֹט אֲלֵהֶם אַל־נָא אֲדֹנָי׃ הִנֵּה־נָא מָצָא עַבְדְּךָ חֵן בְּעֵינֶיךָ וַתַּגְדֵּל יט
חַסְדְּךָ אֲשֶׁר עָשִׂיתָ עִמָּדִי לְהַחֲיוֹת אֶת־נַפְשִׁי וְאָנֹכִי לֹא אוּכַל
לְהִמָּלֵט הָהָרָה פֶּן־תִּדְבָּקַנִי הָרָעָה וָמַתִּי׃ הִנֵּה־נָא הָעִיר הַזֹּאת כ
קְרֹבָה לָנוּס שָׁמָּה וְהִוא מִצְעָר אִמָּלְטָה נָּא שָׁמָּה הֲלֹא מִצְעָר
הִוא וּתְחִי נַפְשִׁי׃ וַיֹּאמֶר אֵלָיו הִנֵּה נָשָׂאתִי פָנֶיךָ גַּם לַדָּבָר הַזֶּה כא רביעי
לְבִלְתִּי הָפְכִּי אֶת־הָעִיר אֲשֶׁר דִּבַּרְתָּ׃ מַהֵר הִמָּלֵט שָׁמָּה כִּי לֹא כב
אוּכַל לַעֲשׂוֹת דָּבָר עַד־בֹּאֲךָ שָׁמָּה עַל־כֵּן קָרָא שֵׁם־הָעִיר צוֹעַר׃
הַשֶּׁמֶשׁ יָצָא עַל־הָאָרֶץ וְלוֹט בָּא צֹעֲרָה׃ וַיהוה הִמְטִיר עַל־ כג כד
סְדֹם וְעַל־עֲמֹרָה גָּפְרִית וָאֵשׁ מֵאֵת יהוה מִן־הַשָּׁמָיִם׃ וַיַּהֲפֹךְ כה
אֶת־הֶעָרִים הָאֵל וְאֵת כָּל־הַכִּכָּר וְאֵת כָּל־יֹשְׁבֵי הֶעָרִים וְצֶמַח
הָאֲדָמָה׃ וַתַּבֵּט אִשְׁתּוֹ מֵאַחֲרָיו וַתְּהִי נְצִיב מֶלַח׃ וַיַּשְׁכֵּם כו כז
אַבְרָהָם בַּבֹּקֶר אֶל־הַמָּקוֹם אֲשֶׁר־עָמַד שָׁם אֶת־פְּנֵי יהוה׃

13 here, because we are about to destroy this place. So great is the outcry against them before the LORD that
14 He has sent us to destroy it." Lot went out and spoke to his sons-in-law, the men who were betrothed to his
daughters, and told them, "Get up and leave this place: the LORD is about to destroy the city!" But his sons-
15 in-law thought him laughable. As dawn was breaking, the angels hurried Lot. "Get up," they said. "Take your
16 wife and your two daughters here, or you will be swept away amid the city's sin." Still he hesitated. So the
men seized him, his wife, and his two daughters by the hand and led them safely outside the city, for the
17 LORD had mercy upon him. As soon as they had brought them out, one said, "Run for your life. Do not look
18 back. Do not stop anywhere in the plain. Flee to the mountains or you will be swept away." But Lot said to
19 them, "No, my lords, please. Your servant has found favor in your eyes, and you have done me great kindness
20 in saving my life. But I cannot flee to the mountains; the disaster would overtake me, and I would die.[38] There
is a town here close enough for refuge. It is small. Let me flee there – is it not small? – so that I might survive."
21 "Very well," he said, "I will grant this request also; I will not overthrow the town of which you speak. But
23 hurry. Flee there, because I cannot do anything until you reach it." That is why the town is called Tzoar.[39] By
24 the time Lot reached Tzoar, the sun had risen over the land. Then the LORD rained down sulfur and fire on
25 Sedom and Amora. Out of the heavens it came from the LORD. He overthrew those cities, and the whole
26 plain, and all the cities' inhabitants, and the vegetation on the land. But Lot's wife looked back – and she

38 | Lot does not regard the mountains as a safe haven from the impending source of destruction.

39 | Tzoar resonates with *mitzar* (small) in verse 20.

ARCHAEOLOGY

19:24–25 Destruction of the cities of the plain

Archaeology has yet to discover direct evidence for the cataclysmic destruction of the cities of the plain, and thus it is difficult to translate the biblical account into contemporary terms.

Some scholars propose an earthquake as the most plausible cause of the destruction. Although there is currently no evidence of a major earthquake during the relevant period, the Dead Sea Rift, a fault system at the boundary between the African Plate to the west and the Arabian Plate to the east, is a place where earthquakes frequently occur.

The most recent major earthquake in the area was in 1927, with its epicenter in Yeriḥo, measuring 6.5 on the Richter scale (categorized as a strong earthquake that can damage even modern well-built structures). Often, geologic fissures or volcanic eruptions caused by earthquakes allow the eruption of petroleum and other noxious gases from within the earth. If these or the chemicals of the area's mineral salts are ignited, a catastrophic fire could result. This may be hinted to in Deuteronomy 29:22, "all its soil a burning waste of sulfur and salt, nothing planted, nothing sprouting, no vegetation growing on it, like the ruins of Sedom and Amora." The exact location of these cities is unclear, and to date, no archaeological evidence has been found of these destroyed cities.

Another suggestion, hotly debated among scholars, is that the destruction was produced by an exploding meteor causing a devastating airburst in the area, although the evidence for a cosmic phenomenon like this occurring there in the Middle Bronze Age is disputed. ▪ ZR

GEOGRAPHY

19:26 The pillar of salt

Lot's wife's punishment seems unusual, reading like an etiological story explaining the salt rock formations in the area of the Dead Sea, some of which appear generally similar to the shape of a person. Josephus writes, "I have seen it, and it remains at this day" (*Antiquities*, 1.203). The earliest reference to this phenomenon outside of Genesis is from the 1st century BCE apocryphal Book of Wisdom 10:7, "a standing pillar of salt is a monument of an unbelieving soul." Today, a pillar of salt on Mount Sedom, near the southwestern part of the Dead Sea, is popularly called "Lot's Wife".

Bereshit Rabba 50:4 explains that she received this punishment for her refusal to provide salt for the guests that Lot would bring home, adhering to the laws of Sedom prohibiting hospitality to strangers.

The motif of punishment for looking back when fleeing a place of doom also appears in the Greek legend of Orpheus and Eurydice, where Orpheus turned back when escaping Hades, thus dooming Eurydice. ▪ ZR

Rock outcropping called "Lot's Wife", Mount Sedom, near the Dead Sea

וַיַּשְׁקֵף עַל־פְּנֵי סְדֹם וַעֲמֹרָה וְעַל כָּל־פְּנֵי אֶרֶץ הַכִּכָּר וַיַּרְא וְהִנֵּה כח
עָלָה קִיטֹר הָאָרֶץ כְּקִיטֹר הַכִּבְשָׁן׃ וַיְהִי בְּשַׁחֵת אֱלֹהִים אֶת־ כט
עָרֵי הַכִּכָּר וַיִּזְכֹּר אֱלֹהִים אֶת־אַבְרָהָם וַיְשַׁלַּח אֶת־לוֹט מִתּוֹךְ
הַהֲפֵכָה בַּהֲפֹךְ אֶת־הֶעָרִים אֲשֶׁר־יָשַׁב בָּהֵן לוֹט׃ וַיַּעַל לוֹט ל
מִצּוֹעַר וַיֵּשֶׁב בָּהָר וּשְׁתֵּי בְנֹתָיו עִמּוֹ כִּי יָרֵא לָשֶׁבֶת בְּצוֹעַר וַיֵּשֶׁב
בַּמְּעָרָה הוּא וּשְׁתֵּי בְנֹתָיו׃ וַתֹּאמֶר הַבְּכִירָה אֶל־הַצְּעִירָה אָבִינוּ לא
זָקֵן וְאִישׁ אֵין בָּאָרֶץ לָבוֹא עָלֵינוּ כְּדֶרֶךְ כָּל־הָאָרֶץ׃ לְכָה נַשְׁקֶה לב
אֶת־אָבִינוּ יַיִן וְנִשְׁכְּבָה עִמּוֹ וּנְחַיֶּה מֵאָבִינוּ זָרַע׃ וַתַּשְׁקֶיןָ אֶת־ לג
אֲבִיהֶן יַיִן בַּלַּיְלָה הוּא וַתָּבֹא הַבְּכִירָה וַתִּשְׁכַּב אֶת־אָבִיהָ וְלֹא־
יָדַע בְּשִׁכְבָהּ וּבְקוּמָהּ׃ וַיְהִי מִמָּחֳרָת וַתֹּאמֶר הַבְּכִירָה אֶל־ לד
הַצְּעִירָה הֵן־שָׁכַבְתִּי אֶמֶשׁ אֶת־אָבִי נַשְׁקֶנּוּ יַיִן גַּם־הַלַּיְלָה וּבֹאִי

27 was turned into a pillar of salt. Avraham rose early the next
morning and returned to the place where he had stood before
28 the Lord. He looked down toward Sedom and Amora and
all the land of the plain, and he saw thick smoke rising from
29 the land like smoke from a kiln. So it was, that when God
destroyed the cities of the plain, He remembered Avraham
and brought Lot out of the overthrow that overturned the
30 cities where Lot had lived. Lot went up from Tzoar and settled
in the hills together with his two daughters because he was
afraid to stay in Tzoar. He and his two daughters settled in a
31 cave. The elder said to the younger, "Our father is old, and
there is no man left on earth to come to us in the normal way
32 of the world. Let us get our father drunk with wine and then
sleep with him, so that we may raise a new generation through
33 our father." That night they gave their father wine to drink.
Then the elder daughter went in and slept with him. He was
34 unaware when she lay down and when she arose. The next
day, the elder said to the younger, "Last night I slept with my

NEAR EAST

19:37–38 Moav and Amon

The Amonites were an ancient Semitic-speaking nation occupying the territory east of the Jordan River, between the valleys of Arnon and Yabok, in modern-day Jordan. Their chief city was Raba (Rabat Amon), site of the modern city Amman, which preserves the ancient name. The constant harassment of the Israelite communities east of the Jordan by the Amonites was part of the impetus behind the unification of the tribes under Sha'ul (as recorded in I Sam. 11:1–15; 12:12), eventually resulting in the formation of the Israelite kingdom. During the reign of King David, the Amonites caused a war in which all their own cities were conquered, and the inhabitants were killed or put to forced labor under David (II Sam. 10:1–19, 12:26–31).

The existence of Amon is attested to in Neo-Assyrian documents dating back to the time of Tiglat-Pileser III (ruled 745–727 BCE), which mention tribute paid by the king of Bit-Amon, and the "sons of Amon" who were ruled by the Assyrians. Documentary evidence of Amonites and Amonite kings is found until the time of Nevukhadnetzar, when they ceased to exist as a significant political entity.

Moav was an ancient kingdom located in the mountainous area on the east bank of the Dead Sea, in modern-day Jordan. In Tanakh, the Moabites are often described as being in conflict with the Israelites (Judges 3:12–30; II Sam. 8:2; II Kings 13:20).

The existence of the Moabite kingdom is attested to by multiple archaeological findings, the most notable being the Mesha Stele (ca. 840 BCE), a Canaanite inscription which tells how Khemosh, the god of Moav, was angry with the Moabites and so he abandoned them and left them to be ruled by Israel. However, later Khemosh assisted King Mesha of Moav to throw off the yoke of Israel and restore their lands. The stele states that "the men of Gad lived in the land of Atarot from ancient times," attesting to the presence of Israelites in the area of Moav (Atarot has been convincingly identified as Khirbet Ataruz, about 15 kilometers/9 miles from Divon, Mesha ov Moav's birthplace). An altar from the 9th century BCE was found there, which has a Moabite inscription written in Old Hebrew script (which was also used by the Moabites).

The Tanakh mentions both King Mesha and his rebellion against Israel (II Kings 3:4–5) and the Moabite god Khemosh (Num. 21:29; Judges 11:24; Jer. 48:7, 13).

Moav disappeared from the historical record during the Persian period. During that time, their territory was overrun by tribes from northern Arabia. Nehemiah 4:1 mentions Arabs and Amonites as enemies of the Jews rather than Moabites. The Amonites are recorded as enemies of the Israelites as late as the Hasmonean period (I Mac. 5:6–7). ▪ ZR

לה שִׁכְבִי עִמּוֹ וּנְחַיֶּה מֵאָבִינוּ זָרַע׃ וַתַּשְׁקֶיןָ גַּם בַּלַּיְלָה הַהוּא אֶת־
אֲבִיהֶן יָיִן וַתָּקָם הַצְּעִירָה וַתִּשְׁכַּב עִמּוֹ וְלֹא־יָדַע בְּשִׁכְבָהּ
לו לז • וּבְקֻמָהּ׃ וַתַּהֲרֶיןָ שְׁתֵּי בְנוֹת־לוֹט מֵאֲבִיהֶן׃ וַתֵּלֶד הַבְּכִירָה בֵּן
לח וַתִּקְרָא שְׁמוֹ מוֹאָב הוּא אֲבִי־מוֹאָב עַד־הַיּוֹם׃ וְהַצְּעִירָה גַם־
הִוא יָלְדָה בֵּן וַתִּקְרָא שְׁמוֹ בֶּן־עַמִּי הוּא אֲבִי בְנֵי־עַמּוֹן עַד־הַיּוֹם׃

father. Let us get him to drink wine again tonight, then you
go in and sleep with him. So may we preserve our family line
through our father." So that night they got their father to drink 35
wine again, and the younger went and slept with him. And
he was unaware when she lay down and when she arose. And 36
so both of Lot's daughters became pregnant by their father.
The elder had a son, whom she named Moav.[40] He is the 37 •
ancestor of the Moabites of today. The younger also had a son, 38
whom she named Ben Ami.[41] And he is the ancestor of the
Amonites of today.

40 | The name Moav resonates with *me'av* (from father).

41 | Literally "son of my kin."

Mesha Stele (reproduction), Diban (ancient Divon), ca. 840 BCE

↗ The green Hills of Shomron, from Yitzhar

The towns that formed the background to the patriarchs' activities lay along this road. From north to south they are: Dotan, Shekhem-Alon Moreh, Luz-Beit El; Ai, Efrat (Beit Leḥem), Migdal Eder, Alonei Mamre, Kiryat Arba (Ḥevron), and Be'er Sheva.

The central hill country, referred to in the Tanakh as "the hill country," "the hill country of Israel," and "that good hill country"' was the center of the patriarchs' activity according to the book of Genesis.

The southern part of this road passes between Ḥevron and Beit El, along the national watershed, while its northern part winds its way through wadis and valleys in Shomron. At Shekhem the road forks at Mount Eival, the highest of the mountains in the Shomron. The eastern branch descends to the Tirtza Valley, and from there ascends to Tubas (biblical Tebetz), and to the Dotan Valley. The western branch descends along Naḥal Shekhem to just below the city of Shomron (Sebaste), and there turns north to the Dotan Valley. A veiled reference to the fork in the main road at Shekhem appears in the description of Yosef wandering there while looking for his brothers (Gen. 37:15–17).

In addition to the north-south road, roads crossed the mountain region from east to west, and at least two of them are described in the stories of the patriarchs. The northern one passed through the Dotan Valley (see "Dotan and the Ishmaelite caravan" on page 226). Farther to the south another east-west road ascended to Shekhem from the Sukkot Valley. A hint to this road may be found in the description of the return of Yaakov to Canaan: Yaakov "arrived safely [*shalem*] at the town of Shekhem" (Gen. 33:18).

Below is a list of places, from north to south, mentioned in the patriarchal narratives, along with a reference to the articles related to those sites.

- Dotan, identified as Tel Dotan: see "Dotan and the Ishmaelite caravan" on page 226.
- Shekhem, situated at Tell Balata: see "Shekhem and the patriarchs" on page 78.
- Beit El and Ai are identified with the villages of Beitin and Deir Dibwan respectively: see "Beit El and Ai" on page 80.
- The place of Raḥel's death and burial: see "Raḥel's grave" on page 218.
- Ḥevron was situated at Tell Rumeida, and the field of the Cave of the Patriarchs is identified in the adjacent valley to the northeast, the Ḥevron Valley (Gen. 37:14: see "Ḥevron" on page 86.

Other sites that are mentioned in the narratives are as follows.

The location of Migdal Eder (Gen. 35:21) is identified south of Beith Leḥem, in the area of Gush Etzion.

Alonei Mamre is traditionally identified with the Roman site Ramath el-Halil, north of Ḥevron, and it is possible that the name is preserved in the nearby Persian-period site Khirbet Nimra. ▪ DR

A geographical overview of the patriarchal narratives

The central hill country, referred to in the Tanakh as "the hill country" (Deut. 1:7, and elsewhere), "the hill country of Israel" (Josh. 11:16), and "that good hill country" (Deut. 3:25), was the center of the patriarchs' activity according to the book of Genesis. Their actions also provide the background for the later conquest of the land by Yehoshua, its settlement, and the eventual rise of the Israelite kingdoms, whose capitals were at the heart of this area (Shilo, Givat Sha'ul, Ḥevron, Jerusalem, Shekhem, Tirtza, and Shomron).

The central hill country is a long ridge along the center of Israel – about 140 kilometers (87 miles) long and 30–50 kilometers (20–30 miles) wide, with summits that reach about 1,000 meters (about 3300 feet). In the south, the hills of Yehuda form a high, fairly continuous plateau, while in the north, the hills of the Shomron are characterized by a varied topography, with high mountains intersected by wide valleys. The valleys of the Shomron are suitable for the development of flourishing agriculture and a prosperous trade network, providing fertile ground (literally and figuratively) for the growth of cities and kingdoms larger and stronger than the ones in Yehuda.

The southern part of the hill country is part of the biblical Negev (see, for example, Josh. 15:19; Judges 1:16), while to its east lie the deserts of Yehuda. This proximity of mountains and desert ensured contact between nomadic pastoralists and sedentary communities since early history, as in the encounters between the patriarchs and the residents of Shekhem and Ḥevron (Gen. 23, 33–34, 37).

The southern part of the hill country is relatively dry (200–300 millimeters annual rainfall), in contrast to the high annual rainfall in its northern part (500–600 millimeters). The difference in rainfall led to the migration of the shepherds with their flocks from the hills of Yehuda to Shomron in the hot summer months. This phenomenon, familiar from antiquity and until today, is reflected in the migration of the sons of Yaakov from Ḥevron to Shekhem and Dotan in search of pasture for their flocks (Gen. 37:12–14).

In biblical times, and particularly in the time of the patriarchs, widespread forests covered the hill country regions (see for example Josh. 17), and they were home to predators such as bears and lions, which have since been hunted out of the Middle East. This zoological reality is reflected in the description of the sale of Yosef, and the reaction of Yaakov on seeing Yosef's blood-stained shirt: "A wild animal must have eaten him! Yosef has been torn limb from limb!" (Gen. 37:33).

A main road, called "the highway leading from Beit El to Shekhem" in the Tanakh (e.g., Judges 21:19) and still in use today, crosses the hill country from north to south. Nowadays it is known as "the Patriarchs' Road" or "the Mountain Road" (Road 60).

Desert of Yehuda, view over the Old City of Jerusalem

כ א וַיִּסַּע מִשָּׁם אַבְרָהָם אַרְצָה הַנֶּגֶב וַיֵּשֶׁב בֵּין־קָדֵשׁ וּבֵין שׁוּר וַיָּגָר
ב בִּגְרָר׃ וַיֹּאמֶר אַבְרָהָם אֶל־שָׂרָה אִשְׁתּוֹ אֲחֹתִי הִוא וַיִּשְׁלַח
ג אֲבִימֶלֶךְ מֶלֶךְ גְּרָר וַיִּקַּח אֶת־שָׂרָה׃ וַיָּבֹא אֱלֹהִים אֶל־אֲבִימֶלֶךְ
בַּחֲלוֹם הַלָּיְלָה וַיֹּאמֶר לוֹ הִנְּךָ מֵת עַל־הָאִשָּׁה אֲשֶׁר־לָקַחְתָּ

20 1 Avraham then journeyed on to the Negev region, settling
between Kadesh and Shur. For a while he lived as a stranger
2 in Gerar. There Avraham said of his wife Sara, "She is my
sister." Avimelekh, king of Gerar, sent for Sara and took her
3 as his own. But God came to Avimelekh in a dream one
night and told him, "You will die because of the woman you

GEOGRAPHY

20:1 Location of Gerar

The identification of Tel Haror as ancient Gerar has been widely, although not universally, accepted based on three principal factors: its location, size, and the nature of its archaeological finds. Situated on the northern bank of Naḥal Gerar in the western Negev desert and strategically located along the main road from Aza to Be'er Sheva, Tel Haror's location is consistent with biblical descriptions of ancient Gerar. Its large size (40 acres), especially compared to other sites in the Negev, further attests to its significance.

The most compelling evidence, however, is the archaeological discoveries themselves. Surveys in the 1950s followed by excavations in the 1980s and early 1990s have yielded a wealth of material finds and structural remains spanning 1,500 years from the Middle Bronze Age (the time of the patriarchs) through the Persian period, including some associated with Iron Age Philistine culture. It should be noted that the Arabic name for the site, Tell Abu Hureyra, does not shed any light on the site's ancient name, as it derives simply from the name of a local Bedouin sheikh buried on the summit of the tell. However, the nearby site of Abu Jerrar, appearing in the 1910 British map of the Negev, does preserve the ancient name Gerar. Also, Tel Haror fits the location of Gerar according to the Onomasticon of Eusebius.

Beginning in the Middle Bronze Age, the overall picture of the site is of a large, well-fortified settlement (with a moat and glacis) with dense occupational remains and monumental architecture consistent with state-level society. Politically, Middle Bronze Age Tel Haror fell within the jurisdiction (at least by the 17th century BCE) of the southern Canaanite kingdom of Sharuhen (also referenced in Josh. 19:6) with its center nearby at either Tell el-Ajjul or Tel Sharuhen, or perhaps even at Tel Haror itself. This political bloc represented the southernmost extension of permanent settlement within Canaan and is noted for its ties to northern Sinai and the Hyksos kingdom in Egypt. ▪ JK

↗ Tel Haror, consensus location of Gerar, aerial view from the southeast

ד וְהִוא בְּעֻלַת בָּעַל׃ וַאֲבִימֶלֶךְ לֹא קָרַב אֵלֶיהָ וַיֹּאמַר אֲדֹנָי הֲגוֹי
ה גַּם־צַדִּיק תַּהֲרֹג׃ הֲלֹא הוּא אָמַר־לִי אֲחֹתִי הִוא וְהִיא־גַם־הִוא
ו אָמְרָה אָחִי הוּא בְּתָם־לְבָבִי וּבְנִקְיֹן כַּפַּי עָשִׂיתִי זֹאת׃ וַיֹּאמֶר
אֵלָיו הָאֱלֹהִים בַּחֲלֹם גַּם אָנֹכִי יָדַעְתִּי כִּי בְתָם־לְבָבְךָ עָשִׂיתָ

have taken. She is already married." Avimelekh had not gone 4
near her, so he said, "Lord, would You destroy an innocent
nation? Did he not tell me, 'She is my sister'? Did she not 5
say, 'He is my brother'? I have acted from an innocent heart,
with clean hands." Then, in the dream, God said to him, "I 6
too knew that you acted from an innocent heart, and so I

NEAR EAST

20:2 She is my sister

See "The sister-wives" on page 82. ▪ ZR

LANGUAGE

20:2 Avimelekh

The name Avimelekh (literally, "my father is king") appears in Tanakh as the personal name of a son of Gidon (Judges 9) and a priest in David's court (I Chr. 18:16). It is a common West Semitic name, appearing as the Ugaritic *abmlk*. The *Amarna letters* include ten letters written to Pharaoh Akhenaten from a vassal, Abimilki, Prince (*surru*) of Tyre (ca. 1347 BCE), whose father was king of Tyre before him. This appellation is also the name given in Psalms 34:1 for the Philistine king called Akhish in I Samuel 21. ▪ ZR

NEAR EAST

20:6 Adultery

Avimelekh protests his innocence in verses. 4–5, indicating that he accepts the fact that adultery is a sin, an attitude reflected in ancient Near Eastern law collections. Yosef also presents this ethical perspective to Potifar's wife: "you are his wife. How could I do so great a wrong? It would be a sin against God!" (Gen. 39:9).

Adultery is labeled an abomination (*toeva*) in Leviticus 18:26 and Ezekiel 22:11 and is also described as one of the sins that defile the land of Israel, causing its inhabitants to be vomited out (Lev. 18:20, 24).

Here, in verse 9, it is called a *ḥataah gedola* (literally, "a great sin," but translated here as "onerous guilt"), a term similar to those found in other societies of the ancient Near East. In the Egyptian *Story of Two Brothers* (ca. 1200 BCE), when the older brother's wife attempts to persuade the younger brother to commit adultery, he responds "What is this great crime which you have said to me?" (iv:1). This term is also used in four Egyptian marriage contracts (ca. 850 BCE), which, from the context, are discussing adultery. In the Akkadian documents concerning the expelled wife of Ammittamru II, king of Ugarit (ruled 1260–1235 BCE), it is stated that she committed a great sin (*ḥitta raba*), which seems to be adultery.

Note that in Tanakh, the other occurrences of this phrase are all in the context of idolatry (Ex. 32:21, 30, 31; II Kings 17:21), which is metaphorically described as adultery in a number of places, most famously in Hosea chapters 2–3. ▪ ZR

Ramesses II killing his enemies before the war god, stele of Ramesses II, Tyre, 13th century BCE

Egyptian marriage contract, Demotic script, Elephantine, 535 BCE

זֹאת וָאֶחְשֹׂךְ גַּם־אָנֹכִי אוֹתְךָ מֵחֲטוֹ־לִי עַל־כֵּן לֹא־נְתַתִּיךָ לִנְגֹּעַ
ז אֵלֶיהָ׃ וְעַתָּה הָשֵׁב אֵשֶׁת־הָאִישׁ כִּי־נָבִיא הוּא וְיִתְפַּלֵּל בַּעַדְךָ
וֶחְיֵה וְאִם־אֵינְךָ מֵשִׁיב דַּע כִּי־מוֹת תָּמוּת אַתָּה וְכָל־אֲשֶׁר־לָךְ׃
ח וַיַּשְׁכֵּם אֲבִימֶלֶךְ בַּבֹּקֶר וַיִּקְרָא לְכָל־עֲבָדָיו וַיְדַבֵּר אֶת־כָּל־
ט הַדְּבָרִים הָאֵלֶּה בְּאָזְנֵיהֶם וַיִּירְאוּ הָאֲנָשִׁים מְאֹד׃ וַיִּקְרָא אֲבִימֶלֶךְ
לְאַבְרָהָם וַיֹּאמֶר לוֹ מֶה־עָשִׂיתָ לָּנוּ וּמֶה־חָטָאתִי לָךְ כִּי־הֵבֵאתָ
עָלַי וְעַל־מַמְלַכְתִּי חֲטָאָה גְדֹלָה מַעֲשִׂים אֲשֶׁר לֹא־יֵעָשׂוּ עָשִׂיתָ

kept you from sinning against Me. That is why I did not let
7 you touch her. But now, give back the man's wife. He is a
prophet. He will pray for you and you will live. But if you do
not give her back, know that you and all your people are to
8 die." Early the next morning, Avimelekh summoned all his
9 servants and told them all this – they were very afraid. Then
Avimelekh summoned Avraham and said, "What have you
done to us? What wrong have I done you? Why have you
brought such onerous guilt upon me and my kingdom? You

NEAR EAST

20:7 Prophet as intercessor

This is the first appearance in Tanakh of the word *navi*. The literal meaning in Hebrew could be "spokesman," which would fit God's description to Moshe of Aharon's role in the interactions with Pharaoh, "I am making you now like a god to Pharaoh, and your brother Aharon will be your prophet (*neviekha*)" (Ex. 7:1). This would indicate that the *navi* is God's spokesman to the people.

The Akkadian cognate *nabu* as a verb has the meaning "to proclaim," but as an adjective also has the sense of "called," which can be used for someone called by the gods. For example, "Hammurabi was called (*nabiu*) by Anu [king of the gods]."

In this verse, *navi* implies the role of intercessor, a role Avraham had played previously with Sedom in Genesis 18:23–32. Jeremiah 15:1 gives Moshe and Shmuel as the primary examples of the *navi* as intercessor, "Even if Moshe and Shmuel were to stand before Me, I would not not show favor to this people." Moshe famously took on this role on behalf of the entire Israelite people at the Golden Calf episode (Ex. 32:10–14, 31–32) and on a number of other occasions (Num. 11:1–3, 14:13–19, 16:22, 21:7). Shmuel interceded on behalf of the Israelites in the face of the Philistine threat (I Sam. 7:8–9), at his farewell speech (I Sam. 12:19, 23), and upon being told that God regretted making Sha'ul king (I Sam. 15:11). ▪ ZR

Assyrian king Ashurnasirpal II performs a ritual before a sacred tree, with a wise winged assistant (*apkallu*) behind him, Northwest Palace Throne Room, Nimrud, 9th century BCE

י עִמָּדִי: וַיֹּאמֶר אֲבִימֶלֶךְ אֶל־אַבְרָהָם מָה רָאִיתָ כִּי עָשִׂיתָ אֶת־
יא הַדָּבָר הַזֶּה: וַיֹּאמֶר אַבְרָהָם כִּי אָמַרְתִּי רַק אֵין־יִרְאַת אֱלֹהִים

have done to me that which should never be done. What 10
were you thinking of," asked Avimelekh, "that you did such a
thing?" Avraham replied, "I thought, 'There is no fear of God 11

NEAR EAST

20:11 Gerar's polytheistic religion

A cultic area has been found at Gerar (Tel Haror) that sheds light on Canaanite ritual practice. While many aspects would not have been *a priori* objectionable, the polytheistic context assumedly rendered the entire ritual experience objectionable to Avraham and precluded his participation while residing in Gerar.

First of all, the sacred area was set apart from the main residential and administrative areas of the settlement by its location in the southwestern part of the town overlooking Naḥal Gerar. The most prominent feature of the sacred landscape was a thick, mudbrick-walled, fortress-like temple. The role of a Canaanite temple was simply as an abode for the deity, and temples in the style of that found at Gerar have been loosely linked to the worship of Baal Hadad, the West Semitic deity of storms, thunder, and rain. The small size of the temple (9 x 15 meters/30 x 50 foot externally yet only 5.5 x 7.6 meters/18 x 25 foot internally) precluded general access and therefore only priests would have entered, conducting a ritual circuit that culminated in direct propitiation in front of the deity's statue in the rear niche.

The general population gathered in the surrounding courtyards (and to a lesser extent nearby auxiliary rooms) to participate in sacred rituals and feasting. Here, they witnessed a cacophony of sounds, smells, sights, and tastes as animals (sheep, goat, and cattle) and birds (ravens and crows) were sacrificed, agricultural products deposited on sacrificial benches, incense burned, food cooked and served, and puppies killed and buried in pits (as part of healing rituals).

While this last element was uncommon in Canaan, the most unusual part of the sacred landscape at Gerar was a fully articulated donkey burial, preserved for many centuries, most likely as a political symbol: the consecration of a treaty of non-aggression. In a letter (ARM 2 37) sent by Ibal-Il to Zimri-lim of Mari, the former reports that he had a young donkey killed in order to establish such a pact of non-aggression between the Hanaeans and the people of Ida-Maras. ▪ JK

↗ Cultic burial of a donkey next to an offering chamber, inset showing skull and bit, Tel Haror, 17th to 16th century BCE

בַּמָּקוֹם הַזֶּה וַהֲרָגוּנִי עַל־דְּבַר אִשְׁתִּי׃ וְגַם־אָמְנָה אֲחֹתִי בַת־אָבִי יב
הִוא אַךְ לֹא בַת־אִמִּי וַתְּהִי־לִי לְאִשָּׁה׃ וַיְהִי כַּאֲשֶׁר הִתְעוּ אֹתִי יג
אֱלֹהִים מִבֵּית אָבִי וָאֹמַר לָהּ זֶה חַסְדֵּךְ אֲשֶׁר תַּעֲשִׂי עִמָּדִי אֶל
כָּל־הַמָּקוֹם אֲשֶׁר נָבוֹא שָׁמָּה אִמְרִי־לִי אָחִי הוּא׃ וַיִּקַּח אֲבִימֶלֶךְ יד
צֹאן וּבָקָר וַעֲבָדִים וּשְׁפָחֹת וַיִּתֵּן לְאַבְרָהָם וַיָּשֶׁב לוֹ אֵת שָׂרָה

12 in this place. They will kill me because of my wife.' Besides,
she really is my sister. She is the daughter of my father though
13 not of my mother, and she became my wife. When God made
me wander from my father's house, I said to her, 'Do me this
kindness: wherever we go, say of me, "He is my brother."'"
14 Avimelekh gave Avraham sheep, cattle, and male and female

NEAR EAST

20:12 Brother-sister incest

Avraham's statement precedes, of course, the law in Leviticus prohibiting sex between a brother and a sister, even if they are merely half siblings, "You shall not expose the nakedness of your sister – whether she is your father's daughter or your mother's" (Lev. 18:9).

In the ancient Near East, incest between brother and sister was common in the Egyptian and Elamite (modern-day Iran, 2nd millennium BCE) monarchies. While the Hammurabi and Hittite laws prohibit certain kinds of incestuous relationships (such as parent-child), brother-sister is not mentioned as outlawed. In her effort to avoid the shame of rape, Tamar protests to Amnon, David's children by different mothers, that their father would permit their marriage (II Sam. 13:13). Yeḥezkel complains about the persistence of this practice, "another in you has forced his sister, the daughter of his father" (Ezek. 22:11). ▪ ZR

↗ Queen Ahmose-Nefertari, sister and chief wife of Ahmose I, 16th century BCE

טו אִשְׁתּוֹ: וַיֹּאמֶר אֲבִימֶלֶךְ הִנֵּה אַרְצִי לְפָנֶיךָ בַּטּוֹב בְּעֵינֶיךָ שֵׁב:
טז • וּלְשָׂרָה אָמַר הִנֵּה נָתַתִּי אֶלֶף כֶּסֶף לְאָחִיךְ הִנֵּה הוּא־לָךְ כְּסוּת
יז עֵינַיִם לְכֹל אֲשֶׁר אִתָּךְ וְאֵת כֹּל וְנֹכָחַת: וַיִּתְפַּלֵּל אַבְרָהָם אֶל־
הָאֱלֹהִים וַיִּרְפָּא אֱלֹהִים אֶת־אֲבִימֶלֶךְ וְאֶת־אִשְׁתּוֹ וְאַמְהֹתָיו
יח וַיֵּלֵדוּ: כִּי־עָצֹר עָצַר יהוה בְּעַד כָּל־רֶחֶם לְבֵית אֲבִימֶלֶךְ עַל־
כא א דְּבַר שָׂרָה אֵשֶׁת אַבְרָהָם: וַיהוה פָּקַד אֶת־שָׂרָה
ב כַּאֲשֶׁר אָמָר וַיַּעַשׂ יהוה לְשָׂרָה כַּאֲשֶׁר דִּבֵּר: וַתַּהַר וַתֵּלֶד שָׂרָה
ג לְאַבְרָהָם בֵּן לִזְקֻנָיו לַמּוֹעֵד אֲשֶׁר־דִּבֶּר אֹתוֹ אֱלֹהִים: וַיִּקְרָא
אַבְרָהָם אֶת־שֶׁם־בְּנוֹ הַנּוֹלַד־לוֹ אֲשֶׁר־יָלְדָה־לּוֹ שָׂרָה יִצְחָק:

slaves, and returned his wife Sara to him. Avimelekh said, 15
"Here is my land. Live wherever you wish." To Sara he said, 16 •
"I am giving your brother a thousand pieces of silver. This
will allay the suspicions of everyone who is with you. You
are fully vindicated." Then Avraham prayed to God, and God 17
healed Avimelekh, his wife, and his female slaves so they
could again have children, for the LORD had prevented all 18
the women in Avimelekh's household from bearing children,
because of Sara, Avraham's wife. The LORD 1 **21**
remembered Sara as He had said He would, and acted for Sara
as He had promised. Sara became pregnant and bore a son to 2
Avraham in his old age at the very time God had promised.
Avraham named his newborn son, whom Sara had borne 3

NEAR EAST

20:16 A thousand pieces of silver

Avimelekh describes his payment as *kesut einayim*, a unique phrase which literally means "a covering of the eyes." This phrase is translated here based on the idea that the payment was made to "allay the suspicions" of people – their eyes would now figuratively be closed to whatever happened between Sara and Avimelekh.

The *Middle Assyrian Laws* include a monetary fine for a man who took a woman on a journey with him, not realizing she was married. "If a man (other than father, brother, or son) has caused a married woman to go on a business trip with him, as long as he did not know that she was married, he is to swear to this effect and pay two talents of lead to the husband. If he did know that she was married, he is to pay this fine and swear, 'I swear that we did not have sex'" (MAL A §22).

The payment here, one thousand pieces (shekels), is a very large amount of silver, equivalent to about 11 kilograms (25 pounds). Note that in those times, a common wage earner would make only ten silver shekels a year, so this compensation is much more than such a person would earn in a lifetime. This same sum is found as part of the bride-price in the short Ugaritic poem *The Betrothal of Yarikh and Nikkal-Ib*, in light of which Avimelekh's payment may perhaps be viewed as a kind of reverse dowry, where he pays restitution money to the woman's family and sends her back to them intact. ▪ ZR

Silver pieces, Tel Megiddo, Israelite, 11th to 10th century BCE

וַיָּמָל אַבְרָהָם אֶת־יִצְחָק בְּנוֹ בֶּן־שְׁמֹנַת יָמִים כַּאֲשֶׁר צִוָּה אֹתוֹ ד
חמישי אֱלֹהִים: וְאַבְרָהָם בֶּן־מְאַת שָׁנָה בְּהִוָּלֶד לוֹ אֵת יִצְחָק בְּנוֹ: ה
וַתֹּאמֶר שָׂרָה צְחֹק עָשָׂה לִי אֱלֹהִים כָּל־הַשֹּׁמֵעַ יִצְחַק־לִי: ו
וַתֹּאמֶר מִי מִלֵּל לְאַבְרָהָם הֵינִיקָה בָנִים שָׂרָה כִּי־יָלַדְתִּי בֵן ז
לִזְקֻנָיו: וַיִּגְדַּל הַיֶּלֶד וַיִּגָּמַל וַיַּעַשׂ אַבְרָהָם מִשְׁתֶּה גָדוֹל בְּיוֹם ח •

4 him, Yitzḥak. And when Yitzḥak his son was eight days old,
5 Avraham circumcised him as God had commanded. Avraham
was one hundred years old when his son Yitzḥak was born
6 to him. Sara said, "God has brought me laughter; all those
7 who hear will laugh with me."[42] Then she said, "Who would
have told Avraham, 'Sara will nurse children'? Yet I have
• 8 borne a son in his old age." The child grew and was weaned;
on the day Yitzḥak was weaned, Avraham held a great feast.

42 | The name Yitzḥak derives from the verb denoting laughter (cf. 17:17–19, 18:12–14).

NEAR EAST

21:8 Age of weaning

Mesopotamian and Egyptian texts suggest that the average age of weaning was between two to three years old. The *Laws of Eshnunna* (ca. 1770 BCE) dictate paying a wet nurse for three years (LE §32). An Old Babylonian text (ca. 1783 BCE) documents that adoptive parents would pay a wet nurse an allowance of barley, oil, and wood for three years to suckle their son. Another Old Babylonian text records an adoptive son being suckled by a wet nurse for two years: "one shekel of silver and the nursing expense for two years." The *Instruction of Any*, dated to Egypt's Eighteenth Dynasty (1550–1292 BCE), states, "Repay your mother for all her care. . . . When you were finally born, she still carried you on her neck, and for three years she suckled you and kept you clean."

The archaeological record, which observes a spike in childhood death from age two or three, also supports the idea that children were weaned at that age, as until then they would receive immunity through breastmilk. During the Middle Bronze Age (1900–1550 BCE) in particular, many children eighteen to thirty-six months old are found buried in jars and placed under house floors. Breastfeeding delayed menstruation, so an extended nursing period functioned as a contraceptive technique as well. ▪ KG

↗ Plaque of a woman nursing her child, southern Mesopotamia, 20th to 16th century BCE

NEAR EAST

21:10 Wives, concubines, and inheritance

Avraham indicated that Yishmael was to be considered his legitimate offspring by naming him (Gen. 16:15) and circumcising him (Gen. 17:23); the text repeatedly refers to Yishmael as Avraham's son (Gen. 17:23, 25, 26, 25:9, 12). While children of a concubine did not necessarily have inheritance rights in the ancient Near East, Avraham's recognition of Yishmael changed his status to that of a legitimate heir. That is why Avraham was so distressed in verse 11 when Sara wanted to deprive Yishmael of his inheritance rights.

This type of situation is explicitly dealt with in the *Laws of Hammurabi* (ca. 1750 BCE): "If his wife bear sons to a man, or his maidservant have borne sons, and the father while still living says to the children whom his maidservant has borne: 'My sons,' and he counts them with the sons of his wife; if then the father dies, then the sons of the wife and of the maidservant shall divide the paternal property in common. The son of the wife is to partition and choose" (LH §170).

However, Sara's demand has a precedent in the *Laws of Lipit-Ishtar* collection (ca. 1870–1860 BCE): "If a man married a wife (and) she bore him children and those children are living, and a slave also bore children for her master (but) the father granted freedom to the slave and her children, the children of the slave shall not divide the estate with the children of their (former) master" (§25). Freeing a slave woman and her children cancels their inheritance rights; this is what Sara asked Avraham to do.

When Sara says, "Drive out (*garsh*) that slave woman," it should be understood as a divorce (as this term is used in Lev. 21:7 and Ezek. 44:22). The verb used for when Avraham "sent her (Hagar) away," *vayeshalkheha*, in verse 14, is also used for both divorce (e.g., Deut. 24:1–4; Is. 50:1; Jer. 3:1; Mal. 2:16) and freeing slaves (Deut. 15:12–13, 18). ▪ ZR

ט הִגָּמֵל אֶת־יִצְחָק׃ וַתֵּרֶא שָׂרָה אֶת־בֶּן־הָגָר הַמִּצְרִית אֲשֶׁר־
י יָלְדָה לְאַבְרָהָם מְצַחֵק׃ וַתֹּאמֶר לְאַבְרָהָם גָּרֵשׁ הָאָמָה הַזֹּאת
וְאֶת־בְּנָהּ כִּי לֹא יִירַשׁ בֶּן־הָאָמָה הַזֹּאת עִם־בְּנִי עִם־יִצְחָק׃
יא יב וַיֵּרַע הַדָּבָר מְאֹד בְּעֵינֵי אַבְרָהָם עַל אוֹדֹת בְּנוֹ׃ וַיֹּאמֶר אֱלֹהִים
אֶל־אַבְרָהָם אַל־יֵרַע בְּעֵינֶיךָ עַל־הַנַּעַר וְעַל־אֲמָתֶךָ כֹּל אֲשֶׁר
יג תֹּאמַר אֵלֶיךָ שָׂרָה שְׁמַע בְּקֹלָהּ כִּי בְיִצְחָק יִקָּרֵא לְךָ זָרַע׃ וְגַם
יד אֶת־בֶּן־הָאָמָה לְגוֹי אֲשִׂימֶנּוּ כִּי זַרְעֲךָ הוּא׃ וַיַּשְׁכֵּם אַבְרָהָם ׀
בַּבֹּקֶר וַיִּקַּח־לֶחֶם וְחֵמַת מַיִם וַיִּתֵּן אֶל־הָגָר שָׂם עַל־שִׁכְמָהּ

9 But Sara saw the son whom Hagar the Egyptian had borne
10 Avraham mocking.[43] She said to Avraham, "Drive out that
slave woman and her son, for the son of that slave woman
must not share the inheritance with my son, with Yitzhak."
11 12 This distressed Avraham greatly because of his son. But God
told Avraham, "Do not be distressed about the boy or about
your slave. Listen to whatever Sara tells you, because it is
through Yitzhak that your descendants will be reckoned.
13 But I will make the slave's son too into a nation, because he is
14 your child." Early the next morning Avraham took bread and
a skin of water and gave them to Hagar. He placed them on her
shoulder, and together with the child, he sent her away. She

43 | Hebrew *metzaḥek* – again bearing a connection to the name Yitzḥak.

Abraham sends Hagar away, from *The Bible and its Story*, by Charles F. Horne and Julius A. Brewer, 1908.

GEOGRAPHY

21:14 Be'er Sheva desert

Be'er Sheva is located on the northern edge of the modern-day Negev desert, the most remote area suitable for human life at the edge of a barren and inhospitable wilderness wherein Hagar and Yishmael wandered – ultimately going even further south to the Wilderness of Paran (Gen. 21:21). This area is distinct from the site of the wells Avraham dug (v. 25), which appears to be closer to Gerar, northwest of Be'er Sheva, nearer to the southwestern foothills of the hill country of Yehuda (the Shefela). That location has more available water, which flows down from the hills and is collected underground in aquifers. ▪ ZR

NEAR EAST

21:14 Divorce from a secondary wife

The text records that Avraham gave Hagar "bread and a skin of water" only when he "sent her away," (i.e., divorced her).

In the ancient Near East, when a second wife was divorced by her husband, even if she was a slave of a low status, certain monetary compensation had to be given. For example, an Old Assyrian (ca. 2025–1765 BCE) contract of a man who already had a wife in Ashur states, "Puzur-Ishtar has taken Ishtar-lamassi, the daughter of Ashur-nada as a slave and he will lead her off to Purushḫandum or to Ḫattum, (the destination of) his journey, and he will let her return to Kanish with him. If he should leave her, he will pay five minas of silver." Another legal document from the same period mentions payment of silver made to an abandoned slave girl, as well as providing for the offspring of that relationship, "Regarding Lamassi, his daughter, whenever Pilaḫ-Ishtar goes to the city he shall take her with him. They (the family of the slave girl) are satisfied (with the payment) for her upbringing and her food. They will demand nothing (more) from him."

The right of the barren primary wife to sell the slave girl who was brought in to provide offspring is found in Neo-Assyrian (911–609 BCE) marriage contracts. For example, "If S. does not become pregnant and does not bear a child, she shall take a slave girl as a replacement for herself. In this way she shall bring forth sons. The sons will be her sons. If she loves (her), she shall protect her. If she hates (her), she shall sell her." ▪ ZR

וְאֶת־הַיֶּלֶד וַיְשַׁלְּחֶהָ וַתֵּלֶךְ וַתֵּתַע בְּמִדְבַּר בְּאֵר שָׁבַע׃ וַיִּכְלוּ טו
הַמַּיִם מִן־הַחֵמֶת וַתַּשְׁלֵךְ אֶת־הַיֶּלֶד תַּחַת אַחַד הַשִּׂיחִם׃ וַתֵּלֶךְ טז
וַתֵּשֶׁב לָהּ מִנֶּגֶד הַרְחֵק כִּמְטַחֲוֵי קֶשֶׁת כִּי אָמְרָה אַל־אֶרְאֶה
בְּמוֹת הַיָּלֶד וַתֵּשֶׁב מִנֶּגֶד וַתִּשָּׂא אֶת־קֹלָהּ וַתֵּבְךְּ׃ וַיִּשְׁמַע אֱלֹהִים יז
אֶת־קוֹל הַנַּעַר וַיִּקְרָא מַלְאַךְ אֱלֹהִים ׀ אֶל־הָגָר מִן־הַשָּׁמַיִם
וַיֹּאמֶר לָהּ מַה־לָּךְ הָגָר אַל־תִּירְאִי כִּי־שָׁמַע אֱלֹהִים אֶל־קוֹל
הַנַּעַר בַּאֲשֶׁר הוּא־שָׁם׃ קוּמִי שְׂאִי אֶת־הַנַּעַר וְהַחֲזִיקִי אֶת־יָדֵךְ יח
בּוֹ כִּי־לְגוֹי גָּדוֹל אֲשִׂימֶנּוּ׃ וַיִּפְקַח אֱלֹהִים אֶת־עֵינֶיהָ וַתֵּרֶא בְּאֵר יט
מָיִם וַתֵּלֶךְ וַתְּמַלֵּא אֶת־הַחֵמֶת מַיִם וַתַּשְׁקְ אֶת־הַנָּעַר׃ וַיְהִי כ
אֱלֹהִים אֶת־הַנַּעַר וַיִּגְדָּל וַיֵּשֶׁב בַּמִּדְבָּר וַיְהִי רֹבֶה קַשָּׁת׃ וַיֵּשֶׁב כא •
בְּמִדְבַּר פָּארָן וַתִּקַּח־לוֹ אִמּוֹ אִשָּׁה מֵאֶרֶץ מִצְרָיִם׃

15 went wandering in the Be'er Sheva desert. When the water in
the skin was all gone, she cast the child away under one of the
16 bushes and went and sat down at a distance, about a bowshot
away, saying, "I cannot watch the child die." Sitting there, at
17 a distance, she raised her voice and wept. God heard the boy
crying, and an angel of God called to Hagar from the heavens
and said to her, "Hagar, what is wrong? Fear not. God has
18 heard the boy's cry there, where he is. Go, raise up the boy and
take him by the hand, for I will make of him a great nation."
19 Then God opened her eyes and she saw a well of water. She
went and filled the skin with water and gave the boy to drink.
20 God was with the boy as he grew. He lived in the desert and
• 21 became an expert with the bow. In the Paran desert he lived,
and his mother took him a wife from Egypt.

GEOGRAPHY

21:21 Wilderness of Paran

The name Paran is preserved in the Arabic name "Wadi Feiran (or Faran)," the largest wadi in the Sinai Peninsula (130 kilometers/81 miles long). The Feiran Oasis, the main oasis in southern Sinai, extends about 4.8 kilometers (3 miles) of the length of the wadi. The name "Paran" was also found in forty-five Nabatean inscriptions from the late Second Temple period, mostly from the Wadi Feiran area. The reason why Wadi Feiran became associated with this area is likely due to Christian pilgrimage in the 4th century CE – there was a circular route that the pilgrims took from Goshen to the Gulf of Suez and then to Santa Catherina (Mount Sinai) and back. In the book of Numbers, the Israelites enter the Wilderness of Paran after leaving Sinai.

The Wilderness of Paran mentioned here must be near the Be'er Sheva desert (21:14). The journey of the spies places the Wilderness of Paran near the Wilderness of Tzin (Numbers 13:3, 21, 26). Neither of these are anywhere near the southern Sinai Peninsula. The only way that this can be explained is that the "wilderness of Paran" must be a general name for a very large area covering most of the southern Sinai Peninsula and the Negev desert. ▪ ZR

Feiran Oasis, from the Matson Collection, 1950–1977

• כב וַיְהִי֙ בָּעֵ֣ת הַהִ֔וא וַיֹּ֣אמֶר אֲבִימֶ֗לֶךְ וּפִיכֹל֙ שַׂר־צְבָא֔וֹ אֶל־אַבְרָהָ֖ם ששי
כג לֵאמֹ֑ר אֱלֹהִ֣ים עִמְּךָ֔ בְּכֹ֥ל אֲשֶׁר־אַתָּ֖ה עֹשֶֽׂה׃ וְעַתָּ֗ה הִשָּׁ֨בְעָה לִּ֤י
בֵֽאלֹהִים֙ הֵ֔נָּה אִם־תִּשְׁקֹ֣ר לִ֔י וּלְנִינִ֖י וּלְנֶכְדִּ֑י כַּחֶ֜סֶד אֲשֶׁר־עָשִׂ֤יתִי
כד עִמְּךָ֙ תַּעֲשֶׂ֣ה עִמָּדִ֔י וְעִם־הָאָ֖רֶץ אֲשֶׁר־גַּ֥רְתָּה בָּֽהּ׃ וַיֹּ֙אמֶר֙ אַבְרָהָ֔ם
כה אָנֹכִ֖י אִשָּׁבֵֽעַ׃ וְהוֹכִ֥חַ אַבְרָהָ֖ם אֶת־אֲבִימֶ֑לֶךְ עַל־אֹדוֹת֙ בְּאֵ֣ר

• 22 At that time, Avimelekh and Pikhol, commander of his troops,
23 said to Avraham, "God is with you in all you do. Now swear
to me here before God that you will not deal falsely with me
or with my children or grandchildren. Show me and the land
where you have lived as a stranger the same kindness I have
24 25 shown to you."[44] Avraham said, "I swear." Then Avraham
rebuked Avimelekh for the well of water that Avimelekh's

44 | See 20:14–16.

NEAR EAST

21:22–32 Avraham's treaty with Avimelekh

Avraham's first acquisition of property in the land of Israel was a result of this transaction with Avimelekh, in which Avraham gave Avimelekh gifts of sheep and cattle, and in return received acknowledgment of his rights to the well he dug, now guaranteed by the king.

In the ancient Near East, there were two broad categories of treaties, "parity treaties" establishing relationships between sovereign powers of equal status, and "vassal treaties" between powers of unequal social and political status. Although it may appear that Avraham gave everything to Avimelekh in this agreement, this was in fact a treaty between equals, as Avimelekh had already gifted sheep, cattle, and slaves to Avraham (Gen. 20:14), as well as the right to settle in the area (20:15), with the addition of water rights in this current agreement.

The area of Be'er Sheva has limited rainfall; its main source of water is wells. Digging a well requires the expertise to identify the location of underground aquifers, and significant labor to build a stable well. Correspondence from the ancient Near East records disputes over water rights between rulers. For example, Old Babylonian letters between Rim-Sin I, ruler of the city-state of Larsa (ruled 1758–1699 BCE), and the king of Eshnunna refer to negotiations lasting a long time, "(Although) we have been (here) five months you still have not granted us the water (rights)," and demands of proof of claims, "If I hear tablets of yours (substantiating the claim) I may grant the water rights. If I do not hear your tablets, I will not grant you the water (rights)."

The presence of Avimelekh's military commander Pikhol (vv. 22, 32) indicates the seriousness of a discussion of water claims, which has the potential to lead to physical conflict. At the same time, Avimelekh comes to make a treaty of amicable relations with Avraham, as the patriarch's prosperity due to obvious divine favor (v. 22) has the potential of threatening the king, who remembers well their previous encounter (20:1–18). ▪ ZR

Well of Milḥan, built during the British Mandate period, no longer in use, Negev desert, 20th century

הַמַּיִם אֲשֶׁר גָּזְלוּ עַבְדֵי אֲבִימֶלֶךְ: וַיֹּאמֶר אֲבִימֶלֶךְ לֹא יָדַעְתִּי כו
מִי עָשָׂה אֶת־הַדָּבָר הַזֶּה וְגַם־אַתָּה לֹא־הִגַּדְתָּ לִּי וְגַם אָנֹכִי לֹא
שָׁמַעְתִּי בִּלְתִּי הַיּוֹם: וַיִּקַּח אַבְרָהָם צֹאן וּבָקָר וַיִּתֵּן לַאֲבִימֶלֶךְ כז
וַיִּכְרְתוּ שְׁנֵיהֶם בְּרִית: וַיַּצֵּב אַבְרָהָם אֶת־שֶׁבַע כִּבְשֹׂת הַצֹּאן כח
לְבַדְּהֶן: וַיֹּאמֶר אֲבִימֶלֶךְ אֶל־אַבְרָהָם מָה הֵנָּה שֶׁבַע כְּבָשֹׂת כט
הָאֵלֶּה אֲשֶׁר הִצַּבְתָּ לְבַדָּנָה: וַיֹּאמֶר כִּי אֶת־שֶׁבַע כְּבָשֹׂת תִּקַּח ל
מִיָּדִי בַּעֲבוּר תִּהְיֶה־לִּי לְעֵדָה כִּי חָפַרְתִּי אֶת־הַבְּאֵר הַזֹּאת:

26 servants had seized. But Avimelekh said, "I do not know who
has done this. You did not tell me; I had not heard about it
27 until today." Avraham then brought sheep and cattle and gave
them to Avimelekh, and the two of them forged a covenant.
28
29 Avraham set apart seven ewe lambs from the flock. Avimelekh
asked him, "What is the meaning of these seven ewe lambs
30 you have set apart?" He replied, "Accept these seven lambs

GEOGRAPHY

21:32 Be'er Sheva

Most scholars associate the biblical Be'er Sheva with Tel Be'er Sheva, an archaeological site containing ruins from an Iron Age town a few kilometers/miles east of the modern city of Be'er Sheva. No physical evidence of a Canaanite settlement in the Middle or Late Bronze Age has been found there, so in the time of Avraham it was not yet a "town."

Other scholars propose that the site should be identified as Tel Sheva, a Bedouin town which has a mound called Bir es-Saba', which also preserves the name Be'er Sheva. However, there have been no finds from the Middle Bronze Age in the excavated area of this site.

Note that the only objects associated in these verses with Be'er Sheva are a newly dug well and a tree (Gen. 21:33), and when Avraham needed to make a treaty, it was with Avimelekh king of Gerar, as there was no ruler of Be'er Sheva or indication of a settled community at the time. The only reference to Be'er Sheva as a "town" in Genesis is 26:33, which may indicate that it was settled by semi-nomads by Mosaic times. ▪ ZR

Tel Be'er Sheva excavations, residential area

לא עַל־כֵּן קָרָא לַמָּקוֹם הַהוּא בְּאֵר שָׁבַע כִּי שָׁם נִשְׁבְּעוּ שְׁנֵיהֶם׃
לב וַיִּכְרְתוּ בְרִית בִּבְאֵר שָׁבַע וַיָּקָם אֲבִימֶלֶךְ וּפִיכֹל שַׂר־צְבָאוֹ

from me as testimony that I dug this well." That is why that 31
place is called Be'er Sheva, because there the two men swore
an oath.[45] Thus they made a pact at Be'er Sheva. And then 32
Avimelekh and Pikhol, commander of his troops, returned to

45 | The name Be'er Sheva resonates with both *sheva* (seven) and *nishbe'u* (swore).

NEAR EAST

21:32 Who were the Philistines in Genesis

The Philistines are first mentioned in Genesis 10:14 in between the Kasluḥim and the Kaftorim. We do not know where the Kasluḥim were located, but Kaftor is understood by most academic scholars to refer to Crete (Jer. 47:4), as the native land of the Philistines (Amos 9:7). Thus, the Philistines may have been viewed as a group of the Kaftorim.

The first extra-biblical mention of the Philistines occurs in the accounts of Ramesses III (ca. 1186–1155 BCE), in his mortuary temple in Medinet Habu, concerning his victorious battles against the invasion of the Sea Peoples in the eighth year of his reign. After their defeat in Egypt, it appears that they settled peaceably in what became their five main cities in Canaan: Ashkelon, Ashdod, Gat, Aza, and Ekron, and they became known as Philistines. The Egyptian Onomasticon of Amenope, from the late 12th to early 11th century BCE, mentions Philistine control of Ashkelon, Ashdod, and Aza, although the archaeological record does not show a destruction level at the time of the Philistine settlement. Nevertheless, the books of Judges and Samuel reveal that the Philistines were major enemies of the Israelites.

In contrast, the relationships between the patriarchs and the Philistines were nothing like those in Judges and Samuel. Although some disputes over water and property took place, no violence is recorded. Indeed, both Avraham and Yitzḥak lived in security in Philistine territory for some time, and the disputes ended when the patriarchs made treaties with the Philistines (21:27–32, 26:26–31). Another difference is that the Philistine King Avimelekh of the patriarchs' time lived in Gerar, which the Tanakh never refers to again as a Philistine town.

Who, then, were the Philistines who interacted with Avraham and Yitzḥak (26:1–31) in Genesis, perhaps some four or five hundred years earlier than the ones in the time of the Judges and of Samuel? The "Phaistos Disc" (ca. 18th to 17th century BCE) found in Minoan Crete shows a warrior with a feather headdress which is very similar to the portrayal of the Philistines in the wall carvings at Medinet Habu. Additionally, finds in Canaan that are typical of Crete have been dated to the Middle Bronze Age. For example, at Tel Haror (20 kilometers/12.5 miles from the Mediterranean Sea and 26 kilometers/16 miles northwest of Be'er Sheva) – identified by a number of scholars as biblical Gerar – a potsherd in the Minoan Crete style was found in a 16th-century BCE temple complex; seeds like those from Crete were found in a storage jar from around the 20th to 18th century BCE at Tel Nami, just south of Haifa; and at Tel Kabri, just south of Akhziv, a painted floor and parts of a wall fresco, both dated to the 17th century BCE and done in Minoan style, were discovered. It appears, then, that groups of traders and immigrants from Crete settled on or near the Canaanite coast during the Middle Bronze Age and intermarried with the natives. That Genesis calls them "Philistines" would have made sense to the Israelites, who were familiar with the peoples who lived in that area (Ex. 13:17).

Interestingly, Midrash Tehillim (first cited in the 11th century CE) on Psalms 60 records an episode that claims that the Philistines of Genesis were a completely different people from those of the books of Judges and Samuel. ▪ JU

Philistine prisoners with feathered headdresses, mortuary temple of Ramesses III, Medinet Habu, 12th century BCE

וַיָּשֻׁבוּ אֶל־אֶרֶץ פְּלִשְׁתִּים: וַיִּטַּע אֶשֶׁל בִּבְאֵר שָׁבַע וַיִּקְרָא־ לג
שָׁם בְּשֵׁם יהוה אֵל עוֹלָם: וַיָּגָר אַבְרָהָם בְּאֶרֶץ פְּלִשְׁתִּים יָמִים לד
רַבִּים:
שביעי וַיְהִי אַחַר הַדְּבָרִים הָאֵלֶּה וְהָאֱלֹהִים נִסָּה אֶת־אַבְרָהָם וַיֹּאמֶר א כב
אֵלָיו אַבְרָהָם וַיֹּאמֶר הִנֵּנִי: וַיֹּאמֶר קַח־נָא אֶת־בִּנְךָ אֶת־יְחִידְךָ ב
אֲשֶׁר־אָהַבְתָּ אֶת־יִצְחָק וְלֶךְ־לְךָ אֶל־אֶרֶץ הַמֹּרִיָּה וְהַעֲלֵהוּ

33 the land of the Philistines. Avraham planted a tamarisk tree
in Be'er Sheva, and there he called on the name of the Lord,
34 the Everlasting God. Avraham stayed on in the land of the
Philistines for many days.
22 1 After these things, God tested Avraham. "Avraham!" He said.
2 And Avraham replied, "Here I am." Then God said, "Take your
son, your only one, the one whom you love – Yitzḥak – and
go to the land of Moria. There, offer him up as a burnt offering

— FLORA AND FAUNA —

21:33 Tamarisk

Tamarisks are a family of common trees and shrubs in the Middle East. Since they have deep roots and are resistant to both saline and alkaline soils, they can grow in sandy areas and areas with a high salt concentration, like the Dead Sea region. The most commonly planted species and the one which grows the tallest (4–15 meters/13–50 feet) is *Tamarix aphylla*, used as both a shade tree and a windbreaker. During the heat of the day, the tamarisk secretes salt, which later dries up. During the night the salt absorbs water from the air, which evaporates in the morning, creating a cooling effect, which helps the tree survive in the hot Middle Eastern climate. ▪ ZR

Tamarisk (*Tamarix aphylla*) growing in the desert sand, Algeria

LANGUAGE

21:33 El olam

The term *el olam*, translated here as "Everlasting God," is unique in Tanakh. El was the name of the chief Canaanite god, who was sometimes referred to as Olam, as in a 7th century BCE Phoenician incantation. Proto-Canaanite inscriptions written by miners at Serabit el-Khadim in the Sinai Peninsula (15th century BCE) include the formula, *el du olam* (El the Ancient One). In contrast to the Canaanite usage, here the phrase *el olam* does not use *el* or *olam* as a proper name of God. In this way, a pagan epithet was repurposed to refer to God by use of an attribute, that is, "the Eternal God." ▪ ZR

Rock inscription, Rod el-'Air, near Serabit el-Khadim, 19th to 18th century BCE

ג שָׁם לְעֹלָה עַל אַחַד הֶהָרִים אֲשֶׁר אֹמַר אֵלֶיךָ׃ וַיַּשְׁכֵּם אַבְרָהָם
בַּבֹּקֶר וַיַּחֲבֹשׁ אֶת־חֲמֹרוֹ וַיִּקַּח אֶת־שְׁנֵי נְעָרָיו אִתּוֹ וְאֵת יִצְחָק
בְּנוֹ וַיְבַקַּע עֲצֵי עֹלָה וַיָּקָם וַיֵּלֶךְ אֶל־הַמָּקוֹם אֲשֶׁר־אָמַר־לוֹ
ד הָאֱלֹהִים׃ בַּיּוֹם הַשְּׁלִישִׁי וַיִּשָּׂא אַבְרָהָם אֶת־עֵינָיו וַיַּרְא אֶת־

on one of the mountains, the one that I will show you." Early 3
the next morning Avraham rose and saddled his donkey. With
him he took two of his young men and Yitzhak his son. He cut
wood for the offering and set out toward the place of which
God had told him. On the third day Avraham looked up and, 4

NEAR EAST

22:2 The land of Moria

In Hebrew, the land of Moria is written with the definite article *heh* at the beginning of the word (*ha-Moria*), indicating that it is not a proper name of a specific location (unlike Mount Sinai for example). This approach is followed by the Aramaic Tanakh (Targum) translations, which translate it as "land of worship" (*ara pulḥana*). Moria would then originate from the verb "to see" (the root *r a [alef] h*, the place that I will show you, or where I will appear to you, as in Bereshit Rabba 55:9) or "to fear" (*y r a [alef]*), the land where people fear God, as in the Targum translations), as both words are prominent in the narrative ("see" in vv. 4, 8, 13, 14; "fear" in v. 12). The text does not indicate the location of this place, or in which direction Avraham journeyed for three days from Be'er Sheva. Avraham seems to be familiar with the location, knowing where to go and that firewood needs to be brought there.

The only other mention of this place is II Chronicles 3:1, which, too, includes "seeing": "Shlomo began to build the House of the Lord in Jerusalem on Mount Moria (*har hamoria*) where He had appeared (*nirah*) to his father David." This reflects the tradition that Moria is the place where the Temple was built.

This association is already hinted at in the second half of verse 14 which states "To this day it is said, 'On the mountain of the Lord, He will be seen (*yeiraeh*).'" This seems to be a reference to Exodus 34:23–24, "Three times a year all the males among you shall appear (*yeiraeh*) before the Master, the Lord, God of Israel...when you go up, three times a year, to appear before the Lord your God," or to Deuteronomy 16:16, "Three times a year all your males shall appear (*yeraeh*) before the Lord your God in the place that He will choose." "The place" is identical to "the place" here in verses 3, 4, 9, 14, to which God has sent Avraham. Thus, this verse is in accord with references in the Torah to the primary place of worship of God, identified only in the prophetic books as Jerusalem, to which the Israelites will go during their three annual pilgrimage festivals. ▪ ZR

↗ View of the Temple Mount from the Haas Promenade, the traditional site where Avraham saw "the place, Jerusalem"

הַמָּקוֹם מֵרָחֹק: וַיֹּאמֶר אַבְרָהָם אֶל־נְעָרָיו שְׁבוּ־לָכֶם פֹּה עִם־ ה
הַחֲמוֹר וַאֲנִי וְהַנַּעַר נֵלְכָה עַד־כֹּה וְנִשְׁתַּחֲוֶה וְנָשׁוּבָה אֲלֵיכֶם:
וַיִּקַּח אַבְרָהָם אֶת־עֲצֵי הָעֹלָה וַיָּשֶׂם עַל־יִצְחָק בְּנוֹ וַיִּקַּח בְּיָדוֹ ו
אֶת־הָאֵשׁ וְאֶת־הַמַּאֲכֶלֶת וַיֵּלְכוּ שְׁנֵיהֶם יַחְדָּו: וַיֹּאמֶר יִצְחָק ז
אֶל־אַבְרָהָם אָבִיו וַיֹּאמֶר אָבִי וַיֹּאמֶר הִנֶּנִּי בְנִי וַיֹּאמֶר הִנֵּה הָאֵשׁ
וְהָעֵצִים וְאַיֵּה הַשֶּׂה לְעֹלָה: וַיֹּאמֶר אַבְרָהָם אֱלֹהִים יִרְאֶה־לּוֹ ח
הַשֶּׂה לְעֹלָה בְּנִי וַיֵּלְכוּ שְׁנֵיהֶם יַחְדָּו: וַיָּבֹאוּ אֶל־הַמָּקוֹם אֲשֶׁר ט
אָמַר־לוֹ הָאֱלֹהִים וַיִּבֶן שָׁם אַבְרָהָם אֶת־הַמִּזְבֵּחַ וַיַּעֲרֹךְ אֶת־
הָעֵצִים וַיַּעֲקֹד אֶת־יִצְחָק בְּנוֹ וַיָּשֶׂם אֹתוֹ עַל־הַמִּזְבֵּחַ מִמַּעַל
לָעֵצִים: וַיִּשְׁלַח אַבְרָהָם אֶת־יָדוֹ וַיִּקַּח אֶת־הַמַּאֲכֶלֶת לִשְׁחֹט י •
אֶת־בְּנוֹ: וַיִּקְרָא אֵלָיו מַלְאַךְ יהוה מִן־הַשָּׁמַיִם וַיֹּאמֶר אַבְרָהָם ׀ יא
אַבְרָהָם וַיֹּאמֶר הִנֵּנִי: וַיֹּאמֶר אַל־תִּשְׁלַח יָדְךָ אֶל־הַנַּעַר וְאַל־ יב
תַּעַשׂ לוֹ מְאוּמָה כִּי ׀ עַתָּה יָדַעְתִּי כִּי־יְרֵא אֱלֹהִים אַתָּה וְלֹא
חָשַׂכְתָּ אֶת־בִּנְךָ אֶת־יְחִידְךָ מִמֶּנִּי: וַיִּשָּׂא אַבְרָהָם אֶת־עֵינָיו יג •
וַיַּרְא וְהִנֵּה־אַיִל אַחַר נֶאֱחַז בַּסְּבַךְ בְּקַרְנָיו וַיֵּלֶךְ אַבְרָהָם וַיִּקַּח

5 in the distance, he saw the place. He told his young men, "Stay
here with the donkey. I and the boy will go there and worship.
6 Then we will come back to you." Avraham took the wood
for the offering and placed it on Yitzḥak his son. He himself
took the fire and the knife. The two of them walked together.
7 Then Yitzḥak said to his father, Avraham, "Father?" Avraham
said, "Here I am, my son." Yitzḥak said, "Here is the fire and
8 the wood, but where is the lamb for the burnt offering?" And
Avraham replied, "God will see to a lamb for an offering, my
9 son." The two of them walked on together. They came to the
place of which God had spoken. There Avraham built an altar
and arranged the wood. Then he bound Yitzḥak his son and
• 10 laid him on the altar on top of the wood. Avraham reached
11 out his hand and took hold of the knife to slay his son. But
an angel of the Lord called out to him from the heavens,
12 "Avraham! Avraham!" He said, "Here I am." "Do not lift your
hand against the boy; do nothing to him, for now I know that
you fear God: for you have not withheld from Me your son,
• 13 your only one." Avraham looked up and saw a ram caught in
a thicket by its horns. Avraham went, took hold of the ram,
14 and offered it up as a burnt offering in place of his son. And

NEAR EAST

22:10 The knife

A rare term is used here for knife, *maakhelet*, literally "a devouring object." Its purpose is to disturb the reader, starkly describing the savagery of the imminent child sacrifice. The term is also used to emphasize the horrific story of the concubine in Giva in Judges 19:29, "When he reached his house, he took a knife (*maakhelet*), seized hold of his concubine and hacked her up, limb by limb, into twelve pieces, and he sent one to each and every region of Israel."

The only other appearance is in Proverbs 30:14 in parallel to the common biblical word for swords or knives, *ḥaravot*: "A generation whose teeth are swords and whose jaws are knives (*maakhalot*) ready to devour the poor from the earth…." The reference to teeth and jaws may allude to double-edged knives or daggers, as in Judges 3:16; Psalms 149:6; Proverbs 5:4 – where the Hebrew for a doubled-edged knife is *ḥerev piphiyot/piyot*, literally, "a knife of mouths."

A wide double-edged bronze dagger that could exemplify such a *maakhelet* was found in a Middle Bronze Age tomb in Ḥevron – dating approximately to the time and location of the patriarchs. ▪ ZR, JU

Bronze dagger with inscription "RN", Canaanite, Lakhish, 16th century BCE

יד אֶת־הָאַ֫יִל וַיַּעֲלֵ֥הוּ לְעֹלָ֖ה תַּ֥חַת בְּנֽוֹ׃ וַיִּקְרָ֧א אַבְרָהָ֛ם שֵֽׁם־הַמָּק֥וֹם
טו הַה֖וּא יהוה ׀ יִרְאֶ֑ה אֲשֶׁר֙ יֵאָמֵ֣ר הַיּ֔וֹם בְּהַ֥ר יהוה יֵרָאֶֽה׃ וַיִּקְרָ֛א
טז מַלְאַ֥ךְ יהוה אֶל־אַבְרָהָ֑ם שֵׁנִ֖ית מִן־הַשָּׁמָֽיִם׃ וַיֹּ֕אמֶר בִּ֥י נִשְׁבַּ֖עְתִּי
נְאֻם־יהוה כִּ֗י יַ֚עַן אֲשֶׁ֤ר עָשִׂ֙יתָ֙ אֶת־הַדָּבָ֣ר הַזֶּ֔ה וְלֹ֥א חָשַׂ֖כְתָּ
יז אֶת־בִּנְךָ֥ אֶת־יְחִידֶֽךָ׃ כִּֽי־בָרֵ֣ךְ אֲבָרֶכְךָ֗ וְהַרְבָּ֨ה אַרְבֶּ֤ה אֶֽת־זַרְעֲךָ֙
כְּכוֹכְבֵ֣י הַשָּׁמַ֔יִם וְכַח֕וֹל אֲשֶׁ֖ר עַל־שְׂפַ֣ת הַיָּ֑ם וְיִרַ֣שׁ זַרְעֲךָ֔ אֵ֖ת
יח שַׁ֥עַר אֹיְבָֽיו׃ וְהִתְבָּרְכ֣וּ בְזַרְעֲךָ֔ כֹּ֖ל גּוֹיֵ֣י הָאָ֑רֶץ עֵ֕קֶב אֲשֶׁ֥ר שָׁמַ֖עְתָּ
יט בְּקֹלִֽי׃ וַיָּ֤שָׁב אַבְרָהָם֙ אֶל־נְעָרָ֔יו וַיָּקֻ֛מוּ וַיֵּלְכ֥וּ יַחְדָּ֖ו אֶל־בְּאֵ֣ר
שָׁ֑בַע וַיֵּ֥שֶׁב אַבְרָהָ֖ם בִּבְאֵ֥ר שָֽׁבַע׃

Avraham named the place The LORD Will See.[46] To this day
it is said, "On the mountain of the LORD, He will be seen."
Then the angel of the LORD called to Avraham from the 15
heavens a second time and said, "By My own Self I swear, 16
says the LORD, that because you have done this and have not
withheld your son, your only one, I will bless you greatly and 17
make your descendants as many as the stars of the heavens,
as the sand on the seashore. Your descendants will possess
their enemies' gate,[47] and through your descendants will all 18
nations of the earth be blessed, because you have listened to
My voice." Avraham returned to his young men, and together 19
they set out and went to Be'er Sheva, and Avraham stayed on
in Be'er Sheva.

46 | Cf. verse 8: "God will see to a lamb for an offering."

47 | That is, their cities.

Scene from the tragedy of Iphigenia, Apulia, Basilicata (Italy), 360-350 BCE

NEAR EAST

22:13 Animal sacrifice in place of a human

In the ancient world, the predominant pagan view of daily animal sacrifices at temples was that they served as meals for the gods. Additionally, people would bring sacrifices for a variety of reasons – from thanking the gods or petitioning them for favors, to trying to appease the gods or to atone for an offense. We do not have ancient Near Eastern evidence of a god wanting a human sacrifice and then accepting an animal substitute. However, in Hittite sources burnt offerings function to deter divine wrath and absolve a person's guilt, parallel to the atonement afforded by the *ola* in Leviticus 1:4. In this view an animal can function as a substitute for a person (such as the expiation of sins on the Day of Atonement – Lev. 16:6, 17, 21–22).

The theme of animal substitution for a human sacrifice is found also in much later classical literature. On his way to the Trojan War, Agamemnon offends the goddess Artemis by killing one of her sacred stags. Artemis retaliates by stopping the Greek troops from reaching Troy unless Agamemnon kills his eldest daughter, Iphigenia. In some versions, Artemis rescues Iphigenia and replaces her with a deer. In the 1st century CE Greek work, *Parallela minora*, attributed to Plutarch, we find, "When a Plague had overspread Sparta, the god gave an oracle that it would cease if they sacrificed a noble maiden each year. Once when Helen had been chosen by lot and had been led forward adorned for the sacrifice, an eagle swooped down, snatched up the sword, carried it to the herds of cattle, and let it fall on a heifer" (§35), which served as her substitute.

In the case of Avraham and Yitzḥak, no offense or appeasement was mentioned as a reason for sacrifice in the first place – rather, God "tested" Avraham (v. 1). ▪ ZR

מפטיר וַיְהִי אַחֲרֵי הַדְּבָרִים הָאֵלֶּה וַיֻּגַּד לְאַבְרָהָם לֵאמֹר הִנֵּה יָלְדָה כ
מִלְכָּה גַם־הִוא בָּנִים לְנָחוֹר אָחִיךָ: אֶת־עוּץ בְּכֹרוֹ וְאֶת־בּוּז אָחִיו כא
וְאֶת־קְמוּאֵל אֲבִי אֲרָם: וְאֶת־כֶּשֶׂד וְאֶת־חֲזוֹ וְאֶת־פִּלְדָּשׁ וְאֶת־ כב
יִדְלָף וְאֵת בְּתוּאֵל: וּבְתוּאֵל יָלַד אֶת־רִבְקָה שְׁמֹנָה אֵלֶּה יָלְדָה כג
מִלְכָּה לְנָחוֹר אֲחִי אַבְרָהָם: וּפִילַגְשׁוֹ וּשְׁמָהּ רְאוּמָה וַתֵּלֶד גַּם־ כד
הִוא אֶת־טֶבַח וְאֶת־גַּחַם וְאֶת־תַּחַשׁ וְאֶת־מַעֲכָה:

20 Some time later, Avraham was told, "Milka too has had
21 children with your brother Naḥor: Utz, his firstborn, his
22 brother Buz, Kemuel, father of Aram, Kesed, Ḥazo, Pildash,
23 Yidlaf, and Betuel." Betuel had a daughter Rivka. Milka bore
24 these eight sons to Avraham's brother Naḥor. His concubine,
named Reuma, also had children: Tevaḥ, Gaḥam, Taḥash,
and Maakha.

Stele with Aramaic inscription, Tayma (Saudi Arabia), 4th to 2nd century BCE

NEAR EAST

22:20–24 Descendants of Naḥor

The names in this genealogical list that can be identified are known as names of tribes or regions, so this list can be understood as a group of peoples linked together by a sense of kinship. For example, Nakhur (Naḥor) is found in the Mari texts as an important town in the upper Euphrates, near Ḥaran.

Utz is the country where Iyov lived (Job 1:1). He was attacked by Sabeans (Job 1:15) and Chaldeans (Job 1:17) which may reflect the state of affairs in northwestern Arabia between 552 and 542 BCE.

Buz is a country in the eastern Arabian Peninsula (Jer. 25:23), where Iyov's friend Elihu was from (Job 32:2). It is found in Assyrian records as Bazu, invaded by Esar Ḥadon in 677 BCE.

Aram is a large region that included a number of Aramaic-speaking tribes and kingdoms. This wide area included most of modern-day Syria, southeastern Turkey, and parts of Lebanon and Iraq, extending beyond the Euphrates River. The period of prominence of these kingdoms impacted the region by causing a shift in the *lingua franca* of the Middle East from Akkadian to Aramean. Anyone from this general area could be considered an Aramean.

Ḥazo is identified with Hazuh, listed in the inscriptions of Esar Ḥadon as a mountainous region next to Bazu. Tevaḥ appears to be the southern Syrian city of Tubihi mentioned in the *Amarna letters* (EA 179). Taḥash is probably Tahsi, an area in Syria also mentioned in the *Amarna letters* (EA 189).

The last child in the list, Maakha, appears in Egyptian lists as a small Aramean kingdom in northern Transjordan, mentioned in Deuteronomy 3:14 as part of the territory conquered by Menashe. In Tanakh, it is also found as the name of one of the Aramean kingdoms in II Samuel 10:6, 8, and as a place called "Aram Maakha" in I Chronicles 19:6. The kingdom of Maakha is normally associated with Avel of Beit Maakha, in the northern Ḥula Valley, identified with Tell Abil el-Qamh near the Israel/Lebanon border, just south of Metula (see "Avel of Beit Maakha" in the Samuel volume of this series on page 354). ▪ ZR

חיי שרה

כג א וַיִּהְיוּ חַיֵּי שָׂרָה מֵאָה שָׁנָה וְעֶשְׂרִים שָׁנָה וְשֶׁבַע שָׁנִים שְׁנֵי חַיֵּי
• ב שָׂרָה׃ וַתָּמָת שָׂרָה בְּקִרְיַת אַרְבַּע הִוא חֶבְרוֹן בְּאֶרֶץ כְּנָעַן וַיָּבֹא
ג אַבְרָהָם לִסְפֹּד לְשָׂרָה וְלִבְכֹּתָהּ׃ וַיָּקָם אַבְרָהָם מֵעַל פְּנֵי מֵתוֹ

23 1 Sara's lifetime – the years of Sara's life – were one hundred
• 2 and twenty-seven. Sara died in Kiryat Arba – that is, Ḥevron –
in the land of Canaan. And Avraham came to mourn for Sara
3 and to weep for her. Then Avraham rose from beside his dead

NEAR EAST

23:2 The death, mourning, and burial of Sara

Sara is the first person whose death, mourning, and burial are described in the Tanakh.

In Bronze Age Israel, the predominant type of burial attested to archaeologically is the cave tomb, such as the one found near Kibbutz Palmaḥim in September, 2022. This type of tomb was intended to be used by an entire clan for burial over many generations – the natural fissures of the cave are enlarged as needed. The deceased would be set out on their backs either on the cave floor or on a rocky bench, and once the flesh decayed the bones were gathered to a place in the periphery of the cave or placed in a receptacle, thus making room for the next body.

Other forms of burial are found in the ancient Near East. A common practice was to bury the dead underneath the floor of their own house. Still, in the case of a distinguished person, burial would take place in a tomb, with even a chapel built at the site. It was important for these tombs to be near where the family lived, since various practices of the ancestor cult necessitated periodic visits to the place of burial. For example, records of the funeral and burial of Geme-Lama, wife of the governor of Lagash (Ur III period, 2112–2004 BCE) included a last meal offered to the deceased at her tomb on the third day of mourning, with subsequent monthly offerings of food and drink taking place at the tomb. Note that these elements of an ancestor cult are completely absent from the accounts of mourning in the Torah.

The Herodian building in Ḥevron, that is called the Tomb of the Patriarchs, is built over a double shaft tomb that is dated from the Middle Bronze Age. Whether or not it is the actual tomb in which Sara is buried, the style is consistent with the burial practices of the time period in which the Torah places the patriarchal narratives. ▪ ZR

↗ Burial benches in a rock hewn tomb, Akeldama (Field of Blood), Jerusalem

וַיְדַבֵּר אֶל־בְּנֵי־חֵת לֵאמֹר: גֵּר־וְתוֹשָׁב אָנֹכִי עִמָּכֶם תְּנוּ לִי ד
אֲחֻזַּת־קֶבֶר עִמָּכֶם וְאֶקְבְּרָה מֵתִי מִלְּפָנָי: וַיַּעֲנוּ בְנֵי־חֵת אֶת־ ה
אַבְרָהָם לֵאמֹר לוֹ: שְׁמָעֵנוּ ׀ אֲדֹנִי נְשִׂיא אֱלֹהִים אַתָּה בְּתוֹכֵנוּ ו
בְּמִבְחַר קְבָרֵינוּ קְבֹר אֶת־מֵתֶךָ אִישׁ מִמֶּנּוּ אֶת־קִבְרוֹ לֹא־יִכְלֶה
מִמְּךָ מִקְּבֹר מֵתֶךָ: וַיָּקָם אַבְרָהָם וַיִּשְׁתַּחוּ לְעַם־הָאָרֶץ לִבְנֵי־ ז
חֵת: וַיְדַבֵּר אִתָּם לֵאמֹר אִם־יֵשׁ אֶת־נַפְשְׁכֶם לִקְבֹּר אֶת־מֵתִי ח
מִלְּפָנַי שְׁמָעוּנִי וּפִגְעוּ־לִי בְּעֶפְרוֹן בֶּן־צֹחַר: וְיִתֶּן־לִי אֶת־מְעָרַת ט
הַמַּכְפֵּלָה אֲשֶׁר־לוֹ אֲשֶׁר בִּקְצֵה שָׂדֵהוּ בְּכֶסֶף מָלֵא יִתְּנֶנָּה לִּי

4 and spoke to the Hittites. He said, "I am a migrant and a
visitor among you. Sell me a burial site here so that I can bury
5 6 my dead." The Hittites answered Avraham, "Hear us, my lord.
You are a prince of God in our midst. Bury your dead in the
choicest of our tombs. None of us will refuse you his tomb to
7 bury your dead." Avraham rose and bowed down to the
8 Hittites, the people of the land, and said to them, "If you are
willing to allow me to bury the dead that lies before me, then
hear me and intercede on my behalf with Efron son of Tzoḥar.
9 Let him sell me the cave of Makhpela that he owns, at the
edge of his field. Ask him to sell it to me at the full price as a

LANGUAGE

23:4 *Ger vetoshav*

The literal translation of *ger vetoshav* is "a migrant and a visitor." *Ger* means "sojourner" or "resident," and almost always refers to a "resident alien," one who is a migrant or who has lived on the land for generations but is a member of a different ethnic group or culture. Therefore, *ger* is often translated as "stranger." Similarly, *toshav* means "resident," or "settler."

The combination *ger vetoshav* is a hendiadys – one idea expressed by two words connected by "and." Sometimes the two words each refer to the same thing, such as the expression "silver and gold," meaning "wealth." In other instances, one word modifies the other. For example, Shakespeare's "sound and fury" really means "furious sound." Here *ger vetoshav* together mean "resident alien" (see Lev. 25:23, 35, 47), which is the meaning of *ger* alone everywhere in the Torah and in most of the rest of Tanakh.

Throughout the ancient Near East, the alien, for all intents and purposes, was legally a totally defenseless element of society, without civil or property rights. All references to aliens in ancient Near Eastern law collections are as slaves (with only one minor exception).

In this verse, Avraham is announcing that he realizes that he is but a resident alien, without normal rights to buy property. The result will be the extraordinarily high price he will have to pay to acquire the cave of Makhpela and the adjoining field (vv. 15–20). According to one recent estimate based upon Ugaritic evidence, four hundred shekels of silver for a property of that approximate size would be a fairly expensive price, equal to USD 624,000 today. In those days, such a cost could have been borne only by nobility or royalty. Even so, Ugarit was a thriving seaport capital of a trade-based kingdom. That same price hundreds of years earlier, for a field outside a town about one-tenth the size of Ugarit in Middle Bronze Canaan, seems all the more exorbitant. ▪ JU

Royal palace entrance, Ugarit, 15th to 13th century BCE

ARCHAEOLOGY

23:9 Family burial caves

Natural or hewn caves used for burial are found throughout ancient Israel. In many Bronze Age burial caves, such as the ones at Ḥatzor and Yeriḥo, the deceased was laid out in the center of the cave. At the site of Eitun, in the hills of Yehuda, roughly shaped benches adorn the cave walls. In one cave, benches were hewn into the rock, and in another cave, they were constructed of stones lining the tomb. The use of benches at Eitun is a forerunner to the bench tomb that became the quintessential form of the Judahite family tomb in the Iron Age. Items of personal adornment often accompanied the body, while multiple ceramic items used for eating and drinking were placed in the chamber as communal grave goods. Once the body decayed the cave was reopened and the bones were pushed aside to the edges, essentially gathering the individual together with their ancestors (here, also 35:27–29, 50:13).

Social-scientific studies note that in reopening and reorganizing the contents, the family burial cave served not only as a place to deposit the deceased, but also as a location for interacting with the memory of the ancestors. Deposition in the family burial tomb was so important, that at times bones were even repatriated so they might be buried with the ancestors (Gen. 49:29–32; Josh. 24:32; Judges 16:31). Burials also played a role in marking territorial boundaries. Yehoshua was buried at the boundary to his ancestral land (Josh. 24:30; Judges 2:8–9). While Raḥel was not buried with the family, her burial was nonetheless important, as it marks the boundary of the territory of Binyamin (Gen. 35:19, 48:7; I Sam. 10:2), according to one potential location of her tomb (see "Raḥel's grave" on page 218). ▪ KG

ARCHAEOLOGY

23:9 Cave of Makhpela

The text in verses 17 and 19 indicates that Makhpela is the name of an area, in which there is a field and a cave. The idea that the word implies something "doubled" is already found in the Septuagint and Targums, and adopted in the Babylonian Talmud, Eruvin 53a: "Rav and Shmuel (disagreed). One said: (It consists of) two rooms, one farther in than the other. And one said: (It consists of) a room and a second story above it." The latter source also suggests that the name refers to the couples buried there.

The traditional location of the cave of Makhpela, known by the Arabs as *haram el-khalil*, "the sacred precinct of the friend (of God, i.e., Avraham)," is surrounded by a stone enclosure erected by Herod as one of the building projects undertaken during his reign (37–4 BCE). This structure stands on top of an earlier structure thought to date from Hasmonean times (2nd century BCE). Later, in the Byzantine era, a roof was made for most of the enclosure, and a church was built on the site. That church was converted into a mosque after the conquest of Israel by Arabs in the 7th century CE, and back into a church when it was taken by the Crusaders in 1100 CE. It was once again turned into a mosque in the 13th century CE under the Mamluks, who built the cenotaphs of the biblical figures now seen inside the structure. During this period, Sultan Baybars forbade entry into the site by Jews and Christians, who were only permitted to go up to the seventh step of the outer wall on the side of the structure leading to the courtyard of the mosque. This situation persisted through the Ottoman period, the British Mandate, and the Jordanian occupation, until finally people of all faiths were allowed to worship at the site when the IDF liberated Ḥevron in 1967. The upper structure currently houses both a synagogue and a mosque, each with its own entrance.

Due to the holiness of the site and sensitive political situation, no archaeological excavation has ever been carried out at the site. Of the two known entrances to the caves below, the better-known one is a shaft covered by a grate near the marker for Avraham; the other is close to the location of the seventh step. Access to them is currently prohibited by the waqf, who was given control of the caves by the Israeli government after 1967, but they were occasionally used to reach the caves in the Crusader period. Most famous is the description of the Jewish traveler Benjamin of Tudela, who visited the site during that period (1170 CE), reporting that beneath

↗ Cave of Makhpela Herodian building, Ḥevron, view from the south

the building was a sequence of three caves, one behind another, and where containers filled with bones are seen in the most internal cave. Occasional visitors to the caves in the 1900s all describe a burial-cave system. Some suggest that the site began as a naturally forming cave (karst) and was later fashioned for use as a burial chamber, perhaps as early as the Middle Bronze Age. Four vessels were removed in 1981 from an oval chamber reached after entering the first cave: fragments from a bowl, a chalice, a jug, and a jar. Using petrography and chemical analysis, scholars determined that they originated from various areas around Ḥevron and Jerusalem. The vessels have been dated to the 8th century BCE, indicating that the cave was already a pilgrimage site during Iron Age II, corresponding to the First Temple period. ▪ ZR

בְּתוֹכְכֶם לַאֲחֻזַּת־קָבֶר׃ וְעֶפְרוֹן יֹשֵׁב בְּתוֹךְ בְּנֵי־חֵת וַיַּעַן עֶפְרוֹן י
הַחִתִּי אֶת־אַבְרָהָם בְּאׇזְנֵי בְנֵי־חֵת לְכֹל בָּאֵי שַׁעַר־עִירוֹ לֵאמֹר׃
לֹא־אֲדֹנִי שְׁמָעֵנִי הַשָּׂדֶה נָתַתִּי לָךְ וְהַמְּעָרָה אֲשֶׁר־בּוֹ לְךָ נְתַתִּיהָ יא
לְעֵינֵי בְנֵי־עַמִּי נְתַתִּיהָ לָּךְ קְבֹר מֵתֶךָ׃ וַיִּשְׁתַּחוּ אַבְרָהָם לִפְנֵי יב
עַם־הָאָרֶץ׃ וַיְדַבֵּר אֶל־עֶפְרוֹן בְּאׇזְנֵי עַם־הָאָרֶץ לֵאמֹר אַךְ יג
אִם־אַתָּה לוּ שְׁמָעֵנִי נָתַתִּי כֶּסֶף הַשָּׂדֶה קַח מִמֶּנִּי וְאֶקְבְּרָה אֶת־
מֵתִי שָׁמָּה׃ וַיַּעַן עֶפְרוֹן אֶת־אַבְרָהָם לֵאמֹר לוֹ׃ אֲדֹנִי שְׁמָעֵנִי יד טו
אֶרֶץ אַרְבַּע מֵאֹת שֶׁקֶל־כֶּסֶף בֵּינִי וּבֵינְךָ מַה־הִוא וְאֶת־מֵתְךָ
קְבֹר׃ וַיִּשְׁמַע אַבְרָהָם אֶל־עֶפְרוֹן וַיִּשְׁקֹל אַבְרָהָם לְעֶפְרֹן אֶת־ טז

10 burial site in your midst." Efron was sitting among the Hittites.
Efron the Hittite answered Avraham in the hearing of all the
11 Hittites who had come to the city gate. He said, "No, my lord,
hear me. I give you the field and I give you the cave that is in
it. In the presence of my people, I give it to you. Bury your
12 dead." Avraham bowed down again before the people of the
13 land and said to Efron in their hearing, "Please, would that
you would hear me. I give you the money for the field. Take
14 it from me so that I can bury my dead there." Efron answered
15 Avraham and said to him, "My lord, hear me. A piece of land
worth four hundred silver shekel – what is that between you
16 and me? Bury your dead." Avraham heard Efron.[48] He
weighed out for him the price he had mentioned in the

48 | Avraham discerned Efron's real intention: that he be paid the specified amount.

NEAR EAST

23:15 Four hundred shekels of silver

Trade in the ancient Near East was facilitated by assigning values to weighed amounts of precious metals. This changed during the Persian period, when coins were introduced. The shekel is the Hebrew form of the Assyrian *siqlu* (based on the Semitic root for weighing), equivalent to the Sumerian *gin*.

In a paper published during the preparation of this volume, researchers determined that the earliest time that silver was used for commercial transactions was in the Middle Bronze Age, in the 17th to 16th century BCE. Previously, scholars assumed that silver was not used for exchange until the Iron Age, in the 11th century BCE. When analyzing silver found in hoards discovered in Megiddo, Gezer, Tell el-Ajjul, and Shilo, the authors of the paper determined that the silver originated from Anatolia or Greece – there are no known silver mines in the Levant – indicating extensive trade with those regions at the time. Silver was not used for day-to-day transactions. Rather, it was the currency exchanged for large purchases, such as the land purchase here. The new analysis reported in 2023 reflects a reality at the time of Avraham that silver was used as a means of exchange for transactions such as this one.

The shekel had varying values depending on the era and region. From Judahite inscribed stone weights, it can be determined that during the period of the monarchy a shekel weighed approximately 11 grams (almost 0.4 ounces). The Mesopotamian shekel, which is what Avraham would have been familiar with, weighed about 8.3–8.5 grams (approximately 0.29 ounces), resulting in 400 shekels being equivalent to about 3.4 kilograms (7.5 pounds) of silver. This is a conservative figure based on the range of shekel values, which could reach double this amount. Even at the low end of shekel values, this sum is a large amount of money considering the average wage was ten shekels a year (see "A thousand pieces of silver" on page 127). ▪ ZR

Hacksilber (silver hoard), Tel el-Ajjul, Aza, 17th century BCE ↘

הַכֶּסֶף אֲשֶׁר דִּבֶּר בְּאׇזְנֵי בְנֵי־חֵת אַרְבַּע מֵאוֹת שֶׁקֶל כֶּסֶף עֹבֵר
יז לַסֹּחֵר׃ וַיָּקׇם ׀ שְׂדֵה עֶפְרוֹן אֲשֶׁר בַּמַּכְפֵּלָה אֲשֶׁר לִפְנֵי מַמְרֵא שני
הַשָּׂדֶה וְהַמְּעָרָה אֲשֶׁר־בּוֹ וְכׇל־הָעֵץ אֲשֶׁר בַּשָּׂדֶה אֲשֶׁר בְּכׇל־
יח גְּבֻלוֹ סָבִיב׃ לְאַבְרָהָם לְמִקְנָה לְעֵינֵי בְנֵי־חֵת בְּכֹל בָּאֵי שַׁעַר־
יט עִירוֹ׃ וְאַחֲרֵי־כֵן קָבַר אַבְרָהָם אֶת־שָׂרָה אִשְׁתּוֹ אֶל־מְעָרַת
כ שְׂדֵה הַמַּכְפֵּלָה עַל־פְּנֵי מַמְרֵא הִוא חֶבְרוֹן בְּאֶרֶץ כְּנָעַן׃ וַיָּקׇם
הַשָּׂדֶה וְהַמְּעָרָה אֲשֶׁר־בּוֹ לְאַבְרָהָם לַאֲחֻזַּת־קָבֶר מֵאֵת בְּנֵי־
כד א חֵת׃ וְאַבְרָהָם זָקֵן בָּא בַּיָּמִים וַיהֹוָה בֵּרַךְ אֶת־
ב אַבְרָהָם בַּכֹּל׃ וַיֹּאמֶר אַבְרָהָם אֶל־עַבְדּוֹ זְקַן בֵּיתוֹ הַמֹּשֵׁל בְּכׇל־
• ג אֲשֶׁר־לוֹ שִׂים־נָא יָדְךָ תַּחַת יְרֵכִי׃ וְאַשְׁבִּיעֲךָ בַּיהֹוָה אֱלֹהֵי
הַשָּׁמַיִם וֵאלֹהֵי הָאָרֶץ אֲשֶׁר לֹא־תִקַּח אִשָּׁה לִבְנִי מִבְּנוֹת הַכְּנַעֲנִי

Hittites' hearing: four hundred silver shekel at the merchants'
standard rate. So Efron's field in Makhpela near Mamre – the 17
field, its cave, and all the trees within the field's borders –
passed to Avraham as his possession, in the presence of all 18
the Hittites who had come to the city gate. Avraham then 19
buried Sara his wife in the cave in the field of Makhpela near
Mamre – that is, Ḥevron – in the land of Canaan. Thus the 20
field and its cave passed from the Hittites to Avraham as a
burial site. Avraham was old, advanced in years, 1 **24**
and the Lord had blessed him in all things. And Avraham 2
said to the senior servant of his household, who was in charge
of all he had, "Place your hand under my thigh.[49] I want you 3 •
to swear by the Lord, God of heaven and earth, that you will

49 | An act sometimes performed in conjunction with an oath.

NEAR EAST

24:3 God of heaven and earth

The phrase "God of heaven and earth" is found only here in the Tanakh, emphasizing God's uniqueness. However, heaven and earth are employed several times in Tanakh as "witnesses" (e.g., Deut. 4:26, 30:19; Is. 1:2). The term is used here to emphasize God's universal sovereignty before Avraham's servant travels to a faraway land. This perspective is in opposition to Mesopotamian pagan beliefs that the gods' powers were restricted to a specific geographic locale.

This phrase is found on an inscription in the central part of the end wall of the tomb of the Egyptian official Meryneith at Saqqara (ca. 1350 BCE), "the living Aten, lord of heaven and earth," in contrast to the more common "lord of heaven" found in other Egyptian inscriptions. As seen with titles such as "Most High" (Gen. 14:18–20, 22), the Tanakh sometimes adopts titles or attributes of pagan gods and "monotheizes" them by applying them to the one, true God. ▪ ZR

Wall relief, tomb of the Egyptian official Meryneith, 14th century BCE

אֲשֶׁר אָנֹכִי יוֹשֵׁב בְּקִרְבּוֹ: כִּי אֶל־אַרְצִי וְאֶל־מוֹלַדְתִּי תֵּלֵךְ וְלָקַחְתָּ ד
אִשָּׁה לִבְנִי לְיִצְחָק: וַיֹּאמֶר אֵלָיו הָעֶבֶד אוּלַי לֹא־תֹאבֶה הָאִשָּׁה ה
לָלֶכֶת אַחֲרַי אֶל־הָאָרֶץ הַזֹּאת הֶהָשֵׁב אָשִׁיב אֶת־בִּנְךָ אֶל־
הָאָרֶץ אֲשֶׁר־יָצָאתָ מִשָּׁם: וַיֹּאמֶר אֵלָיו אַבְרָהָם הִשָּׁמֶר לְךָ ו
פֶּן־תָּשִׁיב אֶת־בְּנִי שָׁמָּה: יְהוָה ׀ אֱלֹהֵי הַשָּׁמַיִם אֲשֶׁר לְקָחַנִי ז

not take a wife for my son from among the daughters of the
4 Canaanites among whom I live. Instead, go to my land and
5 birthplace, and there find a wife for Yitzḥak my son." The
servant asked, "What if the woman does not want to come
back with me to this land? Shall I bring your son back to the
6 land from which you came?" Avraham said to him, "Be sure
7 not to take my son back there. The Lord, God of the heavens,
took me from my father's house and from the land of my birth.

NEAR EAST

24:4 Go to my...birthplace, and there find a wife for...my son

Societies in the ancient Near East practiced endogamy, preferring marriage within the tribe, clan, or social group, ensuring that property and inheritance remains within the clan. With the patriarchs, the concern was to avoid ethnic assimilation with the Canaanites (as seen in Gen. 28:1). Even though Naḥor's family practiced a different religion (see Gen. 31:53), they were preferred to the local Canaanites, since the bride would move away from her family and join her husband's clan to practice his religion.

The idea that a parent initiates the marriage for his child as seen here is also reflected in the *Laws of Hammurabi:* "If a man has betrothed a bride to his son..." (LH §155). The Akkadian legal term here, *aḥazu*, literally means "seize," or "possess," similar to the Hebrew root *l k ḥ*, literally, "take" – translated here as "find." ▪ ZR

Rebecca and Eliezer, Bartolomé Esteban Murillo, ca. 1660 ↘

מִבֵּית אָבִי וּמֵאֶרֶץ מוֹלַדְתִּי וַאֲשֶׁר דִּבֶּר־לִי וַאֲשֶׁר נִשְׁבַּע־לִי לֵאמֹר
לְזַרְעֲךָ אֶתֵּן אֶת־הָאָרֶץ הַזֹּאת הוּא יִשְׁלַח מַלְאָכוֹ לְפָנֶיךָ וְלָקַחְתָּ
ח אִשָּׁה לִבְנִי מִשָּׁם: וְאִם־לֹא תֹאבֶה הָאִשָּׁה לָלֶכֶת אַחֲרֶיךָ וְנִקִּיתָ
ט מִשְּׁבֻעָתִי זֹאת רַק אֶת־בְּנִי לֹא תָשֵׁב שָׁמָּה: וַיָּשֶׂם הָעֶבֶד אֶת־
י • יָדוֹ תַּחַת יֶרֶךְ אַבְרָהָם אֲדֹנָיו וַיִּשָּׁבַע לוֹ עַל־הַדָּבָר הַזֶּה: וַיִּקַּח שלישי
הָעֶבֶד עֲשָׂרָה גְמַלִּים מִגְּמַלֵּי אֲדֹנָיו וַיֵּלֶךְ וְכָל־טוּב אֲדֹנָיו בְּיָדוֹ

He spoke to me and swore to me, 'To your descendants I will
give this land.' He will send His angel before you, and there
you will find a wife for my son. But if the woman does not 8
want to come back with you, then you will be released from
this oath to me. Just do not take my son back there." So the 9
servant placed his hand under his master Avraham's thigh and
swore this by an oath to him. The servant then took ten of his 10 •
master's camels, laden with all his master's bounty, and set

NEAR EAST

24:10 Aram Naharayim

The term *aram naharayim* literally means "Aram [between] the two rivers". However, it was translated in the Septuagint as the proper name Mesopotamia (Greek for "[land] between the rivers"), which was used by ancient Greek writers to refer to the entire area between the Tigris and Euphrates – but that is not accurate in this case, which refers to Aram.

The Aramaic Targums interpreted the term *naharayim* as "the land along the river", meaning "Aram which is on the Euphrates" – an area in central Mesopotamia along the great bend of the Euphrates River, bordered on three sides by the Euphrates turning south and southeast.

The Hurrian state of Mitanni, located in modern-day northern Syria and southeastern Turkey is called Naharin in Egyptian texts going back to the 16th century BCE, and Naharima in the *Amarna letters*. The term Aram Naharayim could therefore be understood as a region identified as "the Naharim part of the area where people speak Aramaic." ▪ ZR

↗ Satellite map from the Copernicus Sentinel-2 satellite of the waters of the Tigris and Euphrates Rivers emptying into the sea, September 2019

וַיָּקָם וַיֵּלֶךְ אֶל־אֲרַם נַהֲרַיִם אֶל־עִיר נָחוֹר׃ וַיַּבְרֵךְ הַגְּמַלִּים מִחוּץ יא
לָעִיר אֶל־בְּאֵר הַמָּיִם לְעֵת עֶרֶב לְעֵת צֵאת הַשֹּׁאֲבֹת׃ וַיֹּאמַר ׀ יב
יְהוָה אֱלֹהֵי אֲדֹנִי אַבְרָהָם הַקְרֵה־נָא לְפָנַי הַיּוֹם וַעֲשֵׂה־חֶסֶד
עִם אֲדֹנִי אַבְרָהָם׃ הִנֵּה אָנֹכִי נִצָּב עַל־עֵין הַמָּיִם וּבְנוֹת אַנְשֵׁי יג
הָעִיר יֹצְאֹת לִשְׁאֹב מָיִם׃ וְהָיָה הַנַּעֲרָ אֲשֶׁר אֹמַר אֵלֶיהָ הַטִּי־נָא יד
כַדֵּךְ וְאֶשְׁתֶּה וְאָמְרָה שְׁתֵה וְגַם־גְּמַלֶּיךָ אַשְׁקֶה אֹתָהּ הֹכַחְתָּ

11 out to Aram Naharayim, to the city of Naḥor. By the well
outside the city, he had the camels kneel. It was evening, the
12 time when the women came out to draw water. "Lord, God
of my master Avraham," he said, "please, grant me success
13 today and show kindness to my master Avraham. I am
standing here by the spring and the daughters of the
14 townspeople are coming out to draw water. If I say to a young
woman, 'Please lower your jar so that I can drink,' and she
replies, 'Drink, and I will water your camels also,' let her be
the one You have chosen for Your servant Yitzḥak. By this I

NEAR EAST

24:11 Women drawing water

This is the first mention in Tanakh of women drawing water. Later examples are found in Genesis 29:2; Exodus 2:16; I Samuel 9:11; and Nahum 3:14. In ancient times, wells required significant labor to build and were often a shared resource. Meetings took place while drawing water at wells, which would serve as a good place for newcomers to learn about the locality and make contacts.

This motif appears in other ancient Near Eastern cultures. For example, women drawing water at a well is mentioned three times in the Ugaritic *Kirta Epic* (KTU 1.14, iii 9), which describes how "the women drawing water will flee from the spring, from the fountain the women filling [jugs]." ▪ ZR

Women at the village well

NEAR EAST

24:12–14 The prayer of Avraham's servant

These verses comprise the first description of an extemporaneous prayer in Tanakh, composed at a critical moment, asking God for assistance and guidance. This informal prose prayer is characteristic of daily life in biblical times. In contrast, the polished and carefully constructed poetic prayers familiar from Psalms and other liturgy are written for others to draw upon as the occasion requires. The theology behind this simple prose prayer is that God is constant, reliable and available, concerned even with the events of the mundane daily life.

This type of artless prayer also demonstrates that prayer is not to be viewed as dependent on a particular type of phrasing to be effective. In contrast, the rigidly fixed formulae of the Babylonian incantations during exorcism rituals are required for the ritual to be validated. In Tanakh, the effectiveness of prayer is due to its content and sincerity, rather than the specific wording, as God "discerns both mind and heart" (Jer. 11:20).

After receiving a positive response to his prayer, Avraham's servant reacts unsurprisingly with another extemporaneous prayer – this time, one of thanks (v. 26). ▪ ZR

Fragment of a talisman used to exorcise the sick, Assyrian

טו לְעַבְדְּךָ לְיִצְחָק וּבָהּ אֵדַע כִּי־עָשִׂיתָ חֶסֶד עִם־אֲדֹנִי: וַיְהִי־הוּא
טֶרֶם כִּלָּה לְדַבֵּר וְהִנֵּה רִבְקָה יֹצֵאת אֲשֶׁר יֻלְּדָה לִבְתוּאֵל בֶּן־
טז מִלְכָּה אֵשֶׁת נָחוֹר אֲחִי אַבְרָהָם וְכַדָּהּ עַל־שִׁכְמָהּ: וְהַנַּעֲרָ טֹבַת
מַרְאֶה מְאֹד בְּתוּלָה וְאִישׁ לֹא יְדָעָהּ וַתֵּרֶד הָעַיְנָה וַתְּמַלֵּא כַדָּהּ
יז וַתָּעַל: וַיָּרָץ הָעֶבֶד לִקְרָאתָהּ וַיֹּאמֶר הַגְמִיאִינִי נָא מְעַט־מַיִם
יח מִכַּדֵּךְ: וַתֹּאמֶר שְׁתֵה אֲדֹנִי וַתְּמַהֵר וַתֹּרֶד כַּדָּהּ עַל־יָדָהּ
• יט וַתַּשְׁקֵהוּ: וַתְּכַל לְהַשְׁקֹתוֹ וַתֹּאמֶר גַּם לִגְמַלֶּיךָ אֶשְׁאָב עַד אִם־
כ כִּלּוּ לִשְׁתֹּת: וַתְּמַהֵר וַתְּעַר כַּדָּהּ אֶל־הַשֹּׁקֶת וַתָּרָץ עוֹד אֶל־
כא הַבְּאֵר לִשְׁאֹב וַתִּשְׁאַב לְכָל־גְּמַלָּיו: וְהָאִישׁ מִשְׁתָּאֵה לָהּ מַחֲרִישׁ

15 will know that You have shown kindness to my master." Before
he had even finished speaking, Rivka, daughter of Betuel son
of Milka, the wife of Avraham's brother Naḥor, came out with
16 her jar on her shoulder. The young woman was very beautiful,
a virgin whom no man had known. She went down to the
17 spring, filled her jar, and came up. The servant ran to meet
her and said, "Please let me sip a little water from your jar."
18 She said, "Drink, my lord," and quickly lowered her jar to her
19 • hand and let him drink. When she had let him drink his fill,
she said, "I will draw water for your camels, too, until they
20 have had enough to drink." Quickly she emptied her jar into
the trough and ran back to the well to draw more water; she
21 drew for all his camels. The man stood gazing at her, silently
wondering whether the Lord had made his journey

Dromedary camels drinking from a well, Sahara desert

— FLORA AND FAUNA —

24:19–22 Camel test

A camel requires about 95 liters (approximately 25 gallons) of water to completely replenish the weight lost over the course of a long journey – yet it only takes a camel approximately ten minutes to drink this quantity of water. The time needed to give each of the ten camels water is compounded due to the size of water jugs of that era. It would take between eight and ten jugs to supply each of the ten camels with water, requiring close to a hundred trips to the well! Even if the camels were partially watered prior to arriving at the well, this would not be known before offering to supply them with water. Thus, the arduous task stipulated by Avraham's servant would certainly establish the good character and generosity of spirit of anyone willing to do this for a total stranger with so many camels. ▪ ZR

לָדַעַת הַהִצְלִיחַ יהוה דַּרְכּוֹ אִם־לֹא: וַיְהִי כַּאֲשֶׁר כִּלּוּ הַגְּמַלִּים כב •
לִשְׁתּוֹת וַיִּקַּח הָאִישׁ נֶזֶם זָהָב בֶּקַע מִשְׁקָלוֹ וּשְׁנֵי צְמִידִים עַל־
יָדֶיהָ עֲשָׂרָה זָהָב מִשְׁקָלָם: וַיֹּאמֶר בַּת־מִי אַתְּ הַגִּידִי נָא לִי הֲיֵשׁ כג
בֵּית־אָבִיךְ מָקוֹם לָנוּ לָלִין: וַתֹּאמֶר אֵלָיו בַּת־בְּתוּאֵל אָנֹכִי כד
בֶּן־מִלְכָּה אֲשֶׁר יָלְדָה לְנָחוֹר: וַתֹּאמֶר אֵלָיו גַּם־תֶּבֶן גַּם־מִסְפּוֹא כה
רביעי רַב עִמָּנוּ גַּם־מָקוֹם לָלוּן: וַיִּקֹּד הָאִישׁ וַיִּשְׁתַּחוּ לַיהוה: וַיֹּאמֶר כו כז
בָּרוּךְ יהוה אֱלֹהֵי אֲדֹנִי אַבְרָהָם אֲשֶׁר לֹא־עָזַב חַסְדּוֹ וַאֲמִתּוֹ
מֵעִם אֲדֹנִי אָנֹכִי בַּדֶּרֶךְ נָחַנִי יהוה בֵּית אֲחֵי אֲדֹנִי: וַתָּרָץ הַנַּעֲרָ כח
וַתַּגֵּד לְבֵית אִמָּהּ כַּדְּבָרִים הָאֵלֶּה: וּלְרִבְקָה אָח וּשְׁמוֹ לָבָן וַיָּרָץ כט
לָבָן אֶל־הָאִישׁ הַחוּצָה אֶל־הָעָיִן: וַיְהִי | כִּרְאֹת אֶת־הַנֶּזֶם וְאֶת־ ל
הַצְּמִדִים עַל־יְדֵי אֲחֹתוֹ וּכְשָׁמְעוֹ אֶת־דִּבְרֵי רִבְקָה אֲחֹתוֹ לֵאמֹר
כֹּה־דִבֶּר אֵלַי הָאִישׁ וַיָּבֹא אֶל־הָאִישׁ וְהִנֵּה עֹמֵד עַל־הַגְּמַלִּים
עַל־הָעָיִן: וַיֹּאמֶר בּוֹא בְּרוּךְ יהוה לָמָּה תַעֲמֹד בַּחוּץ וְאָנֹכִי לא
פִּנִּיתִי הַבַּיִת וּמָקוֹם לַגְּמַלִּים: וַיָּבֹא הָאִישׁ הַבַּיְתָה וַיְפַתַּח לב
הַגְּמַלִּים וַיִּתֵּן תֶּבֶן וּמִסְפּוֹא לַגְּמַלִּים וּמַיִם לִרְחֹץ רַגְלָיו וְרַגְלֵי
וַיּוּשַׂם הָאֲנָשִׁים אֲשֶׁר אִתּוֹ: ויישם לְפָנָיו לֶאֱכֹל וַיֹּאמֶר לֹא אֹכַל עַד לג

• 22 successful. When the camels had finished drinking, the man
took a gold ring weighing a half shekel and two gold bracelets
23 for her arms weighing ten shekel, and he asked, "Whose
daughter are you? Please tell me, is there room in your father's
24 house for us to spend the night?" She answered him, "I am
25 the daughter of Betuel, the son Milka bore to Naḥor." She
added, "We have plenty of straw and fodder, as well as room
26 for you to spend the night." The man bowed low, prostrating
27 himself to the Lord. He said, "Blessed be the Lord, God of
my master Avraham, who has not withheld His kindness and
faithfulness from my master. As for me – the Lord has guided
28 me on the way to the house of my master's close family." The
young woman ran and told all this to her mother's household.
29 Rivka had a brother named Lavan; he ran outside to the man
30 at the spring. He had seen the ring, and the bracelets on his
sister's arms, and had heard his sister Rivka tell what the man
had said to her. He came up to the man who was still standing
31 by the camels at the spring, and said, "Come. The Lord bless
you! Why are you standing outside? I have made room in the
32 house and prepared a place for the camels." So the man
entered the house, the camels were unloaded, straw and
fodder were brought for the camels, and water was brought
33 for him and his men to wash their feet. Food was set before
him to eat, but he said, "I will not eat until I have said what I

NEAR EAST

24:22 Gold ring...gold bracelets

These golden jewelry items represent the first stage of the bride-price that will be completed later (see "Bride-price" on page 150). The term for the gold ring, *nezem*, can refer to a ring worn in the nose or on a finger. Rings like these were popular in biblical times and have been found in many Bronze Age archaeological sites, including Megiddo, Gezer and Lakhish. The bracelets here refer to the bangles worn by women on their arms or wrists; they have also been unearthed in many archaeological sites. These were generally worn in a bunch, which may provide an explanation as why the servant gave more than one. For example, in the "Goddess with a vase" statue from Mari (ca. 2000–1500 BCE), the goddess is shown with three bangles on each wrist. ▪ ZR

↗ Goddess with a vase, Mari, 18th century BCE

לד לה אִם־דִּבַּרְתִּי דְּבָרָי וַיֹּאמֶר דַּבֵּר׃ וַיֹּאמַר עֶבֶד אַבְרָהָם אָנֹכִי׃ וַיהוָה
בֵּרַךְ אֶת־אֲדֹנִי מְאֹד וַיִּגְדָּל וַיִּתֶּן־לוֹ צֹאן וּבָקָר וְכֶסֶף וְזָהָב וַעֲבָדִם
לו וּשְׁפָחֹת וּגְמַלִּים וַחֲמֹרִים׃ וַתֵּלֶד שָׂרָה אֵשֶׁת אֲדֹנִי בֵן לַאדֹנִי
לז אַחֲרֵי זִקְנָתָהּ וַיִּתֶּן־לוֹ אֶת־כָּל־אֲשֶׁר־לוֹ׃ וַיַּשְׁבִּעֵנִי אֲדֹנִי לֵאמֹר
לֹא־תִקַּח אִשָּׁה לִבְנִי מִבְּנוֹת הַכְּנַעֲנִי אֲשֶׁר אָנֹכִי יֹשֵׁב בְּאַרְצוֹ׃
לח אִם־לֹא אֶל־בֵּית־אָבִי תֵּלֵךְ וְאֶל־מִשְׁפַּחְתִּי וְלָקַחְתָּ אִשָּׁה לִבְנִי׃
לט מ וָאֹמַר אֶל־אֲדֹנִי אֻלַי לֹא־תֵלֵךְ הָאִשָּׁה אַחֲרָי׃ וַיֹּאמֶר אֵלָי יְהוָה
אֲשֶׁר־הִתְהַלַּכְתִּי לְפָנָיו יִשְׁלַח מַלְאָכוֹ אִתָּךְ וְהִצְלִיחַ דַּרְכֶּךָ
מא וְלָקַחְתָּ אִשָּׁה לִבְנִי מִמִּשְׁפַּחְתִּי וּמִבֵּית אָבִי׃ אָז תִּנָּקֶה מֵאָלָתִי
כִּי תָבוֹא אֶל־מִשְׁפַּחְתִּי וְאִם־לֹא יִתְּנוּ לָךְ וְהָיִיתָ נָקִי מֵאָלָתִי׃
מב וָאָבֹא הַיּוֹם אֶל־הָעָיִן וָאֹמַר יְהוָה אֱלֹהֵי אֲדֹנִי אַבְרָהָם אִם־
מג יֶשְׁךָ־נָּא מַצְלִיחַ דַּרְכִּי אֲשֶׁר אָנֹכִי הֹלֵךְ עָלֶיהָ׃ הִנֵּה אָנֹכִי נִצָּב
עַל־עֵין הַמָּיִם וְהָיָה הָעַלְמָה הַיֹּצֵאת לִשְׁאֹב וְאָמַרְתִּי אֵלֶיהָ
מד הַשְׁקִינִי־נָא מְעַט־מַיִם מִכַּדֵּךְ׃ וְאָמְרָה אֵלַי גַּם־אַתָּה שְׁתֵה וְגַם
מה לִגְמַלֶּיךָ אֶשְׁאָב הִוא הָאִשָּׁה אֲשֶׁר־הֹכִיחַ יְהוָה לְבֶן־אֲדֹנִי׃ אֲנִי
טֶרֶם אֲכַלֶּה לְדַבֵּר אֶל־לִבִּי וְהִנֵּה רִבְקָה יֹצֵאת וְכַדָּהּ עַל־שִׁכְמָהּ
מו וַתֵּרֶד הָעַיְנָה וַתִּשְׁאָב וָאֹמַר אֵלֶיהָ הַשְׁקִינִי נָא׃ וַתְּמַהֵר וַתּוֹרֶד
כַּדָּהּ מֵעָלֶיהָ וַתֹּאמֶר שְׁתֵה וְגַם־גְּמַלֶּיךָ אַשְׁקֶה וָאֵשְׁתְּ וְגַם
מז הַגְּמַלִּים הִשְׁקָתָה׃ וָאֶשְׁאַל אֹתָהּ וָאֹמַר בַּת־מִי אַתְּ וַתֹּאמֶר
בַּת־בְּתוּאֵל בֶּן־נָחוֹר אֲשֶׁר יָלְדָה־לּוֹ מִלְכָּה וָאָשִׂם הַנֶּזֶם עַל־
מח אַפָּהּ וְהַצְּמִידִים עַל־יָדֶיהָ׃ וָאֶקֹּד וָאֶשְׁתַּחֲוֶה לַיהוָה וָאֲבָרֵךְ
אֶת־יְהוָה אֱלֹהֵי אֲדֹנִי אַבְרָהָם אֲשֶׁר הִנְחַנִי בְּדֶרֶךְ אֱמֶת לָקַחַת

have to say." "Speak, then," said
Lavan. "I am Avraham's servant," 34
he said. "The Lord has blessed 35
my master greatly, and he has
prospered. He has given him
sheep and cattle, silver and gold,
male and female servants, camels
and donkeys. My master's wife 36
Sara bore my master a son in her
old age, and he committed to his
son all that is his. My master made 37
me swear, saying, 'You must not
take a wife for my son from among the daughters of the Canaanites in whose land I live. Instead you 38
must go to my father's house and family and there find a wife for my son.' I asked my master, 'What if 39
the woman does not want to come back with me?' He answered, 'The Lord before whom I have walked 40
will send His angel with you to make your journey a success, so that you may find a wife for my son from
my family and father's house. You are released from this vow only if you come to my family and they 41
refuse to give her to you. Then you are released from my vow.' Today, when I came to the spring, I said, 42
'Lord, God of my master Avraham, if You will, please grant success to this journey on which I have
come. I am standing here by a spring of water. The woman who comes out to draw water, to whom I say, 43
"Please let me sip a little water from your jar," and who says to me, "Drink, and I will also draw for your 44
camels" – let her be the one the Lord has chosen for my master's son.' Before I had even finished speaking 45
to myself, Rivka came out with her jar on her shoulder. She went down to the spring and drew water,
and I asked her, 'Please, let me drink.' She immediately lowered her jar and said, 'Drink, and I will also 46
water your camels.' So I drank, and she gave the camels water too. I asked her, 'Whose daughter are you?' 47
She said, 'The daughter of Betuel son of Naḥor, whom Milka bore to him.' So I placed a ring on her nose
and bracelets on her arms. I bowed low and prostrated myself to the Lord, and blessed the Lord, God 48
of my master Avraham, who led me on the right way to take the daughter of my master's brother for his

אֶת־בַּת־אֲחִי אֲדֹנִי לִבְנוֹ׃ וְעַתָּה אִם־יֶשְׁכֶם עֹשִׂים חֶסֶד וֶאֱמֶת מט
אֶת־אֲדֹנִי הַגִּידוּ לִי וְאִם־לֹא הַגִּידוּ לִי וְאֶפְנֶה עַל־יָמִין אוֹ עַל־
שְׂמֹאל׃ וַיַּעַן לָבָן וּבְתוּאֵל וַיֹּאמְרוּ מֵיְהוָה יָצָא הַדָּבָר לֹא נוּכַל נ
דַּבֵּר אֵלֶיךָ רַע אוֹ־טוֹב׃ הִנֵּה־רִבְקָה לְפָנֶיךָ קַח וָלֵךְ וּתְהִי אִשָּׁה נא
לְבֶן־אֲדֹנֶיךָ כַּאֲשֶׁר דִּבֶּר יְהוָה׃ וַיְהִי כַּאֲשֶׁר שָׁמַע עֶבֶד אַבְרָהָם נב
חמישי אֶת־דִּבְרֵיהֶם וַיִּשְׁתַּחוּ אַרְצָה לַיהוָה׃ וַיּוֹצֵא הָעֶבֶד כְּלֵי־כֶסֶף • נג
וּכְלֵי זָהָב וּבְגָדִים וַיִּתֵּן לְרִבְקָה וּמִגְדָּנֹת נָתַן לְאָחִיהָ וּלְאִמָּהּ׃
וַיֹּאכְלוּ וַיִּשְׁתּוּ הוּא וְהָאֲנָשִׁים אֲשֶׁר־עִמּוֹ וַיָּלִינוּ וַיָּקוּמוּ בַבֹּקֶר נד
וַיֹּאמֶר שַׁלְּחֻנִי לַאדֹנִי׃ וַיֹּאמֶר אָחִיהָ וְאִמָּהּ תֵּשֵׁב הַנַּעֲרָ אִתָּנוּ נה
יָמִים אוֹ עָשׂוֹר אַחַר תֵּלֵךְ׃ וַיֹּאמֶר אֲלֵהֶם אַל־תְּאַחֲרוּ אֹתִי וַיהוָה נו

49 son. Now, if you are willing to show kindness and faithfulness
to my master, tell me; and if not, tell me that, so that I may
50 move on, right or left." Lavan and Betuel answered, "This is
surely from the Lord: there is nothing for us to say to you,
51 bad or good. Here is Rivka in front of you. Take her; go. Let
her be the wife of your master's son, as the Lord has spoken."
52 When Avraham's servant heard these words, he bowed down
• 53 to the ground before the Lord. The servant brought out gold
and silver jewelry and clothes and gave them to Rivka. He
54 also gave costly gifts to her brother and her mother. Then he
and his men ate and drank and spent the night there. When
they got up the next morning he said, "Send me on my way
55 to my master." But her brother and her mother replied, "Let
the young woman stay with us a year or ten months. Then she
56 may go." "Do not delay me," he said, "now that the Lord has

NEAR EAST

24:53 Bride-price

The bride-price was given by the family of the groom to the family of the bride. This is distinct from a dowry, which was given to the bride by her own father (such as in vv. 59 and 61, when Rivka was given a nurse and maids), and remained her personal property, functioning as an inheritance from her family.

Regional and societal variations existed regarding what sorts of gifts were given and when. The Sumerian *nigdea* were gifts presented when the families reached an agreement that their children would marry, as in our verse.

For further discussion on marriage customs in the ancient Near East, see "Bride-price and marriage customs" on page 185.

▪ ZR

Rebecca and Eliezer at the well, Lambert Doomer, 1696

נו • הִצְלִיחַ דַּרְכִּי שַׁלְּחוּנִי וְאֵלְכָה לַאדֹנִי: וַיֹּאמְרוּ נִקְרָא לַנַּעֲרָ
נז וְנִשְׁאֲלָה אֶת־פִּיהָ: וַיִּקְרְאוּ לְרִבְקָה וַיֹּאמְרוּ אֵלֶיהָ הֲתֵלְכִי עִם־
נח הָאִישׁ הַזֶּה וַתֹּאמֶר אֵלֵךְ: וַיְשַׁלְּחוּ אֶת־רִבְקָה אֲחֹתָם וְאֶת־
ס מֵנִקְתָּהּ וְאֶת־עֶבֶד אַבְרָהָם וְאֶת־אֲנָשָׁיו: וַיְבָרֲכוּ אֶת־רִבְקָה
וַיֹּאמְרוּ לָהּ אֲחֹתֵנוּ אַתְּ הֲיִי לְאַלְפֵי רְבָבָה וְיִירַשׁ זַרְעֵךְ אֵת שַׁעַר
סא שֹׂנְאָיו: וַתָּקָם רִבְקָה וְנַעֲרֹתֶיהָ וַתִּרְכַּבְנָה עַל־הַגְּמַלִּים וַתֵּלַכְנָה
סב אַחֲרֵי הָאִישׁ וַיִּקַּח הָעֶבֶד אֶת־רִבְקָה וַיֵּלַךְ: וְיִצְחָק בָּא מִבּוֹא
סג בְּאֵר לַחַי רֹאִי וְהוּא יוֹשֵׁב בְּאֶרֶץ הַנֶּגֶב: וַיֵּצֵא יִצְחָק לָשׂוּחַ
סד בַּשָּׂדֶה לִפְנוֹת עָרֶב וַיִּשָּׂא עֵינָיו וַיַּרְא וְהִנֵּה גְמַלִּים בָּאִים: וַתִּשָּׂא
סה • רִבְקָה אֶת־עֵינֶיהָ וַתֵּרֶא אֶת־יִצְחָק וַתִּפֹּל מֵעַל הַגָּמָל: וַתֹּאמֶר
אֶל־הָעֶבֶד מִי־הָאִישׁ הַלָּזֶה הַהֹלֵךְ בַּשָּׂדֶה לִקְרָאתֵנוּ וַיֹּאמֶר

made my journey a success. Let me leave so that I may go back
to my master." They replied, "Let us call the young woman 57 •
and ask her." So they called Rivka and asked her, "Will you 58
go with this man?" She replied, "I will." So they sent their 59
sister Rivka on her way, together with her nurse and Avraham's
servant and his men. They blessed Rivka and said to her, "Our 60
sister, may you grow into thousands of myriads, and may your
descendants possess their enemies' gates." Then Rivka set off 61
with her maids, riding on camels and following the man. The
servant took Rivka and went. Yitzḥak was just coming back 62
from the direction of Be'er Laḥai Ro'i, for he was then living
in the Negev. He had gone out in the field toward evening to 63
meditate. Looking up, he saw – there were camels approaching.
Rivka too looked up – and saw Yitzḥak. She jumped down 64
from the camel and asked the servant, "Who is that man 65 •
walking in the field toward us?" The servant replied, "That is

NEAR EAST

24:57–58 A woman's choice to marry

In the ancient Near East, two models prevailed for how a marriage match would be conducted. The first was between the two fathers of the bride and groom without any input from the intended couple. The second was an arrangement between the families instigated by the potential groom (as seen in Gen. 34:3–4 and Judges 14:1–2).

In our verses, it appears that Rivka is being asked for her opinion, which may be a unique case due to her moving far away from her family without their immediate protection should the marriage not succeed and help be needed. Note that in verse 55, Rivka's father is not mentioned, and her brother Lavan and her mother conduct the negotiations. That Rivka is asked her opinion in this particular circumstance complements the Sumerian proverb, "Girl, do not let your brother choose for you! Whom do you choose?" ▪ ZR

NEAR EAST

24:65 Veil

In ancient Babylonia and Assyria, a bride would be veiled before her wedding ceremony. The veil was removed by her husband on the wedding night. This scene is depicted on a Hittite vase (ca. 1550 BCE), found near Ankara, which shows a man and a woman sitting opposite each other (see the illustration). With one hand the man lifts up the woman's veil, and with the other, he passes her a drink, a practice familiar even today in Jewish wedding ceremonies.

It may therefore be supposed that the reason Rivka covered herself only when she was about to meet Yitzḥak was to prepare herself for her future husband, who would then remove the veil as an act of marriage. The fact that women were not normally veiled at the time can be deduced from Genesis 12:14 (where the Egyptians could see how Sara looked) and Genesis 38:14 (where Tamar was veiled only as a disguise). ▪ ZR

↗ Groom apparently raising the veil of his bride at a wedding ceremony, decoration on a vase, Hittite, Bitik (near Ankara, Turkey), 16th century BCE

הָעֶבֶד הוּא אֲדֹנִי וַתִּקַּח הַצָּעִיף וַתִּתְכָּס׃ וַיְסַפֵּר הָעֶבֶד לְיִצְחָק סו
אֵת כָּל־הַדְּבָרִים אֲשֶׁר עָשָׂה׃ וַיְבִאֶהָ יִצְחָק הָאֹהֱלָה שָׂרָה אִמּוֹ סז
וַיִּקַּח אֶת־רִבְקָה וַתְּהִי־לוֹ לְאִשָּׁה וַיֶּאֱהָבֶהָ וַיִּנָּחֵם יִצְחָק אַחֲרֵי
אִמּוֹ׃
ששי וַיֹּסֶף אַבְרָהָם וַיִּקַּח אִשָּׁה וּשְׁמָהּ קְטוּרָה׃ וַתֵּלֶד לוֹ אֶת־זִמְרָן א ב • כה
וְאֶת־יָקְשָׁן וְאֶת־מְדָן וְאֶת־מִדְיָן וְאֶת־יִשְׁבָּק וְאֶת־שׁוּחַ׃
וְיָקְשָׁן יָלַד אֶת־שְׁבָא וְאֶת־דְּדָן וּבְנֵי דְדָן הָיוּ אַשּׁוּרִם וּלְטוּשִׁם ג
וּלְאֻמִּים׃ וּבְנֵי מִדְיָן עֵיפָה וָעֵפֶר וַחֲנֹךְ וַאֲבִידָע וְאֶלְדָּעָה כָּל־אֵלֶּה ד

66 my master." And she took her veil and covered herself. The
67 servant told Yitzḥak all he had done. And Yitzḥak brought
her into the tent of his mother Sara. He took Rivka as his wife,
and he loved her. And Yitzḥak was comforted after his
mother's death.
25 • 1 2 Avraham took another wife, whose name was Ketura. She
bore him Zimran, Yokshan, Medan, Midyan, Yishbak, and
3 Shuaḥ; Yokshan was the father of Sheva and Dedan. The
4 sons of Dedan were Ashurim, Letushim, and Leumim. The
sons of Midyan were Eifa, Efer, Ḥanokh, Avida, and Eldaa;

NEAR EAST

25:1–4 The sons of Ketura

Of the sons of Ketura, although Midyan reappears frequently in the Torah and in the Former Prophets, the name does not appear in any known text from the ancient Near East.

By contrast, several other names mentioned here are reflected in ancient Near Eastern texts. Sheva appears as a nomadic desert tribe in the inscriptions of the Assyrian kings Tiglat-Pileser III (745–727 BCE) and Sanḥeriv (704–689 BCE). Similarly, Eifa appears as a desert-dwelling group named Hayappa in the inscriptions of Tiglat-Pileser III and Sargon II (720–705 BCE).

Also recorded in the inscriptions of Tiglat-Pileser III is Adbe'el, son of Yishmael (see Gen. 25:13). This tribe, called Idbi'ilu in Akkadian, formed an alliance with the Assyrians, and was tasked with disrupting traffic hostile to the Assyrians that might pass from Egypt through Sinai to the region near Aza. Nevayot, Kedar, and Massa, mentioned below in verses 13–14, also appear in the inscriptions of these and later Assyrian kings. All these examples show that these descendants of Avraham had evolved into desert tribal entities by the 1st millennium BCE. ▪ ZR

Petroglyph (rock art) of wheeled cart pulled by two horses, Jubbah site, Arabia, ca. 1500 BCE ↘

ה ו בְּנֵ֥י קְטוּרָֽה׃ וַיִּתֵּ֧ן אַבְרָהָ֛ם אֶת־כָּל־אֲשֶׁר־ל֖וֹ לְיִצְחָֽק׃ וְלִבְנֵ֤י
הַפִּֽילַגְשִׁים֙ אֲשֶׁ֣ר לְאַבְרָהָ֔ם נָתַ֥ן אַבְרָהָ֖ם מַתָּנֹ֑ת וַֽיְשַׁלְּחֵ֞ם מֵעַ֨ל
ז יִצְחָ֤ק בְּנוֹ֙ בְּעוֹדֶ֣נּוּ חַ֔י קֵ֖דְמָה אֶל־אֶ֥רֶץ קֶֽדֶם׃ וְאֵ֗לֶּה יְמֵ֛י שְׁנֵֽי־חַיֵּ֥י
ח אַבְרָהָ֖ם אֲשֶׁר־חָ֑י מְאַ֥ת שָׁנָ֛ה וְשִׁבְעִ֥ים שָׁנָ֖ה וְחָמֵ֥שׁ שָׁנִֽים׃ וַיִּגְוַ֨ע

all these were descendants of Ketura. Avraham left all that 5
was his to Yitzḥak – while he was still living he gave gifts to 6
the sons of his concubines and sent them eastward, away
from his son Yitzḥak, to the land of the East. These are the 7
days, the years of Avraham's life: he lived one hundred and
seventy-five years. Avraham breathed his last and died in 8
his ripe old age, aged and satisfied, and was gathered to his

NEAR EAST

25:5–6 Inheritance rights

In this verse, Avraham ensures that Yitzḥak is his only legitimate heir. That Ketura's sons did not receive an inheritance is only somewhat similar to certain laws in the ancient Near East. The *Laws of Hammurabi* state that a father is required to formally adopt children of women other than his wife (that is, concubines and household slaves) in order for them to receive inheritance, "If, however, the father while still living did not say to the sons of the maidservant: 'My sons,' and then the father dies, then the sons of the maidservant shall not share with the sons of the wife" (LH §171). In our verses, the reverse takes place: rather than recognizing the sons of, presumably, a secondary wife, Avraham designates Yitzḥak as his sole heir, sending away Ketura's children to another land in his lifetime.

The gifts of chattel given by Avraham to Ketura's sons is similar with the process for dissolving the inheritance rights of an adopted child in the *Laws of Hammurabi*: "If a man, who had adopted a son and reared him, founded a household, and had children, wish to put this adopted son out, then this son shall not simply go his way. His adoptive father shall give him of his wealth one-third of a child's portion, and then he may go. He shall not give him of the field, garden, and house" (LH §191). Thus, in our verses, Avraham employs multiple mechanisms to make sure that only Yitzḥak will be his sole heir. ▪ ZR

Dialog document concerning succession and inheritance, Neo-Babylonian, Babylon (?), ca. 547 BCE

NEAR EAST

25:8 Gathered to his people

This phrase is found only in the Torah (here, 25:17, 35:29, 49:29, 33; and of Aharon and Moshe in Num. 20:24, 27:13, 31:2; Deut. 32:50). It seems parallel to "lie down with one's fathers" which appears more frequently in both the Torah and the Prophets (Gen. 47:30; Deut. 31:16; II Sam. 7:12; I Kings 1:21; 11:43, etc.). As Nahum Sarna points out, "gathered to his people" does not describe death itself, as that was mentioned earlier in the verse. It does not refer either to burial alongside one's ancestors, since Avraham, Aharon, and Moshe were not buried with their forefathers. It does not even refer to burial in general, as powerfully demonstrated in the case of Yaakov, where he is "gathered to his people" in Genesis 49:33, but only buried later in the land of Israel after a period of mourning in Egypt. Sarna concludes that the phrase indicates a belief in some kind of immortality which continues to exist alongside deceased forefathers in the afterlife. Unlike other ancient Near Eastern cultures, this belief did not lead to any kind of ancestor worship or cult of the dead among the Israelites. ▪ ZR, JU

Bust of an ancestor used in ancestor worship, Egypt, 14th century BCE

וַיָּמָת אַבְרָהָם בְּשֵׂיבָה טוֹבָה זָקֵן וְשָׂבֵעַ וַיֵּאָסֶף אֶל־עַמָּיו׃ וַיִּקְבְּרוּ ט
אֹתוֹ יִצְחָק וְיִשְׁמָעֵאל בָּנָיו אֶל־מְעָרַת הַמַּכְפֵּלָה אֶל־שְׂדֵה
עֶפְרֹן בֶּן־צֹחַר הַחִתִּי אֲשֶׁר עַל־פְּנֵי מַמְרֵא׃ הַשָּׂדֶה אֲשֶׁר־קָנָה י
אַבְרָהָם מֵאֵת בְּנֵי־חֵת שָׁמָּה קֻבַּר אַבְרָהָם וְשָׂרָה אִשְׁתּוֹ׃ וַיְהִי יא
אַחֲרֵי מוֹת אַבְרָהָם וַיְבָרֶךְ אֱלֹהִים אֶת־יִצְחָק בְּנוֹ וַיֵּשֶׁב יִצְחָק
עִם־בְּאֵר לַחַי רֹאִי׃

9 people. His sons, Yitzḥak and Yishmael, buried him in the
cave of Makhpela, near Mamre, in the field of Efron son of
10 Tzoḥar the Hittite – the field Avraham had bought from the
11 Hittites. There Avraham was buried with Sara his wife. After
Avraham's death, God blessed Yitzḥak his son, who was then
living near Be'er Laḥai Ro'i.

NEAR EAST

25:12–18 The sons of Yishmael

Some of the names listed as Yishmael's offspring appear later in extra-biblical sources. They represent various nomadic groups that would become known as Arabs from the 8th century BCE onward.

Nevayot are the Nabaiati mentioned in the records of the Neo-Assyrian kings Tiglat-Pileser III and Ashurbanipal in the 8th and 7th centuries BCE. Kedar is mentioned among the groups from western Mesopotamia that pay tribute to the Tiglat-Pileser III. Both Kedar and Nevayot are mentioned in Isaiah 60:7 as having herds of sheep. Adbe'el is identified with a tribe Tiglat-Pileser III states he placed to guard the border region between the Assyrian territory and Egypt: "I installed Idi-bi'li as a Warden of Marches on the border of Musur (Egypt)."

Mishma is not attested as a people in extra-biblical sources. However, they may be connected to the site Jebel Mishma in Arabia. Duma may be identified with the oasis called Adumatu in the inscriptions of the Neo-Assyrian king Esar Ḥadon, which has been identified with Dumat al-Jandal in northern Saudi Arabia. Massa is also mentioned by Tiglat-Pileser III among other Arabian sites. Tema (also mentioned as a place in Is. 21:14 and Jer. 25:23) is identified with Tayma, a well-known oasis located in northwestern Saudi Arabia, as part of a trade route from the Arabian Peninsula to the Nile Valley as early as the Bronze Age. Yetur is identified with the semi-nomadic Itureans, attested in Greek and early Roman literature, who lived in the area of modern-day Lebanon and Syria.

Collectively, the offspring of Yishmael represent a confederation of various nomadic groups who were understood to share an ancestral kinship with the Israelites. ▪ ZR

↗ Incense burner, Nabatean, from Tayma (Saudi Arabia), 1st century BCE to 1st century CE

יב וְאֵלֶּה תֹּלְדֹת יִשְׁמָעֵאל בֶּן־אַבְרָהָם אֲשֶׁר יָלְדָה הָגָר הַמִּצְרִית שביעי
יג שִׁפְחַת שָׂרָה לְאַבְרָהָם: וְאֵלֶּה שְׁמוֹת בְּנֵי יִשְׁמָעֵאל בִּשְׁמֹתָם
יד לְתוֹלְדֹתָם בְּכֹר יִשְׁמָעֵאל נְבָיֹת וְקֵדָר וְאַדְבְּאֵל וּמִבְשָׂם: וּמִשְׁמָע
טו טז וְדוּמָה וּמַשָּׂא: חֲדַד וְתֵימָא יְטוּר נָפִישׁ וָקֵדְמָה: אֵלֶּה הֵם מפטיר
בְּנֵי יִשְׁמָעֵאל וְאֵלֶּה שְׁמֹתָם בְּחַצְרֵיהֶם וּבְטִירֹתָם שְׁנֵים־עָשָׂר
יז נְשִׂיאִם לְאֻמֹּתָם: וְאֵלֶּה שְׁנֵי חַיֵּי יִשְׁמָעֵאל מְאַת שָׁנָה וּשְׁלֹשִׁים
יח שָׁנָה וְשֶׁבַע שָׁנִים וַיִּגְוַע וַיָּמָת וַיֵּאָסֶף אֶל־עַמָּיו: וַיִּשְׁכְּנוּ מֵחֲוִילָה
עַד־שׁוּר אֲשֶׁר עַל־פְּנֵי מִצְרַיִם בֹּאֲכָה אַשּׁוּרָה עַל־פְּנֵי כָל־אֶחָיו
נָפָל:
יט וְאֵלֶּה תּוֹלְדֹת יִצְחָק בֶּן־אַבְרָהָם אַבְרָהָם הוֹלִיד אֶת־יִצְחָק: וַיְהִי תולדת
יִצְחָק בֶּן־אַרְבָּעִים שָׁנָה בְּקַחְתּוֹ אֶת־רִבְקָה בַּת־בְּתוּאֵל הָאֲרַמִּי
כא מִפַּדַּן אֲרָם אֲחוֹת לָבָן הָאֲרַמִּי לוֹ לְאִשָּׁה: וַיֶּעְתַּר יִצְחָק לַיהוה
לְנֹכַח אִשְׁתּוֹ כִּי עֲקָרָה הִוא וַיֵּעָתֶר לוֹ יהוה וַתַּהַר רִבְקָה אִשְׁתּוֹ:

These are the descendants of Avraham's son Yishmael, whom 12
Sara's maidservant, Hagar the Egyptian, bore to Avraham.
The names of Yishmael's sons, in the order of their birth, 13
are: Nevayot – Yishmael's firstborn, Kedar, Adbe'el, Mivsam,
Mishma, Duma, Massa, Ḥadad, Teima, Yetur, Nafish, and 14 15
Kedma. These were Yishmael's sons, and these are their 16
names by their villages and encampments: twelve princes
and their tribes. These were the years of Yishmael's life: he 17
lived one hundred and thirty-seven years. He breathed his
last and died, and was gathered to his people. The Ishmaelites 18
dwelt from Ḥavila to Shur, up against Egypt, all the way to
Assyria, settling up against all their brothers.
This is the story of Yitzḥak, son of Avraham: Avraham was 19
Yitzḥak's father. When Yitzḥak was forty he married Rivka, 20
daughter of Betuel the Aramean of Padan Aram, sister of
Lavan the Aramean. And Yitzḥak pleaded with the Lord on 21
behalf of his wife, for she was childless. The Lord granted his

GEOGRAPHY

25:20 Padan Aram

Before moving to Canaan, Avraham sojourns in the land around the cities of Ḥaran and Naḥor. The Torah calls this land Padan Aram (Gen. 25:20, 28:2, 5, 7; and more) and Aram Naharayim (see "Aram Naharayim" on page 145). Padan is derived from the Akkadian *padanu* ("way," or "road") or the Aramaic *paddan* ("plow," "yoke of oxen," or "plowed field"). The Arameans appeared in extra-biblical references after 1150 BCE as a distinct population near the upper Euphrates. ▪ YB

Cylinder seal depicting males holding a stylized tree with griffins above horned animals, glazed, Mitanni, 15th to 14th century BCE

כב וַיִּתְרֹצְצוּ הַבָּנִים בְּקִרְבָּהּ וַתֹּאמֶר אִם־כֵּן לָמָּה זֶּה אָנֹכִי וַתֵּלֶךְ
כג לִדְרֹשׁ אֶת־יְהוָה: וַיֹּאמֶר יְהוָה לָהּ שְׁנֵי גיים בְּבִטְנֵךְ וּשְׁנֵי לְאֻמִּים גוֹיִם
כד מִמֵּעַיִךְ יִפָּרֵדוּ וּלְאֹם מִלְאֹם יֶאֱמָץ וְרַב יַעֲבֹד צָעִיר: וַיִּמְלְאוּ יָמֶיהָ
כה לָלֶדֶת וְהִנֵּה תוֹמִם בְּבִטְנָהּ: וַיֵּצֵא הָרִאשׁוֹן אַדְמוֹנִי כֻּלּוֹ כְּאַדֶּרֶת
כו שֵׂעָר וַיִּקְרְאוּ שְׁמוֹ עֵשָׂו: וְאַחֲרֵי־כֵן יָצָא אָחִיו וְיָדוֹ אֹחֶזֶת בַּעֲקֵב
עֵשָׂו וַיִּקְרָא שְׁמוֹ יַעֲקֹב וְיִצְחָק בֶּן־שִׁשִּׁים שָׁנָה בְּלֶדֶת אֹתָם:

22 plea and Rivka became pregnant. But the children clashed
within her. She said, "If this is so, why am I living?" So she
23 went to inquire of the Lord. The Lord said to her, "Two
nations are inside your womb; two peoples are to part from
you. People will overpower people, and the greater shall the
24 younger serve."[50] When the time came for her to give birth,
25 there were twins in her womb. The first came out red. His
whole body was like a hairy cloak, so they named him Esav.[51]
26 Then his brother emerged, his hand grasping Esav's heel, so
he named him Yaakov.[52] Yitzḥak was sixty years old when

50 | The ambiguity as to who will serve whom reflects the Hebrew.

51 | The name Esav may bear the sense of "covered" or "concealed" (cf. Ob. 1:6). The word *se'ar* (hair) resonates with Se'ir, the land inhabited by Esav's descendants.

52 | The name Yaakov resonates with *akev* (heel).

NEAR EAST

25:22 To inquire of the Lord

Rivka here seeks out (the Hebrew root, *d r sh*) divine guidance directly from God, and receives an unambiguous answer in four brief poetic clauses. The Torah does not describe the way Rivka turned to God or how she was answered. However, this same phraseology is used elsewhere in Tanakh to seek an answer from God by consulting a prophet (I Sam. 9:9; I Kings 14:5, 22:8; II Kings 3:11, 8:8, 22:13, 18).

Similar terminology is used consulting a pagan oracle in II Kings 1:2, "He sent messengers, instructing them, 'Go, inquire (*dirshu*) of Baal Zevuv, the god of Ekron, whether I will recover from this injury.'"

Direct questions posed to a deity through an oracle, including direct responses, are also found in the literature of the ancient Near East. In Esar Ḥadon's (Assyria; ruled 681–669 BCE) account of his father asking the gods if Esar Ḥadon was to be his heir despite being the youngest son, "I was (indeed) the(ir) youngest (brother) among my elder brothers, (but) my own father, upon the command of Ashur, Sin, Shamash, Bel and Nebo, the Ishtar of Nineveh (and) the Ishtar of Arbela, has chosen me, in due form and in the presence of all my brothers, saying: 'This is the son to (be elevated to) the position of a successor of mine.' (Then) he put this question before Shamash and Adad by means of an oracle and they answered him: 'He (verily) is your replacement'" (prism B).

However, asking for a response from God in Tanakh does not always mean asking a prophet. In Psalms 34:5, the individual is inquiring of God directly and receives His answer, "I sought (*darashti*) the Lord and He answered me; He saved me from all my fears." Yirmeyahu even promises that God will answer the people in exile, "when you…pray to me, I will hear you…if you seek me (*tidrishuni*) with all your heart…and I…will bring you back to the place from which I have exiled you" (Jer. 29:12–14). The prophet is expanding upon God's promise to the Israelites in Deuteronomy, that if He punishes them with exile, "there, if you seek the Lord your God, you will find Him, if you search (*tidrishenu*) after Him with all your heart… for…He will not forget the covenant that He forged on oath with your ancestors" (Deut. 4:29, 31; compare 30:1–10).

In other words, Rivka may not be seeking a prophetic response, but is simply praying directly to God, and He answers her.
▪ ZR, JU

King Esar Ḥadon and his mother Naqi'a Zakutu in the Temple of Marduk, bronze relief, 7th century BCE

NEAR EAST

25:22–24 Twins in the ancient Near East

Throughout the ancient Near East, reactions to twin births appear to depend upon whether the twins were fraternal or identical. The birth of two identical children was upsetting, as it upended the normal order of things. The Mesopotamian omen series *Shumma Izbu* is a lexical list of birth anomalies. Included in a litany of omens about children born with animal heads and missing limbs are omens about the birth of identical twins, expressing the attitude that the birth of multiples was outside the normal realm. The Egyptian record includes a social correction for "double births," understanding identical twins as a single person, rather than two separate individuals. An oracular decree from the Twenty-Second Dynasty states that a woman shall be saved from "a Horus birth [premature birth], miscarrying, and from giving birth to twins."

Fraternal twins, while still unsettling, were a bit easier to fit into the social order. Notably, the Torah goes out of its way to indicate that Yaakov and Esav looked and acted differently: Esav was red and hairy, made brash decisions, and preferred the outdoors. Yaakov was smooth, clever, and preferred the indoors. Within the biblical text, narratives surrounding the birth of twins stress the birth order and generally include some sort of mix-up, where the elder son is displaced by the younger (Gen. 25:22–34, 27:1–40).

The use of the motif of the younger supplanting the elder is only possible when one can distinguish between the twins. The Ugaritic myth of *The Gracious and Beautiful Gods* describes the birth of twin fraternal deities: Shaḥar ("sunrise" or "break through") and Shalem ("sunset"). These deities were not considered evil or scary. Similarly, the names of Tamar's twins, Peretz (meaning, "breakthrough") and Zeraḥ (meaning, "sunrise" or "wearing the red thread") reflect a positive association with these names (Gen. 3:27–30; there, a mix-up occurs because it is thought that the twin whose hand came out first would be the elder, but the other twin was born first).

Attitudes about the birth of twins is evidenced in the archaeological record as well. Plaques depicting a woman pregnant with two fetuses were likely used as a mediatrix or protective talisman, demonstrating the uncertainty surrounding the impending birth of twins. ▪ KG

Shumma Izbu, Tablet 5, Mesopotamia, 4th to 2nd century BCE

LANGUAGE

25:25–30 Hairiness

Esav's hairiness recalls the character Enkidu in the *Epic of Gilgamesh*, "Shaggy with hair is his whole body. He is endowed with head hair like a woman." The Akkadian word used there for being shaggy, *su-u-ur*, is cognate with the Hebrew *seir*. There too, the abundance of hair is taken to be a sign of a savage and primitive nature, "With the gazelles he feeds on grass. With the wild beasts he jostles at the watering-place."

The theme of twins with opposite personalities and physical characteristics is also found in ancient Greek literature in the description of Amphion and Zethus, twin children of Zeus. Amphion was a singer and musician, depicted as smooth, while Zethus became a hunter and herdsman, depicted as hairy.

In similarity to both Enkidu and Zethus, Esav feels at home in nature, "a skilled hunter, a man of the field" (25:27; compare 27:3). His hairiness is also an allusion to the land of Seir where he would settle (Gen. 32:4), located in the mountainous region on the eastern side of the Arava, between the Dead Sea and the Gulf of Aqaba. Esav's additional name, Edom (25:30), alludes to the nation of Edomites descended from him. The name Esav may itself refer to something concealed or covered, in this context by hair. Such usage is found in Tanakh on occasion, as in Job. 23:9, "He hides (*ba'asoto*) in the north," and may be connected to the Arabic *gh-s-w*, meaning, "to cover" or "envelop." ▪ ZR

Mount of earth housing Mycenean tombs which were later interpreted as being the tombs of Amphion and Zethus, Thiva (Greece)

NEAR EAST

25:27–34 Sale of the birthright

In the ancient Near East, it was taken for granted that the older brother is in a superior position relative to the younger siblings. It is the subtext behind the statement in the Sumerian *Hymn to Enlil* (late 3rd millennium BCE) that Nippur is a particularly gracious city "Where the older brother honors the younger brother, acts humanely (toward him)."

In the ancient Near East, the eldest son was entitled to a double portion of the inheritance. The *Middle Assyrian Laws* state, "If brothers divide the estate of their father…the orchards and wells on the land, [the oldest son] shall choose (and) take two portions [as his share] and then his brothers one after the other shall choose (and) take (theirs). The youngest son shall divide up any cultivated land along with all the (produce of their) labors; the oldest son shall choose (and) take one portion and then cast lots with his brothers for his second portion" (MAL B §1). Although the process is complicated, the eldest ends up with a double portion as was the custom in the ancient Near East at the time.

This double portion was given because the firstborn had greater responsibilities. He was expected to take care of his mother and unwed sisters in the event that his father died; he was primarily responsible for taking care of the rituals accorded to decreased parents.

In the patriarchal period, the privileges of the firstborn could be transferred by a parent, as when Yaakov designates Yehuda and Yosef as leaders (Gen. 49:8, 26), with Reuven losing his position as firstborn (I Chr. 5:1). The inheritance rights of the firstborn were later anchored in Deuteronomy 21:15–17, "If a man has two wives, and loves one but not the other, and if both the loved and unloved bear him sons, but the firstborn is the son of the one unloved, then on the day he bequeaths his possessions to his sons, he may not give the rights of the firstborn to the son of the loved in preference to the son of the unloved, the true firstborn. He must acknowledge the son of his unloved wife as the firstborn, giving him a double portion of all that he has. He is the first fruit of his manhood; the right of the firstborn belongs to him."

Various legal texts from the ancient Near East discuss situations of the adoption of a child and how this would impact the division of inheritance, demonstrating the possibility of some leeway in assigning inheritance rights. The double inheritance portion could be worked out in different ways in this situation. For example, in an Old Babylonian legal text from Mari regarding the adoption of a child, the law ensures that the adopted child will always be regarded as the firstborn, "(As for) Hillalum and Alitum – regardless of how many sons they shall have acquired – Yahatti-el is primary heir, and he shall take a double share of the estate of Hillalum, his father. His younger brothers shall divide (the remainder) in equal shares." On the other hand, a Nuzi adoption document states, "If Shuriha-ilu should have a son of his own, as the principal (son) he shall take a double share; Shennima (the adopted son) shall then be next in order (and) take his proper share." ▪ ZR

וַיִּגְדְּלוּ הַנְּעָרִים וַיְהִי עֵשָׂו אִישׁ יֹדֵעַ צַיִד אִישׁ שָׂדֶה וְיַעֲקֹב אִישׁ כז •
תָּם יֹשֵׁב אֹהָלִים׃ וַיֶּאֱהַב יִצְחָק אֶת־עֵשָׂו כִּי־צַיִד בְּפִיו וְרִבְקָה כח
אֹהֶבֶת אֶת־יַעֲקֹב׃ וַיָּזֶד יַעֲקֹב נָזִיד וַיָּבֹא עֵשָׂו מִן־הַשָּׂדֶה וְהוּא כט
עָיֵף׃ וַיֹּאמֶר עֵשָׂו אֶל־יַעֲקֹב הַלְעִיטֵנִי נָא מִן־הָאָדֹם הָאָדֹם הַזֶּה ל
כִּי עָיֵף אָנֹכִי עַל־כֵּן קָרָא־שְׁמוֹ אֱדוֹם׃ וַיֹּאמֶר יַעֲקֹב מִכְרָה כַיּוֹם לא
אֶת־בְּכֹרָתְךָ לִי׃ וַיֹּאמֶר עֵשָׂו הִנֵּה אָנֹכִי הוֹלֵךְ לָמוּת וְלָמָּה־זֶּה לב
לִי בְּכֹרָה׃ וַיֹּאמֶר יַעֲקֹב הִשָּׁבְעָה לִּי כַּיּוֹם וַיִּשָּׁבַע לוֹ וַיִּמְכֹּר אֶת־ לג
בְּכֹרָתוֹ לְיַעֲקֹב׃ וְיַעֲקֹב נָתַן לְעֵשָׂו לֶחֶם וּנְזִיד עֲדָשִׁים וַיֹּאכַל לד
וַיֵּשְׁתְּ וַיָּקָם וַיֵּלַךְ וַיִּבֶז עֵשָׂו אֶת־הַבְּכֹרָה׃

• 27 they were born. The boys grew up. Esav became a skilled
hunter, a man of the field, while Yaakov was an innocent man
28 who stayed among the tents. Yitzhak loved Esav because he
29 ate of his game, but Rivka loved Yaakov. Once when Yaakov
was cooking a stew, Esav came in exhausted from the field.
30 He said to Yaakov, "Let me gulp down some of that red stuff.
I am starved!" – that is how he came to be named Edom.[53]
31 32 Yaakov said, "First sell me your birthright." And Esav said,
"Look, I am about to die. What use to me is a birthright?"
33 But Yaakov said, "Swear to me first." So he swore, and sold
34 Yaakov his birthright. Yaakov then gave Esav bread and lentil
stew. He ate, drank, got up, and left. Thus – Esav disdained
his birthright.

53 | The name Edom resonates with *adom* (red) here, as well as with *admoni* (red) in verse 25.

Esau Gives up his Birthright; Jacob and Esau with the Bowl of Pottage, stained glass, workshop of Everhard Rensig (?), 1521

↗ Aerial view of et-Tell (Ai?)

There are at least three ways in which what we know…shed[s] light upon the Torah's patriarchal narratives: political control, linguistic developments, and family practices.

and Hebrew. Lacking a better name for this dialect, scholars call it Amorite. Languages related to Amorite are also evidenced in names from Mesopotamia in this period, such as that of the famous king Hammurabi.

The names of the patriarchs and their families fit well in an Amorite context: Semitic names similar to those of Avraham, Yishmael, Lavan, Yaakov, and Binyamin appear in the 18th century BCE texts from Mari in Eastern Syria (similar names also appear at other sites, especially Ebla of the 24th century BCE). Amorite names figure prominently in the foregoing discussion because very few texts were written in Amorite, therefore, the Amorite names preserved in Egyptian hieratic script or in Akkadian cuneiform are among the only clear samples of this language.

↗ Excavations at a Middle Bronze Age site, Tel Kabri, near Nahariya, Israel

In addition to the similarities in names and their apparent language, the general direction of Amorite migration is an additional factor. The Amorite-speaking groups are thought to have emerged in the northern part of the Fertile Crescent around 2000 BCE, moving from there into both Mesopotamia and the Levant, which mirrors Avraham's travels from Ḥaran, in northern Mesopotamia, to Canaan.

A further connection between the patriarchal narratives and the Middle Bronze Age is provided by the similarities in family practices between Mesopotamian texts and those recorded regarding Yaakov's sojourn in Ḥaran. One such practice, known from the *Laws of Hammurabi* and other texts, is the payment the groom must render to the father of the bride, called *terḫatu* in Akkadian. The father of the bride is then bound by custom to hand this payment back to the new couple, so that the woman would have money in reserve. The failure of Lavan to do so explains the complaint of Raḥel and Leah in Genesis 31:14–15 that their father has "spent the money."

Taken together, all of these points demonstrate the interpretive value of placing the patriarchal narratives into the context of what we know about the political geography of Canaan in the Middle and Late Bronze Age, the languages and migration patterns in Canaan and Mesopotamia in this period, and the family practices we know from Mesopotamia. (See also the introduction to this volume). ▪ SZA

Historicity of the patriarchal narratives

Avraham, Yitzḥak, and Yaakov are foundational figures in Jewish thought, and therefore, it would be fascinating to locate clear textual or artifact-based records of their lives, to complement the biblical narrative. Alas, at this point, more than 150 years after archaeological excavations first uncovered Semitic texts from the period 2000–1550 BCE (known as the Middle Bronze Age), no such texts or artifacts have emerged, and it may be unrealistic to expect to find such documents in the future. Instead, rather than searching for direct mentions of the patriarchs, it will be helpful to consider how our knowledge of Canaan in the Middle Bronze Age, the languages spoken then, and the legal structures in use (especially those related to family law) correlate with these narratives.

Before addressing this question, we should explain why we focus on the Middle Bronze Age. This focus is based on several factors. From a combination of archaeological evidence (increased settlement in the hill country of Shomron) and an Egyptian text (the Merenptah Stele), it makes sense to place the exodus from Egypt during the 13th century BCE. Working backward, and assuming a six-generation sojourn in Egypt (based on the genealogy of Tzelofḥad in Numbers 27:1), we can deduce that Yaakov's family arrived in Egypt sometime early in the 15th century BCE (or late in the 16th century). This suggests that the period of the patriarchs covers parts of the late 18th, 17th, and 16th centuries BCE.

There are at least three ways in which what we know of the history of the Near East in this period shed light upon the Torah's patriarchal narratives: political control, linguistic developments, and family practices.

The Egyptian execration texts, which date to the 20th and 19th centuries BCE, inform us about the political organization of Canaan in this period. Various rulers presided over multiple city-states, each of which controlled territory within a radius of between 20 kilometers (12 miles) in the lowlands, and 50 kilometers (30 miles) in the hill country. Although nominally independent, these rulers were subject to the Egyptian kings, who claimed ownership of Canaan (more accurately, the Egyptian kings saw the local city-state rulers as subject to them). This arrangement continued into the 15th and 14th centuries, as we know from the Tanakh and the *Amarna letters*.

Several aspects of this political structure illustrate the background of the patriarchal stories. First of all, in the period under discussion, no central authority ruled Canaan. This explains the patriarchs' travels through Canaan with little hindrance from local rulers. Second, the political bonds between Canaan and Egypt also help explain Avraham's travels to Egypt. Without any difficulty, Avraham is able to travel to Egypt (Gen. 12:10) as a response to famine; two generations later, many people from Canaan make the same trip for similar reasons (Gen. 41:57). The ability of large numbers of people to travel from Canaan to Egypt and back implies a lack of political barriers between the two. Third, the bulk of the patriarchs' activities take place in the central hill country, an area with limited settlement in the Middle Bronze Age, and which seems to have had even fewer people in the Late Bronze Age (1550–1200 BCE). The patriarchs could herd their flocks in this sparsely settled area, and travel to and fro. They encounter local rulers only when their activities required the ruler's permission (as in the narrative of Avraham purchasing land from Efron in chapter 23).

We also have evidence of links between the people of Mesopotamia and those of Canaan in this period. One type of such evidence is the prevalence of names in West Semitic dialects or languages known from both regions. The names found in the execration texts teach us that the people of Canaan spoke a West Semitic dialect, related to both Aramaic

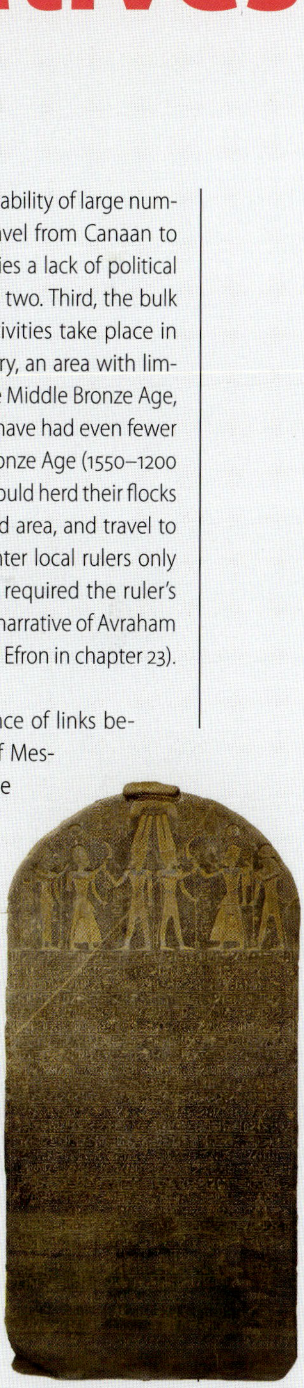

Merenptah Stele, Thebes, end of 13th century BCE

כו א וַיְהִ֤י רָעָב֙ בָּאָ֔רֶץ מִלְּבַד֙ הָרָעָ֣ב הָרִאשׁ֔וֹן אֲשֶׁ֥ר הָיָ֖ה בִּימֵ֣י אַבְרָהָ֑ם
ב וַיֵּ֧לֶךְ יִצְחָ֛ק אֶל־אֲבִימֶ֥לֶךְ מֶֽלֶךְ־פְּלִשְׁתִּ֖ים גְּרָֽרָה׃ וַיֵּרָ֤א אֵלָיו֙
יְהוָ֔ה וַיֹּ֖אמֶר אַל־תֵּרֵ֣ד מִצְרָ֑יְמָה שְׁכֹ֣ן בָּאָ֔רֶץ אֲשֶׁ֖ר אֹמַ֥ר אֵלֶֽיךָ׃

26 1 Another famine afflicted the land, apart from the earlier
famine in Avraham's days, and Yitzḥak went to Avimelekh,
2 king of the Philistines, in Gerar. The LORD had appeared to
him: "Do not go down to Egypt," He had said. "Stay in the

ARCHAEOLOGY

26:1 Gerar as a Philistine city

No later than the end of the 13th century and beginning of the 12th century BCE, an intrusive material culture, which has been identified as "Philistine," was introduced into the land of Israel along the southern coastal plain. This new culture was not homogenous; elements appear to derive from at least three disparate sources tied together by the Mediterranean Sea: Aegean, Anatolian, and Cypriot. Moreover, this intrusive culture, while significant, did not by any means eradicate the local Canaanite culture that itself continued to thrive throughout the period of initial contact and beyond in a manner that indicates cultural co-existence. The practice – in effect since antiquity – of referring to this amalgamated culture as Philistine rather than Canaanite may reflect the higher status and stronger leadership of the newcomers who introduced the local population to exotic practices including rituals with feasting and drinking.

Although the southern coastal plain and its cultural traditions were rebranded as Philistine, it is interesting to note that the five main cities of the region – Aza, Ashkelon, Ashdod, Gat, and Ekron – all retained their original Semitic names. These five cities had all been successful Middle Bronze Age Canaanite polities and were settled by the newcomers specifically for their agricultural potential, established bureaucracies, and civic infrastructure. The same is also true of Gerar. A once-formidable Middle Bronze Age Canaanite city (approximately 24 kilometers/less than 15 miles southeast of Aza), it, too, was rebranded as Philistine with abundant examples of the intrusive richly decorated Philistine pottery. This then is what is meant by Philistine: social, political, and economic integration of the sea-faring newcomers into Canaanite urban life with a concomitant adoption of Philistine ritual and cultural practices by the local inhabitants that occurred gradually over centuries. (See "Who were the Philistines in Genesis" on page 133) ▪ JK

Bridle bit of a donkey, copper, found in situ, Gerar (Tel Haror), 16th to 15th century BCE

NEAR EAST

26:1 Avimelekh

The Avimelekh mentioned in this verse is assumedly not the same king with whom Avraham made a treaty in Genesis 20, as that happened before Yitzḥak was even born. Rather, it appears that Avimelekh was either a common dynastic name or an official title used by Philistine kings, like the term Pharaoh for Egyptian rulers. Evidence of this practice is seen in Psalms 34:1, "Of David, when he feigned insanity before Avimelekh," in reference to Akhish king of Gat (I Sam. 21:13–16). This would be an appropriate term to designate a king in a dynastic monarchy, as it can mean both "my father is king" and "father of a king." ▪ ZR

Ekron royal dedicatory inscription mentions the ruler Akhish, Ekron (Tel Miqne), 7th century BCE

ג גּוּר בָּאָרֶץ הַזֹּאת וְאֶהְיֶה עִמְּךָ וַאֲבָרְכֶךָּ כִּי־לְךָ וּלְזַרְעֲךָ אֶתֵּן
אֶת־כָּל־הָאֲרָצֹת הָאֵל וַהֲקִמֹתִי אֶת־הַשְּׁבֻעָה אֲשֶׁר נִשְׁבַּעְתִּי
ד לְאַבְרָהָם אָבִיךָ׃ וְהִרְבֵּיתִי אֶת־זַרְעֲךָ כְּכוֹכְבֵי הַשָּׁמַיִם וְנָתַתִּי
לְזַרְעֲךָ אֵת כָּל־הָאֲרָצֹת הָאֵל וְהִתְבָּרְכוּ בְזַרְעֲךָ כֹּל גּוֹיֵי הָאָרֶץ׃

3 land I tell you of. Bide in this land and I will be with you and
bless you, for I am going to give all these lands to you and
your descendants, fulfilling the oath I swore to Avraham
4 your father. I will make your descendants as many as the
stars of the heavens, and I will give them all these lands.
All the nations of the earth will bless themselves by your

LANGUAGE

26:2 Stay

"Stay" is the translation here of the Hebrew imperative *shekhon*. The verbal root *sh kh n* is sometimes associated with the noun "tent," so it may connote "to tent," or "to camp" (Gen. 9:27, 35:21–22), and the noun form *mishkan* means "a dwelling place" (most commonly in reference to God's "Tent of Meeting"). In Akkadian, the cognate verb can also mean "to camp," but in the *Amarna letters* (when it does not appear as part of an idiomatic construction), it means "to place," or "to set." Thus, here it should be taken as a general term denoting "to settle," or "to dwell." ▪ JU

LANGUAGE

26:3 Bide

"Bide" is the translation here of the Hebrew imperative *gur*. The verbal root *g v[vav] r* may mean, depending on context, "to reside" or "to sojourn" (for the latter, see Gen. 12:10, 47:4). As seen in the article "*Ger vetoshav*" on page 140, the resident alien had no legal or social rights in the ancient Near East. Therefore, "sojourn" makes sense here as the meaning of *gur* in that God's command, "*Gur* in this land," is immediately followed by, "and I will be with you." That is, God promises to protect Yitzḥak while he dwells in the land of the Philistines. ▪ JU

Tabernacle (*mishkan*), aerial view from southeast, Timna Park

NEAR EAST

26:3 Fulfilling the oath I swore to Avraham your father

In verses 3–5, God reestablishes the promises and the treaty He made with Avraham and with Yitzḥak. An example of a sovereign reestablishing a treaty with a son or even grandson of the loyal vassal he had originally made it with already appears in the historical prologue of the Hittite suzerain-vassal treaty of Mursili II with Duppi-Tesub, king of Amurru (late 14th century BCE):

Treaty between the Hittite King Muwatalli II, son of Mursili II, and the king of Aleppo, Hattusa, ca. 1300 BCE

> My father died, and I sat on the throne of my father. And just as Azira had been in [the time of my father], so he was in my time. When it came about that the kings of Nuhhasse and the king of Kinza became again hostile in my time, Azira, your grandfather, and DU-Tesub, your father… supported only me in (my) overlordship… [just as Azira] went to battle with troops and chariots, DU-Tesub likewise went to battle [with the troops and the chariots of the land of Amurru]. And I, My Majesty, destroyed those [enemies...]
>
> … I, My Majesty, installed you in the position of your father, and for you I made [...], your brothers and the land of Amurru swore allegiance to you.

God's promises to Avraham and Yitzḥak will be passed on to Avraham's grandson, Yaakov (Gen. 28:13–14). ▪ JU

עֵקֶב אֲשֶׁר־שָׁמַע אַבְרָהָם בְּקֹלִי וַיִּשְׁמֹר מִשְׁמַרְתִּי מִצְוֺתַי חֻקּוֹתַי ה
וְתוֹרֹתָי: וַיֵּשֶׁב יִצְחָק בִּגְרָר: וַיִּשְׁאֲלוּ אַנְשֵׁי הַמָּקוֹם לְאִשְׁתּוֹ ו ז שני
וַיֹּאמֶר אֲחֹתִי הִוא כִּי יָרֵא לֵאמֹר אִשְׁתִּי פֶּן־יַהַרְגֻנִי אַנְשֵׁי הַמָּקוֹם
עַל־רִבְקָה כִּי־טוֹבַת מַרְאֶה הִוא: וַיְהִי כִּי־אָרְכוּ־לוֹ שָׁם הַיָּמִים ח
וַיַּשְׁקֵף אֲבִימֶלֶךְ מֶלֶךְ פְּלִשְׁתִּים בְּעַד הַחַלּוֹן וַיַּרְא וְהִנֵּה יִצְחָק
מְצַחֵק אֵת רִבְקָה אִשְׁתּוֹ: וַיִּקְרָא אֲבִימֶלֶךְ לְיִצְחָק וַיֹּאמֶר אַךְ ט
הִנֵּה אִשְׁתְּךָ הִוא וְאֵיךְ אָמַרְתָּ אֲחֹתִי הִוא וַיֹּאמֶר אֵלָיו יִצְחָק
כִּי אָמַרְתִּי פֶּן־אָמוּת עָלֶיהָ: וַיֹּאמֶר אֲבִימֶלֶךְ מַה־זֹּאת עָשִׂיתָ י
לָּנוּ כִּמְעַט שָׁכַב אַחַד הָעָם אֶת־אִשְׁתֶּךָ וְהֵבֵאתָ עָלֵינוּ אָשָׁם:
וַיְצַו אֲבִימֶלֶךְ אֶת־כָּל־הָעָם לֵאמֹר הַנֹּגֵעַ בָּאִישׁ הַזֶּה וּבְאִשְׁתּוֹ יא
מוֹת יוּמָת: וַיִּזְרַע יִצְחָק בָּאָרֶץ הַהִוא וַיִּמְצָא בַּשָּׁנָה הַהִוא מֵאָה יב
שְׁעָרִים וַיְבָרְכֵהוּ יהוה: וַיִּגְדַּל הָאִישׁ וַיֵּלֶךְ הָלוֹךְ וְגָדֵל עַד כִּי־גָדַל יג שלישי
מְאֹד: וַיְהִי־לוֹ מִקְנֵה־צֹאן וּמִקְנֵה בָקָר וַעֲבֻדָּה רַבָּה וַיְקַנְאוּ אֹתוֹ יד

5 descendants, because Avraham listened to My voice and
kept My charge: My commandments, My statutes, and My
6 7 laws." So Yitzḥak now settled in Gerar. The men of the place
inquired after his wife; "She is my sister," he said. He was
terrified to say "She is my wife." "The men of the place might
8 kill me for Rivka," he thought, "she is so beautiful." When he
had already been there for some time, Avimelekh, king of the
Philistines, looked down from a window and saw Yitzḥak
9 enjoying himself with his wife Rivka. Avimelekh summoned
Yitzḥak. "She is your wife," he said. "Why did you say, 'She is
my sister'?" Yitzḥak replied, "I thought I might die because
10 of her." "What is this you have done to us?" said Avimelekh.
"One of the people might have slept with your wife, and you
11 would have brought guilt upon us." Avimelekh then issued
an order to all the people: "Whoever touches this man or
12 his wife shall be put to death." Yitzḥak planted crops in that
land, and that year he reaped a hundredfold because the
13 Lord had blessed him. The man became rich; he prospered
14 more and more until he became very wealthy. He had flocks
and herds and a large retinue of servants, and the Philistines

ARCHAEOLOGY

26:8 Window

Judges 5:28, II Samuel 6:16, and II Kings 9:30 also mention an important figure, albeit a woman, looking out a window. In all of those cases, as well as in our verse, the prefixed definite article, *h*, indicates a specific window ("the window"). This may be referring to the ornate window of the outer court of ancient palaces, used when royal figures showed themselves to the assembled masses on ceremonial occasions and for other ritual purposes. For example, the Hittite *Ritual for the Erection of a New Palace* includes the announcement "Now bring all the king's sons to the palace window!" and the Hittite festival of the warrior god includes sacrifices and libations placed in the palace, "one at the hearth, one at the throne, one at the window, one at the bolt of the door." Ivory plaques of a woman looking out of an elaborately decorated window have been found in the land of Israel and Mesopotamia.

As a palace was usually on high ground, and its window afforded a good view of the surroundings, Avimelekh would have had the opportunity to see something that others could not. ▪ ZR

"Woman at the window," Ivory plaque, Nimrud, 9th to 7th century BCE

NEAR EAST

26:10 Would have brought guilt upon us

The word used for guilt in this verse, *asham*, is a technical cult term primarily used for an unwitting sin as well as for the punishment for such a sin, which is the way Avimelekh uses it in this verse.

The societies of the ancient Near East understood that unintentional sin could evoke divine disfavor and cause disaster. The Royal Library of Ashurbanipal (7th century BCE) contains Babylonian prayers that specifically mention unknown transgressions. The *Prayer to Every God* states, "The sin which I have done, indeed I do not know. The forbidden thing which I have eaten, indeed I do not know. The prohibited (place) on which I have set foot, indeed I do not know." A prayer to the goddess Mullissu states that troubles have afflicted the supplicant due to offenses "which I am or am not aware of…which I may have committed since the time of my youth… whether knowingly or unknowingly, I express my regret." The Akkadian *Dialogue between a Man and His God* from the Old Babylonian period, the earliest known text to address theodicy, similarly states "The wrong I did I do not know!" The Akkadian *Shurpu* incantations (ca. 1350–1050 BCE) consist of a long confessional of sins and unwitting breaches of taboos for situations where the patient was unsure what act of omission he may have committed to offend the gods.

The Torah, though, rejects the view that the expectation of the deity is unknowable. God gives explicit instructions about what He expects of His people. ▪ ZR

Old Babylonian *balag* (prayer set to music) to the goddess Aruru, 19th to 16th century BCE

NEAR EAST

26:12 Reaped a hundredfold

Going back to Neolithic times in the Levant, a lifestyle that combined farming with shepherding was common. Within a single family, some members would tend to the flocks while others farmed the land of their homestead. Even pastoral nomads, who moved their entire households with seasonal migrations, were involved in a certain amount of agriculture. Such small-scale agriculture has been documented among the pastoral nomads of Mari and other groups. Thus, the fact that Yitzḥak planted crops does not imply that he had adopted a sedentary way of life. In his case, the decision to engage in some agriculture was probably due to the local famine where Yitzḥak was camped and the fertile land in the area of Gerar where conditions were better.

Spring flowers in the Gerar riverbed

The region of Gerar is subject to fluctuations in rainfall patterns, with an annual average of 300 milimeters/12 inches. This makes drought a constant threat, potentially resulting in crop failures or low yields. On the other hand, in good years, large harvests of wheat and barley were possible, which are likely the crops referred to in this verse as yielding a hundredfold. In Hebrew, "a hundredfold" is *meah she'arim*; this verse is the source of the name of an ultra-Orthodox neighborhood of Jerusalem, one of the first neighborhoods built outside the Old City walls. ▪ ZR

פְּלִשְׁתִּים: וְכָל־הַבְּאֵרֹת אֲשֶׁר חָפְרוּ עַבְדֵי אָבִיו בִּימֵי אַבְרָהָם טו
אָבִיו סִתְּמוּם פְּלִשְׁתִּים וַיְמַלְאוּם עָפָר: וַיֹּאמֶר אֲבִימֶלֶךְ אֶל־ טז
יִצְחָק לֵךְ מֵעִמָּנוּ כִּי־עָצַמְתָּ מִמֶּנּוּ מְאֹד: וַיֵּלֶךְ מִשָּׁם יִצְחָק וַיִּחַן יז
בְּנַחַל־גְּרָר וַיֵּשֶׁב שָׁם: וַיָּשָׁב יִצְחָק וַיַּחְפֹּר ׀ אֶת־בְּאֵרֹת הַמַּיִם יח
אֲשֶׁר חָפְרוּ בִּימֵי אַבְרָהָם אָבִיו וַיְסַתְּמוּם פְּלִשְׁתִּים אַחֲרֵי מוֹת
אַבְרָהָם וַיִּקְרָא לָהֶן שֵׁמוֹת כַּשֵּׁמֹת אֲשֶׁר־קָרָא לָהֶן אָבִיו:
וַיַּחְפְּרוּ עַבְדֵי־יִצְחָק בַּנָּחַל וַיִּמְצְאוּ־שָׁם בְּאֵר מַיִם חַיִּים: וַיָּרִיבוּ יט כ
רֹעֵי גְרָר עִם־רֹעֵי יִצְחָק לֵאמֹר לָנוּ הַמָּיִם וַיִּקְרָא שֵׁם־הַבְּאֵר
עֵשֶׂק כִּי הִתְעַשְּׂקוּ עִמּוֹ: וַיַּחְפְּרוּ בְּאֵר אַחֶרֶת וַיָּרִיבוּ גַּם־עָלֶיהָ כא

15 envied him. So the Philistines stopped up all the wells that his
father's servants had dug in the time of his father Avraham,
16 filling them with earth. Avimelekh said to Yitzḥak, "Move
away from us. You have become much too powerful for us."
17 So Yitzḥak left and camped in the valley of Gerar and settled
18 there. And he reopened the wells that had been dug in the
time of his father Avraham, which the Philistines had stopped
up after Avraham died, and gave them the same names his
19 father had given them. Yitzḥak's servants dug in the valley
20 and discovered a well of fresh water, but the shepherds of
Gerar quarreled with Yitzḥak's shepherds, claiming that the
water was theirs. So he called the well Esek,[54] because they
21 contended with him there. They dug another well, and there

54 | Meaning "contention."

NEAR EAST

26:15 Stopped up all the wells… filling them with earth

To provide water for their flocks, pastoralists needed to dig wells, which are shafts descending deep into the ground to reach the water stored in an underground aquifer. To prevent the collapse of the shaft, stones were embedded in the sides for support. Wells were usually dug in a wadi bed, where the odds were good for tapping an aquifer. However, winter floods would fill these wells with silt, and it was necessary to clean them out every year once the flooding was over. In this case, the Philistines deliberately filled the wells with dirt, rendering the well useless in an attempt to force Yitzḥak to take his flocks elsewhere.

Evidence of wells in the land of Israel has been found from as early as the Neolithic Age. ▪ ZR

Well shaft, with stones embedded in the sides for support, Tel Lakhish

NEAR EAST

26:17–22 Yitzḥak's wells

Yitzḥak's servants made a valuable discovery of a well that had been dug in the past but since forgotten. By naming it, Yitzḥak established his ownership rights.

Three different places in Tanakh are called Reḥovot. Besides the well in our verses, it is the name of one of the cities established by Ashur in Genesis 10:11 (Reḥovot Ir) and the name of the birthplace of an Edomite king (Gen. 36:37). The word literally means "broad places" and is an appropriate name for any wide-open space.

Reḥovot, the site of Yitzḥak's well, has been identified as Khirbet Ruheibeh about 35 kilometers (21.5 miles) southwest of Be'er Sheva in the Negev desert (not at all where the modern Israeli city of Reḥovot is located). Some scholars dispute this identification, since current finds indicate that this town was founded by Nabateans in the 1st century CE. Still, there are traces of early agricultural settlements and wells in the vicinity. ▪ ZR

כב וַיִּקְרָא שְׁמָהּ שִׂטְנָה: וַיַּעְתֵּק מִשָּׁם וַיַּחְפֹּר בְּאֵר אַחֶרֶת וְלֹא רָבוּ
עָלֶיהָ וַיִּקְרָא שְׁמָהּ רְחֹבוֹת וַיֹּאמֶר כִּי־עַתָּה הִרְחִיב יהוה לָנוּ
כג כד • וּפָרִינוּ בָאָרֶץ: וַיַּעַל מִשָּׁם בְּאֵר שָׁבַע: וַיֵּרָא אֵלָיו יהוה בַּלַּיְלָה רביעי
הַהוּא וַיֹּאמֶר אָנֹכִי אֱלֹהֵי אַבְרָהָם אָבִיךָ אַל־תִּירָא כִּי־אִתְּךָ
אָנֹכִי וּבֵרַכְתִּיךָ וְהִרְבֵּיתִי אֶת־זַרְעֲךָ בַּעֲבוּר אַבְרָהָם עַבְדִּי:
כה וַיִּבֶן שָׁם מִזְבֵּחַ וַיִּקְרָא בְּשֵׁם יהוה וַיֶּט־שָׁם אָהֳלוֹ וַיִּכְרוּ־שָׁם

was a quarrel about that too; so he called it Sitna.[55] He moved 22
on from there and dug another well, and this time they did
not quarrel over it; so he named this one Reḥovot.[56] "Now the
Lord has given us space," he said, "and we will flourish in the
land." From there he went up to Be'er Sheva. That night the 23 24 •
Lord appeared to him and said, "I am the God of your father
Avraham. Do not be afraid, for I am with you. I will bless you
and multiply your descendants for the sake of Avraham My
servant." Yitzḥak built an altar there and called on the name 25
of the Lord. There he pitched his tent, and there his servants

55 | Meaning "hostility."
56 | Meaning "wide spaces."

NEAR EAST

26:24 God of your father

This is the first use of the phrase "God of your father" in the Tanakh. It appears again later in the patriarchal narratives involving God's assurances (Gen. 28:13, 31:5, 31:29, 32:9, 46:1, 46:3). After Genesis, it is found with "father" in the singular only in the episode of Moshe at the burning bush (Ex. 3:6), emphasizing the continuity of God's promises to the patriarchs. Subsequently, the expression shifts to the plural form, referring to the relationship between God and the Israelites as a group ("the God of your fathers" in Ex. 3:15, 16, 4:5).

As Nahum Sarna notes, the fact that "God of your father" is not used concerning Avraham's father, Teraḥ (who, according to Josh. 24:2, was a polytheist), indicates that God's relationship with Avraham represented "a new stage in the history of religion." This expression denotes a special, intimate connection between God and an individual, where God is both protector and patron. It is particularly suited for the patriarchal accounts as these focus on the personal stories of individuals and their relationship with God.

This phrase parallels an expression from the ancient Near East, appearing from the 19th century BCE. For example, a letter in the Mari archives from the king of Qatna to the Old Assyrian king Ishme-Dagan I states as part of an oath, "Had you simply not sent me (anything), by the name of the god of my father my feelings would not have been hurt." It was a common Old Assyrian term for the personal god, such as, "Ilabrat, the god of your father." ▪ ZR

Statuette of a seated god, ivory, Qatna (Tell Mishrife, Syria), ca. 1600 BCE

LANGUAGE

26:28–31 Pact between Yitzḥak and the Philistines

The "pact" of verse 28 is *alah*, literally, "oath." Sha'ul uses the verbal form of the root in I Samuel 14:24 when he puts his men "under oath" not to eat before evening, under penalty of a curse. As in a courtroom oath, the implication is to invoke divine punishment in case of violation. The 7th century BCE Arslan Tash inscription uses the equivalent Phoenician word both as "curse" and "a covenant of the Heavens and Eternal Earth."

The "feast" of verse 30 had a political function as well. In the Tanakh, as elsewhere in the ancient Near East, eating together was a ceremonious conclusion to a treaty (similarly, see Gen. 31:44–54, and "Covenant in the form of a Hittite suzerainty treaty," in the Exodus volume of this series on page 105). ▪ MC

Winged female figure and a "sacred" tree, furniture plaque, Neo-Assyrian, probably from Arslan Tash, 9th to 8th century BCE

עַבְדֵי־יִצְחָק בְּאֵר׃ וַאֲבִימֶלֶךְ הָלַךְ אֵלָיו מִגְּרָר וַאֲחֻזַּת מֵרֵעֵהוּ כו
וּפִיכֹל שַׂר־צְבָאוֹ׃ וַיֹּאמֶר אֲלֵהֶם יִצְחָק מַדּוּעַ בָּאתֶם אֵלָי וְאַתֶּם כז
שְׂנֵאתֶם אֹתִי וַתְּשַׁלְּחוּנִי מֵאִתְּכֶם׃ וַיֹּאמְרוּ רָאוֹ רָאִינוּ כִּי־הָיָה כח
יְהוָה ׀ עִמָּךְ וַנֹּאמֶר תְּהִי נָא אָלָה בֵּינוֹתֵינוּ בֵּינֵינוּ וּבֵינֶךָ וְנִכְרְתָה
בְרִית עִמָּךְ׃ אִם־תַּעֲשֵׂה עִמָּנוּ רָעָה כַּאֲשֶׁר לֹא נְגַעֲנוּךָ וְכַאֲשֶׁר כט
עָשִׂינוּ עִמְּךָ רַק־טוֹב וַנְּשַׁלֵּחֲךָ בְּשָׁלוֹם אַתָּה עַתָּה בְּרוּךְ יְהוָה׃
חמישי וַיַּעַשׂ לָהֶם מִשְׁתֶּה וַיֹּאכְלוּ וַיִּשְׁתּוּ׃ וַיַּשְׁכִּימוּ בַבֹּקֶר וַיִּשָּׁבְעוּ אִישׁ ל לא
לְאָחִיו וַיְשַׁלְּחֵם יִצְחָק וַיֵּלְכוּ מֵאִתּוֹ בְּשָׁלוֹם׃ וַיְהִי ׀ בַּיּוֹם הַהוּא לב
וַיָּבֹאוּ עַבְדֵי יִצְחָק וַיַּגִּדוּ לוֹ עַל־אֹדוֹת הַבְּאֵר אֲשֶׁר חָפָרוּ וַיֹּאמְרוּ
לוֹ מָצָאנוּ מָיִם׃ וַיִּקְרָא אֹתָהּ שִׁבְעָה עַל־כֵּן שֵׁם־הָעִיר בְּאֵר לג
שֶׁבַע עַד הַיּוֹם הַזֶּה׃ וַיְהִי עֵשָׂו בֶּן־אַרְבָּעִים שָׁנָה לד
וַיִּקַּח אִשָּׁה אֶת־יְהוּדִית בַּת־בְּאֵרִי הַחִתִּי וְאֶת־בָּשְׂמַת בַּת־אֵילֹן
הַחִתִּי׃ וַתִּהְיֶיןָ מֹרַת רוּחַ לְיִצְחָק וּלְרִבְקָה׃ לה

26 dug a well. Avimelekh came to him from Gerar, with Aḥuzat
27 his advisor and Pikhol the commander of his troops. Yitzḥak
said to them, "Why have you come to me? You hate me; you
28 sent me away from you." They said, "We have seen clearly that
the LORD is with you, so we say: Let there be a pact between
29 you and us. Let us make a covenant with you that you will do
us no harm, just as we did not touch you, just as we have done
you nothing but good and we sent you on your way in peace.
30 And now – the LORD bless you." Yitzḥak made them a feast,
31 and they ate and drank. Early in the morning they rose and
exchanged oaths, and Yitzḥak sent them on their way. They
32 parted from him in peace. That day, Yitzḥak's servants came
and told him about the well that they had dug; they said, "We
33 have found water." He named it Shiva,[57] which is why the
34 town is called Be'er Sheva to this day.[58] When
Esav was forty years old, he married Yehudit daughter of Be'eri
35 the Hittite, and Basmat daughter of Eilon the Hittite. These
were a source of bitter sorrow to Yitzḥak and Rivka.

57 | The name Shiva resonates with *vayishave'u* (exchanged oaths) in verse 31.
58 | Be'er denotes a well, and Sheva resonates with Shiva and *vayishave'u*.

NEAR EAST

26:34 Hittites

The Hittites were a non-Semitic civilization that flourished in the Middle and Late Bronze Ages in Anatolia. Their capital was Hattusa, in modern-day Turkey. Their empire extended from central Anatolia to the upper Euphrates and northern Levant. After the Hittite empire disintegrated as part of the Bronze Age collapse at the beginning of the 12th century BCE, the Hittites fragmented into the Neo-Hittite city-states, in the area of contemporary northern Syria, which survived until the 8th century BCE.

Some references in Tanakh to Hittites refer to an ethnic group living in Canaan, the "*benei ḥet*" (Gen. 23:6, 27:46). In those passages, the Hittites are depicted as living in Canaan among other peoples. For example, Efron was described as a Hittite who sold the burial plot of the cave of Makhpela to Avraham (Gen. 23:8). On other occasions, the Tanakh uses the term Hittite to refer to the Neo-Hittites, a people with their own country, as in Joshua 1:4, "Your territory shall stretch from the wilderness and Lebanon here to the Great River, the Euphrates River, and all the land of the Hittites", and other places (Judges 1:26; I Kings 10:29; II Kings 7:6). It is unclear if David's officer, Uriya, was part of the Canaanite ethnic group or a Neo-Hittite (see the article "Uriya the Hittite," in the Samuel volume of this series on page 297).

During the Babylonian exile and the early Second Temple period, "Hittite" is also used as a general designation for an ethnic group living in the land of Israel: "Your ancestry and your birth were in the land of the Canaanites; Your father was Amorite, your mother Hittite" (Ezek. 16:3); "They engage in abominations in the manner of the Canaanites, the Hittites…and the Amorites" (Ezra 9:1). By that time, the Hittite empire and Neo-Hittite city states had long ceased to exist. ▪ ZR

NEAR EAST

26:34–35 Esav takes Hittite wives

The "Hittite" wives that Esav takes in this verse are not from the Hittite empire in Anatolia, but from the local clan of Ḥet (23:3, 7; see "Hittites" on this page).

As Nahum Sarna comments, Esav breaks with social convention in the ancient Levant in three ways: (1) he arranges his marriages himself rather than allowing his parents to initiate them; (2) he abandons the custom of endogamy (see "Go to my…birthplace, and there find a wife for…my son" on page 144) by going outside his kinship affiliations to marry; and (3) he denigrates his clan's honor by intermarriage with a local clan. It is thus not surprising that these wives "were a source of bitter sorrow to Yitzḥak and Rivka" (see also 27:46). ▪ JU

Lion Gate, Hittite, Hattusa, 13th century BCE

Entrance to a copper mine, Wadi Faynan, Jordan

excavations of the copper mining and smelting sites in the Arava Valley, in Wadi Faynan, approximately 35 kilometers (21.5 miles) south of the Dead Sea, and in the Timna Valley, about 30 kilometers (18 miles) north of Eilat. Radiocarbon dating of organic finds indicates that the peak of metallurgical activity at these sites took place in the 10th and 9th centuries BCE, even though the copper mines of Timna had been exploited by Egypt in the 13th to 12th century BCE. It is reasonable to assume that Egypt utilized the labor of local nomadic or semi-nomadic groups, including Edomites, without disrupting their social hierarchies. After the collapse of the Egyptian empire in Canaan at the end of the Late Bronze Age, and Egypt's withdrawal from the region, the copper mines were probably operated by the same local nomadic groups that had been employed earlier by the Egyptians; yet, now the wealth produced by the mines bolstered the wealth and social status of those groups' leaders to an extent that turned them into permanent rulers of what can be considered a nomadic kingdom. Some of the finds in the Timna Valley, such as bones of fish imported from the Mediterranean coast and pieces of cloth dyed with the prestigious purple dye produced from marine snails, reflect the prosperity attained by the Edomite rulers. Under their auspices, some fortresses were built at the mining sites, although without residential quarters, and Edom's political control probably extended west to the Negev Highlands. Only after local copper production ceased, in the 8th and 7th centuries BCE, did the people of Edom, living on the Se'ir plateau east of the Arava Valley, turn to sedentary agriculture to sustain themselves.

Ramesses III, detail, facsimile of an illustration from the Harris Papyrus, Thebes, 12th century BCE

Prophets who lived at the time of the Babylonian conquest of Yehuda in 586 BCE – Yeḥezkel and Ovadya – accuse Edom of standing aside while the enemies plundered Jerusalem, and even actively assisting the conquerors. Archaeological evidence supports Edomite movement into southern Yehuda at that time. Cultic and epigraphic finds from Tel Malḥata, Ḥorvat Qitmit, and Ḥorvat Uzza in the Arad Valley, as well as Tel Aro'er south of modern Be'er Sheva, indicate an enduring Edomite presence, even before the downfall of Yehuda.

The story of the beginning of enmity between Yaakov and Esav in Genesis 27 foreshadows these developments. Interestingly, it acknowledges that Yaakov received Yitzḥak's blessing by deception but affirms that once given, the blessing is irreversible. ▪ YB

Israel and Edom

The narrative of chapter 27 of Genesis, where Yaakov tricks his father into blessing him, foreshadows the rivalry between the descendants of Yaakov-Yisrael and Esav-Edom. An interesting parallel to the double names of Yitzḥak's two sons lies in the fact that their bynames, given to them during their lives rather than at birth (Gen. 25:30, 32:28, 35:10), are attested as names of distinct populations in Egyptian sources from the 14th to 12th century BCE – which probably matches the period of the exodus and the giving of the Torah. Yisrael is mentioned in the famous Merenptah Stele (ca. 1213–1203 BCE), and possibly also on a stone statue pedestal (currently housed in the Egyptian Museum in Berlin) dating several decades, or perhaps even around a century, before Merenptah. Edom appears in Papyrus Anastasi VI, also from the reign of Merenptah, where an Egyptian fort commander reports to his superior that he had finished letting the Shasu of Edom pass through his fort, Tjeku (biblical Sukkot), to the pools of Pi-Atum (Pitom). The term "Shasu" is a common Egyptian reference to pastoral nomads of Canaan, and the Edomites' entry into Egypt under Merenptah can be compared with the biblical story of the arrival of Yaakov's family to Egypt a few centuries earlier.

A list of places in western Asia subdued by Amenhotep III (ca. 1387–1349 BCE), recorded on the walls of the temple he built in Soleb and copied on the walls of the temple of Ramesses II (ca. 1279–1213 BCE) in Amara – both now in Sudan – mentions "the land of the Shasu of Sa'arara" beside "the land of the Shasu of Yahwa." The former might be a reference to Se'ir, the mountainous plateau east of the Arava Valley, between the Dead Sea and the Red Sea, settled by Esav-Edom and his descendants (Gen. 36:8–9; Deut. 2:4–12, 22, 29). A more unambiguous reference to Se'ir appears in a letter sent by Abdi-Hepa, the Canaanite king of Jerusalem, to the court of Amenhotep IV/Akhenaten, son of Amenhotep III, in the *Amarna letters* (EA 288, l. 26). A campaign against the Shasu of Se'ir by the pharaoh Ramesses III (ca. 1186–1155 BCE) is recorded in Harris Papyrus I, col. lxxvi, ll. 9–11, and the land of Se'ir is mentioned in an Egyptian literary letter preserved in Papyrus Moscow 127, dated to around 1000 BCE.

None of the above sources speak of a settled population or kingdom in Edom/Se'ir. The question of the emergence of permanent settlement in this region has been significant in archaeological research not only in its own right, but also because state organization has been commonly connected with permanent settlement. Seen from this perspective, there is a contradiction between the Torah's statement about Moshe sending emissaries to the king of Edom (Num. 20:14) and the earliest archaeological indications of a permanent settlement on the plateau of Se'ir, east of the Arava Valley, which belong to the late 8th to 7th century BCE – centuries after Moshe's lifetime. Yet, already the extra-biblical documentary sources suggest that this contradiction is more apparent than real: Edom is attested as a kingdom recognizing Assyrian supremacy via a

The term Shasu is a common Egyptian reference to pastoral nomads of Canaan, and the Edomites' entry into Egypt under Merenptah can be compared with the biblical story of the arrival of Yaakov's family to Egypt a few centuries earlier.

long-distance contact in an inscription of Adad-Nirari III of Assyria (810–783 BCE), about a century before the emergence of permanent agricultural settlement on the plateau of Se'ir. This means that there was some sort of a state in Edom even before the establishment of permanent settlement in that land.

A major step toward solving the riddle of Edomite statehood has been taken in recent years with new archaeological

Fragment of the rare purple fabric, Timna Valley, ca. 1000 BCE

וַיְהִי כִּי־זָקֵן יִצְחָק וַתִּכְהֶיןָ עֵינָיו מֵרְאֹת וַיִּקְרָא אֶת־עֵשָׂו ׀ בְּנוֹ א כז
הַגָּדֹל וַיֹּאמֶר אֵלָיו בְּנִי וַיֹּאמֶר אֵלָיו הִנֵּנִי: וַיֹּאמֶר הִנֵּה־נָא זָקַנְתִּי ב
לֹא יָדַעְתִּי יוֹם מוֹתִי: וְעַתָּה שָׂא־נָא כֵלֶיךָ תֶּלְיְךָ וְקַשְׁתֶּךָ וְצֵא ג
צָיִד הַשָּׂדֶה וְצוּדָה לִּי צידה: וַעֲשֵׂה־לִי מַטְעַמִּים כַּאֲשֶׁר אָהַבְתִּי ד •
וְהָבִיאָה לִּי וְאֹכֵלָה בַּעֲבוּר תְּבָרֶכְךָ נַפְשִׁי בְּטֶרֶם אָמוּת: וְרִבְקָה ה
שֹׁמַעַת בְּדַבֵּר יִצְחָק אֶל־עֵשָׂו בְּנוֹ וַיֵּלֶךְ עֵשָׂו הַשָּׂדֶה לָצוּד צַיִד
לְהָבִיא: וְרִבְקָה אָמְרָה אֶל־יַעֲקֹב בְּנָהּ לֵאמֹר הִנֵּה שָׁמַעְתִּי ו
אֶת־אָבִיךָ מְדַבֵּר אֶל־עֵשָׂו אָחִיךָ לֵאמֹר: הָבִיאָה לִּי צַיִד וַעֲשֵׂה־ ז
לִי מַטְעַמִּים וְאֹכֵלָה וַאֲבָרֶכְכָה לִפְנֵי יהוה לִפְנֵי מוֹתִי: וְעַתָּה ח
בְנִי שְׁמַע בְּקֹלִי לַאֲשֶׁר אֲנִי מְצַוָּה אֹתָךְ: לֶךְ־נָא אֶל־הַצֹּאן ט
וְקַח־לִי מִשָּׁם שְׁנֵי גְּדָיֵי עִזִּים טֹבִים וְאֶעֱשֶׂה אֹתָם מַטְעַמִּים

27 1 When Yitzḥak had grown old, when his eyes had grown so
dim that he could not see, he summoned his elder son Esav.
2 "My son," he said. Esav replied, "Here I am." He said, "I am
3 old, and I do not know when I will die. So now, take your
weapons, your quiver and bow, and go out into the field and
• 4 hunt me some game. Then make me delicious food, prepared
in the way that I love, and bring it to me to eat so that my soul
5 may bless you before I die." When Yitzḥak was speaking to
Esav his son, Rivka was listening. Esav went out into the field
6 to hunt game to bring back. And Rivka said to her son Yaakov,
7 "I overheard your father say to your brother Esav, 'Fetch me
some game and make me delicious food so that I may eat and
8 give you my blessing before the LORD before I die.' Now, my
9 son, listen carefully to my instructions. Go to the flock and
bring me two choice young goats. I will make them into

Funerary stele, with Tembu and his wife (top) and four sons and two daughters (bottom), western Thebes, 15th century BCE

NEAR EAST

27:4–29 Yitzḥak's blessing to Yaakov

Yitzḥak invokes God in his blessing to Yaakov (v. 28). Although God did not command him to give this blessing, once God is invoked, the blessing is irrevocable (v. 37).

This blessing is unique in Genesis, as it does not include the classic promises of offspring and land ownership (which are part of a separate blessing, in 28:3–4). Instead, it focuses on fertility of the land, political power, and God's protection. This blessing effectively transfers leadership of the family clan to Yaakov, a role that otherwise would naturally go to the firstborn son.

Ancient Near Eastern societies had legal provisions for transferring inheritance rights from one son to another. The *Laws of Hammurabi* predicate this on having just cause: "If a man wishes to put his son out of his house, and declares before the judge: 'I want to put my son out,' then the judge shall examine into his reasons. If the son be guilty of no great fault, for which he can be rightfully put out, the father shall not put him out" (LH §168); "If he be guilty of a grave fault, which should rightfully deprive him of the filial relationship, the father shall forgive him the first time; but if he be guilty of a grave fault a second time, the father may deprive his son of all filial relation" (LH §169). Inheritance texts from Emar (14th to 12th century BCE) imply that the primary heir also inherits the father's authority over the rest of the family.

Yitzḥak's blessing is his oral will. When he tells Esav, "I have made him lord over you and given him all his brothers as servants. I have endowed him with grain and wine" (Gen. 27:37), it recalls the ancient Near Eastern legal formula "I have given…," which accorded legal power to an act of speech to bequeath a gift after the speaker's death. When the death of the speaker was not imminent, these testaments were recorded in writing to assure the rights of the inheritors. ▪ ZR

י לְאָבִיךָ כַּאֲשֶׁר אָהֵב׃ וְהֵבֵאתָ לְאָבִיךָ וְאָכָל בַּעֲבֻר אֲשֶׁר יְבָרֶכְךָ
• יא לִפְנֵי מוֹתוֹ׃ וַיֹּאמֶר יַעֲקֹב אֶל־רִבְקָה אִמּוֹ הֵן עֵשָׂו אָחִי אִישׁ
יב שָׂעִר וְאָנֹכִי אִישׁ חָלָק׃ אוּלַי יְמֻשֵּׁנִי אָבִי וְהָיִיתִי בְעֵינָיו כִּמְתַעְתֵּעַ
יג וְהֵבֵאתִי עָלַי קְלָלָה וְלֹא בְרָכָה׃ וַתֹּאמֶר לוֹ אִמּוֹ עָלַי קִלְלָתְךָ
יד בְּנִי אַךְ שְׁמַע בְּקֹלִי וְלֵךְ קַח־לִי׃ וַיֵּלֶךְ וַיִּקַּח וַיָּבֵא לְאִמּוֹ וַתַּעַשׂ
טו אִמּוֹ מַטְעַמִּים כַּאֲשֶׁר אָהֵב אָבִיו׃ וַתִּקַּח רִבְקָה אֶת־בִּגְדֵי עֵשָׂו
בְּנָהּ הַגָּדֹל הַחֲמֻדֹת אֲשֶׁר אִתָּהּ בַּבָּיִת וַתַּלְבֵּשׁ אֶת־יַעֲקֹב בְּנָהּ

delicious food, in the way he loves. Then take it to your father 10
to eat so that he may give you his blessing before he dies."
Yaakov said to Rivka his mother, "My brother Esav is hairy, 11 •
but I have smooth skin. What if my father touches me? I will 12
look to him like a fraud and bring upon myself not a blessing
but a curse." But his mother replied, "Your curse will be on 13
me, my son. Do as I say. Go; fetch them for me." So he went, 14
took the goats, and brought them to his mother, and his
mother prepared delicious food in the way his father loved.
Then Rivka took her elder son Esav's best clothes, which were 15
with her in the house, and put them on Yaakov, her younger

NEAR EAST

27:11–27 Trickery

The theme of using trickery to outwit an opponent appears in the myths of the ancient Near East as a technique to be admired in a hero. For example, in the *Epic of Gilgamesh*, Gilgamesh and Enkidu are trapped in the Forest of Cedar by Huwawa, who Gilgamesh tricks into giving up his auras, thus losing his power. There we also find the Mesopotamian god Ea using craftiness to get around the god Enlil's plan by warning Utanapishtim indirectly about the upcoming flood and telling him how to deceive his suspicious neighbors regarding the upcoming disaster – although no reason is given for Ea's interference. Perhaps, Utnapishtim was simply Ea's favorite human, as he and his wife are eventually granted immortality by the gods, while all other humans are drowned.

However, in our text, Rivka's seemingly successful scheme, with which Yaakov cooperates and even embellishes (by lying while using God's name – v. 20), is implicitly condemned, as the deceivers all received some form of punishment as a consequence of their actions. Rivka had to send Yaakov away, never to see him again, and Yaakov received a measure-for-measure punishment when he was similarly tricked by Lavan: "Yaakov said to Lavan, 'What is this you have done to me? I served you for Raḥel, did I not? Why did you deceive me?' Lavan said, 'This is not done in our country – to marry off the younger before the firstborn'" (Gen. 29:25–26). Yaakov was also deceived by his sons using Yosef's clothing dipped in goat blood (Gen. 37:31–33), just as he deceived his own father with Esav's clothing and goatskins. Furthermore, while the other patriarchs are described as dying in "satisfied" old age (Avraham, Gen. 25:8; Yitzḥak, Gen. 35:29), Yaakov described the years of his life as "few and hard" (the translation "hard," literally, "is bad"; Gen. 47:9).

While Ea's trickery in circumventing Enlil's plan went unpunished in the *Epic of Gilgamesh*, the Torah's message here seems to be quite opposite: God's plan will be fulfilled and cannot be circumvented. Unethical human behavior, even in service of something that a person thinks is good, will be punished. ▪ ZR

↗ Gilgamesh and Enkidu slaying Huwawa at the Forest of Cedar, Iraq, 19th to 17th century BCE

הַקָּטָן׃ וְאֵת עֹרֹת גְּדָיֵי הָעִזִּים הִלְבִּישָׁה עַל־יָדָיו וְעַל חֶלְקַת טז
צַוָּארָיו׃ וַתִּתֵּן אֶת־הַמַּטְעַמִּים וְאֶת־הַלֶּחֶם אֲשֶׁר עָשָׂתָה בְּיַד יז
יַעֲקֹב בְּנָהּ׃ וַיָּבֹא אֶל־אָבִיו וַיֹּאמֶר אָבִי וַיֹּאמֶר הִנֶּנִּי מִי אַתָּה יח
בְּנִי׃ וַיֹּאמֶר יַעֲקֹב אֶל־אָבִיו אָנֹכִי עֵשָׂו בְּכֹרֶךָ עָשִׂיתִי כַּאֲשֶׁר יט
דִּבַּרְתָּ אֵלָי קוּם־נָא שְׁבָה וְאָכְלָה מִצֵּידִי בַּעֲבוּר תְּבָרְכַנִּי נַפְשֶׁךָ׃
וַיֹּאמֶר יִצְחָק אֶל־בְּנוֹ מַה־זֶּה מִהַרְתָּ לִמְצֹא בְּנִי וַיֹּאמֶר כִּי הִקְרָה כ
יהוה אֱלֹהֶיךָ לְפָנָי׃ וַיֹּאמֶר יִצְחָק אֶל־יַעֲקֹב גְּשָׁה־נָּא וַאֲמֻשְׁךָ כא
בְּנִי הַאַתָּה זֶה בְּנִי עֵשָׂו אִם־לֹא׃ וַיִּגַּשׁ יַעֲקֹב אֶל־יִצְחָק אָבִיו כב
וַיְמֻשֵּׁהוּ וַיֹּאמֶר הַקֹּל קוֹל יַעֲקֹב וְהַיָּדַיִם יְדֵי עֵשָׂו׃ וְלֹא הִכִּירוֹ כג
כִּי־הָיוּ יָדָיו כִּידֵי עֵשָׂו אָחִיו שְׂעִרֹת וַיְבָרְכֵהוּ׃ וַיֹּאמֶר אַתָּה זֶה כד
בְּנִי עֵשָׂו וַיֹּאמֶר אָנִי׃ וַיֹּאמֶר הַגִּשָׁה לִּי וְאֹכְלָה מִצֵּיד בְּנִי לְמַעַן כה
תְּבָרֶכְךָ נַפְשִׁי וַיַּגֶּשׁ־לוֹ וַיֹּאכַל וַיָּבֵא לוֹ יַיִן וַיֵּשְׁתְּ׃ וַיֹּאמֶר אֵלָיו כו
יִצְחָק אָבִיו גְּשָׁה־נָּא וּשְׁקָה־לִּי בְּנִי׃ וַיִּגַּשׁ וַיִּשַּׁק־לוֹ וַיָּרַח אֶת־רֵיחַ כז
בְּגָדָיו וַיְבָרְכֵהוּ וַיֹּאמֶר רְאֵה רֵיחַ בְּנִי כְּרֵיחַ שָׂדֶה אֲשֶׁר בֵּרְכוֹ
ששי יהוה׃ וְיִתֶּן־לְךָ הָאֱלֹהִים מִטַּל הַשָּׁמַיִם וּמִשְׁמַנֵּי הָאָרֶץ וְרֹב דָּגָן כח •
וְתִירֹשׁ׃ יַעַבְדוּךָ עַמִּים וְיִשְׁתַּחֲוֻ לְךָ לְאֻמִּים הֱוֵה גְבִיר לְאַחֶיךָ כט

16 son. She put the goatskins on his hands and the smooth part
17 of his neck. She then handed her son Yaakov the delicious
18 food and bread that she had prepared. He went in to his
father; "My father," he said. His father replied, "Here I am.
19 Who are you, my son?" Yaakov said to his father, "I am Esav
your firstborn. I have done as you asked. Please sit up and eat
20 some of my game so that your soul may bless me." Yitzḥak
asked his son, "How did you find it so quickly, my son?" He
21 replied, "The Lord your God brought it about for me." Then
Yitzḥak said to Yaakov, "Come close and let me feel you, my
22 son, to know – are you really my son Esav?" Yaakov came
close to Yitzḥak his father, who felt him and said, "The voice
is the voice of Yaakov, but the hands are the hands of Esav."
23 He did not recognize him, because his hands were hairy like
24 those of his brother Esav. And he blessed him."Are you really
25 my son Esav?" he asked. He replied, "I am." "Then serve me
and let me eat some of my son's game so that my soul may
bless you." He served him food and he ate, he brought him
26 wine and he drank. Then Yaakov's father Yitzḥak said to him,
27 "Come close and kiss me, my son." So he came close and
kissed him, and Yitzḥak smelled the smell of his clothes and
blessed him, saying: "The smell of my son is the smell of a
• 28 field the Lord has blessed. God endow you with dew of
29 heaven, the cream of the land, much grain and wine. May

NEAR EAST

27:28 Dew of heaven

Dew is an extremely important water source for crops during the rainless summer months in the land of Israel. Winds blowing in from the Mediterranean Sea bring moisture, which condenses overnight into a mist that settles as dew on the ground, increasing the water balance in the area and providing much-needed moisture for crops. This phenomenon is also the background for the prominent position of prayers for dew in the liturgy.

The pairing of "dew of heaven, the cream of the land" is also found in Ugaritic literature (*tl shmm* and *shmn artz*). The Ugaritic *Tale of Aqhat*, partially set along the shores of the Sea of Galilee, also notes the significance of dew, "the clouds (that) rain in summer, the dew (that) falls on the fruits" (1, line 40). ▪ ZR

ל וְיִשְׁתַּחֲווּ לְךָ בְּנֵי אִמֶּךָ אֹרְרֶיךָ אָרוּר וּמְבָרְכֶיךָ בָּרוּךְ: וַיְהִי כַּאֲשֶׁר
כִּלָּה יִצְחָק לְבָרֵךְ אֶת־יַעֲקֹב וַיְהִי אַךְ יָצֹא יָצָא יַעֲקֹב מֵאֵת פְּנֵי
לא יִצְחָק אָבִיו וְעֵשָׂו אָחִיו בָּא מִצֵּידוֹ: וַיַּעַשׂ גַּם־הוּא מַטְעַמִּים
וַיָּבֵא לְאָבִיו וַיֹּאמֶר לְאָבִיו יָקֻם אָבִי וְיֹאכַל מִצֵּיד בְּנוֹ בַּעֲבֻר
לב תְּבָרְכַנִּי נַפְשֶׁךָ: וַיֹּאמֶר לוֹ יִצְחָק אָבִיו מִי־אָתָּה וַיֹּאמֶר אֲנִי בִּנְךָ
לג בְּכֹרְךָ עֵשָׂו: וַיֶּחֱרַד יִצְחָק חֲרָדָה גְּדֹלָה עַד־מְאֹד וַיֹּאמֶר מִי־
אֵפוֹא הוּא הַצָּד־צַיִד וַיָּבֵא לִי וָאֹכַל מִכֹּל בְּטֶרֶם תָּבוֹא וָאֲבָרְכֵהוּ
לד גַּם־בָּרוּךְ יִהְיֶה: כִּשְׁמֹעַ עֵשָׂו אֶת־דִּבְרֵי אָבִיו וַיִּצְעַק צְעָקָה גְּדֹלָה
לה וּמָרָה עַד־מְאֹד וַיֹּאמֶר לְאָבִיו בָּרְכֵנִי גַם־אָנִי אָבִי: וַיֹּאמֶר בָּא
לו אָחִיךָ בְּמִרְמָה וַיִּקַּח בִּרְכָתֶךָ: וַיֹּאמֶר הֲכִי קָרָא שְׁמוֹ יַעֲקֹב
וַיַּעְקְבֵנִי זֶה פַעֲמַיִם אֶת־בְּכֹרָתִי לָקָח וְהִנֵּה עַתָּה לָקַח בִּרְכָתִי
לז וַיֹּאמַר הֲלֹא־אָצַלְתָּ לִּי בְּרָכָה: וַיַּעַן יִצְחָק וַיֹּאמֶר לְעֵשָׂו הֵן גְּבִיר
שַׂמְתִּיו לָךְ וְאֶת־כָּל־אֶחָיו נָתַתִּי לוֹ לַעֲבָדִים וְדָגָן וְתִירֹשׁ סְמַכְתִּיו
לח וּלְכָה אֵפוֹא מָה אֶעֱשֶׂה בְּנִי: וַיֹּאמֶר עֵשָׂו אֶל־אָבִיו הַבְרָכָה
אַחַת הִוא־לְךָ אָבִי בָּרְכֵנִי גַם־אָנִי אָבִי וַיִּשָּׂא עֵשָׂו קֹלוֹ וַיֵּבְךְּ:

peoples serve you; may nations bow down to you. Be lord
over your brothers, and may your mother's sons bow down
to you. A curse on those who curse you; on those who bless
you, blessing." Yitzḥak had finished blessing Yaakov, and 30
Yaakov had just left his father Yitzḥak, when his brother Esav
came back from the hunt. He too had prepared delicious food 31
and brought it to his father. And he said to his father, "Let my
father sit up and eat some of his son's game so that your soul
may bless me." "Who are you?" asked his father Yitzḥak. "I 32
am your son, your firstborn, Esav," he replied. Yitzḥak was 33
seized with a violent fit of trembling. "Who then was it that
hunted game and brought it to me? I ate it all before you came,
and I blessed him – and he will be blessed." When Esav heard 34
his father's words, he burst into a loud and bitter cry. He said
to his father, "Bless me, me too, my father!" "Your brother 35
came in deceit and took your blessing," he replied. Esav said, 36
"Is he not rightly named Yaakov? Twice he has supplanted
me.[59] He took my birthright and now he has taken my
blessing." And then, "Do you not have any blessing left for
me?" Yitzḥak answered Esav, "I have made him lord over you 37
and given him all his brothers as servants. I have endowed
him with grain and wine. What then can I do for you, my
son?" Esav said to his father, "Have you only one blessing, 38

Dew drops on purple *catharanthus roseus* flowers, private garden, Israel

59 | Hebrew *vayakeveni*, resonating with the name Yaakov.

וַיַּעַן יִצְחָק אָבִיו וַיֹּאמֶר אֵלָיו הִנֵּה מִשְׁמַנֵּי הָאָרֶץ יִהְיֶה מוֹשָׁבֶךָ לט
וּמִטַּל הַשָּׁמַיִם מֵעָל׃ וְעַל־חַרְבְּךָ תִחְיֶה וְאֶת־אָחִיךָ תַּעֲבֹד וְהָיָה מ
כַּאֲשֶׁר תָּרִיד וּפָרַקְתָּ עֻלּוֹ מֵעַל צַוָּארֶךָ׃ וַיִּשְׂטֹם עֵשָׂו אֶת־יַעֲקֹב מא
עַל־הַבְּרָכָה אֲשֶׁר בֵּרְכוֹ אָבִיו וַיֹּאמֶר עֵשָׂו בְּלִבּוֹ יִקְרְבוּ יְמֵי אֵבֶל
אָבִי וְאַהַרְגָה אֶת־יַעֲקֹב אָחִי׃ וַיֻּגַּד לְרִבְקָה אֶת־דִּבְרֵי עֵשָׂו בְּנָהּ מב
הַגָּדֹל וַתִּשְׁלַח וַתִּקְרָא לְיַעֲקֹב בְּנָהּ הַקָּטָן וַתֹּאמֶר אֵלָיו הִנֵּה
עֵשָׂו אָחִיךָ מִתְנַחֵם לְךָ לְהָרְגֶךָ׃ וְעַתָּה בְנִי שְׁמַע בְּקֹלִי וְקוּם מג
בְּרַח־לְךָ אֶל־לָבָן אָחִי חָרָנָה׃ וְיָשַׁבְתָּ עִמּוֹ יָמִים אֲחָדִים עַד מד
אֲשֶׁר־תָּשׁוּב חֲמַת אָחִיךָ׃ עַד־שׁוּב אַף־אָחִיךָ מִמְּךָ וְשָׁכַח אֵת מה
אֲשֶׁר־עָשִׂיתָ לּוֹ וְשָׁלַחְתִּי וּלְקַחְתִּיךָ מִשָּׁם לָמָה אֶשְׁכַּל גַּם־שְׁנֵיכֶם

father? Bless me, me too, my father!" And Esav wept aloud.
39 His father Yitzḥak answered him and said: "Of the cream of
40 the land your home shall be, of the dew of heaven above. By
your sword you will live, and your brother you will serve; but
when you break loose, you will throw off his yoke from your
41 neck." Esav resented Yaakov because of the blessing his father
had given him. "The days of mourning for my father are
approaching," he said to himself, "and then I will kill my
42 brother Yaakov." When Rivka was told what her elder son
Esav had said, she summoned her younger son Yaakov and
said, "Your brother Esav is consoling himself with the thought
43 of killing you. Now, my son, listen to me. Flee at once to my
44 brother Lavan in Ḥaran. Stay with him a while, until your
45 brother's rage subsides. When your brother is no longer angry

GEOGRAPHY

27:39–40 Yitzḥak's blessing to Esav

The blessings of "cream of the land," and "dew of heaven" which are given to Esav, are similar to the blessings given to Yaakov, but in reverse order. Edom, the ancient kingdom founded by Esav, was located in Transjordan, between Moav to the northeast, the Arava to the west, and the Arabian Desert to the south and east. While most of the kingdom was not fruitful, as the area receives very little dewfall and even less rain, the mountains of Se'ir, in the northwestern part of Edom, do receive sufficient rain, allowing a decent amount of vegetation. This geographic distinction may be reflected in the possibly ambiguous use of the preposition *mem* ("from") before the words for "dew of heaven" and "cream of the land" in the blessings, which can indicate either partaking of these natural blessings or, conversely, being distanced from them.

The reference to breaking the yoke of those who rule over Esav in verse 40 may be a prophetic reference to Edom's revolt in the time of King Yoram (849–842 BCE), after having been a vassal state of Israel since the time of David: "In his time Edom rebelled against Yehuda and appointed their own king. Yoram crossed over to Tza'ir with all his chariots; he advanced at night to attack Edom, who had surrounded him and his chariot officers, but the troops fled back to their homes. And Edom has rebelled against Yehuda ever since" (II Kings 8:20–22). ▪ ZR

Petra, Mount Hor and Akabah, Petra Mountain Ridge, Mount Seir, photograph from 1950–1977

מו יוֹם אֶחָד׃ וַתֹּאמֶר רִבְקָה אֶל־יִצְחָק קַצְתִּי בְחַיַּי מִפְּנֵי בְּנוֹת חֵת
אִם־לֹקֵחַ יַעֲקֹב אִשָּׁה מִבְּנוֹת־חֵת כָּאֵלֶּה מִבְּנוֹת הָאָרֶץ לָמָּה
כח א לִּי חַיִּים׃ וַיִּקְרָא יִצְחָק אֶל־יַעֲקֹב וַיְבָרֶךְ אֹתוֹ וַיְצַוֵּהוּ וַיֹּאמֶר לוֹ
ב לֹא־תִקַּח אִשָּׁה מִבְּנוֹת כְּנָעַן׃ קוּם לֵךְ פַּדֶּנָה אֲרָם בֵּיתָה בְתוּאֵל
ג אֲבִי אִמֶּךָ וְקַח־לְךָ מִשָּׁם אִשָּׁה מִבְּנוֹת לָבָן אֲחִי אִמֶּךָ׃ וְאֵל שַׁדַּי
ד יְבָרֵךְ אֹתְךָ וְיַפְרְךָ וְיַרְבֶּךָ וְהָיִיתָ לִקְהַל עַמִּים׃ וְיִתֶּן־לְךָ אֶת־בִּרְכַּת
אַבְרָהָם לְךָ וּלְזַרְעֲךָ אִתָּךְ לְרִשְׁתְּךָ אֶת־אֶרֶץ מְגֻרֶיךָ אֲשֶׁר־נָתַן
• ה אֱלֹהִים לְאַבְרָהָם׃ וַיִּשְׁלַח יִצְחָק אֶת־יַעֲקֹב וַיֵּלֶךְ פַּדֶּנָה אֲרָם שביעי

with you and has forgotten what you did to him, I will send
word to you to come back. Why should I lose you both in one
day?" Rivka then said to Yitzḥak, "I loathe my life because of 46
these Hittite women. If Yaakov marries a Hittite woman like
them, one of the women of the land, why should I go on
living?" So Yitzḥak called Yaakov to him. He blessed him and 1 28
charged him: "You are not to marry a Canaanite woman. Go 2
at once to Padan Aram, to the house of your mother's father
Betuel, and there marry a daughter of your mother's brother
Lavan. May El Shaddai bless you, make you fertile, and 3
multiply you so that you become a community of peoples.
May He grant Avraham's blessing to you and your descendants, 4
that you may possess the land where you live as a stranger,
which God gave to Avraham." Then Yitzḥak sent Yaakov on 5 •
his way. He went toward Padan Aram, to Lavan son of Betuel

NEAR EAST

28:5 Aramean

"Arameans" is the term given to a diverse group of tribes living in the steppe land on the western side of the upper and middle Euphrates. Although arid, this area does support grazing, which fits the biblical description of the Arameans as having a semi-nomadic pastoral lifestyle.

It is unknown when exactly the Arameans as an ethnic group originated, but the earliest undisputed references to them as a people appear in Assyrian records, in the inscriptions of Tiglat-Pileser I (ca. 1100 BCE) and his successor Ashur-bel-kala (ca. 1074–1056 BCE). Those two kings refer to battles against the Arameans, as a group among the Semitic nomads collectively referred to as the Ahlamu. Later the Arameans rose to prominence among the other tribes, eventually developing a distinct national identity in the early part of the 1st millennium. ▪ ZR

Octagonal prism of Tiglat-Pileser I recounting victories in the Levant, Anu-Adad Temple, Ashur, 1114–1079 BCE

אֶל־לָבָן בֶּן־בְּתוּאֵל הָאֲרַמִּי אֲחִי רִבְקָה אֵם יַעֲקֹב וְעֵשָׂו׃ וַיַּרְא ו
עֵשָׂו כִּי־בֵרַךְ יִצְחָק אֶת־יַעֲקֹב וְשִׁלַּח אֹתוֹ פַּדֶּנָה אֲרָם לָקַחַת־
לוֹ מִשָּׁם אִשָּׁה בְּבָרְכוֹ אֹתוֹ וַיְצַו עָלָיו לֵאמֹר לֹא־תִקַּח אִשָּׁה
מפטיר מִבְּנוֹת כְּנָעַן׃ וַיִּשְׁמַע יַעֲקֹב אֶל־אָבִיו וְאֶל־אִמּוֹ וַיֵּלֶךְ פַּדֶּנָה ז
אֲרָם׃ וַיַּרְא עֵשָׂו כִּי רָעוֹת בְּנוֹת כְּנָעַן בְּעֵינֵי יִצְחָק אָבִיו׃ וַיֵּלֶךְ ח ט
עֵשָׂו אֶל־יִשְׁמָעֵאל וַיִּקַּח אֶת־מָחֲלַת ׀ בַּת־יִשְׁמָעֵאל בֶּן־אַבְרָהָם
ויצא אֲחוֹת נְבָיוֹת עַל־נָשָׁיו לוֹ לְאִשָּׁה׃ וַיֵּצֵא יַעֲקֹב מִבְּאֵר י

the Aramean, brother of Rivka, Yaakov and Esav's mother.
6 Esav learned that Yitzḥak had blessed Yaakov and sent him
to Padan Aram to find a wife, and that when he blessed him,
7 he commanded him not to marry a Canaanite woman, and
that Yaakov had obeyed his father and mother and had gone
8 to Padan Aram. Esav realized then that the Canaanite women
9 displeased his father Yitzḥak. So Esav went to Yishmael and
took Maḥalat, daughter of Avraham's son Yishmael, a sister
10 of Nevayot, to be his wife, with his other wives. Yaakov

NEAR EAST

28:9 Esav and the Ishmaelites

The account of Esav taking a daughter of his uncle Yishmael as a wife indicates a connection between the Edomites and Ishmaelites, also seen in Psalms 83:6–7, "Yes, their hearts conspire as one; they have formed a pact against You: the tents of Edom and the Ishmaelites."

This alliance appears to have functioned as part of the production and distribution of spices along specific trade routes, as early as the Middle Bronze Age. The spices would have come by boat from the shores and islands of the Indian Ocean to the Arabian Peninsula and the Persian Gulf, and then overland through the Fertile Crescent.

The descendants of Nevayot are identified by academic scholars with the Nabaiati mentioned in Assyrian records (see "The sons of Yishmael" on page 154). ▪ ZR

Ruins of the Nabatean Ein Saharonim waystation on the Spice Route from Arabia to Aza

יא שֶׁבַע וַיֵּלֶךְ חָרָנָה: וַיִּפְגַּע בַּמָּקוֹם וַיָּלֶן שָׁם כִּי־בָא הַשֶּׁמֶשׁ וַיִּקַּח

left Be'er Sheva and journeyed toward Ḥaran. In time he 11
chanced upon a certain place and decided to spend the night
there, because the sun had set. He took some stones of the

GEOGRAPHY

28:10 Yaakov's journey from Be'er Sheva to Ḥaran via Beit El

The most likely way for Yaakov to have traveled north from Be'er Sheva to Ḥaran would have been along the main north-south road to Shekhem, which passed through the highlands of Yehuda and Beit El, then crossing the Jordan River. This is also the first stop named when Avram entered Canaan (Gen. 12:6), indicating that this is the way he entered the land, Yaakov probably followed the same route. This is also the route used by Yaakov on his return from Ḥaran (Gen. 33:18), and thus suggests further evidence that this was the route he also used on his way to Ḥaran. This route is expressly noted in Judges 21:19, "the highway leading from Beit El to Shekhem." Beit El guarded the intersection of that highway with the east-west route from Yeriḥo to Afek, as well as a secondary road from Jerusalem. Given the distances involved and the difficulty of traveling at night, Yaakov's stop at Beit El probably took place on the third night of his journey – after traveling about 115 kilometers (71.5 miles). ▪ ZR

↗ The road from Be'er Sheva to Ḥaran

יב מֵאַבְנֵי הַמָּקוֹם וַיָּשֶׂם מְרַאֲשֹׁתָיו וַיִּשְׁכַּב בַּמָּקוֹם הַהוּא: וַיַּחֲלֹם
וְהִנֵּה סֻלָּם מֻצָּב אַרְצָה וְרֹאשׁוֹ מַגִּיעַ הַשָּׁמָיְמָה וְהִנֵּה מַלְאֲכֵי
יג אֱלֹהִים עֹלִים וְיֹרְדִים בּוֹ: וְהִנֵּה יהוה נִצָּב עָלָיו וַיֹּאמַר אֲנִי יהוה
אֱלֹהֵי אַבְרָהָם אָבִיךָ וֵאלֹהֵי יִצְחָק הָאָרֶץ אֲשֶׁר אַתָּה שֹׁכֵב
יד עָלֶיהָ לְךָ אֶתְּנֶנָּה וּלְזַרְעֶךָ: וְהָיָה זַרְעֲךָ כַּעֲפַר הָאָרֶץ וּפָרַצְתָּ
יָמָּה וָקֵדְמָה וְצָפֹנָה וָנֶגְבָּה וְנִבְרְכוּ בְךָ כָּל־מִשְׁפְּחֹת הָאֲדָמָה
טו וּבְזַרְעֶךָ: וְהִנֵּה אָנֹכִי עִמָּךְ וּשְׁמַרְתִּיךָ בְּכֹל אֲשֶׁר־תֵּלֵךְ וַהֲשִׁבֹתִיךָ
אֶל־הָאֲדָמָה הַזֹּאת כִּי לֹא אֶעֱזָבְךָ עַד אֲשֶׁר אִם־עָשִׂיתִי אֵת
טז אֲשֶׁר־דִּבַּרְתִּי לָךְ: וַיִּיקַץ יַעֲקֹב מִשְּׁנָתוֹ וַיֹּאמֶר אָכֵן יֵשׁ יהוה

place and put them under his head, and in that place lay down
12 to sleep. And he dreamed: He saw a ladder set upon the
ground, whose top reached the heavens. On it, angels of God
13 went up and came down. The Lord stood over him there and
said, "I am the Lord, the God of Avraham your father, and
the God of Yitzḥak. The land on which you lie I will give to
14 you and your descendants. Your descendants shall be like the
dust of the earth, and you will spread out to the west, the east,
the north, and the south. Through you and your descendants,
15 all the families of the earth will be blessed. I am with you. I
will protect you wherever you go and I will bring you back to
this land, for I will not leave you until I have done what I have
16 spoken of to you." Then Yaakov awoke from his sleep and said,

NEAR EAST

28:12–17 Yaakov's dream in ancient Near Eastern context

On his way from Be'er Sheva to Aram, Yaakov spends the night at a random place. When, in a dream, he receives a profound message of divine support and blessing there, he recognizes the site as a "House of God" and "gate of the heavens." He sets up a sacred pillar commemorating the revelation and pledges to establish and support the site as a place of worship.

Gudea I, statue dedicated to the god Ningishzida, Neo-Sumerian, Girsu, 22nd century BCE

In the ancient Near East, a person who wanted to discern the will of a deity would customarily engage in "incubation," i.e., sleeping in the precincts of the god's temple, hoping for a nocturnal visit. An allusion to this practice is found in the hymn to the Egyptian goddess Hathor: "I walked about in the Queen's Valley, I spent the night in your forecourt, I drank water while I knelt on my knees." In ancient Mesopotamia, Gudea, king of Lagash, was prompted by an initial dream to incubate a second dream for instructions concerning the construction of a new temple for his god Ningursu. He sacrificed offerings, prayed, and engaged in divination, specifically to receive such a dream revelation. An interesting difference between Genesis 28 and dream incubation in general is that Yaakov's *unsolicited* dream experience establishes Beit El as the site of future worship, as opposed to choosing an established holy site for incubation (compare "Spending a night in the temple" in the Samuel volume of this series on page 29).

The celestial stairway (*sullam*) of Yaakov's dream is termed a "gate of the heavens" (v. 17), similar in function to the ziggurat, known from Mesopotamia (see "Tower of Bavel" on pages 64–65). Remnants of around thirty of these stepped towers have survived. They were built to provide a stairway for the gods to come down and be worshipped in their adjoining temples. The names of these structures reflect their function: in Babylon, the ziggurat was called "the temple (literally, "house") of foundation of heaven and earth"; at Larsa, "temple that links heaven and earth"; and at Sippar, "the temple of the stairway to pure heaven." Similarly, the city name "Babylon" means "gate of gods." The Hebrew *sullam* is cognate to the Akkadian *simmiltu*, meaning "ladder" or "stair," with transposition of letters. One Mesopotamian myth, *Nergal and Ereshkigal*, has the god Nergal descend the "stairway of heaven" to travel from heaven to the underworld.

In Egypt, the high priests of Amun were called the "openers of the gates of heaven." There the gates were physical gates in the temple of Karnak, which led to a hall lined with electrum, a naturally occurring alloy of silver and gold that was so magnificent that it was likened to the horizon of heaven.

The ladder in Yaakov's dream differs from a ziggurat in that it is not a human construction and it does not have the purpose of enabling God to descend to be worshipped. Rather, God's angels ascend and descend it (v. 12). As shown by Israel Prize recipient, Professor Meir Weiss, what is seen in a prophetic dream or vision in the Tanakh is interpreted by what is heard alongside it. Yaakov's dream is explained by God's words, "I am with you. I will protect you wherever you go, and I will bring you back to this land" (v. 15); thus, the angels who had guarded Yaakov until now ascend back to Heaven and are replaced by the angels who will guard Yaakov on his journey. ▪ EG

יז בַּמָּקוֹם הַזֶּה וְאָנֹכִי לֹא יָדָעְתִּי׃ וַיִּירָא וַיֹּאמַר מַה־נּוֹרָא הַמָּקוֹם
יח הַזֶּה אֵין זֶה כִּי אִם־בֵּית אֱלֹהִים וְזֶה שַׁעַר הַשָּׁמָיִם׃ וַיַּשְׁכֵּם יַעֲקֹב
בַּבֹּקֶר וַיִּקַּח אֶת־הָאֶבֶן אֲשֶׁר־שָׂם מְרַאֲשֹׁתָיו וַיָּשֶׂם אֹתָהּ מַצֵּבָה
יט וַיִּצֹק שֶׁמֶן עַל־רֹאשָׁהּ׃ וַיִּקְרָא אֶת־שֵׁם־הַמָּקוֹם הַהוּא בֵּית־אֵל
כ וְאוּלָם לוּז שֵׁם־הָעִיר לָרִאשֹׁנָה׃ וַיִּדַּר יַעֲקֹב נֶדֶר לֵאמֹר אִם־
יִהְיֶה אֱלֹהִים עִמָּדִי וּשְׁמָרַנִי בַּדֶּרֶךְ הַזֶּה אֲשֶׁר אָנֹכִי הוֹלֵךְ וְנָתַן־

"Truly, the Lord is in this place – and I did not know it!" He 17
was afraid and said, "How full of awe is this place! This is none
other than the House of God, and this the gate of the heavens!"
Yaakov rose early the next morning, took the stone he had 18
placed under his head, set it up as a pillar, and poured oil on
top of it. He named the place Beit El;[60] the town was originally 19
called Luz. Yaakov then made a vow. "If God will be with me," 20

60 | Meaning "House of God."

NEAR EAST

28:20–22 Vows to a deity in the ancient Near East

In the ancient Near East, it was common to make a vow to a deity to give them a gift, as a way to secure the god's favor. For example, people would vow to bring a sacrifice or a donation to a temple in order to attain military victory, heal from disease, or achieve romantic success. In the Ugaritic *Kirta Epic*, the god El tells King Kirta that he should wage war against the kingdom of Udum and demand that Hurriya, the daughter of King Pubala of Udum, be given to him as a wife. Kirta vows to give payment far in excess of Hurriya's simple value, if he is successful, "As Ashera of Tyre exists, as Elat of Sidon! If Hurriya to my house I take, bring the lass into my court, her double I'll give in silver, and her treble in gold" (KTU 1.14 iv 201–209).

Vows fitting this structure are found in many places in Tanakh, such as the vows of Yiftaḥ the Gileadite (Judges 11:30–31) and Ḥana (I Sam. 1:11). Yaakov's vow is unique in that God already promised to protect him in verse 15, so his vow has no aspect of bargaining with God. Yaakov's commitment to give a tithe is completely voluntary, an expression of gratitude to God for the promises He already made, if not yet fulfilled. It should be noted, however, that Yaakov does add some elements in his vow; he expands God's general promise of protection to include basic sustenance ("bread to eat and clothes to wear"), and adjusts God's promise of "I will bring you back to this land" (v. 15) to be more specific, "if I return in peace to my father's house."

Yaakov also sets up a pillar here, an element commonly associated with vows in the western region of the ancient Near East. For example, an Egyptian stele from the 13th century BCE was erected by a man named Nebre who had promised to erect a stele if the god Amun-Re saved his son Nachtamu from his illness: "Now, behold, I do what I have said." The Aramaic Melqart Stele (9th century BCE) states, "The stele which Bir-Hadad, son of Ezer, the Damascene, son of the king of Aram, erected to his Lord Melqart, to whom he made a vow and who heard his voice." ZR

↗ Stele dedicated to the gods by Nebre and his son Amenemope, Deir el-Medina, 13th century BCE

לִי לֶחֶם לֶאֱכֹל וּבֶגֶד לִלְבֹּשׁ: וְשַׁבְתִּי בְשָׁלוֹם אֶל־בֵּית אָבִי וְהָיָה כא
יהוה לִי לֵאלֹהִים: וְהָאֶבֶן הַזֹּאת אֲשֶׁר־שַׂמְתִּי מַצֵּבָה יִהְיֶה בֵּית כב •
שני אֱלֹהִים וְכֹל אֲשֶׁר תִּתֶּן־לִי עַשֵּׂר אֲעַשְּׂרֶנּוּ לָךְ: וַיִּשָּׂא יַעֲקֹב רַגְלָיו א כט
וַיֵּלֶךְ אַרְצָה בְנֵי־קֶדֶם: וַיַּרְא וְהִנֵּה בְאֵר בַּשָּׂדֶה וְהִנֵּה־שָׁם שְׁלֹשָׁה ב •
עֶדְרֵי־צֹאן רֹבְצִים עָלֶיהָ כִּי מִן־הַבְּאֵר הַהִוא יַשְׁקוּ הָעֲדָרִים
וְהָאֶבֶן גְּדֹלָה עַל־פִּי הַבְּאֵר: וְנֶאֶסְפוּ־שָׁמָּה כָל־הָעֲדָרִים וְגָלְלוּ ג
אֶת־הָאֶבֶן מֵעַל פִּי הַבְּאֵר וְהִשְׁקוּ אֶת־הַצֹּאן וְהֵשִׁיבוּ אֶת־הָאֶבֶן
עַל־פִּי הַבְּאֵר לִמְקֹמָהּ: וַיֹּאמֶר לָהֶם יַעֲקֹב אַחַי מֵאַיִן אַתֶּם ד

he said, "protecting me on this journey I am taking, giving
21 me bread to eat and clothes to wear, and if I return in peace
• 22 to my father's house, then the LORD will be my God. This
stone I set up as a pillar will become a house of God, and of
29 1 all that You give me I will dedicate a tenth to You." Yaakov
began traveling again and came to the land of the people of
• 2 the East. There he saw a well in a field. Three flocks of sheep
were lying beside it because this was the well from which the
flocks were watered. The top of it was covered with a large
3 stone. When all the flocks were gathered there, the stone
would be rolled from the mouth of the well and the sheep
watered. The stone would then be put back in place on top of
4 the well. Yaakov asked the shepherds, "Brothers, where are

NEAR EAST

28:22 ***Matzeva***

This is the first of several pillars that Yaakov sets up (Gen. 31:45, 35:14, 35:20). *Matzeva* is the term used for an upright stone slab, whether its purpose is religious or political. In this verse the *matzeva* is dedicated as a "house of God," meaning that it represents the Divine Presence there, the same place where Yaakov will fulfill his vow if he returns.

The standing stone, often kept free of decoration even when the stone itself was shaped or worked, is one of the oldest kinds of cultic objects known. Pagan pillars, dating to the 14th millennium BCE and ranging in height from a few centimeters to a few meters (a few inches to a few yards), have been found in the southern Negev and eastern Sinai. In Ḥatzor, pillars were found from both the Canaanite and Israelite periods, possibly representing different concepts for the two societies. Pillars were also found in the "holy of holies" of the Iron Age Israelite temple in Tel Arad.

The *matzeva* as a pagan cultic object is repurposed by Yaakov for worship of the one, true God. Later, it is prohibited in Torah law as not just idolatry but as illegitimate worship of God: "You shall make no idols, nor may you erect any divine image or worship pillar" (Lev. 26:1), and "do not erect a worship pillar, for these are things that the Lord your God hates" (Deut. 16:22). The term is used in Hosea 10:2 to denote a pagan shrine, and in Exodus to describe idolatrous objects that the Israelites are commanded to destroy (Ex. 23:24, 34:13). Whereas in Genesis establishing a *matzeva* is a legitimate practice, it later becomes outlawed to the Israelites as idolatry.

This shift is probably due to the fact that in the ancient world the stones themselves were sometimes seen as containing the essence of a deity, and thus functioned as objects of worship themselves, like a graven image. Although in practice standing stones had a variety of functions, their cultic usage came to be seen by the time of the giving of the Torah as an illegitimate way to relate to God. ▪ ZR

↗ Standing stones, Canaanite, Tel Gezer, 13th century BCE

ה וַיֹּאמְרוּ מֵחָרָן אֲנָחְנוּ: וַיֹּאמֶר לָהֶם הַיְדַעְתֶּם אֶת־לָבָן בֶּן־נָחוֹר
ו וַיֹּאמְרוּ יָדָעְנוּ: וַיֹּאמֶר לָהֶם הֲשָׁלוֹם לוֹ וַיֹּאמְרוּ שָׁלוֹם וְהִנֵּה רָחֵל
ז בִּתּוֹ בָּאָה עִם־הַצֹּאן: וַיֹּאמֶר הֵן עוֹד הַיּוֹם גָּדוֹל לֹא־עֵת הֵאָסֵף
ח הַמִּקְנֶה הַשְׁקוּ הַצֹּאן וּלְכוּ רְעוּ: וַיֹּאמְרוּ לֹא נוּכַל עַד אֲשֶׁר
יֵאָסְפוּ כָּל־הָעֲדָרִים וְגָלְלוּ אֶת־הָאֶבֶן מֵעַל פִּי הַבְּאֵר וְהִשְׁקִינוּ
ט הַצֹּאן: עוֹדֶנּוּ מְדַבֵּר עִמָּם וְרָחֵל ׀ בָּאָה עִם־הַצֹּאן אֲשֶׁר לְאָבִיהָ
י כִּי רֹעָה הִוא: וַיְהִי כַּאֲשֶׁר רָאָה יַעֲקֹב אֶת־רָחֵל בַּת־לָבָן אֲחִי
אִמּוֹ וְאֶת־צֹאן לָבָן אֲחִי אִמּוֹ וַיִּגַּשׁ יַעֲקֹב וַיָּגֶל אֶת־הָאֶבֶן מֵעַל

you from?" "We are from Ḥaran," they replied. He asked, "Do 5
you know Lavan son of Naḥor?" "We know him," they said.
He asked, "Is he well?" "He is well," they said, "and look, here 6
is his daughter Raḥel coming with the sheep." "Look," he said, 7
"it is still broad daylight. It is not yet time to gather in the
animals. Water the flocks and take them back to pasture." But 8
they said, "We cannot do that until all the flocks are gathered
and the stone is rolled from the top of the well. Only then can
we water the flocks." While he was still talking with them, 9
Raḥel came with her father's sheep; she was a shepherdess.
When Yaakov saw Raḥel, daughter of his mother's brother 10
Lavan, with Lavan's sheep, he stepped forward, rolled the
stone from the top of the well, and watered his uncle Lavan's

NEAR EAST

29:2–8 Pacts for herding in the ancient Near East

Herding contracts between the owners of livestock and the herdsmen who took care of them, delineating each party's responsibilities, are well known in the ancient Near East. In areas where the water supply and grazing land were limited, formal and informal contracts were understood to have been made among the local herdsmen themselves to ensure that everyone's herds and flocks could access these vital resources.

These herdsmen were not nomads – the herding and grazing took place in an established territory in the vicinity of their towns or villages. In such situations, the regional well was intended to be used only by the local herdsmen, and outsiders would need to pay to use it. The large stone that covered the well, which could be moved only by many people acting together, ensured that the water would not be stolen and protected it from damage and dirt. ▪ ZR

Well with stone covering, Tekoa

פִּי הַבְּאֵר וַיַּשְׁקְ אֶת־צֹאן לָבָן אֲחִי אִמּוֹ: וַיִּשַּׁק יַעֲקֹב לְרָחֵל יא
וַיִּשָּׂא אֶת־קֹלוֹ וַיֵּבְךְּ: וַיַּגֵּד יַעֲקֹב לְרָחֵל כִּי אֲחִי אָבִיהָ הוּא וְכִי יב

11 12 sheep. And Yaakov kissed Raḥel – and wept aloud. And
Yaakov told Raḥel that he was related to her father: he was

NEAR EAST

29:11 Yaakov kissed Raḥel

Yaakov gives a kiss of greeting to his cousin Raḥel, and he is later kissed in greeting by Lavan. Yaakov's kiss to Raḥel is the only instance in Tanakh of a man kissing a woman who is not his wife or mother; kissing other women was generally considered taboo. But in that time and place, kissing a female relative was not necessarily seen as objectionable.

Even kissing non-relatives was not always particularly problematic in Mesopotamia as long as the woman involved was not actually married. An Old Babylonian letter from Ur reports the unusual case of a woman who was betrothed who defends herself from charges of improper behavior by stating that "when Sin-iddinam (the fiancé) went away from his house, the son of Asqudum sent me a message, 'I want to marry you.' He kissed my lips…I thought this: 'I shall not do anything wrong against Sin-iddinam, who has done no wrong to me.' In my house I have done nothing improper." Since the woman was not yet married, there was no punishment for the kissing. By contrast, kissing a married woman was not tolerated. The *Middle Assyrian Laws* (ca. 1100 BCE) state that in the case of a married woman, "If he should kiss her: they shall draw his lower lip across the blade of an axe and cut it off" (MAL A §9). ▪ ZR

↗ Jacob and Rachel, Erwin Speckter, 1827

NEAR EAST

29:15 Lavan's decision to hire Yaakov

When close family members worked together in the ancient Near East, they did so as partners. This appears to be the initial arrangement between Lavan and Yaakov, as Lavan declares, "You are truly of my own bones, my own flesh" (29:14). After a month, Lavan effectively changes the nature of their work relationship by asking, "If you are my brother, does that mean you should work for me for nothing? Tell me what your hire should be." Lavan feigns concern for Yaakov, telling him that he should stay longer and be paid for his services. This statement can be understood as Lavan asking, "Are you (truly) my brother?" – that is, one who is not paid for his labor but is instead a complete partner as a member of the household? With this statement, essentially questioning Yaakov's close kinship to him, Lavan changes the arrangement from that of family members working together to that of an employer and a wage earner, which characterizes the relationship between Lavan and Yaakov from this point onward.

It was not unusual for a free person to voluntarily join another household as a laborer for a certain amount of time in situations of economic hardship. An example of this kind of agreement is found in a Middle Assyrian letter: "Samas-amranni, son of Erib-ili, of his own volition for ten years shall dwell in the house of Amurru-nasir, son of Assur-iqisa. They shall have him take a wife, (and) in the house of the same Amurru-nasir he shall eat and be clothed. He shall complete ten years, and (then) may take his wife, clothing and contract, and may leave. Who(ever) among them reneges shall pay 5 minas of refined (silver)." ▪ ZR

↗ Contract fragment, cuneiform, Babylonian or Achaemenid, Babylon, 7th to 4th century BCE

יג בֶּן־רִבְקָה הוּא וַתָּרׇץ וַתַּגֵּד לְאָבִיהָ: וַיְהִי כִשְׁמֹעַ לָבָן אֶת־שֵׁמַע ׀
יַעֲקֹב בֶּן־אֲחֹתוֹ וַיָּרׇץ לִקְרָאתוֹ וַיְחַבֶּק־לוֹ וַיְנַשֶּׁק־לוֹ וַיְבִיאֵהוּ
יד אֶל־בֵּיתוֹ וַיְסַפֵּר לְלָבָן אֵת כׇּל־הַדְּבָרִים הָאֵלֶּה: וַיֹּאמֶר לוֹ לָבָן
• טו אַךְ עַצְמִי וּבְשָׂרִי אָתָּה וַיֵּשֶׁב עִמּוֹ חֹדֶשׁ יָמִים: וַיֹּאמֶר לָבָן לְיַעֲקֹב
טז הֲכִי־אָחִי אַתָּה וַעֲבַדְתַּנִי חִנָּם הַגִּידָה לִּי מַה־מַּשְׂכֻּרְתֶּךָ: וּלְלָבָן
יז שְׁתֵּי בָנוֹת שֵׁם הַגְּדֹלָה לֵאָה וְשֵׁם הַקְּטַנָּה רָחֵל: וְעֵינֵי לֵאָה
• יח רַכּוֹת וְרָחֵל הָיְתָה יְפַת־תֹּאַר וִיפַת מַרְאֶה: וַיֶּאֱהַב יַעֲקֹב אֶת־ שלישי

Rivka's son. She ran to tell her father. When Lavan heard the 13
news about Yaakov, his sister's son, he ran to meet him. He
embraced and kissed him and brought him to his house.
Yaakov told Lavan all that had happened. Lavan said to him, 14
"You are truly of my own bones, my own flesh." And Yaakov
stayed with him for a month. Then Lavan said to him, "If you 15 •
are my brother, does that mean you should work for me for
nothing? Tell me what your hire should be." Lavan had two 16
daughters. The elder was called Leah and the younger Raḥel.
Leah had sensitive eyes; Raḥel was beautiful and lovely. 17
And Yaakov was in love with Raḥel, so he said, "I will work 18 •

NEAR EAST

29:18 Bride-price and marriage customs

In this verse, Yaakov offers to work for Lavan for seven years in exchange for his daughter Raḥel. Ultimately, Yaakov worked in Lavan's employ for fourteen years for the right to marry his two daughters Raḥel and Leah. This exchange of wealth, here in the form of labor, for the right to claim a wife, reflects common practice in the ancient Near East. In the Tanakh, the term used is *mohar*, commonly translated as "bride-price." The payment of *mohar* as a necessary step in contracting a marriage is mentioned elsewhere in the Torah in Genesis 34:12 and Exodus 22:15–16. In I Samuel 18:25, Sha'ul invites David to bring him a *mohar* of one hundred Philistine foreskins instead of the conventional silver. In Genesis 24:53, Avraham's servant offered "costly gifts" to Rivka's family when they agreed to her betrothal.

The Mesopotamian equivalent of the biblical *mohar* was the Akkadian *terḫatu*. The *Laws of Hammurabi* obligate the paternal estate to provide a *terḫatu* for every son (in addition to his inheritance share) so that each may acquire a wife (LH §166). The *Middle Assyrian Laws*, for example, decree that if a man divorces his wife, she has the right to keep this sum (MAL A §38).

The "bride-price" is distinct from the dowry, which is paid by the bride's family. Often both the bride-price and dowry were given to the bride so she would have a reserve in case she is widowed or divorced; she could later bequeath it to her children. In Akkadian documents, this wealth was "tied in her hem," and available for her husband's use. Thus, Raḥel and Leah should have received some form of financial compensation for Yaakov's fourteen years of labor. According to Genesis 31:14–16, though, this was not the case. Genesis 31:41 reports that Yaakov's subsequent six years of work paid for the flocks he brought back to Canaan. Thus, Yaakov struggled to build up his own estate in the face of Lavan's callousness.

While the transactional nature of the *mohar* and the English term "bride-price" might suggest that wives were seen as chattel, one should keep in mind that husbands had significant obligations in the maintenance of a wife (Ex. 21:10), and certainly could not sell nor even offer their wives to another man. Further, the Tanakh makes a distinction between a slave-concubine (*shifḥa* or *pileggesh*) and a legitimate wife (*isha*; II Sam. 5:13; I Kings 11:3). The *mohar* or *terḫatu* should be viewed as financial compensation for the loss to her family of the young woman's labor and as purchasing the right to sexual exclusivity and offspring. This is evident in the *Laws of Hammurabi* (LH §163), which stipulates that if a wife dies childless, her husband is entitled to receive back the bride-price. ▪ EG

Bedouin woman "wearing" her dowry

רָחֵל וַיֹּאמֶר אֶעֱבָדְךָ שֶׁבַע שָׁנִים בְּרָחֵל בִּתְּךָ הַקְּטַנָּה׃ וַיֹּאמֶר יט
לָבָן טוֹב תִּתִּי אֹתָהּ לָךְ מִתִּתִּי אֹתָהּ לְאִישׁ אַחֵר שְׁבָה עִמָּדִי׃
וַיַּעֲבֹד יַעֲקֹב בְּרָחֵל שֶׁבַע שָׁנִים וַיִּהְיוּ בְעֵינָיו כְּיָמִים אֲחָדִים כ
בְּאַהֲבָתוֹ אֹתָהּ׃ וַיֹּאמֶר יַעֲקֹב אֶל־לָבָן הָבָה אֶת־אִשְׁתִּי כִּי כא
מָלְאוּ יָמָי וְאָבוֹאָה אֵלֶיהָ׃ וַיֶּאֱסֹף לָבָן אֶת־כָּל־אַנְשֵׁי הַמָּקוֹם כב •
וַיַּעַשׂ מִשְׁתֶּה׃ וַיְהִי בָעֶרֶב וַיִּקַּח אֶת־לֵאָה בִתּוֹ וַיָּבֵא אֹתָהּ אֵלָיו כג
וַיָּבֹא אֵלֶיהָ׃ וַיִּתֵּן לָבָן לָהּ אֶת־זִלְפָּה שִׁפְחָתוֹ לְלֵאָה בִתּוֹ שִׁפְחָה׃ כד

19 for you seven years for your younger daughter Raḥel." Lavan
replied, "Better that I give her to you than to some other man.
20 Stay on with me." So Yaakov worked for Raḥel seven years.
But so great was his love for her that they seemed to him but
21 a few days. Then Yaakov said to Lavan, "Give me my wife – my
• 22 time is done, let me come to her." So Lavan brought together
23 all the local people and made a feast. In the evening he took
his daughter Leah and brought her in to him, and he came to
24 her. Lavan also gave his servant Zilpa to his daughter Leah

NEAR EAST

29:22 Wedding and feast

In the ancient Near East, a wedding feast, although certainly celebrated as a joyful event, primarily marked a social, legal, and economic transaction between two families. Marriages would be arranged by families in binding agreements, sometimes concluded years before the actual ceremony. During that transitional time, the bride was considered to be officially married but stayed with her parents – she did not move to the groom's residence nor was the marriage consummated until the wedding feast.

Lavan's gift of Zilpa as a maid was commonplace in the higher classes of Hurrian society. A 15th century BCE Nuzi tablet, an adoption document that also deals with a marriage involving a local woman of high standing, mentions that "Yalampa has been given as a handmaid to Gilimninu… as long as she is alive she shall honor her." (H67, ll. 35–39). ▪ ZR

Hurrian lion, Nuzi, 15th to 14th century BCE

NEAR EAST

29:26–30 Simultaneous marriage with two sisters

The *Laws of Hammurabi* define the procedure in the case of a father who reneges on delivering his daughter as a bride: "If a man bring chattels into the house of his father-in-law, and pays the purchase price (for his wife): if then the father of the girl says: 'I will not give you my daughter,' he shall give him back all that he brought with him" (LH §160). Here, Lavan gives the excuse that by custom the younger daughter cannot be given in marriage before the older sister. While such a custom has no basis in any recorded ancient Near Eastern practice, being married to two sisters simultaneously is prohibited in the Torah in Leviticus 18:18, as well as in the law collections of the ancient Near East. One known exception is the *Hittite Laws*, which permitted such relations if the sisters were slaves, "If a free man sleeps with slave women who have the same mother… it is not an offense" (HL §194). ▪ ZR

Raḥel (left) and Leah (right) behind Moshe, tomb of Pope Julius II, Michelangelo, 1542–1545

כה וַיְהִי בַבֹּקֶר וְהִנֵּה־הִוא לֵאָה וַיֹּאמֶר אֶל־לָבָן מַה־זֹּאת עָשִׂיתָ
כו לִּי הֲלֹא בְרָחֵל עָבַדְתִּי עִמָּךְ וְלָמָּה רִמִּיתָנִי: וַיֹּאמֶר לָבָן לֹא־
כז יֵעָשֶׂה כֵן בִּמְקוֹמֵנוּ לָתֵת הַצְּעִירָה לִפְנֵי הַבְּכִירָה: מַלֵּא שְׁבֻעַ
זֹאת וְנִתְּנָה לְךָ גַּם־אֶת־זֹאת בַּעֲבֹדָה אֲשֶׁר תַּעֲבֹד עִמָּדִי עוֹד
כח שֶׁבַע־שָׁנִים אֲחֵרוֹת: וַיַּעַשׂ יַעֲקֹב כֵּן וַיְמַלֵּא שְׁבֻעַ זֹאת וַיִּתֶּן־לוֹ
כט אֶת־רָחֵל בִּתּוֹ לוֹ לְאִשָּׁה: וַיִּתֵּן לָבָן לְרָחֵל בִּתּוֹ אֶת־בִּלְהָה
ל שִׁפְחָתוֹ לָהּ לְשִׁפְחָה: וַיָּבֹא גַּם אֶל־רָחֵל וַיֶּאֱהַב גַּם־אֶת־רָחֵל
לא מִלֵּאָה וַיַּעֲבֹד עִמּוֹ עוֹד שֶׁבַע־שָׁנִים אֲחֵרוֹת: וַיַּרְא יהוה כִּי־
לב שְׂנוּאָה לֵאָה וַיִּפְתַּח אֶת־רַחְמָהּ וְרָחֵל עֲקָרָה: וַתַּהַר לֵאָה וַתֵּלֶד
בֵּן וַתִּקְרָא שְׁמוֹ רְאוּבֵן כִּי אָמְרָה כִּי־רָאָה יהוה בְּעָנְיִי כִּי עַתָּה
לג יֶאֱהָבַנִי אִישִׁי: וַתַּהַר עוֹד וַתֵּלֶד בֵּן וַתֹּאמֶר כִּי־שָׁמַע יהוה כִּי־
לד שְׂנוּאָה אָנֹכִי וַיִּתֶּן־לִי גַּם־אֶת־זֶה וַתִּקְרָא שְׁמוֹ שִׁמְעוֹן: וַתַּהַר
עוֹד וַתֵּלֶד בֵּן וַתֹּאמֶר עַתָּה הַפַּעַם יִלָּוֶה אִישִׁי אֵלַי כִּי־יָלַדְתִּי
לה לוֹ שְׁלֹשָׁה בָנִים עַל־כֵּן קָרָא־שְׁמוֹ לֵוִי: וַתַּהַר עוֹד וַתֵּלֶד בֵּן
וַתֹּאמֶר הַפַּעַם אוֹדֶה אֶת־יהוה עַל־כֵּן קָרְאָה שְׁמוֹ יְהוּדָה
ל א וַתַּעֲמֹד מִלֶּדֶת: וַתֵּרֶא רָחֵל כִּי לֹא יָלְדָה לְיַעֲקֹב וַתְּקַנֵּא רָחֵל
בַּאֲחֹתָהּ וַתֹּאמֶר אֶל־יַעֲקֹב הָבָה־לִּי בָנִים וְאִם־אַיִן מֵתָה אָנֹכִי:
ב וַיִּחַר־אַף יַעֲקֹב בְּרָחֵל וַיֹּאמֶר הֲתַחַת אֱלֹהִים אָנֹכִי אֲשֶׁר־מָנַע

as her maid. Then came morning – and it was Leah. Yaakov said to Lavan, "What is this you 25
have done to me? I served you for Raḥel, did I not? Why did you deceive me?" Lavan said, "This 26
is not done in our country – to marry off the younger before the firstborn. Wait until the bridal 27
week of this one is over and then we will give you the other one also, in return for your serving
me another seven years." Yaakov did so. He completed Leah's bridal week; then Lavan gave him 28
his daughter Raḥel as a wife. Lavan gave his servant Bilha to his daughter Raḥel as her maid. 29
And Yaakov came also to Raḥel; and he loved Raḥel more than Leah. And he served him for 30
another seven years. When the Lord saw that Leah was unloved, He opened her womb, but 31
Raḥel was barren. Leah became pregnant and had a son. She named him Reuven, saying, "The 32
Lord has seen my affliction. Now my husband will love me."[61] She became pregnant again and 33
had a son. She said, "The Lord has heard that I am unloved, so He has given me this son also,"
and she named him Shimon.[62] She became pregnant again and had a son and said, "Now that I 34
have borne him three sons, my husband will walk with me." That is why he was named Levi.[63]
She became pregnant again and had a son. She said, "This time I will praise the Lord," so she 35
named him Yehuda.[64] Then she ceased having children. Aware that she had borne Yaakov no 1 **30**
children, Raḥel became envious of her sister. To Yaakov she said, "Give me children! If not, let
me die!" Yaakov grew angry with Raḥel, and said, "Am I in place of God, who has kept you from 2

61 | The name Reuven resonates with *raa* (has seen) and *ben* (son).
62 | The name Shimon resonates with *shama* (has heard).
63 | The name Levi resonates with *yillaveh* (will walk with).
64 | The name Yehuda resonates with *odeh* (I will praise).

מִמֵּךְ פְּרִי־בָטֶן׃ וַתֹּאמֶר הִנֵּה אֲמָתִי בִלְהָה בֹּא אֵלֶיהָ וְתֵלֵד ג
עַל־בִּרְכַּי וְאִבָּנֶה גַם־אָנֹכִי מִמֶּנָּה׃ וַתִּתֶּן־לוֹ אֶת־בִּלְהָה שִׁפְחָתָהּ ד
לְאִשָּׁה וַיָּבֹא אֵלֶיהָ יַעֲקֹב׃ וַתַּהַר בִּלְהָה וַתֵּלֶד לְיַעֲקֹב בֵּן׃ ה
וַתֹּאמֶר רָחֵל דָּנַנִּי אֱלֹהִים וְגַם שָׁמַע בְּקֹלִי וַיִּתֶּן־לִי בֵּן עַל־כֵּן ו
קָרְאָה שְׁמוֹ דָּן׃ וַתַּהַר עוֹד וַתֵּלֶד בִּלְהָה שִׁפְחַת רָחֵל בֵּן שֵׁנִי ז
לְיַעֲקֹב׃ וַתֹּאמֶר רָחֵל נַפְתּוּלֵי אֱלֹהִים ׀ נִפְתַּלְתִּי עִם־אֲחֹתִי ח

3 having children?" "Here is Bilha my slave," she said. "Come
to her. Let her give birth on my knees[65] so that I too can build
4 a family through her." So she gave him her maid Bilha as a
5 wife. Yaakov came to her, and she became pregnant and bore
6 Yaakov a son. Then Raḥel said, "God has vindicated me. He
has listened to my voice and given me a son." So she named
7 him Dan.[66] Bilha, Raḥel's maid, became pregnant again and
8 bore Yaakov a second son. And Raḥel said, "I have struggled
hard with my sister and I have won." So she named him

65 | Meaning "I will raise the child as my own."

66 | The name Dan resonates with *dananni* (has vindicated me).

NEAR EAST

30:3 Let her give birth on my knees

The phrase "Let her give birth on my knees" refers to a symbolic act in the ancient Near East, referenced also in Genesis 50:23: "And the children of Menashe's son Makhir were also born on Yosef's knees." Placing a child on the knees was a demonstration of parenthood or adoption. This act also appears when the gods grant a child to a man in the Hittite story of *Appu and His Two Sons*: "Appu's wife bore a son. The nurse lifted the boy and placed him on Appu's knees."

In the ancient Near East, particularly in Hittite sources, knees represented reproductive power, as in "you two Sarrumanni-deities and one Allanzunni-deity, who have emerged from the deity's knees" (KUB V 1). In Akkadian, *birku* (the term for lap and knee, and cognate of the Hebrew *berekh*) is a euphemism for both male and female reproductive parts, synonymous with "loins"; someone who is impotent was called a person who "has no knees."

Normally it was the father who would place the child on his knees, but here it was important for the adoptive mother, Raḥel, to demonstrate her motherhood to the children of Bilha. ▪ ZR

Study of drapery over the knees of a seated figure, Fra Bartolomeo, 1472–1517

LANGUAGE

30:11 Gad

Gad is a component of a number of names in Tanakh, both of people – the prophet Gad (II Sam. 24:11), Gadiel (Num. 13:10), Gadi (Num. 13:11; II Kings 15:14), and Azgad (Ezra 2:12), and of places, Baal Gad (Josh. 11:17) and Migdal Gad (Josh. 15:37).

This name is a cognate to the god of luck and good fortune in various Near Eastern cultures, found as an element of personal names in Ugaritic, Amorite, and Phoenician, for example, *Abrgd*, *Mlkgd*, *Gdrm*, *Gdazyz*, *Gdnam*. Gad is also mentioned as a pagan deity in Isaiah 65:11: "While you who forsake the Lord, forgetting My holy mountain while laying a table for Gad [Babylonian/Syrian god of fortune], pouring lavish libations to Meni [god of destiny]."

Here, as used by Leah, Gad is an abstract noun simply meaning "good fortune" and divorced from any deification. ▪ ZR

Underground chamber, Hurvat Migdal Gad, near Amatzia (about 8 kilometers/5 miles southeast of Lakhish)

ט גַּם־יָכֹלְתִּי וַתִּקְרָא שְׁמוֹ נַפְתָּלִי׃ וַתֵּרֶא לֵאָה כִּי עָמְדָה מִלֶּדֶת
י וַתִּקַּח אֶת־זִלְפָּה שִׁפְחָתָהּ וַתִּתֵּן אֹתָהּ לְיַעֲקֹב לְאִשָּׁה׃ וַתֵּלֶד
יא זִלְפָּה שִׁפְחַת לֵאָה לְיַעֲקֹב בֵּן׃ וַתֹּאמֶר לֵאָה בגד וַתִּקְרָא אֶת־ בָּא גָד
יב יג שְׁמוֹ גָּד׃ וַתֵּלֶד זִלְפָּה שִׁפְחַת לֵאָה בֵּן שֵׁנִי לְיַעֲקֹב׃ וַתֹּאמֶר לֵאָה
יד בְּאָשְׁרִי כִּי אִשְּׁרוּנִי בָּנוֹת וַתִּקְרָא אֶת־שְׁמוֹ אָשֵׁר׃ וַיֵּלֶךְ רְאוּבֵן רביעי
בִּימֵי קְצִיר־חִטִּים וַיִּמְצָא דוּדָאִים בַּשָּׂדֶה וַיָּבֵא אֹתָם אֶל־לֵאָה
טו אִמּוֹ וַתֹּאמֶר רָחֵל אֶל־לֵאָה תְּנִי־נָא לִי מִדּוּדָאֵי בְּנֵךְ׃ וַתֹּאמֶר
לָהּ הַמְעַט קַחְתֵּךְ אֶת־אִישִׁי וְלָקַחַת גַּם אֶת־דּוּדָאֵי בְּנִי וַתֹּאמֶר
טז רָחֵל לָכֵן יִשְׁכַּב עִמָּךְ הַלַּיְלָה תַּחַת דּוּדָאֵי בְנֵךְ׃ וַיָּבֹא יַעֲקֹב
מִן־הַשָּׂדֶה בָּעֶרֶב וַתֵּצֵא לֵאָה לִקְרָאתוֹ וַתֹּאמֶר אֵלַי תָּבוֹא כִּי

Naftali.[67] Leah realized that she was no longer having children, 9
so she took her maid Zilpa and gave her to Yaakov as a wife.
And Leah's maid Zilpa bore Yaakov a son. Leah said, "Good 10 11
fortune has come!" So she named him Gad.[68] Then Zilpa, 12
Leah's maid, bore Yaakov a second son. Leah said, "How 13
blessed I am; young girls will call me blessed." So she named
him Asher.[69] During the wheat harvest, Reuven went for a 14
walk and found mandrakes in the field. He brought them to
his mother Leah. Raḥel said to Leah, "Please give me some
of your son's mandrakes." She replied, "Is it not enough that 15
you have taken away my husband? Now you want to take my
son's mandrakes too!" "Very well," said Raḥel. "Let him sleep
with you tonight in exchange for your son's mandrakes."
When Yaakov came back from the field that evening, Leah 16
went out to meet him and said, "You are to come to me, for I

67 | The name Naftali resonates with *niftalti* (I have struggled hard).
68 | *Gad* is the word used to denote "good fortune."
69 | The name Asher resonates with *be'oshri* (how blessed I am).

NEAR EAST

30:14–15 Mandrakes

The mandrake root is hallucinogenic and narcotic – it also contains trace amounts of human growth hormone. The shape of the mandrake root made it an optimal choice for sympathetic magic: it looks like a little person. The only Mediterranean species is *Mandragora officinarum*, which grows in areas of North Africa (but was probably imported into Egypt only in the 15th century BCE) and Europe that border the Mediterranean, as well as in Syria, Lebanon, Israel, and Jordan.

The Hebrew term for the mandrake, *dudaim*, sounds like *dodim* ("love"). That association is found in Song of Songs 7:14, "The mandrakes (*dudaim*) impart their scent… my beloved (*dodi*), I have hoarded them for you." That verse also demonstrates the belief (not necessarily backed up by scientific evidence) that the aphrodisiac power of the mandrake was based on its distinctive smell.

In Egypt, in early New Kingdom images, women can be seen holding the fruit of the mandrake, probably imported from Israel or Syria, up to their noses. In Egyptian love poetry, the mandrake metaphorically evokes love, female breasts, and eroticism. For example, in one ancient Egyptian love poem, the male lover wishes that the woman will allow him to bring her mandrakes, "she would smell it/and she would show me the hue of her whole body."

Significantly, the narrative in Genesis polemicizes against the superstitions associated with mandrakes by stating that Raḥel, who got them from Leah, remained barren for a few more years. On the other hand, Leah, who gave them up, had three more children. It is emphasized that Raḥel got pregnant not due to the mandrakes, but only because "God remembered Raḥel and listened to her and enabled her to conceive" (v. 22). ▪ ZR

Mandrake (*mandragora officinarum*) fruits

שָׂכֹר שְׂכַרְתִּיךָ בְּדוּדָאֵי בְּנִי וַיִּשְׁכַּב עִמָּהּ בַּלַּיְלָה הוּא: וַיִּשְׁמַע יז
אֱלֹהִים אֶל־לֵאָה וַתַּהַר וַתֵּלֶד לְיַעֲקֹב בֵּן חֲמִישִׁי: וַתֹּאמֶר לֵאָה יח
נָתַן אֱלֹהִים שְׂכָרִי אֲשֶׁר־נָתַתִּי שִׁפְחָתִי לְאִישִׁי וַתִּקְרָא שְׁמוֹ
יִשָּׂשכָר: וַתַּהַר עוֹד לֵאָה וַתֵּלֶד בֵּן־שִׁשִּׁי לְיַעֲקֹב: וַתֹּאמֶר לֵאָה יט כ
זְבָדַנִי אֱלֹהִים ׀ אֹתִי זֵבֶד טוֹב הַפַּעַם יִזְבְּלֵנִי אִישִׁי כִּי־יָלַדְתִּי לוֹ
שִׁשָּׁה בָנִים וַתִּקְרָא אֶת־שְׁמוֹ זְבֻלוּן: וְאַחַר יָלְדָה בַּת וַתִּקְרָא כא
אֶת־שְׁמָהּ דִּינָה: וַיִּזְכֹּר אֱלֹהִים אֶת־רָחֵל וַיִּשְׁמַע אֵלֶיהָ אֱלֹהִים כב
וַיִּפְתַּח אֶת־רַחְמָהּ: וַתַּהַר וַתֵּלֶד בֵּן וַתֹּאמֶר אָסַף אֱלֹהִים אֶת־ כג

have hired you with my son's mandrakes." So that night he
17 slept with her. God listened to Leah, and she became pregnant
18 and bore Yaakov a fifth son. Leah said, "God has rewarded me
for giving my maid to my husband," so she named him
19 Yissakhar.[70] Leah became pregnant again and bore Yaakov a
20 sixth son. "God has given me a precious gift," said Leah. "This
time my husband will honor me, for I have borne him six
21 sons," so she named him Zevulun.[71] Later she gave birth to a
22 daughter and named her Dina. Then God remembered Raḥel
23 and listened to her and enabled her to conceive. She became
pregnant and gave birth to a son. She said, "God has taken

70 | The name Yissakhar resonates with *natan sekhari* (has rewarded me).

71 | The name Zevulun resonates with *zeved* (gift) and *yizbeleni* (will honor me).

NEAR EAST

30:25 Status of an infertile wife

It is not coincidental that only after Raḥel gives birth to Yosef does Yaakov demand that Lavan let him leave. In the ancient Near East, a woman's status as a wife was at risk if she did not produce an heir. Marriage contacts from Nuzi contain clauses stating that if the bride does not bear children (generally a son/heir), the groom may take an additional wife. In such situations, the first wife could be demoted to the status of concubine or even divorced. Marriage contracts from Late Bronze Age Alalakh set a seven-year limit to determine if the wife is infertile, "[I]f she does not give birth after seven years, he (Idat[ti]) may take a second wife." On the other hand, an Old Assyrian marriage contract allows for only a two-year period of infertility, after which the wife must provide her husband with a concubine. In the cultural context of the ancient Near East, it would not have been advisable for Yaakov to leave with Raḥel before she had a child, as her social standing as a childless wife would be better secured while he still worked for her father. ▪ ZR

Archaeological site of Alalakh (Tel Atchana, Turkey)

NEAR EAST

30:27 Learned by divination

Lavan claims that he learned by divination that he has prospered because of Yaakov. In a general Mesopotamian context, this would most likely be an inquiry through the use of omens, which were used to answer yes/no questions. But for a person who owned or herded flocks, and especially for one inquiring why his herds have prospered, divination may have taken place through reading entrails from a slaughtered animal from the flock, a practice known as extispicy. This incident still does not prove the efficacy of pagan divination, as the text only shows that God can reveal that He is the source of blessing in any way He chooses.

Alternatively, the term *niḥashti* here may have nothing to do with divination, but rather may be a form of the Akkadian term for abundance and plenty (*nuḥshu*), used also for prosperity provided by the gods, so that Lavan's statement could read, "I have prospered; it is because of you that the Lord has blessed me." ▪ ZR

A priest (left) examines the entrails of an animal to predict the future, detail on relief of an Assyrian camp, Nimrud, 9th century BCE

כד חֶרְפָּתִי: וַתִּקְרָא אֶת־שְׁמוֹ יוֹסֵף לֵאמֹר יֹסֵף יְהוָה לִי בֵּן אַחֵר:
כה • וַיְהִי כַּאֲשֶׁר יָלְדָה רָחֵל אֶת־יוֹסֵף וַיֹּאמֶר יַעֲקֹב אֶל־לָבָן שַׁלְּחֵנִי
כו וְאֵלְכָה אֶל־מְקוֹמִי וּלְאַרְצִי: תְּנָה אֶת־נָשַׁי וְאֶת־יְלָדַי אֲשֶׁר
עָבַדְתִּי אֹתְךָ בָּהֵן וְאֵלֵכָה כִּי אַתָּה יָדַעְתָּ אֶת־עֲבֹדָתִי אֲשֶׁר
כז • עֲבַדְתִּיךָ: וַיֹּאמֶר אֵלָיו לָבָן אִם־נָא מָצָאתִי חֵן בְּעֵינֶיךָ נִחַשְׁתִּי
כח כט • וַיְבָרְכֵנִי יְהוָה בִּגְלָלֶךָ: וַיֹּאמַר נָקְבָה שְׂכָרְךָ עָלַי וְאֶתֵּנָה: וַיֹּאמֶר חמישי
אֵלָיו אַתָּה יָדַעְתָּ אֵת אֲשֶׁר עֲבַדְתִּיךָ וְאֵת אֲשֶׁר־הָיָה מִקְנְךָ
ל אִתִּי: כִּי מְעַט אֲשֶׁר־הָיָה לְךָ לְפָנַי וַיִּפְרֹץ לָרֹב וַיְבָרֶךְ יְהוָה אֹתְךָ
לא לְרַגְלִי וְעַתָּה מָתַי אֶעֱשֶׂה גַם־אָנֹכִי לְבֵיתִי: וַיֹּאמֶר מָה אֶתֶּן־לָךְ
וַיֹּאמֶר יַעֲקֹב לֹא־תִתֶּן־לִי מְאוּמָה אִם־תַּעֲשֶׂה־לִּי הַדָּבָר הַזֶּה

away my shame," and she named him Yosef, saying, "May the 24
Lord grant me another son also."[72] After Raḥel had given 25 •
birth to Yosef, Yaakov said to Lavan, "Release me to go home
to my own land. Give me my wives and my children for whom 26
I have worked for you, and let me go. You know very well how
much work I have done for you." But Lavan said to him, "If 27 •
you will allow me to say so, I have learned by divination that
it is because of you that the Lord has blessed me." He added, 28
"Name your hire and I will pay it." Yaakov said, "You know 29 •
well how I have worked for you and how your livestock have
fared under my care. You had little before I came, but it has 30
swelled into much. The Lord has blessed you wherever I have
been. Now, when can I do likewise for my own household?"
Lavan asked, "What shall I give you?" Yaakov replied, "Do 31
not give me anything. If you do this one thing for me, I will

72 | *Yosef* is the word used by Raḥel to denote "grant." The name also resonates with *asaf* (has taken away, v. 23).

Middle Eastern sheep, white wool, darker in head and legs, Qatar

— FLORA AND FAUNA —

30:29–43 Yaakov's sheep

Most Middle Eastern sheep have white wool, with darker areas in the head and legs, whereas goats are brown or black. About a quarter of sheep and goats are speckled or spotted. Lavan removes such animals from the flock assigned to Yaakov (vv. 35–36) based on common knowledge that multicolored animals would breed similar-looking offspring. It was also apparent that occasionally a spotted animal was born to monochrome parents, but the mechanism behind that phenomenon was unclear to them, due to a lack of knowledge concerning genetics.

Yaakov makes sure that the sturdier animals mate together (vv. 41–42). A strong animal may be an indication of hybrid vigor, the phenomenon that a hybrid offspring has improved traits: bigger stature and increased fertility in both sexes, and females going into heat earlier. Even if such an animal were monochrome, its strength and vigor could indicate that it carried the recessive genes for having spots.

Based on this, the true mechanism of producing the speckled and spotted animals by controlled breeding was made known to Yaakov by an angel in a revelatory dream, as he reported to his wives in Genesis 31:10–13. There is no scientific basis for any benefit derived from having sheep look at other sheep or at shoots. ▪ ZR

• לב אָשׁוּבָה אֶרְעֶה צֹאנְךָ אֶשְׁמֹר׃ אֶעֱבֹר בְּכָל־צֹאנְךָ הַיּוֹם הָסֵר
מִשָּׁם כָּל־שֶׂה ׀ נָקֹד וְטָלוּא וְכָל־שֶׂה־חוּם בַּכְּשָׂבִים וְטָלוּא וְנָקֹד
לג בָּעִזִּים וְהָיָה שְׂכָרִי׃ וְעָנְתָה־בִּי צִדְקָתִי בְּיוֹם מָחָר כִּי־תָבוֹא
עַל־שְׂכָרִי לְפָנֶיךָ כֹּל אֲשֶׁר־אֵינֶנּוּ נָקֹד וְטָלוּא בָּעִזִּים וְחוּם
לד לה בַּכְּשָׂבִים גָּנוּב הוּא אִתִּי׃ וַיֹּאמֶר לָבָן הֵן לוּ יְהִי כִדְבָרֶךָ׃ וַיָּסַר
בַּיּוֹם הַהוּא אֶת־הַתְּיָשִׁים הָעֲקֻדִּים וְהַטְּלֻאִים וְאֵת כָּל־הָעִזִּים
הַנְּקֻדּוֹת וְהַטְּלֻאֹת כֹּל אֲשֶׁר־לָבָן בּוֹ וְכָל־חוּם בַּכְּשָׂבִים וַיִּתֵּן
לו בְּיַד־בָּנָיו׃ וַיָּשֶׂם דֶּרֶךְ שְׁלֹשֶׁת יָמִים בֵּינוֹ וּבֵין יַעֲקֹב וְיַעֲקֹב רֹעֶה
לז אֶת־צֹאן לָבָן הַנּוֹתָרֹת׃ וַיִּקַּח־לוֹ יַעֲקֹב מַקַּל לִבְנֶה לַח וְלוּז
וְעַרְמוֹן וַיְפַצֵּל בָּהֵן פְּצָלוֹת לְבָנוֹת מַחְשֹׂף הַלָּבָן אֲשֶׁר עַל־

• 32 continue to shepherd and guard your flocks. Let me go
through all your flocks today and remove every speckled or
spotted sheep, every dark-colored lamb, and every spotted or
33 speckled goat. They shall be my hire. Let my honesty testify
for me in the future, whenever you come to check the wages
you have paid me. Any goat not speckled or spotted or any
lamb not dark colored in my possession shall be considered
34 35 stolen." Lavan said, "Agreed. Let it be as you have said." That
day Lavan removed the streaked or spotted goats, all the
speckled or spotted female goats – every one that had a trace
of white – and every dark-colored lamb. These he placed in
36 the care of his sons. Then he put a three-day-journey's distance
between him and Yaakov. Yaakov tended the rest of Lavan's
37 flock. Yaakov took fresh shoots of poplar, almond, and plane

NEAR EAST

30:32–34 Yaakov's wages

Shepherds in the ancient Near East were usually paid from byproducts of the herd for which they were responsible. These byproducts generally included milk and wool, and could also be a percentage of the new births. The exact amount was not usually stipulated in herding contracts; rather, the standard was that the herdsman could keep animals beyond the normal birthrate of the herd. For example, the Larsa administrative texts include contracts for the herding of state property, where the expected birthrate was eighty lambs for every hundred ewes, with a fifteen percent loss of the original flock allowed without penalty. Any losses beyond that had to be made up by the herdsman himself; conversely, an increase in the herd greater than the standard would function as part of his wages. A different system is reflected in an Old Babylonian contract from Ischali (part of the city-state of Eshnunna), which stipulated that the herdsman could keep twenty percent of the new births. Law collections provide for exceptions where a herdsman was not responsible for a loss, as in the *Laws of Hammurabi*, "If the animal be killed in the stable by god (an accident), or if a lion kill it, the herdsman shall declare his innocence before god, and the owner bears the accident" (LH §266).

Yaakov's arrangement was different, with no percentages agreed upon. He states that an angel promised him in a dream that the streaked and speckled animals would be his earnings (31:10–12). ▪ ZR

↗ Foundation tablet dedicated by King Warad-Sin, Temple of Ninisina, Larsa, ca. 1830 BCE

לח הַמַּקְלוֹת׃ וַיַּצֵּג אֶת־הַמַּקְלוֹת אֲשֶׁר פִּצֵּל בָּרְהָטִים בְּשִׁקְתוֹת
הַמָּיִם אֲשֶׁר תָּבֹאןָ הַצֹּאן לִשְׁתּוֹת לְנֹכַח הַצֹּאן וַיֵּחַמְנָה בְּבֹאָן
לט לִשְׁתּוֹת׃ וַיֶּחֱמוּ הַצֹּאן אֶל־הַמַּקְלוֹת וַתֵּלַדְןָ הַצֹּאן עֲקֻדִּים נְקֻדִּים
מ וּטְלֻאִים׃ וְהַכְּשָׂבִים הִפְרִיד יַעֲקֹב וַיִּתֵּן פְּנֵי הַצֹּאן אֶל־עָקֹד וְכָל־
חוּם בְּצֹאן לָבָן וַיָּשֶׁת לוֹ עֲדָרִים לְבַדּוֹ וְלֹא שָׁתָם עַל־צֹאן לָבָן׃
מא וְהָיָה בְּכָל־יַחֵם הַצֹּאן הַמְקֻשָּׁרוֹת וְשָׂם יַעֲקֹב אֶת־הַמַּקְלוֹת
מב לְעֵינֵי הַצֹּאן בָּרְהָטִים לְיַחְמֵנָּה בַּמַּקְלוֹת׃ וּבְהַעֲטִיף הַצֹּאן לֹא
מג יָשִׂים וְהָיָה הָעֲטֻפִים לְלָבָן וְהַקְּשֻׁרִים לְיַעֲקֹב׃ וַיִּפְרֹץ הָאִישׁ
מְאֹד מְאֹד וַיְהִי־לוֹ צֹאן רַבּוֹת וּשְׁפָחוֹת וַעֲבָדִים וּגְמַלִּים וַחֲמֹרִים׃
לא א וַיִּשְׁמַע אֶת־דִּבְרֵי בְנֵי־לָבָן לֵאמֹר לָקַח יַעֲקֹב אֵת כָּל־אֲשֶׁר
ב לְאָבִינוּ וּמֵאֲשֶׁר לְאָבִינוּ עָשָׂה אֵת כָּל־הַכָּבֹד הַזֶּה׃ וַיַּרְא יַעֲקֹב
ג אֶת־פְּנֵי לָבָן וְהִנֵּה אֵינֶנּוּ עִמּוֹ כִּתְמוֹל שִׁלְשׁוֹם׃ וַיֹּאמֶר יהוה
אֶל־יַעֲקֹב שׁוּב אֶל־אֶרֶץ אֲבוֹתֶיךָ וּלְמוֹלַדְתֶּךָ וְאֶהְיֶה עִמָּךְ׃
ד ה וַיִּשְׁלַח יַעֲקֹב וַיִּקְרָא לְרָחֵל וּלְלֵאָה הַשָּׂדֶה אֶל־צֹאנוֹ׃ וַיֹּאמֶר
לָהֶן רֹאֶה אָנֹכִי אֶת־פְּנֵי אֲבִיכֶן כִּי־אֵינֶנּוּ אֵלַי כִּתְמֹל שִׁלְשֹׁם
ו וֵאלֹהֵי אָבִי הָיָה עִמָּדִי׃ וְאַתֵּנָה יְדַעְתֶּן כִּי בְּכָל־כֹּחִי עָבַדְתִּי
ז אֶת־אֲבִיכֶן׃ וַאֲבִיכֶן הֵתֶל בִּי וְהֶחֱלִף אֶת־מַשְׂכֻּרְתִּי עֲשֶׂרֶת מֹנִים
ח וְלֹא־נְתָנוֹ אֱלֹהִים לְהָרַע עִמָּדִי׃ אִם־כֹּה יֹאמַר נְקֻדִּים יִהְיֶה
שְׂכָרֶךָ וְיָלְדוּ כָל־הַצֹּאן נְקֻדִּים וְאִם־כֹּה יֹאמַר עֲקֻדִּים יִהְיֶה
ט שְׂכָרֶךָ וְיָלְדוּ כָל־הַצֹּאן עֲקֻדִּים׃ וַיַּצֵּל אֱלֹהִים אֶת־מִקְנֵה אֲבִיכֶם
י וַיִּתֶּן־לִי׃ וַיְהִי בְּעֵת יַחֵם הַצֹּאן וָאֶשָּׂא עֵינַי וָאֵרֶא בַּחֲלוֹם וְהִנֵּה
יא הָעַתֻּדִים הָעֹלִים עַל־הַצֹּאן עֲקֻדִּים נְקֻדִּים וּבְרֻדִּים׃ וַיֹּאמֶר אֵלַי

trees and peeled white strips in them,
exposing the white of the shoots. Then 38
he set the peeled shoots in all the water
troughs so that they would be in front
of the flocks when they came to drink.
They would mate when they came to
drink, and since they mated by the 39
shoots, they bore streaked, speckled,
and spotted young.[73] Yaakov set apart 40
the young of the flock, and he made
the others belonging to Lavan face the
streaked and dark-colored animals.
Thus he bred separate flocks for
himself, and he did not let them breed
with Lavan's flocks. Whenever the stronger animals were mating, Yaakov would place the shoots in the 41
troughs facing them so that they mated facing the shoots. But the weaker animals he did not put there, so 42
the weaker went to Lavan and the stronger to Yaakov. Thus the man's wealth swelled into a fortune. He had 43
large flocks, female and male servants, camels and donkeys. Yaakov heard that Lavan's sons were saying, 1 **31**
"Yaakov has taken everything our father owned; of what belonged to our father, he has made all these riches."
And Yaakov saw that Lavan's manner toward him was not what it had been. The LORD said to Yaakov, "Go 2 3
back to the land of your fathers where you were born; I will be with you." So Yaakov sent word to Raḥel and 4
Leah to come out to the field where his flock was. He said to them, "I see that your father's manner toward 5
me is not what it used to be. But the God of my father has been with me. You well know how I have worked 6
for your father with all my strength. Your father cheated me, changing my wages ten times, but God has not 7
let him harm me. If he said, 'The speckled animals shall be your hire,' then all the flock would give birth to 8
speckled young. If he said, 'The streaked animals shall be your hire,' then all the flock would give birth to
streaked young. God has taken your father's livestock and given it to me. Once, during the breeding season, 9 10
I had a dream: I saw that the rams mounting the flock were streaked, speckled, or spotted. And in the dream 11

73 | The animals produced offspring that exhibited the designs seen during the mating process.

מַלְאַךְ הָאֱלֹהִים בַּחֲלוֹם יַעֲקֹב וָאֹמַר הִנֵּנִי: וַיֹּאמֶר שָׂא־נָא עֵינֶיךָ יב
וּרְאֵה כָּל־הָעַתֻּדִים הָעֹלִים עַל־הַצֹּאן עֲקֻדִּים נְקֻדִּים וּבְרֻדִּים
כִּי רָאִיתִי אֵת כָּל־אֲשֶׁר לָבָן עֹשֶׂה לָּךְ: אָנֹכִי הָאֵל בֵּית־אֵל אֲשֶׁר יג
מָשַׁחְתָּ שָּׁם מַצֵּבָה אֲשֶׁר נָדַרְתָּ לִּי שָׁם נֶדֶר עַתָּה קוּם צֵא מִן־
הָאָרֶץ הַזֹּאת וְשׁוּב אֶל־אֶרֶץ מוֹלַדְתֶּךָ: וַתַּעַן רָחֵל וְלֵאָה יד
וַתֹּאמַרְנָה לוֹ הַעוֹד לָנוּ חֵלֶק וְנַחֲלָה בְּבֵית אָבִינוּ: הֲלוֹא נָכְרִיּוֹת טו •
נֶחְשַׁבְנוּ לוֹ כִּי מְכָרָנוּ וַיֹּאכַל גַּם־אָכוֹל אֶת־כַּסְפֵּנוּ: כִּי כָל־הָעֹשֶׁר טז
אֲשֶׁר הִצִּיל אֱלֹהִים מֵאָבִינוּ לָנוּ הוּא וּלְבָנֵינוּ וְעַתָּה כֹּל אֲשֶׁר
ששי אָמַר אֱלֹהִים אֵלֶיךָ עֲשֵׂה: וַיָּקָם יַעֲקֹב וַיִּשָּׂא אֶת־בָּנָיו וְאֶת־נָשָׁיו יז
עַל־הַגְּמַלִּים: וַיִּנְהַג אֶת־כָּל־מִקְנֵהוּ וְאֶת־כָּל־רְכֻשׁוֹ אֲשֶׁר יח
רָכָשׁ מִקְנֵה קִנְיָנוֹ אֲשֶׁר רָכַשׁ בְּפַדַּן אֲרָם לָבוֹא אֶל־יִצְחָק אָבִיו

12 an angel of God said to me, 'Yaakov.' I replied, 'Here I am.' He
said, 'Look up and see that all the rams mounting the flock
are streaked, speckled, or spotted, for I have seen all that
13 Lavan is doing to you. I am the God of Beit El, where you
anointed a pillar and made a vow to Me. Now – leave this land
14 at once and return to the land where you were born.'" Raḥel
and Leah answered him, "Do we still have a share in the
• 15 inheritance of our father's estate? He treats us like strangers.
16 He has sold us and spent the money. All the wealth that God
has taken from our father belongs to us and our children. So
17 do whatever God has told you." So Yaakov put his children
18 and wives on camels and drove all the livestock and wealth
he had accumulated – the livestock he had acquired in Padan

Cassone, Renaissance era chest storing a wife's dowry of clothes and precious objects, Rome, ca. 1500 ↘

NEAR EAST

31:15 He has sold us and spent the money

In the ancient Near East, a father gave his daughter a dowry, generally handed over all at once when she got married. This gift was normally composed of household goods, jewelry, and livestock, but could also include land. In addition to this direct dowry, part of the bride-price paid by the groom was set aside for the bride as a nest egg for her security, functioning as an indirect dowry. Yaakov did not have any money for paying a bride-price, and instead paid Lavan with fourteen years of labor.

When Raḥel and Leah exclaim that their father "treats us like foreigners" (the literal definition of *nakhriyot*, here translated as "strangers"), and has "eaten up our money" (the literal meaning of the phrase translated here as "spent the money"), they are saying that Lavan has violated the local practice by taking for himself the portion of the bride-price expressed in Yaakov's labor that was due them. They assert that essentially, they were not married off by their father so much as sold like slaves. This leaves them vulnerable and unprotected, as aliens are. They see no point in staying with their father's household, as his behavior thus far indicates that they should not expect any sort of inheritance from him in the future either. ▪ ZR

יט אַרְצָה כְּנָעַן׃ וְלָבָן הָלַךְ לִגְזֹז אֶת־צֹאנוֹ וַתִּגְנֹב רָחֵל אֶת־הַתְּרָפִים
כ אֲשֶׁר לְאָבִיהָ׃ וַיִּגְנֹב יַעֲקֹב אֶת־לֵב לָבָן הָאֲרַמִּי עַל־בְּלִי הִגִּיד
כא לוֹ כִּי בֹרֵחַ הוּא׃ וַיִּבְרַח הוּא וְכָל־אֲשֶׁר־לוֹ וַיָּקׇם וַיַּעֲבֹר אֶת־

Aram – heading for his father Yitzḥak in the land of Canaan.
Meanwhile, when Lavan had gone to shear his sheep, Raḥel 19
had stolen her father's household gods. Yaakov deceived 20
Lavan the Aramean by not telling him that he was running
away. He fled with all he had, crossed the Euphrates, and 21

Freshly sheared wool

NEAR EAST

31:19 Sheepshearing in Mesopotamia

It is not a coincidence that Yaakov uses the sheepshearing period to flee across the Euphrates. In shepherding societies, it was one of the most important and labor-intensive times of the year, culminating in prolonged festivities. An Old Babylonian letter from the 18th century BCE states that at a certain time during the shearing, one thousand men was not enough (AbB 2, 25), and a letter from Mari in the same period states that 150 men are insufficient and that 300 or 400 men are needed for a period of three days (ARM 5, 67). Another Mari letter records that due to rain and lack of workers the shearing will take ten or twelve days (ARM 2, 140), rather than five days as planned.

Considering that the shearing would take place at a distance from home and would last for a while, it makes sense that Yaakov takes this opportunity to slip away unnoticed. Lavan finds out only three days later (v. 22). ▪ ZR

NEAR EAST

31:19 Teraphim (*terafim*)

The word *terafim*, translated here as "household gods," is an obscure term that may be a denigrating substitution word, often used in Tanakh when referring to idolatry. This would seem to be the case from the context when the term is used in II Kings 23:24, "household gods, idols (*gilulim*, literally, "dung pellets"), and all the detestable things." In that case, the word may be related to the root *r f h* ("to be weak," or "limp") or *t r f* ("to decay"). Note that Lavan calls these objects "gods" (v. 30), as does Yaakov when speaking with him (v. 32), but the narration always designates them as *terafim* (here and in vv. 34–35).

While in Genesis teraphim are small enough to be hidden in a saddle bag, in I Samuel 19:13, 16, Mikhal uses them to make it appear as though David were in bed, which suggests that sometimes they had a roughly human size and form. In Ezekiel 21:26 and Zechariah 10:2 it appears that teraphim were used for consultation.

These objects have been understood through comparative studies as playing a role in ancient cultic practices, including functioning as physical representations of protective spirits, cultic masks, household deities, deified kings, and ancestor spirits. They were used to both venerate and consult with supernatural forces. In this sense, possession of teraphim indicates access to divine consultation. ▪ ZR

Canaanite gods, Ḥatzor, 15th to 13th century BCE

• כב הַנָּהָר וַיָּשֶׂם אֶת־פָּנָיו הַר הַגִּלְעָד׃ וַיֻּגַּד לְלָבָן בַּיּוֹם הַשְּׁלִישִׁי כִּי
כג בָרַח יַעֲקֹב׃ וַיִּקַּח אֶת־אֶחָיו עִמּוֹ וַיִּרְדֹּף אַחֲרָיו דֶּרֶךְ שִׁבְעַת
כד יָמִים וַיַּדְבֵּק אֹתוֹ בְּהַר הַגִּלְעָד׃ וַיָּבֹא אֱלֹהִים אֶל־לָבָן הָאֲרַמִּי
בַּחֲלֹם הַלָּיְלָה וַיֹּאמֶר לוֹ הִשָּׁמֶר לְךָ פֶּן־תְּדַבֵּר עִם־יַעֲקֹב מִטּוֹב

• 22 headed for the hill country of Gilad. On the third day, Lavan
23 was told that Yaakov had fled. Taking his kinsmen with him,
he pursued him for seven days, catching up with him in the
24 hill country of Gilad. That night God came to Lavan the
Aramean in a dream and said to him, "Take care not to say

NEAR EAST

31:22–23 From Ḥaran to Gilad in seven days

Gilad was the mountainous northern part of the region of Transjordan. Depending on where in Gilad the meeting of Lavan and Yaakov took place, the distance from Ḥaran would have been 480–650 kilometers (300–400 miles). This distance would have been extremely difficult for Yaakov to cover in just ten days (the three days of his head start, and the additional seven days it took Lavan to catch up with him), certainly with a group that included women, children, and flocks, as Yaakov himself states in Genesis 33:13. The maximum realistic distance that could be covered in those circumstances would be close to 16 kilometers (10 miles) a day. The narrative here appears to be using three and seven as typological numbers in describing the journey. These are standard numbers used to describe journeys in other places in Tanakh as well ("three" in Gen. 30:36; Ex. 3:18, 5:3; Num. 10:33, 33:8; "seven" in II Kings 3:9). ▪ ZR

↗ Copy of a detail on a horizontal band, Balawat Gate, palace of Shalmaneser III, Assyria, 9th century BCE

NEAR EAST

31:30 Taking gods to another location

In this verse, Raḥel takes her father's household gods or teraphim. Comparative studies have understood these items as protective spirits, household deities, or ancestor spirits. It is thought that the teraphim might have been used to gain access to divine consultation.

Gods, or cultic images, were generally removed in the context of war. Removal of a god's statue signaled the total defeat of the enemy, as its god was exiled from its land. The Assyrian *Balawat Gate Inscription* records the following: "I [Shalmaneser III] brought back to my presence Ahuni with his troops, his gods, chariots, his horses. I brought (them) to my city Ashur." Similar references to the removal of gods are found in Hittite and Babylonian sources as well. David and his troops took the abandoned gods of the Philistines and carried them away (II Sam. 5:21). The Septuagint adds that David actually destroyed the idols.

Raḥel's removal of Lavan's teraphim is somewhat different as this is a story about a family and not a military battle. Genesis 31:35 does not relate the fate of the teraphim; only that Lavan does not find them. Yet, the larger narrative of territorial gods may help to contextualize why Raḥel might have removed the images. In the ancient Near East, gods were often only thought to have power in their own territory, so Raḥel's moving them to another location would have deprived Lavan of their "power," explicitly his access to divine consultation.

On the other hand, as the teraphim were household gods or related to an ancestor cult, such lesser deities may have still been seen by families as effectual no matter where the families took them. Perhaps Raḥel may have wanted them to prove that she had some inheritance rights, or maybe even to enhance her fertility. However, famed Bible scholar Moshe Greenberg relates this episode to a note that Josephus made (in *Antiquities,* 18.9.5) on ancestral idols. Josephus tells of a widow of a Parthian soldier living in Babylonia who was captured, and took along with her "the ancestral images of the gods belonging to her husband and to herself – for it is the custom among all the people in that country to have objects of worship in their house and to take them along when going abroad." Although Josephus recounts an episode that occurred some 1,500 years after Raḥel, it is the only other reference we have from the ancient Near East to someone taking household idols when going on a long journey. ▪ KG, JU

כה עַד־רָע׃ וַיַּשֵּׂג לָבָן אֶת־יַעֲקֹב וְיַעֲקֹב תָּקַע אֶת־אָהֳלוֹ בָּהָר וְלָבָן
כו תָּקַע אֶת־אֶחָיו בְּהַר הַגִּלְעָד׃ וַיֹּאמֶר לָבָן לְיַעֲקֹב מֶה עָשִׂיתָ
כז וַתִּגְנֹב אֶת־לְבָבִי וַתְּנַהֵג אֶת־בְּנֹתַי כִּשְׁבֻיוֹת חָרֶב׃ לָמָּה נַחְבֵּאתָ
לִבְרֹחַ וַתִּגְנֹב אֹתִי וְלֹא־הִגַּדְתָּ לִּי וָאֲשַׁלֵּחֲךָ בְּשִׂמְחָה וּבְשִׁרִים
כח בְּתֹף וּבְכִנּוֹר׃ וְלֹא נְטַשְׁתַּנִי לְנַשֵּׁק לְבָנַי וְלִבְנֹתָי עַתָּה הִסְכַּלְתָּ
כט עֲשׂוֹ׃ יֶשׁ־לְאֵל יָדִי לַעֲשׂוֹת עִמָּכֶם רָע וֵאלֹהֵי אֲבִיכֶם אֶמֶשׁ ׀
אָמַר אֵלַי לֵאמֹר הִשָּׁמֶר לְךָ מִדַּבֵּר עִם־יַעֲקֹב מִטּוֹב עַד־רָע׃
ל וְעַתָּה הָלֹךְ הָלַכְתָּ כִּי־נִכְסֹף נִכְסַפְתָּה לְבֵית אָבִיךָ לָמָּה גָנַבְתָּ
לא אֶת־אֱלֹהָי׃ וַיַּעַן יַעֲקֹב וַיֹּאמֶר לְלָבָן כִּי יָרֵאתִי כִּי אָמַרְתִּי פֶּן־
לב תִּגְזֹל אֶת־בְּנוֹתֶיךָ מֵעִמִּי׃ עִם אֲשֶׁר תִּמְצָא אֶת־אֱלֹהֶיךָ לֹא יִחְיֶה
נֶגֶד אַחֵינוּ הַכֶּר־לְךָ מָה עִמָּדִי וְקַח־לָךְ וְלֹא־יָדַע יַעֲקֹב כִּי רָחֵל
לג גְּנָבָתַם׃ וַיָּבֹא לָבָן בְּאֹהֶל־יַעֲקֹב ׀ וּבְאֹהֶל לֵאָה וּבְאֹהֶל שְׁתֵּי
לד הָאֲמָהֹת וְלֹא מָצָא וַיֵּצֵא מֵאֹהֶל לֵאָה וַיָּבֹא בְּאֹהֶל רָחֵל׃ וְרָחֵל
לָקְחָה אֶת־הַתְּרָפִים וַתְּשִׂמֵם בְּכַר הַגָּמָל וַתֵּשֶׁב עֲלֵיהֶם וַיְמַשֵּׁשׁ
לה לָבָן אֶת־כָּל־הָאֹהֶל וְלֹא מָצָא׃ וַתֹּאמֶר אֶל־אָבִיהָ אַל־יִחַר

anything to Yaakov for good or for bad." When Lavan 25
overtook him, Yaakov had pitched his tent in the hill country,
and Lavan and his kinsmen too encamped in the hill country
of Gilad. Lavan said to Yaakov, "What have you done? You 26
have deceived me, and carried off my daughters like captives
of the sword. Why did you leave secretly? Why did you 27
deceive me by not telling me? I would have sent you off with
celebration and song, with tambourines and harps. You did 28
not even let me kiss my grandchildren and daughters goodbye.
You have behaved foolishly. I have the power to harm you, 29
but last night your father's God spoke to me and said, 'Take
care not to say anything to Yaakov for good or for bad.' I realize 30
you left because you longed so much for your father's house.
But why did you steal my gods?" Yaakov answered Lavan, 31
saying, "I was afraid; I thought you would take your daughters
away from me by force. But if you find your gods with anyone 32
here, they shall not live. In the presence of our kinsmen, see
if there is anything of yours here, and take it." Yaakov did not
know that Raḥel was the one who had stolen them. So Lavan 33
went into Yaakov's tent, Leah's tent, and the tents of the two
female slaves, but found nothing. Leaving Leah's tent, he
entered Raḥel's. But Raḥel had taken the household gods and 34
put them inside a camel cushion, and was sitting on them;
and Lavan rummaged through the tent but found nothing.
She said to her father, "Do not be angry, my lord, but I cannot 35

NEAR EAST

31:35 The way of women

Menstruation was regarded both in the Torah (Lev. 15:19–23) and in the ancient Near East as a source of contagious impurity, like other bodily fluids, such as semen, secretions, and urine. This is evident in the *Middle Assyrian Palace Decrees*, where menstruating women were considered ritually unclean, and banned from approaching the king when he was making sacrifices (MAPD §7). The Akkadian phrase used in that text to designate a menstruating woman was *la qarabshani* ("unapproachable"). Another Akkadian term used for a menstruating woman is *musukkatu*, meaning, "an unclean woman under a temporary taboo."

In this setting, Lavan would not get too close to Raḥel if he believed that she was indeed menstruating. Additionally, it would be unimaginable to him that she would sit on household idols while in such a state. Nahum Sarna sees Raḥel's behavior as indicative that she saw the teraphim as having no religious value, as otherwise she would not have treated them so disrespectfully. ▪ ZR

Egyptian offering to the god Ra-Horakhty, Egypt, 10th to 8th century BCE

בְּעֵינֵי אֲדֹנִי כִּי לוֹא אוּכַל לָקוּם מִפָּנֶיךָ כִּי־דֶרֶךְ נָשִׁים לִי וַיְחַפֵּשׂ
וְלֹא מָצָא אֶת־הַתְּרָפִים: וַיִּחַר לְיַעֲקֹב וַיָּרֶב בְּלָבָן וַיַּעַן יַעֲקֹב לו
וַיֹּאמֶר לְלָבָן מַה־פִּשְׁעִי מַה חַטָּאתִי כִּי דָלַקְתָּ אַחֲרָי: כִּי־מִשַּׁשְׁתָּ לז
אֶת־כָּל־כֵּלַי מַה־מָּצָאתָ מִכֹּל כְּלֵי־בֵיתֶךָ שִׂים כֹּה נֶגֶד אַחַי וְאַחֶיךָ
וְיוֹכִיחוּ בֵּין שְׁנֵינוּ: זֶה עֶשְׂרִים שָׁנָה אָנֹכִי עִמָּךְ רְחֵלֶיךָ וְעִזֶּיךָ לֹא • לח
שִׁכֵּלוּ וְאֵילֵי צֹאנְךָ לֹא אָכָלְתִּי: טְרֵפָה לֹא־הֵבֵאתִי אֵלֶיךָ אָנֹכִי לט
אֲחַטֶּנָּה מִיָּדִי תְּבַקְשֶׁנָּה גְּנֻבְתִי יוֹם וּגְנֻבְתִי לָיְלָה: הָיִיתִי בַיּוֹם מ
אֲכָלַנִי חֹרֶב וְקֶרַח בַּלָּיְלָה וַתִּדַּד שְׁנָתִי מֵעֵינָי: זֶה־לִּי עֶשְׂרִים מא
שָׁנָה בְּבֵיתֶךָ עֲבַדְתִּיךָ אַרְבַּע־עֶשְׂרֵה שָׁנָה בִּשְׁתֵּי בְנֹתֶיךָ וְשֵׁשׁ

get up for you, for the way of women is with me now." So he
36 searched but did not find his household gods. Yaakov became
indignant and confronted Lavan. "What is my crime?" he
asked Lavan. "What wrong did I do that you come chasing
37 after me? You have rummaged through all my possessions.
What have you found that belongs to your house? Put it here
in front of my kinsmen and yours and let them decide between
• 38 the two of us! For the twenty years I was with you, your sheep
and goats did not miscarry. Not once did I take a ram from
39 your flock as food. I never brought you an animal torn by wild
beasts. I bore the loss myself. Whether it was stolen by day or
40 by night you demanded payment from me. By day I was
ravaged by the heat; at night by the freezing cold. Sleep fled
41 from my eyes. Twenty years I spent working in your
household – fourteen for your two daughters and six for your

↗ Newborn sheep with mother

NEAR EAST

31:38–39 Yaakov's claim of innocence

Ancient Near Eastern law and custom dictated the shepherd's responsibilities,, and detailing the expected birth and death rate among the flock. For example, an account from the ancient Sumerian city of Larsa states, "Entry to the shearing in Year Rim-Sin 22, with eighty female and male lambs born out of one hundred sheep, and fifteen carcasses deducted out of one hundred sheep, and two minas wool the allocation per one sheep," showing that a fifteen percent death rate was accepted as a natural loss. The *Laws of Hammurabi* contain a number of laws on this subject: "If he kill the cattle or sheep that were given to him, he shall compensate the owner with cattle for cattle and sheep for sheep" (LH §263); "If a herdsman, to whom cattle or sheep have been entrusted for watching over, and who has received his wages as agreed upon, and is satisfied, diminishes the number of the cattle or sheep, or makes the increase by birth less, he shall make good the increase or profit which was lost in the terms of settlement" (LH §264); "If the animal be killed in the stable by god (an accident), or if a lion kill it, the herdsman shall declare his innocence before god, and the owner bears the accident in the stable" (LH §266); "If the herdsman overlooks something, and an accident happens in the stable, then the herdsman is at fault for the accident which he has caused in the stable, and he must compensate the owner for the cattle or sheep" (LH §267).

Yaakov's statement that no animals miscarried during his period of service, and that he himself covered any of the flock that were killed by wild animals, therefore indicates that he acted beyond what the law required, implying that Lavan's terms violated the standard agreements between owners and shepherds.
▪ ZR

מב שְׁנֵים בְּצֹאנֶךָ וַתַּחֲלֵף אֶת־מַשְׂכֻּרְתִּי עֲשֶׂרֶת מֹנִים: לוּלֵי אֱלֹהֵי
אָבִי אֱלֹהֵי אַבְרָהָם וּפַחַד יִצְחָק הָיָה לִי כִּי עַתָּה רֵיקָם שִׁלַּחְתָּנִי
מג אֶת־עָנְיִי וְאֶת־יְגִיעַ כַּפַּי רָאָה אֱלֹהִים וַיּוֹכַח אָמֶשׁ: וַיַּעַן לָבָן שביעי
וַיֹּאמֶר אֶל־יַעֲקֹב הַבָּנוֹת בְּנֹתַי וְהַבָּנִים בָּנַי וְהַצֹּאן צֹאנִי וְכֹל
אֲשֶׁר־אַתָּה רֹאֶה לִי הוּא וְלִבְנֹתַי מָה־אֶעֱשֶׂה לָאֵלֶּה הַיּוֹם אוֹ
מד לִבְנֵיהֶן אֲשֶׁר יָלָדוּ: וְעַתָּה לְכָה נִכְרְתָה בְרִית אֲנִי וָאָתָּה וְהָיָה

42 flock – and ten times you changed my wages. Had the God
of my father – the God of Avraham, the Fear of Yitzḥak – not
been with me, you would have sent me away empty-handed.
But God saw my plight and the toil of my hands, and He
43 rebuked you last night." Then Lavan spoke up and said to
Yaakov, "The daughters are my daughters. The children are
my children. The flocks are my flocks. All that you see is mine.
But what can I do now about my daughters or the children
44 they have borne? Come now, let us make a covenant, you and

Cairn (mount of rough stones), Garvera, Surselva, Graubuenden, Switzerland

NEAR EAST

31:44–54 Treaty between Yaakov and Lavan

The pact between Yaakov and Lavan functioned as a parity treaty, a treaty between equals to ensure peaceful coexistence. Lavan now recognized Yaakov as an independent entity of equal status, as symbolized by the large stone functioning as a border between their territories and a commemorative mound of stones having two different names, given by each of the parties in their own language. Note that the term *ed* here, generally translated as "witness," also meant "pact" in Biblical Hebrew (thus the Ark of the Covenant is either *aron habrit* or *aron haedut* and the Tablets of the Covenant are either *luḥot habrit* or *luḥot haedut*) and is cognate with the Akkadian *adu*, a treaty secured by oaths sworn by the gods, as is the case here. The meal at the end (v. 54) commemorates the harmonious conclusion of the treaty ceremony, a standard feature of ancient Near Eastern pacts, seen earlier in Genesis 26:30.

Verse 50 is the only Tanakh verse containing a requirement that a husband may not take additional wives. However, this stipulation is found in a number of ancient Near Eastern texts. For example, a Nuzi marriage contract states, "Naswa, son of Arsenni, has adopted Wullu.... Also he has given his daughter Nuhuia to Wullu to wife; if Wullu shall take another wife he shall vacate the lands and houses of Naswa." In other words, Wullu will be punished by losing any inheritance from Naswa, who in this case is both his adoptive father and his father-in-law. In Yaakov's case, no penalty was stated for noncompliance; rather, God was mentioned as the guarantor. ▪ ZR

לְעֵד בֵּינִי וּבֵינֶךָ: וַיִּקַּח יַעֲקֹב אָבֶן וַיְרִימֶהָ מַצֵּבָה: וַיֹּאמֶר יַעֲקֹב מה מו
לְאֶחָיו לִקְטוּ אֲבָנִים וַיִּקְחוּ אֲבָנִים וַיַּעֲשׂוּ־גָל וַיֹּאכְלוּ שָׁם עַל־
הַגָּל: וַיִּקְרָא־לוֹ לָבָן יְגַר שָׂהֲדוּתָא וְיַעֲקֹב קָרָא לוֹ גַּלְעֵד: וַיֹּאמֶר מז מח
לָבָן הַגַּל הַזֶּה עֵד בֵּינִי וּבֵינְךָ הַיּוֹם עַל־כֵּן קָרָא־שְׁמוֹ גַּלְעֵד:
וְהַמִּצְפָּה אֲשֶׁר אָמַר יִצֶף יהוה בֵּינִי וּבֵינֶךָ כִּי נִסָּתֵר אִישׁ מֵרֵעֵהוּ: מט
אִם־תְּעַנֶּה אֶת־בְּנֹתַי וְאִם־תִּקַּח נָשִׁים עַל־בְּנֹתַי אֵין אִישׁ עִמָּנוּ נ
רְאֵה אֱלֹהִים עֵד בֵּינִי וּבֵינֶךָ: וַיֹּאמֶר לָבָן לְיַעֲקֹב הִנֵּה ׀ הַגַּל הַזֶּה נא
וְהִנֵּה הַמַּצֵּבָה אֲשֶׁר יָרִיתִי בֵּינִי וּבֵינֶךָ: עֵד הַגַּל הַזֶּה וְעֵדָה נב
הַמַּצֵּבָה אִם־אָנִי לֹא־אֶעֱבֹר אֵלֶיךָ אֶת־הַגַּל הַזֶּה וְאִם־אַתָּה
לֹא־תַעֲבֹר אֵלַי אֶת־הַגַּל הַזֶּה וְאֶת־הַמַּצֵּבָה הַזֹּאת לְרָעָה: אֱלֹהֵי נג
אַבְרָהָם וֵאלֹהֵי נָחוֹר יִשְׁפְּטוּ בֵינֵינוּ אֱלֹהֵי אֲבִיהֶם וַיִּשָּׁבַע יַעֲקֹב
בְּפַחַד אָבִיו יִצְחָק: וַיִּזְבַּח יַעֲקֹב זֶבַח בָּהָר וַיִּקְרָא לְאֶחָיו לֶאֱכָל־ נד
לָחֶם וַיֹּאכְלוּ לֶחֶם וַיָּלִינוּ בָּהָר: וַיַּשְׁכֵּם לָבָן בַּבֹּקֶר וַיְנַשֵּׁק לְבָנָיו נה מפטיר
וְלִבְנוֹתָיו וַיְבָרֶךְ אֶתְהֶם וַיֵּלֶךְ וַיָּשָׁב לָבָן לִמְקֹמוֹ:

45 I, and let it be a witness between us." So Yaakov took a stone
46 and set it up as a pillar. Yaakov said to his kinsmen, "Gather
stones." They took stones and made a mound, and there by
47 the mound they ate. Lavan called it Yegar Sahaduta, while
48 Yaakov called it Galed.[74] Lavan said, "This mound is a witness
between me and you this day." That is why it is called Galed.
49 It is also called Mitzpa because he said, "May the Lord keep
watch between me and you when we are out of each other's
50 sight.[75] If you mistreat my daughters or take other wives
besides my daughters, even though no one else is present,
remember that God is the witness between me and you."
51 Lavan said to Yaakov, "Here is the mound and here is the pillar
52 I have set up between us. This mound is a witness, and the
pillar is a witness, that I will not go past this mound on your
side and that you will not go past this mound and pillar on
53 my side with intent to do harm. May the God of Avraham,
the god of Naḥor, and the god of their father be our judge."
54 Yaakov swore by the Fear of his father Yitzḥak. He offered a
sacrifice on the hill and invited his kinsmen to break bread.
55 And they ate and spent the night upon that hill. Lavan rose
early the next morning. He kissed his grandchildren and
daughters goodbye and blessed them. Lavan then left to
return home.

74 | Both names mean "mound of testimony," the former in Aramaic, the latter in Hebrew (cf. also the name Gilad in v. 25).

75 | The name Mitzpa derives from the same root as *yitzef* (keep watch).

↖

Standing stones, Canaanite, Tel Gezer, Middle Bronze Age

וְיַעֲקֹב הָלַךְ לְדַרְכּוֹ וַיִּפְגְּעוּ־בוֹ מַלְאֲכֵי אֱלֹהִים׃ וַיֹּאמֶר יַעֲקֹב א ב • לב
כַּאֲשֶׁר רָאָם מַחֲנֵה אֱלֹהִים זֶה וַיִּקְרָא שֵׁם־הַמָּקוֹם הַהוּא
מַחֲנָיִם׃
וישלח וַיִּשְׁלַח יַעֲקֹב מַלְאָכִים לְפָנָיו אֶל־עֵשָׂו אָחִיו אַרְצָה שֵׂעִיר שְׂדֵה ג •

32 1 Yaakov continued on his way – and angels of God encountered
• 2 him. When he saw them, Yaakov said, "This is God's own
camp," and he named the place Maḥanayim.[76]
• 3 Yaakov sent messengers ahead of him to his brother Esav in

76 | Literally "two camps."

GEOGRAPHY

32:2 Maḥanayim

Maḥanayim was a town in Transjordan on the banks of the Yabok River. It was allotted to Gad (Josh. 13:26, 30), but was also a Levitical town (Josh. 21:36). It appears several times in II Samuel and I Kings as a royal refuge. For example, it was where Ish Boshet was brought in II Samuel 2:8, and where David fled during the rebellion of Avshalom in II Samuel 17:24.

Maḥanayim and the nearby town of Penuel are usually related to the twin ruins of Tell edh-Dhahab al-Garbiyya and Tell edh-Dhahab esh-Sharqiyya, respectively, in the Jordanian archaeological site Tulul edh-Dhahab. The two tells, in an important strategic location, are separated by the Yabok (the Zarqa) River, a short distance from where it meets the Jordan River. Maḥanayim is the dual form of *maḥane* ("camp"), which could indicate a site with two hills. Surveys at both sites revealed Iron Age I and II pottery, which lends support to the identification of Tulul edh-Dhahab with Maḥanayim and Penuel. Both appear as conquered cities on the Karnak relief of Shishak's campaign dated to around 925 BCE. ▪ ZR

Maḥanayim and the fords of the Yabok from the west

ד אֱדוֹם: וַיְצַו אֹתָם לֵאמֹר כֹּה תֹאמְרוּן לַאדֹנִי לְעֵשָׂו כֹּה אָמַר
ה עַבְדְּךָ יַעֲקֹב עִם־לָבָן גַּרְתִּי וָאֵחַר עַד־עָתָּה: וַיְהִי־לִי שׁוֹר וַחֲמוֹר
צֹאן וְעֶבֶד וְשִׁפְחָה וָאֶשְׁלְחָה לְהַגִּיד לַאדֹנִי לִמְצֹא־חֵן בְּעֵינֶיךָ:
ו וַיָּשֻׁבוּ הַמַּלְאָכִים אֶל־יַעֲקֹב לֵאמֹר בָּאנוּ אֶל־אָחִיךָ אֶל־עֵשָׂו
ז וְגַם הֹלֵךְ לִקְרָאתְךָ וְאַרְבַּע־מֵאוֹת אִישׁ עִמּוֹ: וַיִּירָא יַעֲקֹב מְאֹד

the land of Se'ir, the country of Edom. He instructed them, 4
"Say the following to my lord Esav: 'Your servant Yaakov says,
"I have been staying with Lavan; until now I have remained
there. And I have acquired cattle, donkeys, sheep, and male 5
and female servants. I am sending this message to my lord to
find favor in your eyes."'" And when the messengers returned 6
to Yaakov, they said, "We came to your brother Esav. He is on
his way to meet you, and with him, four hundred men."
Yaakov was acutely afraid and distressed. He divided the 7

GEOGRAPHY

32:3 Land of Se'ir, the country of Edom

Se'ir is usually referred to as a mountain or mountainous area (for example, Gen. 14:6, 36:8–9; Deut. 2:1), associated with Edom here and in Judges 5:4. This leads to the identification of Se'ir as the mountainous region in central Edom, running along the eastern side of the Arava, between the Dead Sea and the Gulf of Eilat. Some scholars also include part of the eastern Negev Highlands, west of the Arava Valley, as part of Se'ir. This area is known as Jabel e-Shaira, which preserves the name Se'ir. According to the Torah, Se'ir was originally inhabited by the Horites (Gen. 14:6, 36:21), who were dispossessed by "the descendants of Esav, who live in Se'ir" (Deut. 2:22). Once Se'ir became part of Edom, the two areas, which were somewhat distinct before, became synonymous. ▪ ZR

A view of the mountains of Edom from the Arava Valley

LANGUAGE

32:4–5 Style of Yaakov's message to Esav

The phrasing used in Yaakov's message to Esav conforms to the conventions of the ancient Near East. The introductory phrase, where the recipient of the message is identified, "Say the following to my lord Esav: 'Your servant Yaakov says…'" follows the standard Akkadian epistolary formula, "To my lord X say, so (says) your servant Y." Similarly, the use of the phrase "I am sending this message" in verse 5, without a direct object, literally, "I am sending to tell," parallels the *Lakhish Letters*, "Your servant Hoshaiah [Hoshaya] sent (this letter) to report to my lord Joash [Yoash]" (letter 3:1–2). ▪ ZR

Front side of *Lakhish Letter* 3, Lakhish, 6th century BCE

וַיֵּצֶר לוֹ וַיַּחַץ אֶת־הָעָם אֲשֶׁר־אִתּוֹ וְאֶת־הַצֹּאן וְאֶת־הַבָּקָר
וְהַגְּמַלִּים לִשְׁנֵי מַחֲנוֹת: וַיֹּאמֶר אִם־יָבוֹא עֵשָׂו אֶל־הַמַּחֲנֶה ח
הָאַחַת וְהִכָּהוּ וְהָיָה הַמַּחֲנֶה הַנִּשְׁאָר לִפְלֵיטָה: וַיֹּאמֶר יַעֲקֹב ט
אֱלֹהֵי אָבִי אַבְרָהָם וֵאלֹהֵי אָבִי יִצְחָק יהוה הָאֹמֵר אֵלַי שׁוּב
לְאַרְצְךָ וּלְמוֹלַדְתְּךָ וְאֵיטִיבָה עִמָּךְ: קָטֹנְתִּי מִכֹּל הַחֲסָדִים י
וּמִכָּל־הָאֱמֶת אֲשֶׁר עָשִׂיתָ אֶת־עַבְדֶּךָ כִּי בְמַקְלִי עָבַרְתִּי אֶת־
הַיַּרְדֵּן הַזֶּה וְעַתָּה הָיִיתִי לִשְׁנֵי מַחֲנוֹת: הַצִּילֵנִי נָא מִיַּד אָחִי יא
מִיַּד עֵשָׂו כִּי־יָרֵא אָנֹכִי אֹתוֹ פֶּן־יָבוֹא וְהִכַּנִי אֵם עַל־בָּנִים: וְאַתָּה יב
אָמַרְתָּ הֵיטֵב אֵיטִיב עִמָּךְ וְשַׂמְתִּי אֶת־זַרְעֲךָ כְּחוֹל הַיָּם אֲשֶׁר
לֹא־יִסָּפֵר מֵרֹב: וַיָּלֶן שָׁם בַּלַּיְלָה הַהוּא וַיִּקַּח מִן־הַבָּא בְיָדוֹ יג שני
מִנְחָה לְעֵשָׂו אָחִיו: עִזִּים מָאתַיִם וּתְיָשִׁים עֶשְׂרִים רְחֵלִים יד •
מָאתַיִם וְאֵילִים עֶשְׂרִים: גְּמַלִּים מֵינִיקוֹת וּבְנֵיהֶם שְׁלֹשִׁים פָּרוֹת טו
אַרְבָּעִים וּפָרִים עֲשָׂרָה אֲתֹנֹת עֶשְׂרִים וַעְיָרִם עֲשָׂרָה: וַיִּתֵּן בְּיַד־ טז
עֲבָדָיו עֵדֶר עֵדֶר לְבַדּוֹ וַיֹּאמֶר אֶל־עֲבָדָיו עִבְרוּ לְפָנַי וְרֶוַח תָּשִׂימוּ
בֵּין עֵדֶר וּבֵין עֵדֶר: וַיְצַו אֶת־הָרִאשׁוֹן לֵאמֹר כִּי יִפְגָּשְׁךָ עֵשָׂו יז

people with him into two camps,[77] along with the flocks, the
8 cattle, and the camels. "If Esav comes and attacks one camp,"
9 he thought, "the other camp may still survive." Then Yaakov
prayed, "God of my father Avraham and God of my father
Yitzhak, LORD, You who said to me, 'Go back to the land
10 where you were born and I will deal well with you,' I am
unworthy of all the kindnesses and the faithfulness that You
have bestowed upon Your servant. When I crossed the Jordan
I had only my staff, and now I have become two camps.
11 Rescue me, I pray, from my brother's hand, from the hand of
Esav. I am afraid he will come and kill us all, mothers and
12 children alike. Yet You said, 'I will deal well with you and make
13 your descendants countless, like the sand of the sea.'" He
spent the night there. Then, from what he had at hand, he
• 14 selected a gift for his brother Esav: two hundred female goats,
15 twenty male goats, two hundred ewes, twenty rams, thirty
milk camels and their young, forty cows, ten bulls, twenty
16 female donkeys, and ten male donkeys. He put them in the
care of his servants, each herd by itself, and he told the
servants, "Go on ahead of me. Keep a space between the
17 herds." He instructed the first, "When my brother Esav meets

77 | Cf. previous note.

NEAR EAST

32:14–15 List of Yaakov's gifts

The term *minha* means "gift," but it also has the technical sense of a tribute paid by a subject to an overlord. This sense is reinforced by the political terms used to describe the gifts in verse 18, "They belong to your servant Yaakov; they are a gift sent to my lord Esav."

Tribute was usually paid annually, in addition to payments made directly upon the establishment of a vassal-overlord relationship. Yaakov's gift totaling 220 goats, 220 sheep, 30 camels with their colts, 50 cows and bulls, and 30 donkeys is very large. Although it does not include the gold and silver generally found in ancient tribute lists, it is still larger than what many towns would have been able to pay. By way of comparison, a list of the tribute sent by the town of Hindanu to the Assyrian king Tukulti-Ninurta II (ruled 890–884 BCE) lists 10 minas gold, 2 talents tin, 50 oxen, 14 ducks, 10 minas silver, 30 dromedaries, 30 asses, and 200 sheep. ▪ ZR

Tribute bearer, palace of Nimrud, 883–859 BCE

אָחִ֗י וּשְׁאֵֽלְךָ֙ לֵאמֹ֔ר לְמִי־אַ֙תָּה֙ וְאָ֣נָה תֵלֵ֔ךְ וּלְמִ֖י אֵ֥לֶּה לְפָנֶֽיךָ׃
יח וְאָמַרְתָּ֙ לְעַבְדְּךָ֣ לְיַעֲקֹ֔ב מִנְחָ֥ה הִוא֙ שְׁלוּחָ֔ה לַאדֹנִ֖י לְעֵשָׂ֑ו וְהִנֵּ֥ה
יט גַם־ה֖וּא אַחֲרֵֽינוּ׃ וַיְצַ֞ו גַּ֣ם אֶת־הַשֵּׁנִ֗י גַּ֚ם אֶת־הַשְּׁלִישִׁ֔י גַּ֚ם אֶת־
כָּל־הַהֹ֣לְכִ֔ים אַחֲרֵ֥י הָעֲדָרִ֖ים לֵאמֹ֑ר כַּדָּבָ֤ר הַזֶּה֙ תְּדַבְּר֣וּן אֶל־עֵשָׂ֔ו
כ בְּמֹצַאֲכֶ֖ם אֹתֽוֹ׃ וַאֲמַרְתֶּ֕ם גַּ֗ם הִנֵּ֛ה עַבְדְּךָ֥ יַעֲקֹ֖ב אַחֲרֵ֑ינוּ כִּֽי־אָמַ֞ר
אֲכַפְּרָ֣ה פָנָ֗יו בַּמִּנְחָה֙ הַהֹלֶ֣כֶת לְפָנָ֔י וְאַחֲרֵי־כֵן֙ אֶרְאֶ֣ה פָנָ֔יו אוּלַ֖י
כא יִשָּׂ֥א פָנָֽי׃ וַתַּעֲבֹ֥ר הַמִּנְחָ֖ה עַל־פָּנָ֑יו וְה֛וּא לָ֥ן בַּלַּֽיְלָה־הַה֖וּא
• כב בַּֽמַּחֲנֶֽה׃ וַיָּ֣קָם ׀ בַּלַּ֣יְלָה ה֗וּא וַיִּקַּ֞ח אֶת־שְׁתֵּ֤י נָשָׁיו֙ וְאֶת־שְׁתֵּ֣י

you and asks, 'To whom do you belong? Where are you
going? Who owns all these animals ahead of you?' you must 18
say, 'They belong to your servant Yaakov; they are a gift sent
to my lord Esav – and he is coming behind us.'" He likewise 19
instructed the second and third and all the others who
followed the herds, "You shall say the same thing to Esav
when you meet him. Also say, 'Your servant Yaakov is coming 20
behind us.'" He thought, "I will pacify him with these gifts I
am sending on ahead. Then I will face him. Perhaps he will
accept me." So the gifts went on ahead of him, while he 21
remained in the camp that night. That night Yaakov got up 22 •
and took his two wives, two maidservants, and eleven sons

GEOGRAPHY

32:22 River Yabok

The Yabok, identified with Nahr az-Zarqa ("the blue river") today, is the second largest tributary of the Jordan River. The headwaters of the Zarqa begin just northeast of Amman, rising from the Ain Ghazal spring, a major archaeological site dating back to the Neolithic period. The river flows north before heading west in deep canyons and emptying into the Jordan River. Archaeological finds along the course of the river indicate that the area was rich in flora and fauna in the past. The narrowest and shallowest parts of this river can be crossed by using stepping stones.

In later history, the upper north-south section of the Yabok served as the eastern boundary of the Amonites. The lower east-west section was the boundary between the two Amorite kingdoms of Siḥon and Og. ▪ ZR

↗ Yabok River, near Zarqa, Jordan, 1950–1977

שִׁפְחֹתָיו וְאֶת־אַחַד עָשָׂר יְלָדָיו וַיַּעֲבֹר אֵת מַעֲבַר יַבֹּק׃ וַיִּקָּחֵם כג
וַיַּעֲבִרֵם אֶת־הַנָּחַל וַיַּעֲבֵר אֶת־אֲשֶׁר־לוֹ׃ וַיִּוָּתֵר יַעֲקֹב לְבַדּוֹ כד •
וַיֵּאָבֵק אִישׁ עִמּוֹ עַד עֲלוֹת הַשָּׁחַר׃ וַיַּרְא כִּי לֹא יָכֹל לוֹ וַיִּגַּע כה
בְּכַף־יְרֵכוֹ וַתֵּקַע כַּף־יֶרֶךְ יַעֲקֹב בְּהֵאָבְקוֹ עִמּוֹ׃ וַיֹּאמֶר שַׁלְּחֵנִי כו
כִּי עָלָה הַשָּׁחַר וַיֹּאמֶר לֹא אֲשַׁלֵּחֲךָ כִּי אִם־בֵּרַכְתָּנִי׃ וַיֹּאמֶר כז
אֵלָיו מַה־שְּׁמֶךָ וַיֹּאמֶר יַעֲקֹב׃ וַיֹּאמֶר לֹא יַעֲקֹב יֵאָמֵר עוֹד שִׁמְךָ כח
כִּי אִם־יִשְׂרָאֵל כִּי־שָׂרִיתָ עִם־אֱלֹהִים וְעִם־אֲנָשִׁים וַתּוּכָל׃
וַיִּשְׁאַל יַעֲקֹב וַיֹּאמֶר הַגִּידָה־נָּא שְׁמֶךָ וַיֹּאמֶר לָמָּה זֶּה תִּשְׁאַל כט
שלישי לִשְׁמִי וַיְבָרֶךְ אֹתוֹ שָׁם׃ וַיִּקְרָא יַעֲקֹב שֵׁם הַמָּקוֹם פְּנִיאֵל כִּי־ ל

23 and crossed the ford of the Yabok. He took them and crossed
the stream with them and then brought across all that he had.
• 24 And Yaakov was left alone. And a man wrestled with him until
25 dawn. When he saw that he could not overpower him, the
man wrenched Yaakov's hip in its socket so that the socket of
26 Yaakov's hip was strained as he wrestled with the man. "Let
me go," said the man, "for dawn is breaking." But he replied,
27 "I will not let you go unless you bless me." "What is your
28 name?" asked the man. "Yaakov," he replied. "No longer will
your name be Yaakov, but Yisrael," said the man, "for you have
struggled with God and with men and have prevailed."[78]
29 Yaakov asked, "Please tell me your name." But he said, "Why
30 do you ask my name?" and he blessed him there.[79] Yaakov
named the place Peniel, "for I have seen God face-to-face and

78 | The first part of the name Yisrael resonates with *sarita* (you have struggled). The ending "el" is a divine name.

79 | This response implies that the "man" is an angel; cf. Judges 13:18.

NEAR EAST

32:24–31 Yaakov's struggle with the angel

The motifs of a malevolent supernatural entity who attacks travelers attempting to cross a river, and of beings that have power only at night and are powerless at dawn, are well known in later folklore but are not attested to in the literature of the ancient Near East. Note also that Yaakov's struggle takes place after he has already crossed the river – the supernatural entity here does not seek to impede his crossing and is not associated with the river at all.

The closest thematic parallel is found in a Hittite text describing a festival in honor of Teshub, god of sky, thunder, and storms, and his wife Khebat. As part of a ritual involving the transportation of statues, a human is portrayed as detaining a supernatural being and receiving a blessing, presumably in return for allowing the entity to go. In the rite, the king asks the goddess not to go away. "The goddess (says) as follows: 'If I come back, will you in whatever manner – (such as) with horses and chariots – (strive to) prevail over me?' The king (says) as follows, 'I shall (strive to) prevail over you.' The goddess (says) as follows, 'Ask (something) for yourself' (= make a wish). The king (says) as follows, 'Give me life, health, sons (and) daughters in the future, [strong weapons], and put my enemies under my feet.'"

Basalt stele with a depiction of the storm god Teshub, Gozluhoyuk, Turkey, 8th century BCE

While the Hittite ritual shares strong similarities with Yaakov's wrestling with the angel, the context of the latter episode is different. It is not a repeated ritual, but rather is a unique event in Yaakov's life. While this episode represents God's change of Yaakov's name accompanied by a blessing (reminiscent of God's change of Avram's and Sarai's names), it also occurs at a specific point in time – the night before Yaakov's dreaded meeting with Esav. The purpose of the episode, then, appears to be to give Yaakov confidence that he will successfully survive that encounter, too. After all, Yaakov has now received both proof and God's assurance that he will be able to prevail in all his confrontations with others. Furthermore, unlike the Hittite ritual, which is directed at the monarchy, the Genesis account is directed to the nation that descends from Yaakov and is called by his new name, and the account emphasizes Yaakov's extraordinary relationship with God. • ZR

לא רָאִיתִי אֱלֹהִים פָּנִים אֶל־פָּנִים וַתִּנָּצֵל נַפְשִׁי׃ וַיִּזְרַח־לוֹ הַשֶּׁמֶשׁ
• לב כַּאֲשֶׁר עָבַר אֶת־פְּנוּאֵל וְהוּא צֹלֵעַ עַל־יְרֵכוֹ׃ עַל־כֵּן לֹא־יֹאכְלוּ
בְנֵי־יִשְׂרָאֵל אֶת־גִּיד הַנָּשֶׁה אֲשֶׁר עַל־כַּף הַיָּרֵךְ עַד הַיּוֹם הַזֶּה
לג א כִּי נָגַע בְּכַף־יֶרֶךְ יַעֲקֹב בְּגִיד הַנָּשֶׁה׃ וַיִּשָּׂא יַעֲקֹב עֵינָיו וַיַּרְא
וְהִנֵּה עֵשָׂו בָּא וְעִמּוֹ אַרְבַּע מֵאוֹת אִישׁ וַיַּחַץ אֶת־הַיְלָדִים עַל־
ב לֵאָה וְעַל־רָחֵל וְעַל שְׁתֵּי הַשְּׁפָחוֹת׃ וַיָּשֶׂם אֶת־הַשְּׁפָחוֹת וְאֶת־
יַלְדֵיהֶן רִאשֹׁנָה וְאֶת־לֵאָה וִילָדֶיהָ אַחֲרֹנִים וְאֶת־רָחֵל וְאֶת־יוֹסֵף
• ג אַחֲרֹנִים׃ וְהוּא עָבַר לִפְנֵיהֶם וַיִּשְׁתַּחוּ אַרְצָה שֶׁבַע פְּעָמִים עַד־

31 yet my life has been spared."[80] The sun was rising on him as
32 • he moved on from Penuel, limping on his thigh. That is why,
to this day, the Israelites do not eat the sciatic nerve by the
hip socket: because he wrenched Yaakov's hip socket at the
33 1 sciatic nerve. Yaakov looked up – and saw Esav coming with
his four hundred men. So he divided the children among
2 Leah, Raḥel, and the two maidservants. He put the
maidservants and their children first, Leah and her children
3 • behind, and Raḥel and Yosef at the rear. And he went ahead
of them, bowing down to the ground seven times until he

80 | The first part of the name Peniel resonates with *panim* (face). The ending "el" is a reference to God.

NEAR EAST

33:3 Bowing down to the ground seven times

The bowing here is a full-body prone position on the ground, a symbol of submission to a higher authority. Bowing seven times was customary when Canaanite vassals met or corresponded with the pharaoh, as evidenced by letters found in Ugarit. This is also attested to multiple times in the *Amarna letters* (1360–1332 BCE), for example, "Say to the king of Egypt: Message of Akizzi, your servant. I fall at the feet of my lord, my Storm-god, seven times" (EA 52), and "Rib-Hadda says to [his] lord, king of all countries, Great King, King of Battle: May [the Lady] of Gubla grant power to the king, my lord. I fall at the feet of my lord, my Sun, seven times and seven times" (EA 74). In this instance, Yaakov bows to show his submission to Esav, but the latter refuses to accept his gifts and does so only at Yaakov's insistence (vv. 9–11), perhaps indicating that he is not necessarily interested in Yaakov's submission. ▪ ZR

HALAKHA

32:32 Sciatic nerve

The sciatic nerve is a large nerve found in humans and in vertebrate animals. It is the longest and widest nerve in the human body, running down the back of the leg from alongside the hip joint down to the foot, supplying sensation to that area. Sciatic nerve injuries may result from hip dislocation, trauma, or physical compression at any location along the nerve. Since this part of the hindquarters of an animal is forbidden to be eaten, it must be removed. The removal process is called *nikkur* in halakhic literature, also known as *traibering* in Yiddish, or in English, "porging," from Judeo-Spanish. It is a difficult and expensive procedure, leading to the widespread practice in many Jewish communities of not eating the hindquarters at all. ▪ ZR

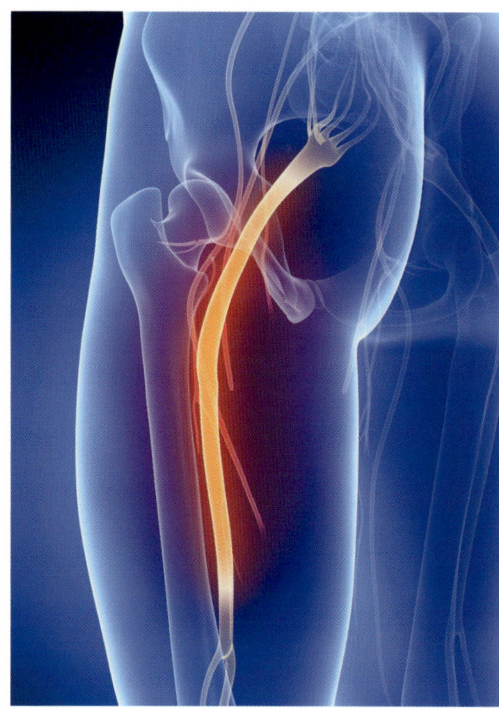

↗ Position of the sciatic nerve in a human

↖ Assyrian king Shalmaneser III receives tribute from Sua, king of Gilzanu, The Black Obelisk, Nimrud, 825 BCE

גִּשְׁתּוֹ עַד־אָחִיו: וַיָּרָץ עֵשָׂו לִקְרָאתוֹ וַיְחַבְּקֵהוּ וַיִּפֹּל עַל־צַוָּארָו ד
וַיִּשָּׁקֵהוּ וַיִּבְכּוּ: וַיִּשָּׂא אֶת־עֵינָיו וַיַּרְא אֶת־הַנָּשִׁים וְאֶת־הַיְלָדִים ה
וַיֹּאמֶר מִי־אֵלֶּה לָּךְ וַיֹּאמַר הַיְלָדִים אֲשֶׁר־חָנַן אֱלֹהִים אֶת־

4 came close to his brother. Esav ran to meet him and embraced
him. He threw his arms around his neck and kissed him, and
5 they wept. Esav looked up and saw the women and children.
He asked, "Who are these with you?" Yaakov answered, "They

NEAR EAST

33:4 Dots above letters in Tanakh

There are fifteen places in Tanakh where dots are marked above certain words: ten in the Torah, four in the Prophets, and one in the Writings. Sometimes the dots appear above all the letters in a word, as is the case here in the word *vayishakehu*, and sometimes above only some of the letters (for example, Gen. 16:5 and 18:9).

Various suggestions have been offered as to the function of these dots. Dots were sometimes used by Greek scribes to call attention to a remarkable passage. This idea apparently is reflected in a well-known rabbinic midrash which provides opposing interpretations for the dots here. "Rabbi Shimon ben Elazar said…it teaches that [Esav] was overcome with compassion in that moment and kissed [Yaakov] with all his heart. Rabbi Yannai said to him…On the contrary, it teaches that [Esav] came not to kiss [Yaakov] but to bite him" (Bereshit Rabba 78:9; "bite" is from the verb *n sh kh,* while "kiss" is from the verb *n sh k*). Thus, the dots here were understood either as emphasizing the extraordinary fact that this was indeed a sincere kiss, or as if indicating that the word was misspelled.

More commonly in early codices, Greek and Latin scribes used dots to indicate letters or words about which there was uncertainty, and which possibly should be erased. Manuscripts of the Septuagint are inconsistent regarding where, if at all, the Hebrew word *vayishakehu*, "and he kissed him," is placed in the verse. This approach is reflected in rabbinic tradition as well: "There are dots above the words… Why? For this is what Ezra said: If Eliyahu comes and says to me: Why did you write it this way? I will say to him: I have already put dots above these words [to indicate I was not certain it was correct]. But if he says to me: You wrote it correctly, then I will remove the dots" (*Avot de Rabbi Natan*, 34).

TFACTVMEST
POST·MORTEM·
MOYSI·SERVI
DNI·VT·LOQVE
RET·DNS·ADIO
SVE·FILIV·NVN·
MINISTRV·MO
YSI·ET·DICET
EI·MOYSES·S
WS·MS·MORTV·
E·SVRGE·ET·TR
SI·IORDANE·IS
TV·TV·ET·OMIS·
POPVLVS·TECV·
IN·TRAM·QVAM·
EGO·DABO·FILIIS
ISRL·OMNE·LO
CV·QVE·CALCA
VERIT·VESTIGI
V·PEDIS·VRI·VOB
TRADA·SICVT·
LOCVT·SV·MOY
SI·A·DESERTO·
ET·LIBANO·VSQ·
AD·FLVM·MAGNV·
EVFRATEN·OIS·
TRA·ETHEORV·

Text from the book of Joshua, *Codex Gigas*, from the monastery of Podlažice, Bohemia (modern-day Czech Republic), Latin, 13th century

Falling on the neck without kissing is found in Genesis 45:14 and 46:29. However, as Ephraim Avigdor Speiser noted, falling on the neck and kissing are found together in early Akkadian literature. For example in the *Enuma Elish Epic*, "Mummu put his arms around Apsu's neck; he sat on his knees kissing him" (I:53–54), in the same sequence that we find here. ▪ ZR

ז עַבְדֶּךָ׃ וַתִּגַּשְׁןָ הַשְּׁפָחוֹת הֵנָּה וְיַלְדֵיהֶן וַתִּשְׁתַּחֲוֶיןָ׃ וַתִּגַּשׁ גַּם־ רביעי
ח לֵאָה וִילָדֶיהָ וַיִּשְׁתַּחֲוּוּ וְאַחַר נִגַּשׁ יוֹסֵף וְרָחֵל וַיִּשְׁתַּחֲוּוּ׃ וַיֹּאמֶר
מִי לְךָ כָּל־הַמַּחֲנֶה הַזֶּה אֲשֶׁר פָּגָשְׁתִּי וַיֹּאמֶר לִמְצֹא־חֵן בְּעֵינֵי
• ט אֲדֹנִי׃ וַיֹּאמֶר עֵשָׂו יֶשׁ־לִי רָב אָחִי יְהִי לְךָ אֲשֶׁר־לָךְ׃ וַיֹּאמֶר
יַעֲקֹב אַל־נָא אִם־נָא מָצָאתִי חֵן בְּעֵינֶיךָ וְלָקַחְתָּ מִנְחָתִי מִיָּדִי

6 are the children God has graciously given your servant." Then
the maidservants and their children came forward and bowed
7 down. Leah and her children came forward and bowed down.
8 And last, Yosef and Raḥel approached and bowed down. Esav
asked, "What did you mean by all the procession that I met
9 before?" He said, "To find favor in your eyes, my lord." But
Esav said, "I have plenty, my brother. Let what is yours remain
10 • yours." "No, please," said Yaakov. "If I have found favor in your
eyes, accept this gift from me, for seeing your face is like seeing

NEAR EAST

33:10–11 Gift giving in the ancient Near East

Yaakov, in addition to acting subserviently to Esav (v. 3), sends him a lavish present of goats, sheep, camels, cows, and donkeys ahead of his arrival, thinking that "I will pacify him with these gifts I am sending on ahead. Then I will face him. Perhaps he will accept me" (Gen. 32:20). Yaakov gives the gift in order to get something in return: he hopes to appease and mend his relationship with his estranged brother. Later in this book, Yaakov sends another gift, this time to the anonymous "man who is lord of the land" (Gen. 42:33 – Yosef) in hopes of gaining favor with him and ensuring the return of Binyamin (Gen. 43:11–14).

The "I give so that you will give back" rationale is common in societies, such as ancient Israel, which have a gift-giving economy. In such societies, a gift calls for a counter-gift. A counter-gift does not have to be in kind; rather, one can choose what to give in return. Refusing to accept the counter-gift would indicate a lack of reciprocity, where the original gift-giver simply refused to respond (showing no respect) or was not able to respond (not behaving according to established social practices). Gift-giving therefore functions as a measure of honor, shame, and rank, and as a means of strengthening ties between two individuals or groups.

Examples of gift exchanges are seen throughout the ancient Near East. In a marriage, the bride-price is given by the groom's family, and the dowry is given by the bride's family. One marriage document from Alalakh even goes so far as to require the return of the gifts in case the union between the families is dissolved (COS 3.101B). Archival letters from Afek (ca. 1200 BCE) discuss matters of state in which gifts strengthen political bonds. In one, the governor Takuhlina sends a request for foodstuffs and, to sweeten the deal, sends a "(peace) gift of greeting for my father of 100 (shekels) of blue wool and 10 (shekels of) red wool" (COS 3.94). Political alliances were also negotiated with gifts, such as a letter (from El Amarna) from Tushratta, king of Mitanni, to Egypt, where he sends many horses, attendants, and chariots, as well as much jewelry, oils, and booty (EA 17).

The parade of gifts that Yaakov sends to Esav is lavish. Initially, Esav refuses the gifts, even as he reacts positively to Yaakov (vv. 4, 9). Only when Yaakov "pressed him" does Esav accept them (v. 11). The latter then offers protection to Yaakov and his family as they cross through Esav's lands (vv. 12, 15), which Yaakov politely declines, while still acting subserviently (vv. 13–15; note his repetitious "my lord"). With the symbolic gift-giving process complete, the two brothers ultimately part ways amicably. ▪ KG

↗ Jacob Sees Esau Coming to Meet Him, James Tissot, ca. 1900

כִּי עַל־כֵּן רָאִיתִי פָנֶיךָ כִּרְאֹת פְּנֵי אֱלֹהִים וַתִּרְצֵנִי׃ קַח־נָא אֶת־ יא
בִּרְכָתִי אֲשֶׁר הֻבָאת לָךְ כִּי־חַנַּנִי אֱלֹהִים וְכִי יֶשׁ־לִי־כֹל וַיִּפְצַר־
בּוֹ וַיִּקָּח׃ וַיֹּאמֶר נִסְעָה וְנֵלֵכָה וְאֵלְכָה לְנֶגְדֶּךָ׃ וַיֹּאמֶר אֵלָיו אֲדֹנִי יב יג
יֹדֵעַ כִּי־הַיְלָדִים רַכִּים וְהַצֹּאן וְהַבָּקָר עָלוֹת עָלָי וּדְפָקוּם יוֹם
אֶחָד וָמֵתוּ כָּל־הַצֹּאן׃ יַעֲבָר־נָא אֲדֹנִי לִפְנֵי עַבְדּוֹ וַאֲנִי אֶתְנָהֲלָה יד
לְאִטִּי לְרֶגֶל הַמְּלָאכָה אֲשֶׁר־לְפָנַי וּלְרֶגֶל הַיְלָדִים עַד אֲשֶׁר־אָבֹא
אֶל־אֲדֹנִי שֵׂעִירָה׃ וַיֹּאמֶר עֵשָׂו אַצִּיגָה־נָּא עִמְּךָ מִן־הָעָם אֲשֶׁר טו
אִתִּי וַיֹּאמֶר לָמָּה זֶּה אֶמְצָא־חֵן בְּעֵינֵי אֲדֹנִי׃ וַיָּשָׁב בַּיּוֹם הַהוּא טז
עֵשָׂו לְדַרְכּוֹ שֵׂעִירָה׃ וְיַעֲקֹב נָסַע סֻכֹּתָה וַיִּבֶן לוֹ בָּיִת וּלְמִקְנֵהוּ יז •
עָשָׂה סֻכֹּת עַל־כֵּן קָרָא שֵׁם־הַמָּקוֹם סֻכּוֹת׃ וַיָּבֹא יח
יַעֲקֹב שָׁלֵם עִיר שְׁכֶם אֲשֶׁר בְּאֶרֶץ כְּנַעַן בְּבֹאוֹ מִפַּדַּן אֲרָם וַיִּחַן

11 the face of God, and you have shown me favor. Please accept
my blessing that was brought to you, for God has been
gracious to me, and I have everything." Yaakov pressed him,
12 and he accepted. Then Esav said, "Let us be on our way. I will
13 go beside you." But Yaakov said, "My lord knows that the
children are fragile, and I must care for the nursing sheep and
cattle. If they are driven hard even for one day, all the flocks
14 will die. Let my lord go on ahead of his servant, and I will go
slowly at the pace of the livestock before me and the pace of
15 the children until I come to my lord in Se'ir." Esav said, "Let
me leave some of my people with you." "Why do that?" he
16 said. "Just let me find favor in the eyes of my lord." So that day
• 17 Esav started back on his way to Se'ir, and Yaakov journeyed
on to Sukkot. There he built himself a house and made huts
for his livestock; that is why he named the place
18 Sukkot.[81] Thus Yaakov, having come from Padan Aram,

81 | Meaning "huts."

NEAR EAST

33:19 *Kesita*

The *kesita*, the unit used to purchase the land mentioned here, is not a coin, as coins did not come into use until the 6th century BCE. The term is also used in Joshua 24:32, recalling this episode, and Job 42:11, where each person who came to comfort Iyov "gave him one *kesita* and one ring of gold." The term is not found in extra-biblical sources.

Based on the context in the book of Job, a *kesita* may be a piece of jewelry, like a ring, that had a customary weight. Shaped silver rings were used for exchange in ancient Egypt. Alternatively, Targum Onkelos, the Septuagint, and the Job Targum translate the word as sheep, reflecting the use of livestock for commercial trade in ancient times. ▪ ZR

GEOGRAPHY

33:17 Sukkot

Based on Judges 8, verses 5 and 8, Sukkot is near the Jordan River and Penuel. The Talmud Yerushalmi identifies Sukkot with Tar'ala (Shevi'it 9:2), itself identified with Deir 'Alla, a large tell in the Jordan Valley on the eastern side of the Jordan River. Excavations have shown that this area was occupied from the Chalcolithic period into the Iron Age. This location is found along the east-west road that connects Canaan with the road leading north to Damascus. This Sukkot is distinct from the Sukkot that is in Egypt – probably associated with the site known to the Egyptians as Tjeku, the first stop on the Israelites' journey out of Egypt (Ex. 12:37). ▪ ZR

Bronze axe head, Tell Deir 'Alla, Middle Bronze Age, 2100–1550 BCE

Scarab ring, glazed steatite scarab set in a bronze band, Egypt, 18th to 17th century BCE

יט • אֶת־פְּנֵי הָעִיר׃ וַיִּקֶן אֶת־חֶלְקַת הַשָּׂדֶה אֲשֶׁר נָטָה־שָׁם אָהֳלוֹ
כ מִיַּד בְּנֵי־חֲמוֹר אֲבִי שְׁכֶם בְּמֵאָה קְשִׂיטָה׃ וַיַּצֶּב־שָׁם מִזְבֵּחַ
לד • א וַיִּקְרָא־לוֹ אֵל אֱלֹהֵי יִשְׂרָאֵל׃ וַתֵּצֵא דִינָה בַּת־לֵאָה חמישי
ב אֲשֶׁר יָלְדָה לְיַעֲקֹב לִרְאוֹת בִּבְנוֹת הָאָרֶץ׃ וַיַּרְא אֹתָהּ שְׁכֶם
בֶּן־חֲמוֹר הַחִוִּי נְשִׂיא הָאָרֶץ וַיִּקַּח אֹתָהּ וַיִּשְׁכַּב אֹתָהּ וַיְעַנֶּהָ׃
ג וַתִּדְבַּק נַפְשׁוֹ בְּדִינָה בַּת־יַעֲקֹב וַיֶּאֱהַב אֶת־הַנַּעֲרָ וַיְדַבֵּר עַל־לֵב
ד הַנַּעֲרָ׃ וַיֹּאמֶר שְׁכֶם אֶל־חֲמוֹר אָבִיו לֵאמֹר קַח־לִי אֶת־הַיַּלְדָּה
ה הַזֹּאת לְאִשָּׁה׃ וְיַעֲקֹב שָׁמַע כִּי טִמֵּא אֶת־דִּינָה בִתּוֹ וּבָנָיו הָיוּ

arrived safely at the town of Shekhem in Canaan, and he set
up camp within sight of the town. He bought the plot of 19 •
ground where he pitched his tent from the sons of Ḥamor,
father of Shekhem, for one hundred *kesita*[82] of silver. There 20
he erected an altar and named it El Elohei Yisrael.[83] Dina, 1 • 34
the daughter whom Leah had borne to Yaakov, went out to
see the daughters of the land. When Shekhem son of Ḥamor 2
the Hivite, prince of the land, saw her, he took hold of her, lay
with her, and violated her. He became deeply drawn to Dina, 3
Yaakov's daughter, and, in love with the young woman, he
spoke to her heart. Shekhem said to his father Ḥamor, "Take 4
this girl as a wife for me." When Yaakov heard that he had 5

82 | Apparently a unit of silver.
83 | Meaning "God, the God of Yisrael."

NEAR EAST

34:1 Dina...went out

The story of Dina in this chapter recounts the harsh circumstances of the encounter between Yaakov's family, now settled near the town of Shekhem, and the local residents. The story begins with the description of Dina as she "went out to see the daughters of the land" (v. 1). Girls of marriageable age were usually not allowed to leave a rural encampment and walk freely, unchaperoned, among foreigners, so Dina's behavior was unconventional. The text expresses criticism regarding Dina's behavior by using the verbal stem *y tz a* [*alef*], "to go out." Like the Akkadian equivalent *waṣu*, the verb can denote inappropriate conduct of a woman (LH §141, §143). The Midrash also viewed Dina's behavior as inappropriate, recalling the resemblance to her mother Leah's behavior (Gen. 30:16) and suggesting she inherited her fondness for "going out" (Bereshit Rabba 80:1). However, other commentators, such as Samson Raphael Hirsch and Malbim, have viewed Dina's behavior as that of an inquisitive girl displaying interest in her local counterparts and eager to make their acquaintance.

Rape of Dinah, Giuliano di Bugiardini, Bologna, 16th century

אֶת־מִקְנֵהוּ בַּשָּׂדֶה וְהֶחֱרִשׁ יַעֲקֹב עַד־בֹּאָם׃ וַיֵּצֵא חֲמוֹר אֲבִי־ ו
שְׁכֶם אֶל־יַעֲקֹב לְדַבֵּר אִתּוֹ׃ וּבְנֵי יַעֲקֹב בָּאוּ מִן־הַשָּׂדֶה כְּשָׁמְעָם ז
וַיִּתְעַצְּבוּ הָאֲנָשִׁים וַיִּחַר לָהֶם מְאֹד כִּי נְבָלָה עָשָׂה בְיִשְׂרָאֵל
לִשְׁכַּב אֶת־בַּת־יַעֲקֹב וְכֵן לֹא יֵעָשֶׂה׃ וַיְדַבֵּר חֲמוֹר אִתָּם לֵאמֹר ח
שְׁכֶם בְּנִי חָשְׁקָה נַפְשׁוֹ בְּבִתְּכֶם תְּנוּ נָא אֹתָהּ לוֹ לְאִשָּׁה׃
וְהִתְחַתְּנוּ אֹתָנוּ בְּנֹתֵיכֶם תִּתְּנוּ־לָנוּ וְאֶת־בְּנֹתֵינוּ תִּקְחוּ לָכֶם׃ ט
וְאִתָּנוּ תֵּשֵׁבוּ וְהָאָרֶץ תִּהְיֶה לִפְנֵיכֶם שְׁבוּ וּסְחָרוּהָ וְהֵאָחֲזוּ בָהּ׃ י
וַיֹּאמֶר שְׁכֶם אֶל־אָבִיהָ וְאֶל־אַחֶיהָ אֶמְצָא־חֵן בְּעֵינֵיכֶם וַאֲשֶׁר יא
תֹּאמְרוּ אֵלַי אֶתֵּן׃ הַרְבּוּ עָלַי מְאֹד מֹהַר וּמַתָּן וְאֶתְּנָה כַּאֲשֶׁר יב

defiled his daughter Dina, his sons were in the field with his
livestock, and so he stayed silent until they came home.
6 Shekhem's father Ḥamor came to Yaakov to speak with him.
7 Meanwhile, Yaakov's sons, having heard what had happened,
came back from the field. They were shocked and furious, for
Shekhem had committed an outrage in Israel by sleeping with
8 Yaakov's daughter. Such a thing cannot be done! But Ḥamor
spoke with them and said, "My son Shekhem has his heart
set upon your daughter. Please give her to him as his wife.
9 Intermarry with us. Give us your daughters and take our
10 daughters for yourselves. Settle with us. The land is open to
11 you. Live here, trade here, acquire property here." Then
Shekhem said to Dina's father and brothers, "Let me but find
12 favor in your eyes and I will give whatever you ask. Set the
bridal price and gifts as high as you like. I will give whatever

LANGUAGE

34:20 Fellow townsmen

The term here for fellow townsmen literally means "men of their city." It refers to a city's assembly, composed of its free citizens, that decides on major public matters. Such political institutions are referred to in the *Amarna letters*. For example, a letter dated to the 14th century BCE from Rib-Addi, the ruler of the Phoenician city of Byblos, to the pharaoh, reports on the local deliberations regarding who the city should align with: "They had a discussion, a[n]d the lords of the city [were jo]ined to the sons of Abdi-Asrati.... Half of the city is on the side of the sons of Abdi-Asirti [difference in spelling in original], and half of it is on the side of my lord" (EA 138). There are also letters to the pharaoh written from organizations of citizens of Tunip in western Syria (EA 59) and Irqata in Lebanon (EA 100); these groups seem to have been temporary republican organizations that governed the city after their king was killed. ▪ ZR

Archaeological site including remains of the Great Temple and the Temple of Ba'alat Gebal (2700 BCE) and the Temple of the Obelisks (1600 BCE), Byblos (Lebanon)

יג תאמרו אלי ותנו-לי את-הנער לאשה: ויענו בני-יעקב את-
שכם ואת-חמור אביו במרמה וידברו אשר טמא את דינה
יד אחתם: ויאמרו אליהם לא נוכל לעשות הדבר הזה לתת
טו את-אחתנו לאיש אשר-לו ערלה כי-חרפה הוא לנו: אך-
טז בזאת נאות לכם אם תהיו כמנו להמל לכם כל-זכר: ונתנו
את-בנתינו לכם ואת-בנתיכם נקח-לנו וישבנו אתכם והיינו
יז לעם אחד: ואם-לא תשמעו אלינו להמול ולקחנו את-בתנו
יח והלכנו: וייטבו דבריהם בעיני חמור ובעיני שכם בן-חמור:
יט ולא-אחר הנער לעשות הדבר כי חפץ בבת-יעקב והוא נכבד
כ מכל בית אביו: ויבא חמור ושכם בנו אל-שער עירם וידברו
כא אל-אנשי עירם לאמר: האנשים האלה שלמים הם אתנו
וישבו בארץ ויסחרו אתה והארץ הנה רחבת-ידים לפניהם
כב את-בנתם נקח-לנו לנשים ואת-בנתינו נתן להם: אך-בזאת
יאתו לנו האנשים לשבת אתנו להיות לעם אחד בהמול לנו
כג כל-זכר כאשר הם נמלים: מקנהם וקנינם וכל-בהמתם הלוא
כד לנו הם אך נאותה להם וישבו אתנו: וישמעו אל-חמור ואל-
שכם בנו כל-יצאי שער עירו וימלו כל-זכר כל-יצאי שער
כה עירו: ויהי ביום השלישי בהיותם כאבים ויקחו שני-בני-יעקב
שמעון ולוי אחי דינה איש חרבו ויבאו על-העיר בטח ויהרגו
כו כל-זכר: ואת-חמור ואת-שכם בנו הרגו לפי-חרב ויקחו את-
כז דינה מבית שכם ויצאו: בני יעקב באו על-החללים ויבזו
כח העיר אשר טמאו אחותם: את-צאנם ואת-בקרם ואת-
כט חמריהם ואת אשר-בעיר ואת-אשר בשדה לקחו: ואת-כל-

you ask of me; only give me the
young woman as my wife."
Yaakov's sons responded to 13
Shekhem and his father Ḥamor,
and they spoke deceptively: he
had, after all, defiled their sister
Dina. They told them, "We cannot 14
do this. To give our sister to an
uncircumcised man would be a
disgrace to us. Only on one 15
condition will we agree with you:
If you become like us, circumcising
all your males, then we will give 16
you our daughters and take your
daughters for ourselves. We will
live with you and become one people. If you do not agree to be circumcised, we will take our daughter 17
and go." Their words gratified Ḥamor and his son Shekhem. The young man, the most honored of his 18 19
father's family, lost no time in doing it, because he longed for Yaakov's daughter. Ḥamor and his son 20
Shekhem came to the town gate and spoke to their fellow townsmen. "These people are friendly toward 21
us," they said. "Let them live in the land and trade in it. We have space enough for them. We can marry
their daughters and they can marry ours. But only on one condition will they agree to dwell with us as 22
one people. Every male among us must be circumcised as they are. Will not their livestock, property, 23
and all their animals be ours? Let us, then, agree to their terms and let them settle among us." All the 24
people who went out by the town gate listened to Ḥamor and his son Shekhem, and all the males who
went out by the town gate were circumcised. On the third day, when the people were weak from pain, 25
two of Yaakov's sons, Shimon and Levi, Dina's brothers, took their swords, entered the unsuspecting
town, and killed every single male. They killed Ḥamor and his son Shekhem by the sword, took Dina 26
from Shekhem's house and left. Yaakov's sons came upon the dead and plundered the town that had 27
defiled their sister. They took their flocks, their cattle, their donkeys, and everything else of theirs in the 28
town and out in the field. Their wealth, their children, and their women they took captive and looted, 29

חֵילָם וְאֶת־כָּל־טַפָּם וְאֶת־נְשֵׁיהֶם שָׁבוּ וַיָּבֹזּוּ וְאֵת כָּל־אֲשֶׁר
בַּבָּיִת׃ וַיֹּאמֶר יַעֲקֹב אֶל־שִׁמְעוֹן וְאֶל־לֵוִי עֲכַרְתֶּם אֹתִי ל
לְהַבְאִישֵׁנִי בְּיֹשֵׁב הָאָרֶץ בַּכְּנַעֲנִי וּבַפְּרִזִּי וַאֲנִי מְתֵי מִסְפָּר וְנֶאֶסְפוּ
עָלַי וְהִכּוּנִי וְנִשְׁמַדְתִּי אֲנִי וּבֵיתִי׃ וַיֹּאמְרוּ הַכְזוֹנָה יַעֲשֶׂה אֶת־ לא
אֲחוֹתֵנוּ׃

לה א וַיֹּאמֶר אֱלֹהִים אֶל־יַעֲקֹב קוּם עֲלֵה בֵית־אֵל וְשֶׁב־שָׁם וַעֲשֵׂה־
שָׁם מִזְבֵּחַ לָאֵל הַנִּרְאֶה אֵלֶיךָ בְּבָרְחֲךָ מִפְּנֵי עֵשָׂו אָחִיךָ׃ וַיֹּאמֶר ב
יַעֲקֹב אֶל־בֵּיתוֹ וְאֶל כָּל־אֲשֶׁר עִמּוֹ הָסִרוּ אֶת־אֱלֹהֵי הַנֵּכָר אֲשֶׁר
בְּתֹכְכֶם וְהִטַּהֲרוּ וְהַחֲלִיפוּ שִׂמְלֹתֵיכֶם׃ וְנָקוּמָה וְנַעֲלֶה בֵּית־אֵל ג
וְאֶעֱשֶׂה־שָּׁם מִזְבֵּחַ לָאֵל הָעֹנֶה אֹתִי בְּיוֹם צָרָתִי וַיְהִי עִמָּדִי בַּדֶּרֶךְ
אֲשֶׁר הָלָכְתִּי׃ וַיִּתְּנוּ אֶל־יַעֲקֹב אֵת כָּל־אֱלֹהֵי הַנֵּכָר אֲשֶׁר בְּיָדָם ד
וְאֶת־הַנְּזָמִים אֲשֶׁר בְּאָזְנֵיהֶם וַיִּטְמֹן אֹתָם יַעֲקֹב תַּחַת הָאֵלָה

30 and all that was in the houses. Yaakov said to Shimon and
Levi, "You have brought trouble upon me – you have made
me odious to the inhabitants of the land, the Canaanites and
Perizzites. I am few in number, and if they join forces and
31 attack me, I and my household will be destroyed." But they
said, "Should our sister be treated like a whore?"

35 1 God said to Yaakov, "Arise, go up to Beit El. Stay there, and
there build an altar to God, who appeared to you as you fled
2 your brother Esav." Yaakov told his household and everyone
with him, "Be rid of the alien gods you have with you. Purify
3 yourselves and change your clothes. Then come, let us go
up to Beit El, and there I will make an altar to God, who
answered me in my time of trouble and who has been with
4 me wherever I have gone." They gave Yaakov all the alien gods
they had, and even the rings in their ears,[84] and Yaakov buried

84 | Earrings may have been associated with idol worship (cf. Ex. 32:2–4).

LANGUAGE

34:30 You have made me odious to the inhabitants of the land

In Hebrew the phrase "you have made me odious" is almost identical to the one in Exodus 5:21, "you have made us repellent in the eyes of Pharaoh and his officials." Both phrases refer literally to making a person stink ("making our smell odious"), employing the verbal form of the root *b a* [*alef*] *sh*. This expression is paralleled in an Egyptian letter from the 13th century BCE, Papyrus Anastasi I, where the senior scribe, Hori, ridicules the work of his fellow scribe, Amenemope, and concludes by saying, "you cannot say, 'You have made my name stink' to others and everyone" (28:6), as Amenemope is responsible for making his own name stink. It also appears in the *Instruction of Any*, an Egyptian wisdom text: "Do not leave when the chiefs enter, lest your name stink." ▪ ZR

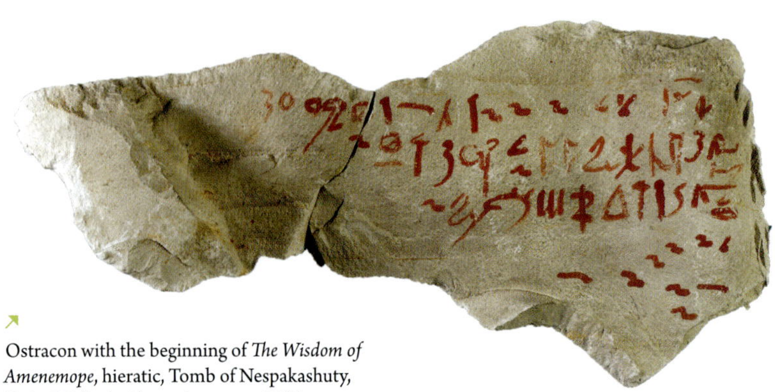

Ostracon with the beginning of *The Wisdom of Amenemope*, hieratic, Tomb of Nespakashuty, Deir el-Bahari, 6th to 5th century BCE

ה אֲשֶׁר עִם־שְׁכֶם: וַיִּסָּעוּ וַיְהִי ׀ חִתַּת אֱלֹהִים עַל־הֶעָרִים אֲשֶׁר
ו סְבִיבוֹתֵיהֶם וְלֹא רָדְפוּ אַחֲרֵי בְּנֵי יַעֲקֹב: וַיָּבֹא יַעֲקֹב לוּזָה אֲשֶׁר

them under a terebinth near Shekhem. As they set out, the 5
terror of God fell on the surrounding towns so that no one
pursued Yaakov's sons. Yaakov and all the people with him 6

↗ Stone lion, Citadel of Zincirli, Neo-Hittite, Sam'al, 10th to 8th century BCE

NEAR EAST

35:2–4 Getting rid of the alien gods

Yaakov now fulfills the vow he made at Beit El in 28:20–21, "if God will be with me, protecting me…and if I return in peace…then the Lord will be my God," by removing the alien cult objects in his camp. Presumably, these include the teraphim that Raḥel stole (which are termed "gods" in 31:30, 32), as well as idols that Yaakov's sons took as booty from Shekhem (34:27, 29). This formal renunciation of alien gods takes place before Yaakov's return to Beit El and is the first time in Tanakh that the inconsistency between the Israelite religion and that of other nations is explicit. Nearly identical phrasing was later used by Yehoshua and Shmuel in their exhortations to the Israelites to "remove the foreign gods" from their midst (compare the Hebrew in Gen. 35:2 with Josh. 24:23; I Sam. 7:3).

Yaakov buries the alien cultic objects "under a terebinth near Shekhem." Interestingly, this is not how such objects are dealt with in the rest of the Tanakh. Deuteronomy 7:5, 25 prescribes the burning of idols and the utter destruction of other objects (see also Ex. 32:20 regarding the destruction of the Golden Calf; I Kings 15:13; II Kings 23:4; I Chr. 14:12). However, in the ancient Near East, burial was one of the methods used to dispose of images in a disgraceful manner, as part of acts of violence perpetrated against statues. The best-known example of this practice is found at Alalakh: a statue of King Idrimi had its head and feet broken off and was buried in a pit following Alalakh's destruction ca. 1200 BCE. Another example is the Iron Age lion pit of Zincirli in southeastern Turkey, in which Hittite portal statues of lions were burned in a pit and then buried there under a heavily trafficked area. Yaakov, then, who was acting before the giving of the Torah on Mount Sinai, was disposing of the alien cultic objects in a manner consistent with ancient Near Eastern practice.

The purification here appears to be connected to the idea that idols are abhorrent (Deut. 7:26) and treated as impure (Is. 30:22). The subsequent changing of clothes demonstrates a transition from one state to another (as in Gen. 41:14; Lev. 6:4, 16:23–24).

When the verse states that "they gave Yaakov all the alien gods they had, and even the rings in their ears," it may be referring to cultic earrings that were decorated with idolatrous imagery (Targum Yerushalmi), per the Aramaic *kedasha* (a holy object), a term corresponding to the Hebrew *nezem*. Alternatively, the verse may be referring to earrings that were in the ears of the idols themselves, an interpretation brought by Ḥizkuni. Examples of such earrings are the ones mentioned in the prayer of the Assyrian king Shalmaneser II (1030–1019 BCE), "they placed earrings of fine gold on its (the idol's) ears" (KAR 98), and the ones typical of cult statutes in the Neo-Sumerian period (ca. 2112–2004 BCE). Idols found with earrings include a seated god from Megiddo with a gold ring in its left ear and an idol from Tell Judeideh in southeastern Turkey with bronze wire earrings. It may have been tempting to remove these earrings and keep them – getting rid of them conforms to the ruling in Deuteronomy 7:25: "Do not covet the silver or gold on them (images) and take it for yourself, because you would be ensnared by it, for it is abhorrent to the Lord your God." ▪ ZR

בְּאֶרֶץ כְּנַעַן הִוא בֵּית־אֵל הוּא וְכָל־הָעָם אֲשֶׁר־עִמּוֹ: וַיִּבֶן שָׁם ז
מִזְבֵּחַ וַיִּקְרָא לַמָּקוֹם אֵל בֵּית־אֵל כִּי שָׁם נִגְלוּ אֵלָיו הָאֱלֹהִים
בְּבָרְחוֹ מִפְּנֵי אָחִיו: וַתָּמָת דְּבֹרָה מֵינֶקֶת רִבְקָה וַתִּקָּבֵר מִתַּחַת ח
לְבֵית־אֵל תַּחַת הָאַלּוֹן וַיִּקְרָא שְׁמוֹ אַלּוֹן בָּכוּת:
וַיֵּרָא אֱלֹהִים אֶל־יַעֲקֹב עוֹד בְּבֹאוֹ מִפַּדַּן אֲרָם וַיְבָרֶךְ אֹתוֹ: ט
וַיֹּאמֶר־לוֹ אֱלֹהִים שִׁמְךָ יַעֲקֹב לֹא־יִקָּרֵא שִׁמְךָ עוֹד יַעֲקֹב כִּי י
אִם־יִשְׂרָאֵל יִהְיֶה שְׁמֶךָ וַיִּקְרָא אֶת־שְׁמוֹ יִשְׂרָאֵל: וַיֹּאמֶר לוֹ יא
אֱלֹהִים אֲנִי אֵל שַׁדַּי פְּרֵה וּרְבֵה גּוֹי וּקְהַל גּוֹיִם יִהְיֶה מִמֶּךָּ וּמְלָכִים
ששי מֵחֲלָצֶיךָ יֵצֵאוּ: וְאֶת־הָאָרֶץ אֲשֶׁר נָתַתִּי לְאַבְרָהָם וּלְיִצְחָק לְךָ יב
אֶתְּנֶנָּה וּלְזַרְעֲךָ אַחֲרֶיךָ אֶתֵּן אֶת־הָאָרֶץ: וַיַּעַל מֵעָלָיו אֱלֹהִים יג

7 came to Luz – that is, Beit El – in the land of Canaan. There
he built an altar and called the place El Beit El,[85] because it
was there that God had revealed Himself to him as he fled his
8 brother. Devora, Rivka's nurse, died and was buried under the
oak outside Beit El. And so it was named Oak of Weeping.
9 After Yaakov had returned from Padan Aram God appeared
10 to him again and blessed him. God said to him, "Your name is
Yaakov; no longer shall you be called Yaakov; Yisrael shall be
11 your name." Thus He named him Yisrael. God said to him: "I
am El Shaddai. Be fertile and multiply. A nation, a community
of nations will come to be from you. Of your loins, kings
12 shall come forth. The land I gave to Avraham and Yitzḥak I
surely give to you; to your descendants after you I will give
13 the land." God went up from him at the place where He had

85 | Literally "God, the House of God."

NEAR EAST

35:14 Libations and pouring oil at a sanctified place

Yaakov sets up a stone pillar here, as he did earlier in Genesis 28:18. On that occasion, he poured oil on top of it. This time, in addition to pouring oil, he offers a libation on the pillar. The term for libation, *nesekh*, is generally used in the Torah for a wine offering poured on an altar. Pouring a libation on a pillar is unusual.

The use of oil and a libation on a pillar is found in an inscription by Sanḥeriv (Assyria, 8th century BCE) upon the building of the royal armory at Nineveh: "A stela with my name inscribed, I set up in it. In the days to come among the kings whose name Ashur and Ishtar shall name for the rule of land and people, when that palace shall have become old and ruined, may some future prince restore its ruins, look upon the stela with my name inscribed (thereon), anoint it with oil, pour out a libation upon it, and return it to its place. (Then) Ashur and Ishtar will hear his prayers" (col. 6, lines 72–80). The implication is that the ceremony will establish a bond between the deity and the person pouring the oil and the libation. This outcome is also implied in the statement of God in Genesis 31:13, "I am the God of Beit El, where you anointed a pillar and made a vow to Me." ▪ ZR

Libation jar with lid, Egyptian alabaster, Fayum Entrance Area, Haraga (Egypt), 19th to 18th century BCE

יד בַּמָּקוֹם אֲשֶׁר־דִּבֶּר אִתּוֹ׃ וַיַּצֵּב יַעֲקֹב מַצֵּבָה בַּמָּקוֹם אֲשֶׁר־דִּבֶּר
טו אִתּוֹ מַצֶּבֶת אָבֶן וַיַּסֵּךְ עָלֶיהָ נֶסֶךְ וַיִּצֹק עָלֶיהָ שָׁמֶן׃ וַיִּקְרָא יַעֲקֹב
טז אֶת־שֵׁם הַמָּקוֹם אֲשֶׁר דִּבֶּר אִתּוֹ שָׁם אֱלֹהִים בֵּית־אֵל׃ וַיִּסְעוּ
מִבֵּית אֵל וַיְהִי־עוֹד כִּבְרַת־הָאָרֶץ לָבוֹא אֶפְרָתָה וַתֵּלֶד רָחֵל
יז וַתְּקַשׁ בְּלִדְתָּהּ׃ וַיְהִי בְהַקְשֹׁתָהּ בְּלִדְתָּהּ וַתֹּאמֶר לָהּ הַמְיַלֶּדֶת
יח אַל־תִּירְאִי כִּי־גַם־זֶה לָךְ בֵּן׃ וַיְהִי בְּצֵאת נַפְשָׁהּ כִּי מֵתָה וַתִּקְרָא
יט שְׁמוֹ בֶּן־אוֹנִי וְאָבִיו קָרָא־לוֹ בִנְיָמִין׃ וַתָּמָת רָחֵל וַתִּקָּבֵר בְּדֶרֶךְ

spoken with him. Yaakov set up a stone pillar at the place 14
where God had talked with him, and on it he offered a libation
and poured oil. And Yaakov named the place where God had 15
spoken to him Beit El.[86] From Beit El they moved on. While 16
they were still some distance from Efrat, Raḥel began to give
birth; her labor pains were intense. When her labor was at 17
its worst, the midwife said to her, "Don't be afraid. You have
another son." But she was dying. With her last breath, she 18
named him Ben Oni;[87] but his father called him Binyamin.[88]
So Raḥel died and was buried on the road to Efrat – that is, 19

86 | Meaning "House of God."

87 | Meaning "son of my sorrow," but it may also denote "son of my strength."

88 | Meaning "son of the right side." The right side signifies strength.

ARCHAEOLOGY

35:16–20 Memorializing the dead

Raḥel is buried on the road, away from the family tomb. Yaakov erects a pillar (*matzeva*) on top of her burial place, presumably to mark the site. The Tanakh mentions the use of pillars and other memorial objects as a means of caring for the dead; for example, Avshalom erected a memorial pillar (*matzevet*) so that his name would be remembered after he died (II Sam. 18:18), and Devora, Rivka's nurse, was buried under an oak tree (Gen. 35:8). Other aspects of caring for the deceased included the invocation of their name (II Sam. 18:18; Is. 56:5; Ruth 4:10), protection or repatriation of human remains (Gen. 49:29–32, 50:12–14; Josh. 24:32), and maintenance of the burial site (Neh. 2:3–5).

Until tombstones became popular in the Greco-Roman period, other means of marking graves were used in the ancient Near East, such as *matzevot* (plural of *matzeva*), and natural markers. In the Ugaritic *Tale of Aqhat* (ca. 1350 BCE), the son of the deceased king is tasked with setting up a stele so that the clan (i.e., the king) would be remembered (CAT 1.17). Other commemorative stelae, or *matzevot*, have been found in connection to Middle Bronze Age burials at Ḥatzor and Megiddo. Sometimes architectural features, such as a threshold, a plastered floor, or a circle of stones would function as burial markers, primarily in connection with Middle Bronze Age infant burials under house floors. ▪ KG

Decorated stele, holy of holies of the Orthostat Temple, Ḥatzor, 15th to 13th century BCE

GEOGRAPHY

35:20 Raḥel's grave

There are two main candidates for the site of Raḥel's grave. The traditional site is Kubbet Raḥil (Arabic for "Raḥel's tomb"), located at the edge of modern-day Beit Leḥem. The tradition of identifying this as the location of Raḥel's grave goes back to at least the 4th century CE, as it is mentioned by both Eusebius and Jerome. However, no remains found at the tomb site date earlier than the Roman period.

Another possibility is the site known as "Qubur Bani Israil" – Arabic for "the tomb of the sons of Israel" – which is located 4 kilometers (2.5 miles) east of biblical Rama. Archaeologically, it comprises a complex of five megalithic structures – probably tombs – that likely date to the Middle Bronze Age based on similarities with structures from this period and the existence of Middle Bronze Age occupation at nearby sites (e.g., Ḥizme/biblical Azmavet). The central and largest megalithic tomb was known as Qubur Um Bani Um Israil, which is Arabic for "the tomb of the mother of the sons of Israel." Upon discovering this site in the late 19th century, many scholars began to identify it with Raḥel's tomb.

The biblical record is unclear about the issue. Verse 16 states that Raḥel died giving birth to Binyamin while on the way from Beit El to Efrat/Beit Leḥem. Some commentators place the grave at the point of departure, closer to Beit El in the north, while others place it near the destination, fitting the traditional site near Efrat/Beit Leḥem.

Noted biblical historian Aaron Demsky has delineated a number of textual and linguistic arguments for the location of Raḥel's grave in the territory of Binyamin. I Samuel 10:2 reports that Raḥel's grave was "on the border of Binyamin." Also, the prophet Yirmeyahu poetically portrays "Raḥel weeping for her children" in Rama (Jer. 31:14), who had been exiled after the Assyrian destruction of the Kingdom of Israel. The exiles would have been traveling north toward the road to Assyria, passing Beit El, and not south passing by Efrat/Beit Leḥem. Furthermore, locating Binyamin's birth near Beit El would connect him to the land his tribe would later possess (Josh. 18:21–28), rather than near Beit Leḥem, in the tribal portion of Yehuda.

Linguistically, among the traditional commentators, there is a difference of opinion about the meaning of the words *kivrat haaretz* in verse 16. The grammarian Menaḥem ben Saruq as well as Ibn Ezra, Targum Yerushalmi, and Rashbam interpret it as denoting a long distance. However, Rashi and many other traditional commentators state the opposite, based on the use of the term in II Kings 5:19.

According to Assyriologist Benno Landsberger, *kivrat haaretz* is cognate with the Akkadian *kima beru*, which reflects a distance, either of astronomy, where it is large, or when qualified, as in *ber qaqqari*, equivalent to "a *beru* of land," where it is short – this is exactly the phrase used in the Torah.

But what is it a short distance from? In the Tanakh and in general, roads in the land of Israel are named after their destination. Verse 20 states that "Raḥel died and was buried on the road to [*derekh*] Efrat." If *kivrat haaretz* in verse 16 describes a short distance, then the verses can be interpreted to indicate a location close to the departure point near Beit El on the road to Efrat. Some researchers propose that there was another town called Efrat in the territory of Binyamin, near Naḥal Prat (Efrat?). In the book of Ruth, Beit Leḥem is usually qualified as "Beit Leḥem Yehuda" to distinguish it from another Beit Leḥem in Binyamin (Ezra 2:21; Neh. 7:26). Others read *derekh Efrat* as indicating a location close to the Efrat in Yehuda, associating it with the road's destination.

Thus, the two potential locations for the grave are based on different readings of this verse. Whether the northern site of Qubur Bani Israil is actually the grave of Raḥel or an unidentified site nearby, most evidence suggests a site in the tribal territory of Binyamin. Alternatively, reading the verses such that the grave is a short distance from Efrat would put the grave at modern-day Raḥel's grave, where it has been commemorated since Byzantine times. ▪ ZR, DAA

↗ Qubur Bani Israil, aerial view from the southeast

כ אֶפְרָתָה הִוא בֵּית לָחֶם: וַיַּצֵּב יַעֲקֹב מַצֵּבָה עַל־קְבֻרָתָהּ הִוא
כא מַצֶּבֶת קְבֻרַת־רָחֵל עַד־הַיּוֹם: וַיִּסַּע יִשְׂרָאֵל וַיֵּט אָהֳלֹה מֵהָלְאָה
כב לְמִגְדַּל־עֵדֶר: וַיְהִי בִּשְׁכֹּן יִשְׂרָאֵל בָּאָרֶץ הַהִוא וַיֵּלֶךְ רְאוּבֵן
וַיִּשְׁכַּב אֶת־בִּלְהָה פִּילֶגֶשׁ אָבִיו וַיִּשְׁמַע יִשְׂרָאֵל
כג וַיִּהְיוּ בְנֵי־יַעֲקֹב שְׁנֵים עָשָׂר: בְּנֵי לֵאָה בְּכוֹר יַעֲקֹב רְאוּבֵן וְשִׁמְעוֹן
כד כה וְלֵוִי וִיהוּדָה וְיִשָּׂשכָר וּזְבוּלֻן: בְּנֵי רָחֵל יוֹסֵף וּבִנְיָמִן: וּבְנֵי בִלְהָה
כו שִׁפְחַת רָחֵל דָּן וְנַפְתָּלִי: וּבְנֵי זִלְפָּה שִׁפְחַת לֵאָה גָּד וְאָשֵׁר אֵלֶּה
כז בְּנֵי יַעֲקֹב אֲשֶׁר יֻלַּד־לוֹ בְּפַדַּן אֲרָם: וַיָּבֹא יַעֲקֹב אֶל־יִצְחָק
אָבִיו מַמְרֵא קִרְיַת הָאַרְבַּע הִוא חֶבְרוֹן אֲשֶׁר־גָּר־שָׁם אַבְרָהָם

20 Beit Leḥem. Yaakov erected a pillar at her grave. To this day,
21 that pillar marks Raḥel's grave. Yisrael traveled on, pitching
22 his tent beyond Migdal Eder. While Yisrael was staying in
that region, Reuven went and lay with his father's concubine
Bilha. And Yisrael heard –[89]
23 Yaakov had twelve sons. The sons of Leah were Reuven,
Yaakov's firstborn, Shimon, Levi, Yehuda, Yissakhar, and
24 25 Zevulun. The sons of Raḥel were Yosef and Binyamin. The
26 sons of Raḥel's maid Bilha were Dan and Naftali. The sons of
Leah's maid Zilpa were Gad and Asher. These were the sons of
27 Yaakov, born to him in Padan Aram. Yaakov came home to his
father Yitzḥak at Mamre, near Kiryat Arba – that is, Ḥevron –

89 | A break appears here in the middle of the verse, implying that the ensuing passage bears a connection to the present one.

Batsheva asks Shlomo whether Adoniya can take Avishag. Shlomo becomes enraged. In the background, Adoniya is stabbed, engraving, 1579

NEAR EAST

35:22 Reuven's adultery with Bilha

Reuven's adultery with Bilha may be seen a deliberate act of rebellion against his father's authority. The Tanakh records several cases of taking a father's or king's concubine in order to demonstrate and induce legitimate succession, since the care of the concubines passed to the next head of the clan or ruler when the previous leader died. To do so while the leader was still alive was an act of subversion and disrespect, such as when Avshalom followed Aḥitofel's advice and "bedded his father's concubines in full view of all Israel" (II Sam. 16:22). Similarly, Ish Boshet suspected Avner of disloyalty when the latter slept with one of Sha'ul's concubines (II Sam. 3:7–8), and Shlomo interpreted Adoniya's request for David's concubine, Avishag, as equivalent to rebellion (I Kings 2:13–25).

The great significance of having intercourse with the king's wife is demonstrated by a Ugaritic text (RS 16.144) which states, "Thus says Arihalbu, king of Ugarit: Whoever, after my death, takes my wife, Kubaba, daughter of Takan, from my brother, may Baal crush him; may he not make great (his) throne, May he not dwell in a (royal) house."

In the case of Reuven, there is an additional element: his action lowers the status of Bilha herself. It is significant that this episode takes place immediately after the text reports on Raḥel's death. By sleeping with Bilha, Reuven ensures that she will not be able to take over Raḥel's position, nor be a rival to his mother, Leah. Since Reuven slept with her, Bilha is off-limits to Yaakov, just as David avoids intimate relations with his concubines after they are defiled by his son Avshalom (II Sam. 20:3). Note that earlier Reuven was involved in the mandrakes episode, in which the mandrakes were used to advance Leah's conjugal rights (Gen. 30:14–16). ▪ ZR

GEOGRAPHY

36:11 Teiman

As elsewhere (for example, in the Table of Nations in Gen. 10), many of the names of Esav's descendants in this chapter became eponymous origins of names of towns.

Similarly, Teiman is unrelated to the modern Hebrew name for Yemen. Rather, it is used as a synonym for Edom as a whole in a number of places in Tanakh (such as Amos 1:12 and Ob. 1:9) indicating that it must have been a place of great importance. Eusebius mentions a town called Theman in the vicinity of Petra where Roman troops were stationed. Although the exact location remains unknown, some scholars identify it with Tawilan, just north of Petra in the hills of contemporary southern Jordan, where a significant amount of early Iron Age Edomite pottery has been found. Others identify it with Shoubak, northeast of Petra, settled by the Edomites in the 2nd millennium BCE. ▪ ZR

Warrior, Edomite pottery, Ḥatzeva, 7th to 6th century BCE

וְיִצְחָק: וַיִּהְיוּ יְמֵי יִצְחָק מְאַת שָׁנָה וּשְׁמֹנִים שָׁנָה: וַיִּגְוַע יִצְחָק כח כט
וַיָּמָת וַיֵּאָסֶף אֶל־עַמָּיו זָקֵן וּשְׂבַע יָמִים וַיִּקְבְּרוּ אֹתוֹ עֵשָׂו וְיַעֲקֹב
בָּנָיו:
לו א ב וְאֵלֶּה תֹּלְדוֹת עֵשָׂו הוּא אֱדוֹם: עֵשָׂו לָקַח אֶת־נָשָׁיו מִבְּנוֹת
כְּנָעַן אֶת־עָדָה בַּת־אֵילוֹן הַחִתִּי וְאֶת־אָהֳלִיבָמָה בַּת־עֲנָה בַּת־
צִבְעוֹן הַחִוִּי: וְאֶת־בָּשְׂמַת בַּת־יִשְׁמָעֵאל אֲחוֹת נְבָיוֹת: וַתֵּלֶד ג ד
עָדָה לְעֵשָׂו אֶת־אֱלִיפָז וּבָשְׂמַת יָלְדָה אֶת־רְעוּאֵל: וְאָהֳלִיבָמָה ה
יָלְדָה אֶת־יעיש וְאֶת־יַעְלָם וְאֶת־קֹרַח אֵלֶּה בְּנֵי עֵשָׂו אֲשֶׁר יְעוּשׁ
יֻלְּדוּ־לוֹ בְּאֶרֶץ כְּנָעַן: וַיִּקַּח עֵשָׂו אֶת־נָשָׁיו וְאֶת־בָּנָיו וְאֶת־בְּנֹתָיו ו
וְאֶת־כָּל־נַפְשׁוֹת בֵּיתוֹ וְאֶת־מִקְנֵהוּ וְאֶת־כָּל־בְּהֶמְתּוֹ וְאֵת
כָּל־קִנְיָנוֹ אֲשֶׁר רָכַשׁ בְּאֶרֶץ כְּנָעַן וַיֵּלֶךְ אֶל־אֶרֶץ מִפְּנֵי יַעֲקֹב
אָחִיו: כִּי־הָיָה רְכוּשָׁם רָב מִשֶּׁבֶת יַחְדָּו וְלֹא יָכְלָה אֶרֶץ מְגוּרֵיהֶם ז
לָשֵׂאת אֹתָם מִפְּנֵי מִקְנֵיהֶם: וַיֵּשֶׁב עֵשָׂו בְּהַר שֵׂעִיר עֵשָׂו הוּא ח
אֱדוֹם: וְאֵלֶּה תֹּלְדוֹת עֵשָׂו אֲבִי אֱדוֹם בְּהַר שֵׂעִיר: אֵלֶּה שְׁמוֹת ט י
בְּנֵי־עֵשָׂו אֱלִיפַז בֶּן־עָדָה אֵשֶׁת עֵשָׂו רְעוּאֵל בֶּן־בָּשְׂמַת אֵשֶׁת
עֵשָׂו: וַיִּהְיוּ בְּנֵי אֱלִיפָז תֵּימָן אוֹמָר צְפוֹ וְגַעְתָּם וּקְנַז: וְתִמְנַע יא יב •

28 where Avraham and Yitzḥak had lived as strangers. Yitzḥak
29 lived one hundred and eighty years. Then he breathed his last,
and died, and was gathered to his people, aged, satisfied with
his years. His sons Esav and Yaakov buried him.
36 1 2 These are the descendants of Esav – that is, Edom. Esav
took wives from among the daughters of Canaan: Ada
daughter of Eilon the Hittite, and Oholivama daughter of
3 Ana, granddaughter of Tzivon the Hivite – and also Basmat,
4 daughter of Yishmael and sister of Nevayot. Ada bore Elifaz
5 to Esav, and Basmat bore Reuel. Oholivama bore Yeush,
Yalam, and Koraḥ. These were the sons of Esav, born in the
6 land of Canaan. Esav took his wives, sons and daughters,
and all the members of his household, together with his
livestock, his other animals, and all the possessions he had
acquired in Canaan, and he moved to another region, away
7 from his brother Yaakov, for their possessions were too great
for them to remain together; because of all their livestock, the
land where they were living could not support them both.
8 So Esav settled in the hill country of Se'ir. Esav is Edom.
9 These, then, are the descendants of Esav, ancestor of the
10 Edomites, in the hill country of Se'ir. These are the names of
Esav's sons: Elifaz, son of Esav's wife Ada, and Reuel, son of
• 11 Esav's wife Basmat. The sons of Elifaz were Teiman, Omar,
12 Tzefo, Gatam, and Kenaz. Timna, a concubine of Esav's son

הָיְתָה פִילֶגֶשׁ לֶאֱלִיפַז בֶּן־עֵשָׂו וַתֵּלֶד לֶאֱלִיפַז אֶת־עֲמָלֵק אֵלֶּה
יג בְּנֵי עָדָה אֵשֶׁת עֵשָׂו׃ וְאֵלֶּה בְּנֵי רְעוּאֵל נַחַת וָזֶרַח שַׁמָּה וּמִזָּה
יד אֵלֶּה הָיוּ בְּנֵי בָשְׂמַת אֵשֶׁת עֵשָׂו׃ וְאֵלֶּה הָיוּ בְּנֵי אָהֳלִיבָמָה בַת־
עֲנָה בַּת־צִבְעוֹן אֵשֶׁת עֵשָׂו וַתֵּלֶד לְעֵשָׂו אֶת־יעיש וְאֶת־יַעְלָם יְעוּשׁ
טו וְאֶת־קֹרַח׃ אֵלֶּה אַלּוּפֵי בְנֵי־עֵשָׂו בְּנֵי אֱלִיפַז בְּכוֹר עֵשָׂו אַלּוּף
טז תֵּימָן אַלּוּף אוֹמָר אַלּוּף צְפוֹ אַלּוּף קְנַז׃ אַלּוּף־קֹרַח אַלּוּף גַּעְתָּם
אַלּוּף עֲמָלֵק אֵלֶּה אַלּוּפֵי אֱלִיפַז בְּאֶרֶץ אֱדוֹם אֵלֶּה בְּנֵי עָדָה׃
יז וְאֵלֶּה בְּנֵי רְעוּאֵל בֶּן־עֵשָׂו אַלּוּף נַחַת אַלּוּף זֶרַח אַלּוּף שַׁמָּה
אַלּוּף מִזָּה אֵלֶּה אַלּוּפֵי רְעוּאֵל בְּאֶרֶץ אֱדוֹם אֵלֶּה בְּנֵי בָשְׂמַת
יח אֵשֶׁת עֵשָׂו׃ וְאֵלֶּה בְּנֵי אָהֳלִיבָמָה אֵשֶׁת עֵשָׂו אַלּוּף יְעוּשׁ אַלּוּף
יַעְלָם אַלּוּף קֹרַח אֵלֶּה אַלּוּפֵי אָהֳלִיבָמָה בַּת־עֲנָה אֵשֶׁת עֵשָׂו׃
יט כ אֵלֶּה בְנֵי־עֵשָׂו וְאֵלֶּה אַלּוּפֵיהֶם הוּא אֱדוֹם׃ אֵלֶּה שביעי
כא בְנֵי־שֵׂעִיר הַחֹרִי יֹשְׁבֵי הָאָרֶץ לוֹטָן וְשׁוֹבָל וְצִבְעוֹן וַעֲנָה׃ וְדִשׁוֹן
כב וְאֵצֶר וְדִישָׁן אֵלֶּה אַלּוּפֵי הַחֹרִי בְּנֵי שֵׂעִיר בְּאֶרֶץ אֱדוֹם׃ וַיִּהְיוּ
כג בְנֵי־לוֹטָן חֹרִי וְהֵימָם וַאֲחוֹת לוֹטָן תִּמְנָע׃ וְאֵלֶּה בְּנֵי שׁוֹבָל
כד עַלְוָן וּמָנַחַת וְעֵיבָל שְׁפוֹ וְאוֹנָם׃ וְאֵלֶּה בְנֵי־צִבְעוֹן וְאַיָּה וַעֲנָה
הוּא עֲנָה אֲשֶׁר מָצָא אֶת־הַיֵּמִם בַּמִּדְבָּר בִּרְעֹתוֹ אֶת־הַחֲמֹרִים
כה כו לְצִבְעוֹן אָבִיו׃ וְאֵלֶּה בְנֵי־עֲנָה דִּשֹׁן וְאָהֳלִיבָמָה בַּת־עֲנָה׃ וְאֵלֶּה
כז בְּנֵי דִישָׁן חֶמְדָּן וְאֶשְׁבָּן וְיִתְרָן וּכְרָן׃ אֵלֶּה בְּנֵי־אֵצֶר בִּלְהָן וְזַעֲוָן
כח כט וַעֲקָן׃ אֵלֶּה בְנֵי־דִישָׁן עוּץ וַאֲרָן׃ אֵלֶּה אַלּוּפֵי הַחֹרִי אַלּוּף לוֹטָן
ל אַלּוּף שׁוֹבָל אַלּוּף צִבְעוֹן אַלּוּף עֲנָה׃ אַלּוּף דִּשֹׁן אַלּוּף אֵצֶר אַלּוּף
דִּישָׁן אֵלֶּה אַלּוּפֵי הַחֹרִי לְאַלֻּפֵיהֶם בְּאֶרֶץ שֵׂעִיר׃

Elifaz, bore him Amalek. These
are the descendants of Esav's
wife Ada. The sons of Reuel were 13
Naḥat, Zeraḥ, Shama, and Miza.
These were the descendants of
Esav's wife Basmat. The sons of 14
Oholivama, daughter of Ana and
granddaughter of Tzivon, Esav's wife, whom she bore to Esav, were Yeush, Yalam, and Koraḥ. These 15
were the tribal chiefs among Esav's descendants. The sons of Elifaz, Esav's firstborn, were the chiefs
Teiman, Omar, Tzefo, Kenaz, Koraḥ, Gatam, and Amalek. These were the chiefs descended from Elifaz 16
in Edom; they were grandsons of Ada. The sons of Esav's son Reuel were the chiefs Naḥat, Zeraḥ, Shama, 17
and Miza. These were the chiefs descended from Reuel in Edom; they were grandsons of Esav's wife
Basmat. The sons of Esav's wife Oholivama were the chiefs Yeush, Yalam, and Koraḥ. These were the 18
chiefs descended from Esav's wife Oholivama daughter of Ana. These were the sons of Esav – that is, 19
Edom – and these were their chiefs. These are the sons of Se'ir the Horite who were settled in 20
the land: Lotan, Shoval, Tzivon, Ana, Dishon, Etzer, and Dishan. These were the chiefs of the Horites, 21
descendants of Se'ir in the land of Edom. Lotan's sons were Ḥori and Heimam. Timna was Lotan's sister. 22
Shoval's sons were Alvan, Manaḥat, Eival, Shefo, and Onam. Tzivon's sons were Aya and Ana. This is the 23 24
Ana who discovered hot springs in the desert while pasturing the donkeys of his father Tzivon. Ana's 25
children were Dishon and Oholivama daughter of Ana. Dishon's sons were Ḥemdan, Eshban, Yitran, 26
and Keran. Etzer's sons were Bilhan, Zaavan, and Akan. Dishan's sons were Utz and Aran. These were 27 28 29
the tribal chiefs of the Horites: chiefs Lotan, Shoval, Tzivon, Ana, Dishon, Etzer, and Dishan. These were 30
the Horite chiefs by their divisions in the land of Se'ir.

לא וְאֵ֙לֶּה֙ הַמְּלָכִ֔ים אֲשֶׁ֥ר מָלְכ֖וּ בְּאֶ֣רֶץ אֱד֑וֹם לִפְנֵ֥י מְלָךְ־מֶ֖לֶךְ לִבְנֵ֥י
לב לג יִשְׂרָאֵֽל׃ וַיִּמְלֹ֣ךְ בֶּֽאֱד֔וֹם בֶּ֖לַע בֶּן־בְּע֑וֹר וְשֵׁ֥ם עִיר֖וֹ דִּנְהָֽבָה׃ וַיָּ֖מָת

31 These were the kings who reigned in Edom before any king
32 reigned over the Israelites. Bela son of Beor became king in
33 Edom. His city was named Dinhava. When Bela died, Yovav

NEAR EAST

36:31 Kings of Edom

Genesis 36:31–39 lists seven kings who "reigned in the land of Edom before any king reigned over the Israelites." Modern scholarship usually identifies ancient kingdoms with sedentary populations who engaged in agriculture, possessing a level of social organization that allowed massive fortifications and monumental structures to be built. By contrast, the Hebrew term for king, *melekh* (and its equivalents in other ancient languages, such as the Akkadian *sharru*), can refer to any ruler of a distinct human population, even in a sparsely populated locale. Kings and queens of Arabs (*aribi*) – nomads of the Syro-Arabian desert – are mentioned in Assyrian royal inscriptions of the 8th to 7th century BCE, and the Cyrus (Koresh) Cylinder speaks of tribute brought by "all the kings of the West Land living in tents."

Edomite goddess, Horvat Qitmit (Desert of Yehuda), 7th to 6th century BCE

With regard to Edom, archaeological evidence from the copper-production sites in the Arava Valley suggests that the local society reached a level of social complexity identified with a polity while retaining a nomadic way of life – making many of their activities archaeologically invisible (see "Israel and Edom" on pages 170–171).

The list here of the kings who ruled Edom anticipates the institution of kingship in Israel, which would emerge around 1000 BCE, and suggests that the Edomite kingship rose earlier. While the findings from the Arava Valley mining area do not suffice to support this chronological precedence, it must be noted that each Edomite king in the list is linked to a different town – probably no more than a nomadic encampment at the time. ▪ YB

GEOGRAPHY

36:33–37 Botzra, Hadad, Midyan, Masreka, Reḥovot HaNahar

Botzra (v. 33) is identified with Busaira, a town located in modern-day Jordan, south of the Dead Sea. It was an important Edomite city, mentioned in a number of places in Tanakh as representative of Edom as a whole (for example, Is. 34:6 and Jer. 49:13). Edomite remains have been found in the area dating as far back as the 7th century BCE.

Hadad (v. 35) is the name of the Mesopotamian/Canaanite storm god. In the Ugaritic *Baal Cycle* stories (ca. 1500–1300 BCE), Hadad is identified with Baal, the chief god of the Canaanite pantheon. Therefore, this king's name may indicate that Baal was worshipped in his locale or by his family.

Scholars understand the Midianites not as a specific group, but rather as an amorphous confederation of nomadic tribes who inhabited a large area. Various Tanakh passages place the Midianites in different locations: Avraham sends the sons of his concubines, including Midyan, eastward from the land of Israel (Gen. 25:2, 6), while Moshe took the flocks of Yitro, priest of Midyan, to *Ḥorev* (Mount Sinai, Ex. 3:1), placing Midianites in or near the Sinai Peninsula. I Kings 11:18 implies that the Midianites occupied an area between Edom and Paran, on the way to Egypt. Midyan is described here (v. 35) as close to Moav. Together, these texts portray the Midianites occupying a wide geographical range, mainly in the relatively unsettled area on the east shore of the Gulf of Aqaba on the Red Sea.

The name Masreka seems to be connected to *sorek* meaning "special vine," indicating an area where grapes are grown. It has been identified with Jebel el-Mushrak in Jordan, located between the Dead Sea and the Gulf of Aqaba.

Reḥovot HaNahar means a "broad place on the river." In Tanakh, "the river" normally means the Euphrates, but that would be too far from Edom. Here, it may refer to Wadi al-Hasa (see "Zered Stream" on page 132 of the Numbers volume of this series) in western Jordan, a 40-kilometer (approximately 25-mile) river that flows all year and forms the natural border between Edom and Moav. The wadi area is used intensely by farmers. ▪ ZR

Colossal statue of the god Hadad with Aramaic inscription, Bit-Gabarri (Turkey), 8th century BCE

לד בֶּלַע וַיִּמְלֹךְ תַּחְתָּיו יוֹבָב בֶּן־זֶרַח מִבָּצְרָה׃ וַיָּמָת יוֹבָב וַיִּמְלֹךְ
לה תַּחְתָּיו חֻשָׁם מֵאֶרֶץ הַתֵּימָנִי׃ וַיָּמָת חֻשָׁם וַיִּמְלֹךְ תַּחְתָּיו הֲדַד
לו בֶּן־בְּדַד הַמַּכֶּה אֶת־מִדְיָן בִּשְׂדֵה מוֹאָב וְשֵׁם עִירוֹ עֲוִית׃ וַיָּמָת
לז הֲדָד וַיִּמְלֹךְ תַּחְתָּיו שַׂמְלָה מִמַּשְׂרֵקָה׃ וַיָּמָת שַׂמְלָה וַיִּמְלֹךְ
לח תַּחְתָּיו שָׁאוּל מֵרְחֹבוֹת הַנָּהָר׃ וַיָּמָת שָׁאוּל וַיִּמְלֹךְ תַּחְתָּיו בַּעַל
לט חָנָן בֶּן־עַכְבּוֹר׃ וַיָּמָת בַּעַל חָנָן בֶּן־עַכְבּוֹר וַיִּמְלֹךְ תַּחְתָּיו הֲדַר
וְשֵׁם עִירוֹ פָּעוּ וְשֵׁם אִשְׁתּוֹ מְהֵיטַבְאֵל בַּת־מַטְרֵד בַּת מֵי זָהָב׃
מפטיר מ וְאֵלֶּה שְׁמוֹת אַלּוּפֵי עֵשָׂו לְמִשְׁפְּחֹתָם לִמְקֹמֹתָם בִּשְׁמֹתָם אַלּוּף
מא תִּמְנָע אַלּוּף עַלְוָה אַלּוּף יְתֵת׃ אַלּוּף אָהֳלִיבָמָה אַלּוּף אֵלָה
מב מג אַלּוּף פִּינֹן׃ אַלּוּף קְנַז אַלּוּף תֵּימָן אַלּוּף מִבְצָר׃ אַלּוּף מַגְדִּיאֵל

son of Zeraḥ from Botzra succeeded him as king. When Yovav 34
died, Ḥusham from the land of the Temanites succeeded
him as king. When Ḥusham died, Hadad son of Bedad, 35
who defeated Midyan in the country of Moav, succeeded
him as king. His city was named Avit. When Hadad died, 36
Samla from Masreka succeeded him as king. When Samla 37
died, Sha'ul from Reḥovot HaNahar succeeded him as king.
When Sha'ul died, Baal Ḥanan son of Akhbor succeeded 38
him as king. When Baal Ḥanan son of Akhbor died, Hadar 39
succeeded him as king. His city was named Pa'u, and his wife's
name was Meheitavel, daughter of Matred, daughter of Mei
Zahav. These were the chiefs descended from Esav, by their 40
clans, localities, and names: the chiefs Timna, Alva, Yetet, 41
Oholivama, Ela, Pinon, Kenaz, Teiman, Mivtzar, Magdiel, 42 43

GEOGRAPHY

36:41 Ela and Pinon

Ela and Pinon mentioned here are eponymous proper names for specific locations. Ela is probably Eilat, mentioned in Deuteronomy 2:8 as a place in the southern boundary of Edom. It is located in modern-day Jordan near Aqaba, opposite the contemporary Israeli city of Eilat. Its location at the northern tip of the Gulf of Eilat made it significant for international trade. The restoration of Eilat was considered a significant achievement of the Judahite monarchy in II Kings 14:22.

Pinon is identified with Punon, one of the stations of the Israelites on their way through the wilderness (Num. 33:42–43). Its name is preserved in the area of Feinan, one of the larger copper mining sites in the ancient Near East. ▪ ZR

Khirbet en-Nahas (Feinan) in the Wadi Feinan region

NEAR EAST

37:2 Bad reports

The noun *dibbatam* in the expression translated here as "bad reports of them," in plural, is actually in the singular in Hebrew, literally, "bad report of them." The unusual syntax precisely matches the usage in Numbers 14:37, where the returning spies bring back adverse *dibba* from Canaan. The word occurs twice more in that story, as well as five other times in the Tanakh – all in the singular.

The related Akkadian noun *dibbu* – derived from and frequently used with the verb *dababu* – sheds some light on the usage here. The basic meaning of the word is "speech," but it is frequently used in contexts of rumor and complaint, such as *bel dababi*, which refers to a litigant in court. It is not surprising that all the occurrences of this word in the Tanakh have a negative flavor, sometimes noted explicitly and sometimes apparent just from context. ▪ MC

אַלּוּף עִירָם אֵלֶּה ׀ אַלּוּפֵי אֱדוֹם לְמֹשְׁבֹתָם בְּאֶרֶץ אֲחֻזָּתָם הוּא
עֵשָׂו אֲבִי אֱדוֹם׃
וישב וַיֵּשֶׁב יַעֲקֹב בְּאֶרֶץ מְגוּרֵי אָבִיו בְּאֶרֶץ כְּנָעַן׃ אֵלֶּה ׀ תֹּלְדוֹת א ב • לז
יַעֲקֹב יוֹסֵף בֶּן־שְׁבַע־עֶשְׂרֵה שָׁנָה הָיָה רֹעֶה אֶת־אֶחָיו בַּצֹּאן
וְהוּא נַעַר אֶת־בְּנֵי בִלְהָה וְאֶת־בְּנֵי זִלְפָּה נְשֵׁי אָבִיו וַיָּבֵא יוֹסֵף
אֶת־דִּבָּתָם רָעָה אֶל־אֲבִיהֶם׃ וְיִשְׂרָאֵל אָהַב אֶת־יוֹסֵף מִכָּל־בָּנָיו ג •

and Iram. These were the chiefs of Edom – of Esav, ancestor of the Edomites – each with their own settlements in the land that they held.
37 1 Yaakov settled where his father had lived as a stranger, in the
• 2 land of Canaan. This is the story of Yaakov. Yosef, seventeen
years old, was shepherding the flock with his brothers, an
assistant to the sons of his father's wives Bilha and Zilpa. And
• 3 Yosef brought his father bad reports of them. Now, Yisrael
loved Yosef more than all his other sons, for he was a child

↗ Joseph relating his dreams to his parents and brothers, Rembrandt, 1633

ד כִּי־בֶן־זְקֻנִים הוּא לוֹ וְעָשָׂה לוֹ כְּתֹנֶת פַּסִּים: וַיִּרְאוּ אֶחָיו כִּי־אֹתוֹ
אָהַב אֲבִיהֶם מִכָּל־אֶחָיו וַיִּשְׂנְאוּ אֹתוֹ וְלֹא יָכְלוּ דַּבְּרוֹ לְשָׁלֹם:
ה ו וַיַּחֲלֹם יוֹסֵף חֲלוֹם וַיַּגֵּד לְאֶחָיו וַיּוֹסִפוּ עוֹד שְׂנֹא אֹתוֹ: וַיֹּאמֶר
ז אֲלֵיהֶם שִׁמְעוּ־נָא הַחֲלוֹם הַזֶּה אֲשֶׁר חָלָמְתִּי: וְהִנֵּה אֲנַחְנוּ
מְאַלְּמִים אֲלֻמִּים בְּתוֹךְ הַשָּׂדֶה וְהִנֵּה קָמָה אֲלֻמָּתִי וְגַם־נִצָּבָה
ח וְהִנֵּה תְסֻבֶּינָה אֲלֻמֹּתֵיכֶם וַתִּשְׁתַּחֲוֶיןָ לַאֲלֻמָּתִי: וַיֹּאמְרוּ לוֹ אֶחָיו
הֲמָלֹךְ תִּמְלֹךְ עָלֵינוּ אִם־מָשׁוֹל תִּמְשֹׁל בָּנוּ וַיּוֹסִפוּ עוֹד שְׂנֹא
ט אֹתוֹ עַל־חֲלֹמֹתָיו וְעַל־דְּבָרָיו: וַיַּחֲלֹם עוֹד חֲלוֹם אַחֵר וַיְסַפֵּר
אֹתוֹ לְאֶחָיו וַיֹּאמֶר הִנֵּה חָלַמְתִּי חֲלוֹם עוֹד וְהִנֵּה הַשֶּׁמֶשׁ וְהַיָּרֵחַ

of his old age; he made him an ornately colored robe. But 4
when his brothers saw that their father loved him more than
any of them, they hated him and could not say a peaceful
word to him. Then Yosef had a dream, and when he told it to 5
his brothers, they hated him still more. "Listen to this dream 6
I had," he said. "We were binding sheaves in the field when 7
my sheaf rose and stood upright and your sheaves gathered
around mine and bowed down to it." His brothers said to him, 8
"Do you mean to be king over us? Do you mean to rule over
us?" Then they hated him even more for his dreams and for
what he said. Then he had another dream and told it to his 9
brothers. "I had another dream," he said. "This time, the sun,

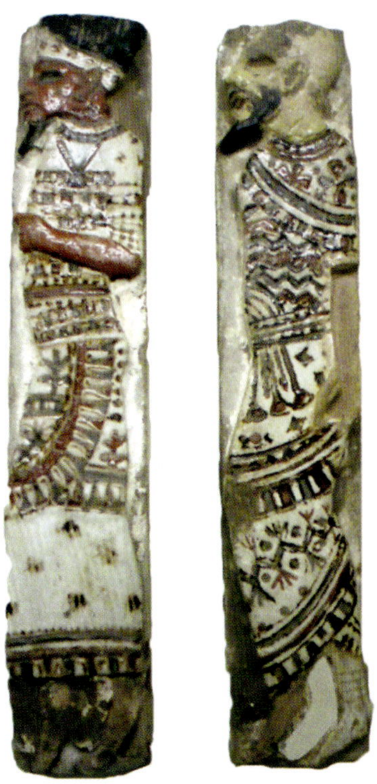

↗ Faience tiles of Philistine and Amorite captives, royal palace adjacent to the Temple of Medinet Habu, reign of Ramesses III, 12th century BCE

NEAR EAST

37:3 Ornately colored robe

Yaakov gives Yosef a *ketonet passim*, translated here as "an ornately colored robe." The only other person in Tanakh who is reported as wearing this kind of garment is David's daughter Tamar in II Samuel 13:18, where we are told that "the virgin daughters of the king wore such robes" (see "The ornate tunic" in the Samuel volume of this series on page 313). The well-known translation of this phrase as "coat of many colors" comes from the Septuagint and the Vulgate.

In Aramaic, *pas* refers to a hand, as in Daniel 5:5. Rabbinic Hebrew uses *pas* like *kaf*, to mean the palm of the hand (e.g., Mishna Megilla 4:8). Therefore, *ketonet passim* may refer to a robe with long sleeves that reach the hand. Similarly, the Septuagint translates the phrase in reference to Tamar as *karpatos*, "reaching the wrist." This kind of garment could be worn by royalty, who did not engage in manual labor and could thus allow their hands to be obstructed by long sleeves. Tile decorations from the palace of Ramesses III (12th century BCE) and Egyptian tomb paintings depict "Asiatics" (i.e., Semites) wearing such wrist-length robes, which, in the illustration here, is also striped (in modern Hebrew, *pas* means "stripe").

The cognate term *lbs psm* has been found in a list of clothing from Ugarit, but its precise meaning there is not obvious from the context. Scholars understand it as related to the Akkadian *pussumu*, meaning "veil" or "gauze," and to *pasamu*, a verb meaning to "conceal," "hide," or "veil"; the Akkadians called the ceremonial robes that were draped over statues of goddesses *pussumu*. Based on this understanding, the Ugaritic term has been translated as a "fine, sleeved robe." ▪ ZR

וְאַחַד עָשָׂר֙ כּוֹכָבִ֔ים מִֽשְׁתַּחֲוִ֖ים לִֽי׃ וַיְסַפֵּ֣ר אֶל־אָבִיו֮ וְאֶל־אֶחָיו֒ י
וַיִּגְעַר־בּ֣וֹ אָבִ֔יו וַיֹּ֣אמֶר ל֔וֹ מָ֛ה הַחֲל֥וֹם הַזֶּ֖ה אֲשֶׁ֣ר חָלָ֑מְתָּ הֲב֣וֹא

10 moon, and eleven stars were bowing down to me." When he
told his father as well as his brothers, his father rebuked him and said, "What kind of dream is this that you have had? Shall we really come, I and your mother and your brothers, to bow

GEOGRAPHY

37:17–25 Dotan and the Ishmaelite caravan

The Dotan Valley (*emek Dotan*) is situated in the northern part of the Shomron highlands, some 23 kilometers (approximately 14 miles) north of Shekhem The depiction of Yaakov's sons shepherding their father's sheep in Dotan fits well with the region's ecology, as many wells and springs are known in this fertile valley and its surroundings. Three key routes pass through the valley, the southernmost of which connects the Yizre'el Valley with the Sharon Plain. It thus makes sense that an Ishmaelite caravan traveling from Gilad toward Egypt would pass by Dotan. The Ishmaelites were Arab traders who made their living by trading and transporting goods – they were experts in crossing large desert territories on camels. The *nekhot* and *lot* (both probably belong to different kinds of resin) and the *tzeri* (perhaps made of the ancient persimmon), mentioned as their cargo, were probably used as medicines for pain relief and healing (see Jer. 51:8).

The ancient site of Dotan is identified with Tel Dotan, located in the southern part of the Dotan Valley. It is situated in a strategic location, serving as the main northern entrance to the Shomron highlands. This fact is supported by the description in II Kings (6:13–14) of the king of Aram coming from the north and laying a siege on the city in his war against the Kingdom of Israel. However, since this is the only other mention of Dotan in the Bible, and Egyptian and Assyrian sources do not mention a place named Dotan, the site probably did not serve as a main administrative center during the Bronze and Iron Ages, and its importance would have been mainly local.

Large-scale archaeological excavations were conducted at Tel Dotan during the 1950s and 1960s, with the earliest remains dated to the Neolithic and Chalcolithic periods. According to the excavation reports, during the Early Bronze Age, the site developed into a fortified city, a common process in Canaan during that time. A later fortified town was dated to the Middle Bronze Age II. Atop the remains of a Late Bronze Age and early Iron Age settlement, large parts of a fortified city from the Iron Age II were exposed. This city was destroyed in the latter part of the 9th century BCE, probably by the Arameans (see also I Kings 22:31–36). The site was later resettled, but it was abandoned once again during the Neo-Assyrian period. ▪ GI

↗ Yosef's journeys in Canaan

יא נָבוֹא אֲנִי וְאִמְּךָ וְאַחֶיךָ לְהִשְׁתַּחֲוֺת לְךָ אָרְצָה: וַיְקַנְאוּ־בוֹ אֶחָיו
יב וְאָבִיו שָׁמַר אֶת־הַדָּבָר: וַיֵּלְכוּ אֶחָיו לִרְעוֹת אֶת־צֹאן אֲבִיהֶם שני
יג בִּשְׁכֶם: וַיֹּאמֶר יִשְׂרָאֵל אֶל־יוֹסֵף הֲלוֹא אַחֶיךָ רֹעִים בִּשְׁכֶם
יד לְכָה וְאֶשְׁלָחֲךָ אֲלֵיהֶם וַיֹּאמֶר לוֹ הִנֵּנִי: וַיֹּאמֶר לוֹ לֶךְ־נָא רְאֵה
אֶת־שְׁלוֹם אַחֶיךָ וְאֶת־שְׁלוֹם הַצֹּאן וַהֲשִׁבֵנִי דָּבָר וַיִּשְׁלָחֵהוּ
טו מֵעֵמֶק חֶבְרוֹן וַיָּבֹא שְׁכֶמָה: וַיִּמְצָאֵהוּ אִישׁ וְהִנֵּה תֹעֶה בַּשָּׂדֶה
טז וַיִּשְׁאָלֵהוּ הָאִישׁ לֵאמֹר מַה־תְּבַקֵּשׁ: וַיֹּאמֶר אֶת־אַחַי אָנֹכִי
יז מְבַקֵּשׁ הַגִּידָה־נָּא לִי אֵיפֹה הֵם רֹעִים: וַיֹּאמֶר הָאִישׁ נָסְעוּ מִזֶּה
כִּי שָׁמַעְתִּי אֹמְרִים נֵלְכָה דֹּתָיְנָה וַיֵּלֶךְ יוֹסֵף אַחַר אֶחָיו וַיִּמְצָאֵם
יח בְּדֹתָן: וַיִּרְאוּ אֹתוֹ מֵרָחֹק וּבְטֶרֶם יִקְרַב אֲלֵיהֶם וַיִּתְנַכְּלוּ אֹתוֹ
יט לַהֲמִיתוֹ: וַיֹּאמְרוּ אִישׁ אֶל־אָחִיו הִנֵּה בַּעַל הַחֲלֹמוֹת הַלָּזֶה
כ בָּא: וְעַתָּה | לְכוּ וְנַהַרְגֵהוּ וְנַשְׁלִכֵהוּ בְּאַחַד הַבֹּרוֹת וְאָמַרְנוּ
כא חַיָּה רָעָה אֲכָלָתְהוּ וְנִרְאֶה מַה־יִּהְיוּ חֲלֹמֹתָיו: וַיִּשְׁמַע רְאוּבֵן
כב וַיַּצִּלֵהוּ מִיָּדָם וַיֹּאמֶר לֹא נַכֶּנּוּ נָפֶשׁ: וַיֹּאמֶר אֲלֵהֶם | רְאוּבֵן אַל־
תִּשְׁפְּכוּ־דָם הַשְׁלִיכוּ אֹתוֹ אֶל־הַבּוֹר הַזֶּה אֲשֶׁר בַּמִּדְבָּר וְיָד
כג אַל־תִּשְׁלְחוּ־בוֹ לְמַעַן הַצִּיל אֹתוֹ מִיָּדָם לַהֲשִׁיבוֹ אֶל־אָבִיו: וַיְהִי שלישי

to the ground before you?" His brothers were jealous of him; 11
but his father kept the matter in mind. When his brothers 12
had gone to pasture their father's flock near Shekhem, Yisrael 13
said to Yosef, "Come, your brothers are pasturing the flocks
near Shekhem; I will send you to them." Yosef said, "Here I
am." He said to him, "Go and see how your brothers and the 14
flocks are doing, and bring me back word," and he sent him
from the Ḥevron Valley, from where he walked to Shekhem.
A man found him wandering lost among the fields and asked 15
him, "What are you looking for?" He replied, "I'm looking 16
for my brothers. Can you tell me where they are pasturing
the sheep?" "They have moved on from here," said the man. 17
"I heard them say, 'Let us go to Dotan.'" So Yosef went after
his brothers and found them at Dotan. They saw him in the 18
distance, and by the time he reached them, they had plotted to
kill him. "Here comes the dreamer!" they said to one another. 19
"Now let us kill him and throw him into one of the pits – we 20
can say that a wild animal ate him – then we shall see what
will come of his dreams!" When Reuven heard this, he tried 21
to save him from them. "Let us not kill him," he said. "Do 22
not shed blood," said Reuven. "Throw him into this pit in the
desert, but do not lay hands on him." His plan was to rescue
him and bring him back to his father. So when Yosef came 23
to his brothers, they stripped him of his robe, the ornately

ARCHAEOLOGY

37:20 Pits (cisterns)

Cisterns were a necessary part of the water infrastructure of ancient Israel, used to collect water during the rainy season for later use in areas where wells could not be dug. The cisterns would need to be maintained and cleaned out regularly, as the collected water would become stagnant – the cistern would fill up with sediment carried by runoff. The inside of a cistern would be coated with plaster in order to prevent the water from seeping into the surrounding rock, a procedure documented from finds dating back to Neolithic times. ▪ ZR

↗ Cistern with plastered walls, Masada, 1st century BCE to 1st century CE

כַּאֲשֶׁר־בָּא יוֹסֵף אֶל־אֶחָיו וַיַּפְשִׁיטוּ אֶת־יוֹסֵף אֶת־כֻּתָּנְתּוֹ אֶת־
כְּתֹנֶת הַפַּסִּים אֲשֶׁר עָלָיו: וַיִּקָּחֻהוּ וַיַּשְׁלִכוּ אֹתוֹ הַבֹּרָה וְהַבּוֹר כד
רֵק אֵין בּוֹ מָיִם: וַיֵּשְׁבוּ לֶאֱכָל־לֶחֶם וַיִּשְׂאוּ עֵינֵיהֶם וַיִּרְאוּ וְהִנֵּה כה •
אֹרְחַת יִשְׁמְעֵאלִים בָּאָה מִגִּלְעָד וּגְמַלֵּיהֶם נֹשְׂאִים נְכֹאת וּצְרִי
וָלֹט הוֹלְכִים לְהוֹרִיד מִצְרָיְמָה: וַיֹּאמֶר יְהוּדָה אֶל־אֶחָיו מַה־בֶּצַע כו
כִּי נַהֲרֹג אֶת־אָחִינוּ וְכִסִּינוּ אֶת־דָּמוֹ: לְכוּ וְנִמְכְּרֶנּוּ לַיִּשְׁמְעֵאלִים כז
וְיָדֵנוּ אַל־תְּהִי־בוֹ כִּי־אָחִינוּ בְשָׂרֵנוּ הוּא וַיִּשְׁמְעוּ אֶחָיו: וַיַּעַבְרוּ כח •
אֲנָשִׁים מִדְיָנִים סֹחֲרִים וַיִּמְשְׁכוּ וַיַּעֲלוּ אֶת־יוֹסֵף מִן־הַבּוֹר וַיִּמְכְּרוּ
אֶת־יוֹסֵף לַיִּשְׁמְעֵאלִים בְּעֶשְׂרִים כָּסֶף וַיָּבִיאוּ אֶת־יוֹסֵף מִצְרָיְמָה:
וַיָּשָׁב רְאוּבֵן אֶל־הַבּוֹר וְהִנֵּה אֵין־יוֹסֵף בַּבּוֹר וַיִּקְרַע אֶת־בְּגָדָיו: כט

24 colored robe he was wearing, and they took him and threw
him into the pit. The pit was empty; there was no water in it.
• 25 And they sat down and ate their meal. Looking up, they saw a
caravan of Ishmaelites coming from Gilad, their camels laden
26 with spices, balm, and myrrh, to be taken to Egypt. Yehuda
said to his brothers, "What do we gain by killing our brother
27 and covering his blood? Let's sell him to the Ishmaelites
and not harm him with our own hands. After all, he is our
• 28 brother, our own flesh and blood." His brothers agreed. Some
Midianite traders passed by and they pulled Yosef up out of
the pit, and they sold him to the Ishmaelites for twenty pieces
29 of silver. They then brought Yosef to Egypt. Reuven returned

NEAR EAST

37:25 Gilad

The brothers were grazing the flocks near Dotan (v. 17), a town in the hilly region south of the Yizre'el Valley that was known for its rich pastures. Gilad was the mountainous region east of the northern part of the Jordan River. Traders traveling south from that region would be using the ancient international trade route known as the Via Maris which dated from the Early Bronze Age and linked Egypt with the northern empires of Syria, Anatolia, and Mesopotamia. This route runs across the Yizre'el Valley on its way to the coastal road near the Mediterranean, the shortest way to get from Canaan to Egypt (as noted in Ex. 13:17).

The route does not pass through the area of Dotan, which is located about 10 kilometers (approximately 6 miles) south of the Yizre'el Valley. However, since Dotan is situated at an elevation of about 200 meters / 656 feet) above the Yizre'el Valley, and the Ishmaelite caravan was traveling west from the Gilad hills toward the Jordan Valley, the brothers would have had time to finish eating before they needed to bring Yosef to a point along the trade route closest to Dotan in order to meet up with the Ishmaelites and make their sale. They were high enough up to see the Ishmaelites long before the Ishmaelites would pass the part of the trade route that was nearest Dotan. Perhaps it was during this interval that Midianites passed by and kidnapped Yosef from the pit (v. 28). ▪ ZR

↗ View of the Gilad mountains across the Jordan Valley

ל לא וַיָּשָׁב אֶל־אֶחָיו וַיֹּאמַר הַיֶּלֶד אֵינֶנּוּ וַאֲנִי אָנָה אֲנִי־בָא: וַיִּקְחוּ
אֶת־כְּתֹנֶת יוֹסֵף וַיִּשְׁחֲטוּ שְׂעִיר עִזִּים וַיִּטְבְּלוּ אֶת־הַכֻּתֹּנֶת בַּדָּם:
לב וַיְשַׁלְּחוּ אֶת־כְּתֹנֶת הַפַּסִּים וַיָּבִיאוּ אֶל־אֲבִיהֶם וַיֹּאמְרוּ זֹאת
לג מָצָאנוּ הַכֶּר־נָא הַכְּתֹנֶת בִּנְךָ הִוא אִם־לֹא: וַיַּכִּירָהּ וַיֹּאמֶר כְּתֹנֶת
לד בְּנִי חַיָּה רָעָה אֲכָלָתְהוּ טָרֹף טֹרַף יוֹסֵף: וַיִּקְרַע יַעֲקֹב שִׂמְלֹתָיו
לה • וַיָּשֶׂם שַׂק בְּמָתְנָיו וַיִּתְאַבֵּל עַל־בְּנוֹ יָמִים רַבִּים: וַיָּקֻמוּ כָל־בָּנָיו

to the pit – and Yosef was not there. He tore his clothes, went 30
back to his brothers, and said, "The boy is gone, and I – where
can I turn?" They took Yosef's robe, slaughtered a goat, and 31
dipped the robe in the blood. They had the ornately colored 32
robe brought to their father, and they said, "We found this.
Try to identify it. Is it your son's robe or not?" He recognized 33
it and said, "It is my son's robe! A wild animal must have eaten
him! Yosef has been torn limb from limb!" Yaakov tore his 34
clothes, put sackcloth on his loins, and mourned for his son
for many days. All his sons and daughters tried to comfort 35 •
him, but he refused to be comforted and said, "I will go down
to Sheol[90] mourning for my son." His father wept for him.

90 | The netherworld.

NEAR EAST

37:28 Twenty pieces of silver

The price of twenty shekels for a slave is found in texts from the early 2nd millennium BCE. The *Laws of Hammurabi* include a few cases where restitution must be made for killing a slave, and the amount given is a third of a mina, which is equivalent to twenty silver shekels. For example, if a person strikes a female slave, "If this maid-servant die, he shall pay one-third of a mina" (LH §214), and in the case of an ox goring a slave, "If he kill a man's slave, he shall pay one-third of a mina" (LH §252). Slave-transaction contracts from Mari and other Old Babylonian documents confirm that, in the 18th century BCE, the prices for a slave ranged from fifteen to thirty shekels. In earlier periods, in the 22nd and 21st centuries BCE, the average price of a slave was eight to ten silver shekels. Documents from Nuzi and Ugarit show that, in the middle and late 2nd millennium, the price went up to thirty silver shekels and rose steadily thereafter. Of course, many additional factors could impact the actual price of a slave in a given time period. ▪ ZR

↗ Treaty for fugitive slaves between Idrimi of Alalakh (now Tell Atchana) and Pillia of Kizzuwatna (now Cilicia), Hittite, Tell Atchana, ca. 1480 BCE

LANGUAGE

37:35 Sheol

In English dictionaries, "Sheol" is listed as a name for the underworld. Up until about 1920, its usage was not uncommon in English. Mark Twain used it in *A Connecticut Yankee in King Arthur's Court*. The English word was simply taken from Hebrew, but the Hebrew word's derivation is unknown. This verse contains the first of the word's sixty-five biblical occurrences.

The image of Sheol as a forbidding, underground location where the soul dwells after death was common in the ancient world – the Septuagint almost always translates it as "Hades" – but in its few occurrences in other Semitic languages it is a loanword from Hebrew, just as it is in English. The word is often paired with *mavet*, "death," and is sometimes personified in the same way that Mot, the god of death, was in Ugaritic literature; see Proverbs 1:12, where Sheol "swallows" those who descend to the grave. In the Tanakh, though, this personification constitutes metaphoric imagery, not theology. ▪ MC

↗ Stele of a Ugaritic god with a feather, Ras Shamra (Ugarit), 15th to 14th century BCE

וְכָל־בְּנֹתָיו לְנַחֲמוֹ וַיְמָאֵן לְהִתְנַחֵם וַיֹּאמֶר כִּי־אֵרֵד אֶל־בְּנִי
אָבֵל שְׁאֹלָה וַיֵּבְךְּ אֹתוֹ אָבִיו: וְהַמְּדָנִים מָכְרוּ אֹתוֹ אֶל־מִצְרָיִם לו
לְפוֹטִיפַר סְרִיס פַּרְעֹה שַׂר הַטַּבָּחִים:
רביעי וַיְהִי בָּעֵת הַהִוא וַיֵּרֶד יְהוּדָה מֵאֵת אֶחָיו וַיֵּט עַד־אִישׁ עֲדֻלָּמִי א לח
וּשְׁמוֹ חִירָה: וַיַּרְא־שָׁם יְהוּדָה בַּת־אִישׁ כְּנַעֲנִי וּשְׁמוֹ שׁוּעַ וַיִּקָּחֶהָ ב
וַיָּבֹא אֵלֶיהָ: וַתַּהַר וַתֵּלֶד בֵּן וַיִּקְרָא אֶת־שְׁמוֹ עֵר: וַתַּהַר עוֹד ג ד
וַתֵּלֶד בֵּן וַתִּקְרָא אֶת־שְׁמוֹ אוֹנָן: וַתֹּסֶף עוֹד וַתֵּלֶד בֵּן וַתִּקְרָא ה
אֶת־שְׁמוֹ שֵׁלָה וְהָיָה בִכְזִיב בְּלִדְתָּהּ אֹתוֹ: וַיִּקַּח יְהוּדָה אִשָּׁה ו
לְעֵר בְּכוֹרוֹ וּשְׁמָהּ תָּמָר: וַיְהִי עֵר בְּכוֹר יְהוּדָה רַע בְּעֵינֵי יְהוָה ז
וַיְמִתֵהוּ יְהוָה: וַיֹּאמֶר יְהוּדָה לְאוֹנָן בֹּא אֶל־אֵשֶׁת אָחִיךָ וְיַבֵּם ח
אֹתָהּ וְהָקֵם זֶרַע לְאָחִיךָ: וַיֵּדַע אוֹנָן כִּי לֹּא לוֹ יִהְיֶה הַזָּרַע וְהָיָה ט
אִם־בָּא אֶל־אֵשֶׁת אָחִיו וְשִׁחֵת אַרְצָה לְבִלְתִּי נְתָן־זֶרַע לְאָחִיו:

36 Meanwhile, the Medanites had sold him in Egypt to Potifar,
one of Pharaoh's officials, captain of the guard.
38 1 Around that time, Yehuda left his brothers and camped near
2 an Adulamite named Ḥira. There, Yehuda met the daughter
of Shua, a Canaanite, and he married her and came to her.
3 4 She became pregnant and had a son, whom he named Er. She
became pregnant again and had another son, and she named
5 him Onan. She had yet another son and named him Shela;
6 Yehuda was in Keziv when she gave birth to him. Yehuda
7 took a wife for his firstborn, Er; her name was Tamar. But Er,
Yehuda's firstborn, was wicked in the Lord's sight, and the
8 Lord took his life. Yehuda then said to Onan, "Go in to your
brother's wife and fulfill your duty as her brother-in-law.[91]
9 Provide children for your brother." But Onan knew that the
children would not be considered his. Whenever he came to
his brother's wife, he let his seed go to waste on the ground so

91 | On levirate marriage, see Deuteronomy 25:5–10.

LANGUAGE

37:36 *saris*

Potifar is described in verse 36 as "one of Pharaoh's officials" – the Hebrew calls him a *saris* of Pharaoh. The Hebrew word comes from the Akkadian *sha-reshi*, "[the one] at the head," that is, a high official. Both languages use the word to refer to governmental and military officers.

In later Hebrew usage, *saris* means "eunuch." This is clearly the meaning in Isaiah 56:3–5, and perhaps in some of the occurrences in Esther as well. Similarly, an Akkadian text states that a wronged husband is permitted to turn the man who slept with his wife into a *sha-reshi*. Apparently in Mesopotamia, sometimes officials were indeed castrated, especially if they might come in contact with the women of the king's harem. However, we know of no such tradition in Egypt. The Septuagint does use "eunuch" here, but, except for Isaiah 56, the Targum avoids using *saris*, which by its time had shifted its meaning almost exclusively to "eunuch." MC

Mummy mask of a high official, probably from the necropolis at Asyut (Egypt), ca. 2000–1980 BCE

GEOGRAPHY

38:1–12 Adulam, Keziv, Timna

The geographic locations where Yehuda lives and travels in this chapter will later be part of the inheritance of the tribe of Yehuda.

Adulam is listed in Joshua 15:35 as a city in the northern lowlands of Yehuda, meaning that Yehuda traveled north and slightly west from the hill country of Ḥevron, where the family was camped (Gen. 37:14). Adulam has been conclusively identified with Tell esh-Sheikh Madhkur, a site at the eastern end of the Ela Valley. Tell esh-Sheikh Madhkur is located next to the spring of Id el-ma, whose name preserves a corrupted form of Adulam. Adulam's primary importance in Tanakh is its pivotal role as David's apparent first base of operations (see II Sam. 23:13; I Chr. 11:15), where, as a fugitive, he made use of the town and its cave.

↗ Adulam (Tell esh-Sheikh Madhkur), aerial view from the northwest

Modern archaeologists identify Timna with Tel Batash, first settled in the Middle Bronze Age, northwest of Beit Shemesh, also in the lowland area. It is found near Khirbet Tibne, which preserves the name. This is apparently a different location than the Timna mentioned in Joshua 15:10, 57, in the hill country of Yehuda, and should also not be confused with the Timna mines in the Negev.

Keziv seems to be another name for Akhziv, listed in Joshua 15:44 as a city in the tribal allotment of Yehuda and called Kozeva in I Chronicles 4:22. This city is distinct from the Akhziv located on the Mediterranean coast in northern Israel. Keziv has been identified with sites in the Ela Valley near the spring called Ain el-Kezbeh, which preserves the ancient name. ▪ ZR

NEAR EAST

38:8 Levirate marriage

The verse refers specifically to levirate marriage (from the Latin, *levir*, meaning "husband's brother"), known in Hebrew as *yibum* – the marriage of the brother of a deceased, heirless husband to his widow. The root *y b m* in reference to the widow's brother-in-law appears in the Tanakh only here and in Deuteronomy 25. Verses 5–6 there state, "When brothers live together, and one of them dies without a son, his widow shall not be married to a stranger outside the family. Her husband's brother shall come to her and take her in marriage, fulfilling the duty of a brother-in-law. The firstborn son whom she bears will perpetuate the name of the dead brother...."

Variations of this practice were known in the ancient Near East before the giving of the Torah. The *Hittite Laws* discuss a similar situation: "If a man has a wife, and the man dies, his brother shall take his widow as wife. (If the brother dies) his father shall take her. When afterward the father dies, his (the father's) brother shall take the woman whom he had" (HL §193). The *Middle Assyrian Laws* discuss a case where a groom dies after a marriage has been arranged, "If a man either pours oil on her head or brings (dishes for) the banquet, (after which) the son to whom he assigned the wife either dies or flees, he shall give her in marriage to whichever of his remaining sons he wishes, from the oldest to the youngest of at least ten years of age" (MAL A §43).

The idea underlying this practice is that once the bride joined a family through marriage, she becomes part of its clan and as such is attached to another male member who will provide for her and protect her. However, in the Torah, the main purpose is to provide an heir to perpetuate the name of the deceased (verses 8 and 9 here). ▪ ZR

וַיֵּ֛רַע בְּעֵינֵ֥י יְהוָ֖ה אֲשֶׁ֣ר עָשָׂ֑ה וַיָּ֖מֶת גַּם־אֹתֽוֹ׃ וַיֹּ֣אמֶר יְהוּדָ֡ה יא
לְתָמָ֨ר כַּלָּת֜וֹ שְׁבִ֧י אַלְמָנָ֣ה בֵית־אָבִ֗יךְ עַד־יִגְדַּל֙ שֵׁלָ֣ה בְנִ֔י כִּ֣י
אָמַ֔ר פֶּן־יָמ֥וּת גַּם־ה֖וּא כְּאֶחָ֑יו וַתֵּ֣לֶךְ תָּמָ֔ר וַתֵּ֖שֶׁב בֵּ֥ית אָבִֽיהָ׃

10 as not to have children in his brother's name. What he did was
11 wicked in the LORD's sight, and so He took his life also. Then
Yehuda said to his daughter-in-law Tamar, "Live as a widow
in your father's house until my son Shela grows up" – for he
thought he too might die like his brothers. So Tamar went to

Mourning widow in front of the mummy, burial chamber of the sculptors Nebamun and Ipuki, near Deir el-Bahari, 13th century BCE

NEAR EAST

38:11 Live as a widow

In the ancient Near East, a widowed woman without children had no independent economic or social status. This situation is reflected in Tanakh as well, with a widow being the exemplar of someone who is helpless, as in "The Lord will extirpate the house of the haughty, but He will secure the widow's boundary stone" (Prov. 15:25), and "Father of orphans, judge of widows, God is in His holy abode" (Ps. 68:6). Babylonian kings would customarily praise themselves by stating that they were the protectors of widows, correcting injustices perpetrated by others.

A widow was dependent on either her husband's family or that of her own father, but her father was not required to take care of her; he could send her off to the care of her father-in-law. Since marriage was viewed as a union not between two individuals, but between two families, the father-in-law could still wield authority over his widowed daughter-in-law. Such dependency is seen, for example, in the *Middle Assyrian Laws,* "If a woman is residing in her own father's house, her husband is dead...[if he so pleases] he shall give her into the protection of the household of her father-in-law. If her husband and her father-in-law are both dead and she has no son, she is indeed a widow: She shall go wherever she pleases" (MAL A §33).

In our narrative, Yehuda uses his position of authority over Tamar to send her back to her father's house (38:11). Apparently while he refuses to accept responsibility for looking after her welfare, he still retains control over her when it comes to meting out punishment (38:24). In this context, Yehuda's confession that Tamar "is more righteous than I" (v. 26) is extraordinary. ▪ ZR

יב וַיִּרְבּוּ הַיָּמִים וַתָּמָת בַּת־שׁוּעַ אֵשֶׁת־יְהוּדָה וַיִּנָּחֶם יְהוּדָה
יג וַיַּעַל עַל־גֹּזְזֵי צֹאנוֹ הוּא וְחִירָה רֵעֵהוּ הָעֲדֻלָּמִי תִּמְנָתָה: וַיֻּגַּד
יד לְתָמָר לֵאמֹר הִנֵּה חָמִיךְ עֹלֶה תִמְנָתָה לָגֹז צֹאנוֹ: וַתָּסַר בִּגְדֵי
אַלְמְנוּתָהּ מֵעָלֶיהָ וַתְּכַס בַּצָּעִיף וַתִּתְעַלָּף וַתֵּשֶׁב בְּפֶתַח עֵינַיִם
אֲשֶׁר עַל־דֶּרֶךְ תִּמְנָתָה כִּי רָאֲתָה כִּי־גָדַל שֵׁלָה וְהִוא לֹא־נִתְּנָה
טו טז לוֹ לְאִשָּׁה: וַיִּרְאֶהָ יְהוּדָה וַיַּחְשְׁבֶהָ לְזוֹנָה כִּי כִסְּתָה פָּנֶיהָ: וַיֵּט
אֵלֶיהָ אֶל־הַדֶּרֶךְ וַיֹּאמֶר הָבָה נָּא אָבוֹא אֵלַיִךְ כִּי לֹא יָדַע כִּי
יז כַלָּתוֹ הִוא וַתֹּאמֶר מַה־תִּתֶּן־לִי כִּי תָבוֹא אֵלָי: וַיֹּאמֶר אָנֹכִי

live in her father's house. A long time passed, and Yehuda's 12
wife, Shua's daughter, died. When he had completed his time
of mourning, he and his neighbor Ḥira the Adulamite went
to join his sheepshearers in Timna. Tamar was told, "Your 13
father-in-law is going to Timna to shear his sheep." And she 14
took off her widow's clothes and covered herself with a veil.
Disguised, she sat at the entrance to Einayim on the road to
Timna, for she had seen that Shela was now grown up and
yet she had not been given to him as a wife. Yehuda saw her 15
and thought she was a prostitute, because she had covered her
face. Not realizing that she was his daughter-in-law, he turned 16
aside to her on the road and said, "Come, let me sleep with
you." She said, "What will you give me to sleep with you?" He 17
said, "I will send you a young goat from my flock." "Only if

NEAR EAST

38:14 Veil

A veil always signified something about the woman's status, although its meaning changed in different periods. Tamar wore a veil to disguise herself, which indicates she was normally unveiled, as was the practice in many societies of the ancient Near East. As noted in the other article titled "Veil" on page 151, a veil was originally worn only at a marriage ceremony, and not by married women afterward.

Much later, by the Middle Assyrian period, the veil was part of the everyday clothing of married women, at least in some regions. The *Middle Assyrian Laws* mandated that prostitutes were forbidden to be veiled, "Married women, widows…must not have their heads uncovered when they go out into the street. Daughters of status must be veiled, whether by a veil, a robe, or a [mantle]; they must not have their heads uncovered…when they go into the street [alone] they are to be veiled…A harlot is not to be veiled; her head must be uncovered" (MAL A §40). In this later time, it appears that wearing a veil publicly was a privilege that indicated high status and may also have functioned as a symbol representing female modesty and chastity, making it inappropriate for prostitutes. ▪ ZR

Judah and Tamar,
Arent de Gelder, ca. 1681

אֲשַׁלַּח גְּדִי־עִזִּים מִן־הַצֹּאן וַתֹּאמֶר אִם־תִּתֵּן עֵרָבוֹן עַד שָׁלְחֶךָ׃
• יח וַיֹּאמֶר מָה הָעֵרָבוֹן אֲשֶׁר אֶתֶּן־לָּךְ וַתֹּאמֶר חֹתָמְךָ וּפְתִילֶךָ
יט וּמַטְּךָ אֲשֶׁר בְּיָדֶךָ וַיִּתֶּן־לָהּ וַיָּבֹא אֵלֶיהָ וַתַּהַר לוֹ׃ וַתָּקָם וַתֵּלֶךְ
כ וַתָּסַר צְעִיפָהּ מֵעָלֶיהָ וַתִּלְבַּשׁ בִּגְדֵי אַלְמְנוּתָהּ׃ וַיִּשְׁלַח יְהוּדָה
אֶת־גְּדִי הָעִזִּים בְּיַד רֵעֵהוּ הָעֲדֻלָּמִי לָקַחַת הָעֵרָבוֹן מִיַּד הָאִשָּׁה
• כא וְלֹא מְצָאָהּ׃ וַיִּשְׁאַל אֶת־אַנְשֵׁי מְקֹמָהּ לֵאמֹר אַיֵּה הַקְּדֵשָׁה
כב הִוא בָעֵינַיִם עַל־הַדָּרֶךְ וַיֹּאמְרוּ לֹא־הָיְתָה בָזֶה קְדֵשָׁה׃ וַיָּשָׁב
אֶל־יְהוּדָה וַיֹּאמֶר לֹא מְצָאתִיהָ וְגַם אַנְשֵׁי הַמָּקוֹם אָמְרוּ לֹא־
כג הָיְתָה בָזֶה קְדֵשָׁה׃ וַיֹּאמֶר יְהוּדָה תִּקַּח־לָהּ פֶּן נִהְיֶה לָבוּז הִנֵּה
• כד שָׁלַחְתִּי הַגְּדִי הַזֶּה וְאַתָּה לֹא מְצָאתָהּ׃ וַיְהִי ׀ כְּמִשְׁלֹשׁ חֳדָשִׁים
וַיֻּגַּד לִיהוּדָה לֵאמֹר זָנְתָה תָּמָר כַּלָּתֶךָ וְגַם הִנֵּה הָרָה לִזְנוּנִים
כה וַיֹּאמֶר יְהוּדָה הוֹצִיאוּהָ וְתִשָּׂרֵף׃ הִוא מוּצֵאת וְהִיא שָׁלְחָה
אֶל־חָמִיהָ לֵאמֹר לְאִישׁ אֲשֶׁר־אֵלֶּה לּוֹ אָנֹכִי הָרָה וַתֹּאמֶר
כו הַכֶּר־נָא לְמִי הַחֹתֶמֶת וְהַפְּתִילִים וְהַמַּטֶּה הָאֵלֶּה׃ וַיַּכֵּר יְהוּדָה
וַיֹּאמֶר צָדְקָה מִמֶּנִּי כִּי־עַל־כֵּן לֹא־נְתַתִּיהָ לְשֵׁלָה בְנִי וְלֹא־יָסַף

you give me something as a pledge until you send it," she said.
• 18 "What pledge should I give you?" he asked. She answered,
"Your seal and cord, and the staff in your hand." He gave
them to her and went in to her – and she became pregnant
19 by him. She got up and left, removed her veil, and put on her
20 widow's clothes again. And Yehuda sent the young goat by
his neighbor the Adulamite, to recover the pledge from the
• 21 woman, but he could not find her. He asked the local men,
"Where is the cult prostitute,[92] the one by the roadside at
22 Einayim?" They said, "No cult prostitute has been here." So he
went back to Yehuda and said, "I could not find her. Besides,
the local men said that there was no cult prostitute there."
23 Yehuda said, "Let her keep what she has or we will become
a laughingstock. I tried to send her this young goat, but you
• 24 could not find her." About three months later, Yehuda was
told, "Your daughter-in-law Tamar has behaved as a loose
woman; in fact she has become pregnant by her harlotry."
25 "Take her out and let her be burned," Yehuda said. As she was
being brought out, she sent her father-in-law a message: "I
am pregnant by the man to whom these belong." She added,
"Please identify to whom this seal and cord and staff belong."
26 Yehuda recognized them and said, "She is more righteous
than I. It was because I did not give her to Shela my son." He

92 | A type of prostitute associated with religious worship.

NEAR EAST

38:18 Your seal and cord, and the staff in your hand

Two of the objects that Tamar requested from Yehuda as a pledge were his seal and his cord.

In the ancient Near East, two types of seals were used: the cylinder seal, rolled on a tablet or a piece of clay (in Mesopotamia and neighboring lands), and the stamp seal, pressed against a piece of clay that was then tied to the object being sealed (in Egypt, the Levant, and Anatolia). A seal was used to identify its owner, and if a seal was lost, a special declaration was issued invalidating it. The cord would likely be used for wearing the seal on one's body, passed through a hole perforated through the seal's sides. ▪ YB

↗ Cylinder seal with hieroglyphics and cuneiform writing, Tell Beit Mirsim, 18th to 17th century BCE

כז כח עוֹד לְדַעְתָּהּ: וַיְהִי בְּעֵת לִדְתָּהּ וְהִנֵּה תְאוֹמִים בְּבִטְנָהּ: וַיְהִי
בְלִדְתָּהּ וַיִּתֶּן־יָד וַתִּקַּח הַמְיַלֶּדֶת וַתִּקְשֹׁר עַל־יָדוֹ שָׁנִי לֵאמֹר
כט זֶה יָצָא רִאשֹׁנָה: וַיְהִי ׀ כְּמֵשִׁיב יָדוֹ וְהִנֵּה יָצָא אָחִיו וַתֹּאמֶר
ל מַה־פָּרַצְתָּ עָלֶיךָ פָּרֶץ וַיִּקְרָא שְׁמוֹ פָּרֶץ: וְאַחַר יָצָא אָחִיו

did not know her intimately again. When the time came for 27
her to give birth, there were twins in her womb. As she was in 28
labor one child put out a hand, so the midwife took a crimson
thread and tied it to his wrist, saying, "This one came out first."
But he pulled his hand back and then his brother came out. 29
She said, "How you have burst through!" So he was named
Peretz.[93] Then his brother came out with the crimson thread 30

93 | Meaning "bursting through."

NEAR EAST

38:21 Cult prostitute

There is much scholarly debate about whether institutionalized cultic prostitution existed in the ancient Near East. Such an institution was theorized by scholars in the past, but no archaeological or textual evidence has been found to support it. While there is ample evidence of sacred marriage rites, these were highly regulated and are not comparable to the idea of a temple prostitute to whom the public has access.

The term used here, *kedesha*, appears to refer to a woman who functioned in the service of a fertility deity, found in Mesopotamian records as a *qadishtu*, literally, a "holy woman." She could be unmarried or married, and could even have children. Among her functions in the 1st millennium BCE was to act as a midwife or wet nurse. In the cult of Adad, a *qadishtu* was also a cult singer. However, there is no evidence that cultic prostitution occurred in the ancient Near East.

Neo-Babylonian temples (mid-1st millennium) did sometimes hire lower-level female personnel out as prostitutes to private citizens in their homes. The income generated thereby went into the temple treasury, and this seems to have been the main impetus for the phenomenon of prostitutes in the service of ancient Near Eastern temples – but these were not cultic acts. In Akkadian literature, "the house of Ishtar" was another name for a brothel, but here as well, the object was not cultic worship.

The Tanakh has a negative view of the *kedesha*, using this term as a synonym for a common prostitute, as found in Deuteronomy 23:18, "No woman of Israel shall be a *kedesha*", and Hosea 4:14, "their men go with the whores and sacrifice with the *kedeshot*." Note that while the people speaking in this chapter of Hosea refer to the woman as a *kedesha*, the narration (v. 15) calls her a *zonah*, a plain prostitute or harlot, reflecting the Israelite opposition to the institution of the *kedesha*. It may also be that *kedesha* is used here as a euphemism. ▪ ZR

↗ Stele for Tashakheper (right, depicted in prayer in front of Osiris and the four sons of Horus), daughter of the priest of Montu, Irethoreru, 7th to 6th century BCE

NEAR EAST

38:24 Let her be burned

The penalty of immolation (death by burning) was rare in the ancient Near East, reserved for the most heinous of sexual offenses. It appears only twice in the *Laws of Hammurabi*, "If anyone be guilty of incest with his mother after his father, both shall be burned" (LH §157), and in the case of a *naditu* (literally, "the fallow"), a woman in Babylonian society who was connected to a particular temple of a male deity, who seems to have been celibate, or at least childless, who "opens a tavern, or enters a tavern to drink" (LH §110). The case of Tamar, who was accused of infidelity, was on par with these crimes.

In the Torah, it appears only in Leviticus 20:14, "If a man marries a woman and also her mother, it is depravity. He and they shall be burned by fire," and 21:9, "If the daughter of a priest profanes herself by immorality, she profanes her father also; she shall be burned with fire." ▪ ZR

Hyksos soldier with a short bow and sword, dagger handle of Abed, soldier of Hyksos Pharaoh Apepi, 16th century BCE

There are obvious similarities between the Torah's description of Yosef becoming the effective ruler of Egypt and the history of the Hyksos rise to power, but there are also obvious gaps.

and Yaakov lived in the Middle Bronze Age, and the Israelites probably entered the land of Israel beginning in the second half of the 13th century BCE.

Nevertheless, identifying Yosef as the vizier of one of the Hyksos rulers presents significant difficulties. First, notable differences exist between the biblical narrative and the events of Hyksos rule. For example, nowhere does the Genesis narrative state that Yosef is part of a larger group of Canaanites who take control of the delta. Secondly, the chronology poses difficulties. If the exodus took place sometime in the 13th century BCE, then Yosef and his brothers should have arrived in Egypt no earlier than the 15th century – but by that time the Hyksos were no longer in power.

No clear resolution has been found to these problems, nor have Egyptian records been discovered that mention Yosef or the specific Pharaoh, Hyksos or otherwise, whom he served. Additionally, we cannot identify Yosef or his Pharaoh with any specific Hyksos ruler. We can say only that the Egyptians were subject to Semite rule of their land for a time, and that the experience of having Semites in prominent positions in Egypt led to enmity against Semites on the part of subsequent rulers.

We would do well to keep in mind that every narrative is a simplification of events. Like any other narrative, the Torah does not aim to give a comprehensive account of everything that occurred, but rather to highlight certain events and to fit those into a pattern that instructs and informs. ▪ SZA

Headband with gazelles and a stag, eastern Delta (?), Fifteenth Dynasty, (Hyksos rule), 17th to 16th century BCE

Yosef in Egypt

From this point to the end of the book of Genesis, the narrative centers around Yosef's high political status, highlighting his role as a non-Egyptian. In Genesis 39:17 and 41:12, Egyptians call him a "Hebrew," and when Yosef's brothers arrive in Egypt, their Hebrew ethnic origins are noted (Gen. 43:32; see "Avram the Hebrew" on page 88). These identifications fit in well with the tendency in ancient Egypt to accentuate the distinction between Egyptians and foreigners, as evidenced in the hieroglyphic inscriptions which affix a determinative to the names of foreign lands and foreign peoples, indicating their separateness. Moreover, Potifar's wife calling Yosef a "Hebrew slave" (39:17) and Yosef's renaming by Pharaoh (41:45) suggest the Egyptians' difficulty with a foreigner holding a position of power in Egypt.

In the long history of Egypt's interactions with foreign peoples, the only period in which control of Egypt passed to Semitic-speaking foreigners was the period of Hyksos rule, during Egypt's Fifteenth Dynasty (ca. 1650–1550 BCE). According to Anson Rainey, however, the Fourteenth Dynasty also had many kings with "largely Semitic names or other Asiatic connections." Hyksos is an Egyptian term meaning "rulers of foreign lands;" Egyptians use it in their texts to refer to the rulers of Canaan.

Rainey reconstructs the events surrounding the Hyksos rule as follows: Powerful groups from Canaan came to Egypt during a period of Egyptian weakness and established a base at Avaris, in the eastern part of the Nile Delta. He avers that "It was not a tribal invasion but rather a force of urbanized warriors launching a new political adventure. They surely must have had the backing of the city-states of southern Canaan in their enterprise."

There are obvious similarities between the Torah's description of Yosef becoming the effective ruler of Egypt and the history of the Hyksos rise to power, but there are also obvious gaps. The Torah makes no clear mention of Yosef as leader of other Canaanite rulers; it notes only that under his rule, "all over the region" (presumably, including Canaan) came to Egypt for food (Gen. 41:57). Yosef is not portrayed as Pharaoh, but only as second-in-command. Nevertheless, the fact remains that Yosef's rise to power as a non-Egyptian corresponds closely with the overall idea of Canaanites rising to power in the Fifteenth Dynasty. Furthermore, Goshen, the area in which he settles his brothers (46:34), was the center of Hyksos political power.

More importantly, the end of the Hyksos rule in Egypt was marked by a period of pride in the return of control to Egyptians. The rulers who ended Hyksos dominion ruled approximately 1550–1450 BCE and emphasized in their rhetoric that "Egypt belongs to the Egyptians." These rulers included Ahmose, Queen Hatshepsut, and her son Thutmose III. The accounts of the latter two are particularly apt, as Rainey translates Hatshepsut's words, "After I had raised up what was formerly torn to pieces…I restored that which had fallen into ruin, since the Semites were in the midst of the northern city, Avaris," and those of Thutmose III, "there was enmity, every man plundering in enmity against his neighbour." These after-the-fact depictions correspond to Pharaoh's fear articulated in Exodus 1:10, "in case they increase, and if war breaks out they may join our enemies." That fear is his justification for oppressing the Israelites (v. 11 there).

Thus, both the narrative of Yosef's rise to power and that of the rise of the Pharaoh "who had not known Yosef" (v. 8 there) may relate to elements in the historical events surrounding the rise and fall of the Hyksos rulers. We cannot ignore these possible connections; they are significant and unique. Furthermore, dating Yosef sometime toward the end of the Hyksos period fits reasonably well with other aspects of the biblical timeline: Avraham, Yitzḥak,

↗ Statue of the physician Sesheshen-sa-Hathor, cartouche of Hyksos pharaoh Amenemhat I on both sides (not visible), Ezbet Rushdi (near Tel el-Dab'a, ancient Avaris), 19th century BCE

חמישי אֲשֶׁר עַל־יָדוֹ הַשָּׁנִי וַיִּקְרָא שְׁמוֹ זָרַח׃ וְיוֹסֵף א לט
הוּרַד מִצְרָיְמָה וַיִּקְנֵהוּ פּוֹטִיפַר סְרִיס פַּרְעֹה שַׂר הַטַּבָּחִים אִישׁ
מִצְרִי מִיַּד הַיִּשְׁמְעֵאלִים אֲשֶׁר הוֹרִדֻהוּ שָׁמָּה׃ וַיְהִי יְהוָה אֶת־ ב •
יוֹסֵף וַיְהִי אִישׁ מַצְלִיחַ וַיְהִי בְּבֵית אֲדֹנָיו הַמִּצְרִי׃ וַיַּרְא אֲדֹנָיו ג
כִּי יְהוָה אִתּוֹ וְכֹל אֲשֶׁר־הוּא עֹשֶׂה יְהוָה מַצְלִיחַ בְּיָדוֹ׃ וַיִּמְצָא ד
יוֹסֵף חֵן בְּעֵינָיו וַיְשָׁרֶת אֹתוֹ וַיַּפְקִדֵהוּ עַל־בֵּיתוֹ וְכָל־יֶשׁ־לוֹ נָתַן
בְּיָדוֹ׃ וַיְהִי מֵאָז הִפְקִיד אֹתוֹ בְּבֵיתוֹ וְעַל כָּל־אֲשֶׁר יֶשׁ־לוֹ וַיְבָרֶךְ ה
יְהוָה אֶת־בֵּית הַמִּצְרִי בִּגְלַל יוֹסֵף וַיְהִי בִּרְכַּת יְהוָה בְּכָל־אֲשֶׁר
יֶשׁ־לוֹ בַּבַּיִת וּבַשָּׂדֶה׃ וַיַּעֲזֹב כָּל־אֲשֶׁר־לוֹ בְּיַד־יוֹסֵף וְלֹא־יָדַע ו
אִתּוֹ מְאוּמָה כִּי אִם־הַלֶּחֶם אֲשֶׁר־הוּא אוֹכֵל וַיְהִי יוֹסֵף יְפֵה־

39 1 on his wrist. He was named Zeraḥ.[93] Meanwhile,
Yosef had been brought down to Egypt. Potifar, an Egyptian,
one of Pharaoh's officials and captain of the guard, had bought
• 2 him from the Ishmaelites who had brought him there. The
Lord was with Yosef, and he became a successful man. He
3 lived in the house of his Egyptian master. And his master
saw that the Lord was with him and that the Lord granted
4 him success in all he did; Yosef found favor in his eyes and
became his personal attendant. Potifar put him in charge of
his household, giving him responsibility for all he owned.
5 From the moment he put him in charge of his household and
all he owned, the Lord blessed the Egyptian's household
because of Yosef. The Lord's blessing was in all he owned,
6 in house and field. And so he left all he had in Yosef's hands
and, with him there, he had no concern for anything but the

93 | The term *zeraḥ* means "shining," an apparent reference to the color of the thread.

EGYPTOLOGY

39:2 He lived in the house of his Egyptian master

In ancient Egypt, slaves were used not only for labor in the fields, but also for professional household tasks, based on the special capabilities they demonstrated. The back of the Brooklyn Papyrus 35.1446 (ca. 1833–1742 BCE) has a list of ninety-five household servants of an Egyptian noblewoman named Senebtisi, seventy-nine of whom have their names preserved. They are listed by name and occupation, including brewer, cook, sandal maker, tutor, and "house man" for the men, and various kinds of weavers and a hairdresser among the women. Forty-five of the slaves on this list have names of Asiatic origin, most performing professional tasks, indicating that Yosef's status in Egypt was not unusual. ▪ ZR

↗ Fragment of the Brooklyn Papyrus 35.1446, Egypt (Thebes?) 19th to 18th century BCE

ז תֹּאַר וִיפֵה מַרְאֶה: וַיְהִי אַחַר הַדְּבָרִים הָאֵלֶּה וַתִּשָּׂא אֵשֶׁת־ ששי
ח אֲדֹנָיו אֶת־עֵינֶיהָ אֶל־יוֹסֵף וַתֹּאמֶר שִׁכְבָה עִמִּי: וַיְמָאֵן ׀ וַיֹּאמֶר
אֶל־אֵשֶׁת אֲדֹנָיו הֵן אֲדֹנִי לֹא־יָדַע אִתִּי מַה־בַּבָּיִת וְכֹל אֲשֶׁר־
ט יֶשׁ־לוֹ נָתַן בְּיָדִי: אֵינֶנּוּ גָדוֹל בַּבַּיִת הַזֶּה מִמֶּנִּי וְלֹא־חָשַׂךְ מִמֶּנִּי
מְאוּמָה כִּי אִם־אוֹתָךְ בַּאֲשֶׁר אַתְּ־אִשְׁתּוֹ וְאֵיךְ אֶעֱשֶׂה הָרָעָה
י הַגְּדֹלָה הַזֹּאת וְחָטָאתִי לֵאלֹהִים: וַיְהִי כְּדַבְּרָהּ אֶל־יוֹסֵף יוֹם ׀
יא יוֹם וְלֹא־שָׁמַע אֵלֶיהָ לִשְׁכַּב אֶצְלָהּ לִהְיוֹת עִמָּהּ: וַיְהִי כְּהַיּוֹם
הַזֶּה וַיָּבֹא הַבַּיְתָה לַעֲשׂוֹת מְלַאכְתּוֹ וְאֵין אִישׁ מֵאַנְשֵׁי הַבַּיִת
יב שָׁם בַּבָּיִת: וַתִּתְפְּשֵׂהוּ בְּבִגְדוֹ לֵאמֹר שִׁכְבָה עִמִּי וַיַּעֲזֹב בִּגְדוֹ

7 food he ate.[94] Now, Yosef was well built and handsome, and
after a while, his master's wife cast her eyes on Yosef. "Lie
8 with me," she said. But he refused. "With me here," he told
her, "my master does not concern himself with the running
9 of the house; he has entrusted me with all that he owns. No
one in this house has greater authority than I. He has withheld
nothing from me except you, because you are his wife. How
could I do so great a wrong? It would be a sin against God!"
10 And though she spoke to Yosef day after day, he would not
11 consent to lie with her or be with her. One day he came into
the house to do his work and none of the other servants were
12 there. She caught him by his cloak and said, "Lie with me!" He

94 | Possibly a euphemism for his wife (cf. v. 9).

NEAR EAST

39:7–20 Yosef and Potifar's wife

The Egyptian *Story of Two Brothers* (ca. 13th century BCE) provides an interesting parallel to the episode here. It begins with the unnamed wife of the older brother, Anubis, attempting to persuade the younger brother, Bata, to commit adultery, to which he responds, "What is this great crime which you have said to me?" (ANET 23–25, iv 1). After this rejection, the wife tells her husband that Bata attempted to seduce her and beat her when she refused. Anubis decides to kill his younger brother but is eventually convinced of his innocence and kills his wife instead.

The relationship between this story and the Yosef narrative is unclear – beyond a well-known ancient literary motif of a wife who wishes to commit adultery, but is spurned by the man she desires. This motif is also found in a version of the Greek myth of Hippolytus and his stepmother Phaedra. As opposed to the Yosef story, the *Story of Two Brothers* includes many mythological elements, such as Bata turning into a bull and a tree, meetings with gods, as well as death and resurrection. ▪ ZR

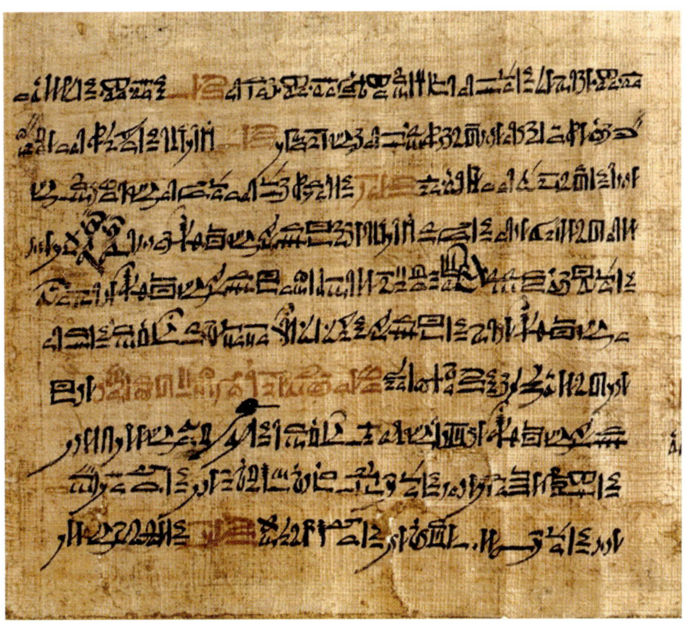

Story of Two Brothers, Egypt, original from 13th century BCE

בְּיָדָהּ וַיָּנׇס וַיֵּצֵא הַחוּצָה׃ וַיְהִי כִּרְאוֹתָהּ כִּי־עָזַב בִּגְדוֹ בְּיָדָהּ יג
וַיָּנׇס הַחוּצָה׃ וַתִּקְרָא לְאַנְשֵׁי בֵיתָהּ וַתֹּאמֶר לָהֶם לֵאמֹר רְאוּ יד
הֵבִיא לָנוּ אִישׁ עִבְרִי לְצַחֶק בָּנוּ בָּא אֵלַי לִשְׁכַּב עִמִּי וָאֶקְרָא
בְּקוֹל גָּדוֹל׃ וַיְהִי כְשׇׁמְעוֹ כִּי־הֲרִימֹתִי קוֹלִי וָאֶקְרָא וַיַּעֲזֹב בִּגְדוֹ טו
אֶצְלִי וַיָּנׇס וַיֵּצֵא הַחוּצָה׃ וַתַּנַּח בִּגְדוֹ אֶצְלָהּ עַד־בּוֹא אֲדֹנָיו טז
אֶל־בֵּיתוֹ׃ וַתְּדַבֵּר אֵלָיו כַּדְּבָרִים הָאֵלֶּה לֵאמֹר בָּא אֵלַי הָעֶבֶד יז
הָעִבְרִי אֲשֶׁר־הֵבֵאתָ לָּנוּ לְצַחֶק בִּי׃ וַיְהִי כַּהֲרִימִי קוֹלִי וָאֶקְרָא יח
וַיַּעֲזֹב בִּגְדוֹ אֶצְלִי וַיָּנׇס הַחוּצָה׃ וַיְהִי כִשְׁמֹעַ אֲדֹנָיו אֶת־דִּבְרֵי יט
אִשְׁתּוֹ אֲשֶׁר דִּבְּרָה אֵלָיו לֵאמֹר כַּדְּבָרִים הָאֵלֶּה עָשָׂה לִי עַבְדֶּךָ
וַיִּחַר אַפּוֹ׃ וַיִּקַּח אֲדֹנֵי יוֹסֵף אֹתוֹ וַיִּתְּנֵהוּ אֶל־בֵּית הַסֹּהַר מְקוֹם כ •
אֲסִירֵי אֲשֶׁר־אסורי הַמֶּלֶךְ אֲסוּרִים וַיְהִי־שָׁם בְּבֵית הַסֹּהַר׃ וַיְהִי יהוה כא
אֶת־יוֹסֵף וַיֵּט אֵלָיו חָסֶד וַיִּתֵּן חִנּוֹ בְּעֵינֵי שַׂר בֵּית־הַסֹּהַר׃ וַיִּתֵּן כב
שַׂר בֵּית־הַסֹּהַר בְּיַד־יוֹסֵף אֵת כׇּל־הָאֲסִירִם אֲשֶׁר בְּבֵית הַסֹּהַר
וְאֵת כׇּל־אֲשֶׁר עֹשִׂים שָׁם הוּא הָיָה עֹשֶׂה׃ אֵין ׀ שַׂר בֵּית־הַסֹּהַר כג
רֹאֶה אֶת־כׇּל־מְאוּמָה בְּיָדוֹ בַּאֲשֶׁר יהוה אִתּוֹ וַאֲשֶׁר־הוּא עֹשֶׂה
יהוה מַצְלִיחַ׃

13 ran away from her and fled outside. When she saw that he
had left his cloak in her hand and had run out of the house,
14 she called out to her servants and said to them, "Look! He
brought us a Hebrew to mock[95] us! He came to me to lie
15 with me, but I screamed. And when he heard me scream
and cry for help, he left his cloak with me and ran outside."
16 She kept his cloak beside her until his master came home.
17 Then she told him the same story: "The Hebrew slave you
18 brought us came to me to mock me. I screamed and called
for help, and he left his cloak with me and ran outside."
19 When his master heard the story his wife told him – "This
• 20 is what your servant did to me!" – he was incensed. Yosef's
master had him put in prison, where the king's prisoners
21 were confined. He remained there in prison. But the LORD
was with Yosef and showed him kindness, granting him
22 favor in the eyes of the prison warden. The warden put
Yosef in charge of all the prisoners in the jail. Everything
23 done there was under his direction. The warden did not
need to pay attention to anything he had entrusted to
him, because the LORD was with him, giving him success
in all he did.

NEAR EAST

39:20 Prison

The punishment of incarceration in prison is unknown in Israelite or ancient Near Eastern law, but is found in numerous Egyptian documents dating back to the Middle Kingdom period. The Great Prison (*hnrt wr*) at Thebes, reported to have been a converted granary, was the most famous prison in ancient Egypt. It appears that prisoners were not differentiated based on their offense.

In the case of Yosef, the prison was located in the master's house, as seen in Genesis 40:7, "He asked Pharaoh's officials who were in custody with him in his master's house." This practice is attested to in an Egyptian papyrus, which refers to "the little prison of the Overseer of the Treasury" (Leiden I.368, 7–9; compare Jer. 37:15). ▪ ZR

Nubian prisoners, Abu Simbel, 13th century BCE

95 | This verb (*letzaḥek*) can have sexual connotations (cf., e.g., v. 17, 21:9, 26:8; Ex. 32:6).

שביעי מ ••א וַיְהִי אַחַר הַדְּבָרִים הָאֵלֶּה חָטְאוּ מַשְׁקֵה מֶלֶךְ־מִצְרַיִם וְהָאֹפֶה

40•• 1 Some time later, the Egyptian kings' cupbearer and baker

EGYPTOLOGY

40:1 Cupbearer and baker

The Egyptian term for the position of royal cupbearer (*wb*^{3}) literally means, "he who opens," as he was responsible for opening the jugs of wine and beer. The title also appears in an expanded form (*wb*^{3} *dp irp*), which means "the opener tasting wine" – reflecting his function of tasting the wine before serving it to the pharaoh.

This position expanded over time beyond being a simple butler. For example, the tomb inscriptions of Dehuty (who served in this capacity during the Eighteenth Dynasty) describe him overseeing the many servants who prepared the pharaoh's food and drinks. In the New Kingdom period, this position included political roles, such as being the king's counselor or secretary. At that time, these officials are often listed first among the royal functionaries.

The position of the baker was significant due to the Egyptian expertise in the preparation of baked goods. Egyptian records have various titles for bakers based on their specialties. In the royal court, the master baker (*'ry rt 'tyw*) was in charge not only of the bread for the pharaoh and the palace, but also of the bread used by priests in temple rituals. • ZR

↗ Wine jar, eastern Delta region, Egypt, 33rd to 30th century BCE

EGYPTOLOGY

40:1–23 Dream interpretation in Egypt

While various means of divination were practiced throughout the ancient Near East, most of the literature regarding dreams and their interpretation (oneiromancy) comes from Egypt. Dream interpretation developed because, while some dreams have a clear and explicitly communicated message (such as Yaakov's dream, Gen. 28), others (like the cupbearer's and baker's dreams in Gen. 40, and Pharaoh's in Gen. 41) contain obscure, perplexing, and troubling symbols.

Two types of dream literature are known from ancient Egypt. In dream narratives, a god appears to tell an individual that he has been chosen as king and requests a specific action. For example, Thutmose IV relates that before he became king, he was hunting at the base of the Sphinx when he fell into a deep sleep. The Sphinx then appeared to him and told him to dust the sand off his image and, when he did so, he was promised kingship. These dreams need little interpretation and serve to emphasize the special relationship between the king and a god. Shlomo's dream (I Kings 3:5–15) is also an example of this genre, although within the unique Israelite religious context.

The second category comprises collections of dream interpretations, which assumed that gods inspired dreams to guide people to take action, as with Pharaoh in Genesis 41. Papyrus Chester Beatty III, believed to derive from an early 2nd-millennium original, is the oldest surviving manual of dream interpretation. The manuscript presents two hundred possible dreams, a judgment of whether each is good or bad, and an interpretation. For example, if a man sees himself submerging in the Nile, it is judged good, as "it means purification from all evil." However, if a man sees himself "looking into a deep well," that is bad, as it means that he will be put in prison.

Nili Shupak, a scholar of the Tanakh and Egyptology, finds many similarities between the dreams in Genesis 40–41 and Egyptian dream collections regarding symbols, irony, and wordplay. She points out that the dream imagery in Genesis 40–41 is reminiscent of the mythology and natural world of Egypt. The motif of seven cows (usually with a bull) is often found on the walls of tombs and temples and associated with the world to come; they represented the ample supply of bread and beer for the deceased. The symbol of the Egyptian god of corn, Npri, was seven ears of grain that appeared on his head or body. The Sehel Inscription tells of a seven-year famine during the reign of Djoser (2267–2248 BCE), who then summons his chief advisor Imhotep for advice. The sage informs Pharaoh that the resolution of the problem lies with the god Khnum who then appears to Djoser in a dream. The priests of Khnum are then given a land grant and the famine ends.

Pharaoh's anxiety over his dreams leads him to summon "all the magicians and sages of Egypt" (41:8). The term for "magician," *ḥartum*, is used also for the court magicians for Pharaoh in Exodus 7–9 and, later, for Babylonian dream interpreters in Daniel 1–2, 4–5. The Hebrew term is probably derived from the title of the Egyptian priest known as the *ḥeri-hab ḥery-tep*, the "chief lector priest," who studied and transmitted magical texts, such as the Chester Beatty III collection. That the Egyptian model influenced Mesopotamia is evident in the Akkadian term for dream interpreter, *hartibi*, derived from the Egyptian term (for further information on this term, see "*Ḥartumim*" on page 246).

In Genesis 40–41, the Torah emphasizes that even the highly sophisticated Egyptian art of dream interpretation is no match for the divine understanding given to a wise and God-fearing Israelite youth (40:8, 41:16). • EG

↗ Votive stele with three Hathor cows, Deir el-Bahari, Thebes, 15th century BCE

לַאֲדֹנֵיהֶם לְמֶלֶךְ מִצְרָיִם: וַיִּקְצֹף פַּרְעֹה עַל שְׁנֵי סָרִיסָיו עַל ב
שַׂר הַמַּשְׁקִים וְעַל שַׂר הָאוֹפִים: וַיִּתֵּן אֹתָם בְּמִשְׁמַר בֵּית שַׂר ג
הַטַּבָּחִים אֶל־בֵּית הַסֹּהַר מְקוֹם אֲשֶׁר יוֹסֵף אָסוּר שָׁם: וַיִּפְקֹד ד
שַׂר הַטַּבָּחִים אֶת־יוֹסֵף אִתָּם וַיְשָׁרֶת אֹתָם וַיִּהְיוּ יָמִים בְּמִשְׁמָר:
וַיַּחַלְמוּ חֲלוֹם שְׁנֵיהֶם אִישׁ חֲלֹמוֹ בְּלַיְלָה אֶחָד אִישׁ כְּפִתְרוֹן ה
חֲלֹמוֹ הַמַּשְׁקֶה וְהָאֹפֶה אֲשֶׁר לְמֶלֶךְ מִצְרַיִם אֲשֶׁר אֲסוּרִים
בְּבֵית הַסֹּהַר: וַיָּבֹא אֲלֵיהֶם יוֹסֵף בַּבֹּקֶר וַיַּרְא אֹתָם וְהִנָּם זֹעֲפִים: ו
וַיִּשְׁאַל אֶת־סְרִיסֵי פַרְעֹה אֲשֶׁר אִתּוֹ בְמִשְׁמַר בֵּית אֲדֹנָיו לֵאמֹר ז
מַדּוּעַ פְּנֵיכֶם רָעִים הַיּוֹם: וַיֹּאמְרוּ אֵלָיו חֲלוֹם חָלַמְנוּ וּפֹתֵר אֵין ח
אֹתוֹ וַיֹּאמֶר אֲלֵהֶם יוֹסֵף הֲלוֹא לֵאלֹהִים פִּתְרֹנִים סַפְּרוּ־נָא
לִי: וַיְסַפֵּר שַׂר־הַמַּשְׁקִים אֶת־חֲלֹמוֹ לְיוֹסֵף וַיֹּאמֶר לוֹ בַּחֲלוֹמִי ט
וְהִנֵּה־גֶפֶן לְפָנָי: וּבַגֶּפֶן שְׁלֹשָׁה שָׂרִיגִם וְהִוא כְפֹרַחַת עָלְתָה י
נִצָּהּ הִבְשִׁילוּ אַשְׁכְּלֹתֶיהָ עֲנָבִים: וְכוֹס פַּרְעֹה בְּיָדִי וָאֶקַּח אֶת־ יא
הָעֲנָבִים וָאֶשְׂחַט אֹתָם אֶל־כּוֹס פַּרְעֹה וָאֶתֵּן אֶת־הַכּוֹס עַל־כַּף
פַּרְעֹה: וַיֹּאמֶר לוֹ יוֹסֵף זֶה פִּתְרֹנוֹ שְׁלֹשֶׁת הַשָּׂרִגִים שְׁלֹשֶׁת יָמִים יב
הֵם: בְּעוֹד ׀ שְׁלֹשֶׁת יָמִים יִשָּׂא פַרְעֹה אֶת־רֹאשֶׁךָ וַהֲשִׁיבְךָ יג
עַל־כַּנֶּךָ וְנָתַתָּ כוֹס־פַּרְעֹה בְּיָדוֹ כַּמִּשְׁפָּט הָרִאשׁוֹן אֲשֶׁר הָיִיתָ
מַשְׁקֵהוּ: כִּי אִם־זְכַרְתַּנִי אִתְּךָ כַּאֲשֶׁר יִיטַב לָךְ וְעָשִׂיתָ־נָּא עִמָּדִי יד
חָסֶד וְהִזְכַּרְתַּנִי אֶל־פַּרְעֹה וְהוֹצֵאתַנִי מִן־הַבַּיִת הַזֶּה: כִּי־גֻנֹּב טו
גֻּנַּבְתִּי מֵאֶרֶץ הָעִבְרִים וְגַם־פֹּה לֹא־עָשִׂיתִי מְאוּמָה כִּי־שָׂמוּ אֹתִי
בַּבּוֹר: וַיַּרְא שַׂר־הָאֹפִים כִּי טוֹב פָּתָר וַיֹּאמֶר אֶל־יוֹסֵף אַף־אֲנִי טז
בַּחֲלוֹמִי וְהִנֵּה שְׁלֹשָׁה סַלֵּי חֹרִי עַל־רֹאשִׁי: וּבַסַּל הָעֶלְיוֹן מִכֹּל יז

gave offense to their master, the
2 king of Egypt. Pharaoh was angry
with the two officials, his chief
3 cupbearer, and his chief baker, and
he placed them in custody in the
house of the captain of the guard,
in the very place where Yosef was
4 confined. The captain of the guard
assigned them to Yosef and it was he who attended them. When they had been in custody for some time,
5 the two of them – the imprisoned cupbearer and baker of the king of Egypt – each had a dream on the
6 same night, each dream seeming to carry its own meaning. When Yosef came to them the next morning,
7 he saw that they were both distressed. He asked Pharaoh's officials who were in custody with him in his
8 master's house, "Why are you looking so troubled today?" "We both had dreams," they told him, "but
there is no one to interpret them." Yosef replied, "Interpretation belongs to God. Tell me your dreams."
9 So the chief cupbearer told his dream to Yosef and said to him, "In my dream I saw a vine in front of me.
10 The vine had three branches. As soon as it budded, it blossomed, and its clusters ripened into grapes.
11 Pharaoh's cup was in my hand; I took the grapes and squeezed them into Pharaoh's cup, and I placed
12 13 the cup in his hand." "This is what it means," Yosef said. "The three branches are three days. In three days
Pharaoh will lift your head and restore you to your position. You will place Pharaoh's cup in his hand
14 again, as you did when you were his cupbearer. When it goes well with you, remember me and do me
15 this kindness: mention me to Pharaoh so as to free me from this place. The truth is that I was kidnapped
16 from the land of the Hebrews. Here too, I have done nothing to deserve being placed in this pit." The
chief baker saw that he had given a favorable interpretation, so he said to Yosef, "I too had a dream. There
17 were three baskets of white bread on my head. In the top basket were all sorts of baked food that Pharaoh

מַאֲכַל פַּרְעֹה מַעֲשֵׂה אֹפֶה וְהָעוֹף אֹכֵל אֹתָם מִן־הַסַּל מֵעַל
יח רֹאשִׁי׃ וַיַּעַן יוֹסֵף וַיֹּאמֶר זֶה פִּתְרֹנוֹ שְׁלֹשֶׁת הַסַּלִּים שְׁלֹשֶׁת
יט יָמִים הֵם׃ בְּעוֹד ׀ שְׁלֹשֶׁת יָמִים יִשָּׂא פַרְעֹה אֶת־רֹאשְׁךָ מֵעָלֶיךָ
• כ וְתָלָה אוֹתְךָ עַל־עֵץ וְאָכַל הָעוֹף אֶת־בְּשָׂרְךָ מֵעָלֶיךָ׃ וַיְהִי ׀ בַּיּוֹם מפטיר
הַשְּׁלִישִׁי יוֹם הֻלֶּדֶת אֶת־פַּרְעֹה וַיַּעַשׂ מִשְׁתֶּה לְכָל־עֲבָדָיו וַיִּשָּׂא
אֶת־רֹאשׁ ׀ שַׂר הַמַּשְׁקִים וְאֶת־רֹאשׁ שַׂר הָאֹפִים בְּתוֹךְ עֲבָדָיו׃

eats, but birds were eating them out of the basket above my
head." "This is what it means," Yosef said. "The three baskets 18
are three days. In three days Pharaoh will lift your head from 19
your body; he will hang you from a stake, and birds will eat
your flesh." The third day was Pharaoh's birthday. He made 20 •
a feast for all his servants, and from among them he singled

EGYPTOLOGY

40:20 Pharaoh's birthday

No evidence has been found for celebrations of the pharaoh's birthday before the 1st millennium BCE; this practice appears to have been introduced in Persian times.

However, another possible meaning exists for the importance of this day. Psalms 2:8–11 seems to be referring to the coronation of a Judahite king, "Just ask of Me – I shall give you nations for your inheritance, estate to the ends of the earth. You will crush them with an iron rod; You will shatter them like pottery. And now, kings, be wise; be warned, judges of the earth: Serve the Lord with reverence and tremble as you exalt." The preceding verse (v. 7) there references a day when the person was fathered, "I tell now of the Lord's decree: He told me, 'You are My child; this very day I fathered you (*yeladetikha*),'" apparently a reference to coronation, metaphorically, a day of rebirth.

Therefore, the verse may be referring to the festival of ascension, when the pharaoh was "reborn" as a divine king, the "Son of Re," the sun god. This was part of the coronation ceremony, after which "Son of Re" was included in the pharaoh's title. Alternately, it may be referring to the "festival of the king's appearance," the anniversary of this ascension. Although there is no evidence that the festivities associated with these occasions involved freeing people from prison, in the Near East the ascension year of a new king was a time when individuals were pardoned, including political enemies. An example of such a pardon is reported in II Kings 25:27: "In the thirty-seventh year following the exile of Yehoyakhin, king of Yehuda, on the twenty-seventh of the twelfth month, Evvil Merodakh, king of Babylon, in the year he became king, granted Yehoyakhin, king of Yehuda, pardon from prison." ▪ ZR

Ramesses II seated with the gods Phah, Amun, and Ra, Great Temple of Ramesses II, Abu Simbel, 13th century BCE

LANGUAGE

41:2 *Ye'or* and reed grass (*aḥu*)

A Torah story set in Egypt would naturally use some Egyptian words appropriate for the story's setting (and for the Torah's original readers); the "reeds" of verses 2 and 18 are *aḥu*, an Egyptian loanword (taken from the plural form of the Egyptian word) that occurs elsewhere in the Tanakh only in Job 8:11, in a context where papyrus is also mentioned. It originally referred to the marshy land affected by the annual inundation of the Nile. The Nile itself, of course, has an Egyptian name as well.

The Hebrew name of the Nile, *ye'or*, is derived from Egyptian *yrw*. Originally a specific name, the Egyptian word eventually simply developed to mean "river." Hebrew too sometimes uses the plural of the word to refer to the multiple branches and canals of the Nile and, extremely rarely, in a non-Egyptian context (Is. 33:21; Job 28:10; Dan. 12:5–7;). This Egyptian loan word is also found in Assyrian as *ya-ra-u*.

The name Nile, used nowadays in Arabic as well, comes to us from Greek via Latin. Its origin is unknown. ▪ ZR, MC

כא וַיָּשֶׁב אֶת־שַׂר הַמַּשְׁקִים עַל־מַשְׁקֵהוּ וַיִּתֵּן הַכּוֹס עַל־כַּף פַּרְעֹה׃
כב כג וְאֵת שַׂר הָאֹפִים תָּלָה כַּאֲשֶׁר פָּתַר לָהֶם יוֹסֵף׃ וְלֹא־זָכַר שַׂר־
הַמַּשְׁקִים אֶת־יוֹסֵף וַיִּשְׁכָּחֵהוּ׃
מא א וַיְהִי מִקֵּץ שְׁנָתַיִם יָמִים וּפַרְעֹה חֹלֵם וְהִנֵּה עֹמֵד עַל־הַיְאֹר׃ מקץ
•• ב וְהִנֵּה מִן־הַיְאֹר עֹלֹת שֶׁבַע פָּרוֹת יְפוֹת מַרְאֶה וּבְרִיאֹת בָּשָׂר
ג וַתִּרְעֶינָה בָּאָחוּ׃ וְהִנֵּה שֶׁבַע פָּרוֹת אֲחֵרוֹת עֹלוֹת אַחֲרֵיהֶן מִן־

21 out his chief cupbearer and chief baker. He restored the chief
cupbearer to his position so that, as before, he placed the cup
22 in Pharaoh's hand. But he hung up the chief baker, as Yosef
23 had predicted. Still, the chief cupbearer did not remember
Yosef; he forgot him.
41 1 Two years passed. Then Pharaoh had a dream: he was standing
•• 2 by the Nile when seven handsome, healthy cows came up out
3 of the river and grazed among the reeds. Then seven other
cows came up from the river after them, ugly and gaunt, and

Nile grasses, Upper Egypt

הַיְאֹר רָעוֹת מַרְאֶה וְדַקּוֹת בָּשָׂר וַתַּעֲמֹדְנָה אֵצֶל הַפָּרוֹת עַל־
ד שְׂפַת הַיְאֹר׃ וַתֹּאכַלְנָה הַפָּרוֹת רָעוֹת הַמַּרְאֶה וְדַקֹּת הַבָּשָׂר
• ה אֵת שֶׁבַע הַפָּרוֹת יְפֹת הַמַּרְאֶה וְהַבְּרִיאֹת וַיִּיקַץ פַּרְעֹה׃ וַיִּישָׁן
וַיַּחֲלֹם שֵׁנִית וְהִנֵּה ׀ שֶׁבַע שִׁבֳּלִים עֹלוֹת בְּקָנֶה אֶחָד בְּרִיאוֹת

stood beside them by the riverbank. The ugly, gaunt cows ate 4
up the seven handsome, healthy cows. Pharaoh awoke. Falling 5 •
back to sleep, he had a second dream: he saw seven ears of

NEAR EAST

41:2 Seven cows

Seven is a common typological number in Egyptian descriptions of dreams: "(He who dreams about) seven – they will rebuke him" (Papyrus Carlsberg XIII a, 2, 1). Seven was also used in various Egyptian rituals and legends, in association with cows in particular. For example, seven Hathors (women who have cow's horns on their heads, representing the Egyptian goddess of fertility, Hathor, often depicted as a cow) arrive to foretell the future of a newborn infant, demonstrating a connection between cows and fertility in Egyptian belief.

Additionally, seven cows and a bull were believed to greet the deceased in the afterlife, a motif often depicted on the walls of temples and tombs. These cows were intended to provide sustenance for the deceased. The *Book of the Dead* states, "I know the names of the seven cows and their bull who give bread and beer, who are beneficial to souls and provide daily portions; may you give bread and beer and make provision for me." Thus, cows carried a particular connotation of sustenance in Egyptian symbolism. It is important to note that while cows were abundant in Egypt and important to the economy, cattle were what the upper class ate; the lower classes consumed sheep (although the ram was a sacred animal of the god Amun, taboos associated with a god only applied to priests and followers of that god – taboos were likely ignored by non-religious and poor people). Therefore, Pharaoh's dream about cows, as opposed to sheep, fits his exalted station. ▪ ZR

NEAR EAST

41:5 He had a second dream

The motif of a double or repeated dream is found in the literature of the ancient Near East, symbolizing the seriousness and urgency of the message contained therein. The Gudea cylinders (ca. 2125 BCE) describe King Gudea of Lagash dreaming that a giant man commands him to build a temple, and a second and third dream provide more details about its construction. In the Babylonian *Poem of the Righteous Sufferer* (*Ludlul bel Nemeqi*, ca. 1307–1282 BCE), the protagonist receives three separate dreams informing him that he has been cleansed from his offense and, significantly, the first one "appeared twice with the same meaning" (III 8). In the *Epic of Gilgamesh*, Gilgamesh has two dreams which his mother interprets as foretelling his meeting with Enkidu. Note also that Yosef's two dreams about his own future set off the chain of events that brought him to Pharaoh's court in Egypt. ▪ ZR

Replica of the *Poem of the Righteous Sufferer*, Nineveh, 7th century BCE

Hathor, the nursing cow goddess, symbol of fertility and nourishment, Hatshepsut mortuary temple, Deir el-Bahari

וְטֹבוֹת: וְהִנֵּה שֶׁבַע שִׁבֳּלִים דַּקּוֹת וּשְׁדוּפֹת קָדִים צֹמְחוֹת ו
אַחֲרֵיהֶן: וַתִּבְלַעְנָה הַשִּׁבֳּלִים הַדַּקּוֹת אֵת שֶׁבַע הַשִּׁבֳּלִים ז
הַבְּרִיאוֹת וְהַמְּלֵאוֹת וַיִּיקַץ פַּרְעֹה וְהִנֵּה חֲלוֹם: וַיְהִי בַבֹּקֶר ח
וַתִּפָּעֶם רוּחוֹ וַיִּשְׁלַח וַיִּקְרָא אֶת־כָּל־חַרְטֻמֵּי מִצְרַיִם וְאֶת־כָּל־
חֲכָמֶיהָ וַיְסַפֵּר פַּרְעֹה לָהֶם אֶת־חֲלֹמוֹ וְאֵין־פּוֹתֵר אוֹתָם לְפַרְעֹה:
וַיְדַבֵּר שַׂר הַמַּשְׁקִים אֶת־פַּרְעֹה לֵאמֹר אֶת־חֲטָאַי אֲנִי מַזְכִּיר ט
הַיּוֹם: פַּרְעֹה קָצַף עַל־עֲבָדָיו וַיִּתֵּן אֹתִי בְּמִשְׁמַר בֵּית שַׂר י
הַטַּבָּחִים אֹתִי וְאֵת שַׂר הָאֹפִים: וַנַּחַלְמָה חֲלוֹם בְּלַיְלָה אֶחָד יא
אֲנִי וָהוּא אִישׁ כְּפִתְרוֹן חֲלֹמוֹ חָלָמְנוּ: וְשָׁם אִתָּנוּ נַעַר עִבְרִי יב

6 grain, ripe and robust, growing on a single stalk. Suddenly,
seven other ears sprouted after them, thin and scorched by
7 the east wind. The thin ears swallowed up the seven ripe, full
8 ears. Pharaoh awoke – and realized it had been a dream. In
the morning his mind was troubled, so he sent for all the
magicians and sages of Egypt. Pharaoh told them his dream,
but no one could offer an interpretation that satisfied him.
9 Then the chief cupbearer said to Pharaoh, "I must recall my
10 sins today. Once, Pharaoh was angry with his servants and
placed me and the chief baker in custody in the house of the
11 captain of the guard. One night he and I each had a dream,
12 and each dream seemed to have its own meaning. With us
was a young Hebrew, a slave of the captain of the guard. We

Detail of dream stele of Thutmose IV making an offering to the Sphinx, granite, Giza Plateau, 1500–1390 BCE

LANGUAGE

41:8 *Ḥartumim*

The "magicians" of verse 8 are *ḥartumim*, a word that occurs in the Tanakh ten times, only in the plural. The word is not Semitic – it is universally acknowledged to derive from an Egyptian term, but which term that is has been surprisingly difficult to determine.

It is generally assumed to be derived from Egyptian *ḥry-tp*, which during the Old Kingdom (3rd millennium BCE) meant "chief" or "head," but by the New Kingdom (second half of the 1st millennium BCE) was often found in combination with the expression *hry-ḥb*, which refers to some sort of priest or magician. The *m* of the Hebrew word would not naturally derive from the *p* of the Egyptian word, and therefore a more recent suggestion is that *ḥartumim* derives from *hry-tm3*, "those on duty." But the *b* of *hry-ḥb* or of the New Kingdom spelling of *ḥry-tp* as *ḥry-tb* might have given rise to the *m* sound in Hebrew.

The *ḥartumim* in Genesis and Exodus play different roles – the former as dream interpreters, the latter as magicians – and these functionaries play both roles in Egyptian texts as well, from as early as the Old Kingdom period (3rd millennium BCE) well into Hellenistic times. The earlier texts present them as scholars and thus experts in ritual and magic. The role of dream interpreter, though found at the earliest stages, grows more prominent in later texts.

The word appears twice (and five times in Aramaic) in the story of Daniel. But the word *ḫarṭibi* is attested in two Akkadian texts, both times in connection with Egyptians, so it was known there as well. The first of these, a tablet in the British Museum, groups the *ḫarṭibi* with exorcists, augurs, and diviners. A. Leo Oppenheim writes in his magisterial work on dream interpretation in the ancient Near East, "Interpreters of dreams had to come from Egypt to be acceptable." ▪ MC

עֶבֶד לְשַׂר הַטַּבָּחִים וַנְּסַפֶּר־לוֹ וַיִּפְתָּר־לָנוּ אֶת־חֲלֹמֹתֵינוּ אִישׁ
יג כַּחֲלֹמוֹ פָּתָר: וַיְהִי כַּאֲשֶׁר פָּתַר־לָנוּ כֵּן הָיָה אֹתִי הֵשִׁיב עַל־כַּנִּי
יד • וְאֹתוֹ תָלָה: וַיִּשְׁלַח פַּרְעֹה וַיִּקְרָא אֶת־יוֹסֵף וַיְרִיצֻהוּ מִן־הַבּוֹר
טו וַיְגַלַּח וַיְחַלֵּף שִׂמְלֹתָיו וַיָּבֹא אֶל־פַּרְעֹה: וַיֹּאמֶר פַּרְעֹה אֶל־יוֹסֵף שני
חֲלוֹם חָלַמְתִּי וּפֹתֵר אֵין אֹתוֹ וַאֲנִי שָׁמַעְתִּי עָלֶיךָ לֵאמֹר תִּשְׁמַע
טז חֲלוֹם לִפְתֹּר אֹתוֹ: וַיַּעַן יוֹסֵף אֶת־פַּרְעֹה לֵאמֹר בִּלְעָדָי אֱלֹהִים
יז יַעֲנֶה אֶת־שְׁלוֹם פַּרְעֹה: וַיְדַבֵּר פַּרְעֹה אֶל־יוֹסֵף בַּחֲלֹמִי הִנְנִי
יח עֹמֵד עַל־שְׂפַת הַיְאֹר: וְהִנֵּה מִן־הַיְאֹר עֹלֹת שֶׁבַע פָּרוֹת בְּרִיאוֹת
יט בָּשָׂר וִיפֹת תֹּאַר וַתִּרְעֶינָה בָּאָחוּ: וְהִנֵּה שֶׁבַע פָּרוֹת אֲחֵרוֹת
עֹלוֹת אַחֲרֵיהֶן דַּלּוֹת וְרָעוֹת תֹּאַר מְאֹד וְרַקּוֹת בָּשָׂר לֹא־רָאִיתִי
כ כָהֵנָּה בְּכָל־אֶרֶץ מִצְרַיִם לָרֹעַ: וַתֹּאכַלְנָה הַפָּרוֹת הָרַקּוֹת
כא וְהָרָעוֹת אֵת שֶׁבַע הַפָּרוֹת הָרִאשֹׁנוֹת הַבְּרִיאֹת: וַתָּבֹאנָה אֶל־
קִרְבֶּנָה וְלֹא נוֹדַע כִּי־בָאוּ אֶל־קִרְבֶּנָה וּמַרְאֵיהֶן רַע כַּאֲשֶׁר
כב בַּתְּחִלָּה וָאִיקָץ: וָאֵרֶא בַּחֲלֹמִי וְהִנֵּה | שֶׁבַע שִׁבֳּלִים עֹלֹת בְּקָנֶה
כג אֶחָד מְלֵאֹת וְטֹבוֹת: וְהִנֵּה שֶׁבַע שִׁבֳּלִים צְנֻמוֹת דַּקּוֹת שְׁדֻפוֹת
כד קָדִים צֹמְחוֹת אַחֲרֵיהֶם: וַתִּבְלַעְןָ הַשִּׁבֳּלִים הַדַּקֹּת אֵת שֶׁבַע
כה הַשִּׁבֳּלִים הַטֹּבוֹת וָאֹמַר אֶל־הַחַרְטֻמִּים וְאֵין מַגִּיד לִי: וַיֹּאמֶר

told him our dreams and he interpreted them for us, telling
each of us the meaning of his dream. Things turned out exactly 13
as he interpreted them to us. I was restored to my position,
and the baker was hung up." So Pharaoh sent for Yosef. He 14 •
was rushed from the dungeon, had his hair cut, changed his
clothes, and came before Pharaoh. Pharaoh said to Yosef, "I 15
had a dream and no one can interpret it; I have heard that
when you hear a dream you can interpret it." "Not I," replied 16
Yosef to Pharaoh. "God will give Pharaoh the answer that he
needs." Pharaoh told Yosef: "In my dream, I was standing by 17
the bank of the Nile when seven handsome, healthy cows 18
came up out of the river and grazed among the reeds. Then 19
after them came seven other cows, scrawny, very sickly, and
thin – I never saw such sickly cows in all Egypt. Then the thin, 20
sickly cows ate up the first seven healthy cows. But when they 21
had eaten them you could not tell that they had eaten them,
for they still looked as bad as before. Then I awoke. In my 22
dream I then saw seven ears of grain, ripe and full, growing
on a single stalk. Suddenly, seven other ears sprouted after 23
them, shriveled, thin, and scorched by the east wind, and the 24
thin ears swallowed the seven good ears. I told this to the
magicians, but none could explain it to me." Yosef said to 25
Pharaoh, "The two dreams of Pharaoh are one and the same.

NEAR EAST

41:14 Hair cut/shaved

While most men in the ancient Near East did not shave, Egyptian men were usually clean shaven and had either closely cropped hair or shaved heads. Wigs made of human hair were sometimes worn, and kings and male deities are depicted with false beards affixed with straps along the side of the face. Such beards were considered a sign of divinity. Fashions changed in different eras – for example, in the Old Kingdom period, elite men were often depicted with short-cropped hair and trimmed moustaches and beards. In the Middle Kingdom period, it was usual for no facial hair to be shown at all. In all eras, natural hair was kept short for hygienic reasons, and the shaving of hair, including body hair, was associated with purity. Foreigners can be distinguished from Egyptians in paintings because they have full beards and longer hair. ▪ ZR

Clean-shaven King Neferhotep, Middle Kingdom (Thirteenth Dynasty), Abydos, 18th century BCE

EGYPTOLOGY

41:27 Seven years of famine

In the ancient Near East, it appears that the conventional way of indicating a very long famine was to say that it lasted seven years. Egyptian texts also refer to famines lasting seven years. The Famine Stele tells of a drought during the reign of Pharaoh Djoser of the Third Dynasty: "Because Hapy (the flooding of the Nile) had failed to come on time for a period of seven years, grain was scant, kernels were dried up, scarce was every kind of food." A seven-year famine also appears in the Ugaritic *Tale of Aqhat*, where Dan'el is warned, "the farmer's nightmare: drought! But this is no ordinary drought. For an epic seven years neither dew nor rain will fall; the wells, deriving their water from the subterranean deeps, will dry up, as will the riverbeds." In the *Epic of Gilgamesh*, the sky god Anu threatens the Sumerian city Uruk with "seven years of empty husks."

Similarly, the prophet Gad in Tanakh presents a seven-year famine as an option for David's punishment (II Sam. 24:13). ▪ ZR

יוֹסֵף אֶל־פַּרְעֹה חֲלוֹם פַּרְעֹה אֶחָד הוּא אֵת אֲשֶׁר הָאֱלֹהִים
עֹשֶׂה הִגִּיד לְפַרְעֹה: שֶׁבַע פָּרֹת הַטֹּבֹת שֶׁבַע שָׁנִים הֵנָּה וְשֶׁבַע כו
הַשִּׁבֳּלִים הַטֹּבֹת שֶׁבַע שָׁנִים הֵנָּה חֲלוֹם אֶחָד הוּא: וְשֶׁבַע הַפָּרוֹת כז •
הָרַקּוֹת וְהָרָעֹת הָעֹלֹת אַחֲרֵיהֶן שֶׁבַע שָׁנִים הֵנָּה וְשֶׁבַע הַשִּׁבֳּלִים
הָרֵקוֹת שְׁדֻפוֹת הַקָּדִים יִהְיוּ שֶׁבַע שְׁנֵי רָעָב: הוּא הַדָּבָר אֲשֶׁר כח
דִּבַּרְתִּי אֶל־פַּרְעֹה אֲשֶׁר הָאֱלֹהִים עֹשֶׂה הֶרְאָה אֶת־פַּרְעֹה: הִנֵּה כט
שֶׁבַע שָׁנִים בָּאוֹת שָׂבָע גָּדוֹל בְּכָל־אֶרֶץ מִצְרָיִם: וְקָמוּ שֶׁבַע ל
שְׁנֵי רָעָב אַחֲרֵיהֶן וְנִשְׁכַּח כָּל־הַשָּׂבָע בְּאֶרֶץ מִצְרָיִם וְכִלָּה הָרָעָב
אֶת־הָאָרֶץ: וְלֹא־יִוָּדַע הַשָּׂבָע בָּאָרֶץ מִפְּנֵי הָרָעָב הַהוּא אַחֲרֵי־ לא
כֵן כִּי־כָבֵד הוּא מְאֹד: וְעַל הִשָּׁנוֹת הַחֲלוֹם אֶל־פַּרְעֹה פַּעֲמָיִם לב
כִּי־נָכוֹן הַדָּבָר מֵעִם הָאֱלֹהִים וּמְמַהֵר הָאֱלֹהִים לַעֲשֹׂתוֹ: וְעַתָּה לג
יֵרֶא פַרְעֹה אִישׁ נָבוֹן וְחָכָם וִישִׁיתֵהוּ עַל־אֶרֶץ מִצְרָיִם: יַעֲשֶׂה לד •
פַרְעֹה וְיַפְקֵד פְּקִדִים עַל־הָאָרֶץ וְחִמֵּשׁ אֶת־אֶרֶץ מִצְרַיִם בְּשֶׁבַע
שְׁנֵי הַשָּׂבָע: וְיִקְבְּצוּ אֶת־כָּל־אֹכֶל הַשָּׁנִים הַטֹּבֹת הַבָּאֹת הָאֵלֶּה לה
וְיִצְבְּרוּ־בָר תַּחַת יַד־פַּרְעֹה אֹכֶל בֶּעָרִים וְשָׁמָרוּ: וְהָיָה הָאֹכֶל לו
לְפִקָּדוֹן לָאָרֶץ לְשֶׁבַע שְׁנֵי הָרָעָב אֲשֶׁר תִּהְיֶיןָ בְּאֶרֶץ מִצְרָיִם

26 God has told Pharaoh what He is about to do. The seven good
cows are seven years, and so too the seven good ears are seven
• 27 years. It is one and the same dream. The seven thin, sickly
cows that came up after them are seven years, as are the seven
empty ears scorched by the east wind. They are seven years
28 of famine. It is as I have told Pharaoh: God has shown Pharaoh
29 what He is about to do. Seven years are coming when there
30 will be great abundance throughout the land of Egypt. But
after them will come seven years of famine, when all the
abundance in Egypt will be forgotten. Famine will ravage the
31 land. So devastating will the famine be that no one in the land
32 will know anything of abundance anymore. As for Pharaoh
having the same dream twice, this means that the matter has
already been decided by God, and He is soon to bring it
33 about. So now let Pharaoh seek out an astute, wise man and
• 34 set him over the land of Egypt. Let Pharaoh appoint overseers
across the land and take a fifth of Egypt's harvest during the
35 seven years of abundance. Let them gather all that food in
these coming good years, storing the grain under Pharaoh's
36 aegis so that there is food under guard in all the cities. The
food should be held in reserve for the land when the seven
years of famine come to Egypt, so that the country is not

Emaciated herdsman, detail from stele of the overseer of the fortress Intef, Egypt, 20th century BCE

לז וְלֹא־תִכָּרֵת הָאָרֶץ בָּרָעָב׃ וַיִּיטַב הַדָּבָר בְּעֵינֵי פַרְעֹה וּבְעֵינֵי
לח כָּל־עֲבָדָיו׃ וַיֹּאמֶר פַּרְעֹה אֶל־עֲבָדָיו הֲנִמְצָא כָזֶה אִישׁ אֲשֶׁר
לט רוּחַ אֱלֹהִים בּוֹ׃ וַיֹּאמֶר פַּרְעֹה אֶל־יוֹסֵף אַחֲרֵי הוֹדִיעַ אֱלֹהִים שלישי
מ • אוֹתְךָ אֶת־כָּל־זֹאת אֵין־נָבוֹן וְחָכָם כָּמוֹךָ׃ אַתָּה תִּהְיֶה עַל־

ruined by the famine." The plan seemed good to Pharaoh and 37
all his officials. Pharaoh said to them, "Could we find another 38
like him, a man who has within him the spirit of God?" So 39
Pharaoh said to Yosef, "Since God has made all this known
to you, there can be no one else as astute or as wise as you.
You shall be in charge of my court, and by your command 40 •
shall all my people be directed. Only the throne itself will

EGYPTOLOGY

41:34–45 Yosef appointed overseer of Egypt

Yosef presents a strategy to minimize the devastating effects of the famine foretold in Pharaoh's dream. His plan stands in contrast to standard convention in the ancient Near East, where negative portents seen in dreams were addressed by invoking supernatural means, such as incantations and rituals. For example, the *Maqlu Series*, an Akkadian incantation text from the 1st millennium BCE, includes, "May the dream I dreamt be made favorable for me" and "I wash my hands, I cleanse my body in the pure spring water that was formed in Eridu. Anything evil, anything unfavorable…the evil of (i.e., portended by) evil, unfavorable dreams, signs, and portents.… With the water of my body and the washing of my hands may it (the various evils) rinse off and come upon a figurine of a substitute."

The appointment of wise overseers is reminiscent of the system put in place under the Middle Kingdom pharaoh, Khakaure Senusret III (reigned 1878–1839 BCE), who innovated the idea of appointing governors responsible for large sections of Egypt. These governors, who were based in the royal court, functioned within two bureaus (*waret*), one for the north and one for the south. He also established other departments, such as a treasury and a separate administration to run the palace. This system increased the size of the bureaucracy and created many new official titles. The execution of his policy demonstrates that periodic shifts in the administrative structure of Egypt occurred. ▪ ZR

Bust of Pharaoh Khakaure Senusret III, Egypt, ca. 1860 BCE

EGYPTOLOGY

41:40 Yosef as commander of the granary

Pharaoh appoints Yosef to be "in charge of my court" and gives him the title, "governor (*shalit*) of the land" (Gen 42:6). Egyptian documents attest that various important governmental roles were carried out by different people who were all considered Pharaoh's second-in-command. The vizier (*tjati*), the highest official under the pharaoh, supervised the running of the country, like a prime minister. The administrative second-in-command was called the chief steward or great overseer of the house (*imi-r pr wr*), in charge of the estates that supplied the palace with food. Additional supervisory roles in particular areas of specialty belonged to others in the position of second-in-command, such as the overseer of the granary, who was responsible for assessing, collecting, registering, storing, and redistributing the grain taxes. This position could be combined with other functions. For example, Khaemhat, an ancient Egyptian official under king Amenhotep III (ca. 1388–1351 BCE), was the royal scribe and also "Overseer of the Double Granary of Upper and Lower Egypt."

Based on his actions in collecting and storing the grain of Egypt (Gen. 41:48–49), as well as distributing it (Gen. 41:55–57), the title of overseer of the granary is consistent with the Torah's description of Yosef's position. Additionally, since Yosef interrogates the brothers, he appears also to be involved in matters of national security. ▪ ZR

Copy of a relief, tomb of Khaemhat, Theban Necropolis, 14th century BCE

בֵּיתִי וְעַל־פִּיךָ יִשַּׁק כׇּל־עַמִּי רַק הַכִּסֵּא אֶגְדַּל מִמֶּךָּ׃ וַיֹּאמֶר מא
פַּרְעֹה אֶל־יוֹסֵף רְאֵה נָתַתִּי אֹתְךָ עַל כׇּל־אֶרֶץ מִצְרָיִם׃ וַיָּסַר מב
פַּרְעֹה אֶת־טַבַּעְתּוֹ מֵעַל יָדוֹ וַיִּתֵּן אֹתָהּ עַל־יַד יוֹסֵף וַיַּלְבֵּשׁ אֹתוֹ
בִּגְדֵי־שֵׁשׁ וַיָּשֶׂם רְבִד הַזָּהָב עַל־צַוָּארוֹ׃ וַיַּרְכֵּב אֹתוֹ בְּמִרְכֶּבֶת מג

41 make me greater than you." Then Pharaoh said to Yosef, "I
42 hereby place you in charge of all the land of Egypt." Pharaoh
removed his signet ring from his hand and placed it on Yosef's.
He had him robed in garments of the finest linen, and placed
43 a gold chain around his neck. He had him ride in the chariot
of his second-in-command, and ahead of him people

NEAR EAST

41:42 Finest linen

Flax was grown extensively along the Nile, and the fine linen produced from it was well known. Proverbs 7:16 refers to Egyptian linen, "I spread my couch with quilts woven from Egyptian linen cords," and Yeshayahu refers to the Egyptian flax workers in his description of the collapse of Egypt, "The many who work combed flax will be shamed" (Is. 19:9).

Rambam notes that "whenever the Torah uses the word *shesh* or *bad*, it is referring to flax (*pishtim*), i.e., linen (*butz*)" (*Mishneh Torah*, Laws of Temple Vessels 8:13). The term used in this verse, *shesh*, is taken from the Egyptian *shs*, used for cloth of exceptional quality. Later Hebrew would use *butz*, the Mesopotamian term, which is the basis for the English word "byssus," via Greek and Latin. While byssus itself originally referred to flax and linen, over time it was extended to refer to any fine and valuable cloth, just as *bad* in Hebrew came to mean any kind of cloth. ▪ ZR

A length of very sheer linen cloth, tomb of Hatnefer and Ramose, Thebes, 15th century BCE

EGYPTOLOGY

41:42–43 Yosef's symbols of rule

Pharaoh rewards Yosef with objects that symbolize his new role as vizier. These objects are known from Egyptian literature and iconography, particularly from the New Kingdom period, as used for the investiture of high officials. These officials were sometimes Semites, not just Egyptians.

The signet ring (Hebrew *taba'at*, Egyptian *gb't*) appears in Old Kingdom texts. A ring bearing the royal seal would enable an official to make decisions and validate documents in the name of the pharaoh. This official was given the title of seal bearer, a known functionary in Egyptian bureaucracy.

Gold signet ring, Amarna (?), 14th century BCE

Clothing of fine linen is known from Egyptian investiture ceremonies as the attire of high officials. For example, Rekh-Mi-Re, the vizier during the reigns of Thutmose III and Amenhotep II (ca. 1400 BCE), writes, "I went forth... clad in fine linen... since I had come forth in the accoutrements [of the vizier]."

The gift of gold was given in particular to members of the inner circle around the pharaoh who otherwise did not have any special social standing or professional background – it was for people the pharaoh himself designated as favorites. This would be appropriate for Yosef, who rose to power after having been a prisoner.

A mark of honor documented from the Amarna period to the Nineteenth Dynasty was to be brought in a chariot all the way home, where family and slaves would greet the honoree with shouts, singing, dancing, and bowing.

Many of these elements can be found in the report of the Assyrian king Ashurbanipal's appointment of Necho as pharaoh in the 7th century BCE, which was done according to Egyptian traditions: "I clad him in a garment with multicolored trimmings, placed a golden chain on him [as the] insignia of his kingship, put golden rings on his hands... I presented him [furthermore] with chariots, horses, and mules as means of transportation [befitting] his position as ruler." ▪ ZR

הַמִּשְׁנֶה אֲשֶׁר־לוֹ וַיִּקְרְאוּ לְפָנָיו אַבְרֵךְ וְנָתוֹן אֹתוֹ עַל כׇּל־אֶרֶץ
מִצְרָיִם: וַיֹּאמֶר פַּרְעֹה אֶל־יוֹסֵף אֲנִי פַרְעֹה וּבִלְעָדֶיךָ לֹא־יָרִים מד
אִישׁ אֶת־יָדוֹ וְאֶת־רַגְלוֹ בְּכׇל־אֶרֶץ מִצְרָיִם: וַיִּקְרָא פַרְעֹה שֵׁם־ מה •
יוֹסֵף צָפְנַת פַּעְנֵחַ וַיִּתֶּן־לוֹ אֶת־אָסְנַת בַּת־פּוֹטִי פֶרַע כֹּהֵן אֹן

proclaimed, "*Avrekh*."[96] Thus was he given authority over all
Egypt. Pharaoh told Yosef, "I am Pharaoh, but without your 44
consent no one will lift hand or foot in all Egypt." And 45 •
Pharaoh gave Yosef the name Tzafenat Paneaḥ[97] and gave him

96 | Possibly meaning "bow" or "kneel," or in Egyptian "make way."

97 | Possibly "interpreter of secrets," or in Egyptian related to a word meaning "life."

NEAR EAST

41:43 *Avrekh*

The word *avrekh* is rendered here in transliteration because its precise meaning remains mysterious. It could be a call (translated into Hebrew) to kneel. The Targum translates this word as "father [Hebrew *av*] of the king [Latin *rex*]," but neither compound words or Latin are a feature of Biblical Hebrew.

Some ancient translations follow the Hebrew of the Samaritan Torah in using a singular verb for "proclaimed" (not plural as in our Torah), so *avrekh* would be the "crier" who led the procession. The Akkadian *abarakku*, "chief steward," could indicate the identity of such a herald. Alternatively, *avrekh* could be a title for Yosef himself (who was put in charge of Pharaoh's court; see v. 40).

Ultimately, it is unclear whether Egyptians adopted *b-r-k* from Semitic languages, with the meaning "render homage," or whether *avrekh* was derived from the Egyptian word *'b-r.k*, "attention!" ▪ MC

NEAR EAST

41:45 Tzafenat Paneaḥ...Asnat... Potifera ...On

The traditional interpretation of Tzafenat Paneaḥ, "the man to whom mysteries are revealed," is provided by Targum Onkelos, and is based on the understanding that the name is derived from Hebrew. Egyptologists have interpreted it as based on either *ḏd p3 nṯr iw.f ꜥnḫ*, "the god speaks [and] he lives," or the Coptic *psotm pheneh*, meaning, "sustainer of life." It is also possible that the form of this Egyptian phrase was transcribed in such a way as to give it meaning in Hebrew as well. If so, it would be similar to the case of the name Moshe, which has Egyptian origins but is provided with a Hebrew meaning in Exodus 2:10 (see "The name 'Moshe'" in the Exodus volume of this series on page 14).

Asnat is a Hebraic form of the Egyptian *js.w-(n)-Nt*, "belonging to Neith," goddess of fate, wisdom, water, rivers, mothers, childbirth, and weaving.

The name Potifera is understood to be the Hebrew transcription of the Egyptian *pa-di-pa-Re*, "he whom Re [the sun god] has given."

The city On is called Heliopolis in Greek. Northeast of modern-day Cairo, it was the center of worship of the sun god, Re. Jeremiah 43:13 refers to it as "the house of the sun (*beit shemesh*), which is in the land of Egypt." The ancient Egyptian name for this city is *Iwnw*, literally, "the pillars," named for the city's impressive columns and colonnades. This name survived in Coptic as *On*, the same term used here. ▪ ZR

↗ The Heliopolis obelisk, photochromic print from a 1905 catalog

NEAR EAST

41:53–54 Famine in Egypt

The northern part of Egypt receives almost no rainfall and is dependent on the annual flooding of the Nile to provide water for agriculture. During the monsoon season, from May to August, the heavy rains from the Upper Nile Basin in the Ethiopian highlands and southern Sudan are carried to the Nile Delta. This natural phenomenon results in the Nile overflowing its banks and covering the adjacent flood plains.

The ancient Egyptians constructed an elaborate irrigation system to distribute these waters. While the flooding could usually be relied upon to occur with regularity, there were years where the rainfall upstream was insufficient for the people's agricultural needs. A few consecutive years of low rainfall could result in a disastrous famine. The ancient Egyptians measured the water level using a "nilometer," a shaft that was marked to indicate how high the water should be to provide adequate water for crops.

Ancient Egyptian inscriptions record years of famine when wheat and barley had to be rationed. For example, the stele of the royal chamberlain, Seneni, from the First Intermediate Period refers to a prolonged famine: "I measured out Upper Egyptian barley as sustenance for this whole town in the gateway of the Count and Chief Priest Djefi, in the painful years of distress. Having acted in the proper manner, I was praised for it by the whole town." ▪ ZR

Nilometer, Elephantine Island (Aswan), Roman era

לאשה ויצא יוסף על־ארץ מצרים: ויוסף בן־שלשים שנה מו
בעמדו לפני פרעה מלך־מצרים ויצא יוסף מלפני פרעה ויעבר
בכל־ארץ מצרים: ותעש הארץ בשבע שני השבע לקמצים: מז
ויקבץ את־כל־אכל ׀ שבע שנים אשר היו בארץ מצרים מח
ויתן־אכל בערים אכל שדה־העיר אשר סביבתיה נתן בתוכה:
ויצבר יוסף בר כחול הים הרבה מאד עד כי־חדל לספר כי־ מט
אין מספר: וליוסף ילד שני בנים בטרם תבוא שנת הרעב נ
אשר ילדה־לו אסנת בת־פוטי פרע כהן און: ויקרא יוסף נא
את־שם הבכור מנשה כי־נשני אלהים את־כל־עמלי ואת
כל־בית אבי: ואת שם השני קרא אפרים כי־הפרני אלהים נב
רביעי בארץ עניי: ותכלינה שבע שני השבע אשר היה בארץ מצרים: נג •
ותחלינה שבע שני הרעב לבוא כאשר אמר יוסף ויהי רעב נד
בכל־הארצות ובכל־ארץ מצרים היה לחם: ותרעב כל־ארץ נה
מצרים ויצעק העם אל־פרעה ללחם ויאמר פרעה לכל־מצרים
לכו אל־יוסף אשר־יאמר לכם תעשו: והרעב היה על כל־פני נו

Asnat, daughter of Potifera, priest of On, as his wife. Thus
46 Yosef went out to oversee Egypt. When he entered the service
of Pharaoh, king of Egypt, Yosef was thirty years old. Leaving
Pharaoh's presence, Yosef traveled throughout the land of
47 Egypt. During the seven years of plenty the land produced in
48 profusion. He gathered all the grain produced during the
seven years of plenty in Egypt and stored it in the cities. In
each city he stored the grain grown in the surrounding fields.
49 Yosef stored so much grain that it was like the sand of the sea.
They had to stop keeping records because it was beyond
50 measure. Before the years of famine came, two sons were born
51 to Yosef by Asnat daughter of Potifera, priest of On. Yosef
named his firstborn Menashe, saying, "God has made me
52 forget all my troubles and all my father's family."[98] The second
son he named Efrayim, saying, "God has made me fruitful in
• 53 the land of my affliction."[99] The seven years of abundance in
54 Egypt came to an end, and the seven years of famine began,
just as Yosef had said they would. There was famine in all the
55 other lands, but throughout Egypt there was food. When all
Egypt began to feel the famine, the people cried to Pharaoh
for food. Pharaoh told all the Egyptians, "Go to Yosef.
56 Whatever he tells you – do." The famine spread over the entire

98 | The name Menashe resonates with *nashani* (made me forget).

99 | The name Efrayim resonates with *hifrani* (made me fruitful).

١٨

הָאָרֶץ וַיִּפְתַּח יוֹסֵף אֶת־כׇּל־אֲשֶׁר בָּהֶם וַיִּשְׁבֹּר לְמִצְרַיִם וַיֶּחֱזַק
הָרָעָב בְּאֶרֶץ מִצְרָיִם: וְכׇל־הָאָרֶץ בָּאוּ מִצְרַיְמָה לִשְׁבֹּר אֶל־יוֹסֵף נז
כִּי־חָזַק הָרָעָב בְּכׇל־הָאָרֶץ: וַיַּרְא יַעֲקֹב כִּי יֶשׁ־שֶׁבֶר בְּמִצְרָיִם א מב
וַיֹּאמֶר יַעֲקֹב לְבָנָיו לָמָּה תִּתְרָאוּ: וַיֹּאמֶר הִנֵּה שָׁמַעְתִּי כִּי יֶשׁ־ ב
שֶׁבֶר בְּמִצְרָיִם רְדוּ־שָׁמָּה וְשִׁבְרוּ־לָנוּ מִשָּׁם וְנִחְיֶה וְלֹא נָמוּת:
וַיֵּרְדוּ אֲחֵי־יוֹסֵף עֲשָׂרָה לִשְׁבֹּר בָּר מִמִּצְרָיִם: וְאֶת־בִּנְיָמִין אֲחִי ג ד
יוֹסֵף לֹא־שָׁלַח יַעֲקֹב אֶת־אֶחָיו כִּי אָמַר פֶּן־יִקְרָאֶנּוּ אָסוֹן: וַיָּבֹאוּ ה
בְּנֵי יִשְׂרָאֵל לִשְׁבֹּר בְּתוֹךְ הַבָּאִים כִּי־הָיָה הָרָעָב בְּאֶרֶץ כְּנָעַן:
וְיוֹסֵף הוּא הַשַּׁלִּיט עַל־הָאָרֶץ הוּא הַמַּשְׁבִּיר לְכׇל־עַם הָאָרֶץ ו
וַיָּבֹאוּ אֲחֵי יוֹסֵף וַיִּשְׁתַּחֲווּ־לוֹ אַפַּיִם אָרְצָה: וַיַּרְא יוֹסֵף אֶת־אֶחָיו ז
וַיַּכִּרֵם וַיִּתְנַכֵּר אֲלֵיהֶם וַיְדַבֵּר אִתָּם קָשׁוֹת וַיֹּאמֶר אֲלֵהֶם מֵאַיִן

country. Yosef then opened all the storehouses and sold grain
to the Egyptians, for the famine was worsening throughout
57 Egypt. People from all over the region came to Egypt to buy
grain from Yosef, because all across the land the famine was
42 1 devastating. Knowing that there was grain in Egypt, Yaakov
said to his sons, "Why do you keep looking at one another?"
2 He said, "I have heard that there is grain in Egypt. Go down
there and buy some for us so that we may live and not die."
3 So ten of Yosef's brothers went down to buy grain in Egypt.
4 But Yaakov did not send Yosef's brother Binyamin with them,
5 for he was afraid that harm might come to him. So Yisrael's
sons were among those who came to buy grain, the famine
6 having reached as far as the land of Canaan. Yosef was the
governor of the land; it was he who dispensed food to all its
people. When Yosef's brothers arrived, they bowed down to
7 him, their faces to the ground. Yosef recognized his brothers
as soon as he saw them, but he acted like a stranger and spoke
harshly to them. "Where have you come from?" he asked.

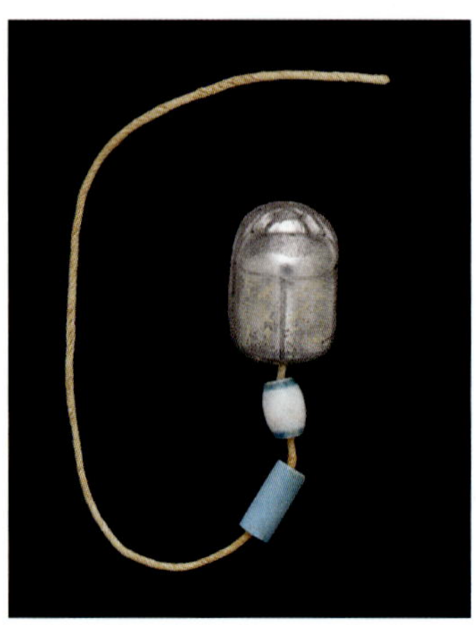

Scarab of the storehouse overseer named Wah, Tomb of Wah, Thebes, 20th century BCE

NEAR EAST

42:9 You are spies

Ancient Egyptians did not distinguish among the peoples of the east – they were all considered Asiatics and generally viewed as uncivilized enemies. The Middle Kingdom literary work, *Instruction of Merikare,* contains a king's advice to his son about how to be a good ruler, including, "Speak thus concerning the barbarian: As for the wretched Asiatic, unpleasant is the place where he is, [with] trouble from water, bare of wood, and the roads thereof awkward by reason of mountains. He does not dwell in one place, being driven hither and yon through want, going about [the desert] on foot. He has been fighting since the time of Horus; he never conquers, yet he is not conquered, and he does not announce a day of fighting, like a thief whom a community has driven out."

Asiatics could enter Egypt along its northeast border, via routes coming through Canaan. It was therefore Egypt's most vulnerable border, and it was the primary border to which frontier guards were assigned to ensure that no suspicious visitors would enter Egypt. Although the term "spies" is used here, it is probably not in the sense of concern about a military invasion, but rather of scouts entering Egypt to lay the groundwork for raids on storehouses. The Middle Kingdom work, *Prophecies of Neferti,* which relates various calamities that were predicted to befall Egypt, speaks of the disasters caused by an influx of Asiatics: "All good things have passed away, the land is burdened with misfortune because of those looking for food, Asiatics roaming the land. Foes have arisen in the east, Asiatics have descended into Egypt." ▪ ZR

ח בָּאתֶם וַיֹּאמְרוּ מֵאֶרֶץ כְּנַעַן לִשְׁבָּר־אֹכֶל׃ וַיַּכֵּר יוֹסֵף אֶת־אֶחָיו
ט וְהֵם לֹא הִכִּרֻהוּ׃ וַיִּזְכֹּר יוֹסֵף אֵת הַחֲלֹמוֹת אֲשֶׁר חָלַם לָהֶם
וַיֹּאמֶר אֲלֵהֶם מְרַגְּלִים אַתֶּם לִרְאוֹת אֶת־עֶרְוַת הָאָרֶץ בָּאתֶם׃
יא וַיֹּאמְרוּ אֵלָיו לֹא אֲדֹנִי וַעֲבָדֶיךָ בָּאוּ לִשְׁבָּר־אֹכֶל׃ כֻּלָּנוּ בְּנֵי
יב אִישׁ־אֶחָד נָחְנוּ כֵּנִים אֲנַחְנוּ לֹא־הָיוּ עֲבָדֶיךָ מְרַגְּלִים׃ וַיֹּאמֶר
יג אֲלֵהֶם לֹא כִּי־עֶרְוַת הָאָרֶץ בָּאתֶם לִרְאוֹת׃ וַיֹּאמְרוּ שְׁנֵים עָשָׂר
עֲבָדֶיךָ אַחִים ׀ אֲנַחְנוּ בְּנֵי אִישׁ־אֶחָד בְּאֶרֶץ כְּנָעַן וְהִנֵּה הַקָּטֹן
יד אֶת־אָבִינוּ הַיּוֹם וְהָאֶחָד אֵינֶנּוּ׃ וַיֹּאמֶר אֲלֵהֶם יוֹסֵף הוּא אֲשֶׁר
טו דִּבַּרְתִּי אֲלֵכֶם לֵאמֹר מְרַגְּלִים אַתֶּם׃ בְּזֹאת תִּבָּחֵנוּ חֵי פַרְעֹה
טז אִם־תֵּצְאוּ מִזֶּה כִּי אִם־בְּבוֹא אֲחִיכֶם הַקָּטֹן הֵנָּה׃ שִׁלְחוּ מִכֶּם
אֶחָד וְיִקַּח אֶת־אֲחִיכֶם וְאַתֶּם הֵאָסְרוּ וְיִבָּחֲנוּ דִּבְרֵיכֶם הַאֱמֶת
יז אִתְּכֶם וְאִם־לֹא חֵי פַרְעֹה כִּי מְרַגְּלִים אַתֶּם׃ וַיֶּאֱסֹף אֹתָם אֶל־
יח מִשְׁמָר שְׁלֹשֶׁת יָמִים׃ וַיֹּאמֶר אֲלֵהֶם יוֹסֵף בַּיּוֹם הַשְּׁלִישִׁי זֹאת
יט עֲשׂוּ וִחְיוּ אֶת־הָאֱלֹהִים אֲנִי יָרֵא׃ אִם־כֵּנִים אַתֶּם אֲחִיכֶם אֶחָד חמישי
יֵאָסֵר בְּבֵית מִשְׁמַרְכֶם וְאַתֶּם לְכוּ הָבִיאוּ שֶׁבֶר רַעֲבוֹן בָּתֵּיכֶם׃
כ וְאֶת־אֲחִיכֶם הַקָּטֹן תָּבִיאוּ אֵלַי וְיֵאָמְנוּ דִבְרֵיכֶם וְלֹא תָמוּתוּ
כא וַיַּעֲשׂוּ־כֵן׃ וַיֹּאמְרוּ אִישׁ אֶל־אָחִיו אֲבָל אֲשֵׁמִים ׀ אֲנַחְנוּ עַל־

8 They replied, "From the land of Canaan – to buy food." Yosef
9 recognized his brothers, but they did not recognize him. Then
Yosef remembered the dreams he had dreamed about them.
"You are spies!" he said. "You have come to see where our
10 land is exposed." "No, my lord," they said. "Your servants have
11 come to buy food. We all are sons of the same man. We are
12 honest men. Your servants are not spies." "Lies," he said. "You
13 have come to see where our land is exposed." "We were once
twelve brothers," they replied, "sons of one man in Canaan.
14 The youngest is now with our father, and one is gone." But
15 Yosef said, "It is as I said to you – you are spies. This is how
you will be tested. By Pharaoh's life, you will not leave this
16 place unless your youngest brother comes here. Let one of
you go and fetch your brother. The rest of you will remain
confined here. This will test whether or not you are telling the
17 truth. If not, by Pharaoh's life, you are spies." He had them
18 placed in custody for three days. On the third day, Yosef said
to them, "If you do this you will live, for I am a God-fearing
19 man. If you are honest, let one of your brothers stay here in
prison while the rest of you go and take back grain for your
20 starving households. Then bring your youngest brother to
me so that your words can be verified and you will not die."
21 They agreed. And they said to one another, "We are guilty,

EGYPTOLOGY

42:15 By Pharaoh's life

Just as an oath in the name of God is considered to be validated by the power of the deity, the same was true for an oath made by the life of a king, as in I Samuel 17:55 and II Samuel 14:19. The Egyptian version of this convention was the formula, "by the life of Pharaoh," who was himself considered a god. Indeed, the standard formula for an assertion of truthful speaking was, "As truly as King X lives, I am telling the truth." Numerous inscriptions have been found using this formula, dating as far back as the 20th century BCE. ▪ ZR

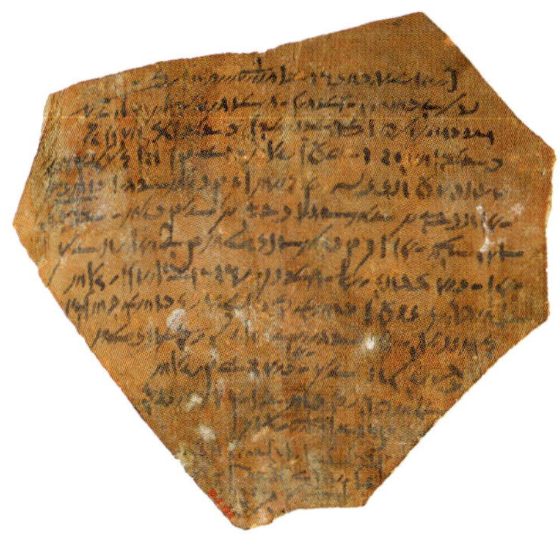

Oath on ostracon, made by a man named Patasetat before the goddess Hathor and authorized by a priest in her temple, Demotic script, possibly Gebelein, 2nd century BCE

אָחִינוּ אֲשֶׁר רָאִינוּ צָרַת נַפְשׁוֹ בְּהִתְחַנְנוֹ אֵלֵינוּ וְלֹא שָׁמָעְנוּ
עַל־כֵּן בָּאָה אֵלֵינוּ הַצָּרָה הַזֹּאת: וַיַּעַן רְאוּבֵן אֹתָם לֵאמֹר הֲלוֹא כב
אָמַרְתִּי אֲלֵיכֶם ׀ לֵאמֹר אַל־תֶּחֶטְאוּ בַיֶּלֶד וְלֹא שְׁמַעְתֶּם וְגַם־
דָּמוֹ הִנֵּה נִדְרָשׁ: וְהֵם לֹא יָדְעוּ כִּי שֹׁמֵעַ יוֹסֵף כִּי הַמֵּלִיץ בֵּינֹתָם: כג
וַיִּסֹּב מֵעֲלֵיהֶם וַיֵּבְךְּ וַיָּשָׁב אֲלֵהֶם וַיְדַבֵּר אֲלֵהֶם וַיִּקַּח מֵאִתָּם כד
אֶת־שִׁמְעוֹן וַיֶּאֱסֹר אֹתוֹ לְעֵינֵיהֶם: וַיְצַו יוֹסֵף וַיְמַלְאוּ אֶת־כְּלֵיהֶם כה
בָּר וּלְהָשִׁיב כַּסְפֵּיהֶם אִישׁ אֶל־שַׂקּוֹ וְלָתֵת לָהֶם צֵדָה לַדָּרֶךְ
וַיַּעַשׂ לָהֶם כֵּן: וַיִּשְׂאוּ אֶת־שִׁבְרָם עַל־חֲמֹרֵיהֶם וַיֵּלְכוּ מִשָּׁם: כו
וַיִּפְתַּח הָאֶחָד אֶת־שַׂקּוֹ לָתֵת מִסְפּוֹא לַחֲמֹרוֹ בַּמָּלוֹן וַיַּרְא אֶת־ כז
כַּסְפּוֹ וְהִנֵּה־הוּא בְּפִי אַמְתַּחְתּוֹ: וַיֹּאמֶר אֶל־אֶחָיו הוּשַׁב כַּסְפִּי כח
וְגַם הִנֵּה בְאַמְתַּחְתִּי וַיֵּצֵא לִבָּם וַיֶּחֶרְדוּ אִישׁ אֶל־אָחִיו לֵאמֹר
מַה־זֹּאת עָשָׂה אֱלֹהִים לָנוּ: וַיָּבֹאוּ אֶל־יַעֲקֹב אֲבִיהֶם אַרְצָה כט
כְּנָעַן וַיַּגִּידוּ לוֹ אֵת כָּל־הַקֹּרֹת אֹתָם לֵאמֹר: דִּבֶּר הָאִישׁ אֲדֹנֵי ל
הָאָרֶץ אִתָּנוּ קָשׁוֹת וַיִּתֵּן אֹתָנוּ כִּמְרַגְּלִים אֶת־הָאָרֶץ: וַנֹּאמֶר לא
אֵלָיו כֵּנִים אֲנָחְנוּ לֹא הָיִינוּ מְרַגְּלִים: שְׁנֵים־עָשָׂר אֲנַחְנוּ אַחִים לב
בְּנֵי אָבִינוּ הָאֶחָד אֵינֶנּוּ וְהַקָּטֹן הַיּוֹם אֶת־אָבִינוּ בְּאֶרֶץ כְּנָעַן:

guilty because of what we did to our brother. We saw his
suffering when he pleaded with us but we did not listen. That
22 is why this trouble has come upon us." Then Reuven spoke
up: "Did I not tell you not to sin against the boy? But you
would not listen. Now comes the reckoning for his blood."
23 They did not realize that Yosef could understand them, for a
24 translator stood between them. And Yosef turned away from
them and wept. Then he turned back to them and spoke again.
He had Shimon taken from them and placed in chains before
25 their eyes. Yosef gave orders to fill their bags with grain and
put each man's money back in his sack. They were to be given
26 provisions for the journey. After this was done for them, they
27 loaded their grain on their donkeys and left. As one of them
was opening his sack to feed his donkey at the place where
they stopped for the night, he saw his money right there at
28 the top of his pack. "My money has been returned!" he told
his brothers. "There it is in my pack!" Their hearts sank.
Trembling, they turned to one another, saying, "What is this
29 that God has done to us?" When they came to their father
Yaakov in the land of Canaan, they told him all that had
30 happened to them. They said, "The man who is the lord of
the land spoke to us harshly. He accused us of spying on the
31 land. We said to him, 'We are honest men; we are not spies.
32 We were twelve brothers, sons of the same father. One is gone,

LANGUAGE

42:27 Pack (*amtaḥat*)

The "sack" of this verse is the Hebrew *sak*, from which the English word is derived. Outside of this story and perhaps Joshua 9:4, it always refers to sackcloth, the material from which sacks are made, and not to the sacks themselves. But this story also employs the word "pack," and this word, *amtaḥat* in Hebrew, is found only in Genesis, chapters 42 through 44. The brothers brought their *amtaḥot* from Canaan, of course; this word does not derive from Egyptian.

Older scholarship maintained that the term derived from the Hebrew root *m t ḥ*, ("stretch,") but the Aramaic translations understand it to mean "burden," and not "bag." In fact, the Assyrian verb derived from *m t ḥ* means not "stretch" but "carry." If the root was used this way in Aramaic too, that would lend support to the Targum and the Peshita translations, where *amtaḥat* is not another word for a container of some kind but a word for what one packs – the contents of the baggage. ▪ MC

Clay figurine, donkey with packs on its back, unfired clay, Temple of Hatshepsut Temenos area, Deir el-Bahari, Thebes, 20th to 15th century BCE

Yosef reunited with Binyamin as the brothers look on, from Hult, Adolf. *Bible Primer, Old Testament.* Rock Island, IL: Augustana Book Concern, 1919.

ויאמר אלינו האיש אדני הארץ בזאת אדע כי כנים אתם לג
אחיכם האחד הניחו אתי ואת־רעבון בתיכם קחו ולכו: והביאו לד
את־אחיכם הקטן אלי ואדעה כי לא מרגלים אתם כי כנים
אתם את־אחיכם אתן לכם ואת־הארץ תסחרו: ויהי הם לה
מריקים שקיהם והנה־איש צרור־כספו בשקו ויראו את־
צררות כספיהם המה ואביהם וייראו: ויאמר אלהם יעקב לו
אביהם אתי שכלתם יוסף איננו ושמעון איננו ואת־בנימן
תקחו עלי היו כלנה: ויאמר ראובן אל־אביו לאמר את־שני לז
בני תמית אם־לא אביאנו אליך תנה אתו על־ידי ואני אשיבנו
אליך: ויאמר לא־ירד בני עמכם כי־אחיו מת והוא לבדו נשאר לח
וקראהו אסון בדרך אשר תלכו־בה והורדתם את־שיבתי
ביגון שאולה: והרעב כבד בארץ: ויהי כאשר כלו לאכל את־ א ב מג
השבר אשר הביאו ממצרים ויאמר אליהם אביהם שבו שברו־
לנו מעט־אכל: ויאמר אליו יהודה לאמר העד העד בנו האיש ג
לאמר לא־תראו פני בלתי אחיכם אתכם: אם־ישך משלח ד
את־אחינו אתנו נרדה ונשברה לך אכל: ואם־אינך משלח ה

33 and the youngest is now with our father in Canaan.' Then the
man who is lord of the land said to us, 'This is how I will know
that you are honest men. Leave one of your brothers with me,
34 take something for your starving households, and go. Then
bring your youngest brother to me. Then I will know that you
are not spies but honest men. And then I will give you back
35 your brother, and you can trade in the land.'" They began
emptying their sacks, and there in each one's sack was his
money bag. When they and their father saw the money bags,
36 they were afraid. Their father Yaakov said to them, "You have
taken my children away from me. Yosef is gone. Shimon is
gone. Now you want to take Binyamin? All this I must suffer!"
37 Reuven said to his father, "You may kill my two sons if I do
not bring him back to you; entrust him to my care and I will
38 bring him back to you." "My son will not go down with you,"
said Yaakov. "His brother is dead, and he is all I have left. If
any harm comes to him on the way, you will bring down my
43 1 gray head in grief to Sheol." The famine in the land continued
2 to be severe. When they had eaten all the grain they had
brought from Egypt, their father said to them, "Go back and
3 buy us some more food." But Yehuda said to him, "The man
warned us, 'Do not appear before me unless your brother is
4 with you.' If you agree to send our brother with us, we will go
5 and buy you food. But if you will not send him, we cannot go.

NEAR EAST

43:9 I myself am the guarantee for his safety

The Hebrew root *a [ayin] r b* is used in Tanakh for a third party's acceptance of legal responsibility for the debt of a borrower; the guarantor will pay back the debt in case the borrower does not. This legal term is found in, "Broken is the person who guaranteed a loan (*arev*) for a stranger" (Prov. 11:15), "Do not be among those who extend their hands as guarantors (*orvim*) for loans" (Prov. 22:26), and elsewhere. It is cognate with the Ugaritic *'rb*, to guarantee, and the Akkadian *erubatu*, a pledge. Here the legal term is used metaphorically, to indicate taking responsibility for someone. Metaphoric usage appears elsewhere in Tanakh as well, as in "Lord, in my oppression, be security to me (*arveni*)" (Is. 38:14). ▪ ZR

Legal debt note, detailing a couple's debt to be paid by the "Sa Parka" festival, Old Assyrian, 19th century BCE

לֹא נֵרֵד כִּי־הָאִישׁ אָמַר אֵלֵינוּ לֹא־תִרְאוּ פָנַי בִּלְתִּי אֲחִיכֶם
ו אִתְּכֶם: וַיֹּאמֶר יִשְׂרָאֵל לָמָה הֲרֵעֹתֶם לִי לְהַגִּיד לָאִישׁ הַעוֹד
ז לָכֶם אָח: וַיֹּאמְרוּ שָׁאוֹל שָׁאַל־הָאִישׁ לָנוּ וּלְמוֹלַדְתֵּנוּ לֵאמֹר
הַעוֹד אֲבִיכֶם חַי הֲיֵשׁ לָכֶם אָח וַנַּגֶּד־לוֹ עַל־פִּי הַדְּבָרִים הָאֵלֶּה
ח הֲיָדוֹעַ נֵדַע כִּי יֹאמַר הוֹרִידוּ אֶת־אֲחִיכֶם: וַיֹּאמֶר יְהוּדָה אֶל־
יִשְׂרָאֵל אָבִיו שִׁלְחָה הַנַּעַר אִתִּי וְנָקוּמָה וְנֵלֵכָה וְנִחְיֶה וְלֹא נָמוּת
ט גַּם־אֲנַחְנוּ גַם־אַתָּה גַּם־טַפֵּנוּ: אָנֹכִי אֶעֶרְבֶנּוּ מִיָּדִי תְּבַקְשֶׁנּוּ
אִם־לֹא הֲבִיאֹתִיו אֵלֶיךָ וְהִצַּגְתִּיו לְפָנֶיךָ וְחָטָאתִי לְךָ כָּל־הַיָּמִים:
י יא כִּי לוּלֵא הִתְמַהְמָהְנוּ כִּי־עַתָּה שַׁבְנוּ זֶה פַעֲמָיִם: וַיֹּאמֶר אֲלֵהֶם
יִשְׂרָאֵל אֲבִיהֶם אִם־כֵּן | אֵפוֹא זֹאת עֲשׂוּ קְחוּ מִזִּמְרַת הָאָרֶץ
בִּכְלֵיכֶם וְהוֹרִידוּ לָאִישׁ מִנְחָה מְעַט צֳרִי וּמְעַט דְּבַשׁ נְכֹאת

The man told us, 'Do not appear before me unless your
brother is with you.'" Yisrael said, "Why did you bring this 6
trouble on me by telling the man you had another brother?"
They replied, "The man kept asking about us and our family: 7
'Is your father still alive?' he asked. 'Do you have a brother?'
We simply answered his questions. How could we know that
he would say, 'Bring your brother here'?" And Yehuda said to 8
his father Yisrael, "Send the boy with me. Let us be on our
way so that we, you, and our children may live and not die. I 9
myself am the guarantee for his safety: you may hold me
personally responsible. If I do not bring him back and set him
before you, I will have sinned against you for all time. We 10
could have been there and back twice if we had not hesitated
so long." And then their father Yisrael said to them, "If that is 11
how it must be, then do this. Take some of the best produce
of the land in your bags, and bring them to the man as a gift –

— FLORA AND FAUNA —

43:11 Yaakov's gifts to "the man"

The balm (*tzori*) mentioned here is understood in most ancient sources to be a type of tree sap that was deemed very effective for healing wounds and fractures, most famously mentioned in Jeremiah 8:22, "Is there no balm in Gilad? Is there no healer there? Why then has there not arisen a cure for my precious people?" The most probable identification of the biblical *tzori* is resin produced from the terebinth (*Pistacia palaestina*) or the mastic tree (*Pistacia lentiscus*).

The honey may refer either to bee honey, or date honey, which is more common in Tanakh. In the Egyptian *Story of Sinuhe* (early 2nd millennium BCE), there is a description of "a good land called Yaa" identified with Israel or southern Syria. This land was very fertile, "Figs were in it and grapes. It had more wine than water. Abundant was its honey, plentiful its oil. All kinds of fruit were in its trees. Barley was there and emmer [wheat]" (ll. 81–84).

The Hebrew terms *nekhot* and *lot* are found in Tanakh only here and in Genesis 37:25, both times together and in the context of balm. *Nekhot* is difficult to precisely identify and may be a general term for spices. Scholars usually identify *lot* as the fragrant resin produced from the pink rock rose (*Cistus creticus*).

Botnim, used in modern Hebrew for peanuts, appears only here in Tanakh. It refers to the edible fruit of one of the shrubs and small trees of the *Pistacia* family, identified in the Aramaic Targums and by Rav Se'adya Gaon as *Pistacia palaestina*. The fruit is small (5 millimeters/0.2 inches in diameter) and spherical, purple when ripe. This tree is not native to Egypt.

Almonds were one of the earliest fruit trees to be domesticated, as they are relatively easy to raise from seeds. They were first domesticated in the Early Bronze Age (ca. 3000 BCE), and were found in Tutankhamun's tomb in Egypt (ca. 1325 BCE), probably imported from the Levant. ▪ ZR

↗ Fruit of the *Pistacia palaestina* tree, Mount Tayasim, Israel

יב וְלֹט בָּטְנִים וּשְׁקֵדִים: וְכֶסֶף מִשְׁנֶה קְחוּ בְיֶדְכֶם וְאֶת־הַכֶּסֶף
הַמּוּשָׁב בְּפִי אַמְתְּחֹתֵיכֶם תָּשִׁיבוּ בְיֶדְכֶם אוּלַי מִשְׁגֶּה הוּא:
יג יד וְאֶת־אֲחִיכֶם קָחוּ וְקוּמוּ שׁוּבוּ אֶל־הָאִישׁ: וְאֵל שַׁדַּי יִתֵּן לָכֶם
רַחֲמִים לִפְנֵי הָאִישׁ וְשִׁלַּח לָכֶם אֶת־אֲחִיכֶם אַחֵר וְאֶת־בִּנְיָמִין
טו וַאֲנִי כַּאֲשֶׁר שָׁכֹלְתִּי שָׁכָלְתִּי: וַיִּקְחוּ הָאֲנָשִׁים אֶת־הַמִּנְחָה הַזֹּאת
וּמִשְׁנֶה־כֶּסֶף לָקְחוּ בְיָדָם וְאֶת־בִּנְיָמִן וַיָּקֻמוּ וַיֵּרְדוּ מִצְרַיִם וַיַּעַמְדוּ
ששי טז לִפְנֵי יוֹסֵף: וַיַּרְא יוֹסֵף אִתָּם אֶת־בִּנְיָמִין וַיֹּאמֶר לַאֲשֶׁר עַל־בֵּיתוֹ
הָבֵא אֶת־הָאֲנָשִׁים הַבָּיְתָה וּטְבֹחַ טֶבַח וְהָכֵן כִּי אִתִּי יֹאכְלוּ
יז הָאֲנָשִׁים בַּצָּהֳרָיִם: וַיַּעַשׂ הָאִישׁ כַּאֲשֶׁר אָמַר יוֹסֵף וַיָּבֵא הָאִישׁ
יח אֶת־הָאֲנָשִׁים בֵּיתָה יוֹסֵף: וַיִּירְאוּ הָאֲנָשִׁים כִּי הוּבְאוּ בֵּית יוֹסֵף
וַיֹּאמְרוּ עַל־דְּבַר הַכֶּסֶף הַשָּׁב בְּאַמְתְּחֹתֵינוּ בַּתְּחִלָּה אֲנַחְנוּ
מוּבָאִים לְהִתְגֹּלֵל עָלֵינוּ וּלְהִתְנַפֵּל עָלֵינוּ וְלָקַחַת אֹתָנוּ לַעֲבָדִים
יט וְאֶת־חֲמֹרֵינוּ: וַיִּגְּשׁוּ אֶל־הָאִישׁ אֲשֶׁר עַל־בֵּית יוֹסֵף וַיְדַבְּרוּ אֵלָיו
כ פֶּתַח הַבָּיִת: וַיֹּאמְרוּ בִּי אֲדֹנִי יָרֹד יָרַדְנוּ בַּתְּחִלָּה לִשְׁבָּר־אֹכֶל:
כא וַיְהִי כִּי־בָאנוּ אֶל־הַמָּלוֹן וַנִּפְתְּחָה אֶת־אַמְתְּחֹתֵינוּ וְהִנֵּה כֶסֶף־
כב אִישׁ בְּפִי אַמְתַּחְתּוֹ כַּסְפֵּנוּ בְּמִשְׁקָלוֹ וַנָּשֶׁב אֹתוֹ בְּיָדֵנוּ: וְכֶסֶף
אַחֵר הוֹרַדְנוּ בְיָדֵנוּ לִשְׁבָּר־אֹכֶל לֹא יָדַעְנוּ מִי־שָׂם כַּסְפֵּנוּ
• כג בְּאַמְתְּחֹתֵינוּ: וַיֹּאמֶר שָׁלוֹם לָכֶם אַל־תִּירָאוּ אֱלֹהֵיכֶם וֵאלֹהֵי
אֲבִיכֶם נָתַן לָכֶם מַטְמוֹן בְּאַמְתְּחֹתֵיכֶם כַּסְפְּכֶם בָּא אֵלָי וַיּוֹצֵא
כד אֲלֵהֶם אֶת־שִׁמְעוֹן: וַיָּבֵא הָאִישׁ אֶת־הָאֲנָשִׁים בֵּיתָה יוֹסֵף
כה וַיִּתֶּן־מַיִם וַיִּרְחֲצוּ רַגְלֵיהֶם וַיִּתֵּן מִסְפּוֹא לַחֲמֹרֵיהֶם: וַיָּכִינוּ אֶת־
הַמִּנְחָה עַד־בּוֹא יוֹסֵף בַּצָּהֳרָיִם כִּי שָׁמְעוּ כִּי־שָׁם יֹאכְלוּ לָחֶם:

a little balm and a little honey,
some spices and myrrh, pistachio
12 nuts and almonds. Take with you
double the money. Return the
money that was put back into your
sacks. Perhaps it was a mistake.
13 14 And take your brother. Go back to the man at once. May El Shaddai grant you mercy before the man,
that he may send your other brother forth to you, and Binyamin. And as for me, if I am to be bereaved,
15 I will be bereaved." So the men took the gift and double the money and set out with Binyamin. They
16 went to Egypt and presented themselves to Yosef. When Yosef saw Binyamin with them, he said to his
house steward, "Take these men to my house. Slaughter an animal and prepare a meal, for they will dine
17 18 with me at noon." The man did as Yosef said and brought them to Yosef's house. The men were frightened
that they were being brought to Yosef's house. They said, "We have been brought here because of the
money that was put back in our sacks the first time. He wants to attack us, seize us as slaves, and take our
19 20 donkeys." So they went up to Yosef's steward and spoke to him at the entrance to the house. "If you
21 please, my lord," they said, "we came here once before to buy food. But at the place where we stopped
for the night, we opened our bags and each of us found his money, in its exact weight, in the mouth of
22 his bag. So we have brought it back with us. We have also brought additional money to buy food. We do
• 23 not know who put our money in our bags." He replied, "All is well. Do not be afraid. Your God, the God
of your father, must have placed a hidden gift in your bags. I received the money you paid." Then he
24 brought Shimon out to them. He brought the brothers into Yosef's house, gave them water to bathe their
25 feet, and had fodder brought for their donkeys. They set out their gifts in preparation for Yosef's arrival

כו וַיָּבֹא יוֹסֵף הַבַּיְתָה וַיָּבִיאוּ לוֹ אֶת־הַמִּנְחָה אֲשֶׁר־בְּיָדָם הַבָּיְתָה
כז וַיִּשְׁתַּחֲווּ־לוֹ אָרְצָה: וַיִּשְׁאַל לָהֶם לְשָׁלוֹם וַיֹּאמֶר הֲשָׁלוֹם אֲבִיכֶם
כח הַזָּקֵן אֲשֶׁר אֲמַרְתֶּם הַעוֹדֶנּוּ חָי: וַיֹּאמְרוּ שָׁלוֹם לְעַבְדְּךָ לְאָבִינוּ
כט עוֹדֶנּוּ חָי וַיִּקְּדוּ וַיִּשְׁתַּחֲוֻ: וַיִּשָּׂא עֵינָיו וַיַּרְא אֶת־בִּנְיָמִין אָחִיו
בֶּן־אִמּוֹ וַיֹּאמֶר הֲזֶה אֲחִיכֶם הַקָּטֹן אֲשֶׁר אֲמַרְתֶּם אֵלָי וַיֹּאמַר
ל אֱלֹהִים יָחְנְךָ בְּנִי: וַיְמַהֵר יוֹסֵף כִּי־נִכְמְרוּ רַחֲמָיו אֶל־אָחִיו וַיְבַקֵּשׁ שביעי
לא לִבְכּוֹת וַיָּבֹא הַחַדְרָה וַיֵּבְךְּ שָׁמָּה: וַיִּרְחַץ פָּנָיו וַיֵּצֵא וַיִּתְאַפַּק

at noon, because they had heard that they were going to eat
there. When Yosef entered the house, they presented him 26
with the gifts they had brought and bowed low to the ground
before him. He asked them how they were. Then he asked, 27
"How is the elderly father about whom you spoke? Is he still
alive?" They said, "Your servant our father is alive and well." 28
They bowed down and prostrated themselves. Then he looked 29
up and saw his brother Binyamin, his mother's son, and asked,
"Is this your youngest brother, the one you mentioned to
me?" And he said, "God be gracious to you, my son." At that, 30
he hurried out, for he was overcome with feeling toward his
brother and was on the verge of tears. He went into a private
room and there he wept. He washed his face and came out, 31

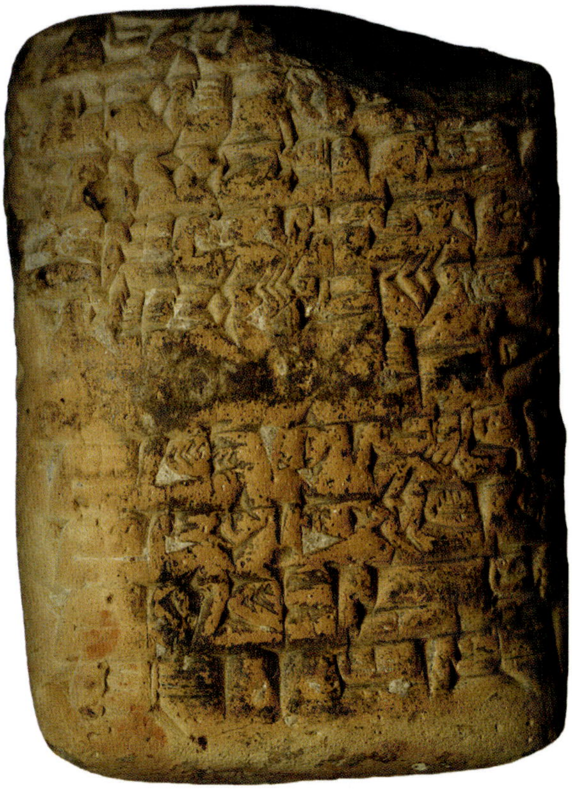

NEAR EAST

43:23 I received the money you paid

The phrase *kaspekhem ba elai*, literally, "your money has come to me," is the Hebrew version of an Aramaic legal formula used by West Semitic traders indicating receipt of full payment. An Old Babylonian receipt clause states that a person "has received (the money), his heart is satisfied," and later Aramaic papyri from Elephantine are similar, "I have received the money and my heart is satisfied therewith." This formula also has the sense of quittance – any further claims are completely renounced, as in the Septuagint's translation, "I have enough of your good money." In our verse, Yosef's steward is using legal language to assure the brothers their account is paid in full and consequently, they will not be punished. ▪ ZR

Receipt of a rent payment in kind to the temple authorities, Umma, Sumer, 20th century BCE

וַיֹּאמֶר שִׂימוּ לָחֶם: וַיָּשִׂימוּ לוֹ לְבַדּוֹ וְלָהֶם לְבַדָּם וְלַמִּצְרִים לב •
הָאֹכְלִים אִתּוֹ לְבַדָּם כִּי לֹא יוּכְלוּן הַמִּצְרִים לֶאֱכֹל אֶת־הָעִבְרִים
לֶחֶם כִּי־תוֹעֵבָה הִוא לְמִצְרָיִם: וַיֵּשְׁבוּ לְפָנָיו הַבְּכֹר כִּבְכֹרָתוֹ לג
וְהַצָּעִיר כִּצְעִרָתוֹ וַיִּתְמְהוּ הָאֲנָשִׁים אִישׁ אֶל־רֵעֵהוּ: וַיִּשָּׂא לד
מַשְׂאֹת מֵאֵת פָּנָיו אֲלֵהֶם וַתֵּרֶב מַשְׂאַת בִּנְיָמִן מִמַּשְׂאֹת כֻּלָּם

• 32 controlling himself. "Serve the food," he said. They served
him apart, them apart, and the Egyptians who ate with him
apart, for the Egyptians could not eat with Hebrews, since to
33 Egyptians that was considered abhorrent. Seated by his
direction in order of age, oldest to youngest, they looked at
34 one another in amazement. He sent them portions from his
table, giving Binyamin five times as much as anyone else. And

EGYPTOLOGY

43:32 Separation between Egyptians and Semites

As Nili Shupak has shown with regard to this and other verses describing "abominations" of the ancient Egyptians, their society prohibited the consumption of certain foods as *bwt* ("abomination") by priests and high-ranking officials, including the pharaoh. These varied in different regions, and included different types of fish, cows, pigs, honey, and leeks.

People who did not abide by these taboos were forbidden to enter the palace. For example, Piye (Piankhi, ruled 744–714 BCE), an ancient Kushite king and founder of the Twenty-Fifth Dynasty of Egypt, wrote that certain defeated local lords were not allowed to enter his place because they "were eaters of fish, which is an abomination in the king's house," with one exception, because "he was pure [*w'b*] and did not eat fish."

Furthermore, in general, it was not customary in ancient Egypt to eat with strangers. When such mixed dining did occur, it was considered exceptional and noteworthy. For example, when the Hittite bride of Ramesses II arrived in Egypt, the Abu Simbel Temple inscription notes that members of both the Egyptian and Hittite entourage were "eating and drinking together with one heart like brothers without bothering one another."

This verse is another example of the use of the term *ivri*, indicating the foreignness of the brothers. Here it reflects the Egyptian separation from the Asiatics while dining. ▪ ZR

Asiatic traders arriving in Egypt, tomb of Khnumhotep II, Beni Hasan, 20th century BCE

מד א חָמֵשׁ יָדוֹת וַיִּשְׁתּוּ וַיִּשְׁכְּרוּ עִמּוֹ׃ וַיְצַו אֶת־אֲשֶׁר עַל־בֵּיתוֹ לֵאמֹר
מַלֵּא אֶת־אַמְתְּחֹת הָאֲנָשִׁים אֹכֶל כַּאֲשֶׁר יוּכְלוּן שְׂאֵת וְשִׂים
ב כֶּסֶף־אִישׁ בְּפִי אַמְתַּחְתּוֹ׃ וְאֶת־גְּבִיעִי גְּבִיעַ הַכֶּסֶף תָּשִׂים בְּפִי
אַמְתַּחַת הַקָּטֹן וְאֵת כֶּסֶף שִׁבְרוֹ וַיַּעַשׂ כִּדְבַר יוֹסֵף אֲשֶׁר דִּבֵּר׃
ג ד הַבֹּקֶר אוֹר וְהָאֲנָשִׁים שֻׁלְּחוּ הֵמָּה וַחֲמֹרֵיהֶם׃ הֵם יָצְאוּ אֶת־הָעִיר
לֹא הִרְחִיקוּ וְיוֹסֵף אָמַר לַאֲשֶׁר עַל־בֵּיתוֹ קוּם רְדֹף אַחֲרֵי
הָאֲנָשִׁים וְהִשַּׂגְתָּם וְאָמַרְתָּ אֲלֵהֶם לָמָּה שִׁלַּמְתֶּם רָעָה תַּחַת

44 1 they drank and grew merry with him. Then Yosef instructed
his steward, "Fill the men's bags with as much food as they
can carry, and put each one's money in the mouth of his bag.
2 Then put my chalice – the silver chalice – in the mouth of the
youngest one's bag, along with the money for his grain." He
3 did as Yosef told him. As morning showed its first light, the
4 men were sent on their way with their donkeys. They had not
gone far from the city when Yosef said to his steward, "Go
after the men at once. When you catch up with them, say to

LANGUAGE

44:2 Chalice (*gavia*)

Gavia, the Hebrew word used in this verse for the "chalice," was long thought to derive from the same Semitic root that creates the word for "hill." Actually, though, it seems to be a loanword from *qbhw*, the Egyptian word for a libation vessel. The *kuba'at* of Isaiah 51:17, 22 may be related to the same Egyptian word.

Except for the "goblets" of wine in Jeremiah 35:5, this word is found only in the description of the cups for the candelabrum in the Tabernacle. The sage Shmuel (BT Menaḥot 28b) passes down a tradition that these were shaped like Alexandrian goblets– which, according to Rashi, are long and narrow; according to Rambam, they are wide on top and narrow at the base. Indeed, the hieroglyph with which the Egyptian word is written could be described in either of these ways. ▪ MC

Two Egyptian priests, one holding a papyrus roll and one holding a libation vessel, tomb painting, Thebes, 14th century BCE

טוֹבָה׃ הֲלוֹא זֶה אֲשֶׁר יִשְׁתֶּה אֲדֹנִי בּוֹ וְהוּא נַחֵשׁ יְנַחֵשׁ בּוֹ ה
הֲרֵעֹתֶם אֲשֶׁר עֲשִׂיתֶם׃ וַיַּשִּׂגֵם וַיְדַבֵּר אֲלֵהֶם אֶת־הַדְּבָרִים ו
הָאֵלֶּה׃ וַיֹּאמְרוּ אֵלָיו לָמָּה יְדַבֵּר אֲדֹנִי כַּדְּבָרִים הָאֵלֶּה חָלִילָה ז
לַעֲבָדֶיךָ מֵעֲשׂוֹת כַּדָּבָר הַזֶּה׃ הֵן כֶּסֶף אֲשֶׁר מָצָאנוּ בְּפִי ח
אַמְתְּחֹתֵינוּ הֱשִׁיבֹנוּ אֵלֶיךָ מֵאֶרֶץ כְּנָעַן וְאֵיךְ נִגְנֹב מִבֵּית אֲדֹנֶיךָ
כֶּסֶף אוֹ זָהָב׃ אֲשֶׁר יִמָּצֵא אִתּוֹ מֵעֲבָדֶיךָ וָמֵת וְגַם־אֲנַחְנוּ נִהְיֶה ט
לַאדֹנִי לַעֲבָדִים׃ וַיֹּאמֶר גַּם־עַתָּה כְדִבְרֵיכֶם כֶּן־הוּא אֲשֶׁר יִמָּצֵא י
אִתּוֹ יִהְיֶה־לִּי עָבֶד וְאַתֶּם תִּהְיוּ נְקִיִּם׃ וַיְמַהֲרוּ וַיּוֹרִדוּ אִישׁ אֶת־ יא
אַמְתַּחְתּוֹ אָרְצָה וַיִּפְתְּחוּ אִישׁ אַמְתַּחְתּוֹ׃ וַיְחַפֵּשׂ בַּגָּדוֹל הֵחֵל יב

5 them, 'Why have you repaid good with evil? Is it not from
this that my master drinks and that he uses for divination? It
6 is a wicked thing you have done.'" He caught up with them
7 and repeated those words to them. But they said to him, "How
can my lord say such things? Heaven forbid that we should
8 do such a thing! Look, we brought back to you from Canaan
the money we found in the mouths of our bags. Why would
9 we steal silver or gold from your master's house? If any of your
servants is found with it, he shall die, and the rest of us will
10 become my lord's slaves." "Let it be as you say," he replied,
"but only the one with whom it is found shall be my slave.
11 The rest of you can go free." Each of them quickly lowered his
12 bag to the ground, and each opened his bag. He searched,

NEAR EAST

44:5 Divination

The text does not specify how a person would use a goblet for divination. However, it appears that this practice is based on the widespread belief that omens could be discerned in the movement or the reflective surface of a liquid, or the shapes produced when liquids are mixed together. In the ancient world, this took various forms: using water (hydromancy), oil (oleomancy), or wine (oenomancy). For example, an Old Babylonian omen collection states that different shapes indicate the presence of different gods: "If the oil, in your pouring water (on it) has taken (the shape of) two horns, (it represents) the presence of Sin… If in your pouring water into the middle of the oil (the oil bubble) came up like a star, (it represents) the presence of Shamash." Even the reflective surface of a highly polished vessel could be used for divination.

This practice is evoked, for example, in the Sumerian proverb, "I looked into the water: [it was] my Fate which was walking there!" It was also recorded in the cuneiform prism where Esar Ḥadon justified rebuilding Babylon after it was destroyed by his father Sanḥeriv. He stated that he used oil divination to make sure that this was the correct course of action. Assyrian texts use the term *apkal shamni*, a "knower of oil," for a diviner, and make reference to a "seer's bowl" (*Shamash Hymn*, l. 155). These practices persisted into Greco-Roman times when bowls of liquids or other reflective surfaces such as primitive mirrors were used to divine the future. ▪ ZR

Divination bowl, bronze, Turkey, 15th century CE

NEAR EAST

44:9 Death penalty for theft

The suggestion of the death penalty for theft might be a rhetorical device as part of a declaration of innocence; it does not necessarily reflect the law of the time.

While no reference to any Egyptian law collection exists prior to ca. 700 BCE, other ancient Near Eastern law collections do contain cases in which the death penalty is given for theft. For example, the *Laws of Hammurabi* state, "If any one steal the property of a temple or of the court, he shall be put to death, and also the one who receives the stolen thing from him shall be put to death" (LH §6), and "If a man commits a robbery and is then seized, that man shall be killed." (LH §22). A different case appears in the *Middle Assyrian Laws*: "If a man is either ill or dead and his wife steal something from his house and give it to either a man or to a woman, or to anyone else, they shall kill the man's wife as well as the receivers [of the stolen goods]" (MAL A §3).

The Torah, though, never imposes a death penalty for a crime against property, as human life and property are not commensurate. ▪ ZR

יג וּבַקָּטֹן כִּלָּה וַיִּמָּצֵא הַגָּבִיעַ בְּאַמְתַּחַת בִּנְיָמִן: וַיִּקְרְעוּ שִׂמְלֹתָם
יד וַיַּעֲמֹס אִישׁ עַל־חֲמֹרוֹ וַיָּשֻׁבוּ הָעִירָה: וַיָּבֹא יְהוּדָה וְאֶחָיו בֵּיתָה מפטיר
טו יוֹסֵף וְהוּא עוֹדֶנּוּ שָׁם וַיִּפְּלוּ לְפָנָיו אָרְצָה: וַיֹּאמֶר לָהֶם יוֹסֵף
מָה־הַמַּעֲשֶׂה הַזֶּה אֲשֶׁר עֲשִׂיתֶם הֲלוֹא יְדַעְתֶּם כִּי־נַחֵשׁ יְנַחֵשׁ
טז אִישׁ אֲשֶׁר כָּמֹנִי: וַיֹּאמֶר יְהוּדָה מַה־נֹּאמַר לַאדֹנִי מַה־נְּדַבֵּר
וּמַה־נִּצְטַדָּק הָאֱלֹהִים מָצָא אֶת־עֲוֺן עֲבָדֶיךָ הִנֶּנּוּ עֲבָדִים לַאדֹנִי
יז גַּם־אֲנַחְנוּ גַּם אֲשֶׁר־נִמְצָא הַגָּבִיעַ בְּיָדוֹ: וַיֹּאמֶר חָלִילָה לִּי
מֵעֲשׂוֹת זֹאת הָאִישׁ אֲשֶׁר נִמְצָא הַגָּבִיעַ בְּיָדוֹ הוּא יִהְיֶה־לִּי
יח עָבֶד וְאַתֶּם עֲלוּ לְשָׁלוֹם אֶל־אֲבִיכֶם: וַיִּגַּשׁ ויגש
אֵלָיו יְהוּדָה וַיֹּאמֶר בִּי אֲדֹנִי יְדַבֶּר־נָא עַבְדְּךָ דָבָר בְּאָזְנֵי אֲדֹנִי
יט וְאַל־יִחַר אַפְּךָ בְּעַבְדֶּךָ כִּי כָמוֹךָ כְּפַרְעֹה: אֲדֹנִי שָׁאַל אֶת־עֲבָדָיו
כ לֵאמֹר הֲיֵשׁ־לָכֶם אָב אוֹ־אָח: וַנֹּאמֶר אֶל־אֲדֹנִי יֶשׁ־לָנוּ אָב
זָקֵן וְיֶלֶד זְקֻנִים קָטָן וְאָחִיו מֵת וַיִּוָּתֵר הוּא לְבַדּוֹ לְאִמּוֹ וְאָבִיו
כא אֲהֵבוֹ: וַתֹּאמֶר אֶל־עֲבָדֶיךָ הוֹרִדֻהוּ אֵלָי וְאָשִׂימָה עֵינִי עָלָיו:
כב וַנֹּאמֶר אֶל־אֲדֹנִי לֹא־יוּכַל הַנַּעַר לַעֲזֹב אֶת־אָבִיו וְעָזַב אֶת־אָבִיו
כג וָמֵת: וַתֹּאמֶר אֶל־עֲבָדֶיךָ אִם־לֹא יֵרֵד אֲחִיכֶם הַקָּטֹן אִתְּכֶם
כד לֹא תֹסִפוּן לִרְאוֹת פָּנָי: וַיְהִי כִּי עָלִינוּ אֶל־עַבְדְּךָ אָבִי וַנַּגֶּד־לוֹ
כה אֵת דִּבְרֵי אֲדֹנִי: וַיֹּאמֶר אָבִינוּ שֻׁבוּ שִׁבְרוּ־לָנוּ מְעַט־אֹכֶל:
כו וַנֹּאמֶר לֹא נוּכַל לָרֶדֶת אִם־יֵשׁ אָחִינוּ הַקָּטֹן אִתָּנוּ וְיָרַדְנוּ כִּי־
כז לֹא נוּכַל לִרְאוֹת פְּנֵי הָאִישׁ וְאָחִינוּ הַקָּטֹן אֵינֶנּוּ אִתָּנוּ: וַיֹּאמֶר
כח עַבְדְּךָ אָבִי אֵלֵינוּ אַתֶּם יְדַעְתֶּם כִּי שְׁנַיִם יָלְדָה־לִּי אִשְׁתִּי: וַיֵּצֵא
הָאֶחָד מֵאִתִּי וָאֹמַר אַךְ טָרֹף טֹרָף וְלֹא רְאִיתִיו עַד־הֵנָּה:

beginning with the oldest and
ending with the youngest. The
chalice was found in Binyamin's
bag. The brothers tore their 13
clothes. Each loaded his donkey
again, and they returned to the
city. Yehuda and his brothers 14
came to Yosef's house – he was
still there – and they threw
themselves on the ground before
him. Yosef said to them, "What is 15
this thing you have done? Do you not know that a man like me can find out the truth by divination?"
Yehuda replied, "What can we say to my lord? What can we speak? How can we prove our innocence? 16
God has uncovered your servants' guilt! We are now my lord's slaves – we and the one in whose
possession the chalice was found." "Heaven forbid that I should do such a thing," he said. "The man in 17
whose possession the chalice was found will become my slave. As for the rest of you, go back to your
father in peace." But Yehuda stepped forward to him. "If you please, my lord," he said, "let your 18
servant speak a word in my lord's hearing. Do not be angry with me, you who are the equal of Pharaoh.
My lord asked his servants, 'Do you have a father or a brother?' And we told my lord, 'We have an elderly 19 20
father and there is a young son, a child of his old age. When his brother died, he was the only one of his
mother's sons left, and his father loves him.' Then you said to your servants, 'Bring him to me that I may 21
set eyes on him.' But we said to my lord, 'The boy cannot leave his father. If he left him, his father would 22
die.' Then you told your servants, 'Unless your youngest brother comes with you, you shall not see my 23
face again.' When we went back to your servant my father, we told him what my lord had said. Then our 24 25
father said, 'Go back and buy a little more food.' We said, 'We cannot go. We can go only if our youngest 26
brother is with us. If he is not with us, we cannot see the man's face.' Then your servant, my father, said 27
to us, 'You know that my wife bore me two sons. One is gone from me, and I said, "He must have been 28

וּלְקַחְתֶּם גַּם־אֶת־זֶה מֵעִם פָּנַי וְקָרָהוּ אָסוֹן וְהוֹרַדְתֶּם אֶת־שֵׂיבָתִי כט
בְּרָעָה שְׁאֹלָה׃ וְעַתָּה כְּבֹאִי אֶל־עַבְדְּךָ אָבִי וְהַנַּעַר אֵינֶנּוּ אִתָּנוּ ל
שני וְנַפְשׁוֹ קְשׁוּרָה בְנַפְשׁוֹ׃ וְהָיָה כִּרְאוֹתוֹ כִּי־אֵין הַנַּעַר וָמֵת וְהוֹרִידוּ לא
עֲבָדֶיךָ אֶת־שֵׂיבַת עַבְדְּךָ אָבִינוּ בְּיָגוֹן שְׁאֹלָה׃ כִּי עַבְדְּךָ עָרַב לב
אֶת־הַנַּעַר מֵעִם אָבִי לֵאמֹר אִם־לֹא אֲבִיאֶנּוּ אֵלֶיךָ וְחָטָאתִי
לְאָבִי כָּל־הַיָּמִים׃ וְעַתָּה יֵשֶׁב־נָא עַבְדְּךָ תַּחַת הַנַּעַר עֶבֶד לַאדֹנִי לג
וְהַנַּעַר יַעַל עִם־אֶחָיו׃ כִּי־אֵיךְ אֶעֱלֶה אֶל־אָבִי וְהַנַּעַר אֵינֶנּוּ לד
אִתִּי פֶּן אֶרְאֶה בָרָע אֲשֶׁר יִמְצָא אֶת־אָבִי׃ וְלֹא־יָכֹל יוֹסֵף א מה
לְהִתְאַפֵּק לְכֹל הַנִּצָּבִים עָלָיו וַיִּקְרָא הוֹצִיאוּ כָל־אִישׁ מֵעָלָי
וְלֹא־עָמַד אִישׁ אִתּוֹ בְּהִתְוַדַּע יוֹסֵף אֶל־אֶחָיו׃ וַיִּתֵּן אֶת־קֹלוֹ ב
בִּבְכִי וַיִּשְׁמְעוּ מִצְרַיִם וַיִּשְׁמַע בֵּית פַּרְעֹה׃ וַיֹּאמֶר יוֹסֵף אֶל־אֶחָיו ג
אֲנִי יוֹסֵף הַעוֹד אָבִי חָי וְלֹא־יָכְלוּ אֶחָיו לַעֲנוֹת אֹתוֹ כִּי נִבְהֲלוּ
מִפָּנָיו׃ וַיֹּאמֶר יוֹסֵף אֶל־אֶחָיו גְּשׁוּ־נָא אֵלַי וַיִּגָּשׁוּ וַיֹּאמֶר אֲנִי ד
יוֹסֵף אֲחִיכֶם אֲשֶׁר־מְכַרְתֶּם אֹתִי מִצְרָיְמָה׃ וְעַתָּה ׀ אַל־תֵּעָצְבוּ ה
וְאַל־יִחַר בְּעֵינֵיכֶם כִּי־מְכַרְתֶּם אֹתִי הֵנָּה כִּי לְמִחְיָה שְׁלָחַנִי
אֱלֹהִים לִפְנֵיכֶם׃ כִּי־זֶה שְׁנָתַיִם הָרָעָב בְּקֶרֶב הָאָרֶץ וְעוֹד חָמֵשׁ ו
שָׁנִים אֲשֶׁר אֵין־חָרִישׁ וְקָצִיר׃ וַיִּשְׁלָחֵנִי אֱלֹהִים לִפְנֵיכֶם לָשׂוּם ז
שלישי לָכֶם שְׁאֵרִית בָּאָרֶץ וּלְהַחֲיוֹת לָכֶם לִפְלֵיטָה גְּדֹלָה׃ וְעַתָּה לֹא־ ח
אַתֶּם שְׁלַחְתֶּם אֹתִי הֵנָּה כִּי הָאֱלֹהִים וַיְשִׂימֵנִי לְאָב לְפַרְעֹה
וּלְאָדוֹן לְכָל־בֵּיתוֹ וּמֹשֵׁל בְּכָל־אֶרֶץ מִצְרָיִם׃ מַהֲרוּ וַעֲלוּ אֶל־ ט
אָבִי וַאֲמַרְתֶּם אֵלָיו כֹּה אָמַר בִּנְךָ יוֹסֵף שָׂמַנִי אֱלֹהִים לְאָדוֹן

torn to pieces." I have not seen him
29 since. If you take this one from me and harm befalls him, you will bring down my gray head in grief
30 to Sheol.' So now, if the boy is not with us when I go back to your servant my father, so bound
31 together are their lives that when he sees that the boy is not with us, he will die. Your servants will have
32 brought down the gray head of your servant, our father, in grief to Sheol. Your servant offered himself to my father as a guarantee for the boy. I said, 'If I do not bring him back to you, I will have sinned against
33 my father for all time.' So, please, let your servant stay as my lord's slave in place of the boy, and let the
34 boy go back with his brothers. For how can I go back to my father if the boy is not with me? I could not
45 1 bear to see the misery that would overwhelm my father!" Yosef could no longer control himself in the company of all his attendants. He cried out, "Have everyone leave my presence!" So no one else was
2 with Yosef when he revealed himself to his brothers. He wept so loudly that the Egyptians could hear
3 him, and the news reached Pharaoh's palace. Yosef said to his brothers, "I am Yosef. Is my father really
4 still alive?" His brothers were so bewildered at his presence that they could not answer him. "Come close to me, please," said Yosef to his brothers. They came close, and he said, "I am your brother Yosef, whom
5 you sold into Egypt. And now, do not be distressed or angry with yourselves that you sold me here, for
6 God sent me ahead of you to save lives. For two years now there has been famine in the land, and for
7 another five years there will be no plowing or reaping. So God sent me ahead of you to ensure your
8 survival in the land, and to save your lives by a great deliverance. So then, it was not you who sent me here, but God. He has made me a father to Pharaoh, lord of his whole household and ruler of all Egypt.
9 Hurry back to my father and tell him, 'This is what your son Yosef says: God has made me lord of all

י לְכָל־מִצְרָיִם רְדָה אֵלַי אַל־תַּעֲמֹד׃ וְיָשַׁבְתָּ בְאֶרֶץ־גֹּשֶׁן וְהָיִיתָ
קָרוֹב אֵלַי אַתָּה וּבָנֶיךָ וּבְנֵי בָנֶיךָ וְצֹאנְךָ וּבְקָרְךָ וְכָל־אֲשֶׁר־לָךְ׃
יא וְכִלְכַּלְתִּי אֹתְךָ שָׁם כִּי־עוֹד חָמֵשׁ שָׁנִים רָעָב פֶּן־תִּוָּרֵשׁ אַתָּה
יב וּבֵיתְךָ וְכָל־אֲשֶׁר־לָךְ׃ וְהִנֵּה עֵינֵיכֶם רֹאוֹת וְעֵינֵי אָחִי בִנְיָמִין
יג כִּי־פִי הַמְדַבֵּר אֲלֵיכֶם׃ וְהִגַּדְתֶּם לְאָבִי אֶת־כָּל־כְּבוֹדִי בְּמִצְרַיִם
יד וְאֵת כָּל־אֲשֶׁר רְאִיתֶם וּמִהַרְתֶּם וְהוֹרַדְתֶּם אֶת־אָבִי הֵנָּה׃ וַיִּפֹּל
טו עַל־צַוְּארֵי בִנְיָמִן־אָחִיו וַיֵּבְךְּ וּבִנְיָמִן בָּכָה עַל־צַוָּארָיו׃ וַיְנַשֵּׁק

10 Egypt. Come down to me without delay. You may live in the
region of Goshen where you will be close to me, you, your
children, and your grandchildren, your flocks and herds and
11 all that is yours. I will provide for you there, for there are still
five years of famine to come. Otherwise you, your household,
12 and all who belong to you will be destitute.' You and my
brother Binyamin can see with your own eyes that it is I who
13 am speaking to you. Tell my father about all the honor
accorded to me in Egypt and about everything you have seen.
14 Hurry now – bring my father here." Then he threw his arms
around his brother Binyamin's neck and wept, and Binyamin
15 wept on his neck; he kissed all his brothers and wept over

EGYPTOLOGY

45:10 Where was Goshen

The name "Goshen" does not appear in any existing ancient Egyptian documents. The area where the Israelites settled is called the region of Ramesses in 47:11, placing Goshen in the Delta region, probably in the area of Wadi Tumilat, a main trade route for caravans traveling eastward from Egypt. This location corresponds with Egyptian records indicating that the biggest concentrations of Semites and Asians in Egypt were in the eastern Delta area, closer to Canaan. These peoples could have included both the Israelites and the mixed multitude who left Egypt with them (Ex. 12:38).

The name Goshen may be connected to the Hebrew term *gush*, meaning a clod of earth (Job 7:5). Goshen is also the name of an area south of Ḥevron in the territory of Yehuda (Josh. 10:41, 11:16). ▪ ZR

Canal, Wadi Tumilat

EGYPTOLOGY

45:22 Gift of clothes

The practice of showing favor through gifts of clothing is well-attested in both Egyptian and Akkadian sources. For example, in the *Amarna letters*, we find that Tushratta, king of Mitanni, sent gifts to Amenhotep IV (ca. 1350 BCE), including, "one shirt, Hurrian-style; one city-shirt; one robe" (EA 27). Such gifts were part of diplomatic protocol, to the extent that the Hittite king Hattushili III (ca. 1267–1237 BCE) complained that the Assyrian king Adad-Nirari I snubbed him by not sending a gift of clothing at his inauguration, "It is the custom that when kings assume kingship, the kings, his equals in rank, send him appropriate [gifts of greeting]. Clothing befitting kingship, and fine [oil] for his anointing. But you did not do this today" (KBo I.14).

Since the quality and technique of manufacture of clothing is a mark of a person's social rank and often signifies their identity, a gift of appropriate clothing indicates that the giver acknowledges the position of the recipient. ▪ ZR

Amarna letter from Tushratta, king of Mitanni, to Amenhotep IV, Tell el-Amarna, ca. 1350 BCE

לְכׇל־אֶחָיו וַיֵּבְךְּ עֲלֵהֶם וְאַחֲרֵי כֵן דִּבְּרוּ אֶחָיו אִתּוֹ: וְהַקֹּל נִשְׁמַע טז
בֵּית פַּרְעֹה לֵאמֹר בָּאוּ אֲחֵי יוֹסֵף וַיִּיטַב בְּעֵינֵי פַרְעֹה וּבְעֵינֵי
עֲבָדָיו: וַיֹּאמֶר פַּרְעֹה אֶל־יוֹסֵף אֱמֹר אֶל־אַחֶיךָ זֹאת עֲשׂוּ טַעֲנוּ יז
אֶת־בְּעִירְכֶם וּלְכוּ־בֹאוּ אַרְצָה כְּנָעַן: וּקְחוּ אֶת־אֲבִיכֶם וְאֶת־ יח
בָּתֵּיכֶם וּבֹאוּ אֵלָי וְאֶתְּנָה לָכֶם אֶת־טוּב אֶרֶץ מִצְרַיִם וְאִכְלוּ
אֶת־חֵלֶב הָאָרֶץ: וְאַתָּה צֻוֵּיתָה זֹאת עֲשׂוּ קְחוּ־לָכֶם מֵאֶרֶץ יט רביעי
מִצְרַיִם עֲגָלוֹת לְטַפְּכֶם וְלִנְשֵׁיכֶם וּנְשָׂאתֶם אֶת־אֲבִיכֶם וּבָאתֶם:
וְעֵינְכֶם אַל־תָּחֹס עַל־כְּלֵיכֶם כִּי־טוּב כׇּל־אֶרֶץ מִצְרַיִם לָכֶם כ
הוּא: וַיַּעֲשׂוּ־כֵן בְּנֵי יִשְׂרָאֵל וַיִּתֵּן לָהֶם יוֹסֵף עֲגָלוֹת עַל־פִּי פַרְעֹה כא
וַיִּתֵּן לָהֶם צֵדָה לַדָּרֶךְ: לְכֻלָּם נָתַן לָאִישׁ חֲלִפוֹת שְׂמָלֹת וּלְבִנְיָמִן כב •
נָתַן שְׁלֹשׁ מֵאוֹת כֶּסֶף וְחָמֵשׁ חֲלִפֹת שְׂמָלֹת: וּלְאָבִיו שָׁלַח כְּזֹאת כג
עֲשָׂרָה חֲמֹרִים נֹשְׂאִים מִטּוּב מִצְרָיִם וְעֶשֶׂר אֲתֹנֹת נֹשְׂאֹת בָּר
וָלֶחֶם וּמָזוֹן לְאָבִיו לַדָּרֶךְ: וַיְשַׁלַּח אֶת־אֶחָיו וַיֵּלֵכוּ וַיֹּאמֶר אֲלֵהֶם כד
אַל־תִּרְגְּזוּ בַּדָּרֶךְ: וַיַּעֲלוּ מִמִּצְרָיִם וַיָּבֹאוּ אֶרֶץ כְּנַעַן אֶל־יַעֲקֹב כה
אֲבִיהֶם: וַיַּגִּדוּ לוֹ לֵאמֹר עוֹד יוֹסֵף חַי וְכִי־הוּא מֹשֵׁל בְּכׇל־אֶרֶץ כו

16 them. Only after that could his brothers speak to him. When
the news reached Pharaoh's palace that Yosef's brothers had
17 come, Pharaoh and his officials were gratified. Pharaoh said
to Yosef, "Tell your brothers, 'Do this: Load your animals and
18 go back to Canaan. Bring your father and your families and
come to me. I will give you the best of the land of Egypt; you
19 shall live off the cream of the land. You are also instructed to
do this: Take wagons from Egypt for your children and wives.
20 Bring your father and come. Do not trouble yourselves about
your belongings, for the best of all Egypt will be yours.'"
21 Yisrael's sons did so. Yosef gave them wagons as Pharaoh had
• 22 ordered, and gave them provisions for the journey. To each
he gave new clothes, but to Binyamin he gave three hundred
23 pieces of silver and five sets of clothes. To his father he sent
the following: ten donkeys loaded with the best things of
Egypt and ten female donkeys loaded with grain, bread, and
24 food for his father's journey. He sent his brothers on their
way; and as they were leaving, he said to them, "Do not
25 quarrel on the way." So they went up out of Egypt and came
26 to their father Yaakov in Canaan. They told him, "Yosef is still
alive; in fact, he is ruler over all Egypt." His heart stood still;

כז מִצְרָיִם וַיָּפָג לִבּוֹ כִּי לֹא־הֶאֱמִין לָהֶם׃ וַיְדַבְּרוּ אֵלָיו אֵת כָּל־דִּבְרֵי
יוֹסֵף אֲשֶׁר דִּבֶּר אֲלֵהֶם וַיַּרְא אֶת־הָעֲגָלוֹת אֲשֶׁר־שָׁלַח יוֹסֵף
כח לָשֵׂאת אֹתוֹ וַתְּחִי רוּחַ יַעֲקֹב אֲבִיהֶם׃ וַיֹּאמֶר יִשְׂרָאֵל רַב עוֹד־ חמישי
מו א יוֹסֵף בְּנִי חָי אֵלְכָה וְאֶרְאֶנּוּ בְּטֶרֶם אָמוּת׃ וַיִּסַּע יִשְׂרָאֵל וְכָל־
אֲשֶׁר־לוֹ וַיָּבֹא בְּאֵרָה שָּׁבַע וַיִּזְבַּח זְבָחִים לֵאלֹהֵי אָבִיו יִצְחָק׃
ב וַיֹּאמֶר אֱלֹהִים ׀ לְיִשְׂרָאֵל בְּמַרְאֹת הַלַּיְלָה וַיֹּאמֶר יַעֲקֹב ׀ יַעֲקֹב
ג וַיֹּאמֶר הִנֵּנִי׃ וַיֹּאמֶר אָנֹכִי הָאֵל אֱלֹהֵי אָבִיךָ אַל־תִּירָא מֵרְדָה
ד • מִצְרַיְמָה כִּי־לְגוֹי גָּדוֹל אֲשִׂימְךָ שָׁם׃ אָנֹכִי אֵרֵד עִמְּךָ מִצְרַיְמָה

27 he did not believe them. But when they told him everything
Yosef had said to them, and when he saw the wagons that
Yosef had sent to carry him back, Yaakov's spirit was filled
28 with new life. Yisrael said, "It is enough: Yosef my son is
46 1 still alive. I must go and see him before I die." So Yisrael set
out with all he had. When he reached Be'er Sheva, he
2 offered up sacrifices to the God of his father Yitzḥak. And
God spoke to Yisrael in a night vision: "Yaakov, Yaakov."
3 He replied, "Here I am." "I am God, the God of your father,"
He said. "Do not be afraid to go down to Egypt, for there
4 • I will make of you a great nation. I Myself will go down to
Egypt with you, and I Myself will also bring you back; and

EGYPTOLOGY

46:4 I Myself will also bring you back – a theological lesson

The Hebrew wording of this phrase is that God literally proclaimed, "I Myself will also surely raise you up." In other words, God promised to return Yaakov to the Promised Land – an allusion to his burial in the cave of Makhpela. That Yaakov would not return alive is indicated by God's next words, "Yosef's hand will close your eyes." In 47:29–31, Yaakov made Yosef swear to bury him in his ancestors' burial place. Yosef appealed to Pharaoh for permission to fulfill his oath to bury his father in Canaan (50:4–5), which Pharaoh granted (50:6).

Although Pharaoh may have thought that his decision is what counts, the Israelite reader knows that Pharaoh – who was, not only a monarch but also an Egyptian deity – was merely a tool in the fulfillment of God's plan, just as a later Pharaoh would be a tool for redeeming the entire nation from Egypt (Ex. 3:8, 17–20, 6:30–7:5). Here, the narrative exemplifies the Torah's monotheistic revolution against paganism. • JU

Entrance to the tombs of Yaakov and Leah, cave of Makhpela, ca. 1950–1977

וְאָנֹכִי אַעַלְךָ גַם־עָלֹה וְיוֹסֵף יָשִׁית יָדוֹ עַל־עֵינֶיךָ׃ וַיָּקָם יַעֲקֹב ה
מִבְּאֵר שָׁבַע וַיִּשְׂאוּ בְנֵי־יִשְׂרָאֵל אֶת־יַעֲקֹב אֲבִיהֶם וְאֶת־טַפָּם
וְאֶת־נְשֵׁיהֶם בָּעֲגָלוֹת אֲשֶׁר־שָׁלַח פַּרְעֹה לָשֵׂאת אֹתוֹ׃ וַיִּקְחוּ ו
אֶת־מִקְנֵיהֶם וְאֶת־רְכוּשָׁם אֲשֶׁר רָכְשׁוּ בְּאֶרֶץ כְּנַעַן וַיָּבֹאוּ
מִצְרָיְמָה יַעֲקֹב וְכָל־זַרְעוֹ אִתּוֹ׃ בָּנָיו וּבְנֵי בָנָיו אִתּוֹ בְּנֹתָיו וּבְנוֹת ז
בָּנָיו וְכָל־זַרְעוֹ הֵבִיא אִתּוֹ מִצְרָיְמָה׃ וְאֵלֶּה שְׁמוֹת ח
בְּנֵי־יִשְׂרָאֵל הַבָּאִים מִצְרַיְמָה יַעֲקֹב וּבָנָיו בְּכֹר יַעֲקֹב רְאוּבֵן׃
וּבְנֵי רְאוּבֵן חֲנוֹךְ וּפַלּוּא וְחֶצְרֹן וְכַרְמִי׃ וּבְנֵי שִׁמְעוֹן יְמוּאֵל וְיָמִין ט י
וְאֹהַד וְיָכִין וְצֹחַר וְשָׁאוּל בֶּן־הַכְּנַעֲנִית׃ וּבְנֵי לֵוִי גֵּרְשׁוֹן קְהָת יא
וּמְרָרִי׃ וּבְנֵי יְהוּדָה עֵר וְאוֹנָן וְשֵׁלָה וָפֶרֶץ וָזָרַח וַיָּמָת עֵר וְאוֹנָן יב
בְּאֶרֶץ כְּנַעַן וַיִּהְיוּ בְנֵי־פֶרֶץ חֶצְרֹן וְחָמוּל׃ וּבְנֵי יִשָּׂשכָר תּוֹלָע יג
וּפֻוָּה וְיוֹב וְשִׁמְרֹן׃ וּבְנֵי זְבֻלוּן סֶרֶד וְאֵלוֹן וְיַחְלְאֵל׃ אֵלֶּה ׀ בְּנֵי יד טו
לֵאָה אֲשֶׁר יָלְדָה לְיַעֲקֹב בְּפַדַּן אֲרָם וְאֵת דִּינָה בִתּוֹ כָּל־נֶפֶשׁ
בָּנָיו וּבְנוֹתָיו שְׁלֹשִׁים וְשָׁלֹשׁ׃ וּבְנֵי גָד צִפְיוֹן וְחַגִּי שׁוּנִי וְאֶצְבֹּן טז
עֵרִי וַאֲרוֹדִי וְאַרְאֵלִי׃ וּבְנֵי אָשֵׁר יִמְנָה וְיִשְׁוָה וְיִשְׁוִי וּבְרִיעָה יז
וְשֶׂרַח אֲחֹתָם וּבְנֵי בְרִיעָה חֶבֶר וּמַלְכִּיאֵל׃ אֵלֶּה בְּנֵי זִלְפָּה יח
אֲשֶׁר־נָתַן לָבָן לְלֵאָה בִתּוֹ וַתֵּלֶד אֶת־אֵלֶּה לְיַעֲקֹב שֵׁשׁ עֶשְׂרֵה
נָפֶשׁ׃ בְּנֵי רָחֵל אֵשֶׁת יַעֲקֹב יוֹסֵף וּבִנְיָמִן׃ וַיִּוָּלֵד לְיוֹסֵף בְּאֶרֶץ יט כ
מִצְרַיִם אֲשֶׁר יָלְדָה־לּוֹ אָסְנַת בַּת־פּוֹטִי פֶרַע כֹּהֵן אֹן אֶת־מְנַשֶּׁה
וְאֶת־אֶפְרָיִם׃ וּבְנֵי בִנְיָמִן בֶּלַע וָבֶכֶר וְאַשְׁבֵּל גֵּרָא וְנַעֲמָן אֵחִי כא
וָרֹאשׁ מֻפִּים וְחֻפִּים וָאָרְדְּ׃ אֵלֶּה בְּנֵי רָחֵל אֲשֶׁר יֻלַּד לְיַעֲקֹב כב
כָּל־נֶפֶשׁ אַרְבָּעָה עָשָׂר׃ וּבְנֵי־דָן חֻשִׁים׃ וּבְנֵי נַפְתָּלִי יַחְצְאֵל וְגוּנִי כג כד

Yosef's hand will close your
5 eyes." Then Yaakov left Be'er
Sheva. Yisrael's sons took their
father Yaakov and their children
and wives in the wagons that
Pharaoh had sent to carry him.
6 They took their livestock and
all the possessions they had
acquired in Canaan. So Yaakov
and all his descendants came to
7 Egypt. He brought with him to
Egypt his sons and grandsons,
daughters and granddaughters,
8 and all his descendants. These are the names of the children of Israel – Yaakov and his
9 descendants – who came to Egypt: Reuven, Yaakov's firstborn, and Reuven's sons, Ḥanokh, Palu,
10 Ḥetzron, and Karmi. Shimon's sons were Yemuel, Yamin, Ohad, Yakhin, Tzoḥar, and Sha'ul, son of the
11 12 Canaanite woman. Levi's sons were Gershon, Kehat, and Merari. Yehuda's sons were Er, Onan, Shela,
Peretz, and Zeraḥ – but Er and Onan had died in Canaan.[100] Peretz's sons were Ḥetzron and Ḥamul.
13 14 15 Yissakhar's sons were Tola, Puva, Yov, and Shimron. Zevulun's sons were Sered, Elon, and Yaḥliel. These
were the sons whom Leah bore to Yaakov in Padan Aram, besides his daughter Dina. In all, male and
16 female, they numbered thirty-three. Gad's sons were Tzifyon, Ḥagi, Shuni, Etzbon, Eri, Arodi, and Areli.
17 Asher's sons were Yimna, Yishva, Yishvi, and Beria. Their sister was Seraḥ. Beria's sons were Ḥever and
18 Malkiel. These were the children of Zilpa, whom Lavan had given to his daughter Leah; these she bore
19 20 to Yaakov – sixteen in all.The sons of Yaakov's wife Raḥel were Yosef and Binyamin. In Egypt Menashe
21 and Efrayim were born to Yosef; Asnat, daughter of Potifera priest of On, bore them to him. Binyamin's
22 sons were Bela, Bekher, Ashbel, Gera, Naaman, Eḥi, Rosh, Mupim, Ḥupim, and Ard. These are the
23 24 children Raḥel bore to Yaakov – fourteen in all. Dan's son was Ḥushim. Naftali's sons were Yaḥtze'el,

100 | See 38:7–10.

כה וְיֵצֶר וְשִׁלֵּם: אֵלֶּה בְּנֵי בִלְהָה אֲשֶׁר־נָתַן לָבָן לְרָחֵל בִּתּוֹ וַתֵּלֶד
כו אֶת־אֵלֶּה לְיַעֲקֹב כָּל־נֶפֶשׁ שִׁבְעָה: כָּל־הַנֶּפֶשׁ הַבָּאָה לְיַעֲקֹב
מִצְרַיְמָה יֹצְאֵי יְרֵכוֹ מִלְּבַד נְשֵׁי בְנֵי־יַעֲקֹב כָּל־נֶפֶשׁ שִׁשִּׁים וָשֵׁשׁ:
• כז וּבְנֵי יוֹסֵף אֲשֶׁר־יֻלַּד־לוֹ בְמִצְרַיִם נֶפֶשׁ שְׁנָיִם כָּל־הַנֶּפֶשׁ לְבֵית־
כח יַעֲקֹב הַבָּאָה מִצְרַיְמָה שִׁבְעִים: וְאֶת־יְהוּדָה שָׁלַח ששי
כט לְפָנָיו אֶל־יוֹסֵף לְהוֹרֹת לְפָנָיו גֹּשְׁנָה וַיָּבֹאוּ אַרְצָה גֹּשֶׁן: וַיֶּאְסֹר
יוֹסֵף מֶרְכַּבְתּוֹ וַיַּעַל לִקְרַאת־יִשְׂרָאֵל אָבִיו גֹּשְׁנָה וַיֵּרָא אֵלָיו
ל וַיִּפֹּל עַל־צַוָּארָיו וַיֵּבְךְּ עַל־צַוָּארָיו עוֹד: וַיֹּאמֶר יִשְׂרָאֵל אֶל־יוֹסֵף
לא אָמוּתָה הַפָּעַם אַחֲרֵי רְאוֹתִי אֶת־פָּנֶיךָ כִּי עוֹדְךָ חָי: וַיֹּאמֶר יוֹסֵף
אֶל־אֶחָיו וְאֶל־בֵּית אָבִיו אֶעֱלֶה וְאַגִּידָה לְפַרְעֹה וְאֹמְרָה אֵלָיו
לב אַחַי וּבֵית־אָבִי אֲשֶׁר בְּאֶרֶץ־כְּנַעַן בָּאוּ אֵלָי: וְהָאֲנָשִׁים רֹעֵי צֹאן
לג כִּי־אַנְשֵׁי מִקְנֶה הָיוּ וְצֹאנָם וּבְקָרָם וְכָל־אֲשֶׁר לָהֶם הֵבִיאוּ: וְהָיָה

Guni, Yetzer, and Shilem. These were the sons born to Yaakov 25
by Bilha, whom Lavan had given to his daughter Raḥel –
seven in all. So the number of people who came to Egypt with 26
Yaakov – his direct descendants, not including his sons'
wives – were sixty-six in all. Yosef's sons, born to him in 27 •
Egypt, were two in number. Thus the total number of Yaakov's
family who came to Egypt was seventy. He sent 28
Yehuda ahead of him to Yosef to show him the way to Goshen.
When they came to the region of Goshen, Yosef harnessed 29
his chariot and rode to Goshen to greet his father Yisrael. He
presented himself to him, threw his arms around his neck,
and wept on his shoulder for a long time. "Now I can die," 30
said Yisrael to Yosef. "I have seen your face! You are still alive!"
Yosef said to his brothers and his father's household, "I will 31
go and speak to Pharaoh. I will tell him, 'My brothers and my
father's household have come to me from Canaan. The men 32
are shepherds. They tend livestock. They have brought their
sheep and cattle and all they have.' When Pharaoh summons 33

NEAR EAST

46:27 Seventy members of Yaakov's family

The number seventy, the stated number of members of Yaakov's family, is complicated by the fact that while the sums given for the offspring of each of Yaakov's wives add up to seventy (Leah – thirty-three, Zilpa – sixteen, Raḥel – fourteen, Bilha – seven), Genesis 46:15 actually lists thirty-four names of Leah's descendants, leading to a total of seventy-one. Furthermore, Genesis 46:26 numbers Yaakov's family as sixty-six, excluding Er and Onan because they died in Canaan, but their exclusion would only have presumed that the original sum was sixty-eight. Presumably, the number sixty-six excluded Yaakov himself and his daughter Dina. Adding them back in yields sixty-eight, but it is not exactly clear how the total of the household reaches seventy in this verse. Various solutions to this problem are given in rabbinic sources.

The simplest understanding is to view the number seventy here as typological, not necessarily meant to be an exact total but rather a symbolic number used to denote a large group and the concept of totality. The motif of seventy important figures associated with a significant person is found multiple times in Tanakh. For example, the seventy descendants of Noaḥ (Gen. 10), the seventy sons of Gidon (Judges 8:30), Avdon, the judge, who "had forty sons and thirty grandsons who rode on seventy donkeys" (Judges 12:14), and the seventy sons of King Aḥav (II Kings 10:1).

This usage is also found in other texts of the ancient Near East. The Ugaritic goddess Athirat (Ashera) has seventy sons, making up the pantheon of gods, although it does not appear that there were seventy uniquely named deities. The leaders of Late Bronze Age Emar in Syria were called "the seventy sons of Emar" (Emar 373:37–38; see also "The seventy nations" on page 58). ▪ ZR

↗ Pendant with Ashera (Athirat) standing on a bull, gold leaf, Ugarit, 1500 to 1300 BCE

לד כִּֽי־יִקְרָא לָכֶם פַּרְעֹה וְאָמַר מַה־מַּעֲשֵׂיכֶם׃ וַאֲמַרְתֶּם אַנְשֵׁי
מִקְנֶה הָיוּ עֲבָדֶיךָ מִנְּעוּרֵינוּ וְעַד־עַתָּה גַּם־אֲנַחְנוּ גַּם־אֲבֹתֵינוּ
בַּעֲבוּר תֵּשְׁבוּ בְּאֶרֶץ גֹּשֶׁן כִּי־תוֹעֲבַת מִצְרַיִם כָּל־רֹעֵה צֹאן׃
מז א וַיָּבֹא יוֹסֵף וַיַּגֵּד לְפַרְעֹה וַיֹּאמֶר אָבִי וְאַחַי וְצֹאנָם וּבְקָרָם וְכָל־
ב אֲשֶׁר לָהֶם בָּאוּ מֵאֶרֶץ כְּנָעַן וְהִנָּם בְּאֶרֶץ גֹּשֶׁן׃ וּמִקְצֵה אֶחָיו
ג לָקַח חֲמִשָּׁה אֲנָשִׁים וַיַּצִּגֵם לִפְנֵי פַרְעֹה׃ וַיֹּאמֶר פַּרְעֹה אֶל־אֶחָיו
מַה־מַּעֲשֵׂיכֶם וַיֹּאמְרוּ אֶל־פַּרְעֹה רֹעֵה צֹאן עֲבָדֶיךָ גַּם־אֲנַחְנוּ
ד גַּם־אֲבוֹתֵינוּ׃ וַיֹּאמְרוּ אֶל־פַּרְעֹה לָגוּר בָּאָרֶץ בָּאנוּ כִּי־אֵין
מִרְעֶה לַצֹּאן אֲשֶׁר לַעֲבָדֶיךָ כִּי־כָבֵד הָרָעָב בְּאֶרֶץ כְּנָעַן וְעַתָּה

34 you and asks, 'What is your occupation?' you should say, 'We
and our fathers have tended livestock all our lives.' Then you
will be allowed to settle in the region of Goshen, because the
47 1 Egyptians abominate all who keep sheep."[101] So Yosef went
and told Pharaoh. He said, "My father and brothers, together
with their flocks, herds, and all they have, have come from
2 Canaan and are now in the region of Goshen." He chose five
3 of his brothers and presented them to Pharaoh. Pharaoh
asked the brothers, "What is your occupation?" They replied,
4 "Your servants are shepherds, as our fathers were before." And
they said to Pharaoh, "We have come to stay for a while in
your land because the famine is severe in Canaan and there
is no pasture for your servants' flocks. Please, then, let your

101 | In other words, because of this consideration, Pharaoh will agree to have you live in a peripheral location such as Goshen.

Depiction of Pharaoh Seti I's campaign in Canaan against the Shasu, Great Hypostyle Hall, Temple of Karnak, Luxor, 13th century BCE

EGYPTOLOGY

46:34 Goshen as a land of herders

The territory of Goshen is located in the eastern part of the Nile Delta. There, pharaohs of the 13th century BCE (Nineteenth Dynasty) built the city of Ramesses on the ruins of Avaris, which had been the capital under the Hyksos. The land of Ramesses is mentioned in Genesis 47:11, and appears identical to the land of Goshen, based on the context.

This region of Egypt had a nomadic Semitic population in the 13th century BCE, and perhaps earlier, according to Papyrus Anastasi VI, a papyrus from this period. The papyrus describes Egyptian attempts to control the migration of a group of Semitic-speaking nomadic herders who were coming into this area from the desert in order to water their flocks. These nomads are called Shasu-Edom, where Shasu is an Egyptian term referring to nomadic Semitic-speaking herders and Edom seems to define the group further by reference to the Edomite people we know from the Torah.

Yosef informs his brothers that "the Egyptians abominate all who keep sheep" (46:34). This fits well with what we know of Egyptian attitudes toward the Semitic-speaking nomadic herders who lived on its borders, and who sometimes entered the territory of Egypt. Aron Pinker summarizes this attitude nicely: "Native Egyptians were farmers – not pastoralists, and disdained shepherds." Similarly, Nili Shupak states: "Shepherding was considered by Egyptians a debased and difficult occupation, and shepherds belonged to the lower social classes." It was deeply ingrained in Egyptian culture to separate from these herders. Yosef, aware of this custom, orders his brothers to emphasize their status as herders, presumably so that they will stay separate from the Egyptians. ▪ SZA

ה יֵשְׁבוּ־נָא עֲבָדֶיךָ בְּאֶרֶץ גֹּשֶׁן: וַיֹּאמֶר פַּרְעֹה אֶל־יוֹסֵף לֵאמֹר
ו אָבִיךָ וְאַחֶיךָ בָּאוּ אֵלֶיךָ: אֶרֶץ מִצְרַיִם לְפָנֶיךָ הִוא בְּמֵיטַב הָאָרֶץ
הוֹשֵׁב אֶת־אָבִיךָ וְאֶת־אַחֶיךָ יֵשְׁבוּ בְּאֶרֶץ גֹּשֶׁן וְאִם־יָדַעְתָּ וְיֶשׁ־
ז בָּם אַנְשֵׁי־חַיִל וְשַׂמְתָּם שָׂרֵי מִקְנֶה עַל־אֲשֶׁר־לִי: וַיָּבֵא יוֹסֵף
אֶת־יַעֲקֹב אָבִיו וַיַּעֲמִדֵהוּ לִפְנֵי פַרְעֹה וַיְבָרֶךְ יַעֲקֹב אֶת־פַּרְעֹה:
ח ט וַיֹּאמֶר פַּרְעֹה אֶל־יַעֲקֹב כַּמָּה יְמֵי שְׁנֵי חַיֶּיךָ: וַיֹּאמֶר יַעֲקֹב אֶל־
פַּרְעֹה יְמֵי שְׁנֵי מְגוּרַי שְׁלֹשִׁים וּמְאַת שָׁנָה מְעַט וְרָעִים הָיוּ יְמֵי
שְׁנֵי חַיַּי וְלֹא הִשִּׂיגוּ אֶת־יְמֵי שְׁנֵי חַיֵּי אֲבֹתַי בִּימֵי מְגוּרֵיהֶם:

servants settle in the region of Goshen." Pharaoh said to Yosef, 5
"Your father and brothers have come to you. The land of 6
Egypt is open before you. Settle your father and brothers in
the best part of the land. Let them live in the region of Goshen,
and if there are able men among them, you may give them
charge of my own livestock." Then Yosef brought his father 7
Yaakov and presented him before Pharaoh. Yaakov blessed
Pharaoh, and Pharaoh asked Yaakov, "How old are you?" 8
Yaakov said to Pharaoh, "The years of my wandering are one 9
hundred and thirty. Few and hard have been the years of my
life, and I have not reached the age my fathers reached in their

EGYPTOLOGY

47:6 *Sarei mikneh*

The term *sarei mikneh*, literally, "officers of livestock," is mentioned multiple times in Egyptian inscriptions. Since the pharaoh owned vast herds of cattle, many people were needed to take care of them. This position was often given to foreigners.

The cattle herders were supervised by the Cattle Accountants, who in turn were supervised by a high official, the Overseer of Cattle. This office was sometimes even held by members of the royal family, such as Amenemhat, a prince of the Eighteenth Dynasty of Egypt, and Amenhotep, described in a stele as a "king's son, overseer of the cattle of Amun." The fact that some of Yosef's brothers were put in charge of the pharaoh's cattle meant that they were government officials and would receive the kind of legal protections not usually accorded to foreign residents who were not in government-appointed positions.

▪ ZR

Scene from the tomb chapel of Nebamun showing the presentation of cattle, Thebes, 14th century BCE

שביעי וַיְבָרֶךְ יַעֲקֹב אֶת־פַּרְעֹה וַיֵּצֵא מִלִּפְנֵי פַרְעֹה׃ וַיּוֹשֵׁב יוֹסֵף אֶת־ יא
אָבִיו וְאֶת־אֶחָיו וַיִּתֵּן לָהֶם אֲחֻזָּה בְּאֶרֶץ מִצְרַיִם בְּמֵיטַב הָאָרֶץ
בְּאֶרֶץ רַעְמְסֵס כַּאֲשֶׁר צִוָּה פַרְעֹה׃ וַיְכַלְכֵּל יוֹסֵף אֶת־אָבִיו יב
וְאֶת־אֶחָיו וְאֵת כָּל־בֵּית אָבִיו לֶחֶם לְפִי הַטָּף׃ וְלֶחֶם אֵין בְּכָל־ יג
הָאָרֶץ כִּי־כָבֵד הָרָעָב מְאֹד וַתֵּלַהּ אֶרֶץ מִצְרַיִם וְאֶרֶץ כְּנַעַן מִפְּנֵי
הָרָעָב׃ וַיְלַקֵּט יוֹסֵף אֶת־כָּל־הַכֶּסֶף הַנִּמְצָא בְאֶרֶץ־מִצְרַיִם יד
וּבְאֶרֶץ כְּנַעַן בַּשֶּׁבֶר אֲשֶׁר־הֵם שֹׁבְרִים וַיָּבֵא יוֹסֵף אֶת־הַכֶּסֶף
בֵּיתָה פַרְעֹה׃ וַיִּתֹּם הַכֶּסֶף מֵאֶרֶץ מִצְרַיִם וּמֵאֶרֶץ כְּנַעַן וַיָּבֹאוּ טו
כָל־מִצְרַיִם אֶל־יוֹסֵף לֵאמֹר הָבָה־לָּנוּ לֶחֶם וְלָמָּה נָמוּת נֶגְדֶּךָ
כִּי אָפֵס כָּסֶף׃ וַיֹּאמֶר יוֹסֵף הָבוּ מִקְנֵיכֶם וְאֶתְּנָה לָכֶם בְּמִקְנֵיכֶם טז
אִם־אָפֵס כָּסֶף׃ וַיָּבִיאוּ אֶת־מִקְנֵיהֶם אֶל־יוֹסֵף וַיִּתֵּן לָהֶם יוֹסֵף יז
לֶחֶם בַּסּוּסִים וּבְמִקְנֵה הַצֹּאן וּבְמִקְנֵה הַבָּקָר וּבַחֲמֹרִים וַיְנַהֲלֵם
בַּלֶּחֶם בְּכָל־מִקְנֵהֶם בַּשָּׁנָה הַהִוא׃ וַתִּתֹּם הַשָּׁנָה הַהִוא וַיָּבֹאוּ יח
אֵלָיו בַּשָּׁנָה הַשֵּׁנִית וַיֹּאמְרוּ לוֹ לֹא־נְכַחֵד מֵאֲדֹנִי כִּי אִם־תַּם
הַכֶּסֶף וּמִקְנֵה הַבְּהֵמָה אֶל־אֲדֹנִי לֹא נִשְׁאַר לִפְנֵי אֲדֹנִי בִּלְתִּי

10 own wanderings." Yaakov blessed Pharaoh and left his
11 presence. Yosef settled his father and brothers, giving them
holdings in the best part of Egypt, in the region of Ramesses,[102]
12 as Pharaoh had instructed. And Yosef provided his father, his
brothers, and all his father's household with food, befitting
13 the numbers of their dependents. And there was no food
across the land, because the famine was so severe. Egypt and
14 Canaan languished because of the famine. Yosef collected all
the money that was to be found in Egypt and Canaan in
payment for the grain the people were buying, and he brought
15 it into Pharaoh's palace. When the money in Egypt and
Canaan was gone, all the Egyptians came to Yosef, saying,
"Give us food. Why should we die before your eyes just
16 because there is no more money left?" "Bring your livestock,"
said Yosef, "and I will sell you food in exchange for your
17 livestock since there is no more money left." So they brought
their livestock to Yosef, and he gave them food in exchange
for horses, sheep, cattle, and donkeys. He supplied them with
18 food that year in exchange for all their livestock. That year
passed, and they came to him the following year and said,
"We cannot hide from my lord that the money is gone and
the livestock belongs to you. There is nothing left for my lord

102 | Ramesses evidently comprised all or part of Goshen.

EGYPTOLOGY

47:11 Region of Ramesses

The place name Ramesses (see also Ex. 1:11, 12:37; Num. 33:3, 5) is the biblical term for the Egyptian Per Ramesses (see "Pithom and Ramesses: language" and "Where did the Israelites live?" in the Exodus volume of this series on page 6). It was the capital constructed by Ramesses II in the 13th century BCE and named after himself, located in the eastern Nile Delta, near the site of the earlier Hyksos capital called Avaris. The city was largely abandoned at the end of the New Kingdom because the Pelusiac branch of the Nile became silted up, resulting in its harbor becoming unusable; the capital was moved to Tanis ca. 1075 BCE.

In the time of Yosef, there was not yet a place named Ramesses. Use of this term anachronistically here makes the area identifiable to the Israelites who received the Torah. ▪ ZR

Statue head of an Asiatic official, Avaris, 18th century BCE

יט אִם־גְּוִיָּתֵנוּ וְאַדְמָתֵנוּ׃ לָמָּה נָמוּת לְעֵינֶיךָ גַּם־אֲנַחְנוּ גַּם־
אַדְמָתֵנוּ קְנֵה־אֹתָנוּ וְאֶת־אַדְמָתֵנוּ בַּלָּחֶם וְנִהְיֶה אֲנַחְנוּ
וְאַדְמָתֵנוּ עֲבָדִים לְפַרְעֹה וְתֶן־זֶרַע וְנִחְיֶה וְלֹא נָמוּת וְהָאֲדָמָה

except our bodies and our land. Why should we and our land 19
die before your eyes? Acquire us and our land in exchange for
food, and we with our land will be slaves to Pharaoh. Give us
seed so that we can live and not die and so that the land does

EGYPTOLOGY

47:17 Horses

This is the first reference to horses in Tanakh, wherein horses are generally mentioned in connection with Egypt, most notably in the instruction for a king, "he must not make the people return to Egypt to acquire more horses" (Deut. 17:16). It is generally accepted that horses were introduced to ancient Egypt in large numbers in the New Kingdom period (ca. 1570–1069 BCE), based on the large number of horse molars found at the Hyksos site of Tell el-Dab'a (ancient Avaris, next to the site of Per Ramesses, the biblical Ramesses). However, this find may indicate that horses were introduced earlier during the Hyksos settlement of the Second Intermediate Period (ca. 1700 BCE).

Horses are mentioned here specifically because of their high value; in ancient Egypt, they were used for military purposes and as symbols of royal power. ▪ ZR

↗ Offering of a chariot and a horse, facsimile by Charles Wilkinson, Tomb of Userhat, Thebes, 15th century BCE

לֹא תֵשָׁם׃ וַיִּקֶן יוֹסֵף אֶת־כׇּל־אַדְמַת מִצְרַיִם לְפַרְעֹה כִּי־מָכְרוּ כ
מִצְרַיִם אִישׁ שָׂדֵהוּ כִּי־חָזַק עֲלֵהֶם הָרָעָב וַתְּהִי הָאָרֶץ לְפַרְעֹה׃
וְאֶת־הָעָם הֶעֱבִיר אֹתוֹ לֶעָרִים מִקְצֵה גְבוּל־מִצְרַיִם וְעַד־קָצֵהוּ׃ כא
רַק אַדְמַת הַכֹּהֲנִים לֹא קָנָה כִּי חֹק לַכֹּהֲנִים מֵאֵת פַּרְעֹה וְאָכְלוּ כב
אֶת־חֻקָּם אֲשֶׁר נָתַן לָהֶם פַּרְעֹה עַל־כֵּן לֹא מָכְרוּ אֶת־אַדְמָתָם׃

20 not become desolate." Thus Yosef acquired all the land of
Egypt for Pharaoh. Each Egyptian sold his field, because the
famine had become too much for them. So the land became
21 Pharaoh's. As for the people, he transferred them town by
22 town from one end of Egypt to the other.[103] The only land he
did not acquire was that of the priests, because they received
an allotment of food from Pharaoh; they were able to live on
the allotment that Pharaoh gave them, and so they did not

103 | To help ensure that the people would not try to reclaim their land.

EGYPTOLOGY

47:20–25 Yosef's reallocation of Egyptian land

Evidence of state-owned real estate in ancient Egypt, in the form of royal vineyards, dates back to the time of King Adj-ib in the First Dynasty (Early Bronze Age). Seals from that period demonstrate the delivery of revenue from these holdings to the king. In practice, most of the land in Egypt became state property after the expulsion of the Hyksos in the middle of the 16th century BCE.

The twenty percent of the yield given in exchange for the seed provided and for the right to harvest state-owned land (vv. 23–24) was not exorbitant by ancient Near Eastern standards. For example, under Hammurabi, the state's share of the harvest from state-owned fields ranged from one-half to two-thirds of the yield, and in Babylon, the standard interest rate on loans of produce was one-third.

During the New Kingdom period, large temples owned and administered extensive tracts of land. The land list in the Harris Papyrus (ca. 1150 BCE) begins with the enumeration of landowners, starting with lands owned by the temples of Amun, Heliopolis, and Memphis, while lands owned by the pharaoh are only listed afterward. This list also sheds light on the Egyptian view of land ownership. Since the land was the property of the gods, it made sense that temples, priests, and the divine pharaoh were viewed as the rightful administrators on behalf of the gods, allotting the land accordingly. Even private property was technically termed a person's "share" in New Kingdom Egypt – a personal right of *use* (but not ownership) of a field granted by the king or a temple.

Yosef's land reforms fit into the establishment of the New Kingdom pharaonic policy after the expulsion of the Hyksos, when the pharaohs seem to have reinstituted their rights to the land while special privileges were accorded to temples and priests. It may be that Yosef was exceptionally instrumental in executing this policy throughout Egypt during the famine. ▪ ZR

Picking grapes, Tomb of Userhat, Thebes, 15th century BCE

כג וַיֹּאמֶר יוֹסֵף אֶל־הָעָם הֵן קָנִיתִי אֶתְכֶם הַיּוֹם וְאֶת־אַדְמַתְכֶם
כד לְפַרְעֹה הֵא־לָכֶם זֶרַע וּזְרַעְתֶּם אֶת־הָאֲדָמָה׃ וְהָיָה בַּתְּבוּאֹת
וּנְתַתֶּם חֲמִישִׁית לְפַרְעֹה וְאַרְבַּע הַיָּדֹת יִהְיֶה לָכֶם לְזֶרַע הַשָּׂדֶה
כה וּלְאָכְלְכֶם וְלַאֲשֶׁר בְּבָתֵּיכֶם וְלֶאֱכֹל לְטַפְּכֶם׃ וַיֹּאמְרוּ הֶחֱיִתָנוּ מפטיר
כו נִמְצָא־חֵן בְּעֵינֵי אֲדֹנִי וְהָיִינוּ עֲבָדִים לְפַרְעֹה׃ וַיָּשֶׂם אֹתָהּ יוֹסֵף
לְחֹק עַד־הַיּוֹם הַזֶּה עַל־אַדְמַת מִצְרַיִם לְפַרְעֹה לַחֹמֶשׁ רַק
כז אַדְמַת הַכֹּהֲנִים לְבַדָּם לֹא הָיְתָה לְפַרְעֹה׃ וַיֵּשֶׁב יִשְׂרָאֵל בְּאֶרֶץ
כח מִצְרַיִם בְּאֶרֶץ גֹּשֶׁן וַיֵּאָחֲזוּ בָהּ וַיִּפְרוּ וַיִּרְבּוּ מְאֹד׃ וַיְחִי יַעֲקֹב ויחי
בְּאֶרֶץ מִצְרַיִם שְׁבַע עֶשְׂרֵה שָׁנָה וַיְהִי יְמֵי־יַעֲקֹב שְׁנֵי חַיָּיו שֶׁבַע
כט שָׁנִים וְאַרְבָּעִים וּמְאַת שָׁנָה׃ וַיִּקְרְבוּ יְמֵי־יִשְׂרָאֵל לָמוּת וַיִּקְרָא ׀
לִבְנוֹ לְיוֹסֵף וַיֹּאמֶר לוֹ אִם־נָא מָצָאתִי חֵן בְּעֵינֶיךָ שִׂים־נָא יָדְךָ
תַּחַת יְרֵכִי וְעָשִׂיתָ עִמָּדִי חֶסֶד וֶאֱמֶת אַל־נָא תִקְבְּרֵנִי בְּמִצְרָיִם׃
ל וְשָׁכַבְתִּי עִם־אֲבֹתַי וּנְשָׂאתַנִי מִמִּצְרַיִם וּקְבַרְתַּנִי בִּקְבֻרָתָם
לא וַיֹּאמַר אָנֹכִי אֶעֱשֶׂה כִדְבָרֶךָ׃ וַיֹּאמֶר הִשָּׁבְעָה לִי וַיִּשָּׁבַע לוֹ
וַיִּשְׁתַּחוּ יִשְׂרָאֵל עַל־רֹאשׁ הַמִּטָּה׃
מח א וַיְהִי אַחֲרֵי הַדְּבָרִים הָאֵלֶּה וַיֹּאמֶר לְיוֹסֵף הִנֵּה אָבִיךָ חֹלֶה וַיִּקַּח
ב אֶת־שְׁנֵי בָנָיו עִמּוֹ אֶת־מְנַשֶּׁה וְאֶת־אֶפְרָיִם׃ וַיַּגֵּד לְיַעֲקֹב וַיֹּאמֶר
הִנֵּה בִּנְךָ יוֹסֵף בָּא אֵלֶיךָ וַיִּתְחַזֵּק יִשְׂרָאֵל וַיֵּשֶׁב עַל־הַמִּטָּה׃
ג וַיֹּאמֶר יַעֲקֹב אֶל־יוֹסֵף אֵל שַׁדַּי נִרְאָה־אֵלַי בְּלוּז בְּאֶרֶץ כְּנָעַן
ד וַיְבָרֶךְ אֹתִי׃ וַיֹּאמֶר אֵלַי הִנְנִי מַפְרְךָ וְהִרְבִּיתִךָ וּנְתַתִּיךָ לִקְהַל

sell their land. Yosef said to the people, "Today I have acquired you and your land for Pharaoh. Here is 23
seed for you to sow the land. When the harvest comes, give one-fifth to Pharaoh. Four-fifths shall be 24
yours as seed for your fields and as food for you, your households, and your children." "You have saved 25
our lives," they said. "May we find favor in the eyes of my lord – we shall be slaves to Pharaoh." So Yosef 26
made it a law, as it is to this day, governing land in Egypt, that one-fifth of all produce belongs to Pharaoh.
Only the land of the priests did not become Pharaoh's. Thus Yisrael settled in the land of Egypt, in the 27
region of Goshen. They acquired holdings in it and were fertile and greatly increased in number. Yaakov 28
lived in Egypt for seventeen years; the years of his life were one hundred and forty-seven. As the time 29
of his death drew near, he summoned his son Yosef and said to him, "If I have found favor in your eyes,
place your hand under my thigh[104] and promise to deal kindly and truly with me: do not bury me in
Egypt. Let me lie with my fathers. Carry me from Egypt and bury me where they are buried." "I will do 30
as you say," he replied. Yaakov said, "Swear to me," and Yosef swore. Then, at the head of the bed, Yisrael 31
bowed.
Some time later, Yosef was told, "Your father is ill." He brought with him his two sons, Menashe and 1 48
Efrayim. And when Yaakov was told, "Your son Yosef has come to see you," Yisrael summoned his 2
strength and sat up in the bed. Yaakov said to Yosef, "El Shaddai appeared to me in Luz in the land 3
of Canaan. He blessed me and said to me, 'I will make you fruitful and increase your numbers. I will 4

104 | Sometimes performed in conjunction with an oath (cf. 24:2).

עַמִּ֑ים וְנָ֨תַתִּ֜י אֶת־הָאָ֧רֶץ הַזֹּ֛את לְזַרְעֲךָ֥ אַחֲרֶ֖יךָ אֲחֻזַּ֥ת עוֹלָֽם׃
ה וְעַתָּ֡ה שְׁנֵֽי־בָנֶ֩יךָ֩ הַנּוֹלָדִ֨ים לְךָ֜ בְּאֶ֣רֶץ מִצְרַ֗יִם עַד־בֹּאִ֥י אֵלֶ֛יךָ
מִצְרַ֖יְמָה לִי־הֵ֑ם אֶפְרַ֨יִם֙ וּמְנַשֶּׁ֔ה כִּרְאוּבֵ֥ן וְשִׁמְע֖וֹן יִֽהְיוּ־לִֽי׃

make you a community of peoples, and I will give this land
5 to your descendants as an everlasting possession.' Now, the
two sons who were born to you in Egypt before I came here
shall be considered mine: Efrayim and Menashe will be like

NEAR EAST

48:5 Yaakov's adoption and blessing of Efrayim and Menashe

Adoption established kinship ties between two individuals who were not directly related by blood. In many cases, the adopted child would enter the new house with the rights of a free-born child; however, in some cases, a child might be adopted with lesser rights. Couples generally adopted children if they had none of their own. Children were needed as heirs, to inherit a person's land, goods, and family name, and were responsible for taking care of aging parents and executing funerary rites. In the *Laws of Hammurabi,* for example, children could also be adopted to learn a family trade (LH §188) or to add labor capacity to the family. Adoption additionally functioned as a social institution to care for unwanted children.

Laws and adoption contracts discuss children adopted as infants. The *Laws of Hammurabi* call this an adoption from "the birth waters" (LH §185). In another example, an Old Babylonian contract states that the infant's mother died, and he was being raised by his older brother and sister until the point that he was adopted: "Ibiq-iltum, the son of Sin-magir, took in adoption the young child pulled from the womb son of Atkalshim (deceased) from his oldest brother Shamash-naṣir and his sister Tarish-matum..." (MAH 15.951). Individuals could also be adopted as adults, a practice known from the city of Nuzi as *ṭuppi marutu/martutu*, "adoption for sonship/daughtership."

The groin, like the breast, was linked to reproduction, and therefore, placing a child on these body parts could symbolically formalize an adoption. The phrase "to place in one's lap" or "to set on one's breast" is found in two Old Babylonian lexical series, and appears in Neo-Babylonian and Assyrian letters, Hittite birth rituals, and Hurrian myths, as well as later Greek sources (ABL 178 r. 5; NA oracles for Esar Ḥadon, the *Annals of Hattusilis*, and the *Iliad* 9:461–470). Such phrases are also linked to adoption in the Tanakh (Gen. 30:3, 50:23; Ruth 4:16). Genesis 48:12, which describes Efrayim and Menashe placed between Yaakov's knees, thus reflects standard ancient Near Eastern adoption practices.

In adopting Yosef's sons, Yaakov first invoked God and then stated that his name shall be called in/on the children, along with the names of Yaakov's forefathers. This is a legal formula transferring the boys into Yaakov's direct family line, as can be seen in Hittite texts and Hurrian myths where the acts of placement on a father's or grandfather's knees, naming, and recognizing the son are all linked together (KUB XXIV 8).

In naming the child, the father also legitimized the child. This practice is similar to Mesopotamian oral statements whereby a man could legitimize children (LH §170–171) and settle disputes over which child would inherit property or servants. Such oral statements had socio-juridical power. Here, the significance is heightened by the fact that Yosef's two sons were adopted by Yaakov, raising Yosef to the status of the firstborn as he received a double portion.

The blessing given to Yosef's sons represents not only adoption but Yaakov's last will and testament. Final words, given close to death or on a deathbed, are found in Mesopotamian legal documents that parcel out land, servants, and household duties. Such texts echo the setting of Genesis 27 and 48.

↗ Old Babylonian legal document for a loan of silver, Kutalla (Tell Sifr), 18th century BCE

When Yaakov blessed Yosef's sons, he placed his right hand on Efrayim's head rather than that of Menashe, his elder brother. The laying on of hands is a transfer ritual. While such rituals are known from Hittite and Mesopotamian texts, they were used there to signify the transfer of sin, illness, guilt, or other maladies. Except for one Egyptian example, the laying on of hands to transfer authority is unique to the Torah. ▪ KG

ו וּמוֹלַדְתְּךָ אֲשֶׁר־הוֹלַדְתָּ אַחֲרֵיהֶם לְךָ יִהְיוּ עַל שֵׁם אֲחֵיהֶם יִקָּרְאוּ
ז בְּנַחֲלָתָם: וַאֲנִי ׀ בְּבֹאִי מִפַּדָּן מֵתָה עָלַי רָחֵל בְּאֶרֶץ כְּנַעַן בַּדֶּרֶךְ
בְּעוֹד כִּבְרַת־אֶרֶץ לָבֹא אֶפְרָתָה וָאֶקְבְּרֶהָ שָּׁם בְּדֶרֶךְ אֶפְרָת
ח הִוא בֵּית לָחֶם: וַיַּרְא יִשְׂרָאֵל אֶת־בְּנֵי יוֹסֵף וַיֹּאמֶר מִי־אֵלֶּה:
ט וַיֹּאמֶר יוֹסֵף אֶל־אָבִיו בָּנַי הֵם אֲשֶׁר־נָתַן־לִי אֱלֹהִים בָּזֶה וַיֹּאמַר
י קָחֶם־נָא אֵלַי וַאֲבָרְכֵם: וְעֵינֵי יִשְׂרָאֵל כָּבְדוּ מִזֹּקֶן לֹא יוּכַל שני
יא לִרְאוֹת וַיַּגֵּשׁ אֹתָם אֵלָיו וַיִּשַּׁק לָהֶם וַיְחַבֵּק לָהֶם: וַיֹּאמֶר יִשְׂרָאֵל
אֶל־יוֹסֵף רְאֹה פָנֶיךָ לֹא פִלָּלְתִּי וְהִנֵּה הֶרְאָה אֹתִי אֱלֹהִים גַּם
יב אֶת־זַרְעֶךָ: וַיּוֹצֵא יוֹסֵף אֹתָם מֵעִם בִּרְכָּיו וַיִּשְׁתַּחוּ לְאַפָּיו אָרְצָה:
יג וַיִּקַּח יוֹסֵף אֶת־שְׁנֵיהֶם אֶת־אֶפְרַיִם בִּימִינוֹ מִשְּׂמֹאל יִשְׂרָאֵל
יד וְאֶת־מְנַשֶּׁה בִשְׂמֹאלוֹ מִימִין יִשְׂרָאֵל וַיַּגֵּשׁ אֵלָיו: וַיִּשְׁלַח יִשְׂרָאֵל
אֶת־יְמִינוֹ וַיָּשֶׁת עַל־רֹאשׁ אֶפְרַיִם וְהוּא הַצָּעִיר וְאֶת־שְׂמֹאלוֹ
טו עַל־רֹאשׁ מְנַשֶּׁה שִׂכֵּל אֶת־יָדָיו כִּי מְנַשֶּׁה הַבְּכוֹר: וַיְבָרֶךְ אֶת־
יוֹסֵף וַיֹּאמַר הָאֱלֹהִים אֲשֶׁר הִתְהַלְּכוּ אֲבֹתַי לְפָנָיו אַבְרָהָם וְיִצְחָק

Reuven and Shimon to me. Any child born to you after shall 6
be yours; in any inheritance they will be reckoned under the
names of their brothers.[105] For I – as I was returning from 7
Padan, Raḥel died beside me in Canaan while we were still
on the way, a short distance from Efrat. And I buried her
there beside the road to Efrat – that is, Beit Leḥem." Then 8
Yisrael looked at Yosef's sons and said, "Who are these?"
Yosef told his father, "They are my sons God has given me 9
here." "Please bring them to me," Yaakov said, "so that I can
bless them." Yisrael's eyes were heavy with age and he could 10
not see. So Yosef brought them close to him, and he kissed
and embraced them. Yisrael said to Yosef, "I never expected 11
to see you again, and now God has shown me your children
as well." Yosef then took them from between his knees and 12
bowed low, his face to the ground. Yosef took both of them, 13
Efrayim on his right to Yisrael's left, and Menashe on his left
to Yisrael's right, and brought them close. Yisrael reached 14
out his right hand and put it on Efrayim's head, even though
he was the younger. And, crossing his hands, he put his left
hand on Menashe's head even though he was the firstborn.
He blessed Yosef and said, "God before whom my fathers 15
walked – Avraham and Yitzḥak – God who has been my

105 | Descendants of Yosef through any other sons would thus be incorporated into the tribes of Efrayim and Menashe.

NEAR EAST

48:15 Ancient Near Eastern metaphor of "shepherd"

In multiple places in Tanakh (Is. 40:11; Jer. 31:9; Ezek. 34:14–15; and famously in Ps. 23), God is described as a shepherd who sustains and guides Israel. This metaphor is also used for Moshe (Is. 63:11; Ps. 77:21), David (II Sam. 5:2, 7:7; Ps. 78:71–72), and other leaders (I Kings 22:17; Jer. 3:15, 23:2; Ezek. 34).

Ramesses II holding a crook and a flail, sandstone, Nubia, 13th century BCE

The association of a leader, particularly a king, with a shepherd was widespread throughout the ancient Near East. Egyptian kings are depicted holding a shepherd's crook as early as the Second Dynasty of the Old Kingdom (ca. 2800 BCE). In Homer's *Iliad*, Nestor recounts the kings he has known, "Never again can I behold such men as Pirithous and Dryas shepherd of his people" (*Iliad* 1:263).

The imagery was especially popular in the areas of the eastern Fertile Crescent, where it was used for Sumerian kings as far back as Lugal-Zage-Si of Umma (reigned ca. 2358–2334 BCE). By the time of the Assyrian empire, it was the standard language used as a synonym for a ruler. In the prologue, Hammurabi states that "I was not careless and I was not negligent towards [my] dark-haired folk whom the god Enlil granted to me, and whose shepherding the God Marduk gave to me," and in the epilogue, he states "The great gods have called me, I am the salvation bearing shepherd." The god Marduk himself is referred to in the *Enuma Elish Epic* as "the star who shepherded the gods like sheep" (VIb to VII). ▪ ZR

הָאֱלֹהִים הָרֹעֶה אֹתִי מֵעוֹדִי עַד־הַיּוֹם הַזֶּה: הַמַּלְאָךְ הַגֹּאֵל טז
אֹתִי מִכָּל־רָע יְבָרֵךְ אֶת־הַנְּעָרִים וְיִקָּרֵא בָהֶם שְׁמִי וְשֵׁם אֲבֹתַי
אַבְרָהָם וְיִצְחָק וְיִדְגּוּ לָרֹב בְּקֶרֶב הָאָרֶץ: וַיַּרְא יוֹסֵף כִּי־יָשִׁית יז שלישי
אָבִיו יַד־יְמִינוֹ עַל־רֹאשׁ אֶפְרַיִם וַיֵּרַע בְּעֵינָיו וַיִּתְמֹךְ יַד־אָבִיו
לְהָסִיר אֹתָהּ מֵעַל רֹאשׁ־אֶפְרַיִם עַל־רֹאשׁ מְנַשֶּׁה: וַיֹּאמֶר יוֹסֵף יח
אֶל־אָבִיו לֹא־כֵן אָבִי כִּי־זֶה הַבְּכֹר שִׂים יְמִינְךָ עַל־רֹאשׁוֹ: וַיְמָאֵן יט
אָבִיו וַיֹּאמֶר יָדַעְתִּי בְנִי יָדַעְתִּי גַּם־הוּא יִהְיֶה־לְּעָם וְגַם־הוּא
יִגְדָּל וְאוּלָם אָחִיו הַקָּטֹן יִגְדַּל מִמֶּנּוּ וְזַרְעוֹ יִהְיֶה מְלֹא־הַגּוֹיִם:
וַיְבָרְכֵם בַּיּוֹם הַהוּא לֵאמוֹר בְּךָ יְבָרֵךְ יִשְׂרָאֵל לֵאמֹר יְשִׂמְךָ כ
אֱלֹהִים כְּאֶפְרַיִם וְכִמְנַשֶּׁה וַיָּשֶׂם אֶת־אֶפְרַיִם לִפְנֵי מְנַשֶּׁה: וַיֹּאמֶר כא
יִשְׂרָאֵל אֶל־יוֹסֵף הִנֵּה אָנֹכִי מֵת וְהָיָה אֱלֹהִים עִמָּכֶם וְהֵשִׁיב
אֶתְכֶם אֶל־אֶרֶץ אֲבֹתֵיכֶם: וַאֲנִי נָתַתִּי לְךָ שְׁכֶם אַחַד עַל־אַחֶיךָ כב
אֲשֶׁר לָקַחְתִּי מִיַּד הָאֱמֹרִי בְּחַרְבִּי וּבְקַשְׁתִּי:
וַיִּקְרָא יַעֲקֹב אֶל־בָּנָיו וַיֹּאמֶר הֵאָסְפוּ וְאַגִּידָה לָכֶם אֵת אֲשֶׁר־ א מט רביעי
יִקְרָא אֶתְכֶם בְּאַחֲרִית הַיָּמִים: הִקָּבְצוּ וְשִׁמְעוּ בְּנֵי יַעֲקֹב וְשִׁמְעוּ ב

16 shepherd all my life to now, the angel who has delivered me
from all harm, may He bless the boys. Through them may my
name be recalled, and the names of my fathers, Avraham and
17 Yitzḥak. May they grow to a multitude upon the land." When
Yosef saw that his father had placed his right hand on Efrayim's
head, he was displeased. He took hold of his father's hand to
18 move it from Efrayim's head to Menashe's head. Yosef said to
his father, "Not so, father. This is the firstborn. Put your right
19 hand on his head." But his father refused: "I know, my son, I
know. He too will be a people, and he too will become great,
but his younger brother will become even greater, and his
20 descendants will become an abundance of nations." On that
day, he blessed them: "By you shall Israel bless,[106] saying: May
God make you like Efrayim and Menashe." He put Efrayim
21 before Menashe. Then Yisrael said to Yosef, "I am about to
die, but God will be with you and will bring you back to the
22 land of your fathers. And to you I give one portion more than
your brothers, which I took from the Amorites by my sword
and my bow."
49 1 Then Yaakov called for his sons and said, "Gather together so
that I can tell you what will happen to you in the days to come.
2 Assemble and listen, Yaakov's sons. Listen to your father

106 | When the Israelites offer blessings, they will invoke Efrayim and Menashe.

LANGUAGE

49:1 In the days to come

The Hebrew phrase is *b'aḥarit hayamim*, "in the days to come," a phrase that eventually came to refer not merely to some indeterminate future point but, in general religious thought, to the eschatological denouement of the human story on earth: "the end of days." However, *aḥarit* in Biblical Hebrew does not lose the original meaning of *aḥar* as "afterward" (see, for example, Gen. 33:2, where Yaakov puts Leah and her children *aḥaronim*, and then puts Raḥel and Yosef even more *aḥaronim*). Yirmeyahu even uses the whole phrase *aḥarit hayamim* simply to mean "in the future," not "at the end of days" (see Jer. 29:11). Yaakov too is speaking about the future, about an epoch that will at some point succeed his own time, and not about what will happen to his sons in their own lives.

This usage seems to match that of the precisely cognate Akkadian phrase *ana aḫrat umee*, referring as it does neither to some random future moment nor to a theologically significant time but instead to a future that is distant but has historical significance. King Shalmaneser I of Assyria (13th century BCE) writes of a military victory: "I gathered up the conquered city's earth and made a heap of it at the gate of my city, Assur, for all the future [*ana aḫrat ume*]." ▪ MC

Limestone stele of the Assyrian king Shalmaneser I, from the Rows of Stelae, Ashur, 13th century BCE

GEOGRAPHY

49:1–33 Blessings for Yaakov's sons

The connection that Yaakov's descendants maintain with the land of Israel is presaged in the blessings Yaakov gives his sons before his death. The blessings to many of the sons are borne out via the particular section of the land of Israel allocated to their tribe in the book of Joshua. It should be noted that the allocation of the land to the tribes is also listed in Numbers 34:16–29 (which lists the tribes from south to north), and in Deuteronomy 34:2.

The settlement of the land by the tribes occurred over a long period of time, in a gradual, complex process. Archaeological evidence does suggest that the Israelite tribes began settling the land in the second half of the 13th century BCE. Settlement commenced in the territory of Menashe and then spread south to Efrayim, Binyamin, and Yehuda, as well as north to Zevulun. Only later were the territories of Yissakhar and Naftali settled (with the exception of Ḥatzor, which the Israelites apparently destroyed and then sparsely resettled in the second half of the 13th century BCE). Archaeological evidence, of course, cannot inform us about the settlement of a single family or a small group of Yaakov's children, but only about large demographic shifts. If Yaakov's children owned estates or houses in the land of Israel, we would not be able to find these in the archaeological record, which provides information only about the settlement of very large groupings. It is therefore impossible to draw definitive conclusions about when precisely each tribe settled its land and what the exact tribal borders were. Nevertheless, the connections between the tribes and their lands are clear in Yaakov's blessings.

In these blessings, Shimon and Levi are grouped together and both tribes are told, "I will divide them up in Yaakov, and scatter them in Israel" (49:7), a clear reference to the allocations of both tribes. Shimon is allocated fourteen cities dispersed in the territory of Yehuda (Josh. 19:1–9), while Levi is allocated cities spread throughout the territory of all the tribes (Josh. 21).

↗ Mount Eival site, evidence of early Israelite settlement

The blessings of two other tribes refer to the agricultural potential of their land. Yehuda is blessed with an abundant grape harvest (49:11). This clearly correlates to the agricultural potential of the magnesium-rich territory around Ḥevron, known until today for its large grapes. Similarly, Asher's blessing (49:20), here translated, "From Asher will come rich food," makes specific reference to the Hebrew root used for oil (*shemen*). The territory of Asher, in the hills of the western Galilee, has land that has been used in all historical periods for olive groves. The phrase "he will proffer the king's delights" may foreshadow the control of this land by the Phoenician kings in Tyre and Sidon (I Kings 9:10–13).

Other statements refer to geographical features of certain tribal lands. The statement "Zevulun will live by the seashore" (49:13) corresponds to the borders described in Joshua 19:10–16, and in particular to the statement in Joshua 19:14 that the territory of Zevulun reaches the Yiftaḥ El Valley. This valley may be identified with modern-day Naḥal Tzippori, whose western edge reaches the plain on the seacoast between Haifa and Akko known today as the Zevulun Valley. Similarly, the blessing of Yosef refers to "blessings of the deep that lies under" (49:25), where the Hebrew word here translated "deep" (*tehom*) refers to subterranean water sources, and the imagery of "breast and womb" refers to the outflow of these sources as springs. Such springs are particularly abundant in the hill-country territory of Efrayim and Menashe, the tribes that descend from Yosef. Furthermore, the city of Shekhem, which was part of Yaakov's gift to Yosef in Genesis 48:22, was at the center of the inheritance of Efrayim and Menashe.

Gad is told that it "will be raided by raiders, but he will then raid at their heels" (49:19). This statement depicts the future reality in the Transjordanian territory of Gad. The Mesha Stele, from the 9th century BCE, recounts that "the men of Gad" had inhabited the territory around Atarot in that region "from time immemorial," and that Moav repeatedly tried to seize that territory.

All of these mentions of territories inhabited by Yaakov's sons show that the specific territories allocated to many of the tribes are predicted in these blessings. ▪ SZA

אֶל־יִשְׂרָאֵל אֲבִיכֶם׃ רְאוּבֵן בְּכֹרִי אַתָּה כֹּחִי וְרֵאשִׁית אוֹנִי יֶתֶר ג
שְׂאֵת וְיֶתֶר עָז׃ פַּחַז כַּמַּיִם אַל־תּוֹתַר כִּי עָלִיתָ מִשְׁכְּבֵי אָבִיךָ ד
אָז חִלַּלְתָּ יְצוּעִי עָלָה׃
שִׁמְעוֹן וְלֵוִי אַחִים כְּלֵי חָמָס מְכֵרֹתֵיהֶם׃ בְּסֹדָם אַל־תָּבֹא נַפְשִׁי ה ו
בִּקְהָלָם אַל־תֵּחַד כְּבֹדִי כִּי בְאַפָּם הָרְגוּ אִישׁ וּבִרְצֹנָם עִקְּרוּ־
שׁוֹר׃ אָרוּר אַפָּם כִּי עָז וְעֶבְרָתָם כִּי קָשָׁתָה אֲחַלְּקֵם בְּיַעֲקֹב ז
וַאֲפִיצֵם בְּיִשְׂרָאֵל׃
יְהוּדָה אַתָּה יוֹדוּךָ אַחֶיךָ יָדְךָ בְּעֹרֶף אֹיְבֶיךָ יִשְׁתַּחֲווּ לְךָ בְּנֵי ח

3 Yisrael. Reuven, you are my firstborn, my strength, first fruit of
4 my manhood, excelling in rank, excelling in power. Unstable
as water, you shall not excel, for you went up onto your father's
bed and defiled it – went up onto my couch.[107]
5 Shimon and Levi are brothers; weapons of violence their
6 wares.[108] Let me never join their council, nor my honor be
of their assembly. For in their anger they killed men; at their
7 whim they hamstrung oxen. Cursed be their anger, for it is
most fierce, and their fury, for it is most cruel. I will divide
them up in Yaakov, and scatter them in Israel.[109]
8 Yehuda, your brothers shall praise you. Your hand will be
on the neck of your foes. To you will your father's sons

107 | See 35:22.
108 | See 34:25–26.
109 | Neither tribe would receive a contiguous portion of territory in the land of Israel.

LANGUAGE

49:4 Unstable (*p ḥ z*)

Forms of the root *p ḥ z* are found in Tanakh to denote reckless (Judges 9:4) or brazen (Zeph. 3:4) people, or the carelessness of false prophecy (Jer. 23:32). It is cognate to the Akkadian *paḫḫuzu* ("scoundrel,") and the Syriac *paḥza* ("indecent.") In Aramaic, it also has the sense of bubbling over or swelling up, making it an appropriate word to use in connection with water to describe Reuven's disgraceful behavior in Genesis 35:22. ▪ ZR

Swell at Shark Island, Kurnell Point, Cronulla NSW, Australia

ט אָבִיךָ: גּוּר אַרְיֵה יְהוּדָה מִטֶּרֶף בְּנִי עָלִיתָ כָּרַע רָבַץ כְּאַרְיֵה
י וּכְלָבִיא מִי יְקִימֶנּוּ: לֹא־יָסוּר שֵׁבֶט מִיהוּדָה וּמְחֹקֵק מִבֵּין רַגְלָיו
יא עַד כִּי־יָבֹא שִׁילֹה וְלוֹ יִקְּהַת עַמִּים: אֹסְרִי לַגֶּפֶן עִירֹה וְלַשֹּׂרֵקָה

9 bow.[110]Yehuda is a lion's cub. From the prey, my son, you have
risen. Like a lion he crouches, lies down, like a lioness; who
10 dares to rouse him? The scepter shall not pass from Yehuda,
nor the staff from between his feet, so that tribute will come to
11 him and the homage of nations be his. He tethers his donkey
to vines, to the vine bough his donkey's colt; he washes his

110 | The tribe of Yehuda would later give rise to King David and his dynasty.

LANGUAGE

49:11 Robe (*sut*)

The term used here for "robe" (*sut*), is unique in Tanakh. It is also found in the Kilamuwa Stele (ca. 830–820 BCE), written in North Phoenician with Aramaic influences. There, the Neo-Hittite King Kilamuwa describes depressed economic conditions, "A young woman was given for a sheep and a young man for a garment." The blessing in our verse speaks of wine in such abundance that it is as plentiful as water. ▪ ZR

Kilamuwa Stele, from one of the palaces at the citadel of Sam'al/Zincirli, 9th century BCE

NEAR EAST

49:9 Lion

The association of royalty with the lion is common throughout the ancient Near East as well as in later history.

In Egypt, the lion was used as a symbol of royal authority, and in Mesopotamian and Akkadian texts kings are commonly described as lions. For example, Hammurabi and Esar Ḥadon were both described as fierce lions, and Shulgi of Ur (reigned 2029–1982 BCE) was described as "the lion with wide-open mouth," "a raging lion," and a "lion with a raised paw" (opening of *Shulgi Hymn C*). Note that this ferociousness stands in contrast with the imagery in our verse depicting the lion after having already brought down its prey. The lion is crouching or lying down, demonstrating quiet power rather than an immediate threat. Additionally, the imagery here includes a cub, whereas the artwork of neighboring cultures portrayed only maned adult male lions. ▪ ZR

The god Meslamtaea facing a lion-shaped griffin, with the seal owner (unnamed) on the left, inscription mentions king Shulgi of Ur, cylinder seal and modern impression, 21st century BCE

LANGUAGE

49:12 Darker (*ḥakhlili*)

The expression *ḥakhlili einayim* only appears in one other place in Tanakh, where it is also used in connection to wine, "To whom bloodshot eyes (*ḥakhlilut einayim*)? To those who linger late for wine" (Prov. 23:29–30). The term is cognate with the Akkadian *ekelu* ("to be dark,") also found in expressions about dark physical features and used in a negative sense to refer to a gloomy day or mood.

In the blessing here, the statement that Yehuda's eyes are "darker than wine" would indicate their sparkling or arresting appearance – a different connotation than the Akkadian expression carried. However, it is also possible to translate this as "dark from wine" and the next phrase as saying that his teeth are "white from milk," in accordance with the explanatory note on the translation. ▪ ZR

NEAR EAST

49:13 Sidon

Sidon is at the northern border of ancient Israel, but the territory of Zevulun was actually further south in the western Lower Galilee. Therefore, the statement that the border of Zevulun will reach Sidon should be understood as a blessing referring to the ideal borders of Zevulun, which were not realized historically. The term Sidonians is used in Tanakh to refer to Phoenicians in general (Deut. 3:9; Judges 3:3; I Kings 5:20), a usage also employed by the Phoenicians themselves who would sometimes refer to the king of Tyre as "King of the Sidonians." ▪ ZR

בְּנִי אֲתֹנוֹ כִּבֵּס בַּיַּיִן לְבֻשׁוֹ וּבְדַם־עֲנָבִים סוּתֹה׃ חַכְלִילִי עֵינַיִם יב
מִיָּיִן וּלְבֶן־שִׁנַּיִם מֵחָלָב׃
זְבוּלֻן לְחוֹף יַמִּים יִשְׁכֹּן וְהוּא לְחוֹף אֳנִיֹּת וְיַרְכָתוֹ עַל־צִידֹן׃ יג
יִשָּׂשכָר חֲמֹר גָּרֶם רֹבֵץ בֵּין הַמִּשְׁפְּתָיִם׃ וַיַּרְא מְנֻחָה כִּי יד טו
טוֹב וְאֶת־הָאָרֶץ כִּי נָעֵמָה וַיֵּט שִׁכְמוֹ לִסְבֹּל וַיְהִי לְמַס־
עֹבֵד׃ דָּן יָדִין עַמּוֹ כְּאַחַד שִׁבְטֵי יִשְׂרָאֵל׃ יְהִי־ טז יז
דָן נָחָשׁ עֲלֵי־דֶרֶךְ שְׁפִיפֹן עֲלֵי־אֹרַח הַנֹּשֵׁךְ עִקְּבֵי־סוּס וַיִּפֹּל
חמישי רֹכְבוֹ אָחוֹר׃ לִישׁוּעָתְךָ קִוִּיתִי יְהוָה׃ גָּד גְּדוּד יח יט

12 clothes in wine, his robe in the blood of grapes.[111] His eyes
are darker than wine, and his teeth whiter than milk.[112]
13 Zevulun will live by the seashore; he will be a haven for ships.
To Sidon his border will reach.
14 Yissakhar is a strong-boned donkey, lying down among the
15 sheep pens. Seeing how good is his resting place, and how
pleasant is the land, he will bend his shoulder to the load, and
16 work like a slave in harness. Dan will seek justice[113]
17 for his people as one of Israel's tribes. Dan: a snake by the
roadside, a viper upon the path that bites the horse's heel,
18 so that its rider falls backward.[114] I wait for Your salvation,
19 Lord. Gad will be raided by raiders, but he then

111 | These images suggest luxuriant wealth.
112 | From the abundance of wine and milk.
113 | The word *yadin* (seek justice) plays on the name Dan.
114 | This image suggests a type of military prowess.

↗ Sidonian burial cave (restored), Maresha (Beit Guvrin), 3rd to 1st century BCE

כ יְגוּדֶנּוּ וְהוּא יָגֻד עָקֵב׃ מֵאָשֵׁר שְׁמֵנָה לַחְמוֹ וְהוּא
כא • יִתֵּן מַעֲדַנֵּי־מֶלֶךְ׃ נַפְתָּלִי אַיָּלָה שְׁלֻחָה הַנֹּתֵן אִמְרֵי־

will raid at their heels.[115] From Asher will come 20
rich food, he will proffer the king's delights. Naftali 21 •

115 | The phrase *gedud yegudenu* (will be raided by raiders) and the word *yagud* (will raid) play on the name Gad.

Workmen hacking up earth and gathering raw clay, initial steps in the production of bricks, Temple of Karnak, 15th century BCE

NEAR EAST

49:15 Like a slave in a harness

The phrase "he will bend his shoulder to the load (*lisbol*)" makes use of the root *s b l*, "to carry a burden." The Akkadian cognate *zabalu* has the meaning of "to transport, carry a load," commonly used in the context of transporting clay, bricks, and straw, making it a particularly appropriate term for the Israelite slave labor in Egypt (Ex. 6:6). A letter from Mari uses the noun *sablum* for corvée labor. *Sevel* is used similarly in I Kings 11:28 and Psalms 81:7; in Nehemiah 4:11, it refers to the basket carried in heavy labor. In Akkadian, the idiom *zabil tupsikki*, literally, "a basket carrier," was used for forced labor in general.

The term *mas oved*, translated here as "slave in harness," and found also in Joshua 16:10 and I Kings 9:21, appears in one of the *Amarna letters* as *massu*, another word for forced labor.

Thus, this verse poetically uses two synonyms for forced labor derived from two different Akkadian dialects, *sevel/sablum* from Mari and *mas/massu* from Amarna. ▪ ZR

LANGUAGE

49:21 Fawns (*imrei*)

The phrase *imrei shafer*, here translated as "loveliest fawns," is unique in Tanakh. Various forms of *imrei* have the meaning of a sheep or lamb in Semitic languages, such as the Ugaritic *imr*, Phoenician *'mr* and Akkadian *immeru*. The entire phrase appears to be cognate with the Akkadian *immir supuri* and Ugaritic *imr shpr*, "sheep of the fold." The reference could be to the wide-open spaces of the tribal territory of Naftali, which are able to contain both wild deer ("a deer set free") as well as domesticated sheep in pens. ▪ ZR

LANGUAGE

49:17 Viper (*shefifon*)

The word "viper" is mentioned here as a translation for *shefifon*, a word found nowhere else in Tanakh. The Septuagint replaces this word with a participle modifying the snake by the roadside, which is "lying in ambush." A similar-sounding Akkadian word with mythological resonance, *shibbu*, is also translated as "viper," and is used as a simile for a king advancing against his enemies. It is tempting also to relate *shefifon* to *shuf*, the verb with which serpents and humans are to strike at each other according to Genesis 3:15. Here, too, the viper "bites the horse's heel."

Others think the word is simply onomatopoeic – the "hisser." This snake has been identified as *vipera cerastes*, a desert serpent known as "the horned viper." As with the American sidewinder, the "horns" are projections over each eye of the snake. Older dictionaries of Biblical Hebrew identified *kerastes* as the Greek translation of *shefifon*. ▪ MC

Horned desert viper (*Vipera cerastes*), Israel

Fawn (*Capra nubiana*), Sde Boker, Israel

שָֽׁפֶר׃ בֵּן פֹּרָת יוֹסֵף בֵּן פֹּרָת עֲלֵי־עָיִן בָּנוֹת כב
צָעֲדָה עֲלֵי־שׁוּר׃ וַיְמָרְרֻהוּ וָרֹבּוּ וַיִּשְׂטְמֻהוּ בַּעֲלֵי חִצִּים׃ וַתֵּשֶׁב כג כד
בְּאֵיתָן קַשְׁתּוֹ וַיָּפֹזּוּ זְרֹעֵי יָדָיו מִידֵי אֲבִיר יַעֲקֹב מִשָּׁם רֹעֶה אֶבֶן
יִשְׂרָאֵל׃ מֵאֵל אָבִיךָ וְיַעְזְרֶךָּ וְאֵת שַׁדַּי וִיבָרְכֶךָּ בִּרְכֹת שָׁמַיִם כה
מֵעָל בִּרְכֹת תְּהוֹם רֹבֶצֶת תָּחַת בִּרְכֹת שָׁדַיִם וָרָחַם׃ בִּרְכֹת כו
אָבִיךָ גָּבְרוּ עַל־בִּרְכֹת הוֹרַי עַד־תַּאֲוַת גִּבְעֹת עוֹלָם תִּהְיֶיןָ
לְרֹאשׁ יוֹסֵף וּלְקָדְקֹד נְזִיר אֶחָיו׃
ששי בִּנְיָמִין זְאֵב יִטְרָף בַּבֹּקֶר יֹאכַל עַד וְלָעֶרֶב יְחַלֵּק שָׁלָל׃ כָּל־אֵלֶּה כז כח
שִׁבְטֵי יִשְׂרָאֵל שְׁנֵים עָשָׂר וְזֹאת אֲשֶׁר־דִּבֶּר לָהֶם אֲבִיהֶם וַיְבָרֶךְ
אוֹתָם אִישׁ אֲשֶׁר כְּבִרְכָתוֹ בֵּרַךְ אֹתָם׃ וַיְצַו אוֹתָם וַיֹּאמֶר אֲלֵהֶם כט

22 is a deer set free, bearing loveliest fawns. Yosef is a
fruitful vine, a fruitful vine by a spring, whose branches spread
23 over a wall. Archers attacked him with bitterness, shot at him,
24 harassed him. But his bow stopped steady, and his arms held
firm because of the hand of the Mighty One of Yaakov, the
25 Shepherd, Yisrael's Rock, because of the God of your father
who will help you, because of Shaddai who will bless you
with blessings of heaven above, blessings of the deep that
26 lies under, blessings of breast and of womb. May your father's
blessing surpass even the blessings of my forebears – to the
bounds of the everlasting hills. May they rest on the head of
Yosef, on the brow of the elect of his brothers.
27 Binyamin is a ravening wolf, devouring prey in the morning,
28 and by evening dividing the plunder." All these are the twelve
tribes of Israel, and this is what their father said to them when
29 he blessed them, giving each his particular blessing. Then he

EGYPTOLOGY

50:2–3 Embalming

The practice of embalming is mentioned in Tanakh only here, in connection with Yaakov, and in verse 26, concerning Yosef.

Egyptian beliefs about the survival of death in the afterlife stressed the preservation of the body; mummification was performed in order to stave off decomposition. The main agent used for embalming was natron, a mineral that absorbs water and acts as a drying agent. Additionally, when exposed to moisture, the chemicals in natron create a hostile environment for bacteria. The internal organs were removed from the body, packed in natron, and then put back inside it. Afterward, the body would be wrapped tightly in linen to preserve its external shape and likeness. In the early Egyptian periods of embalming (ca. 2686–2181 BCE), this process was a luxury only available to nobles and royalty, later becoming more commonplace.

Here, the embalming served a practical purpose, since Yaakov's body was to be transported over a long distance for burial. It was also performed on Yosef, probably because he was also meant to be reinterred in Israel many years later (v. 26). Indeed, the oath to which he obligated the children of Israel, when God would eventually redeem them, was to "carry my bones up from this place" (v. 25). The fact that there was no ritual significance to this embalming is stressed by pointing out that it was performed by physicians rather than priests. ▪ ZR

Egyptian mummy, preserved through embalming, 3rd century BCE to 2nd century CE

אֲנִי֙ נֶאֱסָ֣ף אֶל־עַמִּ֔י קִבְר֥וּ אֹתִ֖י אֶל־אֲבֹתָ֑י אֶל־הַמְּעָרָ֕ה אֲשֶׁ֥ר
ל בִּשְׂדֵ֖ה עֶפְר֥וֹן הַחִתִּֽי׃ בַּמְּעָרָ֞ה אֲשֶׁ֨ר בִּשְׂדֵ֧ה הַמַּכְפֵּלָ֛ה אֲשֶׁר־
עַל־פְּנֵ֥י מַמְרֵ֖א בְּאֶ֣רֶץ כְּנָ֑עַן אֲשֶׁ֨ר קָנָ֤ה אַבְרָהָם֙ אֶת־הַשָּׂדֶ֔ה
לא מֵאֵ֛ת עֶפְרֹ֥ן הַחִתִּ֖י לַאֲחֻזַּת־קָֽבֶר׃ שָׁ֣מָּה קָֽבְר֞וּ אֶת־אַבְרָהָ֗ם וְאֵת֙
שָׂרָ֣ה אִשְׁתּ֔וֹ שָׁ֚מָּה קָבְר֣וּ אֶת־יִצְחָ֔ק וְאֵ֖ת רִבְקָ֣ה אִשְׁתּ֑וֹ וְשָׁ֥מָּה
לב קָבַ֖רְתִּי אֶת־לֵאָֽה׃ מִקְנֵ֥ה הַשָּׂדֶ֛ה וְהַמְּעָרָ֥ה אֲשֶׁר־בּ֖וֹ מֵאֵ֥ת בְּנֵי־
לג חֵֽת׃ וַיְכַ֤ל יַעֲקֹב֙ לְצַוֺּ֣ת אֶת־בָּנָ֔יו וַיֶּאֱסֹ֥ף רַגְלָ֖יו אֶל־הַמִּטָּ֑ה וַיִּגְוַ֖ע
נ א וַיֵּאָ֥סֶף אֶל־עַמָּֽיו׃ וַיִּפֹּ֥ל יוֹסֵ֖ף עַל־פְּנֵ֣י אָבִ֑יו וַיֵּ֥בְךְּ עָלָ֖יו וַיִּשַּׁק־לֽוֹ׃
ב וַיְצַ֨ו יוֹסֵ֤ף אֶת־עֲבָדָיו֙ אֶת־הָרֹ֣פְאִ֔ים לַחֲנֹ֖ט אֶת־אָבִ֑יו וַיַּחַנְט֥וּ
ג הָרֹפְאִ֖ים אֶת־יִשְׂרָאֵֽל׃ וַיִּמְלְאוּ־לוֹ֙ אַרְבָּעִ֣ים י֔וֹם כִּ֛י כֵּ֥ן יִמְלְא֖וּ
ד יְמֵ֣י הַחֲנֻטִ֑ים וַיִּבְכּ֥וּ אֹת֛וֹ מִצְרַ֖יִם שִׁבְעִ֥ים יֽוֹם׃ וַיַּֽעַבְרוּ֙ יְמֵ֣י בְכִית֔וֹ
וַיְדַבֵּ֣ר יוֹסֵ֔ף אֶל־בֵּ֥ית פַּרְעֹ֖ה לֵאמֹ֑ר אִם־נָ֨א מָצָ֤אתִי חֵן֙ בְּעֵ֣ינֵיכֶ֔ם
ה דַּבְּרוּ־נָ֕א בְּאָזְנֵ֥י פַרְעֹ֖ה לֵאמֹֽר׃ אָבִ֞י הִשְׁבִּיעַ֣נִי לֵאמֹ֗ר הִנֵּ֣ה אָנֹכִי֮
מֵת֒ בְּקִבְרִ֗י אֲשֶׁ֨ר כָּרִ֤יתִי לִי֙ בְּאֶ֣רֶץ כְּנַ֔עַן שָׁ֖מָּה תִּקְבְּרֵ֑נִי וְעַתָּ֗ה
ו אֶֽעֱלֶה־נָּ֛א וְאֶקְבְּרָ֥ה אֶת־אָבִ֖י וְאָשֽׁוּבָה׃ וַיֹּ֖אמֶר פַּרְעֹ֑ה עֲלֵ֛ה
ז וּקְבֹ֥ר אֶת־אָבִ֖יךָ כַּאֲשֶׁ֥ר הִשְׁבִּיעֶֽךָ׃ וַיַּ֥עַל יוֹסֵ֖ף לִקְבֹּ֣ר אֶת־אָבִ֑יו

gave them instruction, saying, "I am about to be gathered to
my people. Bury me with my fathers in the cave in the field
of Efron the Hittite, the cave in the field of Makhpela near 30
Mamre in Canaan, which Avraham bought, together with
the field, from Efron the Hittite as a burial place.[116] There 31
Avraham and his wife Sara are buried, there Yitzḥak and his
wife Rivka are buried, and there I buried Leah. The field and 32
the cave in it were bought from the Hittites." There Yaakov 33
finished instructing his sons. And he drew his feet back onto
the bed, breathed his last, and was gathered to his people.
Yosef fell on his father's face and wept over him and kissed him. 1 50
Then Yosef instructed his servants the physicians to embalm 2
his father. So the physicians embalmed Yisrael. It took them 3
forty days; that was the time required for embalming. The
Egyptians mourned him for seventy days. When the period 4
of mourning was over, Yosef spoke to Pharaoh's court: "If I
have found favor in your eyes, please speak to Pharaoh on my
behalf. Tell him, 'My father made me swear an oath, saying, "I 5
am about to die. Bury me in the grave I prepared for myself in
the land of Canaan." Now let me go up and bury my father;
then I will return.'" Pharaoh said, "Go and bury your father as 6
he had you swear." So Yosef went up to bury his father. With 7

116 | See 23:16–18.

NEAR EAST

50:4 Yosef spoke to Pharaoh's court

The reason that Yosef did not go directly to Pharaoh may be because a mourner was not allowed in the palace, a convention also seen with Mordekhai in Esther 4:2, "no one may enter the King's Gate dressed in sackcloth." In the case of Yosef, some scholars suggest that this had to do with Egyptian taboos that kept the Pharaoh away from anyone who had direct contact with a corpse.

Alternatively, it is possible that Yosef was concerned that Pharaoh suspected that he might be planning to return to Canaan permanently with his family, so he needed to get Pharaoh's trusted courtiers on his side as intermediaries for permission. This would also explain the deferential pleading language employed by Yosef here and his assurance to Pharaoh that, after the burial, "I will return" (v. 5). ▪ ZR

Shroud of a man named Hori, depicted at his funerary meal with offerings, Egypt, 13th to 11th century BCE

וַיַּעֲלוּ אִתּוֹ כָּל־עַבְדֵי פַרְעֹה זִקְנֵי בֵיתוֹ וְכֹל זִקְנֵי אֶרֶץ־מִצְרָיִם׃
וְכֹל בֵּית יוֹסֵף וְאֶחָיו וּבֵית אָבִיו רַק טַפָּם וְצֹאנָם וּבְקָרָם עָזְבוּ ח
בְּאֶרֶץ גֹּשֶׁן׃ וַיַּעַל עִמּוֹ גַּם־רֶכֶב גַּם־פָּרָשִׁים וַיְהִי הַמַּחֲנֶה כָּבֵד ט
מְאֹד׃ וַיָּבֹאוּ עַד־גֹּרֶן הָאָטָד אֲשֶׁר בְּעֵבֶר הַיַּרְדֵּן וַיִּסְפְּדוּ־שָׁם י
מִסְפֵּד גָּדוֹל וְכָבֵד מְאֹד וַיַּעַשׂ לְאָבִיו אֵבֶל שִׁבְעַת יָמִים׃ וַיַּרְא יא
יוֹשֵׁב הָאָרֶץ הַכְּנַעֲנִי אֶת־הָאֵבֶל בְּגֹרֶן הָאָטָד וַיֹּאמְרוּ אֵבֶל־
כָּבֵד זֶה לְמִצְרָיִם עַל־כֵּן קָרָא שְׁמָהּ אָבֵל מִצְרַיִם אֲשֶׁר בְּעֵבֶר
הַיַּרְדֵּן׃ וַיַּעֲשׂוּ בָנָיו לוֹ כֵּן כַּאֲשֶׁר צִוָּם׃ וַיִּשְׂאוּ אֹתוֹ בָנָיו אַרְצָה יב יג
כְּנַעַן וַיִּקְבְּרוּ אֹתוֹ בִּמְעָרַת שְׂדֵה הַמַּכְפֵּלָה אֲשֶׁר קָנָה אַבְרָהָם

him went all Pharaoh's officials, the elders of his palace, and all
8 the other elders of Egypt, together with all Yosef's household,
his brothers, and his father's household. They left only their
9 children and flocks and herds in Goshen. With them too went
a chariot brigade and horsemen; it was a very large retinue.
10 When they reached the threshing floor of Atad, beyond
the Jordan, they held a great and solemn lamentation, and
Yosef observed a seven-day period of mourning for his father.
11 When the Canaanites who lived there saw the mourning
at the threshing floor of Atad they said, "Egypt is in deep
mourning here"; that is why the place beyond the Jordan was
12 called Avel Mitzrayim.[117] So his sons did as he had instructed
13 them. They carried him to Canaan and buried him in the cave

117 | Meaning "mourning of Egypt."

GEOGRAPHY

50:10–11 Threshing floor of Atad... beyond the Jordan... Avel Mitzrayim

The location of the threshing floor of Atad is not known. Although the term "beyond the Jordan" (v. 10) can refer to either side of the Jordan River (based on the perspective of the speaker), here it seems to be talking about a place in Canaan (v. 11). According to Nahum Sarna, Atad would probably be somewhere along the International Coastal Route, an ancient trade route dating from the Early Bronze Age linking Egypt with the northern empires of Syria, Anatolia, and Mesopotamia. This route along the Mediterranean coast is the shortest way to get from Egypt to Canaan (as noted in Ex. 13:17).

The word *avel* means "plain," and is found as a component of a number of place names in Tanakh (Num. 33:49; Judges 7:22, 11:33; I Kings 15:20; II Chr. 16:4). Here, it appears to be a play on words, as it also has the meaning of mourning.

Some resemblance to the episode here is provided by the coastal city of Deir al-Balah in modern-day Aza, which dates back to the Late Bronze Age when it served as a fortified outpost for the New Kingdom of Egypt on its frontier with Canaan. Archaeological findings there revealed a large ancient Egyptian cemetery containing graves of Egyptian officials serving in Canaan, as well as those of Canaanite dignitaries who were subjects of Egypt. An earlier place like this fort would have been a logical place for Egyptians to stop to publicly accord respect to Yaakov in his homeland, prior to burial. This type of fort confirms the close contacts the Egyptians had with Canaan along the coastal area near Aza. ▪ ZR

Anthropoid coffin, Deir al-Balah, 13th to 14th century BCE

אֶת־הַשָּׂדֶה לַאֲחֻזַּת־קֶבֶר מֵאֵת עֶפְרֹן הַחִתִּי עַל־פְּנֵי מַמְרֵא׃
יד וַיָּשָׁב יוֹסֵף מִצְרַיְמָה הוּא וְאֶחָיו וְכָל־הָעֹלִים אִתּוֹ לִקְבֹּר אֶת־
טו אָבִיו אַחֲרֵי קָבְרוֹ אֶת־אָבִיו׃ וַיִּרְאוּ אֲחֵי־יוֹסֵף כִּי־מֵת אֲבִיהֶם
וַיֹּאמְרוּ לוּ יִשְׂטְמֵנוּ יוֹסֵף וְהָשֵׁב יָשִׁיב לָנוּ אֵת כָּל־הָרָעָה אֲשֶׁר
טז גָּמַלְנוּ אֹתוֹ׃ וַיְצַוּוּ אֶל־יוֹסֵף לֵאמֹר אָבִיךָ צִוָּה לִפְנֵי מוֹתוֹ לֵאמֹר׃
יז כֹּה־תֹאמְרוּ לְיוֹסֵף אָנָּא שָׂא נָא פֶּשַׁע אַחֶיךָ וְחַטָּאתָם כִּי־רָעָה
גְמָלוּךָ וְעַתָּה שָׂא נָא לְפֶשַׁע עַבְדֵי אֱלֹהֵי אָבִיךָ וַיֵּבְךְּ יוֹסֵף בְּדַבְּרָם
יח אֵלָיו׃ וַיֵּלְכוּ גַּם־אֶחָיו וַיִּפְּלוּ לְפָנָיו וַיֹּאמְרוּ הִנֶּנּוּ לְךָ לַעֲבָדִים׃
יט כ וַיֹּאמֶר אֲלֵהֶם יוֹסֵף אַל־תִּירָאוּ כִּי הֲתַחַת אֱלֹהִים אָנִי׃ וְאַתֶּם
חֲשַׁבְתֶּם עָלַי רָעָה אֱלֹהִים חֲשָׁבָהּ לְטֹבָה לְמַעַן עֲשֹׂה כַּיּוֹם הַזֶּה
כא לְהַחֲיֹת עַם־רָב׃ וְעַתָּה אַל־תִּירָאוּ אָנֹכִי אֲכַלְכֵּל אֶתְכֶם וְאֶת־ שביעי

of the field of Makhpela, near Mamre, which Avraham had
bought as a burial site from Efron the Hittite. After burying 14
his father, Yosef returned to Egypt together with his brothers
and all those who had accompanied him to his father's burial.
When Yosef's brothers knew that their father was dead, they 15
said, "What if Yosef really hates us and decides to pay us back
for all the wrong we did to him?" So they sent word to Yosef 16
saying, "Your father gave these instructions before his death:
'This is what you are to say to Yosef: "Please forgive the crime 17
and sin of your brothers who inflicted such harm upon you."'
That being so, please forgive the crime of these servants of
your father's God." Yosef wept as they spoke to him. Then his 18
brothers came and threw themselves down before him and
said, "We are your slaves." But Yosef said to them, "Do not be 19
afraid. Am I in place of God? You intended to harm me, but 20
God intended it for good, to bring about what is now being
done: the saving of many lives. So, do not be afraid. I myself 21
will provide for you and your children." And he comforted

NEAR EAST

50:10 Seven days of mourning

The seven-day mourning period is also noted for Sha'ul in I Samuel 31:13 and I Chronicles 10:12. Also, Iyov's friends "sat with him on the ground for seven days and seven nights" after his children died (Job 2:13). This mourning period is also found in the Apocrypha, as the mourning period for Yehudit (Judith 16:24), and Sirach 22:12 states "Mourning for the dead, seven days, but for the wicked fool, a whole lifetime."

Seven days may have been the standard mourning period in the ancient Near East. In the *Epic of Gilgamesh*, Gilgamesh weeps for his friend Enkidu for "seven days and seven nights" (X.2.8). The *Curse of Agade* (ca. 2200–2000 BCE) describes a period of seven days and seven nights of lamentation over the destruction of the city of Akkad. The sevenfold offering in the Ugaritic funerary text KTU 1.161 has also been understood as reflecting a seven-day ritual. ▪ ZR

↗ *Curse of Agade*, 22nd to 21st century BCE

טַפְּכֶם וַיְנַחֵם אוֹתָם וַיְדַבֵּר עַל־לִבָּם: וַיֵּשֶׁב יוֹסֵף בְּמִצְרַיִם הוּא • כב
מפטיר וּבֵית אָבִיו וַיְחִי יוֹסֵף מֵאָה וָעֶשֶׂר שָׁנִים: וַיַּרְא יוֹסֵף לְאֶפְרַיִם בְּנֵי • כג

• 22 them and spoke to their hearts. Yosef remained in Egypt
together with his father's family, and he lived one hundred and
• 23 ten years. Yosef saw the third generation of Efrayim's children,
and the children of Menashe's son Makhir were also born on

NEAR EAST

50:22 One hundred and ten years

According to several texts in our possession, 110 years was considered the ideal life span in ancient Egypt.

In the introduction to the Egyptian *Tale of Woe* (ca. 11th to 10th century BCE), we find the blessing, "May he (Atum) cause you to reach 110 years upon earth, your body whole, growing old with a contented heart, without illness in your limbs, but with continuous gladness and joy in your heart and without the weakness of old age." Similarly, an inscription, near the statue of Amenhotep son of Hapu, a public official from the early-mid 14th century BCE, promises that those who provide offerings for him will be rewarded with the same after reaching an old age of 110 years. This age is the Egyptian equivalent of the ideal Israelite life span of 120 years (Gen. 6:3; Deut. 34:7). ▪ ZR

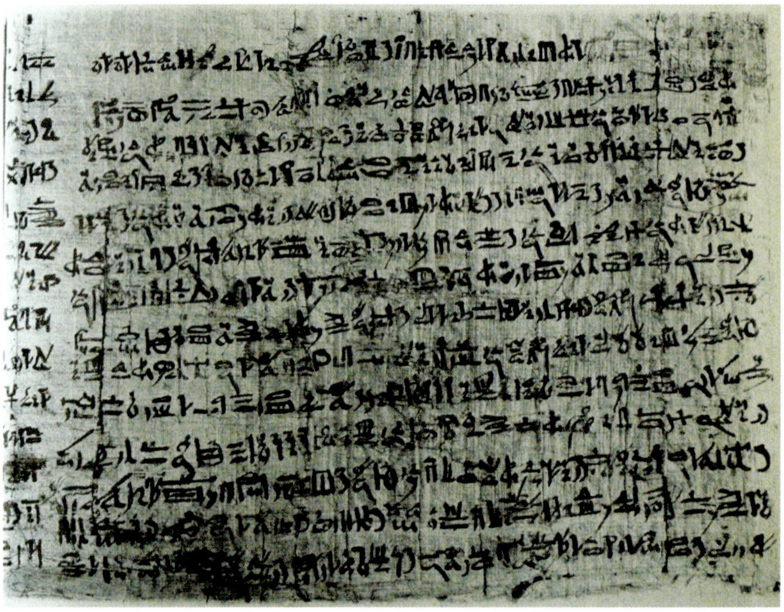

↗ *Tale of Woe*, first page of Papyrus Moscow 127, hieratic, ca. 1000 BCE

NEAR EAST

50:23 Yosef seeing his great-grandchildren

Yosef seeing his great-grandchildren is a sign of divine favor; it is also a reward for righteousness, as indicated concerning Iyov, "He saw his children and grandchildren – four generations" (Job 42:16). This reward is also noted in an Aramaic sepulcher inscription (ca. 7th century BCE) found near Aleppo, which states, "Because of my righteousness before him, he gave me a good name and prolonged my days. On the day I died, my mouth was not closed to words, and with my eyes, what do I see? Children of the fourth generation, who wept for me, being distraught." ▪ ZR

↗ Aramaic inscription to the god Salm, sandstone, Teima (northwestern Arabia), 5th century BCE

כד שִׁלֵּשִׁים גַּם בְּנֵי מָכִיר בֶּן־מְנַשֶּׁה יֻלְּדוּ עַל־בִּרְכֵּי יוֹסֵף׃ וַיֹּאמֶר
יוֹסֵף אֶל־אֶחָיו אָנֹכִי מֵת וֵאלֹהִים פָּקֹד יִפְקֹד אֶתְכֶם וְהֶעֱלָה
אֶתְכֶם מִן־הָאָרֶץ הַזֹּאת אֶל־הָאָרֶץ אֲשֶׁר נִשְׁבַּע לְאַבְרָהָם
כה לְיִצְחָק וּלְיַעֲקֹב׃ וַיַּשְׁבַּע יוֹסֵף אֶת־בְּנֵי יִשְׂרָאֵל לֵאמֹר פָּקֹד יִפְקֹד
• כו אֱלֹהִים אֶתְכֶם וְהַעֲלִתֶם אֶת־עַצְמֹתַי מִזֶּה׃ וַיָּמָת יוֹסֵף בֶּן־מֵאָה
וָעֶשֶׂר שָׁנִים וַיַּחַנְטוּ אֹתוֹ וַיִּישֶׂם בָּאָרוֹן בְּמִצְרָיִם׃

Yosef's knees.[118] Yosef said to his brothers, "I am about to 24
die. But God will surely take note of you and bring you out of
this land to the land He promised to Avraham, Yitzḥak, and
Yaakov." Then Yosef bound the children of Israel by an oath: 25
"When God takes note of you, carry my bones up from this
place." Yosef died at the age of one hundred and ten. He was 26 •
embalmed and placed in a coffin there, in Egypt.

118 | That is, they were born during Yosef's lifetime.

EGYPTOLOGY

50:26 Coffin

This is the only mention of the word "coffin" in Tanakh. The use of a coffin is characteristic of Egyptian burial practices, which prioritized the protection of the dead body in the belief that this would enable the spirit to live on in the afterlife. This protection was accomplished by mummifying the body and placing it in a sealed coffin.

In the early Old Kingdom period, these coffins were plain rectangular chests, but over time they began to be decorated with images and inscriptions having magical significance. By the time of the First Intermediate Period and the Middle Kingdom, spells, known as the Coffin Texts, were written on the inside of coffins. The anthropoid shapes, which displayed an exterior image representing the deceased, were used from the end of the Middle Kingdom period. ▪ ZR

↗
Decorated coffin of Khnumnakht, Meir, Khashaba excavations (?), 19th to 18th century BCE

Tanakh of the Land of Israel	Conventional translation	Hebrew
Moshe	Moses	משה
Noaḥ	Noah	נח
Ovadya	Obadiah	עובדיה
Raḥel	Rachel	רחל
Reuven	Reuben	ראובן
Rivka	Rebecca	רבקה
Sanḥeriv	Sennacherib	סנחריב
Sha'ul	Saul	שאול
Shet	Seth	שת
Shimon	Simeon	שמעון
Shlomo	Solomon	שלמה
Shmuel	Samuel	שמואל
Yaakov	Jacob	יעקב
Yefet	Japheth	יפת
Yeḥezkel	Ezekiel	יחזקאל
Yehoshua	Joshua	יהושע
Yehoyakhin	Jehoiachin	יהויכין
Yehuda	Judah	יהודה
Yeshayahu	Isaiah	ישעיהו
Yiftaḥ	Jephthah	יפתח
Yirmeyahu	Jeremiah	ירמיהו
Yishmael	Ishmael	ישמעאל
Yissakhar	Issachar	יששכר
Yitzḥak	Isaac	יצחק
Yosef	Joseph	יוסף
Zevulun	Zebulun	זבולון

Correspondence between Names

Tanakh of the Land of Israel	Conventional translation	Hebrew
Adoniya	Adonijah	אדניה
Aharon	Aaron	אהרן
Avraham	Abraham	אברהם
Avram	Abram	אברם
Avimelekh	Abimelech	אבימלך
Avshalom	Absalom	אבשלום
Binyamin	Benjamin	בנימין
Dina	Dena	דינה
Efrayim	Ephraim	אפרים
Eliyahu	Elijah	אליהו
Esar Ḥadon	Esarhaddon	אסר חדן
Golyat	Goliath	גלית
Ḥana	Hannah	חנה
Ḥanokh	Enoch	חנוך
Ḥava	Eve	חוה
Hevel	Abel	הבל
Iyov	Job	איוב
Kayin	Cain	קין
Lemekh	Lamech	למך
Malki Tzedek	Melchizedek	מלכי צדק
Menashe	Manassah	מנשה
Metushelaḥ	Methuselah	מתושלח
Mikhal	Michal	מיכל
Moav	Moab	מואב
Mordekhai	Mordecai	מרדכי

List of Contributors

David Arnovitz (DAA) ***Editor in Chief***

Mr. Arnovitz had a successful technology career in Internet security and financial services software in the USA, then made aliyah with his family to Israel in 1999. He took the tour guide course and was in charge of operations for Shalem College, Israel's first liberal arts college and for OurCrowd, a global venture investing platform. He has been Editor in Chief of *The Koren Tanakh of the Land of Israel* since 2016.

Rabbi Dr. Jeremiah Unterman (JU) ***Academic Editor, Biblical Scholarship, Ancient Near East***

Rabbi Dr. Unterman is a resident scholar at the Herzl Institute. He has authored two books, *Justice for All: How the Jewish Bible Revolutionized Ethics* and *From Repentance to Redemption: Jeremiah's Thought in Transition,* and more than a hundred articles in scholarly publications in the USA and Israel. Previously, he was the Director of the Association of Modern Orthodox Day Schools and Yeshiva High Schools, and Adjunct Professor of Bible at Yeshiva University. He has a PhD from the University of California, Berkeley, Judaica Program of the Near Eastern Studies Department, and received rabbinic ordination through private studies in Israel.

Rabbi Dr. Tzvi Hersh Weinreb ***Rabbinic Adviser***

Rabbi Dr. Weinreb is Executive Vice President Emeritus of the Orthodox Union. Rabbi Weinreb received his rabbinic ordination in 1962 from the Rabbi Jacob Joseph Yeshiva in New York and has a PhD in Clinical Psychology from the University of Maryland. He has a unique combination of skills as a pulpit rabbi, scholar, and clinical psychologist. He is the Editor in Chief of the *Koren Talmud Bavli with commentary by Rabbi Adin Steinsaltz*; authored *The Person in the Parsha: Discovering the Human Element in the Weekly Torah Portion*; translated the *Kinot*, the elegies of the Tisha B'Av fast day, for the *Koren Mesorat HaRav Kinot*; and wrote the commentary for the *Rohr Family Edition of Tehillim.*

Rabbi Lord Jonathan Sacks, ***z"l Translator***

Rabbi Lord Sacks was an international religious leader, philosopher, award-winning author and respected moral voice. He was Chief Rabbi of the United Hebrew Congregations of the Commonwealth and has held professorships at several academic institutions including Yeshiva University and King's College London, serving as the Ingeborg and Ira Rennert Global Distinguished Professor at New York University. Rabbi Sacks authored over thirty books, including a new English translation and commentary for the Koren Sacks Siddur, the first new Orthodox siddur in a generation, as well as powerful commentaries for the Rosh Hashana, Yom Kippur, Passover, Shavuot and Sukkot Maḥzorim. Rabbi Sacks was knighted by Queen Elizabeth II in 2005, receiving a life peerage with a seat in the House of Lords.

Prof. Shawn Zelig Aster (SZA) ***Biblical History and Geography***

Prof. Aster is Associate Professor in the Martin (Szusz) Department of Land of Israel Studies and Archaeology at Bar-Ilan University. A specialist in Bible and the biblical period, his work primarily involves prophetic literature, focusing on its historical context, and on connections between biblical Israel and Assyria. His research interests include the history and geography of the Land of Israel in the biblical period, history of the people of Israel in the biblical period, the prophetic literature in its historical context, the Bible and the ancient East.

Dr. Yigal Bloch (YB) ***Ancient Near East***

Dr. Yigal Bloch is a curator at the Bible Lands Museum Jerusalem. He holds a doctorate from the Hebrew University of Jerusalem, and has done post-doctoral research at the University of California, Berkeley, the Hebrew University of Jerusalem, and the University of Haifa. He has published several dozen articles on the Hebrew Bible, Hebrew inscriptions of the biblical period, history and chronology of the ancient Near East. He is the author of two books: *Alphabet Scribes in the Land of Cuneiform* and *The Amorites: A Political History of Mesopotamia in the Early Second Millennium BCE* (jointly with Nathan Wasserman).

Dr. Michael Carasik (MC) ***Ancient Near East, Languages***

Dr. Carasik has a PhD in Bible and the Ancient Near East from Brandeis University and taught at the University of Pennsylvania for twenty years. In addition to articles and reviews, he is the author of *Theologies of the Mind in Biblical Israel* and of a book for general readers called *The Bible's Many Voices*. He is also the creator, editor, and translator of the five-volume *Commentators' Bible*, an English version of the traditional *Mikraot Gedolot* to the Pentateuch and writes the "Torah Talk" and "Bible Guy" Substacks.

Dr. Yitzhaq Feder (YF) ***Biblical and Ancient Near East Ritual***

Dr. Feder received his PhD from Bar-Ilan University and is currently a lecturer in the Department of Biblical Studies at the University of Haifa. He is the author of *Blood Expiation in Hittite and Biblical Ritual: Origins, Context and Meaning* (2011). His latest book, *Purity and Pollution in the Hebrew Bible: From Embodied Experience to Moral Metaphor* (2022), examines the psychological foundations of impurity in ancient Israel.

Dr. Kristine Henriksen Garroway (KG) ***Ancient Near East***

Dr. Garroway is a professor of Hebrew Bible at the Hebrew Union College Jewish Institute of Religion Jack H. Skirball campus in Los Angeles, California. Her background is in Hebrew Bible and ancient Near Eastern archaeology. She is the author of various articles and books, among which are *Children in the Ancient Near Eastern Household* and *Growing Up in Ancient Israel: Children in Material Culture and Biblical Texts.*

Dr. Elaine Adler Goodfriend (EG) ***Biblical Scholarship, Ancient Near East***

Dr. Goodfriend received her PhD in Near Eastern Studies from the University of California, Berkeley. She teaches in the Religious Studies Department at California State University, Northridge, and enjoys writing about the Hebrew Bible and Jewish law.

Prof. Shalom E. Holtz (SH) ***Biblical Scholarship, Ancient Near East***

Prof. Holtz is Professor of Bible at Yeshiva University. He is the author of numerous comparative studies on Mesopotamian civilization as context for biblical interpretation.

Dr. Gilad Itach (GI) ***Archaeology, Geography***

Dr. Itach has a PhD from Bar-Ilan University that focuses on the archaeology, demography, and history of Samaria (Shomron) in the Neo-Assyrian period. He has worked in many roles in the Israel Antiquities Authority, where he is currently employed as a Research Archaeologist for the Central District, participating in excavations around Israel. He has published articles and excavation reports and has presented results at many conferences worldwide.

Dr. Lea Jacobsen (LJ) ***Ancient Near East***

Dr. Jacobsen is a senior lecturer of Bible at Gordon College of Education, Haifa. She holds a PhD from Bar-Ilan University. Her main areas of expertise are biblical law, the laws of the ancient Near East, and law in the biblical narratives. She has published articles in these fields focusing on the relationships between members of the family unit, especially on the relationship between a mother and her offspring.

Dr. Jill C. Katz (JK) ***Biblical Archaeology, Anthropology***

Dr. Katz is Clinical Associate Professor of Archaeology at Yeshiva University, where she teaches archaeology and anthropology with a specialty in biblical archaeology. She has excavated at several sites in Israel, including Ashkelon, Tel Haror/Gerar, and, most recently, Tell es-Safi/Gat. She earned her PhD in Anthropology (Archaeology) from the University of Pennsylvania and is the author of *The Archaeology of Cult in Middle Bronze Age Canaan.*

Dr. Shirly Natan-Yulzary (SNY) ***Ancient Near East***

Dr. Natan-Yulzary is a senior lecturer in Hebrew Bible and Chair of the Department of Biblical Studies at Gordon College of Education, Haifa. She is also a lecturer and instructor at the Department of Jewish Culture at Beit-Berl College of Education. Dr. Natan-Yulzary holds a PhD from Tel Aviv University and specializes in Ugaritic studies. Her research primarily focuses on the poetic texts from Ugarit, including their artistic nature and their relation to narrative and poetic biblical literature. Additionally, she explores the oral aspects of poetic and ritual texts from Ugarit.

Dr. Dvir Raviv (DR) *Archaeology, Geography*

Dr. Raviv has a PhD from the Department of Land of Israel Studies and Archaeology at Bar-Ilan University, where he currently serves as a senior lecturer. He has directed excavations at Tel Tibna and Khirbet Heiva. His primary research interests are in archaeology and historical geography of the land of Israel, concentrating most recently on the Second Temple and Roman periods.

Rabbi Dr. Zvi Ron (ZR) *Biblical Scholarship*

Rabbi Dr. Ron is editor of the *Jewish Bible Quarterly* and has published over sixty scholarly articles on the Bible, pseudepigrapha, Midrash and Jewish customs in *Tradition, Hakirah, Zutot, Sinai, Ha-Ma'ayan, The Review of Rabbinic Judaism, Journal of Jewish Music and Liturgy, Jewish Bible Quarterly* and others. He is also the author of *Sefer Katan v'Gadol* (Hebrew) about all the big and small letters in the Tanakh and *Sefer Ha-Ikkar Chaser* (Hebrew) about variant spellings in the Tanakh.

Glossary

Akkadian was a Semitic language that served as the *lingua franca* of the ancient Near East during the 2nd millennium BCE. Originally spoken by the Babylonian empire, centered in the city of Akkad and its surrounding region, it later divided into two main Mesopotamian dialects: Assyrian in the north and Babylonian in the south.

Amarna is the ruin of Pharaoh Akhenaten's capital city that he established in 1346 BCE. The ***Amarna letters***, a cache of over 300 cuneiform clay tablets, was found there. They record diplomatic correspondence between the Egyptians and representatives in Canaan and Amurru from ca. 1360–1332 BCE during the New Kingdom period. These letters have great significance for biblical studies since they shed light on the culture and language of the Canaanite peoples in pre-biblical times.

The **Amorites** were an ancient Semitic-speaking people from Syria who also occupied large parts of southern Mesopotamia. In the Tanakh, the Amorites are described as occupying the region from the heights west of the Dead Sea to Ḥevron, and Gilad and Bashan east of the Jordan River, ruled by Siḥon and Og.

Aram is the homeland of the **Arameans** and a region, in modern-day Syria, mentioned in the Tanakh. At its height, Aram stretched from the Mount Lebanon range eastward across the Euphrates, including parts of northwestern Mesopotamia on the border of Iraq. Aram Naharayim and Padan Aram are parts of this area mentioned in Tanakh.

Aramaic is a Northwest Semitic language developed among the Arameans of the nation Aram. Old Aramaic (ca. 1200 BCE–200 CE) was adopted as the main language of communication of the Neo-Assyrian empire, and therefore became the *lingua franca* of the ancient Near East throughout the 1st millennium BCE. As such, it influenced Biblical Hebrew. Ancient Aramaic documents are a valuable source for information related to the context of the Tanakh, and considerable portions of Daniel and Ezra were written in Aramaic. Middle Aramaic (ca. 200–1200 CE) includes the Peshita, Targums, and the Aramaic of the Talmuds and the Midrashim.

The **Assyrian periods** are eras when Assyria, a kingdom situated in modern-day northwestern Iraq, was powerful. The proper noun "Assyria," pronounced *ashur* in Akkadian (and Hebrew), also referred to the capital city and the chief god. As this mountainous region was not conducive to the development of agriculture, the Assyrians subsisted primarily on herding and commerce. The **Middle Assyrian period** (ca. 14th to 10th century BCE) is significant for the empire created at that time and the ***Middle Assyrian Laws*** written during the earlier part of that period. The Assyrian civilization underwent a resurgence with the Neo-Assyrian empire (see entry below).

The Ugaritic ***Baal Cycle*** tells of the conflicts of the fertility god Baal with other gods, and Baal's ultimate supremacy over chaos and death. It includes the death of Baal which causes a drought that ends when Baal is resurrected. The story of Baal parallels the yearly cycle of vegetation. The tablets that record these myths date to ca. 14th century BCE but represent a written record of a much older story passed down by oral transmission.

Babylonian Talmud, see Talmud.

Babylonian time periods. The **Old Babylonian period**, roughly 2000–1600 BCE, was an era of great inventions and cultural developments in Mesopotamia. Three different law collections were composed during this period – those of Lipit-Ishtar (Sumerian), Eshnunna (Babylonian), and Hammurabi (Babylonian). The **Neo-Babylonian period** (626–539 BCE) marked the end of Mesopotamian rule over the ancient Near East, due to the Persian conquest. The most famous king of this empire was Nevukhadnetzar II, who invaded Yehuda and destroyed most of its cities and towns. In 586 BCE, he destroyed Jerusalem, burned the First Temple, and exiled most of the Judahite population to Babylonia.

The ***Book of the Dead*** was the New Kingdom body of funerary spells meant to help the dead in their journey through the Realm of the Dead. Usually the texts were written on a papyrus scroll, accompanied by illustrations. The scroll was laid on the mummy's chest or somewhere close to the mummy in the burial chamber. A well-known illustration from the *Book of the Dead* is the Weighing of the Heart, where the heart of the deceased is weighed against the feather of Maat as part of the Judgment of the Dead.

Bronze Age time periods. In the ancient Near East, the **Bronze Age** began with the discovery of the manufacturing process for bronze, a strong metal alloy, by adding tin to copper. The **Early Bronze Age**, 3500–2000 BCE, began with the rise of the Mesopotamian civilization of Sumer. Cultures in this period practiced year-round agriculture, developed writing systems, invented the potter's wheel, created centralized government and written law codes, and founded the first empires. The **Middle Bronze Age**, 2100–1550 BCE, was a period of great wealth and strong self-government of individual city-states in the Levant, with local rulers fortifying their cities and building large scale public buildings, temples and palaces. The **Late Bronze Age**, 1550–1200 BCE, featured individual city-states in the Levant between the empires of Egypt and Hatti. The *Amarna letters* (ca. 1360–1332 BCE) provide much information about regional relationships during this era. The end of the Late Bronze Age marks the collapse of the Hittite empire and the weakening of Egypt, which enabled the emergence of new, smaller kingdoms, such as ancient Israel, in the Iron Age.

The **Byzantine period** began in the 4th century CE with the split of the Roman empire into two parts: the Roman empire centered in Rome in the west, and the Byzantine empire centered in Constantinople (modern-day Istanbul) in the east. The Byzantine era ended with the Ottoman conquest in 1453.

The biblical land of **Canaan** corresponds roughly to the boundaries of the ancient land of Israel plus southern Lebanon today. Archaeological excavations indicate that the **Canaanites** were actually made up of different ethnic groups all living in the same general area. Due to its location at the crossroads of a number of major cultures Canaanite literature and art contain elements from Egyptian, Hurrian, and Mesopotamian cultures, among others.

The **Chalcolithic period** (Copper Age, 4500–3500 BCE) is the archaeological period when copper predominated in metalworking technology. The Chalcolithic period is characterized by rural settlements based on agriculture and livestock, new production technologies, strengthened regional and interregional trade relations and cultural ties, and the first complex and stratified societies.

The **Crusader period** (1095–1291 CE) refers to the time of the series of religious wars undertaken by European Christians to conquer the Holy Land and wrest it from Muslim rule. With the capture of Jerusalem in 1099, the Crusader Kingdom of Jerusalem was established, making the Holy Land a focal point for Christian pilgrimage and the construction of many churches, holy sites, and urban settlements.

A **cylinder seal** is a small round cylinder with engraved characters or images, used to roll an impression on soft clay. It was used as a form of signature in the ancient Near East before the invention of writing.

The **Deir 'Alla inscription**, discovered in Jordan, describes the terrifying visions of Bilam son of Beor which he received from the god El (divinities are also referred to by the words *elohin* and *shagar et Ishtar*). This Bilam appears to be identical to the Bilam of Numbers, indicating that he was a known seer in biblical times. This text dates from 880 to 770 BCE, making it the oldest extant piece of Aramaic literature, albeit containing Canaanite elements.

Early Bronze Age, see Bronze Age.

The **Edomites** were traditional enemies of the Israelites. Edom is located in the southern environs of the Dead Sea. The Edomites attacked Israel when Sha'ul first became king. Later, King David defeated and subjugated them. In Hebrew, the name literally means "red," which may be an allusion to the reddish color of the mountains east of the Jordan River and Arava at sunset. According to the Torah, the Edomites descended from Esav.

Egyptian time periods. The Egyptian **Old Kingdom**, with its capital in Memphis, lasted for more than five hundred years. It began with the Third Dynasty in 2689 BCE and ended with the ephemeral kings of the Seventh and Eighth Dynasties in 2160 BCE. The Fourth Dynasty (2613–2494 BCE) was the age of the great pyramids of Giza, which were built as an expression of royal power and dominion. The Old Kingdom fell into decay and crumbled after the exceptionally long reign (perhaps over 60 years) of King Pepi II of the

Sixth Dynasty. The **First Intermediate Period** (2181–2040) was a period of decentralized control. The Egyptian **Middle Kingdom** lasted for about four hundred years, from 2055 to 1650 BCE. Mentuhotep II, of the Upper Egyptian Eleventh Dynasty who originally ruled from Thebes, reunified Egypt under a single throne in 2055 BCE. After 1650 BCE, Egypt entered into the unstable **Second Intermediate Period** (1650–1550), with the Hyksos ruling in the north, Egyptians continuing to rule at Thebes in the center, and the Nubians ruling in the south. The **New Kingdom**, the imperial time of ancient Egypt, was established by King Ahmose I after the reunification of Egypt under the Theban throne in 1550 BCE. It lasted for about 480 years (Eighteenth to Twentieth Dynasties) until 1069 BCE. The New Kingdom came to an end in a period of worldwide instability in the Late Bronze Age, which, combined with internal political pressures, caused a loss of territory and power.

Elam was a region in the Near East corresponding to modern-day southern Iran whose civilization spanned ca. 3200–540 BCE. The Elamites had a unique language and were among the peoples settled in Shomron by the Assyrians (Ezra 4:9–10). The story of Esther takes place in Susa (Hebrew, *Shushan*), the ancient capital of Elam.

Enuma Elish Epic ("When on high" in Akkadian) is the title and opening words of one of the most famous epics of the ancient Near East. It was composed in Babylonia, telling the story of the creation of the gods and the world. It has similarities with other ancient creation narratives, including that in Genesis.

The ***Epic of Atrahasis*** is a 17th century BCE Akkadian epic which begins before man was created, and includes a version of the Babylonian flood myth, where the gods were angry at the noise made by humanity, thus deciding to wipe them out in a flood. The protagonist is Atrahasis ("exceedingly wise") who is instructed by the god Enki to build an ark. It supplies details which explain the background to the flood story in the *Epic of Gilgamesh*.

The ***Epic of Gilgamesh*** is an ancient Mesopotamian myth about immortality, arguably the most famous literary work from the ancient Near East. Copies or fragments of it were found throughout the Near East, including in Israel. It recounts the adventures of Gilgamesh, king of Uruk, and Enkidu, a wild man who becomes his friend. One part of it recounts a flood story, one of the most significant parallels between ancient Near Eastern mythology and the biblical narrative.

Eshnunna was a city-state in southern Mesopotamia, eventually conquered by Hammurabi and annexed to the Babylonian empire. The ***Laws of Eshnunna***, one of the ancient Near Eastern law collections (ca. 1800 BCE) was composed in Eshnunna a generation prior to Hammurabi's laws. It is similar to other such collections, as well as having interesting comparisons and contrasts to biblical law.

The **Former Prophets** (*Nevi'im Rishonim*) consists of the narrative books of Joshua, Judges, Samuel and Kings. It covers the time period from just after the death of Moshe through the period of the Israelite monarchy until the destruction of the First Temple and subjugation of the Kingdom of Yehuda by the Babylonian empire.

A **glacis** is the surface treatment of a man-made slope made to prevent the erosion of a tell or the lower slope of the fortifications of a city wall. These were made of various materials, such as lime plaster, stones or even beaten earth.

The **Hasmoneans** were a priestly family who led the rebellion against the Seleucid kings in the 2nd century BCE, celebrated in the story of Hanukkah, and established an autonomous Jewish kingdom. The **Hasmonean** period begins with the establishment of its dynasty, which survived for 103 years, and ended with the installation of Herod the Great by the Romans in 37 BCE.

Herod the Great (reigned 37–4 BCE) was installed by the Romans as ruler of Judea. He initiated many monumental construction projects, including the renovation and expansion of the Second Temple, the enclosure of the cave of Makhpelah in Ḥevron, the fortresses at Masada and Herodium, and the establishment of the port and city of Caesarea. The period of his rule is called the **Herodian period**.

The **Hittites** were an Indo-European population that immigrated in the early 2nd millennium BCE to the area of modern-day central Turkey. They called their country the Kingdom of Hattusa (**Hatti** in Akkadian). They established a vast empire, borrowing the cuneiform script from Mesopotamia, and recorded thousands of texts, including a detailed law collection. The two main periods of Hittite history are the Old Kingdom (ca. 1650–1500 BCE) and the New Kingdom (ca. 1400–1180 BCE).

The ***Hittite laws*** are an ancient (ca. 1650–1500 BCE) legal collection written as case laws preserved on a number of cuneiform tablets. They underwent a number of revisions (for example, monetary compensation replacing capital punishment in some cases; changes in prices), indicating that they were in use for the five hundred years of the Hittite kingdom. These laws are often compared to and contrasted with the legal sections of the Torah.

The **Hurrians** were a population that lived in northern Mesopotamia. They established powerful kingdoms, the most famous of which was the Mittani dynasty which ruled over the northern Euphrates-Tigris region between ca. 1600 and 1350 BCE. The *Amarna letters* include correspondence between the Mittani rulers and the Pharaoh.

Iron Age time periods. The **Iron Age** started in the Levant around 1200 BCE when the technique for the production of iron tools and weapons was discovered. Archaeological explorations of this period have shed light on many locations mentioned in the Tanakh. The Iron Age is divided into multiple sub-periods: **Iron Age I** (1200–1000 BCE) is characterized by the decline of the Canaanite culture of the Late Bronze Age and the appearance of new ethnic components, namely the tribes of Israel and the Philistines. **Iron Age II** (1000–586 BCE) begins with the establishment of the United Kingdom (David and Shlomo) and continues with its division into two kingdoms, Israel and Yehuda. This age is further subdivided into **Iron Age IIA** (1000–925 BCE) and **Iron Age IIB–C** (925–586 BCE). The period ends with **Iron Age III** (586–539 BCE), the period of the Babylonian exile.

After the death of King Shlomo (ca. 920 BCE), the United Kingdom was divided into two. The larger, the northern kingdom, was comprised of ten tribes known as the **Kingdom of Israel**, which, before David, had been ruled by the House of Sha'ul. This kingdom was ultimately destroyed by the Assyrians in 721 BCE, and its inhabitants were sent into exile (the "Lost Ten Tribes"). The southern kingdom, consisting of Yehuda and Binyamin, was known as the **Kingdom of Yehuda** and was continuously ruled by the House of David, with Jerusalem as its capital. It was later destroyed by Babylon in 586 BCE and its inhabitants exiled. Many of the exiles and their descendants returned to Israel after the Cyrus Declaration in 539 BCE, allowing the Judahites to return to the land of Israel.

Larsa was an important city-state in ancient Sumer, located in modern day Iraq. Archaeological excavations there found many cuneiform tablets and inscriptions from various periods and different rulers, including Ur-Namma, Hammurabi and Nevukhadnetzar.

Late Bronze Age, see Bronze Age.

Laws of Eshnunna, see Eshnunna.

Laws of Hammurabi, see Hammurabi.

Laws of Ur-Namma (**Ur-Nammu**), see Ur-Namma.

The **Levant** is a geographical term that refers to a part of the ancient Near East, mostly close to the eastern Mediterranean coast. The area of the land of Canaan, or ancient Israel, is often called "the southern Levant."

Lipit-Ishtar was a little-known ruler of Isin in southern Mesopotamia who is most famous for commissioning the ***Laws of Lipit-Ishtar*** collection ca. 1930 BCE. These laws were written in Sumerian, and resemble some statutes found in other ancient Near Eastern law collections and the Torah.

The **Mamluk period** (1250–1517 CE) was the period of Mamluk rule over Egypt, the land of Israel, the Levant and western Arabia. The Mamluks were slave soldiers of Muslim armies who seized control over the political authorities. During their rule in Israel, Muslim settlement was encouraged along with much architectural expansion, particularly of mosques and religious sites. During this period, Jews and Christians, as *dhimmis*, suffered widespread persecution and degradation.

Mari was an important city-state located on the middle Euphrates, on the eastern border of modern-day Syria. In its most significant period, during the early 2nd millennium BCE, Mari was ruled by the Amorite Lim Dynasty. The royal archives of this dynasty shed light on the political affairs of the region at the time.

Mesopotamia is a Greek term meaning "[the land] between the two rivers," referring to two great rivers of the Near East: the Euphrates and the Tigris. The area of Mesopotamia roughly corresponds to modern-day Iraq. Though this term is geographical, it has cultural significance, since it is used to refer to the cultures that lived around the Euphrates and the Tigris: the Sumerians, Akkadians, Babylonians, and Assyrians.

The ***Middle Assyrian Laws*** were composed during the Middle Assyrian period (14th century BCE); they are the only law collection known from Assyria (see entry above). The law collection was inscribed on at least fourteen clay tablets, all of which were found broken. These laws have many similarities to other ancient Near Eastern law collections as well as to biblical law.

Middle Assyrian period, see Assyrian periods.

Middle Bronze Age, see Bronze Age.

Middle Kingdom, see Egyptian time periods.

The **Neolithic period** is the third and last period of the Stone Age. It was during this period that the shift from a hunter-gatherer lifestyle to that of settlements began, including the introduction of farming and domestication of animals. These changes arose in different parts of the world independently of each other, so there are different dates for how long this period lasted. In the Near East, it lasted from around 10,200 BCE, with the earliest framing of cereals in the Levant, to the beginning of the Chalcolithic period (Copper Age) in 4500 BCE.

The **Neo-Assyrian empire** was a Mesopotamian empire lasting from 911–609 BCE – the largest empire in the world up until that time. During this period, the Assyrians perfected methods of imperial rule and employed sophisticated military strategies. In the late 10th century BCE, Assyria began to dominate the ancient Near East as well as surrounding regions, partially due to their iron weaponry. In the late 8th century, Assyria destroyed the Kingdom of Israel and conquered most of Yehuda.

New Kingdom, see Egyptian time periods.

Nuzi was an ancient Mesopotamian city located near the Tigris River. During the excavation of Nuzi, approximately 5,000 ancient tablets, known as the Nuzi texts, were found – mainly routine legal and business documents that contain many parallels to the Tanakh, especially the sections of Genesis describing the patriarchal age.

Old Babylonian period, see Babylonian time periods.

Old Kingdom, see Egyptian time periods.

The **Persian period** in Jewish history began when the Babylonian empire fell to the Persian king Cyrus the Great in 539 BCE. Cyrus allowed the Judahite exiles to return to their homeland and build the Second Temple. This period ended when Persia fell to Alexander the Great in 332 BCE.

The **Philistines** were one of the groups of the Sea Peoples who originated in the Aegean basin and migrated – either by land or sea – to the southern coast of Canaan. According to the Tanakh, the Philistines came from Crete, and founded five major cities: Ashdod, Ashkelon, Ekron, Gath, and Gaza. In the Tanakh, they were among the fiercest enemies of the Israelites.

The **Phoenicians** lived along the Mediterranean coast from present-day southern Syria down through Lebanon to northern Israel. They were a confederation of maritime traders rather than a defined country and were well regarded in the ancient world as merchants, seafarers and explorers. Their major cities were Tyre, Sidon, Byblos, and Arwad. The name Phoenician is a 1st millennium BCE Greek invention, from the word *phoinix*, an allusion to their production of the highly prized

Tyrian purple dye. The **Phoenician** language was Northwest Semitic, similar to ancient Hebrew.

The **Proto-Semitic** language is a hypothetical reconstructed proto-language understood to be the ancestor of all Semitic languages, written in a script known as **Proto-Canaanite**. Different theories suggest that this language originated in the Levant or in North Africa. The earliest attestations of a Semitic language come from names in Sumerian texts dating from the 28th century BCE.

The term **Sages**, or *Ḥazal* (acronym for *ḥakhamim zikhronam livrakha*, "our Sages of blessed memory"), refers to all sages and rabbis cited in the Mishna, Tosefta, and Talmud – who flourished from the 3rd century BCE to the 6th century CE.

The **Second Temple** stood on the Temple Mount in Jerusalem from 516 BCE to 70 CE, known as the **Second Temple period.** It was built by the exiles who returned to Israel from Babylon after the declaration of the Persian king Cyrus the Great. The Second Temple was completely refurbished during the reign of Herod, who converted it into a large and magnificent edifice. The Romans destroyed Jerusalem, including the Second Temple, in 70 CE.

The **Semitic languages** are a group of languages that include Hebrew, Aramaic, and Arabic and the languages of the ancient societies across the Middle East and Asia Minor in the Bronze and Iron Ages. They are broadly divided into the East Semitic languages (Eblaite and Akkadian, both extinct) and West Semitic languages (South Arabian, Ethiopic, Arabic), with the subgroup of Northwest Semitic which includes Hebrew and Aramaic, and extinct languages including Amorite, Ugaritic, Phoenician, and Moabite.

Sumer, in southeastern Iraq just north of the Persian Gulf, was an important civilization in the ancient Near East. The **Sumerian** language was the first to be put into writing, although it was isolated and unrelated to any other known language. The narratives about the patriarchs in the Tanakh mention places and reflect a reality that some scholars relate to Sumerian culture.

The ***Tale of Aqhat*** (ca. 1350 BCE) is a Canaanite myth from the ancient city of Ugarit, one of the longest texts found there. In the story, the god El grants Dan'el a son, Aqhat, in response to his many prayers and offerings. Events lead to a conflict with the goddess Anat, resulting in Aqhat's murder. The text contains many examples of Canaanite ritual performances and their contexts.

Ugarit was an ancient city-state located on the Syrian coast. The royal archives of its capital city, recovered by archaeologists in the early 20th century, shed light on the history and daily life of the region during the 14th century BCE. The **Ugaritic** language is a Northwest Semitic language very similar to ancient Hebrew. Scholars often use Ugaritic literature to better understand biblical vocabulary, imagery, and references to Canaanite polytheism.

Ur-Namma (also known as Ur-Nammu) founded the Third Dynasty of Ur (ca. 2100–2000 BCE), a Sumerian kingdom centered around the capital city of Ur, in what is today southern Iraq. His son and successor, Shulgi, commissioned the ***Laws of Ur-Namma***, the first ancient law collection ever discovered, which modern scholars mistakenly named after his father. Many of the statutes have parallels in later Mesopotamian law collections and in biblical law.

West Semitic languages, see Semitic languages.

Ancient/pre-modern Jewish sources

Benjamin of Tudela (1130–1173 CE) is the most famous of medieval Jewish travelers. He visited Europe, Asia and Africa and described the Jewish communities in the lands he visited. The record of his journeys is also an important source of geographical information.

Ḥizkiya ben Maoaḥ, known as the **Ḥizkuni**, was a 13th century French rabbi and commentator on the Torah.

Rabbi Avraham **Ibn Ezra** was a Spanish poet, astronomer, grammarian and philosopher, who lived from 1089 to 1167. He is best known for his "short" and "long" commentaries on the Torah, focusing on the *peshat* – the plain meaning of the text. Ibn Ezra's greatest claim to fame, though, may well be his lasting contribution in the transmission of the best of Spanish-Jewish exegesis to the Jews of Christian Europe. By the late Middle Ages, he had become an iconic personality for nearly all the intellectual schools of Jewish thought.

Flavius **Josephus** was a 1st century CE Jewish historian. His works, particularly *Antiquities of the Jews*, are valuable sources for the study of early Judaism and even of ancient Israel.

Rabbi Meir Leibush ben Yeḥiel Michel Wisser, known as the **Malbim** (1809–1879), wrote one of the most comprehensive commentaries on Tanakh since medieval times. He was also a major defender of halakha and tradition, which put him in direct confrontation with Reformist innovations.

Philo of Alexandria (ca. 20 BCE–50 CE) was an early Jewish philosopher, the first known to have tried to harmonize the Torah with Greek philosophy. His works on the Bible include the *Quaestiones* ("Inquiries"), short verse-by-verse exposition on Genesis and Exodus; the *Allegorical Commentary* on Genesis; and the *Exposition of the Law* (part of which is the treatise *On the Virtues*, a commentary on Torah law), as well as other historical and philosophical works.

Rabbi Moshe ben Maimon, also known as **Maimonides** or by the acronym **Rambam**, was one of the pivotal figures in Jewish intellectual history, as well as a famous physician. His halakhic code, *Mishneh Torah*, and his philosophical commentary, *Guide of the Perplexed*, are considered foundational Jewish works. He lived in Spain and Egypt from 1135 to 1204.

Rabbi Moshe ben Naḥman, also known as **Naḥmanides** or **Ramban**, lived from 1194 to 1270 in Spain and Israel. He was a leading scholar, philosopher, doctor, and kabbalist, best known for his commentaries on the Talmud and the Torah.

Rashbam (an acronym for Rabbi Shmuel Ben Meir), who lived from 1085 to 1158 in France, was a biblical commentator and Talmudist. He was a grandson and pupil of Rashi, although his interpretation frequently differed from that of his grandfather. His commentary on the Torah is renowned for its emphasis on the plain meaning of the text.

Rashi (an acronym for Rabbi Shlomo Yitzḥaki) lived from 1040 to 1140 in France. He was one of the most influential intellectual giants of Jewish life. He is considered the foremost commentator on the Tanakh and almost all of the Talmud, commentaries included in almost every printed edition of the Tanakh and Talmud to this day.

Menaḥem ben Saruq (ca. 920–970 CE) was lexicographer and poet who composed the *Maḥberet*, the first complete biblical lexicon written entirely in Hebrew. He is often quoted by Rashi and other commentaries when discussing philological matters.

The **Septuagint**, known as the Translation of the Seventy, or LXX, is a Greek translation of the Hebrew Tanakh. According to the *Letter of Aristeas* (apparently, 2nd century BCE), the Tanakh was translated by seventy-two Jewish scholars (six from each tribe) chosen by the High Priest at the request of Ptolemy II Philadelphus. According to tradition, the scholars independently came up with identical Greek translations. However, many differences (small and large) abound between the Septuagint and the Masoretic Text, indicating that the Hebrew texts translated into Greek were not identical to our oldest, complete Hebrew copies of the Tanakh (which come from the 10th century BCE).

Shmuel bar Abba (ca. 165–254 CE) was a first-generation Amora and head of the yeshiva at Nehardea in Babylonia. He is often cited along with Rav, with whom he debated many matters in the Talmud.

Rabbi Yosef **Behkor Shor** was a French talmudic commentator, exegete, and poet of the 12th century CE, known for his brilliant *pshat* (plain meaning of the text) commentary of the Torah.

The **Talmud** is the central text of rabbinic Judaism and the primary source of Jewish religious law, ethics, and theology. The Talmud has two components – the Mishna, originating in the land of Israel ca. 200 CE, a written compendium of rabbinic Judaism's Oral Torah; and the Gemara, written in Hebrew and Aramaic, an elucidation of the Mishna and related writings that often ventures onto other subjects and expounds broadly on the Tanakh. The **Jerusalem Talmud** (also known as **Talmud Yerushalmi** or the **Talmud of the Land of Israel**), was completed late 4th century CE in the land of Israel. The **Babylonian Talmud**, completed ca. 6th century CE in Babylonia, is usually seen as a more authoritative work, although there is significant overlap between them, as well as important differences.

Targum Job is an Aramaic translation of the book of Job, fragments of which were discovered in Qumran in 1956. It is dated to the 1st century BCE and is mentioned as a controversial work in the Talmud, Shabbat 115a.

Targum Onkelos is an Aramaic translation of the Torah, traditionally authored by Onkelos, a famous convert to Judaism ca. 25–120 CE, containing elements which indicate that it was put into writing only after the Mishnaic period. In talmudic times when the commonly spoken language was Aramaic, it was recited alternatively with the Hebrew verses of the Torah during the synagogue service, a practice which continues in Yemenite communities today.

Targum Yonatan (Jonathan) is the Aramaic translation of the Prophets, traditionally authored by Yonatan ben Uzziel, a student of Hillel the Elder, very similar in style to Targum Onkelos, but having more interpretive remarks. By the 4th century CE, it had been redacted under the influence of Babylonian Talmudists and was accepted as the official translation of the Prophets.

Ancient/pre-modern non-Jewish sources

The **Apocrypha** refers to ancient works written in the style of Scripture which were included in the King James Bible but subsequently removed as they were considered non-canonical by the Catholic Church. They were never included in the biblical canon by Jewish authorities. These works were written between 200 BCE and 400 CE, and although not considered holy or inspired, they contain much historical information and insight about how the people of those times regarded the Tanakh.

Eusebius of Caesarea was an early 3rd to 4th century CE bishop, historian of Christianity, exegete, and Christian polemicist. He worked on the textual criticism of the Septuagint, which he revised. One of the valuable aspects of his work are his references to geographic sites mentioned in the Tanakh.

Homer (8th century BCE) was the ancient Greek author to whom the epic poems of the *Iliad* and the *Odyssey* are attributed. These works provided the basis of Greek education and culture in the Classical Age.

Jerome was a Latin priest, theologian, and historian. By 405 CE, he completed the Vulgate, the first Latin translation of the Hebrew of the Tanakh.

The **Samaritan Pentateuch/Torah** is the version of the Torah written in the Samaritan alphabet and used by the Samaritans as their holy scripture. It contains many textual variations from the Masoretic Text, mostly minor changes in spelling but also transposition of passages from Deuteronomy to Exodus. Some of the variants are more significant, such as a commandment to build an altar on Mount Gerizim.

The **Vulgate** (from the Latin *editio vulgata*: "common version") is the Latin Bible used by the Roman Catholic Church, primarily translated from the Hebrew Tanakh by Jerome in the late 4th century CE. Based on this translation, it is possible to determine that the oldest surviving complete manuscripts of the Masoretic Text, dating from nearly 600 years after Jerome, represent a Hebrew text very close to what he used.

Modern scholars

Tzvi Abusch (born 1940) is Professor Emeritus of Assyriology and Ancient Near Eastern Religion at Brandeis University. He has written about Mesopotamian religion, and biblical and Babylonian interconnections.

Robert Alter (born 1935) is a professor of comparative literature at the University of California, Berkeley, who applies literary approaches to the Tanakh. His books introduced English audiences to the idea of approaching the Tanakh as literature, for example, elements such as the type scene. He most recently published a new English translation of the entire Tanakh.

Moshe David (Umberto) Cassuto (1863–1951) was an Italian Bible scholar and rabbi who published a popular commentary on the Tanakh in Hebrew. He wrote detailed commentaries on the beginning of Genesis and Exodus which incorporated information from his studies of the ancient Near East. He was one of the first scholars who recognized the importance of Ugaritic for biblical study.

Aaron Demsky (born 1938) is a biblical historian at Bar-Ilan University. He is known for his studies of proper names (onomastics) and is the founder and director of The Project for the Study of Jewish Names. His Hebrew book, *Literacy in Ancient Israel,* makes important use of ancient Near Eastern materials.

Moshe Greenberg (1928–2010) was a recipient of the Israel Prize for Bible studies. He had a significant influence on modern Jewish academic biblical scholarship, and was well known for his "holistic" method of analysis of biblical texts, his studies on the development of biblical prayer, and his approach to using the Tanakh in modern Israeli education.

Hermann Gunkel (1862–1932) was a German Bible scholar, founder of form criticism, a method of biblical criticism which classifies sections of the text by literary patterns and then attempts to trace each type to its era of oral transmission. Part of this scholarship is identifying elements of folktales that are understood to have been incorporated into the written narrative.

Alexander Heidel (1907–1955) was an Assyriologist and Bible scholar who worked on the *Enuma Elish Epic* and the flood story in the *Epic of Gilgamesh,* noting the comparisons and differences with the Genesis narratives.

Samson Raphael Hirsch (1808–1888) was a prominent German rabbi, who led the Orthodox community of Frankfurt am Main. He is known as a founder of modern Orthodoxy through the *Torah im Derech Eretz* approach which incorporated some secular studies, although always maintaining the primacy of Jewish thought and practice. He was a vociferous opponent of early Reform Judaism. He authored a commentary on the Torah which focused on etymology and philology in order to understand the exact meaning of the Hebrew words, while also emphasizing the meanings and symbols of the commandments as consistent with the rabbinic tradition.

David Tzvi Hoffman (1843–1921) was an Orthodox rabbi, the greatest authority of Jewish law in Germany at that time, and head of the Hildesheimer Rabbinical Seminary in Berlin. He was an original member of the Council of Torah Sages, and was familiar with modern biblical academic scholarship. He wrote a commentary on most of the Torah where he addressed and rebutted the claims of the documentary hypothesis, while focusing on the plain meaning of the text. He also wrote works on the Mishna and responsa on contemporary issues.

Thorkild Jacobsen (1904–1993), was a renowned Danish Sumerologist and Assyriologist at Harvard University. His works are important for understanding Sumerian and Akkadian culture and institutions.

Anne Kilmer (1931–2023) was a pioneering Assyriologist who made significant contributions in the area of Sumero-Babylonian music.

Samuel Noah Kramer (1897–1990) was one of the world's leading experts in Sumerian history and language.

Benno Landsberger (1890–1968) was the founder of the modern study of Assyriology who made groundbreaking contributions in the field of Semitic philology regarding Hebrew-Akkadian and Aramaic-Akkadian comparative semantics and lexicography.

Samuel David Luzzatto, known as **Shadal** (1800–1865), was an Italian Jewish scholar, professor at the Padua rabbinical college, and an expert in Semitic languages who employed modern critical methods to the study of Tanakh. His commentary to the Torah draws on traditional Jewish sources, while focusing on the plain meaning of the text.

A. Leo Oppenheim (1904–1974) was an important Assyriologist and one of the editors of the monumental *Chicago Assyrian Dictionary* (CAD) of the Oriental Institute. He was considered the foremost expert on cuneiform writing in his time and published many works about the daily life and culture of ancient Mesopotamia.

Anson Rainey (1930–2011) was a professor of ancient Near Eastern cultures and Semitic linguistics at Tel Aviv University. He is known for his work on the *Amarna letters* and in the field of biblical geography, most notably *The Sacred Bridge*, co-authored with R. Steven Notley.

Nahum Sarna (1923–2005) was a prominent Bible scholar at Brandeis University whose writings introduced laypeople to modern biblical scholarship. He is best known for his books *Understanding Genesis* (1966) and *Exploring Exodus* (1996), and the *JPS Torah Commentary* to Genesis and Exodus.

Nili Shupak is a professor of Tanakh and Egyptology at Haifa University. She focuses on the genre of ancient wisdom literature and understanding the Tanakh in light of findings from Egyptian sources.

Ephraim Avigdor Speiser (1902–1965) was an Assyriologist and archaeologist who discovered and excavated Tepe Gawra in northern Iraq, an ancient Mesopotamian settlement, one of the earliest sites of human civilization. He is the author of the Genesis volume of the Anchor Bible Commentary series.

Moshe Weinfeld (1925–2009) was a professor of Bible at the Hebrew University of Jerusalem, and the recipient of the Israel Prize in Bible Studies. He was involved in just about every area of Bible scholarship, focusing on the impact of the literature of the ancient Near East on Tanakh, and the connections between the different genres within the Tanakh itself.

Meir Weiss (1902–1998) was a rabbi and professor of Bible at Hebrew University, and recipient of the Israel Prize in Jewish Studies. He introduced his "total interpretation" method of literary analysis into Bible studies in Israel. As such, his teaching and writings influenced the gamut of Israeli biblical studies from secular universities to the Orthodox Herzog College.

Yair Zakovitch (born 1945) is an emeritus professor of Bible at the Hebrew University of Jerusalem, and the recipient of the Israel Prize in Bible Studies. The foremost student of Meir Weiss, his prolific writings focus on what we learn from literary analysis of biblical texts and inner-biblical interpretation.

Abbreviations

Full entries for often-used article source abbreviations

Freedman, David Noel, ed. *The Anchor Bible Dictionary*. 6 vols. New York: Doubleday, 1992.

Hallo, William W., ed. *The Context of Scripture* (*COS*). 4 vols. (Vol. 1: *Canonical Compositions*; Vol. 2: *Monumental Inscriptions from the Biblical World*; Vol. 3: *Archival Documents from the Biblical World*; Vol 4: *Supplements*). Leiden: Brill, 2003–2016.

Koehler, Ludwig and Walter Baumgartner, eds. *The Hebrew and Aramaic Lexicon of the Old Testament (HALOT)*. 2 vols. Leiden: Brill, 2001.

Levine, Baruch A. *Numbers 1–20: A New Translation with Introduction and Commentary, Vol. 4A*. In: *The Anchor Bible*, edited by William Foxwell Albright and David Noel Freedman. New York: Doubleday, 1993.

Milgrom, Jacob. *Leviticus 1–16: A New Translation with Introduction and Commentary, Vol. 3*. In: *The Anchor Bible*, edited by William Foxwell Albright and David Noel Freedman. New York: Doubleday, 1991.

———. *Leviticus 17–22: A New Translation with Introduction and Commentary, Vol. 3A*. In: *The Anchor Bible*, edited by William Foxwell Albright and David Noel Freedman. New York: Doubleday, 2000.

Pritchard, James B., ed. *Ancient Near Eastern Texts Relating to the Old Testament* (*ANET*). Princeton, NJ: Princeton University Press, 1974.

Roth, Martha T., ed.. *Assyrian Dictionary of the Oriental Institute of the University of Chicago* (*CAD*). Chicago, IL: Oriental Institute. 20 vols. 1956–2010.

Sarna, Nahum A. *The JPS Torah Commentary: Genesis*. New York: Jewish Publication Society, 1989.

Speiser, E. A. Genesis: *A New Translation with Introduction and Commentary. In: The Anchor Bible*, edited by Wiliam Foxwell Albright and David Noel Freedman. New York: Doubleday, 1964.

Tawil, Hayim ben Yosef. *An Akkadian Lexical Companion for Biblical Hebrew: Etymological-Semantic and Idiomatic Equivalents with Supplement on Biblical Aramaic*. Jersey City, NJ: Ktav, 2009.

Walton, John H., ed. *Zondervan Illustrated Bible Backgrounds Commentary, Vol. 1*. Grand Rapids, MI: Zondervan, 2009.

Citation abbreviations

ARM Parrot, André and Georges Dossin. *Archives royales de Mari.* 33 vols. Paris: Imprimerie Nationale, 1950–2012.

CTA Herdner, A. *Corpus des tablettes en cunéiforms alphabétiques découvertes à Ras Shamra-Ugari de 1919 à 1939.* Mission de Ras Shamra 10. Paris: P. Geuthner, 1963.

CTH Laroche, E. *Catalogue des textes hittites.* RHA 30. Paris: Klincksieck, 1971.

EA Moran, William L. *The Amarna letters.* Baltimore, MD: Johns Hopkins University Press, 1992.

Emar Arnaud, Daniel. *Textes sumériens et accadiens.* Paris: Éditions Recherche sur les Civilisations, 1985.

KAR Ebeling, E. *Keilschrifttexte aus Assur religiösen* Inhalts. Bd. 1–2. Vol. 28 + 34. Wissenschaftliche Veröffentlichung der Deutschen Orient-Gesellschaft. Leipzig: Hinrichs, 1919, 1923.

KBo, KUB Figulla, H. H. *Keilschrifttexte aus Boghazkoi. Vol. Bd. 1–22.* Wissenschaftliche Veröffentlichung der Deutschen Orient-Gesellschaft. Leipzig: Hinrich, 1916–.

KTU Dietrich, M., O. Loretz and J. Sanmartin. *Die keilalphabbetischen Texte aus Ugarit.* Alter Orient und Altes Testament 24. Neukirchen-Vluyn: Neukirchener, 1976.

CAT ———. *The Cuneiform alphabetic texts: from Ugarit, Ras Ibn Hani and other places* ("CAT"). Münster: Ugarit-Verlag, 1995.

Ancient Near East law texts:

Roth, Martha T. and Harry A. Hoffner. *Law Collections from Mesopotamia and Asia Minor.* Atlanta, GA: Scholars Press, 1995.

MAL Middle Assyrian Laws. In: Roth, 153–194.

MAPD Middle Assyrian Palace Degrees. In: Roth, 195–121.

HL Hittite Laws. In: Roth, 217–249.

LE Laws of Eshnunna. In: Roth, 57–70.

LH Laws of Hammurabi. In: Roth, 71–142.

Ur-Namma Laws of Ur-Namma. In: Roth, 13–22.

Topic Bibliographies

Commentaries on the Book of Genesis

Cassuto, U. *A Commentary on the Book of Genesis*. Abrahams, I., trans. 3 vols. Jerusalem: Magnes Press, 1964.

Kiel, Yehuda. *Da'at Mikra – Breishit*. Jerusalem: Mossad HaRav Kook, 3 vols. 1997–2003 (Hebrew).

Sarna, N. *The JPS Torah Commentary: Genesis*. Philadelphia, PA: The Jewish Publication Society, 1989.

Speiser, E.A. *Genesis: A New Translation with Introduction and Commentary, Vol. 1*. In: *The Anchor Bible*, edited by William Foxwell Albright and David Noel Freedman. New York: Doubleday, 1974.

Walton, John H. *The NIV Application Commentary; Genesis*. Grand Rapids, MI: Zondervan, 2001.

———. "Genesis" In: *Zondervan Illustrated Bible Backgrounds Commentary, Vol. 1*, Grand Rapids, MI: Zondervan, 2009.

Ancient Near East sources

Bryce, Trevor. *The Kingdom of the Hittites*, 2nd ed. New York: Oxford University Press, 2005.

Cross, Frank M. *Canaanite Myth and Hebrew Epic: Essays in the History of the Religion of Israel*. Cambridge, MA: Harvard University Press, 1973.

De Vaux, Roland. *Ancient Israel: Its Life and Instructions*. Grand Rapids, MI: Eerdmans, 1997.

Freedman, David N., ed. *The Anchor Bible Dictionary*. 6 vols. New York: Doubleday, 1992.

Gibson, John C. *Canaanite Myths and Legends*. London: T & T Clark, 2004.

King, Phillip J. and Lawrence E. Stager. *Life in Biblical Israel*. Louisville, KY: Westminster John Knox Press, 2001.

Unterman, Jeremiah. *Justice for All: How the Jewish Bible Revolutionized Ethics*. Philadelphia, PA: Jewish Publication Society, 2017.

Weinfeld, Moshe. *The Place of the Law in the Religion of Ancient Israel*. Leiden: Brill, 2004.

Primary sources, encyclopedias and dictionaries

Achtemeier, Paul J. *HarperCollins Bible Dictionary*. San Francisco, CA: HarperOne, 1996.

Arnaud, Daniel. *Recherches au pays d'Aštata: Emar VI: Les textes sumériens et accadiens*. Paris: Éditions Recherche sur les Civilisations, 1985–1987.

Biggs, Robert D. et. al., ed. *The Assyrian Dictionary of the Oriental Institute of Chicago*. 21 vols. Chicago, IL: The Oriental Institute, 1956–2010.

Botterweck, G. Johannes, Helmer Ringgren, Heinz-Josef Fabry, *Theological Dictionary of the Old Testament*, 13 vols. Grand Rapids. MI: William Eerdmans Publishing Company, 1974–2004.

Dietrich, Manfried, Oswald Loretz, and Joaquin Sanmartin. *The Cuneiform Alphabetic Texts from Ugarit, Ras Ibn Hani, and Other Places*. Münster: Ugarit-Verlag, 1995.

Encyclopedia Biblica (אנציקלופדיה מקראית) 8 vols. Jerusalem: Bialik Institute, 1952–1982.

Fisher, Loren R. and Stan Rummel, eds. *Ras Shamra Parallels: The Texts from Ugarit and the Hebrew Bible*. 3 vols. Rome: Pontifical Biblical Institute, 1972–1981.

Freedman, David Noel, ed. *The Anchor Bible Dictionary*. 6 vols. New York: Doubleday, 1992.

Goetze, Albrecht. *The Laws of Eshnunna*. New Haven, CT: American Schools of Oriental Research, 1956.

Gordon, Cyrus H. *Ugaritic Textbook: Grammar, Texts in Transliteration with Cuneifom Selection.* Rome: Pontificio Istituto Biblico, 1999.

Grayson, Albert Kirk. *Assyrian Royal Inscriptions.* 2 vols. Wiesbaden: O. Harrassowitz, 1972.

Hallo, William W. and K. L. Younger, eds. *The Context of Scripture* (*COS*). 4 vols. Leiden and Boston, MA: Brill, 1997–2017.

Harper, Robert F., trans. *The Code of Hammurabi, King of Babylon.* Chicago, IL: University of Chicago Press, 1904.

Herdner, Andrée. *Corpus des tablettes en cuneiforms alphabétiques découvertes à Ras Shamra-Ugarit de 1220 à 1939*. Paris: Imprimerie nationale, 1963.

Köhler, Ludwig and Walter Baumgartner, eds. *The Hebrew and Aramaic Lexicon of the Old Testament (HALOT).* 4 vols. Translated and edited by M. E. J. Richardson. Leiden: Brill, 1994–2000.

Moran, William L. *The Amarna Letters.* Baltimore, MD: Johns Hopkins University Press, 2000.

Olmo Lete, Gregorio del. and Joaquin Sanmartin. *A Dictionary of the Ugaritic Language in the Alphabetic Tradition.* 2 vols. Translated and edited by Wilfred G. E. Watson. 3rd ed. Leiden: Brill, 2003.

Pritchard, James B. *Ancient Near East in Pictures Relating to the Old Testament. Second Edition With Supplement* (ANEP). Princeton, NJ: Princeton University Press, 1974.

———. *Ancient Near Eastern Texts Relating to the Old Testament, Third Edition with Supplement* (ANET). Princeton, NJ: Princeton University Press, 1969.

Roth, Martha T. and Harry A. Hoffner. *Law Collections from Mesopotamia and Asia Minor.* Atlanta, GA: Scholars Press, 1997.

Tawil, Hayim ben Yosef. *An Akkadian Lexical Companion for Biblical Hebrew: Etymological-Semantic and Idiomatic Equivalents with Supplement on Biblical Aramaic.* Jersey City, NJ: Ktav, 2009.

Article Bibliographies

The Torah and Its Ancient Near Eastern Context

Cline, E. H., ed. *The Oxford Handbook of the Bronze Age Aegean*. Oxford: Oxford University Press, 2010.

Helft, S. N. and W. H. Stiebing, Jr. *Ancient Near Eastern History and Culture*, 3rd ed. New York: Routledge, 2018.

Sasson, J. M., ed. *Civilizations of the Ancient Near East*, 4 vols. New York: Scribners, 1995.

Unterman, Jeremiah. *Justice for All: How the Jewish Bible Revolutionized Ethics*. Philadelphia, PA: Jewish Publication Society, 2017.

———. "Torah." In: *Harper's Bible Dictionary*, edited by Paul J. Achtemeier, 1083–1084. San Francisco, CA: Harper & Row, 1985.

Introduction to the book of Genesis

Cassuto, Umberto. *A Commentary on the Book of Genesis. Part I: From Adam to Noah Genesis I–VI:8*. Translated by Israel Abrahams. Jerusalem: Magnes Press, 1972.

———. *"Abraham and the Promised Land." In: A Commentary on the Book of Genesis. Part II: From Noah to Abraham Genesis VI:9–XI:32*. Translated by Israel Abrahams. Jerusalem: Magnes Press, 1972.

Greenberg, M. "The Vision of Jerusalem in Ezekiel 8–11: A Holistic Interpretation." In: *The Divine Helmsman : Studies on God's Control of Human Events, Presented to Lou H. Silberman*, edited by James Crenshaw and Samuel Sandmel. New York: Ktav, 1980, 149.

Hendel, Ronald S. *Remembering Abraham: Culture, Memory, and History in the Hebrew Bible*, 50–51n26, 52–54. New York: Oxford University Press, 2005.

Kitchen, Kenneth A. "The Patriarchal Age: Myth or History?" *Biblical Archaeology Review* 21(2) 1995: 48–57, 88–95.

Sarna. *The JPS Torah Commentary: Genesis*.

———. *Understanding Genesis: The Heritage of Biblical Israel*. New York: Schocken Books, 1966.

Speiser. *Anchor Bible: Genesis*.

Unterman, Jeremiah. *Justice for All: How the Jewish Bible Revolutionized Ethics*, 1–2. Philadelphia, PA: Jewish Publication Society, 2017.

Walton, John H. "Genesis." In: *Zondervan Illustrated Bible Backgrounds Commentary, Vol. 1*.

1:1 Creation in the ancient Near East and Genesis

Clifford, Richard J. "Creation Accounts in the Ancient Near East." In: *Creation Accounts in the Ancient Near East and the Bible*, 11–133. Washington, DC: Catholic Biblical Association of America, 1994.

———. "Conclusions." In: *Creation Accounts in the Ancient Near East and the Bible*, 198–203. Washington, DC: Catholic Biblical Association of America, 1994.

Heidel, Alexander. "Old Testament Parallels." In: *The Babylonian Genesis*. 2nd ed., 82–140, esp. p. 125. Chicago, IL: University of Chicago Press, 1951.

Lichtheim, Miriam. "The Testament of a Heracleopolitan King: The Instruction Addressed to King

Merikare." In: *Ancient Egyptian Literature, Vol. 1: The Old and Middle Kingdoms,* 97–110, esp. p. 106. Berkeley, CA: University of California Press, 1975.
Sarna. *The JPS Torah Commentary: Genesis,* 7.
Speiser. *Anchor Bible: Genesis,* 10–11.
Unterman, Jeremiah. "The Jewish Bible's Unique Understanding of God: The Ethical Relationship of God to the World and Humanity." In: *Justice for All: How the Jewish Bible Revolutionized Ethics,* 1–14, esp. p. 2–7; 185–188 (notes). Philadelphia, PA: Jewish Publication Society, 2017.
Walton, John H. "Genesis." In: *Zondervan Illustrated Bible Backgrounds Commentary, Vol. 1:* 2–10.

1:1 Heaven and earth

Cassuto, Umberto. "The Story of Creation." In: *A Commentary on the Book of Genesis. Part I: From Adam to Noah Genesis I–VI:8.* Translated by Israel Abrahams, 7–70, esp. p. 20. Jerusalem: Magnes Press, 1972.
Sarna. *The JPS Torah Commentary: Genesis,* 353.
Tawil, Hayim ben Yosef. "ארץ." In: *An Akkadian Lexical Companion for Biblical Hebrew:* 34–36, esp. p. 35.

1:1 The beginning of what

Walton, John H. "Genesis." In: *Zondervan Illustrated Bible Backgrounds Commentary, Vol. 1:* 10–11.

1:2 Pre-existence: void and desolate

Clifford, Richard J. "Creation Accounts in Egyptian Thought." In: *Creation Accounts in the Ancient Near East and in the Bible,* 99–116, esp. p. 102–104. Washington, DC: Catholic Biblical Association, 1994.
Foster, Benjamin R., trans. "Epic of Creation (1.111) (*Enuma Elish*)." In: *COS, Vol. 1:* 390–402, esp. p. 391.
Sarna. *JPS Torah Commentary: Genesis,* 353n6.
Walton, John H. "Genesis." In: *Zondervan Illustrated Bible Backgrounds Commentary, Vol. 1:* 15.

1:2 The deep

Alster, Bendt. "Tiamat." In: *Dictionary of Deities and Demons in the Bible,* edited by Karel van der Toom, Bob Becking, and Pieter W. van der Horst, 867–869, esp. p. 867. Leiden: Brill, 1998.
Lete, Gregorio del Olmo, and Joaquín Sanmartín. "Thm." In: *A Dictionary of the Ugaritic Language in the Alphabetic Tradition. Part Two.* Leiden: Brill, 2004.
Tawil, Hayim ben Yosef. "תהום." In: *An Akkadian Lexical Companion for Biblical Hebrew,* 428–429.

1:2 *Meraḥefet*

Cassuto, Umberto. "The Story of Creation: מרחפת." In: *A Commentary on the Book of Genesis. Part I: From Adam to Noah Genesis I–VI:8.* Translated by Israel Abrahams, 7–70, esp. p. 24–25. Jerusalem: Magnes Press, 1972.
Unterman, Jeremiah. "The Jewish Bible's Unique Understanding of God: The Ethical Relationship of God to the World and Humanity." In: *Justice for All: How the Jewish Bible Revolutionized Ethics,* 1–14, esp. p. 5. Philadelphia, PA: Jewish Publication Society, 2017.

1:3 God said, "Let there be…"

Allen, James P., trans. "From the 'Memphite Theology' (1.15)." In: *COS, Vol. 1:* 21–23, esp. p. 22.
Walton, John H. "Genesis." In: *Zondervan Illustrated Bible Backgrounds Commentary, Vol. 1:* 16.

1:3–4 Light – time and quality

Foster, Benjamin R., trans. "Epic of Creation (1.111) (*Enūma Elish*)." In: *COS, Vol. 1:* 390–402, esp. p. 399.
Kadish, Gerald E. "Time." In: *The Oxford Encyclopedia of Ancient Egypt, Vol. 3,* edited by Donald B. Redford, 405–409, esp. p. 408. Oxford: Oxford University Press, 2001.
Sarna. *The JPS Torah Commentary: Genesis,* 7, 353n11.

Walton, John H. "Genesis." In: *Zondervan Illustrated Bible Backgrounds Commentary, Vol. 1*: 16.
———. The NIV Application Commentary: Genesis, 79–80. Grand Rapids, MI, Zondervan, 2001.

1:6–7 The expanse

Foster, Benjamin R., trans. "Epic of Creation (1.111) (*Enūma Elish*)." In: *COS, Vol. 1*: 390–402, esp. p. 398.
Hoffner, Harry A., Jr. "Song of Ullikummi." In: *Hittite Myths*, edited by Gary M. Beckham, 55–65, esp. p. 64 § 61. Atlanta, GA: SBL Press, 1998.
Horowitz, Wayne." The Geography of the Heavens." In: *Mesopotamian Cosmic Geography*, 243–267, esp. p. 265. Winona Lake, IN: Eisenbrauns, 1998.
Sarna. *The JPS Torah Commentary: Genesis*, 8, 353n15.
Walton, John H. "Genesis." In: *Zondervan Illustrated Bible Backgrounds Commentary, Vol. 1*: 16–18.

1:9 The gathering of waters and the appearance of dry land

Allen, James P., trans. "From Coffin Texts Spell 335 = Book of the Dead Spell 17 (1.10)." In: *COS, Vol. 1*: 15–17, esp. p. 16.
Clifford, Richard J. "Creation Accounts in Mesopotamia: Sumerian Texts.' In: *Creation Accounts in the Ancient Near East and in the Bible*, 13–53, esp. p. 39. Washington, DC: Catholic Biblical Association, 1994.
Walton, John H. "Genesis." In: *Zondervan Illustrated Bible Backgrounds Commentary, Vol. 1*: 18.

1:11–12 Let the earth produce vegetation…and so it was

Clifford, Richard J. "Creation Accounts in Mesopotamia: Sumerian Texts." In: *Creation Accounts in the Ancient Near East and in the Bible*, 13–53, esp. p. 39, 49–50. Washington, DC: Catholic Biblical Association, 1994.
Sarna. *The JPS Torah Commentary: Genesis*, 9.
Walton, John H. "Genesis." In: *Zondervan Illustrated Bible Backgrounds Commentary, Vol. 1*: 18.

1:14 Signs and seasons, days and years

Clifford, Richard J. "Creation Accounts in Mesopotamia: Akadian Texts." In: *Creation Accounts in the Ancient Near East and in the Bible*, 54–98, esp. p. 67. Washington, DC: Catholic Biblical Association, 1994.
Foster, John L. "Morning Hymn to Amun-Ré as Horakhty." In: *Hymns, Prayers and Songs: An Anthology of Ancient Egyptian Lyric Poetry*, edited by Susan Tower Hollis, 71. Atlanta, GA: Scholars Press, 1996.
Koch-Westenholz, Ulla. "The Received Tradition." In: *Mesopotamian Astrology: An Introduction to Babylonian and Assyrian Celestial Divination*, 74–96, esp. p. 77. Copenhagen: Museum Tusculanum Press, 1995.
Walton, John H. "Genesis." In: *Zondervan Illustrated Bible Backgrounds Commentary, Vol. 1*: 18–19.

1:16 Stars

Clifford, Richard J. "Creation Accounts in Mesopotamia: Akadian Texts." In: *Creation Accounts in the Ancient Near East and in the Bible*, 54–98, esp. p. 68. Washington, DC: Catholic Biblical Association, 1994.
Foster, Benjamin R., trans. "Epic of Creation (1.111) (*Enūma Elish*)." In: *COS, Vol. 1*: 390–402, esp. p. 399.
Horowitz, Wayne. "Cosmic Geography in Accounts of Creatrion." In: *Mesopotamian Cosmic Geography*, 107–149, esp. p. 114–115. Winona Lake, IN: Eisenbrauns, 1998.
———. "The Geography of the Sky: The Astrolabes, Mul-Apin, and Related Texts." In: *Mesopotamian Cosmic Geography*, 150–192, esp. p. 170. Winona Lake, IN: Eisenbrauns, 1998.
Walton, John H. "Genesis." In: *Zondervan Illustrated Bible Backgrounds Commentary, Vol. 1*: 19.

1:21 The great sea creatures (*taninim*)

Ayali-Darshan, Noga. *The Storm-God and the Sea: The Origin, Versions, and Diffusion of a Myth throughout the Ancient Near East*. Tübingen: Mohr Siebeck, 2020.

Cross, Frank Moore. "The Divine Warrior." In: *Canaanite Myth and Hebrew Epic: Essays in the History of the Religion of Israel*, 91–111, esp. p. 108. Cambridge, MA: Harvard University Press, 1973.

Talmon, Shemaryahu. "Did There Exist a Biblical National Epic? In: *Literary Studies in the Hebrew Bible: Form and Content - Collected Studies*, 91–111. Jerusalem: Magnes Press, 1993.

קאסוטו, משה דוד. ״שירת העלילה בישרא״ בתוך: מחקרים במקרא ובמזרח הקדום - ספרות מקראית וספרות כנענית. כרך א. תשל״ב (2791), ירושלים, עמ׳ 26 - 09.

1:26–30 The creation and role of humans in the ancient Near East

Walton, John H. "Genesis." In: *Zondervan Illustrated Bible Backgrounds Commentary, Vol. 1:* 1:26; 1:28.

Lichtheim, M. *Ancient Egyptian Literature, vol. 1: The Old and Middle Kingdoms*, 106. Berkeley, CA: University of California, 1975.

Sarna. *The JPS Torah Commentary: Genesis*, 12–13.

Unterman, Jeremiah. *Justice for All: How the Jewish Bible Revolutionized Ethics*, 3–4, 185–187. Philadelphia, PA: Jewish Publication Society, 2017.

2:1–3 The Sabbath in contrast to Mesopotamian divine rest

Hallo, W. W. "New Moons and Sabbaths: A Case-study in the Contrastive Approach." *Hebrew Union College Annual* 48 (1977): 1–18.

Sarna. *The JPS Torah Commentary: Genesis*, 14–15.

Walton, John H. "Genesis." In: *Zondervan Illustrated Bible Backgrounds Commentary, Vol. 1:* 23.

2:1 Array

Tawil, Hayim ben Yosef. " צבא." In: *An Akkadian Lexical Companion for Biblical Hebrew*, 316a.

2:5 No plant has yet sprouted, for the Lord God had not yet brought rain upon the earth

Jacobsen, Thorkild. "The Eridu Genesis." *Journal of Biblical Literature* 100(4) 1981): 513–529, esp. p. 516n7.

Walton, John H. "Genesis." In: *Zondervan Illustrated Bible Backgrounds Commentary, Vol. 1:* 23, 25.

2:6 *Ed*

The Sumerian Dictionary of the University Museum of the University of Pennsylvania. Philadelphia, PA: The Babylonian Section of the University Museum, 1984-1998. Available at: https://www.penn.museum/research/project.php?pid=17#:~:text=ePSD%20is%20an%20online%20lexicon%20of%20Sumerian%2C%20the,outstanding%20collection%20of%20ancient%20scribal%20excercises%20in%20Sumerian. http://psd.museum.upenn.edu/nepsd-frame.html

Tawil, Hayim ben Yosef. "אד." In: *An Akkadian Lexical Companion for Biblical Hebrew*, 6.

Walton, John H. "Genesis." In: *Zondervan Illustrated Bible Backgrounds Commentary, Vol. 1:* 25, 142n107.

2:7 The creation of man from the dust of the earth

Allen, James P., trans. "From Coffin Text Spell 80 (1.8)." In: *COS, Vol. 1:* 11–14, esp. p. 13.

Buyalere, Greta Van, Chikako E. Watanabe, and Mark Altaweel. "'Clay Pit, You Are the Creator of God and Man!': Textual Evidence for the Sources of Raw Clay Used in Mesopotamia." In: *Prince of the Orient: Ancient Near Eastern Studies in Memory of H.I.H. Prince Takahito Mikasa*, edited by Ichiro Nakata, Yoshihiro Nishiaki, Takahiro Odaka, Masamichi Yamada, and Shigeo Yamada, 175–192. Japan: The Society for Near Eastern Studies in Japan, 2019.

Klein, Jacob, trans. "Enki and Ninmah (1.159)." In: *COS, Vol. 1:* 516–518, esp. p. 517.

Lichtheim, Miriam, trans. "Merikare (1.35)." In: *COS, Vol. 1:* 61–66, esp. p. 65.

Mangum, Douglas T. "The Concept of God in Proverbs and Amenemope." Available at: https://www.academia.edu/1315303/The_Concept_of_God_in_Proverbs_and_Amenemope https://www.academia.edu/1315303/The_Concept_of_God_in_Proverbs_and_Amenemope.

Sarna. *The JPS Torah Commentary: Genesis*, 17.

2:8 Ethics of the Garden of Eden versus the quest for immortality in ancient Babylon

Heidel, Alexander. *The Gilgamesh Epic and Old Testament Parallels*, 2nd ed. Chicago, IL: University of Chicago, 1949.
Sarna. *The JPS Torah Commentary: Genesis*, 18.

2:8 Garden

Sarna. *The JPS Torah Commentary: Genesis*, 18.
Katz, D. "Enki and Ninhursaga, Part One: The Story of Dilmun," *Bibliotheca Orientalis* 64 (2007): 568–589; particularly, 569, 575-6.

2:8 Eden

Katz, Dina. "Enki and Ninhursaga, Part One: The Story of Dilmun." *Bibliotheca Orientalis* 64(5–6) 2007, 568–589, esp. p. 569, 575–576.
Sarna. *The JPS Torah Commentary: Genesis*, 18.
Tsumura, David T. "The Earth-Waters Relationship in Gen 2." In: *The Earth and the Waters in Genesis 1 and 2*, 117–139, esp. p. 127–136. Sheffield, England: Sheffield Academic Press, 1989.

2:9 The Tree of Life

Ritner, Robert K., trans. "The Great Cairo Hymn of Praise to Amun-Re (1.25)" *COS, Vol. 1*: 37–40, esp. p. 38.
Walton, John H. "Genesis." In: *Zondervan Illustrated Bible Backgrounds Commentary, Vol. 1*: 28.

2:10 Four headwaters

Muller, W. Max and James G. Scott. *The Mythology of All Races Vol, 12: Egyptian & Indo-Chinese*, edited by Lewis Herbert Gray, 33–67, esp. p. 47. New York: Cooper Square Publishers, 1964.
Walton, John H. "Genesis." In: *Zondervan Illustrated Bible Backgrounds Commentary, Vol. 1*: 28–29.

2:11–14 Pishon, Giḥon, Tigris, and Euphrates

Sarna. *The JPS Torah Commentary: Genesis*, 20.
Walton, John H. "Genesis." In: *Zondervan Illustrated Bible Backgrounds Commentary, Vol. 1*: 30.

2:15 To work it and safeguard it

Clifford, Richard J. "Creation Accounts in Mesopotamia: Sumerian Texts." In: *Creation Accounts in the Ancient Near East and in the Bible*, 13–53, esp. p. 40, 41, 50. Washington, DC: Catholic Biblical Association, 1994.
Sarna. *The JPS Torah Commentary: Genesis*, 20.
Walton, John H. "Genesis." In: *Zondervan Illustrated Bible Backgrounds Commentary, Vol. 1*: 31.

2:20–24 The creation of woman

Alter, Robert. *Genesis: Translation and Commentary*. New York: W. W. Norton, 1996, 9–10.
"Banu." In: *The Asssyrian Dictionary (CAD), Vol. 2: B*, 83–90.
Clifford, Richard J. *Creation Accounts in the Ancient Near East and in the Bible*. Washington DC: Catholic Biblical Association of America, 1994.
Foster, Benjamin R., trans. "Epic of Creation." In: *COS, Vol. 1*: 390–402.
———. "Atra-hasis. (1.130)" In: *COS, Vol. 1*: 450–453.
———. "Gilgamesh (1.132)." In: *COS, Vol. 1*: 458–460.
"Selu." In: *The Assyrian Dictionary (CAD), Vol. 16: S*, 124–126.
Walton, John H. "Understanding the Past: Human Origins and Role." In: *Ancient Near Eastern Thought and the Old Testament*. Grand Rapids, MI: Baker Academic, 2006, 203–215.

2:25 Naked

Clifford, Richard J. "Creation Accounts in Mesopotamia: Sumerian Texts." In: *Creation Accounts in*

the Ancient Near East and in the Bible, 13–53, esp. p. 45. Washington, DC: Catholic Biblical Association, 1994.
Walton, John H. "Genesis." In: *Zondervan Illustrated Bible Backgrounds Commentary, Vol. 1:* 33.

3:1 Slyest

Currid, John D. "The Egyptian Setting of the Serpent Confrontation." In: *Ancient Egypt and the Old Testament*, 83–193, esp. p. 91. Grand Rapids, MI: Baker Publishing Group, 1997.
Teeter, Emily. "Animals in Egyptian Literature." In: *A History of the Animal World in the Ancient Near East*, edited by Billie Jean Collins, 251–270, esp. p. 253–255. Leiden: Brill, 2002,
Walton, John H. "Genesis." In: *Zondervan Illustrated Bible Backgrounds Commentary, Vol. 1:* 33–34.

3:7 Fig leaves

Kislev, Mordechai E., Anat Hartmann, and Ofer Bar-Yosef. "Early Domesticated Fig in the Jordan Valley." *Science* 312(5778) 2006: 1372–1374.
Sarna. *The JPS Torah Commentary: Genesis*, 26.

3:8 The cool of the day

Cassuto, Umberto. "The Story of the Garden of Eden." In: *A Commentary on the Book of Genesis. Part I: From Adam to Noah Genesis I–VI:8*. Translated by Israel Abrahams, 71–177, esp. p. 151. Jerusalem: Magnes Press, 1972.
Naor, R. O. Potchter, H. Shafir, and P. Alpert. (2015). "An Observational Study of the Summer Mediterranean Sea-Breeze-Front Penetration into the Complex Topography of the Jordan-Rift-Valley." *Theoretical and Applied Climatology* 127(1–2): 275–284.
Speiser. *Anchor Bible: Genesis*, 24.

3:14–15 The snake's curse

Der Manuelian, Peter, ed. "Spells for the Spirit's Rebirth (Antechamber, East Gable and Wall)." In: *The Ancient Egyptian Pyramid Texts*. 2nd ed. Translated with an Introduction and Notes by James P. Allen, 50–55, esp. p. 54. Atlanta, GA: Society of Biblical Literature, 2005.
———. "Spells for the Spirit's Rebirth (Antechamber, East Wall)." In: *The Ancient Egyptian Pyramid Texts*. 2nd ed. Translated with an Introduction and Notes by James P. Allen, 88–93, esp. p. 88. Atlanta, GA: Society of Biblical Literature, 2005.
———. "Spells for the Spirit's Rebirth (Antechamber, East Gable and Wall)." In: *The Ancient Egyptian Pyramid Texts*. 2nd ed. Translated with an Introduction and Notes by James P. Allen, 283–289, esp. p. 288. Atlanta, GA: Society of Biblical Literature, 2005.
Walton, John H. "Genesis." In: *Zondervan Illustrated Bible Backgrounds Commentary, Vol. 1:* 35–36.

3:16–19 Punishment of the humans – an etiology

Gunkel, Hermann. *The Legends of Genesis*. Translated by William Herbert Carruth Chicago, IL: Open Court Publishing Company, 1901.
Sarna. *The JPS Torah Commentary: Genesis*, 29.

3:20 Ḥava – mother of all life

Ackerman, Susan. "Asherah/Asherim: Bible." In: *Shalvi/Hyman Encyclopedia of Jewish Women*. 31 December 1999. Jewish Women's Archive. (Viewed on March 8, 2022). Available at: https://jwa.org/encyclopedia/article/asherahasherim-bible.
Kapelrud, A. S. "Chavvah." In: *Theological Dictionary of the Old Testament, Vol. 4*, 257-260, esp. p. 258. Grand Rapids, MI: Eerdmans, 1980,
Sarna. *The JPS Torah Commentary: Genesis*, 29.

3:24 Cherubim (*keruvim*)

Sarna. "Excursus 1: The Cherubim." In: *The JPS Torah Commentary: Genesis*, 375–376.
Tawil, Hayim ben Yosef. "כרוב." In: *An Akkadian Lexical Companion for Biblical Hebrew*, 173.

3:24 Flaming, whirling sword

Albright, W. F. "What Were the Cherubim?" *Biblical Archaeologist* 1(1) 1938: 1–3.
Barnett, Richard D. "Ancient Ivories in the Middle East and Adjacent Countries." *Qedem* 14 (1982): 1–99, esp. p. 43–55, pls. 45–53.
Cagni, Luigi. *The Poem of Erra.* Malibu, CA: Undena, 1977.
Fox, Michael V. *Anchor Bible: Proverbs 1–9, A New Translation with Introduction and Commentary,* 279–281. New York: Doubleday, 2000.
Hendel, Ronald S. "'The Flame of the Whirling Sword': A Note on Genesis 3:24." *Journal of Biblical Literature* 104(4) 1985: 671–674.
Sarna. *The JPS Torah Commentary: Genesis,* 32, 355n1.
Speiser. *Anchor Bible: Genesis,* 24–25.

4:1 With the Lord's help, I have made (*kaniti*)

Sarna. *The JPS Torah Commentary: Genesis,* 32, 355n1, 379.
Fox, Michael V. *Anchor Bible: Proverbs 1–9,* 177. New Haven, CT: Yale University Press, 2000.
Lete, Gregorio del Olmo, and Joaquín Sanmartín. "Thm." In: *A Dictionary of the Ugaritic Language in the Alphabetic Tradition. Part Two.* Leiden: Brill, 2004., s.v. *q-n-y,* 3

4:2 Shepherds and farmers

Kramer, Samuel N. "Inanna Prefers the Farmer." In: *Sumerian Mythology: A Study of Spiritual and Literary Achievement in the Third Millennium B.C.,* Rev. ed., 101–103 New York: Harper and Brothers, 1961.
Sarna. *The JPS Torah Commentary: Genesis,* 32.
Walton, John H. "Genesis." In: *Zondervan Illustrated Bible Backgrounds Commentary, Vol. 1:* 38.

4:3–4 Offering

Milgrom. *The Anchor Bible: Leviticus 1–16,* 195–196.
Walton, John H. "Genesis." In: *Zondervan Illustrated Bible Backgrounds Commentary, Vol. 1:* 38.

4:7 Sin is crouching at the door

Speiser. *Anchor Bible: Genesis,* 33.
Tawil, Hayim ben Yosef. "רבץ." In: *An Akkadian Lexical Companion for Biblical Hebrew,* 358–359.

4:14 Whoever finds me will kill me

Roth, Martha T. "Middle Assyrian Laws." In: *Law Collections from Mesopotamia and Asia Minor,* 153–194, esp. p. 176. Atlanta, GA: Scholars Press, 1995.
Sarna. *The JPS Torah Commentary: Genesis,* 35.
Van den Hout, Th. P. J., trans. "Proclamation of Telipinu (1.76). In: *COS, Vol. 1:* 194–198, esp. p. 198.
Walton, John H. "Genesis." In: *Zondervan Illustrated Bible Backgrounds Commentary, Vol. 1:* 40.

4:17–22 Kayin and the beginnings of civilization

Sarna. *The JPS Torah Commentary: Genesis,* 35–37.
Walton, John H. "Genesis." In: *Zondervan Illustrated Bible Backgrounds Commentary, Vol. 1:* 40–42.

4:17 The first city

Hallo, W. W. "Antediluvian Cities." *Journal of Cuneiform Studies* 23(3) 1971: 57–67: esp. p. 61, 64.
Walton, John H. "Genesis." In: *Zondervan Illustrated Bible Backgrounds Commentary, Vol. 1:* 40–41.

4:19 Married two women

Marsman, Hennie J. *Women in Ugarit and Israel: Their Social and Religious Position in the Context of the Ancient Near East,* 43–471, esp. p. 126–129. Leiden: Brill, 2003.
Roth, Martha T. "Laws of Hammurabi." In: *Law Collections from Mesopotamia and Asia Minor,* 71–142, esp. p. 108. Atlanta, GA: Scholars Press, 1995.
Walton, John H. "Genesis." In: *Zondervan Illustrated Bible Backgrounds Commentary,* Vol. 1: 41.

4:21 The lyre and the pipe

Braun, Joachim. "Introduction." In: *Music in Ancient Israel/Palestine: Archaeological, Written, and Comparative Sources,* 1–45, esp. p. 31–32. Grand Rapids, MI: Eerdmans, 2002.

———. "The Stone Age (Twelfth Millennium–3200 B.C.)." In: *Music in Ancient Israel/Palestine,* 47–65, esp. p. 59–64. Grand Rapids, MI: Eerdmans, 2002.

Goodman, Julianne. "Silver Flute from Ur." Available at: https://pennds.org/nelc133/exhibits/show/object_biographies/ur_flute

Sarna. *The JPS Torah Commentary: Genesis,* 37.

Walton, John H. "Genesis." In: *Zondervan Illustrated Bible Backgrounds Commentary, Vol. 1:* 41.

4:22 Forged ... bronze and iron tools

Maes-Diop, Louise-Marie. In: "Assessment of the Dating of Ancient Relics of Ironworking in Africa: Main Lessons." In: *The Origins of Iron Metallurgy in Africa: New Light on Its Antiquity, West and Central Africa,* edited by Hamady Bacoum,189–193, esp. p. 190. Paris. UNSECO, 2004.

Moorey, P. R. S. "Base Metals." In: *Ancient Mesopotamian Materials and Industries: The Archaeological Evidence,* 240–301, esp. p. 255. Winona Lake, IN: Eisenbrauns, 1999, p. 255.

Sarna. *The JPS Torah Commentary: Genesis,* 38.

Walton, John H. "Genesis." In: *Zondervan Illustrated Bible Backgrounds Commentary, Vol. 1:* 41–42.

4:25–26 When people began to pray in the name of the Lord

Sarna. *The JPS Torah Commentary: Genesis,* 39–40.

Walton, John H. "Genesis." In: *Zondervan Illustrated Bible Backgrounds Commentary, Vol. 1:* 42.

5:1–32 Ten generations

Albright, W. F. "The Babylonian Antediluvian Kings." *Journal of the American Oriental Society* 43 (1923): 323–329.

Cassuto, Umberto. "The Book of the History of Adam." In: *A Commentary on the Book of Genesis. Part I: From Adam to Noah Genesis I–VI:8*. Translated by Israel Abrahams, 249–307, esp. p. 258. Jerusalem: Magnes Press, 1972.

Sarna. *The JPS Torah Commentary: Genesis,* 40–41.

Walton, John H. "Genesis." In: *Zondervan Illustrated Bible Backgrounds Commentary, Vol. 1:* 42 (sidebar: "Sumerian King List and Long Lives.").

5:3 Adam ... had a son in his own likeness and image

Walton, John H. "Genesis." In: *Zondervan Illustrated Bible Backgrounds Commentary, Vol. 1:* 42–43.

5:24 Ḥanokh walked faithfully with God ... God took him

Buber, Solomon, ed. *Pesiqta deRav Kahana*. Lyck: Mekitzei Nirdamim, 1868, 154b–155a.

Cassuto, Umberto. "The Book of the History of Adam." In: *A Commentary on the Book of Genesis. Part I: From Adam to Noah Genesis I–VI:8*. Translated by Israel Abrahams, 249–307, esp. p. 282–283. Jerusalem: Magnes Press, 1972.

Walton, John H. "Genesis." In: *Zondervan Illustrated Bible Backgrounds Commentary, Vol. 1:* 43.

5:29 This one will bring us comfort

Burrows, E. "Notes on Harrian." *The Journal of the Royal Asiatic Society of Great Britain and Ireland* 2 (1925): 287–294, esp. p. 281–282.

Cassuto, Umberto. "The Book of the History of Adam." In: *A Commentary on the Book of Genesis. Part I: From Adam to Noah Genesis I–VI:8*. Translated by Israel Abrahams, 249–307, esp. p. 288. Jerusalem: Magnes Press, 1972.

Sarna. *The JPS Torah Commentary: Genesis,* 44.

6:1–4 *Benei ha'elohim*

Cassuto, Umberto. "The Book of the History of Adam." In: *A Commentary on the Book of Genesis. Part I: From Adam to Noah Genesis I–VI:8*. Translated by Israel Abrahams, 249–307, esp. p. 291–301. Jerusalem: Magnes Press, 1972.

Hoffmann, David Z. *The Book of Genesis: Commentary, Vol. 1:* 129–137. Trans. A. Wasserteil. Bnei Brak, Israel: Nezach, 1969.
Sarna. *The JPS Torah Commentary: Genesis,* 45.

6:4 Nefilim

Kilmer, Anne Draffkorn. "The Mesopotamian Counterparts of the Biblical Nepilim." In: *Perspectives on Language and Text,* edited by Edgar W. Conrad and Edward G. Newing, 39–44. Winona Lake, IN: Eisenbrauns, 1987.
Walton, John H. "Genesis." In: *Zondervan Illustrated Bible Backgrounds Commentary, Vol. 1:* 45–46.

6:5–22 The flood story in the Bible and ancient Mesopotamia

Frymer-Kensky, T. "The Atrahasis Epic and Its Significance for Our Understanding of Genesis 1–9." *Biblical Archaeologist* 40(4) 1977: 147–155.
Heidel, Alexander. *The Gilgamesh Epic and Old Testament Parallels,* 2nd ed. Chicago, IL: University of Chicago, 1949.
Klein, Jacob. "A New Look at the Theological Background of the Mesopotamian and Biblical Flood Stories." *A Common Cultural Heritage: Studies in Mesopotamia and the Biblical World in Honor of Barry L. Eichler,* edited by Grant Frame, Erle Leichty, Karen Sonik, Jeffrey H. Tigay, and Steve Tinney, 151–176. Bethesda, MD: CDL Press, 2011.
Sarna. *The JPS Torah Commentary: Genesis,* 48–50.
———. "Excursus 2: The Chronology of the Flood." *The JPS Torah Commentary: Genesis,* 376.
Unterman, Jeremiah. "The Jewish Bible's Unique Understanding of God: The Ethical Relationship of God to the World and Humanity." In: *Justice for All: How the Jewish Bible Revolutionized Ethics,* 1–14, esp. p. 8–14; 188–190 (notes). Philadelphia, PA: Jewish Publication Society, 2017.
Walton, John H. "Genesis." In: *Zondervan Illustrated Bible Backgrounds Commentary, Vol. 1:* 46–53.

6:14–16 The ark and boats in the ancient Near East

Sarna. *The JPS Torah Commentary: Genesis,* 52.
Walton, John H. "Genesis." In: *Zondervan Illustrated Bible Backgrounds Commentary, Vol. 1:* 46.

6:18 Covenant

Sarna. *The JPS Torah Commentary: Genesis,* 53.

7:2–3 Pure animals and birds

Foster, Benjamin R., trans. "Atra-Hasis (1.130)" In: *COS, Vol. 1:* 450–452, esp. p. 452.
Walton, John H. "Genesis." In: *Zondervan Illustrated Bible Backgrounds Commentary, Vol. 1:* 47.

7:4–12 The numbers seven, forty, six hundred

Carasik, Michael. "Completion of the days of *miluim.*" In: *The Koren Tanakh of the Land of Israel: Leviticus,* 53.
Cole, R. Dennis. "Numbers." In: *Zondervan Illustrated Bible Backgrounds Commentary, Vol. 1:* 359.
Friberg, Jöran. "Numbers and Counting." In: *Anchor Bible Dictionary, Vol. 4,* 1139–1146, esp. p. 1144.
Goodfriend, Elaine. "Seven, the Biblical Number" *Torah.com.* Available at: https://www.thetorah.com/article/seven-the-biblical-number.
Ron, Zvi. "Seven-day fast." In: *The Koren Tanakh of the Land of Israel: I Samuel,* 216.
Walton, John H. "Genesis." In: *Zondervan Illustrated Bible Backgrounds Commentary, Vol. 1:* 51.
———. "Historical Literature." In: *Ancient Israelite Literature in Its Cultural Context,* 111–134, esp. p. 128–129. Grand Rapids, MI: Zondervan, 1990.

8:4 The mountains of Ararat

Sarna. *The JPS Torah Commentary: Genesis,* 57.
Walton, John H. "Genesis." In: *Zondervan Illustrated Bible Backgrounds Commentary, Vol. 1:* 51.

8:11 Freshly picked olive leaf

Sarna. *The JPS Torah Commentary: Genesis*, 58.

Schultz, Colin. "The Oldest Olive Oil Ever Found Is 8,000 Years Old." *Smithsonian Magazine*, December 19, 2014. Available at: https://www.smithsonianmag.com/smart-news/oldest-olive-oil-ever-found-its-8000-years-old-180953678/.

Walton, John H. "Genesis." In: *Zondervan Illustrated Bible Backgrounds Commentary, Vol. 1:* 52.

8:20–21 Noah's sacrifice and God's response

Sarna. *The JPS Torah Commentary: Genesis*, 59.

Walton, John H. "Genesis." In: *Zondervan Illustrated Bible Backgrounds Commentary, Vol. 1:* 52–53.

9:1–7 God's new blessing to humanity

Sarna. *The JPS Torah Commentary: Genesis*, 60–62.

Unterman, Jeremiah. "The Revelation at Sinai: Ethical Implications of the God-Israel Relationship." In: *Justice for All: How the Jewish Bible Revolutionized Ethics*, 15–40, esp. p. 25–30; 195–196 (notes). Philadelphia, PA: Jewish Publication Society, 2017.

Walton, John H. "Genesis." In: *Zondervan Illustrated Bible Backgrounds Commentary, Vol. 1:* 53.

9:18–19 9:8–17 God's eternal covenant with life on Earth

Hendel, Ronald. "The Rainbow in Ancient Context," *TheTorah.com*, 2016, retrieved 12/28/2022, https://thetorah.com/the-rainbow-in-ancient-context.

Sarna. *The JPS Torah Commentary: Genesis*, 62–63.

Unterman, Jeremiah. *Justice for All: How the Jewish Bible Revolutionized Ethics*, 13. Philadelphia, PA: Jewish Publication Society, 2017

Walton, John H. "Genesis." In: *Zondervan Illustrated Bible Backgrounds Commentary, Vol. 1:* 9:13.

9:18–19 Regeneration of humanity

Foster, Benjamin R., trans. "Atra-Hasis (1.130)' In: *COS, Vol. 1*: 450–452, esp. p. 452.

Sarna. *The JPS Torah Commentary: Genesis*, 65.

9:20–21 Viticulture and viniculture

Goor, Asaph. "The History of the Grape-Vine in the Holy Land." *Economic Botany* 20(1) (1966): 46–64.

King, Philip and Lawrence Stager. "The Means of Existence." In: *Life in Biblical Israel*, 85–200, esp. p. 98–101. Louisville, KY: Westminster John Knox Press, 2001.

Sarna. *The JPS Torah Commentary: Genesis*, 65.

Walton, John H. "Genesis." In: *Zondervan Illustrated Bible Backgrounds Commentary, Vol. 1*: 53–54.

9:22–27 Characteristics of Ḥam and Kenaan

Sarna. *The JPS Torah Commentary: Genesis*, 64, 66.

10:1–32 The seventy nations

Hess, Richard. "The Genealogies of Genesis 1–11 and Comparative Literature." *Biblica* 70(2) 1989: 241–254.

Pardee, Dennis, trans. "The Ba'lu Myth (1.86)." In: *COS, Vol. 1*: 241–274.

Sarna. "The Table of Nations." In: *The JPS Torah Commentary: Genesis*, 67–80.

Walton, John H. "Genesis." In: *Zondervan Illustrated Bible Backgrounds Commentary, Vol. 1*: 56–60.

10:2–5 Yefet's sons

Montenegro, Julia and Arcádio del Castillo. "The Location of Tarshish: Critical Considerations." *Revue Biblique* 123(2) 2016: 239–268.

Sarna. "The Japhethites." In: *The JPS Torah Commentary: Genesis*, 70.

Speiser. *Anchor Bible: Genesis*, 65–66.

10:6 The four Hamite groups

Olam HaTanakh Encyclopedia: Genesis. Tel Aviv: Revivim, 1993. 74 (Hebrew).
Sarna. "The Hamites." *The JPS Torah Commentary: Genesis,* 72–77.

10:7 The descendants of Kush: Arabia and Africa

Astour, Michael C. "Sabtah and Sabteca: Ethiopian Pharaoh Names in Genesis 10." *Journal of Biblical Literature* 84(4) 1965: 422–425.
Olam HaTanakh Encyclopedia: Genesis. Tel Aviv: Revivim, 1993. 74 (Hebrew).
Sarna. "The Hamites." In: *The JPS Torah Commentary: Genesis,* 72–77.

10:8–12 The descendants of Kush: Asia

Sarna. *The JPS Torah Commentary: Genesis,* 72–77.
Olam HaTanakh Encyclopedia: Genesis. Tel Aviv: Revivim, 1993. 74 (Hebrew).

10:13–19 The Hamites: Mitzrayim and Kenaan

Olam HaTanakh Encyclopedia: Genesis. Tel Aviv: Revivim, 1993. 74 (Hebrew).
Ron, Zvi. "Amorites." In: *The Koren Tanakh of the Land of Israel: Numbers,* 83.
Sarna. *The JPS Torah Commentary: Genesis,* 72.

10:21–30 The Shemites

MicKinny, Chris. "Finding Mash and His Brothers – The Historical Geography of the Sons of Aram (Gen 10:23; 1 Chr 1:17)." In: *To Explore the Land of Canaan: Studies in Biblical Archaeology in Honor of Jeffrey R. Chadwick,* edited by Aren M. Maeir and George A. Pierce, 37–50, esp. p. 45. Boston, MA: De Gruyter, 2022.
Olam HaTanakh Encyclopedia: Genesis. Tel Aviv: Revivim, 1993. 76 (Hebrew).
"Palgu." In: *The Assyrian Dictionary (CAD), Vol. 12: P,* 62.
Sarna. *The JPS Torah Commentary: Genesis,* 77–80.
Speiser. E. A., trans. "The Epic of Gilgamesh." In: *Ancient Near Eastern Texts Relating to the Old Testament (ANET):* 72–99, esp. p. 88.
———. *Anchor Bible: Genesis,* 70.

11:1–9 Tower of Bavel

George, Andrew. "The Tower of Babel: Archaeology, History and Cuneiform Texts." *Archiv für Orientforschung* 51 (2005): 75–95.
Sarna. *The JPS Torah Commentary: Genesis,* 80–84.
Walton, John H. "Genesis." In: *Zondervan Illustrated Bible Backgrounds Commentary, Vol. 1:* 60–65.

11:2 Shinar

Sarna. *The JPS Torah Commentary: Genesis,* 74, 81.

11:2–3 Making bricks in the valley of Shinar

Sarna. *The JPS Torah Commentary: Genesis,* 81–83, esp. p. 81–82, 357n1.
Walton, John H. "Genesis." In: *Zondervan Illustrated Bible Backgrounds Commentary, Vol. 1:* 60–61.

11:8 They abandoned the building of the city

Beaulieu, Paul-Alain. "Samsu-ditana (1625–1595)." In: *A History of Babylon, 2200 BC–AD 75.* Medford, MA: John Wiley and Sons, 2018, p. 117–119.
Sarna. *The JPS Torah Commentary: Genesis,* 84.

11:9 Bavel…because the Lord confused the language

"Balālu." In: *Concise Dictionary of Akkadian,* edited by Jeremy Black, Andrew George, and Nicholas Postgate, 36. Wiesbaden, Harrassowitz, 2000.
"בלל." In: *Dictionary of Classical Hebrew Revised,* edited by David J. A. Clines, 22–23. Sheffield, UK: Sheffield Phoenix Press, 2019.
"בלל." In: *The Hebrew and Aramaic Lexicon of the Old Testament. Vol. 1,* 104–108.

Sarna. *The JPS Torah Commentary: Genesis*, 84.

11:10–26 From Shem to Avram

Hess, Richard S. "Terah." In: *Anchor Bible Dictionary, Vol. 6*, 387–388.
———. "Nahor." In: *Anchor Bible Dictionary, Vol. 4*, 996–997.
———. "Serug." In: *Anchor Bible Dictionary, Vol. 5*, 1117–1118.
Kobayashi, Yoshitaka. "Haran" (Place). In: *Anchor Bible Dictionary, Vol. 3*, 58–59.
Rainey, Anson and R. Steven Notley. "The Ancient World View." In: *The Sacred Bridge: Carta's Atlas of the Biblical World*, 25–29, esp. p. 27. Jerusalem: Carta, 2006.
Sarna. *The JPS Torah Commentary: Genesis*, 84–88.
Speiser. *Anchor Bible: Genesis*, 78.
Walton, John H. "Genesis." In: *Zondervan Illustrated Bible Backgrounds Commentary, Vol. 1*: 65–67.

11:28 Ur Kasdim

Rendsburg, Gary. Ur Kasdim: Where Is Abraham's Birthplace?, *The Torah.com* Available at: https://www.thetorah.com/article/ur-kasdim-where-is-abrahams-birthplacehttps://www.thetorah.com/article/ur-kasdim-where-is-abrahams-birthplace.
Sarna. *The JPS Torah Commentary: Genesis*, 84–86.
Walton, John H. "Genesis." In: *Zondervan Illustrated Bible Backgrounds Commentary, Vol. 1*: 65–68.

12 The religious revolution of God's personal relationship with Avraham

Abusch, Tzvi. "Witchcraft and the Anger of the Personal God." *Mesopotamian Magic: Textual, Historical, and Interpretative Perspectives*, edited by Tzvi Abusch and Karel van der Toorn, 83–121, esp. p. 105–107. Groningen: Styx, 1999.
———. "Ghost and God: Some Observations on a Babylonian Understanding of Human Nature." In: *Self, Soul and Body in Religious Experience*, edited by Albert I. Baumgarten, 363–383, esp. p. 378–381. Leiden: Brill, 1998.
Eshel, Tzilla. "How Silver Was Used for Payment." *TheTorah.com*. Available at: https://www.thetorah.com/article/how-silver-was-used-for-payment.
Jacobsen, Thorkild. "Second Millennium Metaphors. The Gods as Parents: Rise of Personal Religion." In: *The Treasures of Darkness: A History of Mesopotamian Religion*, 145–164, esp. p. 147, 155–157, 159, 164. New Haven, CT: Yale University Press, 1976.
Sarna. *The JPS Torah Commentary: Genesis*, 88–90, esp. p. 88–89.
Toorn, K. van der. "The Veneration of Family Gods: A Local Focus of Identity." In: *Family Religion in Babylonia, Syria and Israel*, 66–93, esp. p. 73–84. Leiden: Brill, 1996.
Unterman, Jeremiah. "*Ger vetoshav*." In: *The Koren Tanakh of the Land of Israel: Genesis*, 140.
———. "Providing for the Disadvantaged: The Stranger, the Poor, the Widow, and the Orphan." In: *Justice for All: How the Jewish Bible Revolutionized Ethics*, 41–84, esp. p. 42–45; 202–204 (notes). Philadelphia, PA: Jewish Publication Society, 2017.
Walton, John H. "Genesis." In: *Zondervan Illustrated Bible Backgrounds Commentary, Vol. 1*: 69, sidebar. "Personal God in Mesopotamia."

12:1 Go – from your land, your birthplace, and your father's house

Sarna. *The JPS Torah Commentary: Genesis*, 88–89.
Toorn, K. van der. "The Veneration of Family Gods: A Local Focus of Identity." In: *Family Religion in Babylonia, Syria and Israel*, 66–93, esp. p. 66–72. Leiden: Brill, 1996,
Walton, John H. "Genesis." In: *Zondervan Illustrated Bible Backgrounds Commentary, Vol. 1*: 68–69.

12:2 I will make you a great nation, and I will bless you and will make your name great

Assmann, Jan. "The 'Name Formula'" In: *The Search for God in Ancient Egypt*, 83–86, esp. p. 84–85. Ithaca, NY; Cornell University Press, 2001.
Sarna. *The JPS Torah Commentary: Genesis*, 89.

Walton, John H. "Genesis." In: *Zondervan Illustrated Bible Backgrounds Commentary, Vol. 1:* 69.

12:5 Canaan

Na'aman, Nadav. "The Canaanites and Their Land." In: *Canaan in the 2nd Millennium BCE: Collected Essays, Vol. 2,* 110–133. Winona Lake, IN: Eisenbrauns, 2005.

Rainey, Anson F. and R. Steven Notley. "The Land Bridge." In: *The Sacred Bridge: Carta's Atlas of the Biblical World,* 30–42, esp. p. 34–36. Jerusalem: Carta, 2006.

Walton, John H. "Genesis." In: *Zondervan Illustrated Bible Backgrounds Commentary, Vol. 1:* 69–70.

12:6 Canaanites

Cassuto, Umberto. "Abraham and the Promised Land." In: *A Commentary on the Book of Genesis. Part II: From Noah to Abraham Genesis VI:9–XI:32.* Translated by Israel Abrahams, 291–369, esp. p. 327–328. Jerusalem: Magnes Press, 1972.

Killebrew, Anne E. "Canaan and Canaanites: An Ethnic Mosaic." In: *Biblical Peoples and Ethnicity: An Archaeological Study of Egyptians, Canaanites, Philistines, and Early Israel 1300–1100 B.C.E,* 93–148, esp. p. 94, 95. Atlanta, GA: SBL Press, 2005.

Levin, Yigal. "Who Was Living in the Land When Abraham Arrived?" *The Torah.com.* Available at: https://www.thetorah.com/article/who-was-living-in-the-land-when-abraham-arrived.

Walton, John H. "Genesis." In: *Zondervan Illustrated Bible Backgrounds Commentary, Vol. 1:* 72.

12:6 Oak of Moreh

Jacob, Irene and Jacob, Walter. "Flora." In: *Anchor Bible Dictionary, Vol. 2,* 803–817, esp. p. 806.

Sarna. *The JPS Torah Commentary: Genesis,* 91.

12:6 Shekhem and the patriarchs

Campbell, Edward F., Jr. and James F. Ross. "The Excavation of Shechem and the Biblical Tradition." *The Biblical Archaeologist.* 26(1) 1963: 1–27.

Magen, I. "Shechem: Tel Balatah." In: *Encyclopedia of Archaeological Excavations in the Holy Land.* Vol. 4, edited by Michael Avi-Yona and Ephraim Stern, 1345–1359, esp. p. 1346–1352. Jerusalem: The Israel Exploration Society and Carta, 1993.

Meitlis, Itzhak. *Excavating the Bible: New Archaeological Evidence for the Historical Reliability of Scripture.* Baltimore, MD: Eshel Books, 2012.

12:7 Promise of land

Nissinen, Martti. "Nur-sin to Zimri-lim." In: *Prophets and Prophecy in the Ancient Near East,* 17–20, esp. p. 17, 19. Atlanta, GA: SBL Press, 2019.

Sarna. *The JPS Torah Commentary: Genesis,* 91–92.

Unterman, Jeremiah. "The Primacy of Morality over Ritual: A Prophetic Innovation." In: *Justice for All: How the Jewish Bible Revolutionized Ethics,* 85–108, esp. p. 90. Philadelphia, PA: Jewish Publication Society, 2017.

12:7 There he built an altar to the Lord

Sarna. *The JPS Torah Commentary: Genesis,* 92–93,

———. "Excursus 22: Bethel." In: *The JPS Torah Commentary: Genesis,* 398–400.

Walton, John H. "Genesis." In: *Zondervan Illustrated Bible Backgrounds Commentary, Vol. 1:* 72–73.

12:8 Beit El and Ai

Callaway, Joseph. "Ai." In: *The New Encyclopedia of Archaeological Excavations in the Holy Land, Vol. 1,* edited by Ephraim Stern, 39–45. Jerusalem: The Israel Exploration Society & Carta, 1993.

Kelso, James L. 1993. "Bethel." In: *The New Encyclopedia of Archaeological Excavations in the Holy Land,* edited by Ephraim Stern, *Vol. 1,* 192–194. Jerusalem: The Israel Exploration Society & Carta, 1993.

Tavger, Aharon. "E.P. 914 east of Beitin and the Location of the Ancient Cult Site of Bethel." In: *In the Highland's Depth* (IHD) 5(2015): 49–69 (Hebrew).

12:9 Negev

Cavanagh, Mark, Ben-Yosef, Erez and Langgut, Dafna. "Fuel exploitation and environmental degradation at the Iron Age copper industry of the Timna Valley, southern Israel." Scientific Reports 12(1) 2022: 15434.

Evenari, Michael, Leslie Shanan, and Naphtali Tadmor. "The Negev: A Dessert." In: *The Negev: The Challenge of a Desert*, 29–38, esp. p. 30–33. Cambridge, MA: Harvard University Press, 1982.

Rosen, Steven A. "Negeb." In: *Anchor Bible Dictionary, Vol. 4*, 1061–1064.

Sarna. *The JPS Torah Commentary: Genesis*, 92.

Walton, John H. "Genesis." In: *Zondervan Illustrated Bible Backgrounds Commentary, Vol. 1*: 73.

12:10 Egypt

Sarna. *The JPS Torah Commentary: Genesis*, 93 (last two full paragraphs).

Walton, John H. "Genesis." In: *Zondervan Illustrated Bible Backgrounds Commentary, Vol. 1*: 74.

Wilson, John W. "The Pursuit of Runaway Slaves." In: *Ancient Near Eastern Texts Relating to the Old Testament (ANET)*: 259

12:10 Famine in the land

Sarna. *The JPS Torah Commentary: Genesis*, 93.

Walton, John H. "Genesis." In: *Zondervan Illustrated Bible Backgrounds Commentary, Vol. 1*: 73–74, 147n296–299.

Weiss, H., Courty, M-A., Wetterstrom, W., Guichard, F., Senior, L., Meadow, R. and Curnow, A. (1993). "The Genesis and Collapse of Third Millennium North Mesopotamian Civilization." *Science* 261(5124) 1993: 995–1004.

Wilford, John Noble. "Collapse of Earliest Known Empire Is Linked to Long, Harsh Drought." *New York Times*, August 24, 1993.

12:13 The sister-wives

Eichler, Barry L. "On Reading Genesis 12:10–20." In: *Tehilla le-Moshe: Biblical and Judaic Studies in Honor of Moshe Greenberg*, edited by Mordechai Cogan, Barry L. Eichler, and Jeffrey H. Tigay, 23–38. Winona Lake, IN: Eisenbrauns, 1997.

Weinfeld, Moshe. "Sarah and Abimelech (Genesis 20) Against the Background of an Assyrian Law and the Genesis Apocryphon." In: *Mélanges bibliques et orientaux en l'honneur de M. Mathias Delcor*, edited by A. Caquot, S. Légasse, and M. Tardieu, 431–436. Neukirchen-Vluyn: Neukirchener Verlag, 1985.

12:16 Domestication of camels

Free, Joseph P. "Avraham's Camels." *Journal of Near Eastern Studies* 3(3) 1944: 187–193.

Heide, Martin. "The Domestication of the Camel: Biological, Archaeological, and Inscriptional Evidence from Mesopotamia, Egypt, Israel, and Arabia, and Literary Evidence from the Bible." *Ugarit-Forschungen* 42 (2010): 148–184.

Horowitz, Wayne. "The Ship of the Desert, the Donkey of the Sea": The Camel in Early Mesopotamia Revisited." In: *Birkat Shalom: Studies in the Bible, Ancient Near Eastern Literature, and Postbiblical Judaism Presented to Shalom M. Paul on the Occasion of His Seventieth Birthday. Vol. 2*, edited by Chaim Cohen, Victor Avigdor Hurowitz, Avi M. Hurvitz, Yochanan Muffs, Baruch J. Schwartz, and Jeffrey H. Tigay, 597–612. Winona Lake, IN: Eisenbrauns, 2008.

"Ibilu." In: *The Assyrian Dictionary (CAD), Vol. 7: I and J.*

Leiman, S. Z. "The Camel in the Patriarchal Narrative." *The Yavneh Review* 6 (1967): 16–26.

Ripinsky, Michael. "The Camel in Dynastic Egypt." *The Journal of Egyptian Archaeology* 71 (1985): 134–141.

Speiser. *Anchor Bible: Genesis*, 90.

Wapnish, Paula. "Camel Caravans and Camel Pastoralists at Tell Jemmeh." *The Journal of the Ancient Near Eastern Society* 13(1) 1981: 101–121.

13:6–7 Dispute between shepherds

Sarna. *The JPS Torah Commentary: Genesis*, 93.

Walton, John H. "Genesis." In: *Zondervan Illustrated Bible Backgrounds Commentary, Vol. 1:* 75.

13:10 Sedom, Tzoar, and the "Five Cities"

Collins, Steven. *The Tall al-Hammam Excavations.* Winona Lake, IN: Eisenbrauns, 2015.
Juda, Uri. *Sedom: A New Identification.* Unpublished M.A. thesis, Bar-Ilan University, 2017.
Konstantinos D. Politis. *Ancient Landscapes of Zoara I: Surveys and Excavations at the Ghor As-Safi in Jordan, 1997–2018.* New York: Routledge, 2020.

13:14–17 Gift of land to Avram

Sarna. *The JPS Torah Commentary: Genesis,* 99–100.
Walton, John H. "Genesis." In: *Zondervan Illustrated Bible Backgrounds Commentary, Vol. 1:* 76–77, 147n305–306.
Weinfeld, M. "The Covenant of Grant in the Old Testament and in the Ancient Near East." *Journal of the American Oriental Society* 90(2) 1970: 184–203.

13:18 Ḥevron

Sarna. *The JPS Torah Commentary: Genesis,* 101.
Walton, John H. "Genesis." In: *Zondervan Illustrated Bible Backgrounds Commentary, Vol. 1:* 77, 147n307–311.

14:1 War of the four and five kings

"Apilu." In: *The Assyrian Dictionary (CAD), Vol. 2: A,* 170.
"Aplu." In: *The Assyrian Dictionary (CAD), Vol. 2: A,* 173–176.
Millard, Alan, trans. "The Weidner Chronicle (1.138)." In: *COS, Vol. 1:* 468–470.
Rainey, Anson F. and R. Steven Notley. "Excursus 7.2: The Apiru – A Social Phenomenon." In: *The Sacred Bridge: Carta's Atlas of the Biblical World.* Jerusalem: Carta, 2006, 88–90.
———. "Crisis and Transition: Twelfth Century BCE." In: *The Sacred Bridge: Carta's Atlas of the Biblical World,* 104–130, esp. p. 113–116. Jerusalem: Carta, 2006.
Sarna. *The JPS Torah Commentary: Genesis*: 103–110, 377–382.
Speiser. *Anchor Bible: Genesis,* 105–109.

14:13 Avram the Hebrew

Sarna. *The JPS Torah Commentary: Genesis,* 101–107. 388–379.
Speiser. *Anchor Bible: Genesis,* 103.
Walton, John H. "Genesis." In: *Zondervan Illustrated Bible Backgrounds Commentary, Vol. 1:* 14:13.

14:13 Mamre, Eshkol, Aner

Hess, Richard S., trans. "The Agreement Between Ir-Addu and Niqmepa (*AT* 2) (2.128)" In: *COS, Vol.* 2: 329–331, esp. p. 330.
Sarna. *The JPS Torah Commentary: Genesis,* 107.
Speiser. *Anchor Bible: Genesis,* 103.

14:14 Three hundred eighteen trained men

Heimpel, Wolfgang."Translation of Texts from ARM 26/1." In: *Letters to the King of Mari: A New Translation, with Historical Introduction,* 173–283, esp. p. 241. Winona Lake, IN: Eisenbrauns, 2003.
———. "Translation of Texts from ARM 26/2." *Letters to the King of Mari: A New Translation, with Historical Introduction,* 284–410, esp. p. 404. Winona Lake, IN: Eisenbrauns, 2003.
Sarna. *The JPS Torah Commentary: Genesis,* 108.
Walton, John H. "Genesis." In: *Zondervan Illustrated Bible Backgrounds Commentary, Vol. 1:* 81.

14:14 Redemption of captives

Sarna. *The JPS Torah Commentary: Genesis,* 379–380.

14:14 Pursuit as far as Dan

Luzzatto, Shmuel David. *The Commentary of Shadal on the Five Books of the Torah.* Tel Aviv: Devir, 1971 (Hebrew).

Pritchard, James B. *Ancient Near Eastern Text relating to the Old Testament.* 2nd edition, 1955, 242, 329.
Sarna. *The JPS Torah Commentary: Genesis,* 107–108.
"The Site of Tel Dan." Available at: https://www.teldanexcavations.com/the-site-of-tel-dan-https://www.teldanexcavations.com/the-site-of-tel-dan.
Walton, John H. "Genesis." In: *Zondervan Illustrated Bible Backgrounds Commentary, Vol. 1:* 81.

14:17 Shaveh Valley

Astour, Michael C. "Shaveh, Valley of." In: *Anchor Bible Dictionary, Vol.* 5, 1168.
Sarna. *The JPS Torah Commentary: Genesis,* 109.

14:18 Malki Tzedek, king of Shalem

Astour, Michael C. "Some New Divine Names from Ugarit." *Journal of the American Oriental Society* 86(3) 1966: 277–284, esp. p. 282–283.
Sarna. "Excursus 6: Melchizedek." In: *The JPS Torah Commentary: Genesis,* 380.
———. *The JPS Torah Commentary: Genesis,* 109–110.
Walton, John H. "Genesis." In: *Zondervan Illustrated Bible Backgrounds Commentary, Vol. 1:* 81–82.
———. "Melchizedek in Later Traditions." In: *Zondervan Illustrated Bible Backgrounds Commentary, Vol. 1:* 82.

14:18 Priest of God Most High

Rosenthal, Franz, trans. "The Treaty between *KTK* and Arpad." In: *Ancient Near Eastern Texts Relating to the Old Testament (ANET):* 659–661, esp. p. 659.
Sarna. "Excursus 7: 'El 'Elyon." In: *The JPS Torah Commentary: Genesis,* 381.
———. *The JPS Torah Commentary: Genesis,* 110.
Speiser. *Anchor Bible: Genesis,* 104, 109.
Walton, John H. "Genesis." In: *Zondervan Illustrated Bible Backgrounds Commentary, Vol. 1:* 81–82.

14:20 A tenth

Sarna. *The JPS Torah Commentary: Genesis,* 110.
Walton, John H. "Genesis." In: *Zondervan Illustrated Bible Backgrounds Commentary, Vol. 1:* 83.

14:22 Maker of heaven and earth

Handy, Lowell K. "The Elkunirsh Myth." In: *Among the Host of Heaven: The Syro-Palestinian Pantheon as Bureaucracy,* 34–36. Winona Lake, IN: Eisenbrauns, 1994.
Rosenthal, Franz, trans. "Building Inscriptions." In: *Ancient Near Eastern Texts Relating to the Old Testament (ANET):* 653–655, esp. p. 654.
Sarna. "Creator of Heaven and Earth." In: *The JPS Torah Commentary: Genesis,* 382.
Speiser. *Anchor Bible: Genesis,* 104.

14:24 Sharing the spoils

Elgavish, David. "The Division of the Spoils of War in the Bible and the Ancient Near East." *Zeitschrift für altorientalische und biblische Rechtsgeschichte (ZAR)* 8 (2002): 242–273, esp. p. 255–265.
Greenstein, Edward and David Marcus. "The Akkadian Inscription of Idrimi." *Journal of the Ancient Near Eastern Society* 8(1) 1976: 59–96, esp. p. 67.
Oppenheim, A. Leo, trans. "The Story of Idrimi, King of Alalakh." In: *Ancient Near Eastern Texts Relating to the Old Testament with Supplement,* edited by James B. Pritchard, 557–558, esp. p. 558. Princeton, NJ: Princeton University Press, 1969.
Ron, Zvi "Sharing the Spoils." In: *The Koren Tanakh of the Land of Israel: Samuel,* 211.

15:1 A vision

Nissinen, Martti. "Ancient Near Eastern Sources." In: *Ancient Prophecy: Near Eastern, Biblical, and Greek Perspectives,* 57–115, esp. p. 72, 77–78. New York: Oxford University Press, 2018.
Walton, John H. "Genesis." In: *Zondervan Illustrated Bible Backgrounds Commentary, Vol. 1:* 84, 148n341–342.

15:1 Do not be afraid

Conrad, Edgar W. "The 'Fear Not' Oracles in Second Isaiah." *Vetus Testamentum* 34(2) 1984: 129–152.

Nissinen, Martti. "Ancient Near Eastern Sources." In: *Ancient Prophecy: Near Eastern, Biblical, and Greek Perspectives*, 57–115, esp. p. 107, 109. New York: Oxford University Press, 2018.

Pfeiffer, Robert H., trans. "Akkadian Oracles and Prophesies." In: *Ancient Near Eastern Texts Relating to the Old Testament (ANET)*: 449–452, esp. p. 450.

Rosenthal, Franz, trans. "Cultic Inscriptions." In: *Ancient Near Eastern Texts Relating to the Old Testament (ANET)*: 655–658, esp. p. 655.

Sarna. *The JPS Torah Commentary: Genesis*, 112.

15:2 Childless

Milgrom, *The Anchor Bible: Leviticus*, 17–22, p. 1757–1758.

Pardee, Dennis, trans. "The Aqhatu Legend (1.103)." In: *COS, Vol. 1*: 343–356, esp. p. 344.

Tawil, Hayim ben Yosef. "רחם." In: *An Akkadian Lexical Companion for Biblical Hebrew*, 361–362, esp. p. 362.

Unterman, Jeremiah. "Barrenness in the ancient Near East." In: *The Koren Tanakh of the Land of Israel: Samuel*, 8.

15:2 Damascus

Cross, Frank Moore. "The Stele Dedicated to Melcarth by Ben-Hadad of Damascus." *Bulletin of the American Schools of Oriental Research*, 205 (1972): 36–42, esp. p. 41–42.

Pitard, Wayne T. "Damascus." In: *Anchor Bible Dictionary, Vol. 2*, 5–6.

Sarna. "Excursus 9: Ben Meshek – Dammesek 'Eli'ezer." *The JPS Torah Commentary: Genesis*, 382–383, esp. p. 383.

15:2–3 Adopting Eliezer

Garroway, Kristine Henriksen. "Adoption." In: *Children in the Ancient Near Eastern Household*, 48–91, esp. p. 68–85. Winona Lake, IN: Eisenbrauns, 2014.

Porten, Bezalel, trans. "Testament of Manumission (3.74)." In: *COS, Vol. 3*: 178–180.

Sarna, Nahum M. "Abraham's heir" In: *Understanding Genesis: The Heritage of Biblical Israel.* New York: Schocken Books, 1966, 122–123.

Steinberg, Naomi. *Kinship and Marriage in Genesis: A Household Economics Perspective.* Minneapolis, MN: Fortress Press, 1993, 60–61.

Suurmeijer, Guido. "'He Took Him as His Son,' Adoption in Old Babylonian Sippar." *Revue d'Assyroiologie et d'archaéologie orientale* 104(1) 2010: 9–40.

Walton, John H. "Genesis." In: *Zondervan Illustrated Bible Backgrounds Commentary, Vol. 1*: 84.

15:5 Innumerability of the stars in Mesopotamia

Held, Moshe. "A Faithful Lover in an Old Babylonian Dialogue." *Journal of Cuneiform Studies* 15, no. 1 (1961): 1–26, esp. p. 9.

Reiner, Erica. "Divination." In: *Astral Magic in Babylonia*, 61–80, esp. p. 67. Philadelphia, PA: The American Philosophical Society, 1995.

Walton, John H. "Genesis." In: *Zondervan Illustrated Bible Backgrounds Commentary, Vol. 1*: 84–85, 148n346–347.

15:9–17 The ritual acts of the covenant between the parts

Collins, Billy Jean, trans. "*The Ritual Between the Pieces* (1.61)." In: *COS, Vol. 1*: 160–161.

Hasel, Gerhard F. "The Meaning of the Animal Rite in Genesis 15." *Journal for the Study of the Old Testament* 6(19) (1981): 61–78.

Weinfeld, M. "The Covenant of Grant in the Old Testament and the Ancient Near East." *Journal of the American Oriental Society* 90(2) 1970, 184–203, esp. p. 196.

Zakovitch, Yair. "The Pattern of the Numerical Sequence Three-Four in the Bible." PhD dissertation, Hebrew University, 1977, p. 150–157.

15:18 The River of Egypt to... Euphrates

Sarna. *The JPS Torah Commentary: Genesis*, 117.
Walton, John H. "Genesis." In: *Zondervan Illustrated Bible Backgrounds Commentary, Vol. 1*: 86.

15:19–21 The ten nations of the covenant between the parts

Amzallag, Nissim. "Why Is the Cain Genealogy (Gen. 4:17–24) Integrated into the Book of Genesis?" *Ancient Near Eastern Studies* 55 (2018): 23–50.
Baker, David W. "Girgashite." In: *Anchor Bible Dictionary, Vol. 2*, 1028.
Ishida, Tomoo. "The Structure and Historical Implications of the Lists of Pre-Israelite Nations." *Biblica* 60(4) (1979): 461–490.
Rainey, Anson F. and R. Steven Notley. *The Sacred Bridge: Carta's Atlas of the Biblical World*. Jerusalem: Carta, 2006.
Singer, Itamar. "The Hittites and the Bible Revisited." In: *The Calm before the Storm: Selected Writings of Itamar Singer on the End of the Late Bronze Age in Anatolia and the Levant*, edited by Billy Jean Collins, 525–560. Atlanta, GA: Society of Biblical Literature, 2011.
Wasserman Nathan and Yigal Bloch, *The Amorites: Mesopotamia in the Early Second Millennium BCE*. Jerusalem: Carmel, 2019 (Hebrew).

16:2 Concubinage for the purpose of child-bearing

Finkelstein, J. J., trans. "Additional Mesopotamian Legal Documents." In: *Ancient Near Eastern Texts Relating to the Old Testament (ANET)*: 542–547, p. 543.
———. "Sumerian Laws." In: *Ancient Near Eastern Texts Relating to the Old Testament (ANET)*: 525–526, esp. p. 525.
Garroway, Kristine Henriksen. "What to Expect When You are (Not) Expecting." In: *Growing Up in Ancient Israel: Children in Material Culture and Biblical Texts*. Atlanta, GA: SBL Press, 2018.
Kramer, S. N., trans. "Lipit–Ishtar Lawcode." In: *Ancient Near Eastern Texts Relating to the Old Testament (ANET)*: 159–161, esp. p. 160.
Meeks, Theophile J., trans. "The Code of Hammurabi." In: *Ancient Near Eastern Texts Relating to the Old Testament (ANET)*: 163–180, esp. p. 172.
Sarna. *The JPS Torah Commentary: Genesis*, 118–120.
———. "Hagar the concubine." In: *Understanding Genesis: The Heritage of Biblical Israel*. New York: Schocken Books, 1966, 127–129.
Stol, Marten. "A Second Wife." In: *Women in the Ancient Near East*, 165–192, esp. p. 168–170. Boston, MA: De Gruyter, 2016.
Thompson, Thomas. "Nuzi and the Patriarchal Narratives." In: *The Historicity of the Patriarchal Narratives: The Quest for Historical Abraham*, 196–297, esp. p. 252–297. Boston, MA: DeGruyter, 2016.
Van Seters, John. "The Problem of Childlessness in near Eastern Law and the Patriarchs of Israel." *Journal of Biblical Literature* 87(4) 1968: 401–408.
Walton, John H. "Genesis." In: *Zondervan Illustrated Bible Backgrounds Commentary, Vol. 1*: 86–87.

16:7 Geography of Hagar's journey

Douglas, J. D., and Merrill C. Tenney, *Zondervan Illustrated Bible Dictionary*, 176, 184. Grand Rapids, MI: Zondervan, 2011.
Hoffmeier, James K. and Stephen O. Moshier. "'A Highway out of Egypt:' The Main Road from Egypt to Canaan." In: *Desert Road Archaeology in Ancient Egypt and Beyond*, edited by Frank Foerster and Heiko Riemer, 485–510, esp. p. 485–486. Cologne: Heinrich Barth Institute, 2013.

16:7 Angel of the Lord

Ginsberg, H. L., trans. "Poems about Baal and Anath." In: *Ancient Near Eastern Texts Relating to the Old Testament (ANET)*:129–142, esp. p. 135.
Hélena von Heijne, Camilla. "The Ambiguous Identity of the Angel." In: *The Messenger of the Lord in Early Jewish Interpretations of Genesis*, 49–120, esp. p. 49–52. Berlin: De Gruyter, 2010.
Sarna. "Excursus 10: Angelology." In: *The JPS Torah Commentary: Genesis*, 383–384.

Walton, John H. "Genesis." In: *Zondervan Illustrated Bible Backgrounds Commentary, Vol. 1:* 87–88, 149n365–368.

16:12 Wild donkey

Firmage, Edwin. "Zoology." In: *Anchor Bible Dictionary, Vol. 6,* 1109–1167, esp. p. 1135–1136.
"Onager." Available at: https://en.wikipedia.org/wiki/Onager.
Sarna. *The JPS Torah Commentary: Genesis,* 121, 360n.10.

17:1 El Shaddai

Kramer, S. N., trans. "Hymn to Enlil, the All-Beneficent." In: *Ancient Near Eastern Texts Relating to the Old Testament (ANET):* 573–576, esp. p. 575–576.
Knauf, E. A. "Shadday." *Dictionary of Deities and Demons in the Bible,* edited by K. van der Toorn, Bob Becking, and Pieter Willem van der Horst. Leiden: Brill, 1995, 749–751.
Niehr, H. "*Shadday.*" In: *Theological Dictionary of the Old Testament, Vol.14: D, Vol. 14,* 420–421, bottom of 422–424 (Deir Alla inscriptions).
Ron, Zvi. "Shaddai." In: The *Koren Tanakh of the Land of Israel: Numbers,* 159.
Sarna. "Excursus 11: 'El Shaddai." In: *The JPS Torah Commentary: Genesis,* 384–385.
"Šādu." In: *The Assyrian Dictionary (CAD), Vol. 16:* 57–59.
"שדי." In: *The Hebrew and Aramaic Lexicon of the Old Testament, Vol. 4,* 1420–1422.
Wagner, S. "Darash." In: *Theological Dictionary of the Old Testament, Vol. 3: D,* 293–307, esp. p. 298–305. Grand Rapids, MI: Eerdmans, 1974.
Walton, John H. "Genesis." In: *Zondervan Illustrated Bible Backgrounds Commentary, Vol. 1:* 88.

17:1 Walk before Me

Sarna. *The JPS Torah Commentary: Genesis,* 123.
Weinfeld, M. "The Covenant of Grant in the Old Testament and in the Ancient Near East." *Journal of the American Oriental Society* 90(2) 1970: 184–203.

17:5 Your name will be Avraham

Sarna. *The JPS Torah Commentary: Genesis,* 124.
Walton, John H. "Genesis." In: *Zondervan Illustrated Bible Backgrounds Commentary, Vol. 1:* 88–89, 149n373–374.

17:10 Circumcision

Faust, Avraham. "The Bible, Archaeology, and the Practice of Circumcision in Israelite and Philistine Societies." *Journal of Biblical Literature* 134(2) 2015: 273–290, esp. p. 273–278.
———. "Excursus 12: Circumcision." In: *The JPS Torah Commentary: Genesis,* 385–387.
Goetze, Albrecht, trans. "Instructions for Temple Officials." In: *Ancient Near Eastern Texts Relating to the Old Testament (ANET):* 207–210, esp. p. 208.
Klein, Neria. "Circumcision in the ancient Near East." In: *The Koren Tanakh of the Land of Israel: Exodus,* 28.
Sarna. *The JPS Torah Commentary: Genesis,* 125–126.
Shalomi-Hen, Racheli "Circumcision in Egypt." In: *The Koren Tanakh of the Land of Israel: Exodus,* 70.
Walton, John H. "Genesis." In: *Zondervan Illustrated Bible Backgrounds Commentary, Vol. 1:* 89, 149n375–378.

17:15–16 Sara... kings of peoples shall descend from her

Sarna. *The JPS Torah Commentary: Genesis,* 126, 360n7.

17:16 I will... give you a son by her

Dalley, Stephanie, trans. "Etana (1.131)." In: *COS Vol. 1:* 453–457, esp. p. 456.
Millard, Alan, trans. "Appu and His Two Sons (1.158)." In: *COS, Vol. 1:* 153–155, esp. p. 154.
Roth, Martha, trans. "The Kirta Epic (1.102)." In: *COS, Vol. 1:* 335–353, esp. p. 344.
Walton, John H. "Genesis." In: *Zondervan Illustrated Bible Backgrounds Commentary, Vol. 1:* 89–90.

18:22–23 Avraham intercedes for Sedom and Amora

Sarna. *The JPS Torah Commentary: Genesis*, 131–134.

Singer, Itamar. "Mursili's Hymn and Prayer to the Sun-Goddess of Arinna (CTH 376.A)." In: *Hittite Prayers*, edited by Harry A. Hoffner, 49–54, esp. p. 52–53. Atlanta, GA: Society of Biblical Literature, 2002.

Tiemeyer, Lena-Sofia. "Were the Neo-Assyrian Prophets Intercessors? A Comparative Study of Neo-Assyrian and Hebrew Texts." In: *"Thus Speaks Ishtar of Arbela:" Prophecy in Israel, Assyria, and Egypt in the Neo-Assyrian Period*, edited by Robert P. Gordon and Hans M. Barstad, 253–272. Winona Lake, IN: Eisenbrauns, 2013.

Unterman, Jeremiah. "The Prophet as intercessor." In: *The Koren Tanakh of the Land of Israel: Samuel*, 104.

———. *Justice for All: How the Jewish Bible Revolutionized Ethics*, 231–232n31. Philadelphia, PA: Jewish Publication Society, 2017.

Walton, John H. "Genesis." In: *Zondervan Illustrated Bible Backgrounds Commentary, Vol. 1:* 91–92, 150n389–390.

19:1 In the city gate

King, Philip and Lawrence Stager. "Patrimonial Kingdom." In: *Life in Biblical Israel*, 221–258, esp. p. 234–236. Louisville, KY: Westminster John Knox Press, 2001.

Morschauser, Scott. "'Hospitality,' Hostiles and Hostages: On the Legal Background to Genesis 19:1–9." *Journal for the Study of the Old Testament* 27(4) 2003: 461–485, esp. p. 465–467.

Sarna. *The JPS Torah Commentary: Genesis*, 134–135, 360 (general footnote at start of chapter and n1).

Walton, John H. "Genesis." In: *Zondervan Illustrated Bible Backgrounds Commentary, Vol. 1:* 92, 150n391–392.

19:2 House ... square

"Canaanite Life: Houses, Food, Tools, Music and Games." Available at: https://factsanddetails.com/world/cat55/sub389/entry-5702.html.

Holladay, John S. "House, Israelite." In: *Anchor Bible Dictionary, Vol. 3*, 308–318.

Sarna. *The JPS Torah Commentary: Genesis*, 135, 360n4.

19:3 Unleavened bread

King, Philip and Lawrence Stager. "The Israelite House and Household." In: *Life in Biblical Israel*, 21–84, esp. p. 65–67. Louisville, KY: Westminster John Knox Press, 2001.

Sarna. *The JPS Torah Commentary: Genesis*, 135.

19:11 Struck ... with blindness

Goetze, Albrecht, trans. "The Soldiers' Oath." In: *Ancient Near Eastern Texts Relating to the Old Testament (ANET):* 353–354, esp. p. 354.

Meek, Theophile J., trans. "The Code of Hammurabi." In: *Ancient Near Eastern Texts Relating to the Old Testament (ANET):* 163–180, esp. p. 165.

Scurlock, JoAnn and Burton Andersen. "Eyes, Ears, and Nose." In: *Diagnoses in Assyrian and Babylonian Medicine*, 185–207, esp. p. 195–196. Chicago, IL: University of Illinois Press, 2005,

"Sinhurma." In: *The Assyrian Dictionary (CAD), Vol. 15: S*, 285.

Stol, Marten. "Blindness and Night-Blindness in Akkadian." *Journal of Near Eastern Studies* 45(4) 1986: 295–299, esp. p. 296–297.

Walton, John H. "Genesis." In: *Zondervan Illustrated Bible Backgrounds Commentary, Vol. 1:* 93.

19:24–25 Destruction of the cities of the plain

Bunch Ted E., Malcom A. LeCompte, A Victor Adedeji, James H. Wittke, T. David Burleigh, Robert E. Hermes, Charles Mooney, et al. "A Tunguska sized airburst destroyed Tall el-Hammam a Middle Bronze Age city in the Jordan Valley near the Dead Sea." *Scientific Reports*, 11(1) 2021: 18632.

Jaret, Steven J. and R. Scott Harris. "No mineralogic or geochemical evidence of impact at Tall el-Hammam, a Middle Bronze Age city in the Jordan Valley near the Dead Sea." *Scientific Reports* 12 (2022): 5189.

Nissenbaum, Arie. (1994). "Sodom, Gomorrah and the other lost cities of the plain – a climatic perspective." *Climatic Change* 26 (1994): 435–446.

Sarna. *The JPS Torah Commentary: Genesis*, 138–139.

Walton, John H. "Genesis." In: *Zondervan Illustrated Bible Backgrounds Commentary, Vol. 1:* 93.

19:26 The pillar of salt

Alter, Robert. *Genesis: Translation and Commentary*. New York: W. W. Norton, 1996, 89.

Sarna. *The JPS Torah Commentary: Genesis*, 138.

19:37–38 Moav and Amon

Ron, Ziv. "Moav." In: *The Koren Tanakh of the Land of Israel: Numbers*, 132.

Tarragon, Jean-Michel de. "Ammon." In: *Anchor Bible Dictionary, Vol. 1*, 194–195.

20 A geographical overview of the patriarchal narratives

Harel, Menasha. *Journeys and Battles in Ancient Times*. Tel Aviv, Ministry of Defence Printing House, 1980. (Hebrew).

Rainey Anson F. and R. Steven Notley. *The Sacred Bridge: Carta's Atlas of the Biblical World*. Jerusalem: Carta, 2006.

Tavger Aharon. "And He Called the Name of that Place Bethel" (Gen 28: 19): Historical-Geography and Archaeology of the Sanctuary of Bethel. In: *The History of the Jacob Cycle (Genesis 25–35)*, edited by Benedikt Hensel, 201–222. Mohr Siebeck, 2021.

20:1 Location of Gerar

Katz, Jill. *The Archaeology of Cult in Middle Bronze Age Canaan: The Sacred Area at Tel Haror, Israel*. Piscataway, NJ: Gorgias Press, 2009.

Kempinski, Aaron. The Hyksos: A View from Northern Canaan and Syria. In The Hyksos: New Historical and Archaeological Perspectives, edited by Eliezer D. Oren, 327–334. Philadelphia, PA: University of Pennsylvania Museum, 1997.

Oren, Eliezer D. "The 'Kingdom of Sharuhen' and the Hyksos Kingdom." In: *The Hyksos: New Historical and Archaeological Perspectives*, edited by Eliezer D. Oren, 253–283. Philadelphia, PA: University of Pennsylvania Museum, 1997.

20:2 Avimelekh

Sarna. *The JPS Torah Commentary: Genesis*, 141.

20:6 Adultery

Goodfriend, Elaine A. "Adultery." In: *Anchor Bible Dictionary, Vol. 2*, 82–86.

Moran, W. L. "The Scandal of the 'Great Sin' at Ugarit." *Journal of Near Eastern Studies* 18(4) 1959, 280–281.

Rabinowitz, Jacob J. "The 'Great Sin' in Ancient Egyptian Marriage Contracts." *Journal of Near Eastern Studies* 18(1) 1959: 73.

Sarna. *The JPS Torah Commentary: Genesis*, 1

Wilson, John A. "Heroic Tales-Exploits of Gods and Human Beings: The Story of Two Brothers." In: *Ancient Near Eastern Texts Relating to the Old Testament (ANET):* 23–25, esp. p. 24

20:7 Prophet as intercessor

King, Leonard W. *The Letters and Inscriptions of Hammurabi, King of Babylon*. London: Fb&c Limited, 2018.

"Nabu." In: *The Assyrian Dictionary (CAD), Vol. 11, part 1: N*, 31, 32

Sarna. *The JPS Torah Commentary: Genesis*, 142.

Tiemeyer, Lina-Sophia. "Were the Neo-Assyrian Prophets Intercessors? A Comparative Study of Neo-Assyrian and Hebrew Texts." *"Thus Speaks Ishtar of Arbela": Prophecy in Israel,*

Assyria, and Egypt in the Neo-Assyrian Period, edited by Robert P. Gordon and Hans M. Barstad, 253–272. Winona Lake, IN: Eisenbrauns, 2013.

Unterman, Jeremiah. "The Prophet as intercessor." In: *The Koren Tanakh of the Land of Israel: Samuel,* 104.

20:11 Gerar's polytheistic religion

Katz, Jill. "Conclusion." In: *The Archaeology of Cult in Middle Bronze Age Canaan: The Sacred Area at Tel Haror, Israel,* 161–168, esp. p. 168. Piscataway, NJ: Gorgias Press, 2013.

Kempinski, Aaron. *The Hyksos: A View from Northern Canaan and Syria.* In: *The Hyksos: New Historical and Archaeological Perspectives,* edited by Eliezer D. Oren, 327–334, esp. p. 330. Philadelphia: University of Pennsylvania Museum, 1997.

Oren, Eliezer D. "The 'Kingdom of Sharuhen' and the Hyksos Kingdom." In: *The Hyksos: New Historical and Archaeological Perspectives,* edited by Eliezer D. Oren, 253–283. Philadelphia: University of Pennsylvania Museum, 1997.

20:12 Brother-sister incest

Ehrlich, Carl S. "Brother-sister incest." In: *The Koren Tanakh of the Land of Israel: Leviticus,* 127.

Jacobsen, Lea. "Incest and rape." In: *The Koren Tanakh of the Land of Israel: Samuel,* 309.

Sarna. *The JPS Torah Commentary: Genesis,* 143.

20:16 A thousand pieces of silver

Sarna. *The JPS Torah Commentary: Genesis,* 144, 361n10.

Walton, John H. "Genesis." In: *Zondervan Illustrated Bible Backgrounds Commentary, Vol. 1:* 95, 150n403.

Weinfeld, Moshe. "Sarah and Abimelech (Genesis 20) Against the Background of an Assyrian Law and the Genesis Apocryphon." In: *Mélanges bibliques et orientaux en l'honneur de M. Mathias Delcor.* edited by A. Caquot, S. Légasse et M. Tardieu, 431–436. Kevelaer: Vluyn, 1985.

21:8 Age of weaning

Garroway, Kristine Henriksen. "The Newborn: Postpartum Rituals and Practices." In: *Growing Up in Ancient Israel: Children in Material Culture and Biblical Texts,* 79–110, esp. p. 95–100. Atlanta, GA: SBL Press, 2018.

Gruber, Mayer I. "Breast-Feeding Practice in Biblical Israel and in Old Babylonian Mesopotamia." *Journal of the Ancient Near Eastern Society* 19(1) 1989: 61–83. esp. p. 77–78.

Lichtheim, Miriam. "The Instruction of Any." In: *Ancient Egyptian Literature Volume II: The New Kingdom,* 135–145, esp. p. 141. Berkeley, CA: University of California Press, 2006.

Pinch, Geraldine. "Private Life in Ancient Egypt." In: *Civilizations of the Ancient Near East. Vol. 1,* edited by Jack Sasson, 363–381, esp. p. 376. Peabody, MA: Hendrickson, 2000.

21:10 Wives, concubines, and inheritance

King, L. W., trans. "The Code of Hammurabi." In: *Encyclopedia Britannica,* 11th edition. Worchester, MA: Horace Everett Hooper, 1915.

Kramer, S. N., trans. "Lipit-Ishtar Lawcode." In: *Ancient Near Eastern Texts Relating to the Old Testament (ANET):* 159–161, esp. p. 160.

Sarna. *The JPS Torah Commentary: Genesis,* 146–147, 361n4.

Walton, John H. "Genesis." In: *Zondervan Illustrated Bible Backgrounds Commentary, Vol. 1:* 95, 150n405–406.

21:14 Divorce from a secondary wife

Stol, Marten. "A Second Wife." In: *Women in the Ancient Near East,* 165–192, esp. p. 180–185, 187, 189–190. Boston, MA: De Gruyter, 2016.

———. "Marriage Between Equals." In: *Women in the Ancient Near East,* 200–204, esp. p. 203. Boston, MA: De Gruyter, 2016.

21:14 Be'er Sheva desert

Aharoni, Yohanan. *Land of the Bible: A Historical Geography.* London: Burns & Oates, 1974.

Rainey Anson F. and R. Steven Notley. *The Sacred Bridge: Carta's Atlas of the Biblical World.* Jerusalem: Carta, 2006.
Walton, John H. "Genesis." In: *Zondervan Illustrated Bible Backgrounds Commentary, Vol. 1:* 95–96.

21:21 Wilderness of Paran

Avner, Uzi. "Nabataeans in Southern Sinai." *Aram* 27: 1–2 (2015): 397–429, esp. p. 406.
Rainey, Anson F. and R. Steven Notley. "Territorial States: Tenth Century BCE." In: *The Sacred Bridge: Carta's Atlas of the Biblical World,* 157–189, esp. p. 168. Jerusalem: Carta, 2006.
Ron, Zvi. "Wilderness of Paran." In: *Koren Tanakh of the Land of Israel: Numbers,* 57.

21:22–32 Avraham's treaty with Avimelekh

Rowton, M. B. "Watercourses and Water Rights in the Official Correspondence from Larsa and Isin." *Journal of Cuneiform Studies* 21 (1969): 267–274, esp. p. 269–270.
Sarna. *The JPS Torah Commentary: Genesis,* 148–149.
Walton, John H. "Genesis." In: *Zondervan Illustrated Bible Backgrounds Commentary, Vol. 1:* 96, 150n407–408.

21:32 Be'er Sheva

Sarna. "Excursus 14: Beer–sheba." In: *The JPS Torah Commentary: Genesis,* 389.

21:32 Who were the Philistines in Genesis

Kitchen, K. "Founding Fathers or Fleeting Phantoms – The Patriarchs." In: *On the Reliability of the Old Testament,* 313–372, esp. p. 339–341. Grand Rapids, MI: W. B. Eerdmans, 2003.
Wood, Bryant G. "The Genesis Philistines." *Associates for Biblical Research Newsletter* (March, 2006); retrieved 12–11–2022. Available at: at: https://biblearchaeology.org/research/chronological-categories/patriarchal-era/3640-the-genesis-philistines

21:33 *El olam*

Cross, Frank M. "The Epithets of 'El." In: *Canaanite Myth and Hebrew Epic,* 15–19, esp. p. 17–19. Harvard, MA: Cambridge University Press, 1973.
Sarna. *The JPS Torah Commentary: Genesis,* 148–150, esp. p. 149–150.
Walton, John H. "Genesis." In: *Zondervan Illustrated Bible Backgrounds Commentary, Vol. 1:* 96, 150n411.

21:33 Tamarisk

Jacob, Irene and Jacob, Walter. "Flora." In: *Anchor Bible Dictionary, Vol. 2,* 803–817, esp. p. 896.
"Tamarix." Available at: https://en.wikipedia.org/wiki/Tamarix.

22:2 The land of Moria

Sarna. "Excursus 16: The Land of Moriah." In: *The JPS Torah Commentary: Genesis,* 391–392.
Walton, John H. "Genesis." In: *Zondervan Illustrated Bible Backgrounds Commentary, Vol. 1:* 96–97.

22:10 The knife

Unterman, Jeremiah. "The Literary Influence of 'the Binding of Isaac' (Genesis 22) on 'the Outrage at Gibeah' (Judges 19)." *Hebrew Annual Review* 4 (1980): 161–166.
Walton, John H. "Genesis." In: *Zondervan Illustrated Bible Backgrounds Commentary, Vol. 1:* 98, 150n413.

22:13 Animal sacrificed in place of a human

Gaster, Theodore. "The Patriarchs." In: *Myth, Legend, and Custom in the Old Testament,* 139–222, esp. p.162. New York: Harper & Row, 1969.
Lewis, Juan "Agnus vicarius, a substitute for child sacrifice?" In: *L'epigrafia del Nord Africa: Novità, riletture, nuove sintesi. Vol. XXI,* edited by Samir Aounallah, and Attilio Mastino, 373–380, 2020.
Milgrom, *The Anchor Bible: Leviticus 1–16,* 174–175

Walton, John H. "Genesis." In: *Zondervan Illustrated Bible Backgrounds Commentary, Vol. 1:* 98, 150n414.

22:20–24 Descendants of Naḥor

Knauf, Ernst A. "Buz." In: *Anchor Bible Dictionary, Vol. 1*, 794.
———. "Uz." In: *Anchor Bible Dictionary, Vol. 6*, 770–771.
Moran, William L., ed and trans. "A treacherous brother." In: *The Amarna Letters*. Baltimore, MD: Johns Hopkins University Press, 1992, 262.
———. "Etakkama of Qadesh." In: *The Amarna Letters*. Baltimore, MD: Johns Hopkins University Press, 1992, 269–270.
Rainey, Anson F. and R. Steven Notley. "Crisis and Transition: Twelfth Century BCE." In: *The Sacred Bridge: Carta's Atlas of the Biblical World*, 104–130, esp. p. 112. Jerusalem: Carta, 2006.
Sarna. *The JPS Torah Commentary: Genesis*, 154–156.

23:2 The death, mourning, and burial of Sara

Bloch-Smith, Elizabeth. "Death and Burial in Eighth-Century Judah." In: *Archaeology and History of Eighth-Century Judah*, edited by Zev I. Farber and Jacob L. Wright, 365–678, esp. p. 365–366. Atlanta, GA: SBL Press, 2018.
Schuster, Ruth. "Intact Burial Cave from Time of Ramesses II Discovered on Israeli Coast." *Haaretz*, September 18, 2022.
Stol, Marten. "Her Physical Life." In: *Women in the Ancient Near* East, 436–458, esp. p. 456–458. Boston, MA: De Gruyter, 2016,
Walton, John H. "Genesis." In: *Zondervan Illustrated Bible Backgrounds Commentary, Vol. 1:* 99–100, 150n427–428.

23:4 *Ger vetoshav*

Eshel, Tzilla. "How Silver Was Used for Payment," *TheTorah.com*, 2018. https://www.thetorah.com/article/how-silver-was-used-for-payment (retrieved 7/7/2022).
Unterman, Jeremiah. *Justice for All: How the Jewish Bible Revolutionized Ethics*, 42-45, 202-204. Philadelphia, PA: Jewish Publication Society, 2017.

23:9 Family burial caves

Bloch-Smith, Elizabeth. "Cave, Chamber and Shaft Tombs." In: *Judahite Burial Practices and Beliefs about the Dead*. Sheffield, UK: Sheffield Academic Press. 1992, 36–43.
Brichto, Herbert Chanan. "Kin, Cult, Land and Afterlife–A Biblical Complex." *Hebrew Union College Annual* 44 (1973): 1–54.
Cradic, Melissa. "Embodiments of Death: The funerary Sequence and Commemoration in the Bronze Age Levant." *Bulletin of the American Schools of Oriental Research* 377 (2017): 219–248.
Gonen. Rivka. *Burial Practices and Cultural Diversity in Late Bronze Age Canaan*. Winona Lake, IN: Eisenbrauns, 1979.
Stavrakopoulou, Francesca. *Land of Our Fathers: The Roles of Ancestor Veneration in Biblical Land Claims*. New York: T & T Clark, 2010.

23:9 Cave of Makhpela

Arnon, Noam. *The Cave of Makhpelah: History of the Site from its Beginnings until Late Antiquity*. Doctoral dissertation summary (Hebrew). Available at: http://hebron.org.il/blog/7/1273.
Sarna. *The JPS Torah Commentary: Genesis*, 156–161.
Tercatin, Rossella. "Tomb of Patriarchs Pilgrimage Site in First Temple Times, Pottery Suggests." *Jerusalem Post*, July 5, 2020. Available at: https://www.jpost.com/israel-news/tomb-of-patriarchs-popular-site-in-first-temple-times-pottery-suggests-633960.
Walton, John H. "Genesis." In: *Zondervan Illustrated Bible Backgrounds Commentary, Vol. 1:* 100.
Westbrook, Raymond. "Purchase of the Cave of Machpelah." In: *Property and the Family in Biblical Law*, 24–35. Sheffield, England: JSOT Press, 1991.

23:15 Four hundred shekels of silver

Dilke, Oswald Ashton Wentworth. "Calculations for Trade and Commerce." In: *Mathematics and Measurement*, 46–52. Berkeley, CA: University of California Press, 1987.

Walton, John H. "Genesis." In: *Zondervan Illustrated Bible Backgrounds Commentary, Vol. 1:* 100.

24:3 God of heaven and earth

Raven, Maarten J. and René van Walsem. "The Reliefs, Paintings, and Inscriptions." In: *The Tomb of Meryneith at Saqqara*, 77–186, esp. p. 131. Turnhout, Belgium, Brepols, 2014.

Sarna. *The JPS Torah Commentary: Genesis*, 162.

24:4 Go to my…birthplace, and there find a wife for…my son

Sarna. *The JPS Torah Commentary: Genesis*, 162, 362n7.

Walton, John H. "Genesis." In: *Zondervan Illustrated Bible Backgrounds Commentary, Vol. 1:* 100.

24:10 Aram Naharayim

Sarna. *The JPS Torah Commentary: Genesis*, 163–164.

Speiser. *Genesis*, 179.

24:11 Women drawing water

Unterman, Jeremiah. "Women drawing water." In: *The Koren Tanakh of the Land of Israel: Exodus*, 16.

Sarna. *The JPS Torah Commentary: Genesis*, 164.

24:12–14 The prayer of Avraham's servant

Greenberg, Moshe. "Lecture Two." In: *Biblical Prose Prayer as a Window to the Popular Religion of Ancient Israel*. Berkeley, CA: University of California Press, 1983, 30–31.

———. "Lecture Three." In: *Biblical Prose Prayer as a Window to the Popular Religion of Ancient Israel*. Berkeley, CA: University of California Press, 1983, 48 n2, 57n6.

Sarna. *The JPS Torah Commentary: Genesis*, 164.

Tigay, Jeffrey H. "Review of *Biblical Prose Prayer*." *Journal of American Oriental Society* 105(1) 1985: 155–156.

24:19–22 Camel test

Sarna. *The JPS Torah Commentary: Genesis*, 164.

Walton, John H. "Genesis." In: *Zondervan Illustrated Bible Backgrounds Commentary, Vol. 1:* 101.

24:22 Gold ring…gold bracelets

Platt, Elizabeth E. "Jewelry, Ancient Israelite." In: *Anchor Bible Dictionary, Vol.* 3, 823–834, esp. p. 825–826.

Walton, John H. "Genesis." In: *Zondervan Illustrated Bible Backgrounds Commentary, Vol. 1:* 101–102.

24:53 Bride-price

Sarna. *The JPS Torah Commentary: Genesis*, 168, 362n19.

Stol, Marten. "The Bridal Price." In: *Women in the Ancient Near East*, 112–146. Boston, MA: De Gruyter, 2016.

Walton, John H. "Genesis." In: *Zondervan Illustrated Bible Backgrounds Commentary, Vol. 1:* 102, 151n427–434.

24:57–58 A woman's choice to marry

Stol, Marten. "Marriage." In: *Women in the Ancient Near East*, 60–111, esp. p. 72–76. Boston, MA: De Gruyter, 2016.

Toorn, K. van der. "A Second Home: The Wedding." In: *From Her Cradle to Her Grave: The Role of Religion in the Life of the Israelite and the Babylonian Woman*, 59–76, esp. p. 64–65. Sheffield, England: JSOT, 1995.

Walton, John H. "Genesis." In: *Zondervan Illustrated Bible Backgrounds Commentary, Vol. 1:* 102.

24:65 Veil

Sarna. *The JPS Torah Commentary: Genesis*, 170.

Stol, Marten. "Her Outward Appearance." In: *Women in the Ancient Near East*, 7–59, esp. p. 22–28. Boston, MA: De Gruyter, 2016.

Walton, John H. "Genesis." In: *Zondervan Illustrated Bible Backgrounds Commentary, Vol. 1:* 102–103, 151n436–440.

25:1–4 The sons of Ketura

Eph'al, Israel. "The Sons of Qeturah and the Sons of Ishmael (In the Biblical Genealogy Lists. In: *The Ancient Arabs: Nomads on the Borders of the Fertile Crescent 9th-5th Centuries B.C.*, 231–240. Jerusalem: Magnes Press, 1982.

Royal Inscriptions of the Neo-Assyrian Period. Accessed February 13, 2023. Available at: http://oracc.museum.upenn.edu/rinap/news/.

25:5–6 Inheritance rights

King, L. W., trans. "The Code of Hammurabi." In: *Encyclopedia Britannica*, 11th edition. Worchester, MA: Horace Everett Hooper, 1915.

Sarna. *The JPS Torah Commentary: Genesis*, 173.

Stol, Marten. "Concubines." In: *Women in the Ancient Near East*, 193–199, esp. p. 195–197. Boston, MA: De Gruyter, 2016.

Walton, John H. "Genesis." In: *Zondervan Illustrated Bible Backgrounds Commentary, Vol. 1:* 103.

Westbrook, Raymond. "Undivided Inheritance." In: *Property and the Family in Biblical Law*, 118–141, esp. p. 123n2. Sheffield, England: JSOT Press, 1991.

25:8 Gathered to his people

Sarna. *The JPS Torah Commentary: Genesis*, 174.

Walton, John H. "Genesis." In: *Zondervan Illustrated Bible Backgrounds Commentary, Vol. 1:* 103.

25:12–18 The sons of Yishmael

Eph'al, Israel. "The Sons of Qeturah and the Sons of Ishmael (In the Biblical Genealogy Lists. In: *The Ancient Arabs: Nomads on the Borders of the Fertile Crescent 9th-5th Centuries B.C.*, 231–240. Jerusalem: Magnes Press, 1982.

McKinny, Chris. "'He Will Father Twelve Princes' (Gen 17:20) - A Historical Geographical Assessment of Ishmael and His Descendants." In: *Lexham Geographic Commentary on the Pentateuch*, edited by Barry Beitzel, 3. Bellingham, WA: Lexham Press, 2022.

Oppenheim, A. Leo, trans. "Texts from Hammurabi to the Downfall of the Assyrian Empire." In: *Ancient Near Eastern Texts Relating to the Old Testament (ANET):* 269–301, esp. p. 282.

Sarna. "The Line of Ishmael." In: *The JPS Torah Commentary: Genesis*, 175–177.

———. *The JPS Torah Commentary: Genesis*, 170–173.

Smith, Robert H. "Arabia." In: *Anchor Bible Dictionary, Vol. 1*, 324–327.

Walton, John H. "Genesis." In: *Zondervan Illustrated Bible Backgrounds Commentary, Vol. 1:* 103–104.

25:20 Padan Aram

Lipiński, Edward. *The Aramaeans: Their Ancient History, Culture, Religion*. Leuven: Peeters, 2000.

Niehr, Herbert (ed.). *The Aramaeans in Ancient Syria*. Leiden: Brill, 2014.

Pitard, Wayne T. "Paddan-Aram." In: *Anchor Bible Dictionary, Vol. 5*, 55.

Sarna. *The JPS Torah Commentary: Genesis*, 178.

Younger, K. Lawson. "The Origins of the Aramaeans." In: *A Political History of the Arameans from Their Origins to the End of Their Polities*, 35–108, esp. p. 96. 99. Atlanta, GA: Society of Biblical Literature, 2016,

Zadok, Ran. "The Aramean Infiltration and Diffusion in the Upper Jazira, ca. 1150–930 BCE." In: *The Ancient Near East in the 12th-10th Centuries BCE: Culture and History. Proceedings of the International Conference held at the University of Haifa, 2-5 May, 2010*, edited by Gershon Galil, Ayelet Gilboa, Aren M. Maeir and Dan'el Kahn, 569–579. Münster: Ugarit-Verlag, 2012.

25:22 To inquire of the Lord

Oppenheim, A. Leo, trans. "Texts from Hammurabi to the Downfall of the Assyrian Empire." In: *Ancient Near Eastern Texts Relating to the Old Testament (ANET)*: 269–301, esp. p. 289.
Sarna. *The JPS Torah Commentary: Genesis*, 179.
Wagner, S. "Darash." In: *Theological Dictionary of the Old Testament, Vol. 3: D*, 293–307, esp. p. 298–305. Grand Rapids, MI: Eerdmans, 1974.

25:22–24 Twins in the ancient Near East

Bains, John. "Egyptian Twins." *Orientalia* 54(4) 1985: 461–482.
Garroway, Kristine Henriksen. "How to Birth a Baby." In: *Growing Up in Ancient Israel: Children in Material Culture and Biblical Texts*, 49–79, esp. p. 66–75. Atlanta, GA: SBL Press, 2018.
Leichty, Erle. *The Omen Series Shumma Izbu*. Locust Valley, NY: Augustin, 1970.
Margalith, Othniel. "A New Type of Asherah-Figurine?" *Vetus Testamentum* 44 (1994): 109–115, esp. p. 113.
Roubach, Sharon. "Two Who Donned the Veil: The Image of Twins in the Bible." *Beit Mikra* 183 (2005): 366–390 (Hebrew).

25:25–30 Hairiness

Gaster, Theodore. "The Patriarchs." In: *Myth, Legend, and Custom in the Old Testament*, 139–222, esp. p. 161, 367–368note. New York: Harper & Row, 1969.
Harris, J. Rendal. *The Cult of the Heavenly Twins*. Cambridge: Cambridge University Press, 1906, p. 46, 91.
Sarna. *The JPS Torah Commentary: Genesis*, 180–181(vv. 25, 27), 363n39–40.
Speiser. E. A., trans. "The Epic of Gilgamesh." In: *Ancient Near Eastern Texts Relating to the Old Testament (ANET)*: 72–99, esp. p. 74.

25:27–34 Sale of the birthright

Finkelstein, J. J., trans. "Additional Mesopotamian Legal Documents." In: *Ancient Near Eastern Texts Relating to the Old Testament (ANET)*: 545.
Greenspahn, Frederick E. *When Brothers Dwell Together: The Preeminence of Younger Siblings in the Hebrew Bible*. Oxford: Oxford University Press, 1994.
Kramer, S. N., trans. "Hymn to Enlil, the All-Beneficent." In: *Ancient Near Eastern Texts Relating to the Old Testament (ANET)*: 573–576, esp. p. 574.
Meek, Theophile J., trans. "The Middle Assyrian Laws." In: *Ancient Near Eastern Texts Relating to the Old Testament (ANET)*: 180–188, esp. p. 185.
———. "Mesopotamian Legal Documents." In: *Ancient Near Eastern Texts Relating to the Old Testament (ANET)*: 217–223, esp. p. 219–220.
Sarna. *The JPS Torah Commentary: Genesis*, 180–181, 363n1
Walton, John H. "Genesis." In: *Zondervan Illustrated Bible Backgrounds Commentary, Vol. 1*: 104–105.

26 Historicity of the patriarchal narratives

Malamat, Abraham. *The History of Biblical Israel*. Boston, MA: Brill, 2004.
Rainey, Anson F. and R. Steven Notley, *The Sacred Bridge: Carta's Atlas of the Biblical World*. Jerusalem: Carta, 2006.
Speiser. *Anchor Bible: Genesis*, 86.

26:1 Gerar as a Philistine city

Katz, Jill. "The Sacred Area of Tal Haror." In: *The Archaeology of Cult in Middle Bronze Age Canaan: The Sacred Area at Tel Haror*, Israel, 29–120, esp. p. 29, 30, 31, 35. Piscataway, NJ: Gorgias Press, 2009.
Kempinski, Aaron. "The Hyksos: A View from Northern Canaan and Syria. In: *The Hyksos: New Historical and Archaeological Perspectives*, edited by Eliezer D. Oren, 327–334. Philadelphia, PA: University of Pennsylvania Museum, 1997.
Oren, Eliezer D. "The "Kingdom of Sharuhen" and the Hyksos Kingdom." In: *The Hyksos: New Historical and Archaeological Perspectives*, edited by Eliezer D. Oren, 253–283. Philadelphia, PA: University of Pennsylvania Museum, 1997.

26:1 Avimelekh

Sarna. *The JPS Torah Commentary: Genesis*, 183.

26:2 Stay

Sarna. *The JPS Torah Commentary: Genesis*, 363n2.

Tawil, Hayim ben Yosef. "מבוע." In: *An Akkadian Lexical Companion for Biblical Hebrew*: 196–197.

26:3 Bide

Sarna. *The JPS Torah Commentary: Genesis*, 183.

Unterman, Jeremiah. "Providing for the Disadvantaged: The Stranger, the Poor, the Widow, and the Orphan." In: *Justice for All: How the Jewish Bible Revolutionized Ethics*, 41–84, esp. p. 44. Philadelphia, PA: Jewish Publication Society, 2017.

26:3 Fulfilling the oath I swore to Avraham your father

Singer, Itamar, trans. "Treaty between Murshili and Duppi-Teshub (2.17B)" In: *COS, Vol. 2*: 96.

26:8 Window

Amin, Osama Shukir Muhammed. "Ivory Plaque of Woman at the Window." *World History Encyclopedia*. July 26, 2014. Available at: https://www.worldhistory.org/image/2872/ivory-plaque-of-woman-at-the-window https://www.worldhistory.org/image/2872/ivory-plaque-of-woman-at-the-window/.

Goetze, Albrecht, trans. "The Festival of the Warrior-God." In: *Ancient Near Eastern Texts Relating to the Old Testament (ANET)*: 358–361, esp. p. 359.

———. "Ritual for the Erection of a New Palace." In: *Ancient Near Eastern Texts Relating to the Old Testament (ANET)*: 357–358, esp. p. 357.

Livingstone, Alasdair, trans. "An Assurbanipal Prayer for Mullissu (1.144). In: *COS, Vol. 1*: 475 § 5–10.

Milgrom. *The Anchor Bible: Leviticus 1–16*, 361–362.

———. "Extra-Biblical Confirmation." In: *Cult and Conscience: The Asham and the Priestly Doctrine of* Repentance, 76–80, esp. p. 77–78. Leiden: Brill, 1976.

Ron, Zvi and Unterman, Jeremiah. "Accidental sins of commission." In: *The Koren Tanakh of the Land of Israel: Leviticus*, 33.

Sarna. *The JPS Torah Commentary: Genesis*, 184.

———. *The JPS Torah Commentary: Genesis*, 184–185.

26:10 Would have brought guilt upon us

Foster, Benjamin R., trans. "Dialogue Between a Man and His God (1.151). In: *COS, Vol. 1*:485 §13.

Livingstone, Alasdair, trans. "An Assurbanipal Prayer for Mullissu (1.144). In: *COS, Vol. 1*: 475 § 5–10.

Milgrom. *The Anchor Bible: Leviticus 1–16*, 361–2.

———. *Cult and Conscience: The Asham and the Priestly Doctrine of Repentance*, 77–78. Leiden: Brill, 1976.

Ron, Zvi and Unterman, Jeremiah. "Accidental sins of commission." In: *The Koren Tanakh of the Land of Israel: Leviticus*, 33.

Sarna. *The JPS Torah Commentary: Genesis*, 184–5

26:12 Reaped a hundredfold

King, Philip and Lawrence Stager. "The Means of Existence." In: *Life in Biblical Israel*, 85–200, esp. p. 111–112. Louisville, KY: Westminster John Knox Press, 2001.

Oren, Eliezer. "Ziklag: A Biblical City on the Edge of the Negev." *The Biblical Archaeologist* 45(3) 1982: 155–166, esp. p. 157.

Sarna. *The JPS Torah Commentary: Genesis*, 185, 364n9.

26:15 Stopped up all the wells ... filling them with earth

King, Philip and Lawrence Stager. "The Means of Existence." In: *Life in Biblical Israel*, 85–200, esp. p. 123–126. Louisville, KY: Westminster John Knox Press, 2001.

Lynch, Avraham and Helaine Selin, H. "Water Systems in Bronze and Iron Age Israel." In: *Encyclopaedia of the History of Science, Technology, and Medicine in Non-Western Cultures*, edited by Helaine Selin, 1–7. Springer, Dordrecht, 2016.
Sarna. *The JPS Torah Commentary: Genesis*, 185.

26:17–22 Yitzḥak's wells

Sarna. *The JPS Torah Commentary: Genesis*, 186.
Tanakh Lametayel, 411. Jerusalem: Koren, 2022.

26:24 God of your father

Jacobsen, Thorkild. "Second Millennium Metaphors. The God as Parents: Rise of Personal Religion." In: *The Treasures of Darkness: A History of Mesopotamian Religion*, 145–164, esp. p. 159. New Haven, CT: Yale University Press, 1976.
Moran, William J. "The God of My Father." In: *Ancient Near Eastern Texts Relating to the Old Testament (ANET)*: 628–629.
Sarna. "Excursus 20: God of the Father." In: *The JPS Torah Commentary: Genesis*, 396–397.

26:28–31 Pact between Yitzḥak and the Philistines

Conklin, Blane. "Arslan Tash I and other Vestiges of a Particular Syrian Incantatory Thread" *Biblica* 84(1) 2003: 89–101, esp. p. 98.
McCarter, P. Kyle, trans. "An Amulet from Arslan Tash (2.86)" In: *COS, Vol. 2*: 222–223, esp. p. 222.
Zevit, Ziony. "A Phoenician Inscription and Biblical Covenant Theology." *Israel Exploration Journal* 27(2–3) 1977: 110–118, esp. p. 117.

26:34–35 Hittites

Ron, Zvi. "Uriya the Hittite." In: *The Koren Tanakh of the Land of Israel: Samuel*. 297.

26:34 Esav takes Hittite wives

Sarna. *The JPS Torah Commentary: Genesis*, 189.

27 Israel and Edom

Aḥituv, Shmuel. *Echoes from the Past: Hebrew and Cognate Inscriptions from the Biblical Period*, Jerusalem: Carta, 2008.
Beit-Arie, Itzhak. "Judean–Edomite Rivalry in the Negev." *Qadmoniot* 126 (2003): 66–76 (Hebrew).
Ben-Yosef, Erez. "The Central Timna Valley Project: Research Design and Preliminary Results." In: *Mining for Ancient Copper: Essays in Memory of Benno Rothenberg*, edited by Erez Ben-Yosef, 28–63. Winona Lake, IN: Eisenbrauns, Tel Aviv: Institute of Archaeology of the Tel Aviv University, 2018.
———. "The Architectural Bias in Current Biblical Archaeology." *Vetus Testamentum* 69(3) 2019: 361–387.
———. "Rethinking the Social Complexity of Early Iron Age Nomads." *Jerusalem Journal of Archaeology* 1 (2021): 155–179.
Bienkowski, Piotr (ed.), *Early Edom and Moab: The Beginning of the Iron Age in Southern Jordan*. Sheffield, England: J. R. Collis, 1992.
Eph'al, Israel. "The Origins of Idumaea." *Qadmoniot* 126 (2003): 77–79 (Hebrew)
Levy, Thomas E., Mohammad Najjar and Erez Ben-Yosef (eds.), *New Insights into the Iron Age and Archaeology of Edom, Southern Jordan*, Los Angeles, CA: The Cotsen Institute of Archaeology Press, 2014.
Rainey, Anson F. *The El-Amarna Correspondence: A New Edition of Cuneiform Letters from the Site of El-Amarna Based on Collation of All Extant Tablets*, edited by W. M. Schniedewind and Z. Cochavi-Rainey. Leiden: Brill, 2015.
Rainey Anson F. and R. Steven Notley. *The Sacred Bridge: Carta's Atlas of the Biblical World*, Jerusalem: Carta, 2006.
Sukenik, Naaama, David Iluz, Zohar Amar, Alexander Varvak, Orit Shamir and Erez Ben–Yosef. "Early Evidence of Royal Purple–Dyed Textile from Timna Valley (Israel)." *PLOS*

ONE 16(1) 2021. January 28, 2021. Available at: https://journals.plos.org/plosone/article?id=10.1371/journal.pone.0245897https://journals.plos.org/plosone/article?id=10.1371/journal.pone.0245897.

Van der Veen, Peter, Christopher Theis and Manfred Görg. "Israel in Canaan (Long) Before Pharaoh Merenptah? A Fresh Look at the Berlin Statue Pedestal Relief 21687." *Journal of Ancient Egyptian Interconnections* 2(4) 2010: 15–25.

Zucconi, Laura M. "From the Wilderness of Zin alongside Edom: Edomite Territory in the Eastern Negev during the Eighth–Sixth Centuries B.C.E." In: *Milk and Honey: Essays on Ancient Israel and the Bible in Appreciation of the Judaic Studies Program at the University of California, San Diego*, edited by Sarah Malena and David Miano, 241–256. Winona Lake, IN: Eisenbrauns, 2007.

27:4 Yitzḥak's blessing to Yaakov

King, L. W., trans. "The Code of Hammurabi." In: *Encyclopedia Britannica*, 11th edition. Worchester, MA: Horace Everett Hooper, 1915.

Sarna. *The JPS Torah Commentary: Genesis*, 190, 194.

Toorn, K. van der. "A Hidden Heritage: The Israelite Cult of the Dead." In: *Family Religion in Babylonia, Syria and Israel*, 206–235, esp. p. 223. Leiden: Brill, 1996.

Walton, John H. "Genesis." In: *Zondervan Illustrated Bible Backgrounds Commentary, Vol. 1*: 105–106.

Westbrook, Raymond. "The Character of Ancient Near Eastern Law." In: *A History of Ancient Near Eastern Law*, edited by Raymond Westbrook, 1–90, esp. p. 56–59. Leiden: Brill, 2003.

27:11–27 Trickery

Sarna. "Excursus 21: Jacob: The Moral Issue." In: *The JPS Torah Commentary: Genesis*, 397–398.

27:28 Dew of heaven

Gordon, Cyrus H. "Linguistices Affinities." In: *Ugaritic Textbook*, 144–148, esp. 145. Rome, Pontifical Biblical Institute, 1965.

———. "Syntax and the Poetic Structure." In: *Ugaritic Textbook*, 144–148, esp. 141. Rome, Pontifical Biblical Institute, 1965.

Sarna. *The JPS Torah Commentary: Genesis*, 192–193.

27:39–40 Yitzḥak's blessing to Esav

Sarna. *The JPS Torah Commentary: Genesis*, 194.

28:5 Aramean

Schniedewind, William M. "The Rise of the Aramean States." In: *Mesopotamia and the Bible*, edited by Mark W. Chavalas and K. L. Younger, 276–287, esp. p. 276–279. Grand Rapids, MI: Baker, 2002.

Walton, John H. "Genesis." In: *Zondervan Illustrated Bible Backgrounds Commentary, Vol. 1*: 106, 151n457–459.

28:9 Esav and the Ishmaelites

Sarna. *The JPS Torah Commentary: Genesis*, 196–197.

28:10 Yaakov's journey from Be'er Sheva to Ḥaran via Beit El

Dorsey, David A. "The National (Beersheba-Jerusalem-Jenin) and Its Alternatives. In: *The Roads and Highways of Ancient Israel*, 117–146, esp. p. 134. Eugene, OR: Wipf and Stock, 2018.

Walton, John H. "Genesis." In: *Zondervan Illustrated Bible Backgrounds Commentary, Vol. 1*: 106.

28:12–17 Yaakov's dream in ancient Near Eastern context

Averbeck, Richard E., trans. "The Cylinders of Gudea (2.155)" In: *COS, Vol. 2*: 417–433.

Borghouts, Joris F. "Witchcraft, Magic, and Divination in Ancient Egypt." In: *Civilizations of the Ancient Near East, Vol. 3*, edited by Jack M. Sasson,1775–1785, esp. p. 1783. Peabody, MA: Hendrickson, 2000.

Dalley, Stephanie, trans. "Nergal and Ereshkigal, standard version. In: *Myths from Mesopotamia*:

Creation, The Flood, Gilgamesh, and Others, 163–177, esp. p. 173. Oxford: Oxford University Press, 1989.
Masparo, Gaston. *Guide to the Cairo Museum*. Cairo: French Institute of Oriental Archeology, 1903. 221–222, 230–235. Available at: https://scholarship.rice.edu/jsp/xml/1911/13080/1540/MusCa1903.tei-timea.html.
Sarna. *The JPS Torah Commentary: Genesis*, 198–200.
"Simmiltu." In: *The Assyrian Dictionary (CAD), Vol. 15: S*: 273.
Walton, John H. "Genesis." In: *Zondervan Illustrated Bible Backgrounds Commentary, Vol. 1:* 106–107.

28:20–22 Vows to a deity in the ancient Near East

Cartledge, Tony W. "The Literary Function of Vows in Hebrew Narrative." In: *Vows in the Hebrew Bible and the Ancient Near East*, 162–199, esp. p. 170. Sheffield, UK: Sheffield Academic Press, 1992, p. 170.
Ron, Zvi. "Vows in the ancient Near East." In: *The Koren Tanakh of the Land of Israel: Numbers*, 189.
Sarna. *The JPS Torah Commentary: Genesis*, 200–201.
Walton, John H. "Genesis." In: *Zondervan Illustrated Bible Backgrounds Commentary, Vol. 1:* 108.

28:22 *Matzeva*

Ron, Zvi. "Sacred pillar." In: *The Koren Tanakh of the Land of Israel: Leviticus*, 196.
Sarna. *The JPS Torah Commentary: Genesis*, 201.
Walton, John H. "Genesis." In: *Zondervan Illustrated Bible Backgrounds Commentary, Vol. 1:* 107–108.

29:2–8 Pacts for herding in the ancient Near East

Sarna. *The JPS Torah Commentary: Genesis*, 202.
Walton, John H. "Genesis." In: *Zondervan Illustrated Bible Backgrounds Commentary, Vol. 1:* 108.

29:11 Yaakov kissed Raḥel

Sarna. *The JPS Torah Commentary: Genesis*, 203.
Speiser. *Anchor Bible: Genesis*, 223.
Stol, Marten. "Adultery." In: *Women in the Ancient Near* East, 256–263, esp. p. 257. Boston, MA: De Gruyter, 2016.
———. "The Middle Assyrian Law-book about Women." In: *Women in the Ancient Near East*. Boston, MA: De Gruyter, 2016, 662–683, p. 663.

29:15 Lavan's decision to hire Yaakov

Sarna. *The JPS Torah Commentary: Genesis*, 203, 204 (v.18), 365n9.
Postgate, J. N. "On Some Assyrian Ladies." *Iraq* 41(2) 1979: 89–103, esp. p. 93–94.
Walton, John H. "Genesis." In: *Zondervan Illustrated Bible Backgrounds Commentary, Vol. 1:* 108–109, 152n475.

29:18 Bride-price and marriage customs

Postgate. J. N. "On Some Assyrian Ladies." *Iraq* 41(2) 1979: 89–103.
Roth, Martha T. *Law Collections from Mesopotamia and Asia-Minor*. Atlanta, GA: Scholars' Press, 1995.
Sarna. *The JPS Torah Commentary: Genesis*, 204.
Stol, Marten. "The Marriage Gifts." In: *Women in the Ancient Near East*, 112–146. Boston, MA: De Gruyter, 2016.
"*Terḫatu.*" In: *The Assyrian Dictionary (CAD), Vol. 18: T*, 350–354.
Westbrook, Raymond and Bruce Wells. "Status and Family." In: *Everyday Law in Biblical Israel: An Introduction*, 53–68. Louisville, KY: Westminster John Knox, 2009.

29:22 Wedding and feast

Marsman, Hennie J. *Women in Ugarit: Their Social and Religious Position in the Context of the Ancient Near East*, 43–471, esp. p. 86–87. Leiden: Brill, 2003

Speiser. ***Anchor Bible: Genesis***, 227.

———. "New Kirkuk Documents Relating to Family Laws." *The Annual of the American Schools of Oriental Research* (AASOR) 10(1928): 1–73, esp. text number 2, p. 22, 32.

Walton, John H. "Genesis." In: *Zondervan Illustrated Bible Backgrounds Commentary, Vol. 1:* 109, 152n477–482.

29:26–30 Simultaneous marriage with two sisters

Carasik, Michael. "To be a rival (*litzror*)." In: *The Koren Tanakh of the Land of Israel: Leviticus*, 131.

King, L. W., trans. "The Code of Hammurabi." In: *Encyclopedia Britannica*, 11th edition. Worchester, MA: Horace Everett Hooper, 1915.

Roth, Martha T. "Hittite Laws." In: *Law Collections from Mesopotamia and Asia Minor*, 256–263, esp. p. 257. Atlanta, GA: Scholars Press, 1995.

Walton, John H. "Genesis." In: *Zondervan Illustrated Bible Backgrounds Commentary, Vol. 1:* 109, 152n483.

30:3 Let her give birth on my knees

"Birku." *In: The Assyrian Dictionary (CAD), Vol. 3: B*, 255, 257.

Hoffner, Harry A., trans. "Appu and His Two Sons (1.58)' In: *COS, Vol. 1:* 153–155, esp. p. 154.

Sarna. *The JPS Torah Commentary: Genesis*, 207–208.

Speiser. *Anchor Bible: Genesis*, 230.

30:11 Gad

Batto, B. F. "Curse אלה." In: *Dictionary of Deities and Demons in the Bible*, edited by Karel van der Toom, Bob Becking, and Pieter W. van der Horst, 338–405, esp. p. 339. Leiden: Brill, 1995.

Sarna. *The JPS Torah Commentary: Genesis*, 208.

30:14–15 Mandrakes

Biggs, Robert D. "Medicine, Surgery, and Public Health in Ancient Mesopotamia." In: *Civilizations of the Ancient Near East, Vol.* 3, edited by Jack M. Sasson,1911–1924, esp. p. 1917. Peabody, MA: Hendrickson, 2000.

Casini, Emanuele. "Rethinking the Multifaceted Aspects of Mandrake in Ancient Egypt." *Egitto e Vicino Oriente* 41 (2018): 101–116, esp. p. 102.

Garroway, Kristine Henriksen. "What to Expect When You are (Not) Expecting." In: *Growing Up in Ancient Israel: Children in Material Culture and Biblical Texts*, 256–263, esp. p. 257. Atlanta, GA: SBL Press.

Keel, Othmar. "If You were Only My Brother." In: *The Song of Songs: A Continental* Commentary. 256–263, esp. p. 257. Minneapolis, MN: Fortress, 1994.

Reiner, Erica. "Babylonian Birth Prognoses." *Zeitschrift* für *Assyrologie und vorderasiatische Archäeologie* 72(1) 1982: 124–138.

Sarna. *The JPS Torah Commentary: Genesis*, 209.

Stol, Marten. "Magic and the Divine." In: *Birth in Babylonia and the Bible: Its Mediterranean Setting*, 112–146, esp. p. 133–135. Groningen: Styx. 2000.

Walton, John H. "Genesis." In: *Zondervan Illustrated Bible Backgrounds Commentary, Vol. 1:* 109–110, 152–153n485–489.

30:25 Status of an infertile wife

Hess, Richard S., trans. "Seven Years of Barrenness Before a Second Wife (at 93) (3.101C)." In: *COS, Vol.* 3: 252.

Marsman, Hennie J. "The Social Position of Women." In: *Women in Ugarit: Their Social and Religious Position in the Context of the Ancient Near East*, 43–471, esp. p. 197. Leiden: Brill, 2003.

Stol, Marten. "A Second Wife." In: *Women in the Ancient Near East*, 112–146, esp. p. 133–135. Boston, MA: De Gruyter, 2016.

Walton, John H. "Genesis." In: *Zondervan Illustrated Bible Backgrounds Commentary, Vol. 1:* 110, 153n490.

30:27 Learned by divination

"Nuhsu." In: *The Assyrian Dictionary (CAD), Vol. 11, part 2: N.* 319–320.
Sarna. *The JPS Torah Commentary: Genesis*, 211.
Speiser. *Anchor Bible: Genesis*, 236.
Walton, John H. "Genesis." In: *Zondervan Illustrated Bible Backgrounds Commentary, Vol. 1:* 110.

30:29–43 Yaakov's sheep

Feliks, Yehuda. "Nature and the Land in the Tanakh: Chapters in Biblical Ecology." In: Olam HaTanakh Encyclopedia. Tel Aviv: Revivim, 1993. 31–36, 181–182 (Hebrew).
Sarna. *The JPS Torah Commentary: Genesis*, 212.

30:32–34 Yaakov's wages

Morrison, Martha A. "The Jacob and Laban Narrative in Light of Near Eastern Sources." *The Biblical Archaeologist* 46(3) 1983: 155–164, esp. p. 156–157.
Walton, John H. "Genesis." In: *Zondervan Illustrated Bible Backgrounds Commentary, Vol. 1:* 110, 153n492–493.

31:15 He has sold us and spent the money

Alter, Robert. *Genesis: Translation and Commentary*. New York: W.W. Norton, 1996, 168.
Marsman, Hennie J. "The Social Position of Women." In: *Women in Ugarit: Their Social and Religious Position in the Context of the Ancient Near East*, 43–471, esp. p. 103. Leiden: Brill, 2003.
Sarna. *The JPS Torah Commentary: Genesis*, 215.
Speiser. *Anchor Bible: Genesis*, 245.
Stol, Marten. "The Marriage Gifts. In: *Women in the Ancient Near East*, 112–146, esp. p. 133–135. Boston, MA: De Gruyter, 2016.
Walton, John H. "Genesis." In: *Zondervan Illustrated Bible Backgrounds Commentary, Vol. 1:* 111.

31:19 Sheepshearing in Mesopotamia

Frankena, R. "Some Remarks on the Semitic Background of Genesis XXIX–XXXI" In: *The Witness of Tradition: Papers Read at the Joint British–Dutch Old Testament Conference Held at Woudschoten*, edited by C. Van Der Woude, 53–64, esp. p. 56. Leiden: Brill, 1972.
Sarna. *The JPS Torah Commentary: Genesis*, 216.

31:19 Teraphim (*terafim*)

Flynn, Shawn W. "The Teraphim in Light of Mesopotamian and Egyptian Evidence." *The Catholic Biblical Quarterly* 74(4) 2012: 694–711.
Garroway, Kristine Henriksen. "Household Gods." In: *The Koren Tanakh of the Land of Israel: Samuel*: 155.
Sarna. *The JPS Torah Commentary: Genesis*, 216.
Speiser. *Anchor Bible: Genesis*, 245.
Walton, John H. "Genesis." In: *Zondervan Illustrated Bible Backgrounds Commentary, Vol. 1:* 111, 112.

31:22–23 From Ḥaran to Gilad in seven days

Sarna. *The JPS Torah Commentary: Genesis*, 217.
Walton, John H. "Genesis." In: *Zondervan Illustrated Bible Backgrounds Commentary, Vol. 1:* 111, 113, 153n499–502.

31:30 Taking gods to another location

Flynn, S. W. "The Teraphim in Light of Mesopotamian and Egyptian Evidence." *The Catholic Biblical Quarterly* 74(4) 2012: 694–711.
Garroway, Kristine Henriksen. "Household Gods." In: *The Koren Tanakh of the Land of Israel: Samuel*: 155.
Greenberg, M. "Another Look at Rachel's Theft of the Teraphim." *Journal of Biblical Literature* 81(3) 1962: 239–248.
Hoffner, Harry A., trans. "Proclamation of Anita of Kuššar (1.72). In: *COS, Vol. 1*: 182–184, esp. p. 183.
Paul, S. "Daniel 11:8" In: *Commentary on Daniel* (unpublished manuscript).

Sarna. *The JPS Torah Commentary: Genesis*, 216.
Speiser. *Anchor Bible: Genesis*, 245n19.
Walton, John H. "Genesis." In: *Zondervan Illustrated Bible Backgrounds Commentary, Vol. 1*: 98–99.
Wiseman, Donald J. "B.M. 21901." In: *Chronicles of Chaldean Kings (626–556) in the British Museum*, 54–64, esp. p. 54–55. London, Trustees of the British Museum, 1961.
———. "B.M. 21946." In: *Chronicles of Chaldean Kings (626–556) in the British Museum*, 60–74, esp. p. 70. London, Trustees of the British Museum, 1961.

31:35 The way of women

"Musukku." In: *The Assyrian Dictionary (CAD), Vol. 10, part 2: M*, 239.
Peled, Ilan. "The menstruant." In: *The Koren Tanakh of the Land of Israel: Leviticus*, 103.
Sarna. *The JPS Torah Commentary: Genesis*, 219.
Walton, John H. "Genesis." In: *Zondervan Illustrated Bible Backgrounds Commentary, Vol. 1*: 113, 153n503–504.

31:38–39 Yaakov's claim of innocence

King, L. W., trans. "The Code of Hammurabi." In: *Encyclopedia Britannica*, 11th edition. Worchester, MA: Horace Everett Hooper, 1915.
Postgate, J. N. "Crops and livestock." In: *Early Mesopotamia: Society and economy at the dawn of history*, 157–172, esp. p. 160–161 (text 8:4). New York: Routledge, 1994.
Sarna. *The JPS Torah Commentary: Genesis*, 220, 366n15–16.
Walton, John H. "Genesis." In: *Zondervan Illustrated Bible Backgrounds Commentary, Vol. 1*: 113–114, 153n505–507.

31:44–54 Treaty between Yaakov and Lavan

"Adu." In: *The Assyrian Dictionary (CAD), Vol. 1, part 1: A*, 131.
Sarna. *The JPS Torah Commentary: Genesis*, 221–222.
Thompson, Thomas L. "Nuzi and the Patriarchal Narratives." In: *The Historicity of the Patriarchal Narratives: The Quest for the Historical Abraham*, 196–297, esp. p. 270. Berlin: Walter de Gruyter, 1974.
Walton, John H. "Genesis." In: *Zondervan Illustrated Bible Backgrounds Commentary, Vol. 1*: 114, 153n508–509.

32:2 Maḥanayim

McKinney, Chris. "Maḥanayim." In: *The Koren Tanakh of the Land of Israel: Samuel*: 229.
Sarna. *The JPS Torah Commentary: Genesis*, 223.
Walton, John H. "Genesis." In: *Zondervan Illustrated Bible Backgrounds Commentary, Vol. 1*: 114–115, 153n510.

32:3 Land of Se'ir, the country of Edom

Knauf, Ernest Axel. "Seir." In: *Anchor Bible Dictionary, Vol. 5*, 1072–1073.
Rainey, Anson F. and R. Steven Notley. "The Land Bridge." In: *The Sacred Bridge: Carta's Atlas of the Biblical World*, Jerusalem: Carta, 2006, 30–42, esp. p. 41 (map on 38).
Walton, John H. "Genesis." In: *Zondervan Illustrated Bible Backgrounds Commentary, Vol. 1*: 115.

32:4–5 Style of Yaakov's message to Esav

Sarna. *The JPS Torah Commentary: Genesis*, 366n7.
Speiser. *Anchor Bible: Genesis*, 254.

32:14–15 List of Yaakov's gifts

Alter, Robert. *Genesis: Translation and Commentary*, 179. New York: W. W. Norton, 1996.
Walton, John H. "Genesis." In: *Zondervan Illustrated Bible Backgrounds Commentary, Vol. 1*: 115, 116(sidebar), 153n12–513.

32:22–23 River Yabok

Aharoni, Yohanan. "The Land of Many Contrasts." In: The Land of the Bible: A Historical Geography, 21–42, esp. p. 34. Philadelphia, PA: The Westminster Press, 1979.

Rainey Anson F. and R. Steven Notley. *The Sacred Bridge: Carta's Atlas of the Biblical World*. Jerusalem: Carta, 2006.
Ron, Zvi. "Yabok." In: *The Koren Tanakh of the Land of Israel: Numbers*, 137.
Sarna. *The JPS Torah Commentary: Genesis*, 226, 228.

32:24–31 Yaakov's struggle with the angel

Sarna. "Excursus 24: Jacob's Struggle with the Angel." In: *The JPS Torah Commentary: Genesis*, 403–404.
Tsevat, Matitiahu. "Two Old Testament Stories and Their Hittite Analogues." *Journal of the American Oriental Society* 103(1) 1983: 321–326, esp. p. 321–322.
Walton, John H. "Genesis." In: *Zondervan Illustrated Bible Backgrounds Commentary, Vol. 1*: 115, 153n515–519.

32:32 Sciatic nerve

Zivotofsky, Ari. "What's the Truth about Nikkur Achoraim?" *OUKosher.org*, September 2006. Available at: https://oukosher.org/blog/consumer-kosher/whats-the-truth-about-nikkur-achoraim.

33:3 Bowing down to the ground seven times

Moran, William L., ed and trans. "The loyalty of Qatna." In: *The Amarna Letters*. Baltimore, MD: Johns Hopkins University Press, 1992, 123.
———. "Like a bird in a trap." In: *The Amarna Letters*. Baltimore, MD: Johns Hopkins University Press, 1992, 142.
Sarna. *The JPS Torah Commentary: Genesis*, 229, 366n1.
Walton, John H. "Genesis." In: *Zondervan Illustrated Bible Backgrounds Commentary, Vol. 1*: 116, 153n520.

33:4 Dots above letters in Tanakh

Butin, Romain. *The Ten Nequdoth of the Torah: Or the Meaning and Purpose of the Extraordinary Points of the Pentateuch (Massoretic Text); A Contribution to the History of Text Criticism Among the Ancient Jews*. New York: Ktav, 1969, xi–xiii, 73–75, 123.
Lambert, Wilfred G., trans. "Enuma Elish." In: *Babylonian Creation Myths*. University Park, PA: Penn State University Press, 2013, 3–133.
Lieberman, Saul. "Critical Marks in the Hebrew Bible." In: *Hellenism in Jewish Palestine*, 38–46, esp. p. 43–46. New York: Jewish Theological Seminary, 1950.
Sarna. *The JPS Torah Commentary: Genesis*, 366n3.
Speiser. *Anchor Bible: Genesis*, 259.
Yeivin, Israel. "The Writing of the Biblical Text." In: *Introduction to the Tiberian Masorah*, translated and edited by E.J. Revell, 36–49, esp. p. 44–45. Missoula, MT: Scholars Press, 1980.

33:10–11 Gift giving in the ancient Near East

Garroway, Kristine Henriksen. "Joseph's Coat: Giving Gifts to Children in the Hebrew Bible." *AVAR* 1(2) 2002: 185–211. esp. p. 139–165.
Hallo, William W, trans. "The Letter of Takuhlina (3.94)." In: *COS, Vol.* 3: 243–244.
Hess, Richard S., trans. "Marriage Customs (AT 92) (3.101B)." In: *COS, Vol.* 3: 251–252.
Matthews, Victor H. "The Unwanted Gift: Implication of Obligatory Gift Giving in Ancient Israel." *Semeia* 87 (1999): 91–104.
Moran, William, trans. "Letter of Tushratta, King of Mitanni (EA 17) (3.92D)." In: *COS, Vol. 3*: 239–240.
Satlow, Michael ed. *The Gift in Antiquity*. Hoboken, NJ: Wiley-Blackwell, 2013.
Stansell, Gary. "The Gift in Ancient Israel." *Semeia* 87 (1999): 65–90.

33:17 Sukkot

Sarna. *The JPS Torah Commentary: Genesis*, 231.
Walton, John H. "Genesis." In: *Zondervan Illustrated Bible Backgrounds Commentary, Vol. 1*: 116–117.

33:19 *Kesita*

Sarna. *The JPS Torah Commentary: Genesis*, 232, 367n13.
Walton, John H. "Genesis." In: *Zondervan Illustrated Bible Backgrounds Commentary, Vol. 1:* 117–118, 153–154n524–525.

34:1 Dina...went out

Sarna. *The JPS Torah Commentary: Genesis*, 233, 367n3.

34:20 Fellow townsmen

Moran, William L. "From the citizens of Tunip." In: *The Amarna Letters*. Baltimore, MD: Johns Hopkins University Press, 1992, 130–131.
———. "De profundis." In: *The Amarna Letters*, 222–225. Baltimore, MD: Johns Hopkins University Press, 1992.
Sarna. *The JPS Torah Commentary: Genesis*, 237.

34:30 You have made me odious to the inhabitants of the land

Allen, James P., trans. "The Craft of the Scribe (3.22) In: *COS, Vol. 3*: 9–14, esp. p. 14.
Lichtheim, Miriam, trans. "Instructions of Any (1.46)." In: *COS, Vol. 1*: 110–115, esp. p. 111.

35:2–4 Getting rid of the alien gods

Bachhuber, Christoph. "The Lion Pit and other Ambiguous Violence against Statues at Iron Age Zincirli" In: *Visual Histories of the Classical World: Essays in Honour of R.R.R. Smith*, edited by Catherine M. Draycott, Rubina Raja, Katherine Welch and William T. Wootton, 76–86, esp. p. 77–79. Turnhout: Brepols, 2018.
Hallo, William W. "Cult Statue and Divine Image: A Preliminary Study." In: *Scripture in Context II More Essays on the Comparative Method*, edited by William W. Hallo, James C. Moyer, and Leo G. Perdue, 1–17, esp. p. 15–17. Winona Lake, IN: Eisenbrauns, 1983.
Hurowitz, Victor Avigdor. "Who Lost an Earring: Genesis 35:4 Reconsidered." *The Catholic Biblical Quarterly* 62(1) 2000: 28–32.
Sarna. *The JPS Torah Commentary: Genesis*, 239–240.
Walton, John H. "Genesis." In: *Zondervan Illustrated Bible Backgrounds Commentary, Vol. 1:* 118–119.

35:14 Libations and pouring oil at a sanctified place

Luckenbill, Daniel David. "The 'Bit–Kutalli' or Armory." In: *The Annals of Sennacherib*, 128–134, esp. p. 130. Chicago, IL: University of Chicago Press, 1924.
Sarna. *The JPS Torah Commentary: Genesis*, 200, 242, 368n11.

35:16–20 Memorializing the dead

Aja, Adam J. "Grid 38." In: *Ashkelon 7: The Iron Age I*, 20-126. Winona Lake, IN: Eisenbrauns.
Martin, Mario A.S., Melissa S. Cradic and Rachel Kalisher. "Area K: Intramural Pit and Jar Burials (Level K-10)." In: *Megiddo VI the 2010–2014 Seasons*, edited by I. Finkelstein and Mario A. S. Martin, 224–305. Tel Aviv: Emery and Claire Yass Publications in Archaeology and Winona Lake, IN: Eisenbrauns, 2022.
Sonia, Kerry M. *Caring for the Dead in Ancient Israel*. Atlanta, GA: SBL Press, 2020.
Suriano, Matthew J. *A History of Death in the Hebrew Bible*. New York: Oxford University Press, 2018.
Xella, Paolo. "Death and Afterlife in Canaanite and Hebrew Thought." In: *Civilizations of the Ancient Near East, Vol. 3*, edited by Jack M. Sasson, 2059–2070, esp. p. 2064. Peabody, MA: Hendrickson, 2000.

35:20 Raḥel's grave

Elitzur, Yoel "Solving the Signs of Sha'ul and the Problem of Rachel's Burial." *Sinai*, Vol. 82 (1983). Available at: https://www.daat.ac.il/he-il/kitveyet/sinai/elizur-pesher.htm (Hebrew). https://www.daat.ac.il/daat/tanach/tora/rachel/elitzur2.htm
Etshalom, Yitzchak. "The Location of Rachel's Tomb: Parshas Yayechi" In: The Torah.com. Available at: https://torah.org/torah-portion/mikra-5774-vayechi. https://torah.org/torah-portion/mikra-5774-vayechi/

McKinny, Chris. "Raḥel's tomb." In: *The Koren Tanakh of the Land of Israel: Samuel*, 88.
Sarna. "Excursus 27: Ephrath, Rachel's Tomb, and Migdal-eder." In: *The JPS Torah Commentary: Genesis*, 407–408.

35:22 Reuven's adultery with Bilha

Sarna. "Reuben's Wanton Challenge." In: *The JPS Torah Commentary: Genesis*, 244–245.
Tsevat, Matitiahu. "Marriage and Monarchical Legitimacy in Ugarit and Israel." *Journal of Semantic Studies* 3(3) 1958: 237–243.
Walton, Andrew. "Sleeping with a King's concubine." In: *The Koren Tanakh of the Land of Israel: Samuel*, 236.
Walton, John H. "Genesis." In: *Zondervan Illustrated Bible Backgrounds Commentary, Vol. 1:* 120, 154n538–539.

36:11 Teiman

Ron, Zvi. "Midianites." In: *The Koren Tanakh of the Land of Israel: Numbers*, 58.
Sarna. *The JPS Torah Commentary: Genesis*, 249.
Speiser. *Anchor Bible: Genesis*, 279.

36:31–39 Kings of Edom

Ben-Yosef, Erez. "Rethinking the Social Complexity of Early Iron Age Nomads." *Jerusalem Journal of Archaeology* 1 (2021): 155–179.
———. "The Architectural Bias in Current Biblical Archaeology." *Vetus Testamentum* 69(3) 2019: 361–387.
Eph'al, Israel. *The Ancient Arabs: Nomads on the Borders of the Fertile Crescent, 9th–5th Centuries BC*, Jerusalem: Magnes Press, 1982.
Knauf, Ernst A. "Qaus in Ägypten." *Göttinger Miszellen* 73 (1984): 33–36.
Millard, Alan R. "Assyrian Involvement in Edom." In: *Early Edom and Moab: The Beginning of the Iron Age in Southern Jordan*, edited by Piotr Bienkowski, 35–39. Sheffield, UK: J. R. Collis, 1992.

36:33–37 Botzra, Hada, Midyan, Masreka

Sarna. *The JPS Torah Commentary: Genesis*, 252.
Speiser. *Anchor Bible: Genesis*, 280.

36:41 Ela and Pinon

Sarna. *The JPS Torah Commentary: Genesis*, 253.

37:2 Bad reports

Ron, Zvi. "Adverse report (*dibbah*)." In: *The Koren Tanakh of the Land of Israel: Numbers*, 85.
Tawil, Hayim ben Yosef. "דבה." In: *An Akkadian Lexical Companion for Biblical Hebrew*, 71.

37:3 Ornately colored robe

Carasik, Michael. "The ornate tunic." In: *The Koren Tanakh of the Land of Israel: II Samuel*, 13:18.
אנציקלופדיה עולם התנ"ך: בראשית. תל אביב: הוצאת רביבים, 1993.
"*Pasamu*." In: *The Assyrian Dictionary (CAD), Vol. 12: P*, 217.
"*Pussunu*." In: *The Assyrian Dictionary (CAD), Vol. 12: P*, 537.
Sarna. *The JPS Torah Commentary: Genesis*, 255.
Speiser. *Anchor Bible: Genesis*, 289–290.
Walton, John H. "Genesis." In: *Zondervan Illustrated Bible Backgrounds Commentary, Vol. 1:* 120–121.
Watson, Wilfred G. E. "Terms for Textiles, Clothing, Hides, Wool and Accessories in Ugaritic: An Etymological Study." *Aula Orientalis* 36(2) 2018: 359–396, esp. p. 367, 378, 383, 387.

37:17–25 Dotan and the Ishmaelite caravan

Dorsey, David A. *The Roads and Highways of Ancient Israel*. Baltimore, MD: The Johns Hopkins University Press, 1991.

Eph'al, Israel. *The Ancient Arabs: Nomads on the Borders of the Fertile Crescent, 9th–5th Centuries B.C.* Leiden, Brill, 1982.
Master, Daniel M. "Tell Dothan." In: *The Oxford Encyclopedia of the Bible and Archaeology. Vol. 2*, edited by Daniel M. Master, 388–393. Oxford: Oxford University Press, 2013.
———. John M. Monson, Egon H. E. Lass, and George A. Pierce. *Dothan I: Remains from the Tell (1953–1964)*. Winona Lake, IN: Eisenbrauns, 2005.
Ussishkin, David. "Dothan." In: *The New Encyclopedia of Archaeological Excavations in the Holy Land, Vol. 1*, edited by Ephraim Stern, 372–373. Jerusalem: The Israel Exploration Society & Carta, 1993.

37:20 Pits (cisterns)

Tuk, Tsvika. "Touring Israel's Ancient Water Systems." In: *Cura aquarum in Israel II: Water in Antiquity: Proceedings of the 15th International Conference on the History of Water Management and Hydraulic Engineering in the Mediterranean Region, Israel, 14 – 20 October 2012*, 85-106, esp. p. 98. Siegburg, DWhG, 2014.
Walton, John H. "Genesis." In: *Zondervan Illustrated Bible Backgrounds Commentary, Vol. 1:* 123.

37:25 Gilad

Leibtag, Menachem. "Who Really Sold Yosef." Available at: https://www.hatanakh.com/sites/herzog/files/herzog/Who%20Really%20Sold%20Yosef.docx.pdf.
Sarna. *The JPS Torah Commentary: Genesis*, 260.

37:28 Twenty pieces of silver

King, L. W., trans. "The Code of Hammurabi." In: *Encyclopedia Britannica*, 11th edition. Worchester, MA: Horace Everett Hooper, 1915.
Kitchen, K. "Founding Fathers or Fleeting Phantoms – The Patriarchs." In: *On the Reliability of the Old Testament*, 313–372, esp. p. 344–345; 576n118–123. Grand Rapids, MI: W.B. Eerdmans, 2003.
Walton, John H. "Genesis." In: *Zondervan Illustrated Bible Backgrounds Commentary, Vol. 1:* 124, 154n550.

37:35 Sheol

Barstad, H. M. "Sheol." In: *Dictionary of Deities and Demons in the Bible*, edited by Karel van der Toom, Bob Becking, and Pieter W. van der Horst, 1452–1457. Leiden: Brill, 1998.
Lewis, Theodore J. "Dead, Abode of the." In: *Anchor Bible Dictionary, Vol. 2*, 101–105.
"שְׁאוֹל" In: *The Hebrew and Aramaic Lexicon of the Old Testament, Vol. 4*, 1368–1370.

37:36 *Saris*

Carasik, Michael. "Officials or eunuchs?" In: *The Koren Tanakh of the Land of Israel: Samuel*, 8:15.
Sarna. *The JPS Torah Commentary: Genesis*, 263.

38:1–12 Adulam, Keziv, Timna

McKinny, Chris. "Adulam." In: *The Koren Tanakh of the Land of Israel:* I Samuel, 166.
McKinny, Chris and Cassuto, Deborah. "Looms on Location: Textile Production in the Shephelah and the Identity of Beth-ashbea (1 Chr 4:21)." Presented at SBL Annual Meeting. December 10, 2020 (virtual meeting).
Sarna. *The JPS Torah Commentary: Genesis*, 265, 267.

38:8 Levirate marriage

Roth, Martha T. "Middle Assyrian Laws (MAL) (ca. 1076 B.C.E., Assur)." In: *Law Collections from Mesopotamia and Asia Minor*153–194, esp. p. 169. Atlanta, GA: Scholars Press, 1995.
———. "Hittite Laws." In: *Law Collections from Mesopotamia and Asia Minor*, 213–243, esp. p. 236. Atlanta, GA: Scholars Press, 1995.
Sarna. *The JPS Torah Commentary: Genesis*, 266–267.
Tigay, Jeffrey H. "Excursus 23: Levirate Marriage." In: *The JPS Torah Commentary: Deuteronomy*, 482–483.

Walton, John H. "Genesis." In: *Zondervan Illustrated Bible Backgrounds Commentary, Vol. 1:* 124–126.

38:11 Live as a widow

Marsman, Hennie J. "The Social Position of Women." In: *Women in Ugarit: Their Social and Religious Position in the Context of the Ancient Near East,* 43–471, esp. p. 292. Leiden: Brill, 2003.

Stol, Marten. 'The Widow." In: *Women in the Ancient Near East,* 275–295, esp. p. 275–276. Boston, MA: De Gruyter, 2016.

Walton, John H. "Genesis." In: *Zondervan Illustrated Bible Backgrounds Commentary, Vol. 1:* 126, 155n561.

38:14 Veil

Marsman, Hennie J. "The Social Position of Women." In: *Women in Ugarit: Their Social and Religious Position in the Context of the Ancient Near East,* 43–471, esp. p. 123. Leiden: Brill, 2003.

Sarna. *The JPS Torah Commentary: Genesis,* 268.

Stol, Marten. "Her Outward Appearance." In: *Women in the Ancient Near East,* 7–59, esp. p. 24–25. Boston, MA: De Gruyter, 2016.

Toorn, Karel van der. "The Significance of the Veil in the Ancient Near East." In: *Pomegranates and Golden Bells: Studies in Biblical, Jewish, and Near Eastern Ritual, Law, and Literature in Honor of Jacob Milgrom,* edited by David P. Wright, David Noel Freedman, and Avi Hurvitz, 327–340, esp. p. 338. Winona Lake, IN: Eisenbrauns, 1995

38:18 Your seal and cord, and the staff in your hand

Sarna. *The JPS Torah Commentary: Genesis,* 268.

Walton, John H. "Genesis." In: *Zondervan Illustrated Bible Backgrounds Commentary, Vol. 1:* 127.

38:21 Cult prostitute

Marsman, Hennie J. "The Social Position of Women." In: *Women in Ugarit: Their Social and Religious Position in the Context of the Ancient Near East,* 43–471, esp. p. 292. Leiden: Brill, 2003.

———. "The Religious Position of Women." In: *Women in Ugarit: Their Social and Religious Position in the Context of the Ancient Near East,* 473–626, esp. p. 498–499. Leiden: Brill, 2003.

Sarna. *The JPS Torah Commentary: Genesis,* 269.

Stol, Marten. "Temple Prostitution." In: *Women in the Ancient Near East,* 419–435. Boston, MA: De Gruyter, 2016.

———. "Married Holy Women." In: *Women in the Ancient Near East,* 605–616, esp. p. 608–614. Boston, MA: De Gruyter, 2016.

Tawil, Hayim ben Yosef. "קדשה." In: *An Akkadian Lexical Companion for Biblical Hebrew:* 335–336, esp. p. 335.

Van der Toorn, Karel. "Prostitution (Cultic)." In: *Anchor Bible Dictionary, Vol. 5,* 510–513, esp. p. 512–513.

Walton, John H. "Genesis." In: *Zondervan Illustrated Bible Backgrounds Commentary, Vol. 1:* 126–127, 155n568, 570.

38:24 Let her be burned

Driver, G. R. and Miles, John C., trans. "Laws of Hammu-rabi." In: *The Babylonian Laws. Vol. 2,* §§110, §§157. Oxford, Clarendon Press, 1955.

Walton, John H. "Genesis." In: *Zondervan Illustrated Bible Backgrounds Commentary, Vol. 1:* 127, 155n571.

39:1–23 Yosef in Egypt

Rainey Anson F. and R. Steven Notley. *The Sacred Bridge: Carta's Atlas of the Biblical World,* Jerusalem: Carta, 2006.

Rendsburg, Gary. The Joseph Story: Ancient Literary Art at Its Best. *The Torah.com.* Available at: https://www.thetorah.com/article/the-joseph-story-ancient-literary-art-at-its-best https://www.thetorah.com/article/the-joseph-story-ancient-literary-art-at-its-best.

39:2 He lived in the house of his Egyptian master

Hayes, William C. "The List of Servants." In: *A Papyrus of the Late Middle Kingdom in the Brooklyn Museum*, 87–109, esp. p. 90, 103, 108. Brooklyn: Brooklyn Museum, 1972,

39:7–20 Yosef and Potifar's wife

Sarna. "Excursus 29: Joseph and Potiphar's Wife." In" *The JPS Torah Commentary: Genesis*, 410.

Wilson, John A., trans. "The Story of Two Brothers." In: *Ancient Near Eastern Texts Relating to the Old Testament (ANET)*: 23–25, esp. p. 24.

39:20 Prison

Peters, Edward. "Prison before Prison: The Ancient and Medieval Worlds." In: *The Oxford History of the Prison: The Practice of Punishment in Western Society*, edited by Norval Morris and David J. Rothman, 3–47, esp. p. 8–9. Oxford: Oxford University Press, 1998.

Sarna. *The JPS Torah Commentary: Genesis*, 276.

———. *The JPS Torah Commentary: Genesis*, 276–277.

Shupak, Nili. "A Fresh Look at the Dreams of the Officials and of Pharaoh in the Story of Joseph (Genesis 40–41) in the Light of Egyptian Dreams." *Journal of the Ancient Near Eastern Society* 30(1) 2006: 103–138, esp. p. 128–130.

40:1–23 Dream interpretation in Egypt

"Hartibi." *In: The Assyrian Dictionary (CAD), Vol.* 6: H, 116.

Hoffmeier, James K. "Joseph in Egypt." In: *Israel in Egypt: The Evidence for the Authenticity of the Exodus Tradition*, 77–106, esp. p. 88–89. New York: Oxford University Press, 1999.

Ritner, Robert K, trans. "Dream Oracles (1.33)." In: *COS, Vol. 1*: 52–54.

Shupak, N. "A Fresh Look at the Dreams of the Officials and of Pharaoh in the Story of Joseph (Genesis 40–41) in the Light of Egyptian Dreams." *Journal of the Ancient Near Eastern Society* 30(1) 2006: 103–138.

40:1 Cupbearer and baker

Sarna. *The JPS Torah Commentary: Genesis.*

Shupak, N. "A Fresh Look at the Dreams of the Officials and of Pharaoh in the Story of Joseph (Genesis 40-41) in the Light of Egyptian Dreams." *Journal of the Ancient Near Eastern Society* 30 (1) 2006: 128–130.

40:20 Pharaoh's birthday

Hoffmeier, James K. "Joseph in Egypt." In: *Israel in Egypt: The Evidence for the Authenticity of the Exodus Tradition*, 77–106, esp. p. 89–91. New York: Oxford University Press, 1997.

Walton, John H. "Genesis." In: *Zondervan Illustrated Bible Backgrounds Commentary, Vol. 1*: 129.

41:2 *Ye'or* and reed grass (*aḥu*)

"יְאֹר." In: *The Hebrew and Aramaic Lexicon of the Old Testament. Vol.* 2, 381–382.

Lambdin, Thomas O. "Egyptian Loan Words in the Old Testament." *Journal of the American Oriental Society* 73(3) 1953: 145–155, esp. p. 146, 151.

Noonan, Benjamin. "אחו." In: *Non-Semitic Loanwords in the Hebrew Bible: A Lexicon of Hebrew*. University Park, PA: Pennsylvania State University Press, 2021.

———. "יאור." In: *Non-Semitic Loanwords in the Hebrew Bible: A Lexicon of Hebrew*. University Park, PA: Pennsylvania State University Press, 2021.

Shupak, Nili. "A Fresh Look at the Dreams of the Officials and of Pharaoh in the Story of Joseph (Genesis 40–41) in the Light of Egyptian Dreams." *Journal of the Ancient Near Eastern Society* 30(1) 2006: 103–138.

41:2 Seven cows

Sarna. *The JPS Torah Commentary: Genesis*, 281.

Shupak, Nili. "A Fresh Look at the Dreams of the Officials and of Pharaoh in the Story of Joseph (Genesis 40–41) in the Light of Egyptian Dreams." *Journal of the Ancient Near Eastern Society* 30(1) 2006: 103–138, esp. p. 121, 122, 131.

41:5 He had a second dream

Pfeiffer, Robert H., trans. In: *Ancient Near Eastern Texts Relating to the Old Testament (ANET):* 434–437, esp. p. 436.

Walton, John H. "Genesis." In: *Zondervan Illustrated Bible Backgrounds Commentary, Vol. 1:* 129–130.

41:8 *Ḥartumim*

Goedicke, Hans. "Hartummîm." *Orientalia* 65(1) 1996: 24–30.

"Hartibi." In: *The Assyrian Dictionary (CAD), Vol. 6*: H, 16.

Noonan, Benjamin. "חַרְטֹם." In: *Non-Semitic Loanwords in the Hebrew Bible: A Lexicon of Hebrew.* University Park, PA: Pennsylvania State University Press, 2021.

Oppenheim, A. Leo. "The Interpretation of Dreams in the Ancient Near East. With a Translation of the Assyrian Dream-Book" *Transactions of the American Philosophical Society* 46(3) 1956: 179–373, esp. p. 238–239.

Quaegebeur, Jan. "On the Egyptian Equivalent of Biblical Hartummím." In: *Pharaonic Egypt: The Bible and Christianity*, 162–172. Jerusalem: Magnes Press, 1985.

Shupak, Nili. "A fresh look at the dreams of the officials and of Pharaoh in the story of Joseph (Genesis 40–41) in the light of Egyptian dreams." *Journal of the Ancient Near Eastern Society (JANES)* 30(1) 2006: 103–138.

Tawil, Hayim ben Yosef. "חַרְטֹם." In: *An Akkadian Lexical Companion for Biblical Hebrew*, 120.

41:14 Hair cut/shaved

Fried, Lisbeth S. "Why Did Joseph Shave." *Biblical Archaeology Review* 33(4) 2007: 36–41, 74.

Green, Lyn. "Hairstyles." In: *The Oxford Encyclopedia of Ancient Egypt, Vol. 2*, edited by Donald B. Radford, 73–76. Oxford: Oxford University Press, 2001.

Sarna. *The JPS Torah Commentary: Genesis*, 283.

Walton, John H. "Genesis." In: *Zondervan Illustrated Bible Backgrounds Commentary, Vol. 1:* 130.

41:27 Seven years of famine

Bar, Shaul. "Pharaoh' Dreams." In: *A Letter That Has Not Been Read: Dreams in the Hebrew Bible*, 54–59, esp. p. 58. Cincinnati, OH: HUC Press, 2001.

Sarna. *The JPS Torah Commentary: Genesis*, 290.

Walton, John H. "Genesis." In: *Zondervan Illustrated Bible Backgrounds Commentary, Vol. 1:* 130–131.

41:34–45 Yosef appointed overseer of Egypt

Abusch, Tzvi. "Introduction." In: *The Witchcraft Series Maqlu*, 1–43, esp. p. 28, 32. Atlanta, GA: SBL Press, 2015.

Callender, Gae. "The Middle Kingdom Renaissance." in *The Oxford History of Ancient Egypt*, edited by Ian Shaw, 148–217, esp. p. 164. New York: Oxford University Press, 2000.

Walton, John H. "Genesis." In: *Zondervan Illustrated Bible Backgrounds Commentary, Vol. 1:* 131.

———. "Genesis." In: *Zondervan Illustrated Bible Backgrounds Commentary, Vol. 1:* 131–132.

41:40 Yosef as commander of the granary

Walton, John H. "Genesis." In: *Zondervan Illustrated Bible Backgrounds Commentary, Vol. 1:* 131–132.

Ward, W. "The Egyptian Office of Joseph." *Journal of Semitic Studies* 5(2) 1960: 144–150.

41:42 Finest linen

"Byssus." In: *Oxford University Dictionary. Vol. 2*. Oxford: Oxford University Press, 1992.

King, Philip and Lawrence Stager. "The Means of Existence." In: *Life in Biblical Israel*, 85–200, esp. p. 148–152. Louisville, KY: Westminster John Knox Press, 2001.

Unterman, Jeremiah. "Egyptian agricultural cycle." In: *The Koren Tanakh of the Land of Israel: Exodus*, 53.

Sarna. *The JPS Torah Commentary: Genesis*, 286.

41:42–43 Yosef's symbols of rule

Oppenheim, A. Leo. "Texts from the Beginnings to the First Dynasty of Babylon." In: *Ancient Near Eastern Texts Relating to the Old Testament (ANET)*: 265–301, esp. 294–301.

Sarna. *The JPS Torah Commentary: Genesis*, 286–287, 369n16.

Shupak, Nili. "The Egyptian Background of the Joseph Story: Selected Issues Revisited" In: *"An Excellent Fortress for His Armies, a Refuge for the People": Egyptological, Archaeological, and Biblical Studies in Honor of James K. Hoffmeier*, 340–352, esp. p. 344–346. University Park, PA: Eisenbrauns, 2020.

Speiser. *Anchor Bible: Genesis*, 316–317.

Walton, John H. "Genesis." In: *Zondervan Illustrated Bible Backgrounds Commentary, Vol. 1*: 132.

Wilson, John A., trans. "The Vizier of Egypt." In: *Ancient Near Eastern Texts Relating to the Old Testament (ANET)*: 212–214, esp. p. 213.

41:43 *Avrekh*

Mankowski, Paul W. "אברך." In: *Akkadian Loanwords in Biblical Hebrew*, 16–20. Leiden: Brill, 2000.

Tigay, Jeffrey H. "Abrech." In: *Encyclopedia Judaica. Vol. 2*. Jerusalem: Keter, 1971, 174.

41:45 Tzafenat Paneaḥ … Asnat … Potifera … On

Sarna. *The JPS Torah Commentary: Genesis*, 287–288.

41:53–54 Famine in Egypt

Katary, Sally. "Nilometer." In: *The Encyclopedia of Ancient History*, edited by Roger S. Bagnall, Kai Brodersen, Craige B. Champion, Andrew Erskine and Sabine R. Huebner, 4794–4795. Malden, MA: Wiley-Blackwell, 2013.

Lichtheim, Miriam. "Stela of the Steward Seneni of Copus." In: *Ancient Egyptian Literature Volume I: The Old and Middle Kingdoms Egyptian Literature Volume I: The Old and Middle Kingdoms*. Berkeley, CA: University of California Press, 1975, 89–90.

Sarna. "The Onset of Famine." In: *The JPS Torah Commentary: Genesis*, 290–291.

42:9 You are spies

Cooney, Kathlyn M. "The New Kingdom of Egypt under the Ramesside Dynasty." In: *The Oxford History of the Ancient Near East. Volume III, From the Hyksos to the late second millennium BC*, edited by Karen Radner, Nadine Moeller, and D. T. Potts, 251–366, esp. p. 290. New York: Oxford University Press, 2022.

Lichtheim, Miriam, trans. "Merikare (1.35)" In: *COS, Vol. 1*: 61–66.

Sarna. *The JPS Torah Commentary: Genesis*, 293.

Shupak, Nili, trans. "The Prophecies of Neferti (1.45)" In. *COS, Vol. 1*: 106–110.

Walton, John H. "Genesis." In: *Zondervan Illustrated Bible Backgrounds Commentary, Vol. 1*: 132.

42:15 By Pharaoh's life

Sarna. *The JPS Torah Commentary: Genesis*, 294.

Wilson, John A. "The Oath in Ancient Egypt." *Journal of Near Eastern Studies* 7(3) 1948: 129–156.

42:27 Pack (*amtaḥat*)

Elman, Yaakov. "The Rebirth of Omnisignificant Biblical Exegesis in the Nineteenth and Twentieth Centuries." *Jewish Studies, an Internet Journal* 2 (2003): 199–249, esp. p. 233. Available at: http://www.biu.ac.il/JS/JSIJ/2-2003/Elman.doc.

Greenfield, Jonas C. "The Etymology of אַמְתַּחַת." *Zeitschrift für die Alttestamentlichw Wissenschaft* 77(1) 1965: 90–92.

43:9 I myself am the guarantee for his safety

Sarna. *The JPS Torah Commentary: Genesis*, 298.

Tawil, Hayim ben Yosef. "ערבה." In: *An Akkadian Lexical Companion for Biblical Hebrew*, 284.

43:11 Yaakov's gifts to "the man"

"Almond." In: *Encyclopedia of Cultivated Plants: From Acacia to Zinniap: Vol. 1*, edited by Christopher Cumo, 15–17, esp. p. 16. Santa Barbara, CA: ABC-CLIO, 2013.

Amar, Zohar. "Appendix on plants." In: *The Koren Israel Humash: Bereshit, with Rashi/Onkelos*, 16. Jerusalem: Koren, 2016.

———. *Tanakh La Metayyel*, 86, 100. Jerusalem: Koren, 2016.

Dershowitz, Idan. "Flowing with Fat and (Bee) Honey: Evidence from Ancient Egypt." *Vetus Testamentum* 64(4) 2014: 665–667.

Lichtham, Miriam, trans. "Sinuhe (1.38)" In: *COS, Vol. 1*: 77–82, esp. p. 79.

Sarna. *The JPS Torah Commentary: Genesis*, 299,

43:23 I received the money you paid

Muffs, Yochanan. "Two Comparative Lexical Studies." *Journal of the Ancient Near Eastern Society* 5(1) 1973: 287–298, esp. p. 288–291.

Sarna. *The JPS Torah Commentary: Genesis*, 301.

43:32 Separation between Egyptians and Semites

Sarna. *The JPS Torah Commentary: Genesis*, 302 plus his Excursus 4.

Shupak, Nili. "The Egyptian Background of the Joseph Story: Selected Issues Revisited." In: *"An Excellent Fortress for His Armies, a Refuge for the People": Egyptological, Archaeological, and Biblical Studies in Honor of James K. Hoffmeier*, 340–353, esp. p. 346–350. University Park, PA: Eisenbrauns, 2020.

44:2 Chalice (*gavia*)

"גביע." In: *The Hebrew and Aramaic Lexicon of the Old Testament, Vol. 1*, 175.

Noonan, Benjamin J. "גביע." In: *Non-Semitic Loanwords in the Hebrew Bible: A Lexicon of Hebrew*. University Park, PA: Pennsylvania State University Press, 2021.

44:5 Divination

Cryer, Frederick H. "Oil Omens." In: *Divination in Ancient Israel and its Near Eastern* Environment, 145–148, esp. p. 146–147. Sheffield, UK: JSOT Press, 1994.

Sarna. *The JPS Torah Commentary: Genesis*, 304.

44:9 Death penalty for theft

Roth, Martha T. "Laws of Hammurabi." In: *Law Collections from Mesopotamia and Asia Minor*, 71–142, esp. p. 82, 83. Atlanta, GA: Scholars Press, 1995.

———. "Middle Assyrian Laws." In: *Law Collections from Mesopotamia and Asia Minor*, 153–194, esp. p. 155. Atlanta, GA: Scholars Press, 1995.

Sarna. *The JPS Torah Commentary: Genesis*, 304.

45:10 Where was Goshen

Sarna. *The JPS Torah Commentary: Genesis*, 309–310.

Walton, John H. "Genesis." In: *Zondervan Illustrated Bible Backgrounds Commentary, Vol. 1:* 133.

45:22 Gift of clothes

Bryce, Trevor. "The Club of Royal Brothers." In: *Letters of the Great Kings of the Ancient Near East: The Royal Correspondence of the Late Bronze Age*, 70–88, esp. p. 77. London: Routledge, 2003.

King, Philip and Lawrence Stager. "Culture and Expressive Life." In: *Life in Biblical Israel*, 259–315, esp. p. 259–275. Louisville, KY: Westminster John Knox Press, 2001.

Moran, William L. *The Amarna Letters*. Baltimore, MD: Johns Hopkins University Press, 1992.

Perazzone Rivero, Emma. "Gift-exchange in the Amarna Letters: A Concise Study of the Letters from the Great Kings." In: *Trabajos de Egiptología/Papers on Ancient Egypt*, 139–159, esp.

p. 149. San Cristóbal de La Laguna: Universidad de La Laguna, Centro de Estudios Africanos, 2021. Available at: https://riull.ull.es/xmlui/bitstream/handle/915/27345/TdE_12_%282021%29_07.pdf?sequence=1

Sarna. *The JPS Torah Commentary: Genesis*, 311, 370n6.

46:27 Seventy members of Yaakov's family

Gollub, David. "The Seventy Israelites Who Went to Egypt." *Jewish Bible Quarterly*, 48(3) 2020: 196–198.

Pope, M. H. "Seven, Seventh, Seventy." In: *The Interpreter's Dictionary of the Bible: An Illustrated Encyclopedia, Vol. 4*, edited by George Arthur Buttrick, 294–295, esp. p. 295. New York: Abingdon Press, 1962.

Ron, Zvi. "Seventy." In: *The Koren Tanakh of the Land of Israel: Numbers*, 66.

Sarna. *The JPS Torah Commentary: Genesis*, 317.

46:34 Goshen as a land of herders

Allen, James P., trans. "A Report of Bedouin (3.5) (Papyrus Anastasi VI) In: *COS, Vol. 3*: 16–17.

Pinker, Aron. "'Abomination to Egyptians' in Genesis 43:32, 46:34, and Exodus 8:22." *Old Testament Essays* 22(1) 2009: 151–174, esp. p. 166.

Shupak, Nili. "Abominations of Egypt: New Light on an Old Problem." In: *Marbeh Ḥokmah: Studies in the Bible and the Ancient Near East in Loving Memory of Victor Avigdor Hurowitz*, edited by S. Yona, M. I., Greenstein, P. Gruber, P. Machinist, and S. M. Paul, 271–294, esp. p. 284–288.Winona Lake, IN: Eisenbrauns, 2015.

47:6 *Sarei mikneh*

Hayes, William C. "The Thutmoside Pharaohs: Thut-mose I to Hat-shepsut." In: *The Scepter of Egypt: A Background for the Study of the Egyptian Antiquities in the Metropolitan Museum of Art, Vol. 2*, 74–113, esp. p. 77, 78. New York: Metropolitan Museum of Art, 1990

———. "Private Works of Art and Craftsmanship Produced during the Thutmoside Period." In: *The Scepter of Egypt: A Background for the Study of the Egyptian Antiquities in the Metropolitan Museum of Art, Vol. 2*, 156–230, esp. p. 166, 168. New York: Metropolitan Museum of Art, 1990.

Sarna. *The JPS Torah Commentary: Genesis*, 319.

47:11 Region of Ramesses

Sarna. *The JPS Torah Commentary: Genesis*, 320

Walton, John H. "Genesis." In: *Zondervan Illustrated Bible Backgrounds Commentary, Vol. 1*: 134, 156n605.

47:17 Horses

Hill, Lauren. "Horses in Ancient Egypt." In: *Garstang Museum of Archaeology and the University of Liverpool*. Available at: https://garstangmuseum.wordpress.com/2018/04/13/horses-in-ancient-egypt/comment-page-1/

Sarna. *The JPS Torah Commentary: Genesis*, 321.

47:20–25 Yosef's reallocation of Egyptian land

Römer, M. "Landholding." In: *The Oxford Encyclopedia of Ancient Egypt, Vol. 2*, edited by Donald B. Radford, 256–257. Oxford: Oxford University Press, 2001.

Sarna. *The JPS Torah Commentary: Genesis*, 320–323.

Walton, John H. "Genesis." In: *Zondervan Illustrated Bible Backgrounds Commentary, Vol. 1*: 134–135.

———. "Genesis." In: *Zondervan Illustrated Bible Backgrounds Commentary, Vol. 1*: 135.

48:5 Yaakov's adoption and blessing of Efrayim and Menashe

Barmash, Pamela. "Adoption." In: *Oxford Encyclopedia of the Bible and Law,* edited by Brent A, Strawn, 1–9. Oxford: Oxford University Press, 2015.
Birku." In: *The Assyrian Dictionary (CAD), Vol.* 2: B, 256.
Chapman, Cynthia R. "'Oh that you were like a brother to me, one who had nurse at my mother's breasts:' Breast Milk as a Kinship–Forging Substance." *Journal of Hebrew Scriptures* 12 article 7 (2012): 1–41. Available at: https://doi.org/10.5508/jhs.2012.v12.a7
Chiera, Edward. *Excavations at Nuzi, Vol. 1: Texts of Varied Contents,* 67. Cambridge, MA: Harvard University Press, 1929.
Harper, Robert Francis. "[182.] K. 1058." In: *Assyrian and Babylonian Letters: Belonging to the Kouyunjik Collecftions of the British Museum* (ABL), 178. Chicago. IL: University Press of Chicago, 1893.
Hoffner, Harry A. Jr. "Birth and Name–Giving in Hittite Texts." *Journal of Near Eastern Studies* 27(3) 1968: 198–203.
Knobloch, Frederick. "Adoption." In: *Anchor Bible Dictionary, Vol. 1,* 76–79.
"Musée d'Art et d'Histoire, Geneva, Switzerland - Collections." Cuneiform Digital Library Initiative. August 23, 2023. Available at: https://cdli.mpiwg-berlin.mpg.de/collections/293.
Sarna. *The JPS Torah Commentary: Genesis,* 325–326.
Shalom, M. Paul. "Adoption Formulae: A Study of Cuneiform and Biblical Legal Clauses." *Maarav* 2 (1979): 173–185.
Strassmaier, J. N. *Inschriften von Nabuchodonosor, Köing von Babylon* (604–651 v. Chr.), 439. Leipzig: Pfeiffer, 1889.
Suurmeijer, Guido. "'He took him as his son'. Adoption in old Babylonian Sippar." *Revue de assyriologie* 104(2010–2011): 9–40. Available at: https://www.cairn.info/revue-d-assyriologie–2010–1–page–9.htm
Tigay, Jeffrey T. "Adoption." In: *Encyclopedia Judaica,* Vol. 2: A, 298–302. Jerusalem: Keter, 1971.
Westbrook, Raymond. "Adoption." In: *A History of Ancient Near Eastern Law,* 50–54. Leiden, Brill, 2003.
Wilson, John A., trans. "Egyptian Documents." In: *Ancient Near Eastern Texts Relating to the Old Testament (ANET):* 220.

48:15 Ancient Near Eastern metaphor of "shepherd"

Ron, Zvi. "The metaphor of shepherd as leader." In: *The Koren Tanakh of the Land of Israel: Numbers,* 177.
Sarna. *The JPS Torah Commentary: Genesis,* 328.

49:1 In the days to come

"Ahratu." In: *The Assyrian Dictionary (CAD), Vol.* 1: A, 194a
Sarna. *The JPS Torah Commentary: Genesis,* 332.

49:1–33 Blessings for Yaakov's sons

Ahituv, Shmuel. *Echoes from the Past: Hebrew and Cognate Inscriptions from the Biblical Period.* Jerusalem: Carta, 2008.
Gal, Zvi and Yardena Alexandre, with contributions by U. Baruch, *Horbat Rosh Zayit : An Iron Age Storage Fort and Villa.* Jerusalem: Israel Antiquities Authority, 2000.

49:4 Unstable (*p ḥ z*)

Sarna. *The JPS Torah Commentary: Genesis,* 333.
Tawil, Hayim ben Yosef. "פחז."In: *An Akkadian Lexical Companion for Biblical Hebrew,* 294.

49:9 Lion

Walton, John H. "Genesis." In: *Zondervan Illustrated Bible Backgrounds Commentary, Vol. 1:* 135–136.
Watanabe, Chikako E. *Animal Symbolism in Mesopotamia: A Contextual Approach,* 42-50. Vienna: Institut für Orientalistik der Universität Wien, 2002.

49:11 Robe (*sut*)

Lawson Younger, K., trans. The Kulamuwa Inscription (2.30). In: *COS, Vol. 2*: 147–148, esp. p. 147.

Sarna. *The JPS Torah Commentary: Genesis*, 371n27.

49:12 Darker (*ḥakhlili*)

"Ekehu." In: *The Assyrian Dictionary (CAD), Vol.* 4: E, 64.

Sarna. *The JPS Torah Commentary: Genesis*, 337, 371n28.

Tawil, Hayim ben Yosef. "חכלילי." In: *An Akkadian Lexical Companion for Biblical Hebrew*: 106–107.

49:13 Sidon

Boyes. Philip J. "'The King of the Sidonians': Phoenician Ideologies and the Myth of the Kingdom of Tyre–Sidon." *Bulletin of the American Schools of Oriental Research* 365 (2012): 33–44.

Sarna. *The JPS Torah Commentary: Genesis*, 338.

Walton, John H. "Genesis." In: *Zondervan Illustrated Bible Backgrounds Commentary, Vol. 1*: 136–137.

49:15 Like a slave in a harness

Albright, W. F., trans. "The Amarna Letters." In: *Ancient Near Eastern Texts Relating to the Old Testament (ANET)*: 483–490, esp. p. 484.

Held, Moshe. "The Root ZBL/SBL in Akkadian, Ugaritic and Biblical Hebrew." *Journal of the American Oriental Society* 88(1) 1968: 90–96.

Sarna. *The JPS Torah Commentary: Genesis*, 339–340, 372n36.

49:17 Viper (*shefifon*)

"שפיפון." In: *The Hebrew and Aramaic Lexicon of the Old Testament. Vol.4*, 1628–1629.

"Šibbu." In: *The Assyrian Dictionary (CAD), Vol.* 16, 375.

49:21 Fawns (*imrei*)

Gevirtz, Stanley. "Naphthali in 'The Blessing of Jacob.'" *Journal of Biblical Literature* 103(4) 1984: 513–521.

Sarna. *The JPS Torah Commentary: Genesis*, 342, 372n42.

50:2–3 Embalming

Jones, Richard N. "Embalming." In: *Anchor Bible Dictionary, Vol.* 2, 490–496.

Walton, John H. "Genesis." In: *Zondervan Illustrated Bible Backgrounds Commentary, Vol. 1*: 137, 137 (sidebar).

50:4 Yosef spoke to Pharaoh's court

Alter, Robert. *Genesis: Translation and Commentary*, 303. New York, W. W. Norton, 1996.

Sarna. *The JPS Torah Commentary: Genesis*, 347–349, esp. p. 348

Speiser. *Anchor Bible: Genesis*, 377.

50:10–11 Threshing floor of Atad . . . beyond the Jordan . . . Avel Mitzrayim

Sarna. *The JPS Torah Commentary: Genesis*, 347–349, esp. p. 348–349.

50:10 Seven days of mourning

Klingbeil, Gerald A. "Ritual Time." In: *A Comparative Study of the Ritual of Ordination as Found in Leviticus 8 and Emar 369*, 166–174, esp. p. 174. Lewiston, NY: E. Mellen Press, 1998.

Sarna. *The JPS Torah Commentary: Genesis*, 347–349, esp. p. 349, 372n6.

Xuan Huong Thi Pham. "The Mourning Rites of the Ancient Near East." In: *Mourning in the Ancient Near East and the Hebrew Bible*,16–23, esp. p. 16,17, 23. Sheffield, England: Sheffield Academic Press, 1999.

50:22 One hundred and ten years

Janssen, Josef M. A. "On the Ideal Lifetime of the Egyptians." Leiden: Rijksmuseum van Oudheden te Leiden, Leiden, 1950, 33–44.

Sarna. *The JPS Torah Commentary: Genesis,* 349–351, esp. p. 350.
Walton, John H. "Genesis." In: *Zondervan Illustrated Bible Backgrounds Commentary, Vol. 1:* 137.

50:23 Yosef seeing his great-grandchildren

Rosenthal, Franz, trans. "Canaanite and Aramaic Inscriptions: Agbar, Priest of the Moon–God in Nerab." In: *Ancient Near Eastern Texts Relating to the Old Testament (ANET):* 661–662.
Sarna. *The JPS Torah Commentary: Genesis,* 349–351, esp. p. 350–351.

50:26 Coffin

Sarna. *The JPS Torah Commentary: Genesis.*
MacLeod, Caroline Arbuckle. "The Development of the Egyptian Coffin." *American Research Center in Egypt,* https://www.arce.org/resource/development-egyptian-coffin.

Image Credits

Shu amulet on page 4, © Metropolitan Museum of Art, accession number 89.2.287, Gift of Joseph W. Drexel, 1889, metmuseum.org / CC0 1.0 DEED

Nun lifts solar barque, top on page 5, Scanned from The Complete Gods and Goddesses of Ancient Egypt by Richard H. Wilkinson, p. 117; artwork from the *Book of the Dead of Anhai* / Public domain

Marduk and Tiamat, bottom on page 5, From Layard, Austen Henry, ed. *Monuments of Nineveh, Second Series*, London: J. Murray, 1853. plate 5. Drawing by L. Grune / Public domain

Young doves, bottom left on page 6, Courtesy of Sarang / Public domain

Ramesses II and Ptah, bottom right on page 6, © Richard Mortel from Riyadh, Saudi Arabia / (CC BY 2.0)

Sun god with Akhenaten, bottom on page 7, © ArchaiOptix / (CC BY-SA 4.0)

Phoenician gold crown, right on page 7, Courtesy of The Walters Art Museum / (CC BY-SA 3.0)

Hathor Temple relief on page 8, © Olaf Tausch / (CC BY 3.0)

Shrine of Amun-Re on page 9, © Olaf Tausch / (CC BY 3.0)

Mul Apin fragment on page 10, © Zunkir / (CC BY-SA 4.0)

Crocodile god on page 11, Courtesy of The Walters Art Museum, acquired by Henry Walters, 1912 / (CC0 1.0)

Thutmose IV on page 12, © Rama / (CC BY-SA 3.0 FR)

Sacred basin on page 13, © Osama Shukir Muhammed Amin FRCP(Glasg) / (CC BY-SA 4.0)

Agricultural scenes Nakht tomb, bottom on page 15, © Metropolitan Museum of Art, Rogers Fund, 1915, metmuseum.org

Amun-Re with ankh to Ramesses II's nose on page 15, © Djehouty / (CC BY-SA 4.0)

Ninhursag temple panel on page 18, © Vassil / (CC0 1.0)

Investiture of Zimri-lim, center left on page 19 © Rama / (CC BY-SA 2.0 FR)

Fountain of the Four Rivers, bottom on page 19, © George M. Groutas / (CC BY 2.0)

Cow Temple of Ninmah on page 20, © Osama Shukir Muhammed Amin FRCP(Glasg) / (CC BY-SA 4.0)

Deucalion and Pyrrha on page 21, © Rijksmuseum / (CC0 1.0 Universal Public Domain Dedication)

Thutmose III with uraeus crown on page 22, © Tim Evanson from Cleveland Heights, Ohio, USA / (CC BY-SA 2.0)

Fig and fig leaf, bottom on page 23, © William Creswell from Seattle, Washington, USA / (CC BY 2.0)

Late afternoon in Jerusalem, right on page 23, United States Library of Congress's Prints and Photographs, Matson Collection, Public domain, digital ID matpc.14973

Pepi II relief, bottom left on page 24, © Osama Shukir Muhammed Amin FRCP(Glasgow) / (CC BY-SA 4.0)

Banishment of Adam and Eve, right on page 24, The Library of Congress (CC0 1.0) / Public domain

Jar with Ashera trees on page 25, © פעמי-עליון / (CC BY-SA 4.0)
Bronze Age sickle-shaped sword, left on page 26, © The Metropolitan Museum of Art, Gift of J. Pierpont Morgan, 1911, metmuseum.org
Winged bull statues, right on page 26, © Poulpy / (CC BY-SA 3.0)
Inanna Prefers the Farmer on page 27, © Osama Shukir Muhammed Amin FRCP(Glasgow) / (CC BY-SA 4.0)
Rekhmire and mother receive offerings on page 28, © Metropolitan Museum of Art, Rogers Fund, 1930, metmuseum.org (CC0)
Nergal plaque on page 29, © Osama Shukir Muhammed Amin FRCP(Glasg) / (CC BY-SA 4.0)
Irrigation remains on page 30, © shankar s. / (CC BY 2.0)
Inscription from Eridu, left on page 31, © Osama Shukir Muhammed Amin FRCP(Glasg) / (CC BY-SA 4.0)
Nuzi tablet, right on page 31, © Daderot / (CC0 1.0)
Tel Megiddo, left on page 32, © Avram Graicer / (CC BY-SA 3.0)
Chalcolithic copper mine, right on page 32, © Zairon / (CC BY-SA 4.0)
Temple of Baalat Gebal on page 33, © Joseph Azzam / (CC BY-SA 3.0)
Sumerian King List on page 34, © Gts-tg / (CC BY-SA 4.0)
Hurrian incense container on page 36, © Osama Shukir Muhammed Amin FRCP(Glasg) / (CC BY-SA 4.0)
Cylinder seal with Canaanite god on page 37, © Zunkir / (CC BY-SA 4.0)
Ninsun bas relief on page 38, © Rama / (CC BY-SA 2.0 FR)
Noah's ark on page 39, Courtesy Sotheby's Paris, 23 Juni 2011 Lot 30, Public domain
Ea statue, right on page 40, © Osama Shukir Muhammed Amin FRCP(Glasg) / (CC BY-SA 4.0)
Epic of Gilgamesh from Megiddo, bottom on page 40, © Todd Bolen / BiblePlaces.com
Epic of Atrahasis on page 41, Courtesy of Daderot / Public domain
Ancient Egyptian boat on page 42, © Ovedc / (CC BY-SA 4.0)
Hittite/Egypt treaty on page 43, © Olaf Tausch / (CC BY 3.0)
Cow slaughter on page 44, © Anastasia Petrova / Shutterstock
Votive stele from the Temple of Ningirsu on page 45, © Osama Shukir Muhammed Amin FRCP(Glasg) / (CC BY-SA 4.0)
Mount Ararat on page 47, © Serouj Ourishian / (CC BY-SA 4.0)
Croatia olive tree on page 48, © Palauenco5 / (CC BY-SA 4.0)
Ishtar on a lion on page 49, © Osama Shukir Muhammed Amin FRCP(Glasg) / (CC BY-SA 4.0)
Cave painting hunting scene on page 50, Courtesy of Nathan McCord, U.S. Marine Corps / Public domain
Kadesh treaty on page 51, © Osama Shukir Muhammed Amin FRCP(Glasg) / (CC BY-SA 4.0)
Deucalion and Pyrrha on page 52, Peter Paul Rubens, 1636, Museo del Prado artwork ID: 0851e122-93c1-44b4-9e94-23fd1c4edae9 / Public domain
Aegean grapevine on page 53, © Norbert Nagel / (CC BY-SA 3.0)
Stele of Canaan military campaign on page 54, © Oren Rozen / (CC BY-SA 4.0)
Noah with Grapes on page 55, © Georges Seguin (Okki) / (CC BY-SA 1.0)
Seventy nations on pages 56–57, Prepared by A.D. Riddle for Koren Publishers Jerusalem
Elamite seal on page 58, © ALFGRN / (CC BY-SA 2.0)
Alashiya (Cyprus) tablet, bottom on page 59, © Osama Shukir Muhammed Amin FRCP(Glasg) / (CC BY-SA 4.0)
Nubian mirror, right on page 59, © Hans Ollermann / (CC BY-SA 2.0), Museum of Fine Arts, Boston, mfa.org
Shabaka sphinx head on page 60, © woodsboy2011 / (CC BY-SA 2.0)
Ishtar gate 1932, top of page 61, Matson (G. Eric and Edith) Photograph collection at the Library of Congress. Public domain
Cretan pottery, bottom on page 61, © Zde / (CC BY-SA 4.0)
Elamite inscription on page 63, © Zunkir / (CC BY-SA 4.0)
Tower of Babel by Bruegel the Elder, top of page 64, Kunsthistorisches Museum Accession number GG_1026, bAGKOdJfvfAhYQ— Google Arts & Culture Project / Public domain
Borsippa ziggurat, bottom on page 64, © MohammadHuzam / (CC BY-SA 4.0)

Brick mentioning Esagila on page 65, © Daderot / (CC0 1.0)
Kassite-era ziggurat, left center on page 66, © Osama Shukir Muhammed Amin FRCP(Glasg) / (CC BY-SA 4.0)
Mud brick Amar-Sin, bottom on page 66, © Osama Shukir Muhammed Amin FRCP(Glasg) / (CC BY-SA 4.0)
Ziggurat of Ur on page 67, © Simon Edge / Shutterstock
Temple Tel Haran on page 69, © A.D. Riddle / BiblePlaces.com
Ur from the air on page 70, From History and monuments of Ur, by Gadd, C. J. 1927. Royal Air Force official / Public domain
Abraham Leaves Ḥaran on page 71, Courtesy of Rijksmuseum, Accession number SK-A-3377, www.rijksmuseum.nl, Public domain
Fertility figurine, left on page 72, © The Walters Art Museum, Museum purchase [formerly part of the Walters Collection], 1941, thewalters.org / (CC0 1.0)
Head of a god, right on page 72, © The Metropolitan Museum of Art, Rogers Fund, 1907, metmuseum.org / (CC0 1.0)
Ashur relief on page 73, © Osama Shukir Muhammed Amin FRCP(Glasg) / (CC BY-SA 4.0)
Avraham in the land of Israel on page 74, Map by A. D. Riddle for Koren Publishers Jerusalem
Edfu Temple of Horus on page 75, © CL-Medien / Shutterstock
Ḥatzor ruler on page 76, © Gary Todd from Xinzheng, China / (CC0 1.0)
Israel oak, left on page 77, © Layue / Shutterstock
Canaanite tower, right on page 77, © Mujaddara / (CC BY-SA 3.0)
Middle Bronze Age wall, Shekhem on page 78, © A.D. Riddle / BiblePlaces.com
Zimri-lim tablet, bottom on page 79, © Motty / Louvre Museum ARK ID: 010144876 / (CC BY-SA 3.0)
Megiddo altar, center on page 79, © Vinicius Moreira da Silva / Shutterstock
Burj Beitin lintel on page 80, © Bukvoed / (CC BY 4.0)
Ramon Crater, top on page 81, © kavram / Shutterstock
Famine stele, bottom on page 81, © Morburre / (CC BY-SA 3.0)
Nuzi tablets on page 82, © Dima Moroz / Shutterstock
Dromedary camel on page 83, © Photoestetica / Shutterstock
Sheep grazing on page 84, © Noa Steiner Pikiwiki Israel / (CC BY 2.5)
Dead Sea cave on page 85, © Bukvoed / (CC BY 3.0)
Hittite tablet, left on page 86, © Rama / Louvre Museum ARK ID: 010144666 / (CC BY-SA 2.0 FR)
Tel Rumeida, right on page 86, © Altosvic / Shutterstock
Amar-Sin nail and tablet on page 87, © Mbzt / (CC BY 3.0)
Letter from Abdi-Hepa on page 88, © Osama Shukir Muhammed Amin FRCP(Glasg) / (CC BY-SA 4.0)
Niqmepa seal on page 89, © Mbzt / Louvre Museum Accession number AO 27986 / (CC BY-SA 4.0)
Gravestone of Rabbi Meir of Rothenberg, left on page 90, Courtesy of Ramessos / Public domain
Execration figurines, right on page 90, © U0045269 / (CC BY-SA 4.0)
Tel Dan Canaanite gate on page 91, © Hanay / (CC BY-SA 3.0)
Hinnom and Kidron, center on page 92, © Yehuda asulin / (CC BY-SA 3.0)
Yehimilk inscription, bottom on page 92, Unknown (ancient Phoenician) /(CC BY-SA 4.0)
Canaanite god El, top on page 93, © Mary Harrsch / (CC BY-SA 4.0)
Melchizedek and Abraham, bottom on page 93, © anagoria / Germanisches National Museum / Public domain
Temple of Baal Shamin on page 94, © Sasha Isachenko / (CC BY-SA 4.0)
Mursili II prayer tablet, center on page 95, © Osama Shukir Muhammed Amin FRCP(Glasg) / (CC BY-SA 4.0)
Zakkur Stele, right on page 95, © Rama / (CC BY-SA 2.0 FR)
Tale of Aqhat, top on page 96, © Rama / (CC BY-SA 2.0 FR)
Thutmose III, bottom on page 96, © RPBaiao /Shutterstock
Aramaic adoption contract on page 97, © Brooklyn Museum, Bequest of Theodora Wilbour from the collection of her father, Charles Edwin Wilbour, brooklynmuseum.org

Mul Apin tablet, left on page 98, © Zunkir / (CC BY-SA 4.0)
Old illustration, right on page 98, Illustration from *Figures de la Bible*, illustrated by Gerard Hoet and others. The Hague: P. de Hondt, 1728. / Public domain
Letter from Akhenaten to Aziru on page 100, © Osama Shukir Muhammed Amin FRCP(Glasg) / (CC BY-SA 4.0)
Foundation cones on page 101, © Osama Shukir Muhammed Amin FRCP(Glasg) / (CC BY-SA 4.0)
Routes between Canaan and Egypt on page 102, Map by J. Rosenberg for Koren Publishers Jerusalem
Hagar and the Angel on page 103, © Rama / (CC BY-SA 2.0 FR)
Onager on page 104, © Sergei25 / Shutterstock
Enlil statue on page 105, © Osama Shukir Muhammed Amin FRCP(Glasg) / (CC BY-SA 4.0)
Akhenaten statue on page 106, © Prof. Mortel / (CC BY 2.0)
Circumcision relief Saqqara on page 107, © Wellcome Library, London / (CC BY 4.0)
Etana cylinder seal on page 109, © Zunkir / (CC BY-SA 4.0)
Hittite sun god on page 111, © Klaus-Peter Simon / (CC BY-SA 3.0)
Ashkelon gate on page 112, © Ian Scott / (CC BY-SA 2.0)
Four room house model on page 113, © Daderot / (CC0 1.0)
Flat bread on page 114, © ozrimoz / Shutterstock
Blind musician on page 115, The Yorck Project (2002), *10.000 Meisterwerke der Malerei* (DVD-ROM), distributed by DIRECTMEDIA Publishing GmbH, ISBN: 3936122202 / Public domain
Lot's wife on page 117, © Kylie Nicholson / Shutterstock
Mesha Stele on page 119, © Mbzt / (CC BY-SA 4.0)
Hills of Shomron on page 120, © שליו / Public domain
Desert of Yehuda on page 121, © AVRAM GRAICER / (CC BY-SA 3.0)
Tel Haror (Gerar) aerial view on page 122, © Bill Schlegel / BiblePlaces.com
Ramesses II Stele, right on page 123, © RomanDeckert / (CC BY-SA 4.0)
Egyptian marriage contract left on page 123, © Anagoria / (CC BY 3.0)
Ashurnasirpal II ritual on page 124, © Osama Shukir Muhammed Amin FRCP(Glasg) / (CC BY-SA 4.0)
Donkey burial on page 125, Plos One open access online magazine, https://doi.org/10.1371/journal.pone.0058648.g002
Queen Ahmose-Nefertari on page 126, © Vassil / (CC0 1.0) Public Domain Dedication
Megiddo silver on page 127, © Courtesy of the Israel Antiquities Authority, photo by Klara Amit, IAA number: B-405655
Woman nursing her child on page 128, © Osama Shukir Muhammed Amin FRCP(Glasg) / (CC BY-SA 4.0)
Abraham sends Hagar away on page 129, Courtesy of the Internet Archive
Feiran Oasis on page 130, Matson Collection at the Library of Congress, Public domain
Milḥan well on page 131, © יאיר ליברמן / (CC BY-SA 4.0)
Tel Be'er Sheva on page 132, © Mboesch / (CC BY-SA 4.0)
Philistine prisoners on page 133, © Rémih / (CC BY-SA 3.0)
Tamarisk, left on page 134, © Anthere / (CC BY-SA 3.0)
Serabit el-Khadim inscription, right on page 134, © Einsamer Schütze / (CC BY-SA 4.0)
Temple Mount from Tayelet on page 135, © emkaplin / Shutterstock
Lakhish dagger on page 136, © A.D. Riddle / BiblePlaces.com
Tragedy of Iphigenia on page 137, © José Luis Filpo Cabana / (CC BY-SA 4.0)
Aramaic stele on page 138, © Nesnad / (CC BY 4.0)
Rock hewn tomb on page 139, Matson (G. Eric and Edith) Photograph collection at the Library of Congress / Public domain
Ugarit palace entrance on page 140, © Disdero / (CC BY 3.0)
Cave of Makhpela on page 141, © Djampa / (CC BY-SA 4.0)
Silver hoard on page 142, © Courtesy of the Israel Antiquities Authority, photo by Mariana Saltzberger, IAA number: B-25017
Meryneith tomb relief on page 143, © Ivan Sebborn / Alamy Stock Photo
Rebecca and Eliezer on page 144, Museo Nacional del Prado / Public domain

Tigris and Euphrates satellite map on page 145, © ESA 2000 - 2023
Women at the well, left on page 146, © Todd Bolen / BiblePlaces.com
Exorcism talisman, right on page 146, © Wellcome Images / (CC BY 4.0)
Camels drinking on page 147, © Mieszko9 / Shutterstock
Goddess with a vase on page 148, © robsonc / (CC BY-SA 2.0 DEED)
Rebecca and Eliezer at the well on page 150, © The Metropolitan Museum of Art, metmuseum.org / (CC0 1.0)
Veiling on vase on page 151, © Dosseman / (CC BY-SA 4.0)
Rock art on page 152, © Prof. Mortel / (CC BY 2.0)
Inheritance tablet, center on page 153, Courtesy of the Metropolitan Museum of Art, Purchase, 1886, metmuseum.org (CC0 1.0)
Ancestor worship bust, bottom right on page 153, © Rama / (CC BY-SA 3.0 FR)
Incense burner on page 154, © Wolfgang Sauber / (CC BY-SA 3.0)
Mitanni cylinder seal on page 155, Walters Art Museum, thewalters.org / Public domain
Esar Ḥadon and his mother on page 156, Louvre Museum, Purchase, 1954 / Public domain
Shumma Izbu tablet, top on page 157, © Metropolitan Museum of Art, accession number 86.11.383a, Purchase, 1886, metmuseum.org / (CC0 1.0)
Tombs of Amphion and Zethus, bottom on page 157, © Vanbasten 23 / (CC BY-SA 3.0)
Esau Gives up his Birthright on page 159, Courtesy of Google Cultural Institute, Victoria and Albert Museum accession number C.120-1945/ Public domain
Et-Tell, top on page 160, Courtesy Dvir Raviv
Tel Kabri excavations, bottom on page 160, © Hanay / (CC BY-SA 3.0)
Merenptah Stele on page 161, © Olaf Tausch / (CC BY 3.0)
Gerar (Tel Haror) donkey bit, center on page 162, Plos One online open access magazine, https://journals.plos.org/plosone/article?id=10.1371/journal.pone.0058648
Ekron inscription, bottom on page 162, © Oren Rozen / (CC BY-SA 4.0)
Tabernacle model Timna, bottom on page 163, © Bill Schlegel / BiblePlaces.com
Aleppo treaty, top on page 163, © Zunkir / (CC BY-SA 4.0)
Woman at the window on page 164, © Osama Shukir Muhammed Amin FRCP(Glasg) / (CC BY-SA 4.0)
Balag, top on page 165, Courtesy of Metropolitan Museum of Art, Purchase 1886 / Public domain (CC0 1.0)
Gerar riverbed, bottom on page 165, © Yehudit Garinkol Pikiwiki Israel / (CC BY 2.5)
Lakhish well on page 166, © Bukvoed / (CC BY 4.0)
Qatna god statue on page 167, © Jastrow / Louvre Museum ARK ID: 010164868, Purchase, 1902 / Public domain
Arslan Tash plaque on page 168, @ Metropolitan Museum of Art, Fletcher Fund, 1957 / (CC0 1.0)
Lion Gate Hattusa on page 169, © Murat Özsoy 1958 / (CC BY-SA 4.0)
Mine Wadi Faynan, top on page 170, © Following Hadrian / (CC BY-SA 2.0)
Harris Papyrus, bottom on page 170, © rowanwindwhistler / (CC BY-SA 2.0)
Purple fabric from Timna on page 171, © Courtesy of the Israel Antiquities Authority, photo by Dafna Gazit
Funerary stele on page 172, Courtesy of the Walters Art Museum / Public domain
Slaying Huwawa on page 173, © Osama Shukir Muhammed Amin FRCP(Glasg) / (CC BY-SA 4.0)
Dew on flowers on page 175, Courtesy of Shanigut / Public domain
Mount Seir on page 176, Matson (G. Eric and Edith) Photograph collection at the Library of Congress / Public domain
Octagonal prism on page 177, © A.D. Riddle / BiblePlaces.com
Ein Saharonim on page 178, © Andrew Shiva / Wikipedia / (CC BY-SA 4.0)
The road from Be'er Sheva to Ḥaran on page 179, Map by A. D. Riddle for Koren Publishers Jerusalem
Gudea I on page 180, Courtesy of Jastrow / Public domain
Nebre stele on page 181, © Siren-Com / (CC BY-SA 4.0)
Gezer standing stones on page 182, © Mboesch / (CC BY-SA 4.0)
Tekoa well on page 183, © Todd Bolen / BiblePlaces.com

Jacob and Rachel painting, top on page 184, Courtesy of Hamburger Kunsthalle / Public domain
Contract tablet fragment, bottom on page 184, © Metropolitan Museum of Art, Purchase, 1886 / (CC0 1.0)
Dowry jewelry on page 185, © www.LifeintheHolyLand.com / BiblePlaces
Hurrian lion, left on page 186, © A.D. Riddle / BiblePlaces.com
Raḥel and Leah behind Moshe, bottom on page 186, © Luciano Tronati / (CC BY-SA 4.0)
Knees study, left on page 188, © Metropolitan Museum of Art, Bequest of Walter C. Baker, 1971 / (CC0 1.0)
Hurvat Migdal Gad, right on page 188, © Bukvoed / (CC BY 4.0)
Mandrake fruits on page 189, © Carstor / (CC BY-SA 3.0)
Alalakh archaeology site, left on page 190, © Nicoleon / (CC BY-SA 4.0)
Divination by entrails, right on page 190, © Osama Shukir Muhammed Amin FRCP(Glasg) / (CC BY-SA 4.0)
Middle Eastern sheep on page 191, © Shine Achari / Shutterstock
Larsa tablet on page 192, © Mbzt / (CC BY 3.0)
Marriage chest on page 194, © Cleveland Museum of Art, Bequest of John L. Severance / (CC0 1.0)
Wool, left on page 195, © ymgerman / Shutterstock
Canaanite gods, right on page 195, © Fabien Gatti / (CC BY-SA 4.0)
Balawat Gate on page 196, © Osama Shukir Muhammed Amin FRCP(Glasg) / (CC BY-SA 4.0)
Egyptian offering on page 197, © Rama / (CC BY-SA 2.0 FR)
Newborn sheep on page 198, © Try_my_best / Shutterstock
Swiss cairn on page 199, © Tinelot Wittermans / (CC BY-SA 3.0)
Standing stones on page 201, © Mboesch / (CC BY-SA 4.0)
Maḥanayim and Yabok River on page 202, © Todd Bolen / BiblePlaces.com
Edom mountains, left on page 203, © Todd Bolen / BiblePlaces.com
Lakhish Letter 3, right on page 203, Courtesy of NenyaAleks / Public domain
Tribute bearer on page 204, © Gary Todd / (CC0 1.0)
Yabok River on page 205, Courtesy of Matson Collection, Library of Congress / Public domain
Stele depicting Teshub on page 206, © Cynthia Burdge / (CC BY 4.0)
Sciatic nerve, right on page 207, © SciePro / Shutterstock
Bowing, left on page 207, © Osama Shukir Muhammed Amin FRCP(Glasg) / (CC BY-SA 4.0)
Codex Gigas on page 208, Courtesy of Benedictine monastery of Podlažice / Public domain
Tissot, Jacob and Esau on page 209, © The Jewish Museum, New York, Accession Number: X1952-117 / Public domain
Axe head, top on page 210, © Todd Bolen / BiblePlaces.com
Scarab ring, bottom on page 210, Courtesy of Walters Art Museum, Gift of the children of Robert Garrett, 1964 / Public domain
Rape of Dinah on page 211, © Shakko, Kunsthistorisches Museum, Inv. Nr. 1554 / Public domain
Byblos ruins on page 212, © Vyacheslav Argenberg / http://www.vascoplanet.com / (CC BY 4.0)
Ostracon Amenemope on page 213, © Metropolitan Museum of Art, Rogers Fund, 1926 / (CC0 1.0)
Neo-Hittite stone lion on page 215, © Gary Todd / (CC0 1.0)
Libation jar on page 216, © Metropolitan Museum of Art, Purchase, Lila Acheson Wallace Gift, 2014, metmuseum.org (CC0)
Ḥatzor stele on page 217, © Gary Todd / (CC0 1.0)
Qubur Bani Israil on page 218, © Bill Schlegel / BiblePlaces.com
Batsheva and Shlomo on page 219, Rijksmuseum, Aankoop uit het F.G. Waller-Fonds / (CC0 1.0)
Edomite pottery warrior on page 220, © Gary Todd from Xinzheng, China / (CC0 1.0)
Edomite goddess, left on page 222, © Anagoria / (CC BY 3.0)
Hadad statue, right on page 222, © Osama Shukir Muhammed Amin FRCP(Glasg) / (CC BY-SA 4.0)
Wadi Feinan on page 223, © Erez Ben-Yosef and the Central Timna Valley Project
Rembrandt, Joseph on page 224, © Rijksmuseum, accession number SK-A-3477, Purchased by the

Rijksmuseum Amsterdam with support of the Vereniging Rembrandt and the Stichting tot Bevordering van de Belangen van het Rijksmuseum / (CC0 1.0)
Faience tiles on page 225, © Captmondo / (CC BY-SA 3.0)
Yosef's journeys on page 226, Map by A. D. Riddle for Koren Publishers Jerusalem
Cisterns on page 227, © Rafael Dias Katayama / Shutterstock
Gilad mountains on page 228, © יאיר דב / (CC BY-SA 4.0)
Fugitive slave treaty, left on page 229, © Fæ / (CC BY-SA 3.0)
Ugaritic god stele, right on page 229, © Rama / (CC BY-SA 2.0 FR)
Mask of high official on page 230, Courtesy of Walters Art Museum, Purchase, 2001 / Public domain
Adulam on page 231, © Bill Schlegel / BiblePlaces.com
Mourning widow on page 232, Courtesy of The Yorck Project (2002) / Public domain
Judah and Tamar painting on page 233, Mauritshuis Collection , National Gallery London / Public domain
Cylinder seal on page 234, © Courtesy of the Israel Antiquities Authority, photo by Klara Amit, IAA Number: B-39037
Daughter of a priest on page 235, © Khruner / (CC BY-SA 4.0)
Hyksos dagger, top on page 236, © Udimu / GNU Free Documentation License 1.2 (color photograph), original black and white image: Georges Émile Jules Daressy (19 March 1864 – 28 February 1938) (Public domain)
Hyksos headband, bottom on page 236, © Metropolitan Museum of Art / (CC0 1.0), Purchase, Lila Acheson Wallace Gift, 1968, metmuseum.org
Hyksos physician on page 237, © Khruner / (CC BY-SA 4.0)
Brooklyn Papyrus on page 238, Brooklyn Museum, Gift of Theodora Wilbour
Story of Two Brothers on page 239, © Historic Images / Alamy Stock Photo
Cows votive stele, top on page 240, © Metropolitan Museum of Art, Rogers Fund, 1923 / (CC0 1.0)
Nubian prisoners, bottom on page 240, © Aidan McRae Thomson / (CC BY-SA 2.0)
Wine jar on page 241, © Metropolitan Museum of Art, Gift of Ernst E. Kofler, 1961 / (CC0 1.0)
Ramesses II with gods on page 243, © Ahmed Emad Hamdy / (CC BY-SA 4.0)
Nile grasses on page 244, © Mmelouk / (CC BY-SA 4.0)
Hathor relief, left on page 245, © Storm Is Me / Shutterstock
Poem of the Righteous Sufferer, right on page 245, © Zunkir / (CC BY-SA 4.0)
Dream stele on page 246, © user Captmondo / (CC BY-SA 3.0)
Clean-shaven king on page 247, © Daderot / (CC0 1.0)
Emaciated herdsman on page 248, © Metropolitan Museum of Art, Harris Brisbane Dick Fund, 1957 / (CC0 1.0)
Bust of Senusret III, left on page 249, © Miguel Hermoso Cuesta / (CC BY-SA 4.0)
Relief from tomb of Khaemhat, right on page 249, © Sailko / (CC BY-SA 3.0)
Linen cloth, left on page 250, © Metropolitan Museum of Art, Rogers Fund, 1936 / (CC0 1.0)
Gold signet ring, right on page 250, © Metropolitan Museum of Art, Rogers Fund, 1924 / (CC0 1.0)
Heliopolis obelisk on page 251, Photoglob Co., publisher, Library of Congress / Public domain
Aswan nilometer on page 253, © Olaf Tausch / (CC BY 3.0)
Overseer's scarab on page 254, © Metropolitan Museum of Art, Rogers Fund and Edward S. Harkness Gift, 1940 / (CC0 1.0)
Temple oath on page 255, © Metropolitan Museum of Art, Rogers Fund, 1921 / (CC0 1.0)
Donkey with packs on page 256, Courtesy of Metropolitan Museum of Art, Rogers Fund 1912 / (CC0 1.0)
Yosef reunited with Binyamin on page 257, courtesy of the Library of Congress / (CC0 1.0)
Debt tablet on page 258, © Osama Shukir Muhammed Amin FRCP(Glasg) / (CC BY-SA 4.0)
Pistacia palaestina fruit on page 259, © Uzi Paz Pikiwiki Israel / (CC BY 2.5)
Rent receipt on page 261, Photographs by UBC Library Digitization CentrePhotos
Asiatic traders on page 262, © A.D. Riddle / BiblePlaces.com
Priest with libation vessel on page 263, Israel Museum / Public domain
Turkish divination bowl on page 264, © Wellcome Images, Turkey / (CC BY 4.0)
Wadi Tumilat on page 267, © Todd Bolen / BiblePlaces.com

Tushratta *Amarna letter* on page 268, © Osama Shukir Muhammed Amin FRCP(Glasg) / (CC BY-SA 4.0)
Yaakov and Leah tomb on page 269, Matson Collection, matpc.23168, United States Library of Congress's Prints and Photographs division, Public domain
Ugarit Ashera pendant on page 271, © A.D. Riddle / BiblePlaces.com
Shasu campaign on page 272, © A.D. Riddle / BiblePlaces.com
Cattle presentation on page 273, © Didia / (CC BY-SA 3.0)
Asiatic official Avaris on page 274, © Einsamer Schütze / (CC BY-SA 3.0)
Offering of horse on page 275, Courtesy of Metropolitan Museum of Art, Rogers Fund, 1930 / Public domain
Picking grapes on page 276, The Yorck Project, distributed by DIRECTMEDIA Publishing GmbH / Public domain
Old Babylonian contract on page 278, © Zunkir / (CC BY-SA 4.0)
Ramesses II with crook on page 279, © Osama Shukir Muhammed Amin FRCP(Glasg) / (CC BY-SA 4.0)
Shalmaneser I Stele on page 280, © Osama Shukir Muhammed Amin FRCP(Glasg) / (CC BY-SA 4.0)
Mount Eival on page 281, © Bukvoed / (CC BY 4.0)
Swell on page 282, © James W Webb / (CC BY-SA 4.0)
Cylinder seal with Shulgi of Ur, bottom on page 283, © Zunkir / (CC BY-SA 4.0)
Kilamuwa Stele, right on page 283, © Dosseman / (CC BY-SA 4.0)
Sidonian burial cave on page 284, © Carole Raddato / (CC BY-SA 2.0)
Workmen, top on page 285, Cleveland Museum of Art, Purchase from the J. H. Wade Fund / Public domain
Viper, middle right on page 285, © מינוזיג - MinoZig / (CC BY-SA 4.0)
Fawn, bottom right on page 285, © מינוזיג - MinoZig / (CC BY-SA 4.0)
Mummy on page 286, © C Watts / (CC BY 2.0)
Shroud on page 287, Metropolitan Museum of Art, Fletcher Fund, 1944 / Public domain
Anthropoid coffin on page 288, © yoav dothan, Israel Museum Archaeology Wing / GNU Free Documentation License 1.2
Curse of Agade on page 289, © Zunkir / (CC BY-SA 4.0)
Tale of Woe, top on page 290, From Caminos, Ricardo A. A *Tale of Woe*. Plate 3. Oxford: Griffith Institute, 1977. From a Hieratic Papyrus (Moscow 127) in the A. S. Pushkin Museum of Fine Arts in Moscow.
Aramaic inscription, bottom on page 290, Marie-Lan Nguyen / Wikimedia Commons (Public domain)
Decorated coffin on page 291, The Metropolitan Museum of Art, Rogers Fund, 1915, metmuseum.org / (CC0 1.0)

Index